Using *Texas Write Source*

Your *Texas Write Source* book is loaded with information to help you learn about writing. One section that will be especially helpful to you is the "Proofreader's Guide" at the back of the book. The "Proofreader's Guide" covers all of the rules for language.

The book also includes units covering the types of writing that you may have to complete on district or state writing tests. At the end of each unit, there are samples and tips for writing in social studies, science, and math.

Texas Write Source will help you with other learning skills, too—test taking, note taking, listening, and speaking. This help makes *Texas Write Source* a valuable writing and learning guide in all of your classes.

Your *Texas Write Source* guides . . .

With practice, you will be able to use the guides explained below to quickly find information in this book.

The **CONTENTS** lists the six major sections in the book and the chapters found in each section.

The **INDEX** (starting on page 809) lists the topics covered in the book in alphabetical order. Use the index when you are interested in a specific topic.

The **COLOR CODING** used for "Basic Grammar and Writing," "A Writer's Resource," and the "Proofreader's Guide" make these important sections easy to find.

The **SPECIAL PAGE REFERENCES** in the book tell you where to turn for additional information about a specific topic.

If at first you're not sure how to find something in *Texas Write Source*, ask your teacher for help. With a little practice, you will find everything quickly and easily.

TEXAS WRITE SOURCE

Authors
Dave Kemper, Patrick Sebranek, and Verne Meyer

Consulting Author
Gretchen Bernabei

Illustrator
Chris Krenzke

GREAT SOURCE®

HOUGHTON MIFFLIN HARCOURT

TEXAS WRITE SOURCE Online

www.hmheducation.com/tx/writesource

Printed in the U.S.A.

ISBN-13 978-0-547-39480-0

1 2 3 4 5 6 7 8 9 10 0914 19 18 17 16 15 14 13 12 11 10

Quick Guide

contents

Texas Write Source

The Forms of Writing

DESCRIPTIVE WRITING

NARRATIVE WRITING

EXPOSITORY WRITING

PERSUASIVE WRITING

RESPONDING TO TEXTS

CREATIVE WRITING

RESEARCH WRITING

The Tools of Language

Basic Grammar and Writing

WORKING WITH WORDS

BUILDING EFFECTIVE SENTENCES

CONSTRUCTING STRONG PARAGRAPHS

A Writer's Resource

Proofreader's Guide

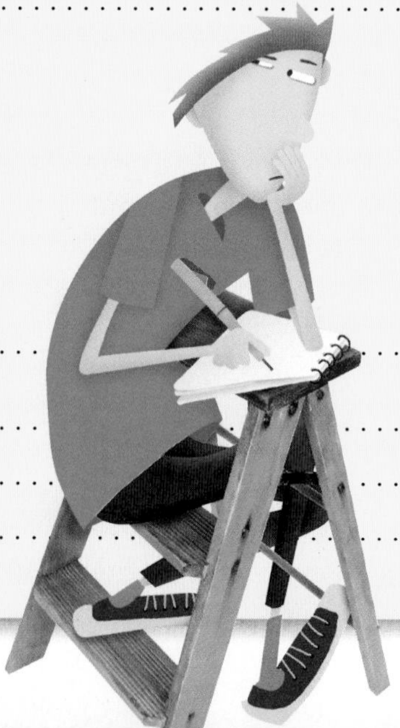

Why Write?

When Walter was a toddler, his mother passed away. His father was too poor to raise him, so he ended up as a foster child. He also suffered from a speech impairment. Walter didn't have much going for him, did he?

Of course, he hated to speak in front of the class in school. Then in fifth grade, Walter was asked to read something he had written for a speech assignment. His own writing contained words that he was able to pronounce. Afterward, he felt much better about himself and continued to write stories and poems. So began the incredible writing life of Walter Dean Myers, the award-winning author of *Hoops* and *Fast Sam, Cool Clyde, and Stuff.*

We now know how important writing has been to Walter Dean Myers. Read on to find out how writing can be important to you.

What's Ahead

- **Reasons to Write**
- **Starting Points for Writing**

Reasons to Write

Why should you write? Actually, there are many good reasons to write, and four of the most important are listed below. If you write for one or more of these reasons, you can expect good things to happen.

Writing for All the Right Reasons

You can write about your experiences by keeping a personal journal. Just set aside 10 or 15 minutes every day and write about the people, places, and events in your life.

tip Writing in a personal journal helps you make sense of everything that is happening in your world. It also helps you gain confidence in your ability to write.

To Learn

Writing about new or complex ideas presented in your classes will help you to understand the ideas better. It's best to do this kind of writing in a special notebook or learning log. Think of the writing that you do in a learning log as an ongoing conversation about the subjects you are studying.

To Show Your Understanding

You are assigned paragraphs, essays, and reports to see how well you are learning. You are also asked to answer prompts on assessment tests. These types of assignments require that you (1) understand your subjects, and (2) use your best writing skills.

To Share Ideas

Writing narratives, stories, and poems allows you to use your imagination and creativity. These forms of writing are meant to be shared.

Write to learn. Write nonstop for 5 to 8 minutes about one of your classes. Discuss any new concepts you may be covering in that class. Decide how this new information relates to what you already know. Try to sort out any ideas that confuse you.

Starting Points for Writing

Every day you do things that you feel good about. You hear things that make you angry. You become curious about how something works. These common, everyday thoughts and happenings make excellent starting points for writing. The list of prompts below will also help you get started on your own writing.

Writing Prompts

Best and Worst, First and Last

My worst day
My craziest experience
The hardest thing I've ever done
My best moment
My greatest creation

Inside Education

My best class ever
Dear Blackboard,
A good assembly
I memorized every word.
A classmate I admire

Where? What? Why?

Where do I draw the line?
What should everyone know?
What should I do next?
Why are people always in such a rush?

It could only happen to me!

It sounds crazy, but . . .
Putting my foot in my mouth
Guess what I just heard?
Creepy, crawly things
Whatever happened to my . . .
I got so mad when . . .

As My World Turns

My secret snacks
A day in the life of my pet
When I played the rebel
When I'm in charge
The last time I went shopping, I . . .

Find a topic. On a piece of paper titled "Writing Prompts," list the five headings shown above—"Best and Worst, First and Last," "Inside Education," and so on. Leave space between each heading, and write one or two new prompts under each. Add others to the list throughout the school year. Use these prompts as starting points for your personal writing.

publish EDIT draft

The Writing Process

Writing Focus

Learning Language

Work with a partner. Read the meanings and share answers to the questions.

1. A **purpose** is the reason why you do something.
   What is the purpose of going to school?
2. Writing that has **coherence** is logically organized; it "sticks together" well.
   If instructions you are reading do not have coherence, what is likely to happen?
3. **Conventions** are rules that tell how things should be done.
   What are some conventions that you know for capitalization or punctuation?
4. To **beat the odds** means to overcome a difficult challenge.
   Describe a time when you beat the odds.

prewrite. revise

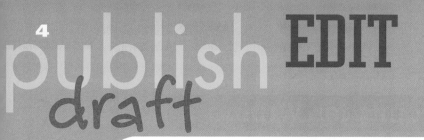

Understanding the Writing Process

Take your time. These three words may be the best advice you will ever receive when it comes to writing. No one can write well by trying to do everything at once. As author Lloyd Alexander says, "Unless you're a genius, I don't see how you could get everything right the first time."

To do your best work, you need to take your writing through a series of steps—the writing process. The steps are *prewriting, drafting, revising, editing,* and *publishing.* As you complete each step, your writing will get closer and closer to a finished product that will please both you and your readers.

This chapter will help you learn more about the writing process and build some valuable writing habits.

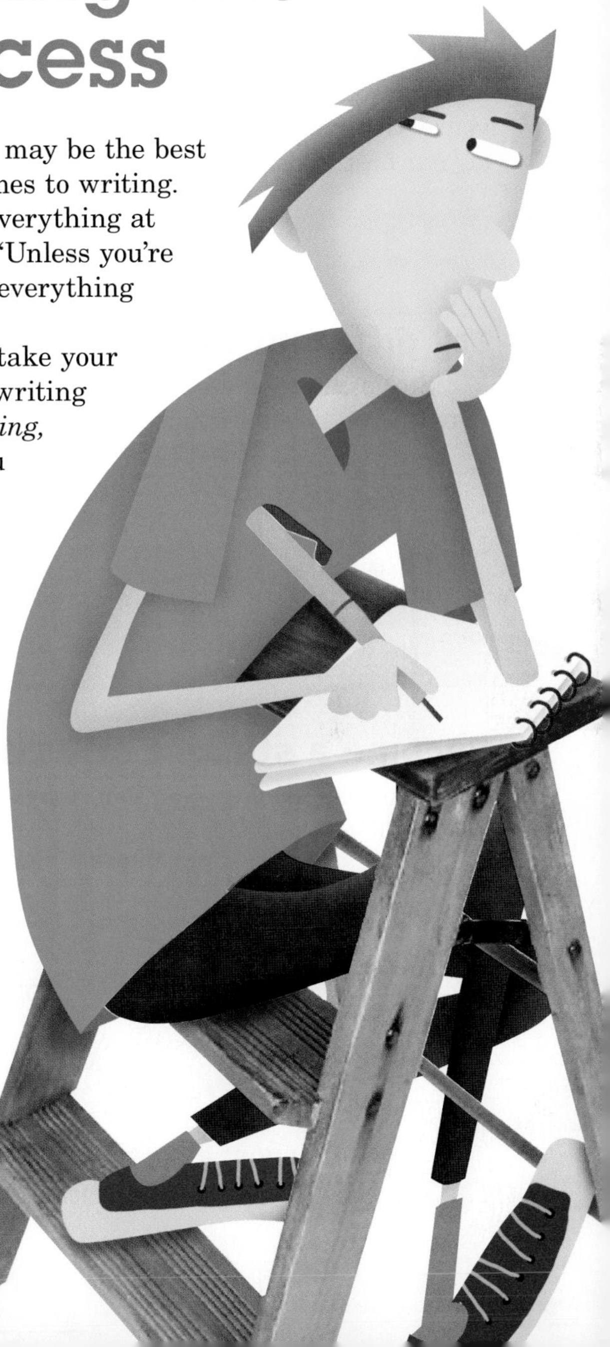

What's Ahead

- **Building Good Writing Habits**
- **The Writing Process**
- **The Process in Action**
- **Getting the Big Picture**

ELPS 2G, 2H, 3E, 3G, 3H

Building Good Writing Habits

Someone once said that writing is too much fun to be left to professional writers. This is very true, especially when you make writing an important part of your life. If you're ready to get into writing, follow the tips below.

Write as well as you can each time you write.

You will feel good about your writing if it is the result of your best efforts.

> Quality is its own reward.
>
> —William Zinsser

Try different forms of writing.

Stories, letters, e-mail messages, essays, poems—they all have something to teach you about writing.

> I wrote my first poems and short stories perched on a fire escape high above the backyards.
>
> —Sharon Bell Mathis

Become a student of writing.

Learn as much as you can about writing, including the traits of effective writing. (See pages **33–44**.)

> Good writing is about making good choices when it comes to picking the tools you plan to work with.
>
> —Stephen King

Write about a quotation. Write for 5 minutes about one of the quotations above. Consider what it means to you. Discuss your thoughts with a partner.

The Writing Process

The best writers use the writing process to help them complete their work. The steps in the process are described below.

The Steps in the Writing Process

Prewriting

Prewrite

At the start of an assignment, you think about the purpose and audience to decide on the best writing form. Then you select a topic, collect details about the topic, and plan how to use them.

Drafting

Draft

During this step, you complete the first draft using the prewriting plan as a guide. This draft is your *first* chance to get everything down on paper while thinking about the purpose, audience, and genre.

Revising

Revise

After reviewing the first draft, you think about how well the questions of purpose, audience, and genre were addressed. Then you change the parts of your writing that may be confusing or incomplete. A wise writer will ask at least one other person to review the draft.

Editing

Edit

You then check your revised writing for correctness before preparing a neat final copy. You proofread the final copy for errors before sharing or publishing it.

Publishing

Publish

This is the final step in the writing process. Publishing is an opportunity to share your work with others.

TEKS 7.14A, 7.14C

The Process in Action

Prewriting Selecting a Topic

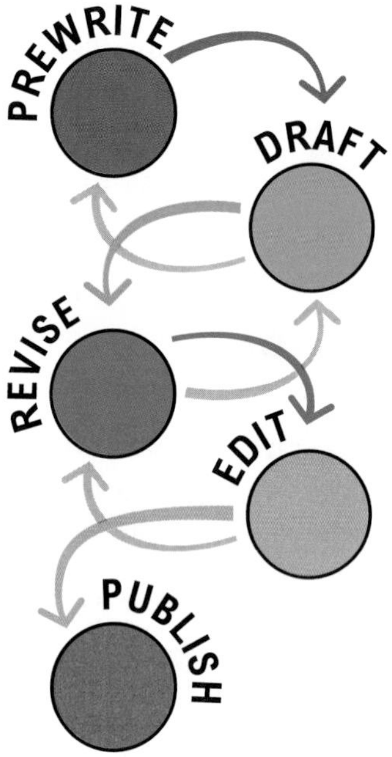

- Think about your writing assignment.
  - **What do you want to do in your writing (share, inform, persuade, entertain, be creative)?**
  - **Who is your audience?**
  - **What form of writing are you using?**

  These are your questions of purpose, audience, and form.
- Select a specific topic that really interests you.

Gathering Details

- Learn as much as you can about the topic before you start writing.
- Consider what to emphasize in the writing—either an interesting part of the topic or your personal feelings about it. This will be the focus, or thesis, of your writing.
- Decide which details you want to include in your writing. Also decide on the best way to organize the details.

Drafting Developing the First Draft

- When you write your first draft, concentrate on getting your ideas on paper. Don't try to produce a perfect piece of writing.
- Use the details you collected and your prewriting plan as general guides, but feel free to add new ideas as you go along.
- Make sure your writing has a beginning, a middle, and an ending.
- Think about your purpose, audience, and form as you write.

TEKS 7.14C
ELPS 3E, 3G

Revising Improving Your Writing

- Review your first draft after setting it aside for a while.
- Think about how well you addressed questions of purpose, audience, and form.
- Use these questions as a general revising guide:
  - **Are the ideas clear and well thought out?**
  - **Have you stated a main idea?**
  - **Do all the parts of the writing support the main idea?**
  - **Are the ideas presented in the best order?**
  - **Does one sentence lead to the next?**
  - **Does the writing express your personality and individuality?**
  - **Have you chosen colorful and expressive words?**
  - **Have you written in a style that will really connect with your audience?**
- Try to have at least one other person review your work.
- Make as many changes as necessary to improve your first draft.

Editing Checking for Conventions

- Edit for correctness by checking for grammar, mechanics, and spelling errors. Also ask someone else to check your writing for errors.
- Then prepare a neat final copy of your writing. Proofread this copy for errors before sharing it.

Publishing Sharing Your Writing

- Share your finished work with your classmates, teacher, friends, and family members.
- Consider including the writing in your portfolio.
- Think about submitting your writing to your school newspaper or another publication.

Consider the process. **Each step in the writing process is important. However, some experts say that prewriting and revising are especially important steps. In a brief paragraph, explain the importance of either prewriting or revising. Share your thoughts with a classmate.**

Getting the Big Picture

Many questions will come to mind each time you write. What is my purpose for writing? What is my main idea? What is the best way to organize and develop my ideas? How can I express my personality, or individual voice, in my writing? Are my grammar, capitalization, punctuation, and spelling correct?

Luckily, you won't have to answer these questions all at once. Instead, you can deal with them as they become important at different times in the writing process. *Remember:* The writing process helps you slow down and think about what you are writing. You can give each of the traits, the five qualities of writing listed below, the proper attention.

- ☐ Focus and Coherence
- ☐ Organization
- ☐ Development of Ideas
- ☐ Voice
- ☐ Conventions

Use the writing process. Imagine that you are working on a writing assignment. On your own paper, match each activity on the left to its proper place in the writing process on the right.

___	1. Review the first draft for voice. ("Voice" relates to the writer's personality.)	A. Prewriting
___	2. Gather the important ideas about a topic.	B. Drafting
___	3. Share the final copy with classmates.	C. Revising
___	4. Double-check the spelling of all names.	D. Editing
___	5. Write a beginning that gets the reader's attention.	E. Publishing

One Writer's Process

Many people dream about becoming "black belts" in judo, but not everyone succeeds at it. Why? Because mastering a martial art is a lot tougher than just putting on a belt. It takes discipline, courage, and a great deal of determination.

Writing well takes these same three qualities. If you have the *discipline* to search for interesting topics and gather plenty of details, your writing will be full of great ideas. If you then have the *courage* to pour words onto a blank page—or computer screen—you'll watch your ideas come to life. Finally, if you have the *determination* to revise and edit your writing, it will be unbeatable.

This chapter shows you how seventh-grader Kaylie Campos used the writing process to write an imaginative story about the sport of judo. As you will see, Kaylie is well on her way to becoming a skilled writer.

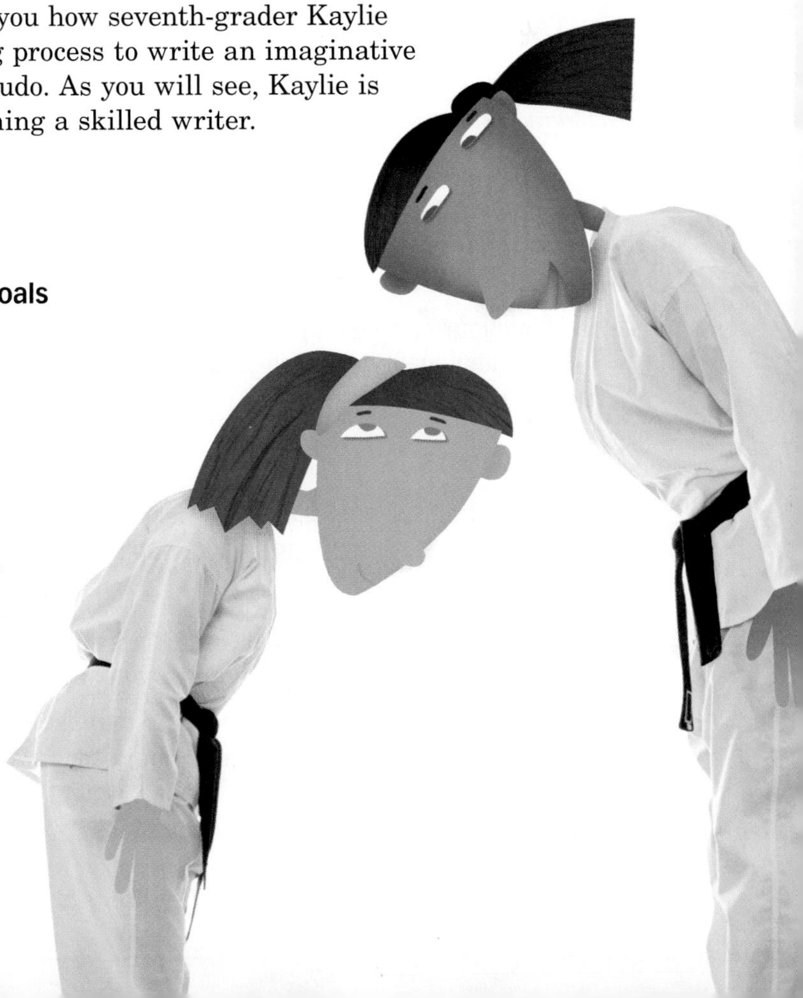

What's Ahead

- **Previewing the Goals**
- **Prewriting**
- **Drafting**
- **Revising**
- **Editing**
- **Publishing**
- **Evaluating and Reflecting on the Final Copy**

ELPS 2G, 2I, 3D, 3E, 3G, 4C, 4G, 4I, 4K

Previewing the Goals

Before Kaylie began writing, she looked at the goals for her creative writing assignment, which are shown below. These goals helped her get started.

Goals of Creative Writing

Focus and Coherence

Include the important details that will help your reader follow your story. Leave out unnecessary details, sentences, or paragraphs that might distract your reader from the main point you are trying to communicate.

Organization

Organize your story so that one event leads to another event. Each sentence you write should move the story forward.

Development of Ideas

Think carefully about what you include in your story. Include enough information about characters, events, and the setting so readers will feel like they are there.

Voice

Write your story using language that expresses your personality and individuality. Choose colorful words to make your story come alive.

Conventions

Make sure that you follow the rules for correct grammar, sentence structure, punctuation, capitalization, and spelling.

Try It To understand the important goals for Kaylie's assignment, answer the following questions. Explain your answers to a partner:

1. What kind of subject should Kaylie select? Why?
2. What should she include in her story? What should she leave out?
3. How should she develop her ideas?
4. What kind of language and words should she use?

ELPS 2C, 2G, 2H, 2I, 3D, 3E, 4C, 4G, 4I, 4K

evising

After Kaylie finished her first draft, she looked again at the goals on page and used them as a revising guide. Her thoughts, which are shown below, you what changes she planned to make.

Focus and Coherence

Include the important details that will help your reader follow your story. Leave out unnecessary details, sentences, or paragraphs that might distract your reader from the main point you are trying to make.

"I need to look at the details I included to make sure they are not confusing."

Organization

Organize the story so that one event leads to another. Each sentence you write should move the story forward.

"I need to add more details to support my main points."

Try It Team up with a partner to review Kaylie's first draft. Brainstorm and write down some words Kaylie could use in her story to make the writing sound more like how kids talk.

Prewriting **Selecting a Topic**

Kaylie was given the following assignment: Write an imaginative story involving sports that entertains readers. To select a sport to use in her story, Kaylie listed sports that she had tried and ones that she thought would interest readers.

swimming	*judo* *	*biking*
soccer	*volleyball*	*aerobics*

Kaylie chose judo because it is her favorite sport and the one that she knows most about.

Try It List your own possible activities on a piece of paper and put a star next to the one that would make the best topic. Write a brief paragraph (several sentences) explaining why you would write about this topic.

Gathering and Organizing Details

Next, Kaylie listed the main character, plot idea, and setting for her story:

main character: a kid like me
plot idea: main character faces a challenge
setting: a judo tournament

Sequence Chart

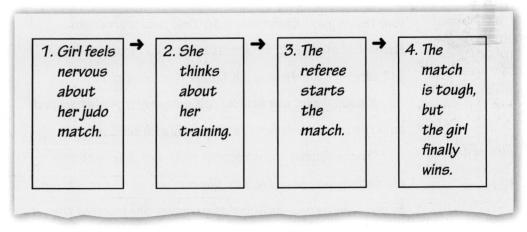

1. Girl feels nervous about her judo match. → *2. She thinks about her training.* → *3. The referee starts the match.* → *4. The match is tough, but the girl finally wins.*

Try It Make a sequence chart like the one Kaylie used. Fill it in with plot events that you could use to write a story.

Drafting Developing Your First Draft

Kaylie sat down to write her essay. She used the ideas she gathered on her sequence chart as a basic guide. Her head was full of thoughts, and she wanted to get them all down on paper. **(There are errors in Kaylie's first draft.)**

The first two paragraphs introduce the main character and describe the setting.

The second two paragraphs describe the conflict, or the problem that the character faces.

The third paragraph shows the character's thoughts about solving the problem.

No Chance at All

Rachel Lopez was feeling extremely nervous, frightened, and wary as she looked across the mat at the judo tournament at her much taller and heavier opponent, a girl named LeAnne who was from Lubbock or someplace out west. Rachel was convinced that her match against the girl was hopeless—why even try? "She looks about six feet tall," Rachel thought. "How am I ever going to beet her?" Rachel thought about what she had done earlier in the morning. She ate a good breakfast and did some stretching exercises. Now here she was.

the last thing Ms. Morita said to Rachel was, "Rememmber your techniques." Rachel was in her first judo tournament. Rachel had study judo for almost a year at a dojo. Ms Morita had decided Rachel was ready for her first competition.

Rachels heart was beating against her ribs. And struggled to keep her emotions from running away with her

"Focus, Rachel, she whispered to herself. She went over the techniques she had lerned. She mastered different throws. Silently, she names the different grapples. She pictured the break-fall techniques.

ELPS 2C, 2G, 2H, 3E, 3G, 4G

This paragraph shows the character addressing the problem.

The second, third, and fourth paragraphs describe important events of the story.

The fourth paragraph includes the climax, or high point of interest or tension, in the story.

"I can do this," she tell herself. "If I can overc can overcome that girl across the mat."

The referree signaled for the two girls to come center of the mat Rachel and her opponent bowed to other, and the match begin.

The two girl's circles each other carefully. Suddenly, Rachel's opponent reach for her and they became all tang up. Rachel felt that the tall girl was like a big spidder with hairy long arms and legs every where. Rachel found herself face-down on the mat face-down. As her opponent strained t flip her over and win the match, but Rachel heard Ms. Morita shouting to her, "Techniques, Rachel. Use what you know!"

Rachel looped her leg under her opponent's leg and applied pressure, it took all her strength to force the girl up and over. In an instant, Rachel was on top, and the tall girl was struggling to escape. But Rachel has used her favorite grapp to control the girl and forcing her sholders to the mat.

Rachel realized that the girls height and size had wo aginst her. Once she was down, she couldn't excape. As Morita hugged Rachel. She said, "With your technique that big girl didn't have no chance"

Try It On page 13, Kaylie used a sequence cha How did she use the sequence of events to w a partner and listen to your partner's respo

R

12
te

ELPS 2C, 2G, 2I, 3D, 3E, 4C, 4G, 4I, 4K

Reviewing Kaylie's First Revision

After Kaylie reviewed her first draft, she made the following revisions, or changes.

Removing unnecessary details helps focus the story.

Moving the sentence to the end of the paragraph makes more sense.

Including more information about the different techniques helps develop the ideas.

Rachel Lopez swalowed hard and looked across the mat at her opponent.

~~Rachel Lopez was feeling extremely nervous, frightened, and wary as she looked across the mat at the judo tournament at her much taller and heavier opponent, a girl named LeAnne who was from Lubbock or someplace out west. Rachel was convinced that her match against the girl was hopeless—why even try?~~ "She looks about six feet tall," Rachel thought. "How am I ever going to beet her?" Rachel thought about what she had done earlier in the morning. She ate a good breakfast and did some stretching exercises. Now here she was.

the last thing Ms. Morita said to Rachel was, "Rememmber your techniques." Rachel was in in her first judo tournament. Rachel had study judo for almost a year at a dojo. Ms Morita had decided Rachel was ready for her first competition.

Rachels heart was beating against her ribs. And struggled to keep her emotions from running away with her "Focus, Rachel, she whispered to herself. She went over the techniques she had lerned. She mastered different throws~~.~~ —the ways to take down her opponent. Silently, she names the different grapples. She pictured the break-fall techniques~~.~~ that would help her avoid injery when she was thrown.

Try It Review Kaylie's changes. Identify two changes that seem the most effective. Explain your choices to a partner.

TEKS 7.14E
ELPS 2C, 2G, 2I, 3D, 3E, 3G, 4C, 4I, 4K

Revising Using a Peer Response Sheet

One of Kaylie's classmates read her story. He used a rubric like the one on pages 48–49 and spotted more places that could use improvements. Kaylie's classmate wrote his comments on a "Peer Response Sheet."

Peer Response Sheet

Writer: *Kaylie Campos* Responder: *Chris Williams*

Title: *No Chance at All*

What I liked about your writing:

** You chose a great subject for your story.*

** I can tell you know a lot about judo.*

** I like knowing what the character is thinking.*

Changes I would suggest:

** The beginning is a little confusing. Could you remove unnecessary details?*

** Who is Ms. Morita?*

** You might tell a little bit more about what judo is.*

Try It Review the classmate's suggestions for improvements listed above. Which one do you think is the most important? Explain to a partner. Also add one suggestion of your own. Think about the focus and coherence and organization in the writing.

TEKS 7.14E
ELPS 2C, 2G, 2I, 3D, 3E, 3G, 4C, 4I, 4K

Revising Using a Peer Response Sheet

One of Kaylie's classmates read her story. He used a rubric like the one on pages 48–49 and spotted more places that could use improvements. Kaylie's classmate wrote his comments on a "Peer Response Sheet."

Peer Response Sheet

Writer: *Kaylie Campos* Responder: *Chris Williams*

Title: *No Chance at All*

What I liked about your writing:

** You chose a great subject for your story.*

** I can tell you know a lot about judo.*

** I like knowing what the character is thinking.*

Changes I would suggest:

** The beginning is a little confusing. Could you remove unnecessary details?*

** Who is Ms. Morita?*

** You might tell a little bit more about what judo is.*

Try It Review the classmate's suggestions for improvements listed above. Which one do you think is the most important? Explain to a partner. Also add one suggestion of your own. Think about the focus and coherence and organization in the writing.

ELPS 2C, 2G, 2I, 3D, 3E, 4C, 4G, 4I, 4K

Reviewing Kaylie's First Revision

After Kaylie reviewed her first draft, she made the following revisions, or changes.

Removing unnecessary details helps focus the story.

Moving the sentence to the end of the paragraph makes more sense.

Including more information about the different techniques helps develop the ideas.

Rachel Lopez swalowed hard and looked across the mat at her opponent.

~~Rachel Lopez was feeling extremely nervous, frightened, and wary as she looked across the mat at the judo tournament at her much taller and heavier opponent, a girl named LeAnne who was from Lubbock or someplace out west. Rachel was convinced that her match against the girl was hopeless—why even try?~~ "She looks about six feet tall," Rachel thought. "How am I ever going to beet her?" Rachel thought about what she had done earlier in the morning. She ate a good breakfast and did some stretching exercises. Now here she was.

the last thing Ms. Morita said to Rachel was, "Rememmber your techniques." Rachel was in in her first judo tournament. Rachel had study judo for almost a year at a dojo. Ms Morita had decided Rachel was ready for her first competition.

Rachels heart was beating against her ribs. And struggled to keep her emotions from running away with her "Focus, Rachel, she whispered to herself. She went over the techniques she had lerned. She mastered different throws—the ways to take down her opponent. Silently, she names the different grapples. She pictured the break-fall techniques that would help her avoid injery when she was thrown.

Try It Review Kaylie's changes. Identify two changes that seem the most effective. Explain your choices to a partner.

ELPS 2C, 2G, 2H, 3E, 3G, 4G

This paragraph shows the character addressing the problem.

"I can do this," she tell herself. "If I can overcome my fear. I can overcome that girl across the mat."

The referree signaled for the two girls to come to the center of the mat Rachel and her opponent bowed to each other, and the match begin.

The second, third, and fourth paragraphs describe important events of the story.

The two girl's circles each other carefully. Suddenly, Rachel's opponent reach for her and they became all tangled up. Rachel felt that the tall girl was like a big spidder with big hairy long arms and legs every where. Rachel found herself face-down on the mat face-down. As her opponent strained to flip her over and win the match, but Rachel heard Ms. Morita shouting to her, "Techniques, Rachel. Use what you know!"

The fourth paragraph includes the climax, or high point of interest or tension, in the story.

Rachel looped her leg under her opponent's leg and applied pressure, it took all her strength to force the girl up and over. In an instant, Rachel was on top, and the tall girl was struggling to escape. But Rachel has used her favorite grapple to control the girl and forcing her sholders to the mat.

Rachel realized that the girls height and size had worked aginst her. Once she was down, she couldn't excape. As Ms. Morita hugged Rachel. She said, "With your techniques, Rachel, that big girl didn't have no chance"

Try It On page 13, Kaylie used a sequence chart to plan her story. How did she use the sequence of events to write the story? Explain to a partner and listen to your partner's response.

ELPS 2C, 2G, 2H, 2I, 3D, 3E, 4C, 4G, 4I, 4K

Revising

After Kaylie finished her first draft, she looked again at the goals on page 12 and used them as a revising guide. Her thoughts, which are shown below, tell you what changes she planned to make.

Focus and Coherence

Include the important details that will help your reader follow your story. Leave out unnecessary details, sentences, or paragraphs that might distract your reader from the main point you are trying to make.

"I need to look at the details I included to make sure they are not confusing."

Organization

Organize the story so that one event leads to another. Each sentence you write should move the story forward.

"I need to add more details to support my main points."

Try It Team up with a partner to review Kaylie's first draft. Brainstorm and write down some words Kaylie could use in her story to make the writing sound more like how kids talk.

Prewriting Selecting a Topic

Kaylie was given the following assignment: Write an imaginative story involving sports that entertains readers. To select a sport to use in her story, Kaylie listed sports that she had tried and ones that she thought would interest readers.

swimming	*judo**	*biking*
soccer	*volleyball*	*aerobics*

Kaylie chose judo because it is her favorite sport and the one that she knows most about.

Try It List your own possible activities on a piece of paper and put a star next to the one that would make the best topic. Write a brief paragraph (several sentences) explaining why you would write about this topic.

Gathering and Organizing Details

Next, Kaylie listed the main character, plot idea, and setting for her story:

main character: a kid like me
plot idea: main character faces a challenge
setting: a judo tournament

Sequence Chart

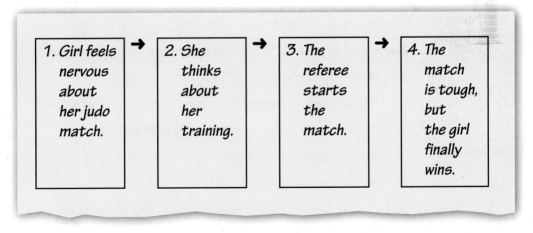

1. Girl feels nervous about her judo match. →	*2. She thinks about her training.* →	*3. The referee starts the match.* →	*4. The match is tough, but the girl finally wins.*

Try It Make a sequence chart like the one Kaylie used. Fill it in with plot events that you could use to write a story.

Drafting Developing Your First Draft

Kaylie sat down to write her essay. She used the ideas she gathered on her sequence chart as a basic guide. Her head was full of thoughts, and she wanted to get them all down on paper. **(There are errors in Kaylie's first draft.)**

The first two paragraphs introduce the main character and describe the setting.

The second two paragraphs describe the conflict, or the problem that the character faces.

The third paragraph shows the character's thoughts about solving the problem.

No Chance at All

Rachel Lopez was feeling extremely nervous, frightened, and wary as she looked across the mat at the judo tournament at her much taller and heavier opponent, a girl named LeAnne who was from Lubbock or someplace out west. Rachel was convinced that her match against the girl was hopeless—why even try? "She looks about six feet tall," Rachel thought. "How am I ever going to beet her?" Rachel thought about what she had done earlier in the morning. She ate a good breakfast and did some stretching exercises. Now here she was.

the last thing Ms. Morita said to Rachel was, "Rememmber your techniques." Rachel was in her first judo tournament. Rachel had study judo for almost a year at a dojo. Ms Morita had decided Rachel was ready for her first competition.

Rachels heart was beating against her ribs. And struggled to keep her emotions from running away with her

"Focus, Rachel, she whispered to herself. She went over the techniques she had lerned. She mastered different throws. Silently, she names the different grapples. She pictured the break-fall techniques.

TEKS 7.14E
ELPS 2G, 2H, 2I, 3D, 3E, 3G, 3H

Revising with a Peer Response Sheet

Using the comments made by her classmate, Kaylie revised her story again. These changes made her essay even more effective.

The beginning is a little confusing. Could you remove unnecessary details?

You might tell a little bit more about what judo is.

Who is Ms. Morita?

Rachel Lopez swalowed hard and looked across the mat at her opponent. "She looks about six feet tall," Rachel thought. "How am I ever going to beet her?" ~~Rachel thought about what she had done earlier in the morning. She ate a good breakfast and did some stretching exercises. Now here she was.~~

Rachel was in in her first judo tournament. [Judo is a japanese sport that stresses fitness, self-discipline, and character development.] Rachel had study judo for almost a year at a dojo. [Her teacher,] Ms Morita, had decided Rachel was ready for her first competition. the last thing Ms. Morita said to Rachel was, "Rememmber your techniques."

Rachels heart was beating against her ribs. And struggled to keep her emotions from running away with her "Focus, Rachel, she whispered to herself. She went over the techniques she had lerned. She mastered different throws—the ways to take down her opponent. Silently, she names the different grapples. She pictured the break-fall techniques that would help her avoid injery when she were thrown.

Try It Have you ever used peer responding during a writing assignment? Consider why peer responding is (or can be) helpful. Explain. Discuss your experience with your classmates and listen to their descriptions.

TEKS 7.15A(v)
ELPS 3E, 4C

Revising

Once Kaylie finished revising her focus and coherence and organization, she began checking the style and tone of her writing. She considered what she should change to make it more appealing to her readers. She wanted to make sure her readers could feel, see, and hear what Rachel felt as she took part in her first judo tournament.

Development of Ideas

Think carefully about what you include in your story. Include enough information about characters, events, and the setting so readers will feel like they are there.

"I could add more specific words to create a vivid picture for my reader."

Voice

Write your story using language that expresses your personality and individuality. Choose colorful words to make your story come alive.

"I need to make sure this story sounds like me. I think I'll add a little more about how Rachel was feeling."

Try IT Team up with a partner to review Kaylie's revised writing on page 19 for style. Identify two nouns, two verbs, or two adjectives that could be more specific, vivid, or colorful. Then find one or two sentences that could be improved.

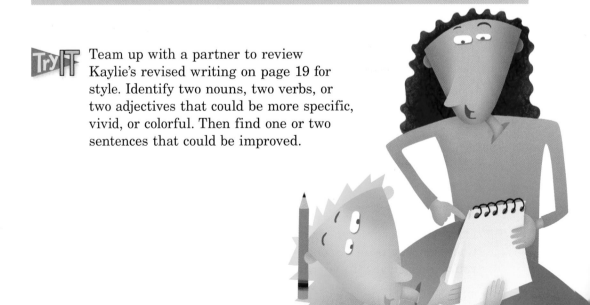

Checking Kaylie's Improvements in Style

Kaylie's next step was to concentrate on the style or sound of her ideas. She paid special attention to the effectiveness of the words and the sentences.

> The word choice is improved.

> Difficult words are defined to help the reader understand.

> Using transitions improves the flow of the story.

> Using colorful words helps the story come alive.

stared
Rachel Lopez swalowed hard and ~~looked~~ across the mat at
her opponent. "She looks about six feet tall," Rachel thought.
"How am I ever going to beet her?"

competing
Rachel was ~~in~~ in her first judo tournament. Judo is a
japanese sport that stresses fitness, self-discipline, and
character development. Rachel had study judo for almost a year
, which is a special school
at a dojo. Her teacher, Ms Morita, had decided Rachel was ready
for her first competition. the last thing Ms. Morita said to
before she left the bench to meet her first opponent
Rachel was, "Rememmber your techniques."
"How will my techniques help me beat a girl who's almost twice my size," Rachel wondered. "I don't have a chance."
Rachels heart was beating against her ribs. And struggled
like a hammer
to keep her emotions from running away with her

In her mind, she
"Focus, Rachel, she whispered to herself. ~~She~~ went over the
techniques she had lerned. She mastered different throws—
the ways to take down her opponent. Silently, she names the
, or ways to control an opponent.
different grapples. She pictured the break-fall techniques that
would help her avoid injery when she were thrown.

Try It Compare your comments about the style of Kaylie's writing (page 20) with the changes she has made. How are those changes alike or different from your recommendations?

ELPS 3E, 4G

Editing Checking for Conventions

Once Kaylie was pleased with the way her story read, she checked her work for conventions. (Conventions deal with the rules for correct grammar, mechanics, sentence structure, and spelling.)

Conventions

Make sure that you follow the rules for grammar, sentence structure, punctuation, capitalization, and spelling.

"I'll check word by word and look at how I used grammar and mechanics."

For help with writing rules, Kaylie turned to the "Proofreader's Guide" in the back of her *Write Source* book. She also used the editing checklist shown below.

Editing Checklist

GRAMMAR

_____ **1.** Do I use correct forms of verbs (*had gone,* not *had went*)?
_____ **2.** Do my subjects and verbs agree in number? (*Each* of them *has* a chance to win.)
_____ **3.** Do I use the right word (*to, too, two*)?

MECHANICS

_____ **4.** Do I use end punctuation after all my sentences?
_____ **5.** Do I use commas correctly?
_____ **6.** Do I use apostrophes to show possession (*a boy's bike*)?
_____ **7.** Do I capitalize the first word in each sentence?

SENTENCE STRUCTURE

_____ **8.** Do I avoid sentence fragments and run-on sentences?

SPELLING

_____ **9.** Have I spelled all my words correctly?
_____ **10.** Have I double-checked words my spell-checker might miss?

Try It Team up with a partner. Using the checklist above, find two or three errors in Kaylie's revised draft on page 21.

Checking Kaylie's Editing for Conventions

Before writing a final copy, Kaylie checked her essay for conventions—grammar, mechanics, sentence structure, and spelling. (See inside the back cover of this book for a list of the common editing and proofreading marks.)

Corrections are made to spelling.

Capitalization and punctuation errors are corrected.

Errors in sentence structure are corrected.

Rachel Lopez ~~swalowed~~ swallowed hard and stared across the mat at her opponent. "She looks about six feet tall," Rachel thought. "How am I ever going to ~~beet~~ beat her?"

Rachel was competing in her first judo tournament. Judo is a japanese sport that stresses fitness, self-discipline, and character development. Rachel had ~~study~~ studied judo for almost a year at a dojo, which is a special school. Her teacher, Ms Morita, had decided Rachel was ready for her first competition. the last thing Ms. Morita said to Rachel before she left the bench to meet her first opponent was, "Remember your techniques."

"How will my techniques help me beat a girl who's almost twice my size," ? Rachel wondered. "I don't have a chance." Rachels heart was beating like a hammer against her ribs. ~~And~~ She struggled to keep her emotions from running away with her

"Focus, Rachel, " she whispered to herself. In her mind, she went over the techniques she had ~~lerned~~ learned. She mastered different throws—the ways to take down her opponent. ~~Silently, she~~ named names the different grapples, or ways to control an opponent. She pictured the break-fall techniques that...

Try It Review Kaylie's editing for conventions in the paragraphs above. Did you find some of the same errors when you edited her earlier draft on page 21?

Publishing Sharing Your Writing

Kaylie used the tips below to help her write the final copy of her story. (See pages 25–26.)

Focus on Presentation

Tips for Handwritten Copies

- Use blue or black ink and write neatly.
- Write your name following your teacher's instructions.
- Skip a line and center your title; skip another line and start your writing.
- Indent every paragraph and leave a one-inch margin on all four sides.
- Write your last name and page number on every page after page 1.

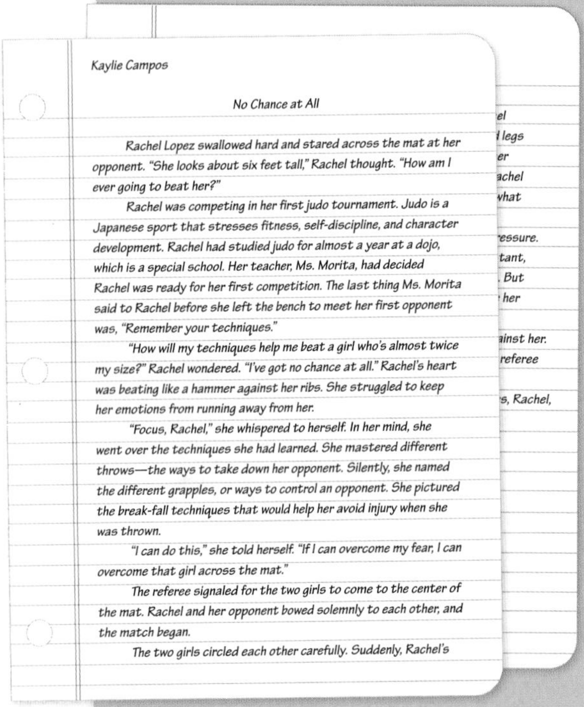
Kaylie Campos

No Chance at All

Rachel Lopez swallowed hard and stared across the mat at her opponent. "She looks about six feet tall," Rachel thought. "How am I ever going to beat her?"

Rachel was competing in her first judo tournament. Judo is a Japanese sport that stresses fitness, self-discipline, and character development. Rachel had studied judo for almost a year at a dojo, which is a special school. Her teacher, Ms. Morita, had decided Rachel was ready for her first competition. The last thing Ms. Morita said to Rachel before she left the bench to meet her first opponent was, "Remember your techniques."

"How will my techniques help me beat a girl who's almost twice my size?" Rachel wondered. "I've got no chance at all." Rachel's heart was beating like a hammer against her ribs. She struggled to keep her emotions from running away from her.

"Focus, Rachel," she whispered to herself. In her mind, she went over the techniques she had learned. She mastered different throws—the ways to take down her opponent. Silently, she named the different grapples, or ways to control an opponent. She pictured the break-fall techniques that would help her avoid injury when she was thrown.

"I can do this," she told herself. "If I can overcome my fear, I can overcome that girl across the mat."

The referee signaled for the two girls to come to the center of the mat. Rachel and her opponent bowed solemnly to each other, and the match began.

The two girls circled each other carefully. Suddenly, Rachel's

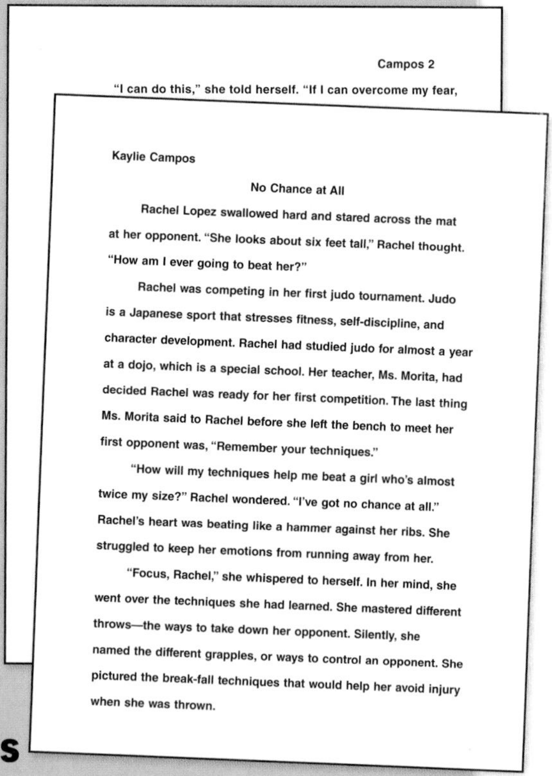
Campos 2

"I can do this," she told herself. "If I can overcome my fear,

Kaylie Campos

No Chance at All

Rachel Lopez swallowed hard and stared across the mat at her opponent. "She looks about six feet tall," Rachel thought. "How am I ever going to beat her?"

Rachel was competing in her first judo tournament. Judo is a Japanese sport that stresses fitness, self-discipline, and character development. Rachel had studied judo for almost a year at a dojo, which is a special school. Her teacher, Ms. Morita, had decided Rachel was ready for her first competition. The last thing Ms. Morita said to Rachel before she left the bench to meet her first opponent was, "Remember your techniques."

"How will my techniques help me beat a girl who's almost twice my size?" Rachel wondered. "I've got no chance at all." Rachel's heart was beating like a hammer against her ribs. She struggled to keep her emotions from running away from her.

"Focus, Rachel," she whispered to herself. In her mind, she went over the techniques she had learned. She mastered different throws—the ways to take down her opponent. Silently, she named the different grapples, or ways to control an opponent. She pictured the break-fall techniques that would help her avoid injury when she was thrown.

Tips for Computer Copies

- Use an easy-to-read font and a 12-point type size.
- Double-space and leave a one-inch margin around each page.

Kaylie's Final Copy

Kaylie was proud of her final story. She had shared her favorite sport with her readers through an interesting and memorable character.

Kaylie Campos

No Chance at All

Rachel Lopez swallowed hard and stared across the mat at her opponent. "She looks about six feet tall," Rachel thought. "How am I ever going to beat her?"

Rachel was competing in her first judo tournament. Judo is a Japanese sport that stresses fitness, self-discipline, and character development. Rachel had studied judo for almost a year at a dojo, which is a special school. Her teacher, Ms. Morita, had decided Rachel was ready for her first competition. The last thing Ms. Morita said to Rachel before she left the bench to meet her first opponent was, "Remember your techniques."

"How will my techniques help me beat a girl who's almost twice my size?" Rachel wondered. "I've got no chance at all." Rachel's heart was beating like a hammer against her ribs. She struggled to keep her emotions from running away from her.

"Focus, Rachel," she whispered to herself. In her mind, she went over the techniques she had learned. She mastered different throws—the ways to take down her opponent. Silently, she named the different grapples, or ways to control an opponent. She pictured the break-fall techniques that would help her avoid injury when she was thrown.

"I can do this," she told herself. "If I can overcome my fear, I can overcome that girl across the mat."

The referee signaled for the two girls to come to the center of the mat. Rachel and her opponent bowed solemnly to each other, and the match began.

The two girls circled each other carefully. Suddenly, Rachel's opponent reached for her and they became tangled up. Rachel felt that the tall girl was like a big spider with long arms and legs everywhere. Rachel found herself face-down on the mat as her opponent strained to flip her over and win the match. But Rachel heard Ms. Morita shouting to her, "Techniques, Rachel. Use what you know!"

Rachel looped her leg under her opponent's leg and applied pressure. It took all her strength to force the girl up and over. In an instant, Rachel was on top, and the tall girl was struggling to escape. But Rachel used her favorite grapple to control the girl and force her shoulders to the mat.

Rachel realized that the girl's height and size had worked against her. Once she was down, she couldn't escape. A second later, the referee signaled that the match was over.

As Ms. Morita hugged Rachel, she said, "With your techniques, Rachel, that big girl had no chance at all!"

Evaluating and Reflecting on the Final Copy

Kaylie's teacher used a rubric like the one that appears on pages 48–49 to assess Kaylie's final copy. The very best score that a writer can receive is 4. The teacher also wrote comments on factors that contribute to the total impression the writing makes.

4 Score

Your story is very effective. The reader feels like he or she is right there on the mat at the tournament with Rachel. Your dialogue, inner thoughts, sentences, and word choices really develop your ideas. You stay focused on your main idea, and the events of your story are well organized and easy to follow. I can tell you worked hard to create your unique voice, and it shows. Finally, I like the way your ending refers to the title and to the beginning—good organization and focus. Your grammar, mechanics, and spelling are all very good. Good work, Kaylie!

Review the assessment. Do you agree with the comments and score made by Kaylie's teacher? Why or why not? Explain your feelings to a partner.

Evaluating and Reflecting on the Writing

Kaylie put a lot of time and effort into her imaginative story. When she was finished she took some time to score and think about her writing.

Kaylie Campos

My Imaginative Story

1. *The best score for my imaginative story is . . .*
   4

2. *It's the best score because . . .*
   I really thought about all the traits and included them in my story.

3. *The best part of my story is . . .*
   how the beginning and ending relate to each other.

4. *The part that still needs work is . . .*
   the action. I think I could add more about the physical part of the match.

5. *The main thing I learned about writing an imaginative story is . . .*
   it is good to jump right into the action of your story. This helps capture your reader's interest.

ELPS 2C, 3E, 3G, 4G

Peer Responding

In 1609, Galileo started experimenting with lenses and tubes. He was trying to create an instrument that would magnify things that were very small or very far away. He and others eventually devised microscopes and telescopes. With these two tools, people suddenly could see their world in a whole new way.

Sometimes a classmate can act as a microscope or telescope for your writing. Through another person's eyes, you can see things in your writing that you never knew were there. A peer response can point out not only what could be improved but also what is already working well!

Learning Language

Work with a partner. Read the meanings and share answers to the questions.

1. Your **peers** are other people like you in the same situation. **Who are some people you consider your peers? Why?**
2. A **response** is an answer, either with words or actions. **Imagine that you got an invitation to your favorite theme park or water park. What would your response be?**
3. A **role** is a part that you play in a situation. **What role does a team captain play?**

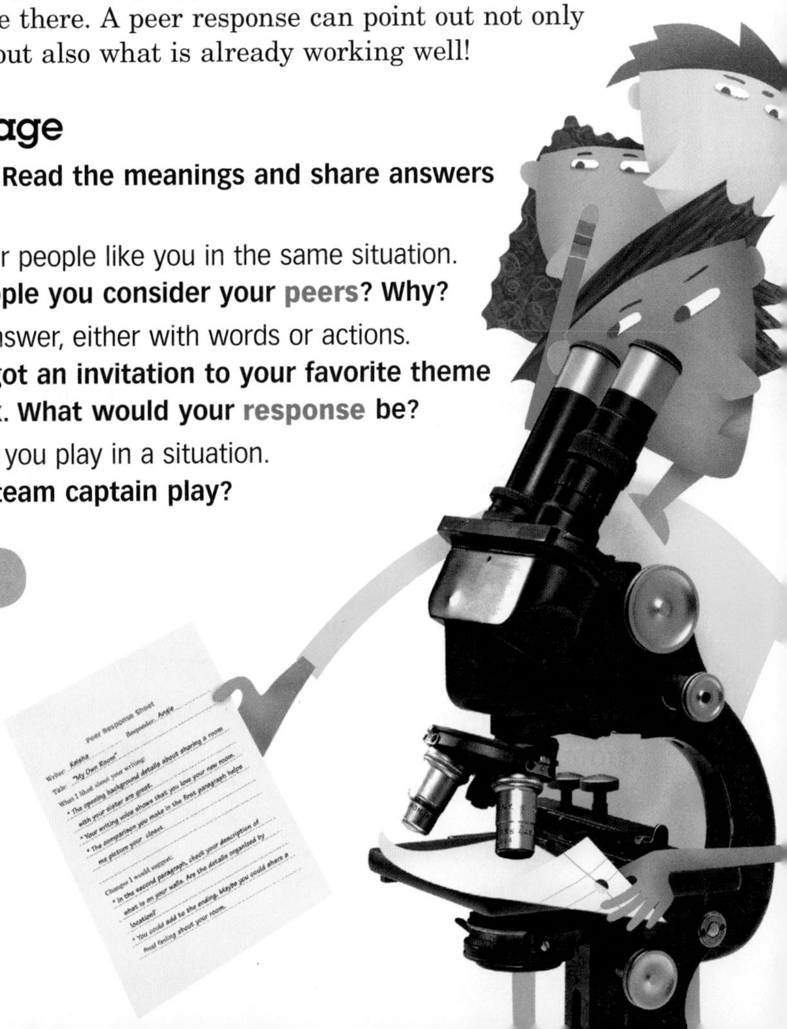

What's Ahead

- **Peer-Responding Guidelines**
- **Sample Peer Response Sheet**

TEKS 7.14E
ELPS 2I, 3G, 4G

Peer-Responding Guidelines

At first, you may work with only one person: a teacher or a classmate. This person does not expect your writing to be perfect. He or she knows that you are still working on your paper.

Later, you may have a chance to work with a small group. After a while, you will find that responding to someone's writing is much easier than you thought it would be.

The Author's Role

Select a piece of writing to share and make a copy of it for each group member.

Guidelines	Sample Responses
• **Introduce your piece of writing.** But don't say too much about it.	*This story is about a strange thing that happened one night in a spooky old house.*
• **Read your writing out loud.** Or ask group members to read it silently.	*Everyone in town always walked a little faster when they passed the old Morris place. . . .*
• **Invite your group members to comment.** Listen carefully.	*Okay, everyone, now it's your turn to talk. I'm listening.*
• **Take notes** so you will remember what was said.	*I should double-check the detail about the clock.*
• **Answer all questions** the best you can. Be open and polite.	*The bird wasn't making the noise, but I see how you might think that.*
• **Ask for help from your group** with any writing problems you are having.	*What do you think of my title? Does the ending seem too unreal?*

TEKS 7.14E
ELPS 2I, 3E, 3G

The Responder's Role

Responders should show an interest in the author's writing and treat it with respect.

Guidelines	Sample Responses
Listen carefully. Take notes so that you can make helpful comments.	*Notes: At what time does the story take place? Is it night?*
Look for what is good about the writing. Give some positive comments. Be sincere.	*Your use of kids' dialogue is very good.*
Tell what you think could be improved. Be polite when you make suggestions.	*Could you add more details about the spooky old house?*
Ask questions if you need more information.	*What happened to the barking dog at the neighbor's house?*
Make other suggestions. Help the writer improve her or his work.	*How about including a full moon?*

Helpful Comments

In all your comments, be as specific as you can be. This will help the writer make the best changes.

Instead of . . .	Try something like . . .
Your writing is boring.	**Most of your sentences begin with "There" or "It."**
I can't understand one part.	**The part about the creaking stairs is not very clear.**
What about the final sentence?	**Perhaps you should check the wording of the final sentence.**

Try It In a class discussion, share your experiences with peer responding. When have you participated in peer responding? Was it helpful? What would you do differently next time?

TEKS 7.14E
ELPS 3G, 4G

Sample Peer Response Sheet

Your teacher may want you and a classmate to react to each other's first draft by completing a response sheet like the one below. (Sample comments are included.)

Peer Response Sheet

Writer: *Keisha* Responder: *Angie*

Title: *My Own Room*

What I liked about your writing:

** In the opening, the background details about sharing a room with your sister are great.*

** Your writing voice shows that you love your new room.*

** The comparison you make in the first paragraph helps me picture your closet.*

Changes I would suggest:

** In the second paragraph, check your description of what is on your walls. Are the details organized by location?*

** You could add to the ending. Could you share a final feeling about your room?*

Practice. Exchange a recent first draft with a classmate.

1. Read the draft once to get an overall feel for it. Read it again to determine the strengths and weaknesses.
2. Fill out a response sheet like the one above.
3. Use the feedback from your peers to revise your writing.

Understanding the Traits of Writing

When a dedicated hairstylist gives a haircut, she has two people to please—the customer, so the person comes back for more haircuts, and herself, because this is her chosen profession.

This holds true for professional writers, too. First, they want to please the readers so that they become loyal fans, and second, they want to please themselves because their writing reflects directly on their own thoughts and feelings.

Good writers know that they must pay careful attention to the *focus and coherence, organization, development of ideas, voice,* and *conventions* in everything they write. You should do the same in each of your writing assignments. This chapter discusses the five traits found in all good writing. Once you understand them, you will know how to make your own essays and stories the best they can be.

What's Ahead

- **Introducing the Texas Traits**
- **Understanding Focus and Coherence**
- **Understanding Organization**
- **Understanding Development of Ideas**
- **Understanding Voice**
- **Understanding Conventions**

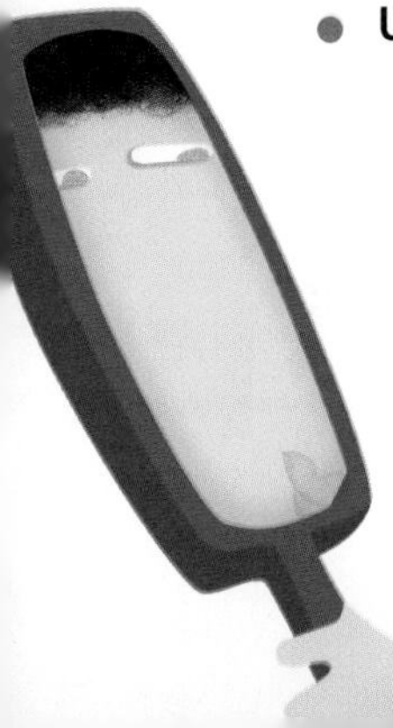

ELPS 4C

Introducing the Texas Traits

Writing is made up of five main traits, or qualities. Each of these traits is important for every essay, story, or report that you develop. This page explains how the traits work in the best writing.

Focus and Coherence

Effective writing has a clear focus and purpose—what the writer is trying to say. Good writing doesn't include unnecessary ideas. It stays on the topic.

Organization

Strong writing has a clear beginning, middle, and ending. The overall writing is well organized and easy to follow. It includes transitions that connect one idea to another.

Development of Ideas

Effective writing develops and extends ideas. Good writing shows that the writer has thought deeply about the subject. It does not include vague or general ramblings.

Voice

The best writing reveals the writer's voice, or special way of saying things. It showcases his or her unique viewpoints. The voice also fits the audience and purpose.

Conventions

Carefully edited writing is easy to understand. Good writing follows the rules for grammar, mechanics, sentence structure, and spelling.

One additional trait to consider is the **presentation** of your writing. Good writing looks neat and follows guidelines for margins, spacing, indenting, and so on. The way the writing looks on the page attracts the reader and makes him or her *want* to read on.

Texas Traits Understanding Focus and Coherence

Writing that has one main idea—and in which everything is related to that idea—is focused and coherent. The one main idea of a piece of writing is sometimes called a focus statement or controlling idea. If your writing has coherence, it is easy to follow and understand.

How can I make my writing focused and coherent?

Think about what it means when we say a photograph is "out of focus." It means the edges of things are blurry, not sharp. You can't tell what's in the photo. You can't tell where one thing ends and another begins. It's the same way with writing. If your writing gets out of focus, your reader will have a hard time telling what it is about.

How can I choose an appropriate topic?

Good writing topics are neither too general nor too specific. They cover just the right amount of information for the assignment.

Sample Assignment: Share an unforgettable experience—a specific event that has meant a lot to you.

	Possible Topics
• ***Too Broad***	Being a baseball fan
• ***Too Narrow***	Buying a pack of baseball cards
• ***Just Right***	Visiting the Astros' training camp

The following topic statement puts the topic in clear focus. It states the main idea and also focuses in on the special part you want to write about.

Focus Statement:
During my visit to the Astros' training camp (topic), *I was able to get autographs from my two favorite players* (the special focus).

Try It Identify a specific topic and write an effective focus statement based on the following assignment: Recall an unforgettable experience—a specific event that has meant a lot to you.

How many main points do I need to support my main idea?

In most cases, you should have two or three main points to support your main idea. Each of these points will need supporting details. Here's how it might work for the focus statement on the previous page.

> **Focus Statement:** *During my visit to the Astros' training camp, I was able to get autographs from my two favorite players.*

Main supporting points:

- Waiting in the parking lot for players to arrive at the ballpark
- Getting an autograph from one of my favorite players
- Getting an autograph from another favorite player

How do I use details to support my main idea?

Specific details will help hold your readers' interest. These details will also help you keep your writing focused and coherent. On the other hand, including details that don't relate to your main idea will harm the focus of your writing and make it harder for readers to follow.

Here are some details that keep the focus on the main idea:

- My favorite player got out of a white van.
- I was so excited to see him I dropped my pen in a puddle.
- He's played in the All-Star game three years in a row.

Here are some unnecessary or unrelated details that don't focus on the main idea:

- I play first base on our baseball team.
- Two different companies print baseball cards.
- I hate white vans because they show dirt so easily.

Try It Write a focus statement for this assignment prompt: Recall an unforgettable experience—a specific event that has meant a lot to you. Then add three main points you could cover in the assignment.

ELPS 4C

Texas Traits

Understanding Organization

Strong writing is well organized from start to finish. Writer Stephen Tchudi (pronounced "Judy") calls organizing a paper the "framing" process: "Just as a carpenter puts up a frame of a house before tacking on the outside walls, a writer needs to build a frame for a paper."

How should I organize my writing assignments?

Everything you write—essays, reports, stories—should have a beginning, middle, and ending. The graphic below shows the shape of effective writing.

Beginning

Start with interesting information and state the focus (underlined).

> Last year my grandma gave me the best present ever. She took me to two baseball spring training camps. <u>During my visit to the Astros' site, I was able to get autographs from two of my favorite players.</u>

Middle

Present the main supporting points and details.

> We arrived at the Astros' camp early and waited in the parking lot. . . .
>
> All of a sudden, a fancy white van pulled into the area reserved for the players. . . .
>
> A few minutes later, a red sports car pulled into the players' lot. . .

Ending

Review the essay and offer a final thought.

> Lucky me! I got autographs from my two favorite players . . .
>
> I guess you could say the ball took a lucky bounce—right to me!

TEKS 7.14C, 7.17A(v)
ELPS 4C, 4K

How can transitions help me organize my writing?

Linking words and phrases (transitions) can help you organize the details in your narratives, descriptions, and essays. (Also see pages **634–635**.)

Descriptions: You can use the following transitions, which show location, to arrange details in your descriptions.

above	across	below	in the front	on the right	near	in the back

In the front of the snack shop is a small counter surrounded by rows of candy bars. Across from the counter, bags of pretzels and popcorn are neatly stacked. In the back of the shop, a cooler contains sports drinks and water . . .

Personal narratives: You can use the following transitions, which show time, to arrange details in your narratives. These types of transitions also work well for "how-to" or procedure essays.

after	before	during	first	second	today	next	then

Next I got my favorite player's autograph. It was so amazing. I was speechless. Then I watched for other players to arrive just for the fun of it. . . .

Comparison-contrast essays: You can use the following transitions to organize comparisons.

(when comparing)	like	also	both	in the same way	similarly
(when contrasting)	but	still	yet	on the other hand	unlike

Both red blood cells and white blood cells play important roles. Red blood cells transport oxygen throughout your body, and white blood cells protect your body against infection. Unlike red blood cells, most white blood cells live only a few days.

Persuasive essays: You can use the following transitions to organize the details in your persuasive essays.

first of all	in addition	equally as important	most importantly

First of all, carrying out the death penalty is a very slow process. . . . In addition, capital punishment is very expensive. . . . Most importantly, many people believe that capital punishment is morally wrong. . . .

Try It Review a narrative, a description, or an essay that you have written. Underline any transitions that you find. Do they organize your writing, making it easier to follow? Could you add any more transitions?

Texas Traits

Understanding Development of Ideas

Ideas are the beginning and the end of good writing. That is why the best writers are constantly thinking of good ideas for their stories and essays. Author Jane Yolen knows the importance of good ideas: "I keep an idea file. I always scribble down ideas when I get them."

How can I choose details to develop ideas?

On pages 36 and 37, you learned how to choose details to support your main points. This is really another way of describing how you develop ideas.

Think of a main idea for a piece of writing as a cake before it is decorated. Without the frosting and toppings, it's just a cake. But when you decorate it, you are adding "details" that help make it a perfect cake for a special person. Your idea for a piece of writing needs to be decorated, too. The "toppings" you place on your idea are thoughtful and specific details.

Here is a table that shows how adding details can help deepen and support an idea.

Type of writing/Idea	Specific details
Persuasive essay/Kids should try to eat healthy snacks.	* Snack foods contain too much sugar and fat. * Healthy snacks include raw fruits, vegetables, and whole grains. * Here's how I made the switch to healthy snacks…
Description/Sunrise at Padre Island National Seashore	* miles of sugary white sand * gentle waves lapping the shore * seabirds frantically hunting for food in the foaming surf
Personal narrative/A Day to Remember	* My brother woke me up early … * Entering the auditorium, I saw . . . * When my name was announced and the audience cheered . . .

How do I add my personal touch?

You can develop your ideas by approaching them in a unique or personal way. Use your own special insight, or understanding, to present the ideas in a new light. For example, which paragraph below packs more punch and makes you want to read on?

> Have you ever wondered what it would be like to boogie onstage at a concert? Well, I used to wonder too. Why don't I wonder any more? I actually did it. It makes an interesting story, how I wound up on stage with the superstar!

> A contest was held last year. Kids were asked to write an essay explaining why they should be chosen to appear onstage in an ensemble dance routine with a famous singer. I was one of the winners.

How can I show a unique perspective about an idea?

Another way to develop your ideas is to take an unusual perspective, or point of view. You could write a story about giving your cat a bath from your point of view. You could also try telling the story from the unhappy cat's perspective.

> I carried Muffin to the sink. I checked to make sure the water wasn't too warm or too cold. Then I added some baby shampoo and watched the suds form. "Come on, Muffin," I said gently. "I know you don't like getting a bath, but you need one."

> There it is, right in front of me. I try to struggle free, but Latika holds me tight. Her words are soothing, but they strike fear in my heart. Closer, closer, I come to the sudsy mess. You don't understand! It took me months to get this nice and dirty. No, no... yoowwwwwlllll!

Try It Review a narrative, description, or essay that you have written. Work with a partner. Describe how you could revise it to present a different perspective or viewpoint.

Texas Traits

Understanding Voice

Writer Donald Murray says that voice is the "person in the writing." When the writer's voice or personality is strong, the reader stays interested. Something about the writer's way of using words attracts the reader.

How can I write with voice?

To have voice, you must be honest and sincere in what you write.

This passage lacks voice because you can't hear the writer.

> Coach Brown requires us to complete pull-ups in a very specific way. He doesn't allow any unnecessary movements. He positions himself close to the bar with a yardstick in hand. As soon as there is any movement . . .

This passage has voice because you can hear the writer.

> For Coach Brown, there is only one way to complete a pull-up—his way. For one thing, he doesn't allow any kicking, wriggling, or squirming. He stands right next to the bar and taps us if . . .

Is audience important when thinking about voice?

Your audience is very important because it impacts the tone of your voice. For example, in a letter to the school board, you would try to sound formal and respectful. In a personal narrative shared with classmates, you would try to sound more casual and relaxed.

Audience Adults (school administrators, businesspeople, city officials)
Voice Serious, formal, respectful, and thoughtful
Art classes greatly benefit all students. . . .

Audience Peers (classmates, friends, and students in other schools)
Voice Engaging, usually informal, casual, and relaxed
Art classes give kids a chance to be creative. . . .

Try It Write a brief note to a teacher explaining something that you really like about class. Then write another note, this time to a friend in the class, about the same topic. The tone of each note should be different.

ELPS 2G, 2H, 2I, 3D, 3E, 3G, 3H

How can I find the right tone?

Tone is the writer's attitude toward the subject. It is part of your voice when you are writing. Effective writing communicates its author's attitude about the subject—admiring, respectful, amused, scornful, afraid, nostalgic, enthusiastic, bored, and so on. Can you identify the writers' tones in these two reviews?

(Yawn) Sorry. Last night, I watched the premiere of the new TV show, Misfit Middle School. I have one question: Which genius TV producer decided the world needed yet another show about goofy but street-smart teenagers, serious teachers, and clueless parents? As if the 96 current shows like this didn't cover the subject...

Run, don't walk, to the cinema to catch the new spy thriller Nine Lives to Live! Better yet, rent a helicopter to get there before the crowds discover this one. And once you're there, DO NOT TAKE YOUR EYES OFF THE SCREEN FOR ONE SECOND. If you do, you'll miss something important and incredible!

How do I build sentences?

Sentence structure is the way you write your sentences. They can be short and choppy or long and elegant. They can all begin the same way or they can vary. You can use sentence structure to express your individual voice. How would you describe the voices behind these two passages?

Here comes the pitch. Alvarez swings. He hits it. Long fly ball to center. The fielder goes back. Back. Back. He jumps. He hits the wall. He's got it! Game over!

When training dolphins, patience is key. The process cannot be rushed, nor can it be hurried, and there is no short cut. Establishing trust between human and animal is the only path to success in this challenging effort.

Remember, to a reader, your writing is you. You put your best foot forward when you meet someone in person. You can do the same when you write if you create your own individual, authentic voice.

Try It Write a paragraph of several sentences. Ask a partner to describe your voice. Then have your partner rewrite your paragraph, keeping the same subject, to communicate a different voice.

Texas Traits

Understanding Conventions

Good writing follows the conventions, or basic rules, of the language. These rules cover grammar, mechanics, sentence structure, and spelling. When you follow these rules, the reader will find your writing much easier to understand and enjoy.

How can I make sure my writing follows the rules?

A checklist like the one below can guide you as you look over your writing for errors. When you are not sure about a certain rule, refer to the "Proofreader's Guide" (pages 640–797).

Conventions

GRAMMAR

_____ **1.** Do I use correct forms of verbs (*had gone,* not *had went*)?
_____ **2.** Do my subjects and verbs agree in number (*Each of them has a chance to win*)?
_____ **3.** Do I use the right word (*to, two, too*)?

MECHANICS

_____ **4.** Do I use end punctuation after all my sentences?
_____ **5.** Do I use commas correctly?
_____ **6.** Do I use apostrophes to show possession (*a girl's shoe*)?
_____ **7.** Do I capitalize all proper nouns?

SENTENCE STRUCTURE

_____ **8.** Do I avoid sentence fragments and run-on sentences?

SPELLING

_____ **9.** Have I spelled every word correctly?
_____ **10.** Have I double-checked words my spell-checker might miss?

tip Have at least one other person check your writing for conventions. Professional writers have trained editors to help them with this step in the process. You should ask your classmates, teachers, and family members for help.

How can I avoid common mistakes using conventions?

Grammar

Make sure that pronouns agree in number and gender (male, female, or neutral) with their antecedents.

Incorrect	Each student should bring their homework by Friday.
Correct	Each student should bring his or her homework by Friday.

The possessive pronoun must agree in number with its antecedent. In the first sentence, the antecedent is singular: each student. Therefore, the possessive pronoun must also be singular: his, her, or its.

Mechanics

Use an apostrophe to show possession.

Incorrect	Marias rabbit	the teachers car	Americas pride
Correct	Maria's rabbit	the teacher's car	America's pride

Sentence Structure

Every sentence must have a subject and a verb. Sentences that lack subjects or verbs are called sentence fragments.

Incorrect	Sipped lemonade under the tree.
Incorrect	The girl with the cap.
Correct	The girl with the cap sipped lemonade under the tree.

Spelling

Words that have the same pronunciation, but different spellings and meanings, can be tricky. If you're in doubt, look the word up in the dictionary. These three words are often confused:

there: a place. *Put the flag over there.*

their: a possessive pronoun. *Their car needs a wash.*

they're: a contraction meaning "they are." *They're late, as usual!*

Evaluating Your Writing

Some things you read are red-hot, and other things leave you cold. The problem is that you can't use a thermometer to measure how "hot" a piece of writing is. Instead, you measure writing by using a rubric.

A rubric is a chart that lists the main traits of writing. This chapter explains how to use a rubric and "heat up" your writing.

What's Ahead

- **Understanding Holistic Scoring**
- **Reading a Rubric**
- **Model Essays**
- **Evaluating an Essay**

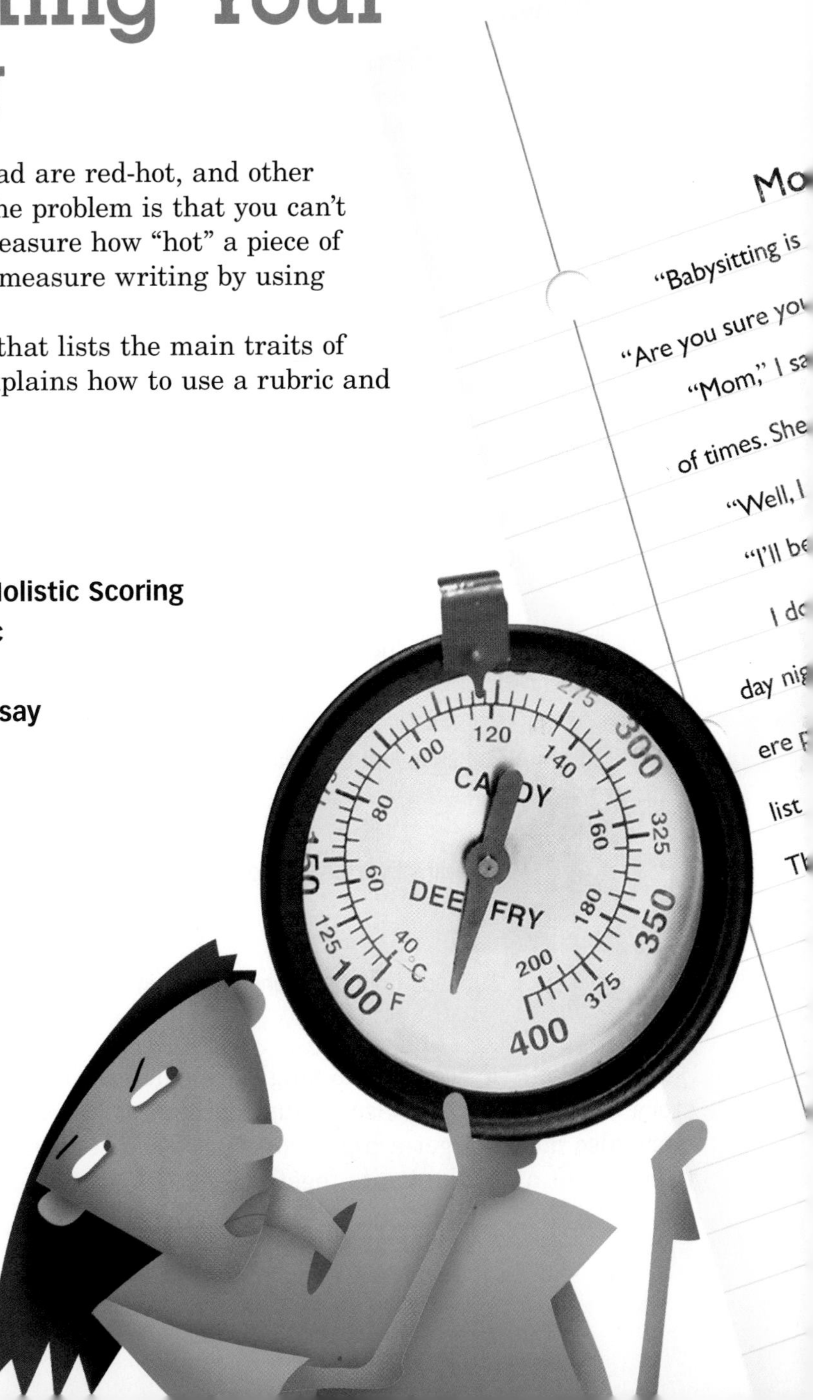

ELPS 4C, 4K

Understanding Holistic Scoring

Read the following expression:

"The whole is greater than the sum of its parts."

Do you know what this means? Think about looking at a face. When you respond to a face, you don't usually think separately about its shape, features, color, and expression. You don't separately evaluate the nose, lips, and ears, and whether you like its freckles or not. You think of the face as a whole. You evaluate the overall impression it makes on you.

The same is true for a piece of writing. You can evaluate it as a whole, or holistically. With holistic evaluation, you follow these steps:

- Think about how well the story addresses the five traits of writing.
- Ask: What is the total impression the story makes on the reader?
- Assign a score of 1, 2, 3, or 4 that stands for the overall quality of the writing.

With holistic scoring, you do not give a separate score for each trait. You give a single score, using these guidelines:

4 A **4** means that the writing is strong in **all** of the traits.

3 A **3** means that the writing is strong in **most** of the traits.

2 A **2** means that the writing is strong in **some** of the traits.

1 A **1** means that the writing is weak in **most** of the traits.

With holistic scoring, no single trait determines the score. For example, a story does not get a low score just because it has many mechanical errors. A story also does not get a high score just because it is well organized. You must think about all of the traits together.

Try It Reread a story you have written. When you think about it as a whole, should it receive a score of 1, 2, 3, or 4?

ELPS 3D, 3G, 3H, 4C, 4G, 4K

Reading a Rubric

For the rubrics in this book, the four score points are color coded. There is a description for each rating to help you evaluate your writing.

The *Write Source* Scoring Rubric

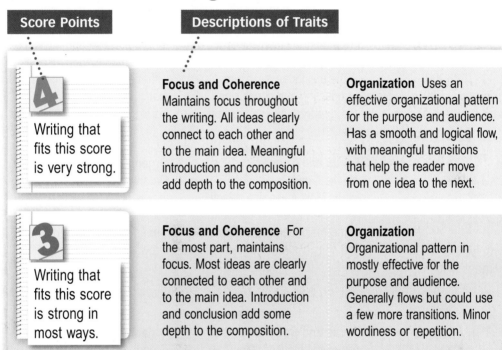

Score Points	Descriptions of Traits	
4 Writing that fits this score is very strong.	**Focus and Coherence** Maintains focus throughout the writing. All ideas clearly connect to each other and to the main idea. Meaningful introduction and conclusion add depth to the composition.	**Organization** Uses an effective organizational pattern for the purpose and audience. Has a smooth and logical flow, with meaningful transitions that help the reader move from one idea to the next.
3 Writing that fits this score is strong in most ways.	**Focus and Coherence** For the most part, maintains focus. Most ideas are clearly connected to each other and to the main idea. Introduction and conclusion add some depth to the composition.	**Organization** Organizational pattern in mostly effective for the purpose and audience. Generally flows but could use a few more transitions. Minor wordiness or repetition.

Guiding Your Writing

Learning how to use a rubric helps you . . .

- think like a writer—understanding your goal,
- make meaningful changes in your writing—using the traits of writing, and
- assess your final copies—rating their strengths and weaknesses.

Reflect on your work with rubrics. On your own paper, explain your experience with rubrics. When have you used them? How well did they work for you? What have they taught you about writing? If you've never used a rubric, explain how you have generally evaluated your writing. Share your thoughts with your class.

ELPS 4C, 4K

Texas Traits

The *Write Source* Scoring Rubric

Use the descriptions for each score to holistically evaluate your writing or that of your peers.

Score	Focus and Coherence	Organization
4 Writing that fits this score is very strong.	**Focus and Coherence** Maintains focus throughout the writing. All ideas clearly connect to each other and to the main idea. Meaningful introduction and conclusion add depth to the composition.	**Organization** Uses an effective organizational pattern for the purpose and audience. Has a smooth and logical flow, with meaningful transitions that help the reader move from one idea to the next.
3 Writing that fits this score is strong in most ways.	**Focus and Coherence** For the most part, maintains focus. Most ideas are clearly connected to each other and to the main idea. Introduction and conclusion add some depth to the composition.	**Organization** Organizational pattern is mostly effective for the purpose and audience. Generally flows but could use a few more transitions. Minor wordiness or repetition.
2 Writing that fits this score is strong in a few ways.	**Focus and Coherence** Is somewhat focused. May suddenly shift from one idea to another, but the ideas are related. Some ideas do not add to the writing. Introduction and conclusion do not add depth.	**Organization** Organizational pattern may not suit the purpose and audience. Thoughts do not always flow clearly or logically. Wordiness or repetition may interfere with ideas.
1 Writing that fits this score is weak.	**Focus and Coherence** Lacks focus. Includes a large amount of information not connected to the main idea. Is missing an introduction and/or a conclusion.	**Organization** Has no clear organizational pattern or logical flow of ideas. Has no transitions or uses ones that do not make sense. Wordiness and repetition interfere with ideas.

Development of Ideas Supports all ideas thoroughly and with specific detail. Shows deep or creative thinking that adds to the overall quality of the writing.	**Voice** Engages the reader throughout the writing. Sounds authentic and original; expresses the writer's personality or unique viewpoint.	**Conventions** Shows a strong command of grammar, sentence structure, mechanics, and spelling.
Development of Ideas Supports all ideas, but some need to be developed more thoroughly. Development may be thoughtful but may not show creative thinking.	**Voice** Engages the reader for most of the writing. Sounds authentic and original and expresses the writer's unique viewpoint.	**Conventions** Includes only minor errors in grammar, sentence structure, capitalization, punctuation, and spelling.
Development of Ideas Support is general or shows little depth of thinking. Support may be only a list. Information may be missing. The message may be unclear.	**Voice** Engages the reader in some parts of the writing. Sounds authentic and original in only a few places. Does not express a unique viewpoint.	**Conventions** Several errors in grammar, sentence structure, mechanics, and spelling. Errors may interfere with the reader's understanding.
Development of Ideas Does not support ideas or provides only general and unclear support. Important information may be left out. The message is unclear.	**Voice** Does not engage the reader. Does not sound authentic and original. Does not express a unique viewpoint.	**Conventions** Major errors in grammar, sentence structure, mechanics, and spelling. These problems interfere with the reader's understanding.

ELPS 4I, 4K

Model Essays

To learn how to evaluate an essay, you'll use the scoring rubric on pages 48–49 and the essays that follow. These essays are examples of writing for each score on the rubric.

Notice that this first essay received a score of 4. Read the description for a score of 4 on pages 48–49. Then read the essay. Use the same steps to study the other examples. Always remember to think about the overall quality of the writing. (The essay does contain a few errors.)

Writing that fits a score of 4 is very strong.

4

Inner thoughts help readers understand how the character feels.

Specific details add realism to the story.

Inner thoughts help add voice.

First Flight

Geri was nervous—very nervous. Was it her imagination, or was her hand really quivering? "It must be from gripping the arm of my seat so hard," she told herself. She stretched her arm out toward the empty seat next to her.

To take her mind off what she was about to experience, she looked around. There were people everywhere, and they all seemed completely at ease. Some were reading newspapers or books, others had on headphones. A few well-dressed men and women were even talking into their cellphones.

"Don't they know they're about to shoot off into the air?" she thought. "Take off right into the sky with nothing holding them up but some skinny metal wings? How can they be so calm?"

Geri was flying in a plane for the first time. When she first found out she would be flying from the Dallas/Fort Worth Airport to visit her cousins in New York, she was excited. But over the next few weeks, she began to feel wary of the flight.

The writer clearly identifies the character's problem.

Idea is developed through the character's words and actions.

Ending shows resolution to the problem.

Visions of the terrible things that could happen flitted through her head. She even thought about asking her mom if she could just skip the visit. But she decided not to, she couldn't let everyone know she was afraid of flying.

So, here she was. The plane was almost full. At the last minute before the attendants shut the big doors, a boy several years younger than her made his way down the isle. He plopped his backpack on the floor and took the seat next to Geri. He looked at Geri and smiled weakly.

Geri smiled back.

The video showed passengers what to do in case of an emergency. Geri glanced at the boy next to her. She thought he must have been about nine or ten. To her amazement, the boy looked even more frightened than Geri felt. He looked like he was about to cry.

"Hey," Geri said. 'It'll be OK. Flying is really safe."

The boy looked around like a scared animal as the plane began to taxi down the runway. Geri took a deep breath.

She leaned toward the little boy. "I'll tell you a secret," she said. "I've never flown before. Would it be OK if you held my hand while we take off? I'd feel a whole lot better."

The little boy slipped his hand into Geris. The plane lifted off the ground. "I'm flying," she said, looking out the window.

"We're flying," answered the boy.

ELPS 4I, 4K

Writing that fits a score of 3 is strong in most ways.

3

The Old Picture

Specific details and tone develop the writer's voice.

Description helps readers see the setting.

Correct use of quotation marks show dialogue.

It was a Saturday morning, the day that Felipe had not been looking foreward to one bit. What was the reason? His dad had said that was the day they must clean out the attic in their house.

The attic was filled with boxes, bags, old furniture, old records, and books. Not to mention the clothes! There were things up there that no one would ever wear in a milion years. Their family stored stuff there that they didn't think they would want but that they couldn't bare to throw away. Like a lot of families!

Felipe helped his dad pull down the door in the ceiling that led up to the attic. Pulled on the rope and down came the door. He unfolded a little wooden ladder and they climbed up. Felipe had to hold on to the raling because it was pretty steep.

The attic was tall in the middle, but it was low on the sides. This was because the roof on their house was pointy. Felipe looked around at all the stuff there. Then his dad said, "OK, where should we begin?"

Felipe said, "I don't know, how about we look at stuff and descide if we want to keep it or throw it away."

"That's a good idea."

They started to look at the old clothes hanging on hangers and put some of the stuff in a pile to give to charity and some of the stuff they wanted to keep after all.

Transitions help the story flow smoothly.

After a while, Felipe asked, "What is in those boxes over there?"

His dad looked at the boxes. Then he replied, "Old pictures of the family."

Felipe walked over to the boxes and opened one up. He pulled out a bunch of old photos. He new who some of the people were but not other people. Some of them were wearing funny old clothes—like the stuff in the attic.

Felipe held up one old picture. It showed a little boy standing by a poney. It was at a fair or circus or something. Felipe figured it was a picture of him because the boy looked like him and the same hair color.

"Look Dad," Felipe called holding up the picture. "Here's one of me with a poney. Do you remember when this was cause I don't."

His dad walked over to Felipe and looked at the picture. Then he laughed.

A surprise ending gives meaning to the title.

"Yes, it looks like you with the poney," he said. "But you know what, it's not you, it's me. This picture was taking more than 30 years ago when I was a little boy!"

ELPS 4I, 4K

Writing that fits a score of 2 is strong in some ways.

2

Organization could be tighter.

Lack of focus weakens the story.

Details add realism to the story.

There are several errors in conventions.

Some events have been left out.

Rafting on the River

It was May and Tina's family want to go on a raft trip. It was on the Blanco River. They lived in Austin and this river not to far from their house in Austin. They all got in the car and drive to the Blanco River place where you can get on the raft tour. It's a jeep. Yes, said Tina, rafting is really cool!

After they rode to the river in their car they paid and got life jakets and even helmets so they won't get hurt if they crash or fall out on a rock or log. Tinas helmet was brite red. Then the guide tell them about the trip they were going to take.

"It is a Class 3 water, so there could be some big splashes and somebody might fall out" the guide said. "If one of you falls out, dont worry because I can save you no problem." The guide laughed a big laugh because he thought one of them was going to fall out and he could save them.

The sky was very blue and not a cloud. It was gorgous. The water was calm mostly but also rough sometimes.

Then the going got rough and the guide said, "Don't forget I can save you if one you fall out of the raft." Yeah, right Tina thought.

Just then the raft tipped over on a big wet rock and guess who falls out? Not Tina or her family but the guide hisself! He looked funny! He thought he would save them but they have to save him!

Writing that fits a score of 1 is weak.

1

The Dirty Dog—Not!

Organization is confusing.

Many events were left out.

Some ideas are repeated over and over.

There are many errors in conventions.

James and Shaun decided, we need some money. So they start a dog washing bisness. In there naborhood. There plan will be to wash dogs of people for three dollars a dog. They want to buy video games. That game is awesome!

So then people bring they dogs to james and Shaun dog washing place. At Shauns house by the back yard where the hose is. Shaun said, "I hope we get lots of people and the dogs because games are not cheap are they."

You are right, Shaun, James said.

The next dog was pretty big and white and gray spots on the legs and head. He was Alicias dog Hugo. In you go Hugo James said. We are going to make a lot of money cause dogs are so dirty around here, and it's the rain that makes them all muddy, so we can make money for sure.

"Yeh, like Hugo. How much does a game cost, do you know? Shaun said."

The two boys scrub and scrub at Hugo but he does not get mad or bark, hes a very good dog and Alicia is right there just in case.

"This dirt spot on Hugos head will not come out said James. "Let me see it, James"

Shaun looks at the spot on Hugo head and then he laugh like crazy. Boy are you dumb, that is not dirt that is a spot! You will not wash it off! you will not wash it off in a hunderd years if you keep trying! Then the two boys just laufed.

ELPS 4G, 4I, 4K

Evaluating an Essay

As you read through the essay below, pay attention to the strengths and weaknesses in the writing. Then follow the directions at the bottom of the page. **(This writing does contain errors.)**

Moms Can Be Right

"Baby-sitting is alot harder then it looks," my mom said. "Are you sure you want your first job to be for three kids?"

"Mom," I said, "I'll be fine. I've gone baby-sitting with Ellie a bunch of times. She and I have taken care of there kids before."

"Well, I really think you should have some jobs with one child."

"I'll be fine," I said. "You'll see."

I don't know if I could of been more wrong! I showed up on Friday night just as planned. The boys were already changed into there pjs and I just had to watch them. Mrs. Taylor ran thru the list of things they could and couldn't do and then headed for an office party.

The first twenty minutes was fine but then the show they were watching ended. So they got out some toys and started playing. Alex was good and wanted to sit on my lap, so I let him.

Then Robbie was in tears. Robbie screamed and yelled but Max just smiled and run into another room. I couldn't get up fast enough because Alex didn't want me to. He kept crawling up on me.

I had only just gotten them to bed when the Taylor's walked back in. I hadn't even got a chance to clean up. Their place was a total mess. They didn't say anything, but I could tell they weren't too happy. They paid me and I felt bad for not listening to my mom.

Use the scoring rubric. **Assess the narrative essay you have just read using the rubric on pages 48–49 as a guide. Record your rating and comments on a separate sheet of paper.**

ELPS 2C, 3D, 4G

Publishing Your Writing

Publishing refers to the ways that you can present your finished writing. Sharing a story in class is one form of publishing. Posting a poem on your own Web site is another form. In one way, publishing is the most important step in the writing process because it helps you take pride in your work.

Your writing is ready for publication when it reflects your true thoughts and feelings from start to finish. Your writing must also be as close to error-free as you can make it.

This chapter will help you get your writing ready to publish and give you a variety of publishing ideas. (Also see "Creating a Portfolio" on pages 65–69.)

Learning Language

Work with a partner. Read the meanings and share answers to the questions.

1. **Publishing** is making your work available for others to see.
   What are some different ways of publishing your work?
2. **Graphic devices**, such as charts and graphs, can help information stand out.
   What kinds of graphic devices have you seen or used?
3. A **Web site** is a location on the Internet that has specific information.
   Have you visited Web sites to find facts? Which ones?

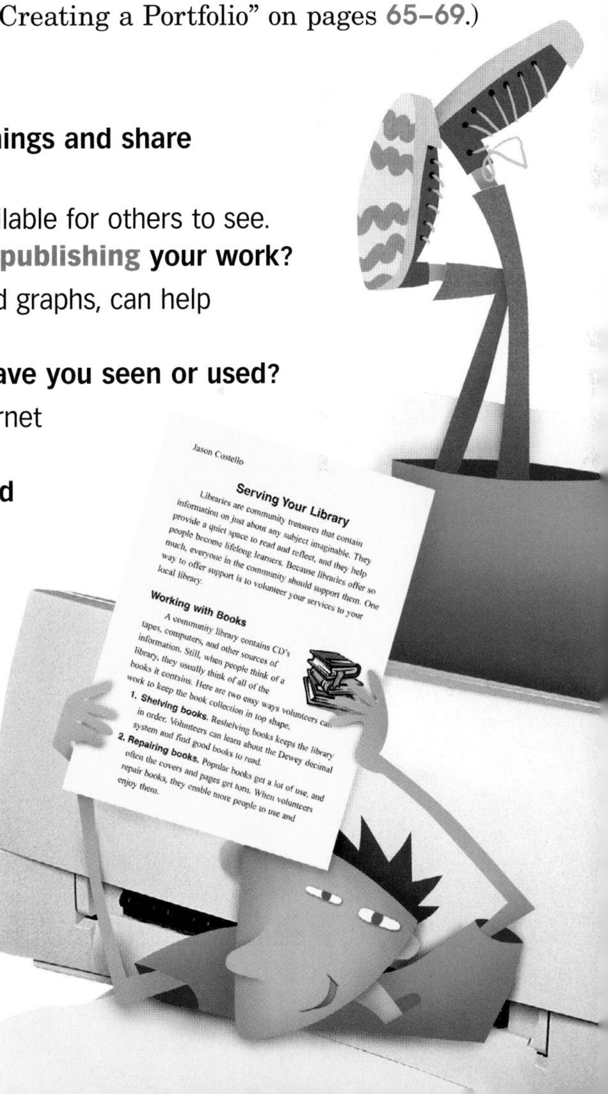

What's Ahead

- Sharing Your Writing
- Preparing to Publish
- Designing Your Writing
- Making Your Own Web Site
- Publishing Online

ELPS 3H

Sharing Your Writing

Some publishing ideas are easy to carry out, like sharing your writing with your classmates. Other publishing ideas take more time and effort, like entering a writing contest. Try a number of these publishing ideas during the school year. All of them will help you grow as a writer.

Performing

- Sharing with Classmates
- Reading to Various Audiences
- Preparing a Multimedia Presentation
- Videotaping for Special Audiences
- Performing Onstage

In School

- School Newspapers
- School Literary Magazines
- Classroom Collections
- Writing Portfolios

Self-Publishing

- Family Newsletters
- Greeting Cards
- Bound Writings
- Online Publications

Posting

- Classroom Bulletin Boards
- School or Public Libraries
- Hallway Display Cases
- Business Windows
- Clinic Waiting Rooms
- Literary/Art Fairs

Sending It Out

- Local Newspapers
- Area Historical Society
- Young Writers' Conferences
- Magazines and Contests
- Various Web Sites

Plan your publishing. Identify one piece of writing that you would like to perform. Explain to a partner why and how you would perform this writing. Then identify another piece that you would like to send out. Explain why you would send this writing out and where you would send it.

Preparing to Publish

Your writing is ready to publish when it is clear, complete, and correct. Getting your writing to this point requires careful revising and editing. Follow the tips below to prepare your writing for publication.

Publishing Tips

- **Ask for advice during the writing process.**
  Be sure your writing answers any questions your readers may have about your topic.
- **Check for focus and coherence, organization, development of ideas, and voice.**
  Every part of your writing should be clear and complete.
- **Work with your writing.**
  Continue working until you feel good about your writing from beginning to end.
- **Check your writing for conventions.**
  In addition, ask at least one classmate to check your work for this trait. Another person can catch errors that you miss.
- **Prepare a neat finished piece.**
  Use a pen (blue or black ink) and one side of the paper if you are writing by hand. If you are writing with a computer, use a font that is easy to read. Double-space your writing.
- **Know your options.**
  Explore different ways to publish your writing. (See page 58.) As you become more confident in your writing ability, you will become more interested in publishing your writing.
- **Follow all publication guidelines.**
  Just as your teacher wants assignments presented in a certain way, so do the newspapers, magazines, and Web sites that review the writing you submit.

Save all drafts for each writing project. This will help you keep track of the changes you have made. If you are preparing a portfolio, you may be required to include early drafts as well as finished pieces.

ELPS 2H, 3E, 4K

Designing Your Writing

When you write, always focus on the content or information first. Then think about how you want your paper to look. For handwritten papers, write neatly in blue or black ink on clean paper. When using a computer, follow the guidelines below.

Typography

- Use an easy-to-read font. Generally, a serif font is best for the body, and a sans serif font is used for contrast in headings.

  The letters of serif fonts have "tails"—as in this sentence.

  The letters of sans serif fonts are plain—as in this sentence.

- Use a title and headings. Headings break writing into smaller parts, making the writing easier to follow.

Spacing and Margins

- Use one-inch margins on all sides of your paper.
- Indent the first line of every paragraph.
- Use one space after every period and comma.
- Avoid awkward breaks between pages. Don't leave a heading or the first line of a paragraph at the bottom of a page or a column. Never split a hyphenated word between pages or columns.

Graphic Devices

- If possible, use bulleted lists in your writing. Often, a series of items works best as a bulleted list (like the ones on this page).
- Include graphics where appropriate. A table, a chart, or an illustration can help make a point clearer. But keep each graphic small enough so that it doesn't dominate the page. A larger graphic can be displayed by itself on a separate page.

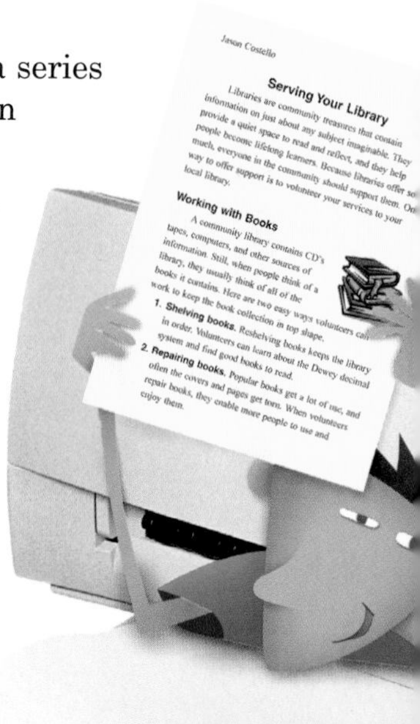

Share effective design. Find an article in a magazine or newspaper that contains many design features. Share the article with the class and identify the features. Do all of the features work effectively?

Computer Design in Action

The following two pages show a well-designed student essay. The side notes explain all of the design features.

The title is 18-point type.

The main text is 12-point type and double-spaced.

Headings are 14-point type.

A graphic is inserted for visual interest.

Numbered lists identify options.

Jason Costello

Serving Your Library

Libraries are community treasures that contain information on just about any subject imaginable. They provide a quiet space to read and reflect, and they help people become lifelong learners. Because libraries offer so much, everyone in the community should support them. One way to offer support is to volunteer your services to your local library.

Working with Books

A community library contains CDs, tapes, computers, and other sources of information. Still, when people think of a library, they usually think of all the books it contains. Here are two easy ways volunteers can work to keep the book collection in top shape.

1. **Shelving books.** Reshelving books keeps the library in order. Volunteers can learn about the Dewey decimal system and find good books to read.
2. **Repairing books.** Popular books get a lot of use, and often the covers and pages get torn. When volunteers repair books, they enable more people to use and enjoy them.

The writer's last name and the page number appear on every page starting with page 2.

A bulleted list helps organize the essay.

Margins are at least one inch all around.

Costello 2

Working with People

Another way to help out at the library is to work with others. Volunteers can use their people skills in one of the following ways:

- **Reading out loud.** Most libraries have children's story hours and need extra people to read to children. This is a good choice for people who like entertaining others.
- **Being read to.** Sometimes children have trouble reading, and it may be helpful for them to read out loud to another person. Volunteers can be good listeners and help struggling readers improve.
- **Matching people with materials.** Another volunteer job is helping people locate books or other library resources.

Finding Your Place

Stop in and have a talk with your local librarian after deciding which services you can offer. See how you can volunteer to make your library the best it can be for everyone in your community.

Design a page. Create an effective design for an essay or a report you've already written. Share your design with a classmate to get some feedback: Does your design make the writing clear and easy to follow? Does your design distract the reader in any way?

Making Your Own Web Site

You can make your own Web site if your family has an Internet account. Ask your provider how to get started. If you are using a school account, ask your teacher for help. Then start designing your site. Use the questions and answers below as a starting point.

How do I plan my site?

Think about the purpose of your Web site and how many pages you need. Will one page be enough space, or will you require several pages? Check out other sites for ideas. Then make sketches to plan your pages.

How do I make the pages?

Start each page as a text file by using your computer. Many new word processing programs let you save a file as a Web page. If yours doesn't, you will have to add HTML (Hypertext Markup Language) codes to format the text and make links to graphics and other pages. You can find instructions for HTML on the Internet or at the library.

How do I know whether my pages work?

You should always test your pages. Using your browser, open your first page. Then follow the links to make sure they work correctly and that all the pages look right.

How do I get my pages on the Internet?

You must upload your finished pages to the Internet. (Ask your Internet provider how to do this.) After the upload, visit your site to make sure it still works. Also, check it from other computers if possible.

How do I let people know about my site?

Once your site is up, e-mail your friends and tell them to visit it!

Try It Visit a number of different sites for ideas. On your own paper, answer these questions about each one: What is especially good about this site? What could be better? Also talk about these sites with your classmates and friends. When designing your own pages, refer to your research for ideas.

Publishing Online

The Internet offers many publishing opportunities, including online magazines and writing contests. The information below will help you submit your writing on the Internet. (At home, always get a parent's approval first. In school, follow all guidelines for computer use.)

How should I get started?

Check with your teacher to see if your school has its own Web site where you can post your work. Also ask your teacher about other Web sites. There are a number of online magazines that accept student writing. Visit some of these magazines to learn about the types of writing they usually publish.

How do I search for possible sites?

Use a search engine to find places to publish. Some search engines offer their own student links.

How do I submit my work?

Before you do anything, make sure that you understand the publishing guidelines for each site. Be sure to share this information with your teacher and your parents. Then follow these steps:

- **Send your writing in the correct form.**
  Some sites have online forms. Others will ask you to send your writing by mail or e-mail. Always explain why you are sending your writing.
- **Give the publisher information for contacting you.**
  However, don't give your home address or any other personal information unless your parents approve.
- **Be patient.**
  A site may contact you within a week to confirm that your work has arrived. However, it may be several weeks before you hear whether your writing will be used or not.

Search for Web sites. Use the guidelines above to search the Internet for sites that publish student work. Create a list of sites to share with the class. When you complete writing assignments, consider submitting your work for publication using one of the Web sites from your class list.

ELPS 2C, 3E, 4G

Creating a Portfolio

Would it be fair if people judged your overall writing ability by looking at the very first thing that you wrote in the fall? Not at all. It would be like meeting someone for the first time as you shuffled down to breakfast, sleepy. Obviously, you would not make your best impression at such a moment.

Your writing skills can be judged best by looking at a collection of your writing developed throughout a grading period. This type of collection is often called a *writing portfolio*, and it gives a clear, complete picture of you as a writer.

This chapter will help you develop a writing portfolio. It includes information about the types and parts of portfolios, plus planning ideas.

Learning Language

Work with a partner. Read the meanings and share answers to the questions.

1. A portfolio is a collection of a person's work.
   Which pieces of writing would you put in your portfolio? Why?
2. Your best work belongs in a showcase for others to admire.
   What kinds of collections might you find in a showcase?
3. A reflection is a personal thought about something that you did in the past.
   Share a reflection about something important that you have done.

What's Ahead

- **Types of Portfolios**
- **Parts of a Portfolio**
- **Planning Ideas**
- **Sample Portfolio Reflections**

Types of Portfolios

There are four basic types of portfolios you should know about: a showcase portfolio, a growth portfolio, a personal portfolio, and an electronic portfolio.

Showcase Portfolio

A showcase portfolio presents the best writing you have done in school. A showcase is the most common type of portfolio and is usually put together for evaluation at the end of a grading period.

Growth Portfolio

A growth portfolio shows your progress as a writer. It contains many writing assignments and shows how your writing skills are developing:

- writing beginnings and endings,
- writing with voice,
- using specific details, and
- using transitions.

Personal Portfolio

A personal portfolio contains writing you want to keep and share with others. Many professional people—including writers, artists, and musicians—keep personal portfolios. You can arrange this type of portfolio according to different types of writing, different themes, and so on.

Electronic Portfolio

An electronic portfolio is any type of portfolio (showcase, growth, or personal) available on a CD or a Web site. Besides your writing, you can include graphics, video, and sound with this type of portfolio. This makes your writing available to friends and family members no matter where they are!

Rate your growth. On your own paper, list two or three skills that show how your overall writing ability is developing. Also list one or two skills that you need to work on. Make sure to review several pieces of writing before you make your choices.

Parts of a Portfolio

A showcase portfolio is one of the most common types of portfolios used in schools. It may contain the parts listed below, but always check with your teacher to be sure.

- A **table of contents** lists the writing samples you have included in your portfolio.
- A **brief essay** or **letter** introduces your portfolio—telling how you put it together, how you feel about it, and what it means to you.
- A **collection of writing samples** presents your best work. Your teacher may require that you include all of your prewriting, drafting, and revising for one or more of your writings.
- A **cover sheet for each sample** explains why you selected it.
- **Evaluations, reflections,** or **checklists** identify the basic skills you have mastered, as well as those skills that you still need to work on.

Gathering Tips

- **Keep track of all your work.** Include prewriting notes, first drafts, and revisions for each writing assignment. Then, when you put together a portfolio, you will have everything that you need.
- **Store all of your writing in a pocket folder or computer file.** This will help you keep track of your writing as you build your portfolio.
- **Set a schedule for working on your portfolio.** You can't put together a good portfolio by waiting until the last minute.
- **Take pride in your work.** Make sure that your portfolio shows you at your best.

Write a cover sheet. Think of the best piece of writing you've done this year. Why is it your best piece? What parts are especially good? How did other people react to the writing? Then write a sample cover sheet for this writing, explaining why you would include it in your portfolio.

Planning Ideas

The following tips will help you choose your best pieces of writing to include in your portfolio.

1 Be patient.

Don't make quick decisions about which pieces of writing to include in your portfolio. Just keep gathering everything—including all of your drafts—until you are ready to review all of your writing assignments.

2 Make good decisions.

When it's time to choose writing for your portfolio, review each piece. Remember the feelings that you had during each assignment. Which piece makes you feel the best? Which one did your readers like the best? Which one taught you the most?

3 Reflect on your choices.

Read the sample reflections on page 69. Then answer these questions about your writing:

- Why did I choose this piece?
- Why did I write this piece? (What was my purpose?)
- How did I write it? (What was my process?)
- What does it show about my writing ability?
- How did my peers react to this writing?
- What would I do differently next time?
- What have I learned since writing it?

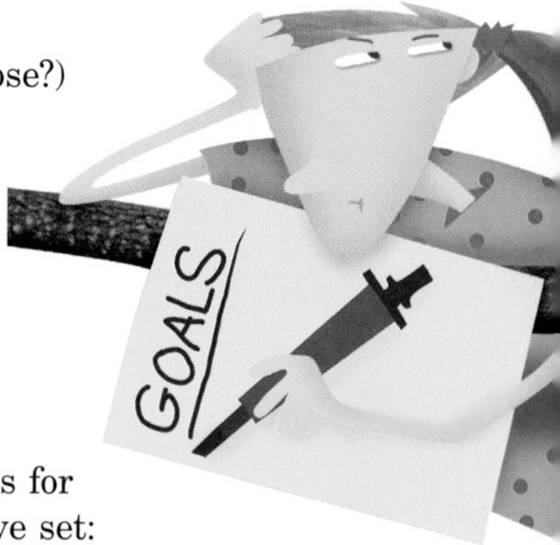

4 Set future writing goals.

After putting your portfolio together, set some goals for the future. Here are some goals that other students have set:

I will write about topics that really interest me.

I will spend more time on my beginnings and endings.

I will make sure that my sentences read smoothly.

I will support my main points with convincing details.

Plan a portfolio cover. On a piece of plain paper, design a cover for a portfolio folder. Include your name and an interesting title. Add sketches or photos related to your writing, your classes, your favorite hobby, and so on.

Sample Portfolio Reflections

When you take time to reflect on your writing assignments, think about the process that you used to develop each one. Also think about what you might do differently next time. The following samples will help you with your own reflections.

Student Reflections

If I had to write another comparison essay, I would think more carefully about my topics. To make effective comparisons, there must be a number of meaningful similarities and differences to write about. I would also do a lot more research before I started my writing. When my classmates rated my essay, I could tell that they had a lot of questions about the information I included. Next time, I will seek their advice much earlier in the writing process.

—Anna Hernandez

My persuasive essay on proposing a solution turned out really well. This happened because I felt so strongly about my topic. I really do think that students would become better writers if we had a writing lab open before and after school. I learned from this essay that the words and ideas come easy if I have strong feelings about a topic. I also learned that these strong feelings helped make my writing voice sound really convincing. —Roy Baker

Professional Reflections

I wrote *Mad Merlin* by combining legends of Camelot with histories and myths. As I look back at the novel, though, I see it is mostly about my own life. Good fiction is that way—creative in the details, but otherwise full of truth.

—J. Robert King

With each book I write, I become more and more convinced that the books have a life of their own, quite apart from me. —Madeleine L'Engle

SPECIFY

picture

ELPS 2C, 3E, 4G

TEXAS WRITE SOURCE Online

www.hmheducation.com/tx/writesource

Descriptive Writing

Writing Focus

- **Descriptive Paragraph**
- **Descriptive Essay**

Learning Language

Work with a partner. Read the meanings and share answers to the prompts.

1. A **description** tells what something is like.
   Give a description of an item in the room.
2. If something is your **favorite**, it means you like it best.
   What is your favorite meal?
3. **Sensory details** are words that describe how something looks, smells, sounds, feels, or tastes.
   Use sensory details to describe your favorite season.
4. Your **home away from home** is a place where you feel as comfortable and relaxed as you do when you are in your own home.
   Describe one place that is a home away from home for you.

express

describe

portray

Descriptive Writing

Descriptive Paragraph

All kids have a favorite place where they like to spend time, either alone or with their friends. It could be a room at home, a particular spot in the park, or maybe a neighborhood restaurant with the "World's Juiciest Burgers."

In this chapter, you will write a paragraph to describe a favorite place. You will need to use plenty of sensory details to re-create this place. Your goal is to help readers see the sights, smell the aromas, feel the atmosphere, and hear the sounds as if the readers were right there with you.

Writing Guidelines

Subject: A favorite place
Purpose: To describe one of your favorite places
Form: Descriptive paragraph
Audience: Classmates

ELPS 4G

Descriptive Paragraph

In a descriptive paragraph, you use details to paint a vivid picture of one person, place, thing, or event. You start with a **topic sentence** that tells what the paragraph is about. Then, in the **body** of the paragraph, you add the specific details. The **closing sentence** brings the description to an end.

Topic Sentence

Body

Closing Sentence

Bob's Deli

When I walk through the door at Bob's Deli, familiar sights and smells greet me. As usual, Bob is wiping the counter, even though it's spotless. "Hey, you," he says. He greets all his regular customers this way. Above him on the wall, giant pictures of sandwiches and salads make me even hungrier than I already am. At least six kinds of pie fill a round display case that stands next to the counter. It looks as though someone has already had a piece of the lemon meringue. A sign on the cash register announces today's special—a bowl of vegetable beef soup and half a sandwich. I sit down at the cold, shiny chrome counter and watch Bob pour a thick smoothie into a tall glass. As he plops a fresh strawberry on top, my stomach growls, and I am ready to place my order.

Respond to the reading. On your own paper, answer the following questions.

- ☐ **Development of Ideas (1) What details did the writer use to "paint" a picture? Name three of them.**
- ☐ **Organization (2) Which order of location pattern did the writer use (left to right, right to left, top to bottom, far to near)?**
- ☐ **Voice (3) What phrases show that the writer really likes Bob's Deli? List two of them.**

Prewriting Selecting a Topic

To get started, think about places you could write about. Clustering is one way to begin. The writer of the paragraph on page 72 used a cluster like the one below to remember some favorite places.

Cluster

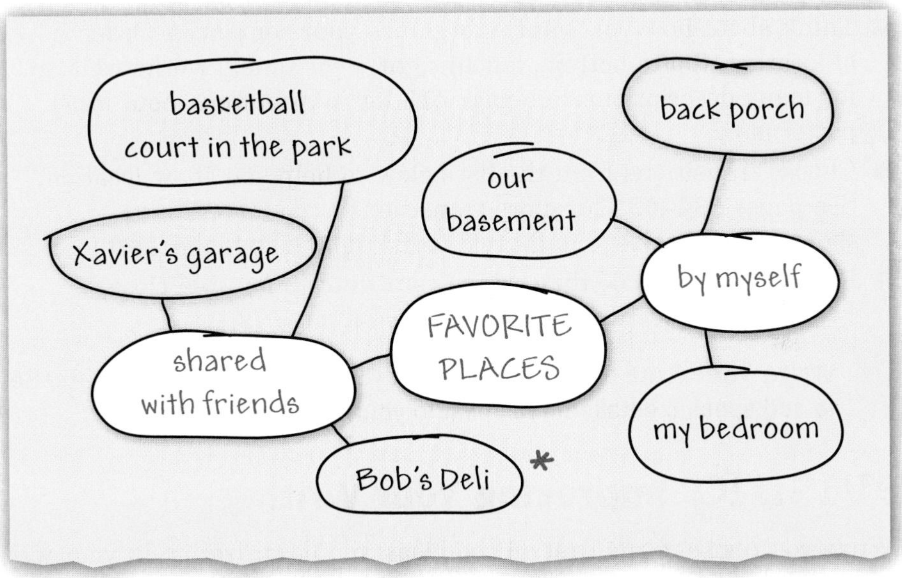

Prewrite **Select a topic. Create your own cluster to identify possible places to write about in your paragraph. Then "star" one place you'd like to describe.**

Gathering Details

Collect plenty of sensory details about your topic, even though you might not use all of them in your paragraph. Choose details that will help you create a clear, vivid description.

Prewrite **Collect your details. Use the following questions to help you remember important details.**

- **What are the main sights and sounds?**
- **Are there any parts in this place that stand out?**
- **What colors are important?**
- **What smells and tastes do you connect with this place?**
- **What feelings do you have about it?**
- **What happens in this place?**

TEKS 7.14B, 7.14C

Drafting Creating Your First Draft

The goal of a first draft is to get all of your ideas and details down on paper. Remember that everything does not have to be perfect in a first draft. You can make as many changes as you want later on.

- Start your paragraph with a topic sentence that identifies a favorite place and interests your reader.
- Think about how you want to organize your sentences. Order of location (top to bottom, left to right, near to far) works well for many descriptions. See page 613 for information about other patterns.
- Choose transitions from the list below to help you show location. See pages 634–635 for more transitions.
  above, below, beside   to the left, to the right   on top of, next to
- End with a sentence that brings your description to a close. See the closing sentence in the model on page 72.

Draft **Write your first draft.** Use the guidelines above when you write. Be sure to add specific details that appeal to your reader's senses.

Revising Improving Your Writing

When you revise, focus first on the ideas and organization in your writing. You may move, delete, or change parts of your writing as necessary.

Revise **Revise your paragraph.** Use the following questions as a guide.

1. Does my topic sentence identify the place I'm describing?
2. Have I included enough sensory details?
3. Have I put the details in the best order?
4. Do I use specific nouns, verbs, and adjectives?
5. Do I use complete sentences that read smoothly?

Editing Checking for Conventions

Carefully edit your revised paragraph for grammar, punctuation, capitalization, and spelling.

Edit **Proofread and edit your work.** Use the conventions checklist on page 128 as you edit. Then write a neat final copy.

Descriptive Writing

Describing a Place

"Ah, my room. . . . Let me show you around. Do you see how I display all my stylish clothes across the floor? Do you hear the gentle snoring of my dog Urfie as he warms the foot of my bed? Do you detect that strange odor coming from the closet? Ah hah! That must be my gym shoes."

When you describe a familiar place, you take your reader on a tour using your best words. Your goal is to let the reader see the things around you, hear what is happening, and maybe even smell the gym shoes!

Writing Guidelines

Subject: A place you know well
Purpose: To describe a familiar place
Form: Descriptive essay
Audience: Classmates

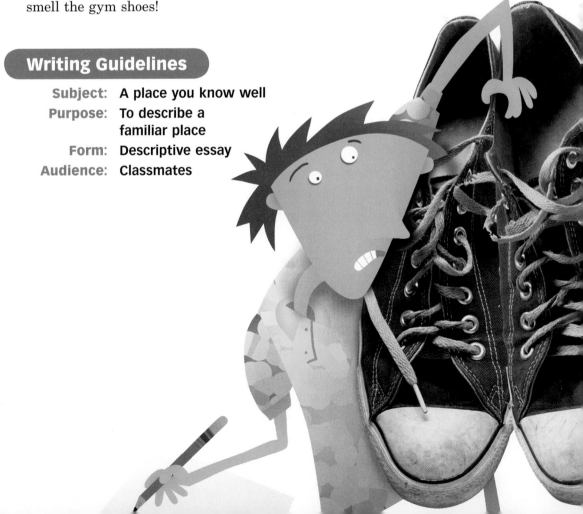

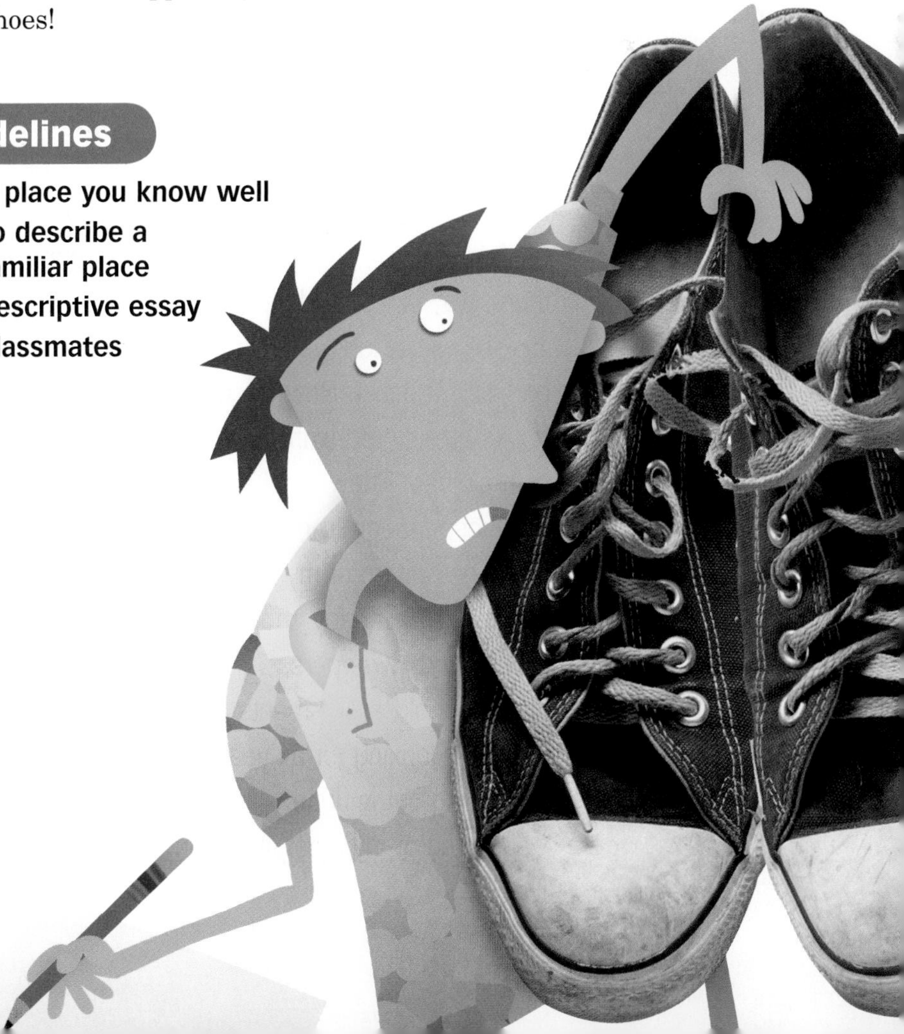

Descriptive Essay

In the sample essay that follows, the writer describes his locker. As you read the description, look at the notes in the left margin. They explain the important parts of the essay.

Beginning
The beginning shows why this place is special.

Middle
The middle paragraphs describe the locker from top to bottom.

My Home Away from Home

Blue metal lockers line the hallways in our school. Each locker is identical except for the brass number attached to the door. Locker number 379 is mine. This locker is my home away from home for the year.

When I click open my locker, the smell of peanut butter escapes from a brown paper lunch bag on the top shelf. Under the bag, the sleeve of my old olive green sweatshirt dangles off the shelf. On top of everything is my favorite blue cap. Some magazines that I've shoved up there, way in the back, almost hide my dead CD player.

All winter long, my ski jacket was stuffed in the middle part of my locker. Now the only things hanging on the hooks are my red warm-up jacket and my bag full of dirty gym clothes. Phew. That smell mixed with the peanut butter is almost enough to make me gag.

The bottom of my locker is like a mini dump site. It is filled with my muddy shoes, broken pencils, and a pile of sticky candy wrappers. Buried underneath all of that are dozens of old assignments and, probably, some things I've been looking for all year. I'll know for sure when I dig everything out in June.

Some of my most important stuff is attached to the

Middle
Special attention is given to the locker door.

inside of my locker door. Near the top, I've taped two pictures of my favorite rock group. Around the edges, I've jammed in a bunch of notes from my friends. Below the notes, a collection of fridge magnets from my favorite pizza places hold up a huge photo of me with the 10-pound bass I landed last summer.

Ending
The ending gives more insight into the writer's personality.

On the last day of school, I'll take down the pictures and throw out the candy wrappers and trash. I'll stuff all the important things into my backpack and grab those smelly gym clothes. When I close my locker for the last time and head for home, it will feel as if I've just completed another chapter in my life.

Respond to the reading. **Answer the following questions about the essay.**

- ☐ **Development of Ideas** **(1) What comparison does the writer make to introduce the topic? (2) Which details rely on a sense other than sight? Name two.**
- ☐ **Organization** **(3) How is the essay organized?**
- ☐ **Voice** **(4) Which details reveal the most about the writer's personality?**

TEKS 7.14A
ELPS 4G

Prewriting Selecting a Topic

The topic for your essay should be a place that is very familiar to you. Make sure that you choose a place that isn't too big or too small. Think of places that you can describe in a few paragraphs with many interesting details. A topic chart like the one below can help you organize your thoughts.

Topic Chart

Places	*Specific Topics*
Home	*– my bedroom* *– our backyard* *– the kitchen*
School	*– my locker* *– the music room* *– the office*
Other	*– Rico's Pizza* *– my grandma's kitchen* *– the city beach*

Prewrite **Create a topic chart.** Make a chart like the one above, using *Home, School,* and *Other.* Think of two or three specific topics for each category. Circle the one specific topic that you would like to write about.

Gathering Details

One way to gather details is to make a list of sensory details. Sensory details help the reader see, feel, smell, taste, and hear what is being described.

Prewrite **Collect details.** Gather sensory details for your description by answering the following questions.

1. What do you see when you look around your place? (Think about colors, shapes, and sizes.)
2. What sounds do you hear?
3. What smells do you notice?
4. What textures can you touch?
5. What tastes or feelings come to mind?

Organizing Your Details

You can use order of location (spatial order) to arrange the details in a description. For example, you may decide to organize the details from top to bottom or from left to right or farthest to nearest. The writer of the essay on pages 76–77 organized the details from top to bottom on a list.

Organizing List

1. *Open the locker door.*
2. *Describe what's on the top shelf.*
3. *Tell what's hanging in the middle part.*
4. *Draw a mental picture of what's on the bottom.*
5. *Describe the inside of the locker door.*
6. *Share the details of the last day of school.*

Prewrite **Organize your details.** Decide which order works best for your description (top to bottom, left to right, far to near). Then write an organizing list like the one above for your essay.

Using Similes and Metaphors

Similes and metaphors can make descriptive writing clearer and more creative. They can help readers see the description in their minds. The writer of the essay on pages 76–77 uses a metaphor in the opening paragraph and a simile in the third middle paragraph.

- A **simile** compares two different things using *like* or *as*.

  The bottom of my locker is like a mini dump site.

- A **metaphor** compares two different things without using *like* or *as*.

  This locker is my home away from home for the year.

Try It Write a simile and a metaphor to compare your place with other things. If you like how your comparisons turn out, include them in your essay.

Drafting Starting Your Descriptive Essay

The beginning paragraph should get your reader's attention and identify your topic—a familiar place. Here are two ways to get started.

Beginning Paragraph

- **Put yourself in the description.** You can do this by serving as the narrator. This means that you will use "I" and describe the place through your eyes.

The writer tells how she feels.

When I stand on our back step and look out, I see more than just a backyard. I see my family's "summer home," a small, relaxing plot of land protected by a redwood fence.

- **Begin with background information.** This information will help your reader better understand or appreciate your topic.

The writer shows why this place is special.

When my mom's job forced us to move into the city, she decided to create a quiet place for us to relax. That's just what she did in our backyard. With a lot of work, we now have a peaceful "getaway" to enjoy.

Using Words with Feeling

Don't settle for just any word to capture the description of the place you are describing. Use words that have the right meaning and the right feeling, or connotation. (*Connotation* means "the feeling that a word suggests.")

The writer of each of the beginning paragraphs above uses words like "summer home," "relaxing," "quiet," and "peaceful" because they all have the right feeling—the backyard is a place to unwind and enjoy yourself.

Draft

Write your beginning paragraph. Write a beginning that catches your reader's interest and focuses on your topic. Make sure to use words with the right feeling. If you don't like how your first opening turns out, try again.

Developing the Middle Part

In the middle paragraphs of the essay, describe your familiar place. Use your organizing list from page 79 as a guide for your writing. Be sure to use a variety of sentence types.

Middle Paragraphs

In the middle paragraphs, the writer first describes the three sides of the backyard before focusing on the lawn in the center.

Each middle paragraph focuses on a different part of the yard.

The underlined phrases show the organization of the essay.

Sentence variety helps to keep the reader's interest.

Along the fence at the left side of the yard are my mom's famous red rosebushes. They explode with color all summer long. A flat stone walkway running in front of the bushes makes it easy to admire and smell the flowers. These stones are smooth and warm against my bare feet.

Against the back fence is a small white shed. The shed holds my mom's garden tools and an old push mower. It also holds our bicycles and a lot of sports equipment, including my favorite basketball. On rainy days, I like to stand in the shed and hear the raindrops hitting the metal roof.

My mother's vegetable garden runs next to the fence on the right side of the yard. Mom always plants beans in that space. As the bean plants grow, she carefully ties them to stakes to keep them from falling over. In the front of this garden is a row of golden yellow marigolds. Their distinct smell is supposed to keep the rabbits away from the beans.

At the heart of our yard is the lawn itself. A crab apple tree towers over the back of the yard and provides plenty of shade. In front of the tree is a wooden lawn swing that gets plenty of use, especially in the evening. To the right of the swing is a yellow plastic sandbox where my little brother and sister play for hours at a time.

Draft

Write your middle paragraphs. Use sensory details in your paragraphs to help the reader imagine how your place looks, feels, sounds, and smells. Vary your sentence types to keep the reader interested.

Drafting Ending Your Essay

The ending paragraph should clearly signal that your description is complete. In the last sentence or two, leave your reader with a final idea or image—something that will keep her or him thinking about your topic.

Ending Paragraph

The writer makes a final comment about the topic.

Beyond my yard lies a busy city. On hot summer nights, when we relax in the yard, I can hear the rush of freeway traffic and the call of far-off train whistles. I'm sure that someday I'll join the traffic or follow the train whistles, but for now, I'm happy right here.

Draft **Write your ending paragraph.** Use interesting details that will keep this place in your reader's memory for some time.

Revising and Editing

You can improve your first draft by adding, deleting, or changing some details. Keep these questions in mind when you revise.

Revise **Revise your first draft.** Revise your first draft using the questions below as a guide.

- ☐ **Focus and Coherence** Do I have a clear, focused topic? Do all the parts of my essay support my topic?
- ☐ **Organization** Do I use order of location to organize the details?
- ☐ **Development of Ideas** Have I included enough sensory details about the place? Do the ideas flow smoothly and give the reader a mental picture of my place?
- ☐ **Voice** Do I sound like I really care about the subject and the reader?

Edit **Edit your description.** Once you have completed your revising, use the checklist on page 128 to correct any errors in your essay. Then write a neat final copy to share.

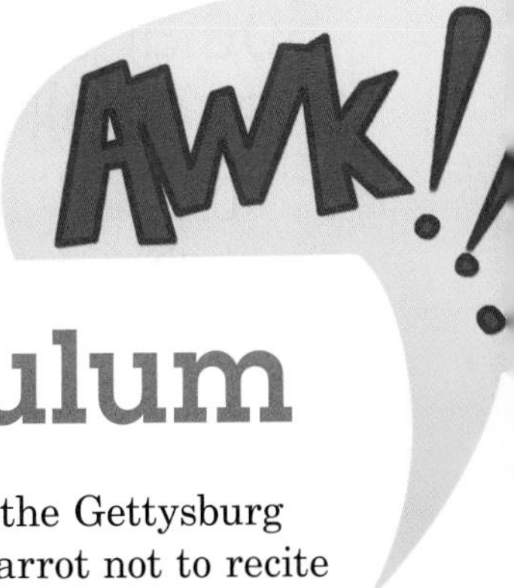

Descriptive Writing

Across the Curriculum

Wouldn't it be great if you could teach a parrot to recite the Gettysburg Address? Wouldn't it be even better if you could teach your parrot not to recite the speech all day and all night? Finally, wouldn't it be the greatest if you could write an ad that describes your parrot so well that a kind and caring bird lover comes to buy him? Descriptive writing can be useful.

Sometimes, descriptive writing can also be useful in completing class assignments. For example, in social studies, you could describe a famous person or place. In math, you could describe a geometric object, or in science, you could describe the result of a lab experiment.

What's Ahead

- **Social Studies:** Describing a Famous Place
- **Math:** Writing a Geometric Riddle
- **Science:** Writing a Lab Report
- **Practical Writing:** Writing a Personal Letter

Social Studies:
Describing a Famous Place

Use descriptive writing when you need to explain the features of a place. Think about a structure or natural wonder that you have read about or visited. The writer below chose to write about the Caverns of Sonora.

The **beginning** shares important background information.

The **middle** describes the place from location to location.

The **ending** gives the reader something to think about.

The Caverns of Sonora

Every day, visitors to the Caverns of Sonora enter a cave that is over a million years old. The caverns, which look like they belong on another planet, are named to match the interesting formations inside.

One of the first rooms on the tour is called the War Club room. Mineral deposits shaped like battle weapons line the floor and ceiling. Rough textures and amber colors make the formations look like stone.

The Valley of Ice comes next. In this Arctic-like room, icicle formations hang from the ceiling and the look of windswept snow covers the walls and floor. The white color comes from the purity of the minerals.

Beyond the valley lies the Butterfly formation, the only one like it in the world. It is made of two growths coming out from the wall to meet together. The result is a beautiful crystal butterfly.

The tour ends with a walk through the famous Crystal Palace. Stepping into this beautiful room is like taking a walk through a crystal-lined geode.

These are just a few of the natural wonders that can be found at the Caverns of Sonora. The million years of history are a sight to be seen.

TEKS 7.17A(iii)
ELPS 3H

Writing Tips

Before you write . . .

- **Choose a famous place that interests you.**
  Select a place related to a subject you are studying in social studies class.
- **Do your research.**
  Learn about your place. Look at pictures of it and read about its history and culture.
- **Take notes.**
  Collect important details that will help create a clear description in the reader's mind.

During your writing . . .

- **Write a clear beginning, middle, and ending.**
  Begin with a little-known fact or a comparison. In the middle, describe the place using precise words. End with a final thought that inspires your reader to find out even more.
- **Organize your thoughts.**
  Describe your place in order of location, from top to bottom, from left to right, or from near to far. Make sure that the information from paragraph to paragraph is consistent.
- **Use an engaging voice.**
  Your writing should give the impression that you know a lot about the place and are interested in it.

After you've written a first draft . . .

- **Check for completeness.**
  Make sure that you have included details that allow the reader to imagine your place in his or her mind. Check for inconsistencies.
- **Check for correctness.**
  Proofread your essay to make sure there are no mistakes in grammar, punctuation, capitalization, or spelling.

Try It Choose a famous place that interests you and learn more about it. Then write a consistent, clear description to share with your classmates.

Math: Writing a Geometric Riddle

Descriptive writing can be used to write about objects. Below, a student writes a riddle for math class using geometric terms.

The writer uses personification to describe the object.

The writer rhymes the second and fourth lines.

An Ancient Wonder

I stand upon a giant square
And have four triangle faces.
My polyhedron family
Lives near a large oasis.
What am I?

Answer: An Egyptian pyramid

More About Riddles

Riddles are rewarding mental exercises. They encourage you to use your imagination and build new language skills. Riddles are also creative forms of descriptive writing. The simplest form of riddle, the "What Am I?" riddle, has been around for a long time. Court jesters used this type of riddle to entertain kings and queens for centuries.

TEKS 7.15B(i)
ELPS 3E

Writing Tips

Before you write . . .

- **Think about different geometric shapes and figures.** There are many to choose from, such as the triangle, rectangle, square, parallelogram, pentagon, cube, and sphere.
- **Look at the world around you.** Choose an object to describe that contains specific geometric shapes and figures. The object is the answer to your riddle.
- **Study your object.** Read about your object and answer the 5 Ws to gather information for your description.
- **Jot down details.** Write down specific words and phrases to describe your object. Be sure to include some geometric terms. Begin to think about rhyming words as you do this.

During your writing . . .

- **Be creative.** Think of different ways to write your riddle. Here are a few suggestions.

  Use metaphors. Compare the object to something else.

  Use personification. Describe the object as if it were a living thing.

  Create a surprise ending. Let the ending take a funny or unexpected twist.

  Make it rhyme. Try to make your riddle rhyme. Look at poems and study different rhyme schemes. Try to make the words and phrases you write fit into a rhyme scheme.

After you've written a first draft . . .

- **Check for completeness.** Have you used the best words to describe your object? Have you included enough information for readers to answer the riddle?
- **Check for correctness.** Are the words spelled correctly? Do you use the correct words *(angle, angel; right, write)*?

Try It Write a geometric riddle of your own following the tips above. Make the riddle rhyme. Share your riddle with your classmates.

Science: Writing a Lab Report

In science class, you may be asked to write a lab report. The student report below describes which variables (variety of conditions) make mold grow fastest on bread.

In the **beginning** the purpose is stated, variables are listed, and a hypothesis is given.

A Moldy Problem

PURPOSE: Find out what conditions will make mold grow fastest on bread.

VARIABLES: Temperature and moisture

HYPOTHESIS: Mold will grow fastest on bread that is kept warm and moist.

The **middle** clearly describes the experiment and what the writer observed.

EXPERIMENT: Four slices of freshly baked white bread were put into sandwich bags and labeled A, B, C, and D. A small amount (2 T.) of water was placed in Bags A and B. Bag A was placed inside a warm, dark cabinet. Bag B was placed in the refrigerator. Bags C and D got no water. Bag C was placed in the refrigerator, and Bag D was placed inside the warm, dark cabinet. The bags were checked daily for one week, and any changes were observed.

OBSERVATIONS: Nothing happened until the fifth day. The slices of bread in the refrigerator appeared fresh. The dry bread in the cabinet had no mold. The moist bread in the warm cabinet was starting to grow spots of greenish-gray mold on the crust.

The **ending** reports the writer's conclusion.

CONCLUSION: The hypothesis that mold will grow fastest on bread that is kept warm and moist was correct. It was expected that the mold would appear sooner than it did.

Writing Tips

Before you write . . .

- **Choose a topic that interests you.**
  Select a science topic related to a subject you are studying in school.
- **Research your topic and plan your experiment.**
  Read about your topic and jot down important details. Then decide what your experiment will be.

During your writing . . .

- **State the purpose, the variables, and your hypothesis.**
  Write a statement that describes what you want to do. Tell which variable(s) you will test. Then write a hypothesis telling what you think you will find out from your experiment.
- **Organize your details.**
  Use time order to describe the procedure you followed (what happened first, second, next, and so on).
- **Use strong, colorful words.**
  A good description contains strong verbs, and specific nouns, adjectives, and adverbs.
- **Clearly state your observations and conclusion.**
  Your observations should describe what happened during your experiment. Your conclusion should tell whether or not your hypothesis was correct.

Time line

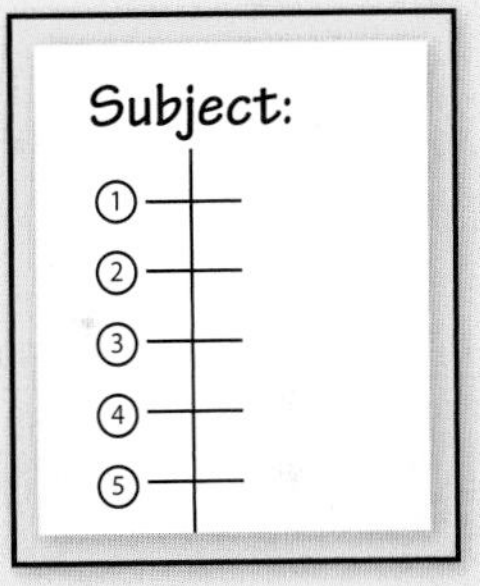

After you've written a first draft . . .

- **Check for completeness.**
  Be sure that you have clearly stated the purpose, variables, hypothesis, and conclusion. Check your experiment and observation. Be sure you include all the important details.
- **Check for correctness.**
  Proofread your report for grammar, punctuation, capitalization, and spelling.

Try It Select and perform a science experiment. Then describe it in a lab report using the tips above as a guide.

TEKS 7.17B

Practical Writing:
Writing a Personal Letter

In everyday life, you will find descriptive writing used in many ways. A personal letter can contain descriptive writing to share an opinion, express a complaint, or ask for information. Read the student-written letter below.

The heading includes your address and the date, and the salutation identifies the person you are writing to.

123 Blue Heron Lane
Dallas, TX 75243

May 15, 2011

Dear Inez,

The beginning introduces the writer, explains the issue, and includes an opinion.

Thank you for agreeing to help me with my new hamster, Stella. She is doing very well.

I need to buy a new cage. I prefer the cages that are multi-level. I especially like the brightly colored ones with tubes. They look like little spaceships!

The middle describes the complaint and asks for information.

The first cage I bought had a huge flaw. The flimsy water bottle it came with leaked everywhere. The shavings at the bottom of the cage were a soaked, smelly mess. The pet store told me that there had been other similar complaints. I decided to find a better cage.

I was wondering if you could send me the information about the cage that you are using for your hamster. If I remember correctly, it is three levels and plastic. I would like to know the model and brand name of the cage, the size, and the price.

Thanks again for your help. Stella and I feel much better having your advice. I look forward to hearing from you soon.

The closing and signature complete the letter.

Sincerely,

Crisanna

TEKS 7.17B

Writing Tips

Before you write . . .

- **Choose an audience.**
  Choose a friend or relative to write to.
- **Select a topic for your letter.**
  Pick an issue that you have an opinion about. Think of a complaint or problem with this particular issue. Then decide on information that you can request related to the issue.
- **List specific information to request.**
  Make a list of the specific details you will need to include when asking for information. This might include model numbers, prices, sizes, or amounts.

During your writing . . .

- **Organize your thoughts.**
  Identify your issue and state your opinion. Then state your complaint.
- **Use colorful words.**
  A good description contains strong verbs and specific nouns, adjectives, and adverbs. Specific details will also help you request the information you want.
- **Be concise and focused.**
  Stay on topic when you write your letter. Do not include unnecessary details that take you away from the issue that you are describing.

After you've written a first draft . . .

- **Check for completeness.**
  Did you explain your issue? Did you state your opinion clearly? Have you asked for the necessary information? Is your writing clear and focused?
- **Check for correctness.**
  Proofread your letter to make sure there are no mistakes in grammar, capitalization, punctuation, or spelling.

Try It Write a personal letter. State an opinion and/or complaint and request information about your topic. Use the tips above as a guide.

tell
relate

ELPS 2C, 3D, 3E, 4G

TEXAS WRITE SOURCE Online
www.hmheducation.com/tx/writesource

Narrative Writing

Writing Focus

- Narrative Paragraph
- Personal Narrative
- Phase Autobiography

Grammar Focus

- Misplaced Modifiers
- Adverbial Clauses

Learning Language

Work with a partner. Read the meanings and share answers to the questions

1. A narrative is a story.
   What are some narratives that you have read?
2. An experience is one or more events.
   Tell about an interesting experience you have had.
3. A transition is a word or phrase that ties ideas together.
   Explain how you would use the words *next, finally,* and *suddenly* as transitions.

narrate
remember
share

Narrative Writing

Narrative Paragraph

Think of a time when something really exciting happened to you. Maybe you won a basketball game, or caught a big fish, or got an "A" on a tough test. Now imagine telling a friend all about it. That's what a "narrative" is—a story about something that has happened. We all tell such stories at one time or another.

In this chapter, you will write a paragraph that tells about a great moment in your life. Once you are finished, you and your classmates can share these personal stories with each other.

Writing Guidelines

Subject: A great moment
Purpose: To entertain
Form: Narrative paragraph
Audience: Classmates

ELPS 4G

Narrative Paragraph

By remembering the great experiences in your life and telling stories about them, you can relive those moments over and over. In the following narrative paragraph, Devon opens with a **topic sentence** that identifies the experience. Next, the **body** of his paragraph recalls the events. Finally, the **closing sentence** tells how the experience ended.

Topic Sentence

Body

Closing Sentence

Getting Game

The teachers were winning the annual student-faculty basketball game 42 to 40. One minute remained, and Coach Williams had the ball. He tried to dodge around me at midcourt, but I reached in and swatted the ball away from him. The crowd roared as the ball bounced toward our basket, but Mrs. Jenkins was too quick. She snatched the ball up. Ten seconds remained on the clock. Mrs. Jenkins tried to pass, but one of my teammates knocked the ball right into my hands. Two seconds remained, and Coach Williams was guarding me. In desperation, I hurled a half-court shot over his head. The ball sailed up—beautiful—and the crowd held its breath. BUZZ! With a silent swish, the shot dropped through the hoop. Our score flipped to 43. The stands erupted, and Coach Williams gave me a high five, saying, "I guess I've found next year's shooting guard."

Respond to the reading. Answer the following questions on your own paper.

- ☐ **Focus and Coherence (1) What unforgettable experience does the writer share?**
- ☐ **Organization (2) How are the events organized?**
- ☐ **Voice (3) Which details show the writer's personality? Name two.**

TEKS 7.14A
ELPS 4G

Prewriting Selecting a Topic

How do you choose a great moment to write about? Devon used a listing strategy to help him think about exciting moments he had experienced. Part of his list follows.

Topics List

Rode the "Plunge"
Got a first at the solo and ensemble contest
Fed a sea lion
Scored the winning shot in basketball
Did my first gainer dive

List your ideas. **On your own paper, write a list of exciting experiences or great moments you have had. Choose one experience to write about.**

Gathering Details

To collect details for his narrative paragraph, Devon decided to make a time line. Not every detail ended up in the final draft, but the time line did give Devon a good plan for starting to write.

Time Line

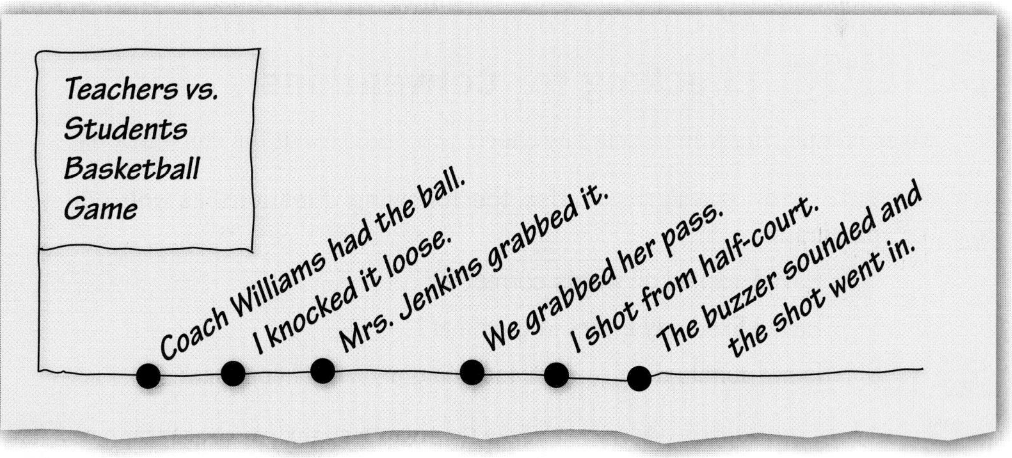
Teachers vs. Students Basketball Game
Coach Williams had the ball.
I knocked it loose.
Mrs. Jenkins grabbed it.
We grabbed her pass.
I shot from half-court.
The buzzer sounded and the shot went in.

List your details. **Make a time line of details for the event you will write about. Make sure to list them in the correct order.**

Drafting Creating Your First Draft

A narrative paragraph has a topic sentence, a body, and a closing sentence. Each part serves a different purpose.

- The topic sentence introduces the narrative.
- The body uses details to describe what happened.
- The closing sentence wraps up the narrative.

Draft **Write your first draft.** **Review your time line and then write your narrative paragraph. Include details to make your readers feel that they are experiencing the event for themselves.**

Revising Improving Your Paragraph

In a piece of writing as short as a narrative paragraph, it's important for every sentence to work well. Keep these tips in mind as you revise.

- **Revise with a reader's eye.** Pretend you are reading the paragraph for the first time. What parts work well? What parts still need work?
- **Keep the action moving.** Use strong action verbs and specific nouns to hold the reader's interest. Cut any unnecessary details.
- **Build to a climax.** Make the events in your paragraph lead up to a moment of crisis. Then resolve the crisis at the end.

Revise **Revise your paragraph.** **Revise with an eye for focus and coherence, organization, development of ideas, and voice. Make sure your narrative grabs the reader's interest and holds it to the end.**

Editing Checking for Conventions

After completing your revision, check your narrative for conventions.

Edit **Edit your paragraph.** **Use the following questions as you edit your paragraph.**

1. **Have I spelled all words correctly?**
2. **Have I fixed any errors in grammar?**
3. **Is my punctuation correct, including my use of commas?**

Edit **Proofread your narrative.** **Take the time to check your paragraph carefully for any errors. Then make a clean final copy to share with your classmates.**

Narrative Writing

Personal Narrative

"The writer steps up to the plate. She looks cool and focused. She takes a couple of practice swings with her pencil, and then settles in. Here comes the first idea. The writer takes a swing at it by starting her first sentence . . . , but then decides to cross it out. She gets ready for the next idea. She swings. Crack! The idea is a real hit, and the writer is off and running with her story."

Writing a personal narrative can be just as exciting as playing baseball. All kinds of ideas will enter your mind; it's your job to connect with the best ones. Personal narratives allow readers to experience the thrill of your life stories and learn from them just as you did. They will cheer whenever you make a hit.

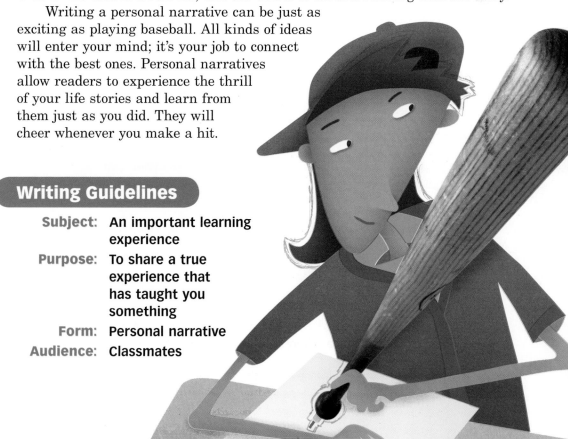

Writing Guidelines

Subject: An important learning experience

Purpose: To share a true experience that has taught you something

Form: Personal narrative

Audience: Classmates

Texas Traits

Understanding Your Goal

Your goal in this chapter is to write an essay about a personal experience that taught you something. As you write, keep in mind the five traits of good writing. These traits will help you to plan, create, and evaluate your personal narrative. Look at the rubric on pages 48–49 to assess your work.

Traits of Narrative Writing

Focus and Coherence

Decide on your controlling, or main, idea. Stay focused on your topic. Be sure that every sentence supports your main idea.

Organization

Put the events in chronological (time) order with a beginning, middle, and ending.

Development of Ideas

Make sure your ideas are developed in a clear and logical way that makes sense to your reader.

Voice

Write in a way that sounds like you and expresses your own personality and viewpoint.

Conventions

Be sure that your grammar, punctuation, capitalization, sentence structure, and spelling are correct.

Literature Connection: You can find a personal narrative in "My First Free Summer" by Julia Alvarez.

Personal Narrative

In this personal narrative, the student writer remembers an experience from his first day in middle school. The key parts of the narrative are described in the left margin.

Beginning
The beginning starts in the middle of an action and then gives the reader background information.

Middle
The middle includes the writer's feelings.

Home Team or Visitor?

"Time to leave!" my mother yelled up the stairs.

My heart kicked against my ribs. This was it—my first day at school in Chicago! Before this, we had lived in a town that had a total population of 2,114. I could walk from the cornfields at one end of town to the bean fields at the other end in 20 minutes. Mom had changed jobs, though, and now we were Chicagoans. I had no idea what to expect from this big-city school.

I took one last look in the mirror. My brand-new Chicago Cubs jersey looked great with my faded jeans and new tennis shoes. I slapped my old Cubs cap on my head, snatched my backpack from the kitchen table, and ran for the waiting school bus.

When the bus came, it was nearly full. I walked down the aisle slowly, looking for an empty seat. I felt as if everybody was staring at me, even though most of them were busy talking to each other. However, as I glanced toward the back, I noticed a couple of guys laughing. They were pointing at me.

"Hey, it looks like we have a super fan riding on our bus today!" one of them shouted over the noise.

At that moment, everyone got quiet and all eyes were glued on me. I could feel my face getting hot. The last thing I wanted to be was the center of attention.

ELPS 4G

Middle
The middle includes dialogue that connects the action and gives information.

Suddenly, this big kid stood up and said, "Slide in here." I was glad to get out of the aisle, away from all those eyes. I slid in next to the window and breathed a sigh of relief. The big kid sat down beside me, and the bus started moving.

"I'm Alberto," he said, shaking my hand. "Don't let those two bother you. You'll soon find out that they're some of the biggest baseball fans in our school."

"I'm Lewis," I said.

Alberto grinned and said, "You know, you do kind of look like a tourist."

We both laughed, and suddenly I felt a lot better. Right then I decided that the next day I'd wear the same kind of clothes I had worn at my old school. I wouldn't worry about fitting into the city scene.

Ending
The ending tells what the writer learned from his experience.

I thought I needed to impress everyone, but I learned that it's always best to just be myself. I also realized that every day is full of surprises. How could I know that in the middle of an embarrassing moment, I'd meet someone like Alberto, who would become a great friend?

Respond to the reading. What makes "Home Team or Visitor?" a well-written narrative? To find out, answer the following questions.

- ☐ **Focus and Coherence** (1) What specific experience does the writer choose to share with the reader?
- ☐ **Organization** (2) How does the writer organize the narrative? (3) What is the purpose of the ending?
- ☐ **Voice** (4) What words and phrases show how the writer feels about this experience?

Go Online!

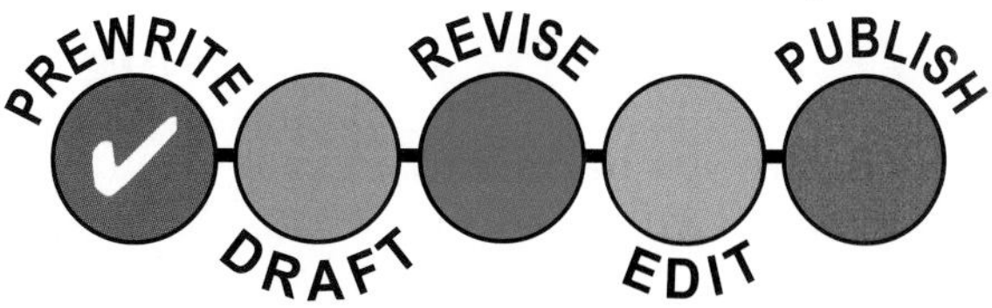

Prewriting

Choosing a topic that interests you can make all the difference in your personal narrative. Along with choosing an interesting topic, you will also gather and organize details in this prewriting section.

Keys to Effective Prewriting

1. *Select a topic that both you and your reader will enjoy.*
2. *Focus on your topic by thinking about your experience.*
3. *Answer the 5 W and H questions to help you remember the details.*
4. *Make a list of the events in chronological (time) order.*
5. *Make a graphic organizer to record details about what you saw, heard, smelled, tasted, and felt.*
6. *Plan how to add dialogue in your narrative.*

TEKS 7.14A

Prewriting Selecting a Topic

Before you begin writing, you need to choose a topic that both you and your reader will enjoy. One writer began thinking about topics by completing the following sentence starters.

Sentence Starters

1. *I was being helpful when . . .*
   — *I kept the little kids away from the fire equipment.* *
   — *I helped my uncle install a CD player in his car.*
2. *I was inspired when . . .*
   — *I saw how well everyone liked my science-fair project.*
   — *the guest speaker from Kenya spoke to our class.*
3. *I was exhausted when . . .*
   — *I came home from my cousin's sleepover.*
   — *I hiked up the giant sand dunes.* *
4. *I was excited when . . .*
   — *my uncle from Puerto Rico visited us.*
   — *I placed third in the gymnastics competition.* *

Prewrite

Use a brainstorming method. On your own paper, finish the sentence starters, or complete a web using the idea starters above. Put stars next to three ideas you think would make the most interesting personal narratives.

Texas Traits

Focus on the Texas Traits

Focus and Coherence Choose an event that stands out and has many clear details that you remember. If that event still feels real to you, then it will also feel real to your reader.

Focusing on Your Topic

You've identified some possible experiences to write about. Now you need to focus on how much you remember about those experiences. Below, a writer used a chart to list three interesting experiences and the lessons learned.

Focus Chart

My Experiences		*Lessons I Learned*
Climbing the sand dunes	→	*I shouldn't hike alone.*
Watching the warehouse burn	→	*I want to be a firefighter.*
Placing in a competition	→	*The more I practice, the better I perform.*

Prewrite **Focus on a topic.** **Using your three starred ideas from the activity on page 102, make a chart like the one above. Then choose one experience and write a topic sentence for your narrative.**

Remembering the Details

Isabella used two gathering techniques. First, she wrote freely, and then she answered the 5 W and H questions.

Freewriting

My brother was shouting. I heard sirens. Fire trucks flew past. I ran down to the corner. Smoke was coming out of the warehouse's windows. One firefighter asked me to help her. I did. I kept watching her. I'd like to be a firefighter.

Who was in the experience?—my brother, the firefighter, me
What happened?—a warehouse caught on fire
When did it happen?—last summer
Where did it happen?—in my neighborhood
Why did I get interested?—a firefighter asked for help
How did I change?—now want to be a firefighter

Prewrite **Remember your details.** **Write nonstop about your topic for 5 minutes. Also answer the 5 W and H questions about your topic.**

Prewriting Putting Events in Order

Once you've gathered your details, it's time to put the main events in order. Most narratives are organized in chronological (time) order. That means the events, or scenes, appear in the order in which they happened. Isabella used a quick list to get her events in order.

Quick List

Watching the Fire

1. *My brother started shouting.*
2. *The sirens got louder.*
3. *Fire trucks flew past our apartment.*
4. *I ran down to the corner.*
5. *The warehouse was burning.*
6. *A woman firefighter asked me for my help.*
7. *I kept the little kids away.*
8. *I watched how she handled the equipment.*

Lesson Learned: I'd like to be a firefighter someday.

Prewrite **Make your quick list like the one above. Look back at your details to get started. List the main scenes of your experience. Then add the lesson you learned. You may find that you need to add more information.**

Texas Traits

Focus on the Texas Traits

Organization As you begin your first draft, keep in mind that the beginning, the middle, and the ending are equally important. Think about how to link each part of your narrative to the next to create a logical sequence.

Gathering Sensory Details

Sensory details help the reader see, hear, smell, taste, and feel what is being described. The chart below shows some of the sensory details Isabella remembered.

Sensory Detail Chart

I saw...	*I heard...*	*I smelled...*	*I felt...*
racing fire trucks	screaming sirens	smoke	the spray of water
shooting flames	firefighters shouting orders	burning tires	waves of heat
dark smoke	shattering windows	chemical fumes	
heavy hoses	noisy kids	exhaust fumes	
leaning ladders			

Prewrite **Create a sensory detail chart.** **Make a chart of sensory details for your experience. As you gather details for your narrative, think about the importance of and reasons for the characters' actions and the consequences that result. Refer to the events in your quick list from page 104. Write down some reasons and consequences for the events.**

TEKS 7.15A(v)

Prewriting Adding Dialogue

There are many different reasons to use dialogue, or conversation, in your narrative. You can use it to show a speaker's personality, to keep the action moving, or to add information. The chart below shows different ways the writer can express the same idea.

Use dialogue to . . .	Without Dialogue	With Dialogue
Show a speaker's personality	One of the kids started shouting that I looked like a super fan.	"Hey, it looks like we have a super fan riding on our bus today!" one of them shouted over the noise.
Keep the action moving	Suddenly this big kid stood up and told me to slide in next to him. I was glad to get away from all those eyes.	Suddenly, this big kid stood up and said, "Slide in here." I was glad to get out of the aisle, away from all those eyes.
Add information	The big kid told me his name and not to be bothered by the other kids. I told him my name, too.	"I'm Alberto," he said, shaking my hand. "Don't let those two bother you. . . ." "I'm Lewis," I said.

Prewrite

Plan some dialogue for your narrative. Plan to use dialogue in at least three places in your essay—one time for each of the ways listed above. (See page 618 for more about punctuating dialogue.)

TEKS 7.14C
ELPS 4G

Go Online!

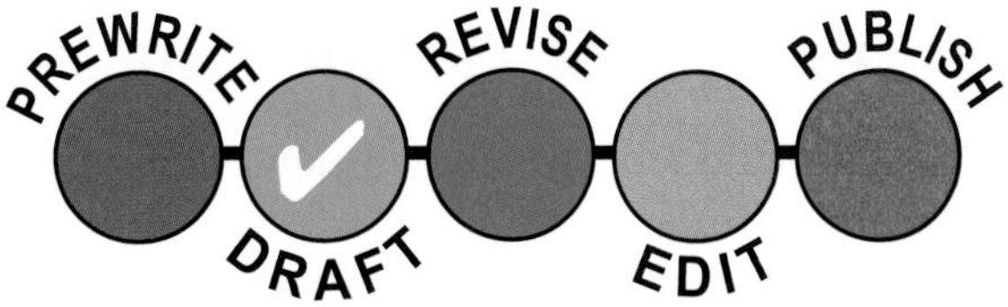

Drafting

After you have finished gathering and organizing ideas, you are ready to begin the first draft of your narrative. Write as if you were telling a friend about your experience.

Keys to Effective Drafting

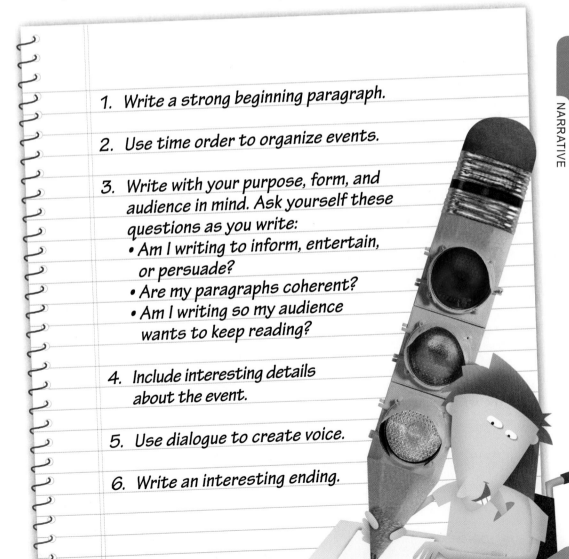

1. Write a strong beginning paragraph.
2. Use time order to organize events.
3. Write with your purpose, form, and audience in mind. Ask yourself these questions as you write:
   - Am I writing to inform, entertain, or persuade?
   - Are my paragraphs coherent?
   - Am I writing so my audience wants to keep reading?
4. Include interesting details about the event.
5. Use dialogue to create voice.
6. Write an interesting ending.

TEKS 7.14B
ELPS 4C

Drafting Getting the Big Picture

The chart below shows how a personal narrative is put together. Notice how the details in the middle and ending all build upon the topic shown in the beginning. The story unfolds from beginning to middle to end. Before you begin to write your first draft, be sure you have gathered enough details about your experience and organized the events in chronological order.

Beginning

The **beginning** introduces the topic and grabs the reader's attention. The details that follow will build from this topic to create a coherent story.

Opening Sentences

"Something's burning. I hear sirens. Something's burning!" Marcus shouted . . .

Middle

The **middle** gives details that appeal to the senses and tells what happened first, second, and so on. It also uses dialogue to show personalities and to keep the action going.

I rushed to the corner . . .

The firefighter shouted thanks . . .

Suddenly, giant flames shot . . .

I kept watching the firefighters . . .

Ending

The **ending** reflects on the experience and tells what the writer learned.

Closing Sentences

I now had a dream. I wanted to be a firefighter. I knew that, someday, I wanted to be the person opening a hydrant to help put out a fire.

Starting Your Personal Narrative

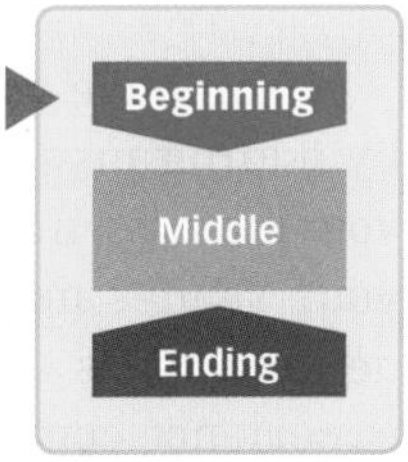

Now that you have a plan, you can begin writing about your experience. Your first paragraph should get your reader's attention and introduce your topic. Make the topic general so that you can add details that build upon this idea. Don't give away the story at the beginning. You want to encourage the reader to continue reading. You can begin your narrative in several different ways.

- **Start with interesting details.**

  It's common to hear sirens wailing through the city. In fact, I usually don't pay attention to them. Then one day the sirens came screaming right past my apartment and stopped at the corner.

- **Use sensory details to grab the reader's attention.**

  When was the last time you were at the scene of a fire? Every time I think about the warehouse fire, I remember the thick smoke reaching into the air and the stench of burning tires.

- **Begin with a person speaking.**

  "Something's burning. I hear sirens. Something's burning!" Marcus shouted.

Beginning Paragraph

The writer grabs the reader's attention with dialogue.

The writer introduces her experience.

"Something's burning. I hear sirens. Something's burning!" Marcus shouted. I usually don't pay too much attention to my little brother. However, as the wailing sirens got louder, I thought maybe this time he was right. Just then, two fire trucks flew past our apartment building. I bolted out the front door and immediately felt my heart pumping fast. The trucks had stopped at the end of our block.

Draft

Write your beginning. On your own paper, write the beginning for your narrative. Try using one of the three suggestions above. Your beginning should be a starting point on which the events can build.

TEKS 7.14B, 7.16

Drafting Developing the Middle Part

You have your reader's attention. Now you need to keep it by adding just the right details. Remember that even though you may be interested in every little thing that happened, your reader may not be. Your writing should have a clearly defined focus and include only those details that make your experience come alive. Here are a few things to remember as you write your middle paragraphs.

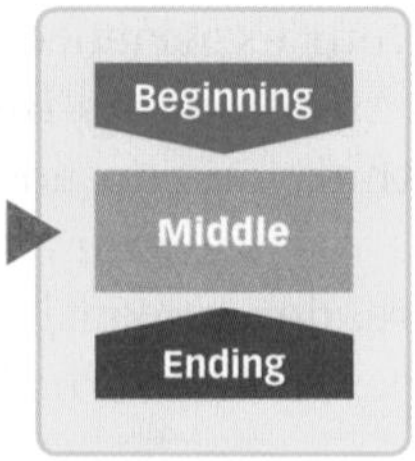

- **Put your events in the order in which they happened.**
- **Appeal to your reader's senses.**
- **Create a clear picture with action words.**
- **Use dialogue to show a speaker's personality, to keep the action moving, or to add information.**

Middle Paragraphs

I rushed to the corner and saw the firefighters charging toward the abandoned warehouse across the street. A firefighter in a bulky coat, a yellow helmet, and big boots was attaching a huge snakelike hose to the hydrant. "Do me a favor," she said. "Stand back and keep those kids away from my rig." I could see a group of neighborhood kids, including my brother, running up to the fire truck.

Dialogue moves the action along.

"Marcus, Paulo, Maria!" I shouted. "You and your friends come here and stay away from that truck!"

The firefighter shouted thanks as she ran toward the burning, smoking warehouse. Then more sirens screamed to the scene. Suddenly, giant flames shot into the sky, and a dark tower of smoke swirled into the air like a tornado. Above the shouts of firefighters, an

Sensory details let the reader "see" and "hear" the experience.

Sensory details capture the excitement.

Dialogue adds information.

Dialogue shows personality.

explosion rocked the ground, and windows shattered. I watched my firefighter friend handle the hose as the powerful spray of water poured down on the blaze. "Some of those firemen aren't men," Marcus said, tugging on my shirt.

"You're right, Marcus, but they are all working together to put out the fire." I kept watching the firefighters wrestling with the huge hoses, smashing holes in the smoking roof, and climbing the leaning ladders.

"Bet you couldn't do that," Marcus said.

"Bet I could!" I answered.

Another important element to consider in a personal narrative is how you tell your reader about the consequences of or reasons for each action. Remember the following points as you write your middle paragraphs.

- **Think about the consequences of or reasons for each action. Make these ideas clear to the reader.**
- **What would you like the reader to learn from your experience? Use the actions and consequences to relay this message.**

Draft

Write your middle paragraphs. As you begin to write your middle paragraphs, be sure you look at all of the details you collected. Tell your reader about consequences of and reasons for each action. Make sure that the details you use show a clearly defined focus for your narrative.

TEKS 7.14C
ELPS 4G

Drafting Ending Your Personal Narrative

There are two important things to remember as you get ready to write your ending: (1) reflect on the experience, and (2) share what you learned from it. *Note:* The writer of this model used dialogue to add a final detail.

Beginning
Middle
Ending

Ending Paragraph

The writer tells the reader what she learned from her experience.

By early evening the firefighters had gone, but the people were still standing around on the sidewalk talking about the fire. I heard a man say, "Some squirrels chewed on electrical wires." Maybe tomorrow things would get back to normal, but I would never be the same. I now had a dream. I wanted to be a firefighter. I knew that, someday, I wanted to be the person opening a hydrant to help put out a fire.

Draft **Write your ending.** In a final paragraph, tell the reader what you learned from your experience. Remember to keep it simple but interesting.

Draft **Form a complete first draft.** Think about how well questions of form, purpose, and audience have been addressed before you revise your work.

Drafting Tips

- **If you are having trouble writing your ending, wait awhile.** Then read through the narrative aloud. Think about all the ways this experience is important and how it has changed you.

Go Online!

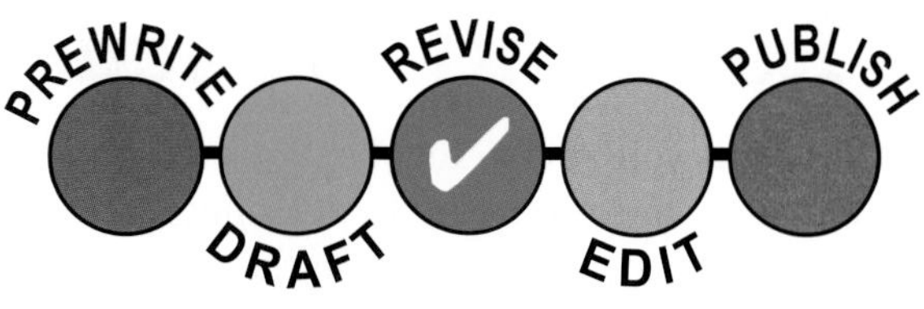

Revising

As you revise, you get the chance to take your essay to the next level. You've already written about the major ideas. Now it's time to add, delete, or move certain parts in order to make your narrative even better.

Keys to Effective Revising

1. *Revise for focus and coherence, organization, development of ideas, and voice.*
2. *Read your beginning and ending to make sure they are strong.*
3. *Read your narrative aloud to yourself. Listen to make sure your writing voice sounds like you.*
4. *Check that your writing has a consistent point of view.*
5. *Ask a classmate to read and respond to your narrative.*
6. *Make sure you have used words that create vivid images.*
7. *Make any revisions that need to be made.*

TEKS 7.14C
ELPS 4G

Texas Traits

Revising for Focus and Coherence

When you revise for *focus and coherence*, you make sure you have written about only one event or experience. All details, information, and dialogue in your personal narrative should be about that one event. The point of view should remain the same throughout your writing. Your narrative should also have a strong beginning and ending. These help your reader want to read your narrative and take away something memorable from it.

Have I focused on one experience?

You know you have focused on one experience if all the ideas in your narrative are about that experience. Don't include anything that does not relate to that experience.

Is my point of view consistent?

You are the person who is telling the story. Remember this as you revise your story. Use words like *I, me,* and *mine*. Change statements that are not from your point of view.

Try It Read the paragraph and identify the unforgettable experience. Find any inconsistencies in point of view. Then tell which ideas do not belong.

I could hear the barking before my dad even opened the door. I have to admit, I was more excited about getting a new dog than I had been about anything in a long time. While Dad was talking to the shelter official, all I could think about was what my new pet would look like and what name I'd choose. Mom wanted us to get a cat last year, but we found out I was allergic. As soon as an attendant opened the door to the kennel, you could hear the dogs really let loose. Some howled. Some yipped. You listened to the noise of barking until the sounds echoed off the concrete walls. Every year hundreds of dogs end up in shelters. Dad looked at me and said, "Well, let's see what kind of man's best friend we can find today."

Revise **Check your narrative.** Read through your first draft. Make sure all of your details, events, and dialogue are about your one experience. Check that there is a consistent point of view.

Has the purpose of my narrative remained the same?

The purpose of a narrative is to tell a story, or entertain. When you revise for purpose, you make sure that your writing tells a story, rather than explains, informs, or persuades. You can check on this by asking yourself the following questions.

1. Does the writing sound as if someone is telling a story?
2. Have I done any writing that distracts from the story?
3. Is every part of my narrative entertaining?

Revise **Check your purpose. Read your narrative aloud and listen for anything that does not entertain or add to the story. Omit those sentences and revise as needed.**

Have I kept my audience in mind?

Remember who your reader is. The style and tone of your writing are meant to engage your reader. If the writing becomes flat or boring, your reader will lose interest. To make sure you have kept your audience in mind, think about the following questions.

1. Do any of the words or sentences sound as if I'm talking to someone different from my intended reader?
2. Are the tone and style of my writing consistent from paragraph to paragraph?

Revise **Check your audience. Ask a partner to read your narrative and respond to any words or sentences that do not make sense or are flat and boring. Revise those parts.**

Have I written a narrative essay?

Remind yourself that a narrative essay is an essay that tells a story about an individual experience or event. Ask yourself:

1. Does my essay tell a story about one event or experience?
2. Does the narrative read like a story or something else?

Revise **Check your genre. As you read your narrative, make notes next to any writing that does not sound like it would be part of a story. Revise or omit those sentences.**

TEKS 7.14C, 7.19A(viii)

Texas Traits

Revising for Organization

Your narrative needs to have a strong beginning, middle, and ending. As you revise for *organization*, use the suggestions included below.

Did I choose the best way to begin my narrative?

You can check how well your beginning works by answering the following questions. (See page 109 for ideas.)

1. What method do I use to grab the reader's attention?
2. As I read over my narrative again, can I see that a different beginning would work better? (If you answered "yes" to this question, try another beginning.)

Revise **Reread your opening. Make any necessary changes to improve your beginning.**

How do I know if the middle is well organized?

Your middle is well organized if you put your events in the order in which they happened. It's also important that your middle be organized in such as way that your reader can move through it easily. Transition words can help tie ideas, sentences, and paragraphs together. The transitions below tie things together by time and work well in narratives.

before	while	immediately	soon	then
during	suddenly	next	later	after
finally	when	afterward	until	as soon as

As you read the middle of your narrative, you can ask yourself these questions.

1. Where does my reader need help to know when something happens?
2. What are the best transition words to use in those places?

Revise **Revise for transitions. As you read your narrative, think about places where adding a transition would help your reader follow the events or connect ideas.**

Does my ending work well?

You will know whether your ending is successful after you answer the following questions.

1. Does my narrative end soon after the most important or intense moment?
2. Does my whole narrative lead up to the lesson I learned?
3. Will the reader be left with unanswered questions? (If you answered "yes," make changes to bring the reader to a satisfying ending.)

Revise **Check your ending. Use the questions listed above to see if you have written a winning ending.**

Organization
Transitions are added to move the events along.

The firefighter shouted thanks as she ran toward the burning, smoking warehouse. Then more sirens screamed to the scene. Suddenly, giant flames shot into the sky, and a dark tower of smoke swirled into the air like a tornado. Above the shouts of firefighters, an explosion rocked the ground, and windows shattered. I watched my firefighter . . .

TEKS 7.14C
ELPS 4G

Texas Traits

Revising for Development of Ideas

When you revise for *ideas,* be sure you have focused on one experience. Check to see that you use a variety of sensory details to create vivid images.

Have I used a variety of sensory details?

You have used a variety of sensory details if you have appealed to most of the reader's senses and if you have created vivid images.

Try It In the paragraph below, some of the sensory details have been underlined. Identify each numbered detail, using "S" for See, "H" for Hear, "F" for Feel, or "SM" for Smell.

With a groan, I pulled on my heavy backpack (F) and headed off barefoot up the giant sand hills (S) at Sleeping Bear Dunes. At first, I thought this hike would be easy. Then, about halfway up, I began huffing and puffing (1) like an old steam engine (2). My feet sank deep into the cold (3) white sand (4). Although my leg muscles were burning (5), I kept trudging up and up. Once at the top, I saw the icy-blue lake (6) and enjoyed the cool breeze (7) blowing a fresh scent (8) my way.

Revise **Check your sensory details.** Read through your first draft. Underline and label each sensory detail, using the following labels: "S"—See, "H"—Hear, "SM"—Smell, "T"—Taste, and "F"—Feel. Have you included a variety of sensory details? Have you used sensory details in your beginning, middle, and ending? Have you created vivid images?

Do I "show" instead of "tell"?

If you have created a detailed picture of your experience by using vivid descriptions in your writing, then you have *shown* your ideas.

Telling: **I saw damage from the tornado.**

Showing: **The tornado ruined our street. The winds roared out of the southwest about 3:00 p.m. and hit us hard. Along our street, all the houses are now missing either a roof or a front porch. A huge oak tree smashed down on four parked cars. Broken glass, tree limbs, and dangling electrical wires made moving on our street impossible. No one was seriously injured, although two people were taken to the clinic for cuts.**

Try It Use one of the following sentences for a topic sentence. Write a paragraph full of details that *show* rather than *tell*.

1. Yesterday's class was a blast.
2. My mother works very hard.

Revise **Review your details.** **Make sure your details "show" your ideas. Use action verbs and concrete nouns.**

Development of Ideas
Sensory details are checked for vivid pictures that "show" the experience.

"Something's burning. I hear sirens. Something's burning!" Marcus shouted. I usually don't pay too much attention to my little brother. However, as the wailing sirens got louder, I thought maybe this time he was right. Just then, two fire trucks flew past our apartment building. I bolted out the . . .

(Annotations: "Something's burning" — SM—Smell; "I hear sirens" — H—Hear; "Marcus shouted" — H—Hear; "wailing sirens got louder" — H—Hear; "two fire trucks flew past" — S—See)

Revising for Voice

When you revise for *voice*, check to make sure your writer's voice is sincere and shows feelings. Also make sure that the dialogue you use helps to reveal each speaker's personality.

Is my personal voice heard in my narrative?

Your voice will come through if you express yourself sincerely and with real feelings. This is usually not difficult to do when you are sharing a personal experience. On the other hand, writers sometimes turn uninteresting, or dull, as soon as they put pen to paper (or fingers to the keyboard).

Writing That Lacks Voice: Uninteresting/Dull

When we walked home, I saw the moon. The night was foggy. I heard one dog bark and then others.

Writing That Contains Voice: Sincere and Full of Real Feelings

While we were walking home, I looked up and saw the moon through the fog. Off in the distance, I heard a dog bark and then a chorus of barks. I felt a shiver crawl up my spine. It was probably just the cold.

Try It Write the first part of your narrative in the form of an e-mail message or a note to your closest friend. "Talk" to this person as if she or he were sitting right next to you. Afterward, underline any thoughts and feelings that sound like the real you.

Revise **Check for voice.** Rewrite any parts of your narrative that don't sound like the real you. Consider adding some of the thoughts and feelings you underlined in the previous activity.

Does my dialogue show each speaker's personality?

Your dialogue shows each speaker's personality if it sounds natural and expresses true thoughts and feelings. Dialogue that works well helps the reader get to know each speaker. (See page 618.)

Sample Dialogue: Shows Each Speaker's Personality

"Well, don't just stand there. Grab a shovel. We've got a garden to plant," Mrs. Walters, our next-door neighbor, bellowed at me.

"Me? Garden? I don't think so," I replied.

"Here. Put on these gloves. We don't want to hurt those tender hands of yours," she said.

"Come on, Mrs. Walters. I don't do gardens," I pleaded.

"Nonsense. Your mother said that you needed a project, so let's get to work," she barked.

Revise

Check the dialogue in your narrative. Do I include enough dialogue? Does it sound realistic and show each speaker's personality? If you can't answer "yes" to these questions, revise the dialogue in your narrative.

Voice
Dialogue helps reveal the personality of the writer and of Marcus.

I kept watching the firefighters wrestling with the huge hoses, smashing holes in the smoking roof, and climbing the leaning ladders.

"Bet you couldn't do that," Marcus said.

"Bet I could!" I answered.

Texas Traits

Revising Using a Checklist

Revise

Check your revising. On a piece of paper, write the numbers 1 to 10. If you can answer "yes" to a question, put a check mark next to that number. If not, continue to work with that part of your essay.

Focus and Coherence

_____ **1.** Do all the details and events tell about my one experience?

_____ **2.** Have I kept my purpose, audience, and genre in mind?

Organization

_____ **3.** Have I placed all the events in their correct time order?

_____ **4.** Does my beginning grab the reader's attention and interest?

_____ **5.** Have I used transition words to help my reader follow the story?

_____ **6.** Do I have a strong ending?

Development of Ideas

_____ **7.** Did I include enough vivid details?

_____ **8.** Did I "show" instead of "tell"?

Voice

_____ **9.** Can the reader hear my personal voice in the narrative?

_____ **10.** Does the dialogue show the speaker's personality?

Revise

Make a clean copy. When you've finished revising your essay, make a clean copy before you begin to edit.

Go Online!

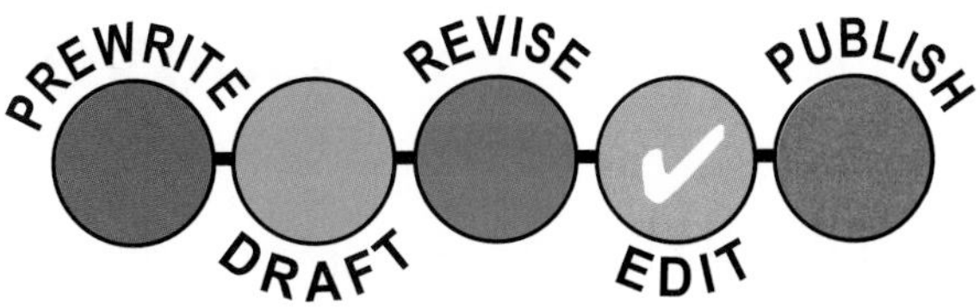

Editing

Editing is the next step in the writing process. When you edit, you are checking to make sure you have followed the rules for grammar, mechanics, sentence structure, and spelling. These rules are called the conventions of writing.

Keys to Effective Editing

1. *Use a dictionary, a thesaurus, and the "Proofreader's Guide" in the back of this book.*
2. *Check for any words or phrases that may be confusing to your reader.*
3. *Edit on a printed copy if you use a computer. Then make your changes to the document on the computer.*
4. *Use the editing marks shown inside the back cover of this book.*
5. *Ask someone else to check your writing for errors, too.*

TEKS 7.19C

Texas Traits Editing for Conventions

Grammar

When you edit for grammar, you make sure you use nouns, verbs, pronouns, adjectives, adverbs, and all other parts of speech correctly.

Did I place the modifiers correctly?

Modifiers, especially adjective and adverb phrases and clauses, need to be placed where they do not confuse your reader.

A misplaced modifier is one that modifies the wrong noun or pronoun or is unclear about which noun it is modifying.

Misplaced modifier: **I made a fruit salad for my sister with extra strawberries.**

Corrected: **I made a fruit salad with extra strawberries for my sister.**

A dangling modifier is placed so that the reader is unsure which noun or pronoun is being modified—or the noun or pronoun may be missing altogether.

Dangling modifier: **Presenting the flag to the school, the principal thanked the officer.**

Corrected: **The principal thanked the officer for presenting the flag to the school.**

Dangling modifier: **After pitching for six innings, the coach sent Rafael in to finish the game.**

Corrected: **The coach sent Rafael in to finish the game after Julian had pitched for six innings.**

GRAMMAR Try It Rewrite the following sentences to put the modifiers in the correct place.

1. The neighbor gave a dozen apples to my grandmother with the stems removed.
2. Screaming at the top of his lungs, Pablo gave his baby brother a toy to play with.
3. Before reading the newspaper, the dog carried it to his bed.

Edit **Edit your modifiers.** **Carefully review your sentences for misplaced or dangling modifiers and correct all that you find.**

TEKS 7.19A(iii)
ELPS 2G, 2I, 3E, 3H

How can adverbial clauses improve my writing?

A clause that modifies a verb, an adjective, or an adverb is called an adverbial clause. These clauses begin with such words as

after	although	as	as if	as soon as	because
before	if	since	so that	than	that
though	unless	until	when	whenever	where
wherever	while				

Adverbial clauses are powerful additions to your writing that help further describe when, where, why, how, or to what extent. Compare the following sentences.

Without an Adverbial Clause

The dogs barked louder.

With an Adverbial Clause

The dogs barked louder when we walked into the kennel.

GRAMMAR Try It

Combine the following sentences to make one stronger sentence by using an adverbial clause.

1. He didn't want to go to the concert. Sam went anyway.
2. I'll apologize for the mistake. You say you're sorry first.
3. Quentin had to print his report again. It was smudged the first time.

Edit

Use adverbial clauses. Edit your sentences to add adverbial clauses where they will make your writing stronger.

Learning Language

Misplaced modifiers may confuse your readers and make your writing less interesting. To help put your modifiers in the correct place, make sure the modifier is close to the word you want to modify. Work with a partner to rearrange the words in the following sentences so that they make more sense.

1. I ate a hot bowl of posole for dinner.
2. We saw a dog behind the house playing with a stick.
3. On the bus, Regina found a blue man's hat.

TEKS 7.19A(i)

Sentence Structure

When you edit for *sentence structure*, you correct errors in sentences. You can also make sure you have used a variety of sentence types to make your writing more interesting.

How can participles improve my writing?

Participles are powerful adjectives that help writers strengthen their sentences. They are formed by adding *–ing* and *–ed* to verbs. Compare the following sentences.

Without a Participle

The leaves decay and fill the forest with a rich smell. (verb)

With a Participle

The rich smell of decaying leaves fills the forest. (participle)

Try It Change the verbs in the parentheses into participles by adding *–ing* or *–ed*. For each item, write the participle along with the noun it modifies. Then write a sentence using the new word group. The first one has been done for you.

1. (close) door
   closing door; The squeaky sound of the closing door startled Juan.
2. (crackle) campfire
3. (laugh) children
4. (whine) puppies
5. (surprise) faces
6. (annoy) sounds

Edit **Check your use of participles. Edit your sentences to add participles where they will make your writing stronger.**

TEKS 7.14C

How can I use simple sentences effectively?

A good writer will vary his or her sentence structure by using a mix of simple, compound, and complex sentences. A simple sentence has one subject and one verb and is usually short. You can sometimes use simple sentences to draw attention to important details in your writing. Look at the simple sentences below to see how they are used effectively.

> Our school has a fascinating name that is connected to a mystery. Long before the school was built, maybe even before my grandparents were born, Native Americans had discovered a strange pit on the land. The pit held broken bones. Maybe an ancient hunter had dug the pit to trap animals, which would fall into it and break their bones when they hit the bottom. Maybe the pit had been a dump where a long-ago tribe had thrown their garbage. The mystery of the pit was never solved, but it did provide a name for our school. Its name is Broken Bone School.

NARRATIVE

Try It Revise each compound or complex sentence below to make two simple sentences.

1. My best friend came to the party early, but my sister arrived late.
2. I've worked all day, so I need a break.
3. When the school bus rounded the curve, four deer ran into the woods.
4. The telephone rang in the middle of the night, and it woke me from my sleep.

Edit **Check your sentence structure.** Edit your sentences to vary the structure and to create short sentences that draw attention to important facts or details.

Editing Using a Checklist

Edit

Check your editing. On a piece of paper, write the numbers 1 to 10. If you can answer "yes" to a question, put a check mark next to that number. If not, continue to work on parts of your essay that are not checked off.

Conventions

GRAMMAR

____ **1.** Have I placed my modifiers correctly?

____ **2.** Have I effectively used adverbial clauses?

MECHANICS

____ **3.** Do I use end punctuation after all my sentences?

____ **4.** Do I use commas after introductory word groups and transitions?

____ **5.** Do I use commas between equal adjectives?

____ **6.** Do I punctuate dialogue correctly?

____ **7.** Do I use apostrophes to show possession (*the dog's toy*)?

SENTENCE STRUCTURE

____ **8.** Have I used simple sentences effectively?

SPELLING

____ **9.** Have I spelled all my words correctly?

____ **10.** Have I double-checked the words my spell-checker may have missed?

Creating a Title

- **Use strong, vivid words: Best Friend Rescue**
- Give the words rhythm: A Day of Sun, Sand, and Survival
- Be imaginative: **Camping Equals Disaster**

TEKS 7.14E

Go Online!

Publishing

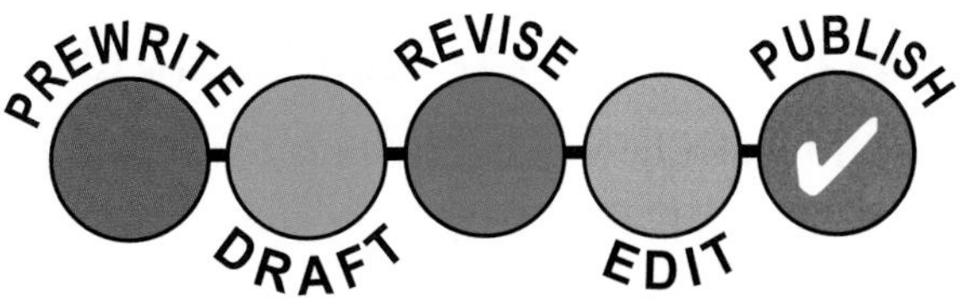

Sharing Your Narrative

After you have worked hard to improve your narrative, make a neat, final copy to share. Think about your audience, and choose a format that will grab their attention and hold their interest. Read the suggestions below for publishing your narrative.

Publish **Make a final copy.** Choose an appropriate format for your audience. Use the guidelines below or develop your own format. Create a clean copy of your narrative and carefully proofread it.

Focus on Presentation

- Use blue or black ink and write neatly.
- Write your name in the upper left corner of page 1.
- Skip a line and center your title; skip another line and start your writing.
- Double-space your essay.
- Indent every paragraph and leave a one-inch margin on all four sides.
- Write your last name and the page number in the upper right corner of every page after the first one.

Go Online!
Upload your personal narrative for others to read.

Read to an Adult
Share your narrative with an adult. Have the adult tell you what he or she liked best.

Create an Illustrated Book
Make a neat copy of your essay, including illustrations of the main events. Add a cover and share your book with younger students.

NARRATIVE

ELPS 4I, 4K

Evaluating a Narrative

To learn how to evaluate a narrative, you'll use the scoring rubric on pages 48–49 and the narratives that follow. These narratives are examples of writing for each score on the rubric.

Notice that this first personal narrative received a score of 4. Read the description for a score of 4 on pages 48–49. Then read the narrative. Use the same steps to study the other examples. Always remember to think about the overall quality of the writing.

Writing that fits a score of 4 is very strong.

4

The clearly defined focus grabs readers' attention.

Dialogue shows individuals' voices.

The Day I Lost My Key

"When can I get a key? When can I get a key?"

That was a question I kept asking my parents. The answer was always, "When you're older." Sometimes it was, "When you're in seventh grade." Then I got to seventh grade and to my surprise they gave me a key instead of saying, "When you're in eighth grade."

For an hour I couldn't stop looking at my shiny steel key. Through the house I strolled, locking and unlocking all the doors—the front door, the side door, the door to the backyard. Then I stuck it in my pocket—or at least I thought I did. However, the next time I wanted to lock and unlock something, it wasn't there.

I panicked. I walked through the house as fast as a race-walker. I investigated all the furniture, floors, shelves, and closets. The key was nowhere to be found.

"Why am I not surprised?" my dad said.

"Well, this is what happens," my mom said.

They told me in order to get a new key I would have to do extra chores. I knew that was coming. Not that I mind chores. I just mind being told I have to do them in order to get something I should have anyway—like my own key. Most of my friends already had keys.

Consistent point of view expresses the narrator's feelings.

I almost felt like crying. Why do I lose things? Why can't I find a place for something and just put it there so I'll always know where it is? But I thought I did that! How had the key jumped from my pocket to somewhere invisible?

I sat at the kitchen table with my head in my hands for about fifteen minutes. My dad came over and asked me about every single place I should have looked. I had looked in all of them. My mom came over and told me it wasn't a tragedy to go another year without a key. That really helped.

Sensory details make the reader want to know what happens next.

I gave up. I threw myself onto the living room rug and buried my face in the brown and black wool. Then I figured it would be better to breathe without wool in my nose, so I turned my head to the left, which is the direction of the sofa. And underneath it was—da-da-ta-da! The key.

The writer communicates the reasons for actions and consequences.

Dad thinks I never put the key in my pocket, I just think I remember doing that. Instead, he thinks I was playing with it and let it drop and my attention went somewhere else. Unfortunately, that sounds like me.

The ending wraps up a coherent sequence of events.

However, I'll never do it again! My key is on a key ring now, and I always keep it in my right front pocket. I don't use it much, because somebody is usually home when I get home, but it's nice to know it's there. It will never stray from my sight—I think.

ELPS 4I, 4K

Writing that fits a score of 3 is strong.

3

Beginning introduces the experience.

Unnecessary details weaken coherence.

Voice shows sincere, real feelings.

Vivid images bring the scene to life.

My First Snow

I never saw snow until I was eight years old. You don't see snow very much in McAllen. I had heard about snow all my life. I wondered, "What is it like?" I wondered what it looked like, felt like, and tasted like.

Then I got my chance. On the winter break my family went to Wisconsin. Why? The answer is that Mom's best friend lives their and she hadn't seen her in about five years. They were best friends when they were kids but now that they're adults they don't see each other very often.

We flew north in a small plane that only has four seats across. Finally we landed. Guess what? There was snow on the ground! Not on the runways but on the grass outside the airport.

I wooped with joy. Snow at last! It was frustrating because I couldn't run out to the field yet. I had to wait. At last we got to Rosa's house, Mom's friend. She has two children, one was younger than me and the other was older than me. I was in the middle. I was glad the first thing Robert said was "Let's go play outside."

"Can we play in the snow?" I asked eagerly. As a result, they laughed as if I had said something silly. I was a little embarrassed but it was OK. They knew I had never seen snow. Soon they enjoyed teaching me about what to do in the snow. We went to a park that was near their house. It had a hill and pine trees. People were sliding down the hill on big blue saucers. Robert and Roxanne let me try their saucer. (We brought it from their house.) That was the greatest moment of my life. I will always remember sliding down the hill rocking

Small errors don't affect the reader's understanding.

The ending makes a contrast that is related to the narrative's focus.

to and fro, spinning and trying to steer with my hands on the snow. I was wearing a pair of Robert's gloves. I had a spill and got snow all over my face and that was just as good as staying on it.

Our second event was having a snowball fight. Robert called to his friends "This kids never saw snow before!" "Get him!" his friends said. Robert and Roxanne were on my side as they pelted me with snowballs. They hurt more than I thought they would but that's OK. I learned how to make a really good snowball and I enjoyed throwing them fast into someone's chest and seeing their reacion.

Two more things we did were making snow angels and a snowman. However we did not complete the snowman because we were tired. Rosa made us all cocoa and we sat at her fireplace watching the fire. I had never done that before, and it's also a very nice thing to do when it snows. All in all, it was one of my favorite days ever.

Writing that fits a score of 2 is strong in some ways.

2

Voice sounds real but unemotional.

Errors in spelling and grammar distract the reader.

The writer is telling, rather than showing with details.

Time-order transitions help the reader.

Riding the Steam Train

In the Hill Country they have the Steam Train that people go to and ride and one day my friend Paulas father took me, Susana and Paula to ride on it. I didn't know anything about it before I went there. I knew we were going there but I didn't know anything about the train exept it's name, but now I can tell you all about it. You see there are people who love old trains. I wouldn't exactly say I love them but now, that I've been on that ride, I like them, but I would not particly choose to go on one again very soon. Maybe every couple of years.

There's this assosiation that keeps the trains sparkling clean just like they were new. They have different kind of cars and seats, some are very fancy but wouldn't you know it Paulas father got the cheapest tickets with no AC. Well, anyway we saw the hill country which is pretty. Secondly we got to feel what an old fashion train feels like. It's a little bumpy and noisy but I liked it. Third we got off at a old train station. There wasn't much to do but it was nice to get out and strech our legs. We continued down the tracks. The whole train ride took three hours. Paulas father loved it more than we did. I would definately recommend this train ride if you are looking for something to do and you like the hill country and trains.

ELPS 4I, 4K

Writing that fits a score of 1 is weak.

1

The writer starts at the end of the story.

The writing jumps from topic to topic without coherence.

The voice sounds uninterested.

The writer makes many errors in conventions.

The Hurrican

The Hurrican wasn't as bad as they said. No houses were destroyd. We live rite near the beech. So we had to prepare, Weve been living here 100 years. Not me, my family. We now what to do in a hurrican. You put bords on the windows that's the main thing dad says. Also your glass doors. He went out to trim the trees. So that they woodnt damage the house. Then you got to get your supplys. We got enough for a week. Including

cans & boxes of food & dog food
bottles of water & diet soda
took all our medicine in a box
radio & batterys
propane stove, flashlite

Also lots of other stuff. Didnt have to use any of it. We waited. I seen news vans on our street. We live rite near the beech. The hurrican came in. Sky was dark. Wind got fast. Trees bending. A lot of rain that fell sideways. But it was all right. No houses broken just a few boats. Nobody got killed. We lost power for one day. We did not have to eat the stuff we brot down to the seller for a weak. Did not have to use the flashlite or propane. There were people who evakouated from this Hurrican but they just had to come back. They should not have evakouated thats what I learned.

Evaluating and Reflecting on Your Writing

You've put a lot of time and effort into your personal narrative. Now take some time to score and think about your writing. On your own paper, finish each sentence starter below. To score your writing, refer to the scoring rubric on pages 48–49 and the examples you just read.

My Personal Narrative

1. *The best score for my personal narrative is . . .*

2. *It's the best score because . . .*

3. *The best part of my narrative is . . .*

4. *The part that still needs work is . . .*

5. *The main thing I learned about writing a personal narrative is . . .*

Narrative Writing

Phase Autobiography

The *Saturn V* rocket that carried the first astronauts to the moon used three stages. The first stage was basically an engine with a big fuel tank of hydrogen and oxygen. Its job was to push the rocket past the atmosphere. The second stage propelled the rocket into space, toward the moon. The third stage of the rocket included the space capsule and the landing module. Each stage had its own purpose.

Our lives also have stages, or phases. Each phase serves a different purpose. In a phase autobiography, you tell about a stage or phase in your own life and what effect it has had on you. Your goal is to entertain your readers while showing them a little bit about who you are.

Writing Guidelines

Subject: A time of personal change
Purpose: To tell about a phase in your life
Form: Phase autobiography
Audience: Classmates

Phase Autobiography

We all go through phases or stages. Sometimes those stages are school related, like graduating from elementary school and beginning middle school. Other stages are more personal, like moving to a new town, learning to play chess, or making a new friend. A phase autobiography tells how events over a period of time affect a person. In the following sample, Andy tells about a summer he spent drawing.

Beginning
The beginning introduces the stage.

Middle
The middle provides details about the stage.

Rocket to Mars

At the beginning of last summer, my dad gave me a sketchbook. At first I wondered what I would do with it. I wasn't planning to be an artist or anything, and I figured I'd catch up on a few TV shows. Then Dad lost his job. He was home all day every day, and the TV was his. We were living in a small apartment in Brooklyn, and Dad and I were always stumbling over each other. Since I couldn't watch my shows, I started drawing. With just a pencil and my sketchbook, I could be in another world. And that world was full of rockets.

The first drawing in my sketchbook showed a needle-tipped rocket just as it was bounding from the launchpad. I sketched in ice cracking from the hull and falling toward the firestorm below. It was a rocket caught in the moment of breaking free. The next pages had more rockets blasting off, ripping through clouds, and reaching for the stars.

"We're just about out of money, Son," Dad told me one day. "We can't afford to stay here. We're going to have to move."

ELPS 4G

Middle
A series of events occurs during this stage.

Suddenly, I couldn't draw rockets. Each time I tried, the hull would shift this way or that. Nothing was sleek anymore, but clunky and bent. My rockets evolved into space stations—pages and pages of space stations. They just floated there above the earth. I'd put little windows in them, and inside you could see me sitting at a table, drawing pictures, or Dad tending pots with space plants in them.

"Son, I got a new job!" Dad told me near the end of summer. "We don't have to move after all!"

Dad started his new job, and I had the TV back. The funny thing was, I didn't care about watching TV so much anymore. I was too busy drawing. My space stations got land put under them, and they became Mars bases. And I drew my dad and me standing outside, waving, next to a field of space plants.

Ending
The ending shows how the person changed.

Now I'm taking art classes in school, learning to draw people. One of these days, maybe I'll be an artist for NASA.

Respond to the reading. Answer the following questions on your own paper.

- ☐ **Organization** (1) What problem is identified in the beginning? (2) How is this problem resolved in the end?
- ☐ **Development of Ideas** (3) What details does Andy provide about his art and his home during this phase?
- ☐ **Voice** (4) What words and phrases give you clues about Andy's personality? Name two.

TEKS 7.14A

Prewriting Selecting a Topic

You've been through many stages in your life, but which one should you write about? A life map can help you decide on a topic.

A life map begins at your birth and continues to the present. The pictures represent important events in your life, and the numbers or dates indicate your age or the year for each event. Andy made the following life map.

Life Map

Prewrite

Make a life map. Draw your own life map. Then review it, looking for a stage to write about. The stage must include a number of events over a period of time. For example, Andy could have written about learning to swim or spending the summer with his uncle. Select a stage to write about.

Gathering Details

To write your phase autobiography, you'll need to communicate the importance of or reasons for actions and consequences. Every action in a story or narrative has a consequence. Each consequence affects the story and its eventual outcome.

Andy used an Action/Consequence Chart to show the reasons for each event in his phase autobiography. This chart helped Andy gather details for his writing.

Action/Consequence Chart

	ACTION	CONSEQUENCE
1	*Dad lost his job.*	*He stayed home and watched TV.*
2	*I couldn't watch TV.*	*I began to draw in my sketchbook.*
3	*Dad said we'd have to move.*	*I couldn't draw rockets anymore.*
4	*Dad got a new job.*	*I started drawing again.*

Prewrite

Make a chart. Put together a chart of actions and consequences of the stage you've chosen for your autobiography. Start with the first pair and then list others in the order they happened.

Another good way to gather details for a narrative is to make a 5 Ws chart. Label the columns *Who? What? When? Where?* and *Why?* Then fill in the table with answers to those questions. (See page 611.)

TEKS 7.15A(i), 7.15A(ii), 7.16

Drafting Creating Your First Draft

With your Action/Consequence Chart in mind, begin writing your phase autobiography. Use the tips below to guide your writing.

Beginning

Draw the reader in and introduce the stage you are describing.

- **Set the scene.** Give the time and place and describe the first action and its consequence. Andy, for example, starts by saying at the beginning of summer his dad gave him a sketchbook.
- **Move the story forward with details.** Show the consequences of actions and how one leads to another. For example, Andy doesn't know what he's going to do with the sketchbook, but he starts to draw in it when he can't watch TV.

Middle

Let your story unfold and keep it interesting and imaginative.

- **Keep the action well-paced.** Keep things happening in your story to sustain the interest of your reader. Leave out unneeded details.
- **Remain focused on your story.** Don't stray away from your main characters and action.
- **Make your story engaging.** Create characters and situations that your reader can relate to. Make your reader care about what happens to your characters. In Andy's story, the reader cares when Andy's dad loses his job and then nearly loses their home.

Ending

Describe how the stage ends. Consider using one of the following approaches for your ending.

- **Reveal why the phase was important.** Make sure your reader understands the significance of this phase.
- **Tell how the experience changed you.** Tell what you learned from the phase or how you are different because of it.

Draft

Write the first draft. Review your chart and then write your phase autobiography. Make sure to keep your narrative focused and interesting for the reader.

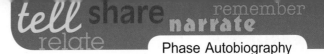

Revising Improving Your Writing

Revise your first draft with the following traits in mind.

- ☐ **Focus and Coherence** Have you focused only on the stage you have chosen and details that explain this stage?
- ☐ **Organization** Does each paragraph build on the one before it?
- ☐ **Development of Ideas** Have you "fleshed out" the ideas in your narrative and made them clear to the reader?
- ☐ **Voice** Does your writing sound authentic and natural? Does it express your personality?

Voice
This change shows more of the writer's personality.

Focus and Coherence
A detail that weakens focus is cut.

Development of Ideas
Combining two sentences helps make the writer's thinking more clear.

Organization
A sentence is moved for better order.

At the beginning of last summer,
~~When the hot season arrived,~~ my dad gave me a sketchbook. At first I wondered what I would do with it. ~~Who gives a kid a sketchbook?~~ I wasn't planning to be an artist or anything. and I figured I'd catch up on a few TV shows. Then Dad lost his job. He was home all day every day, and the TV was his. We were living in a small apartment in Brooklyn, and Dad and I were always stumbling over each other. With just a pencil and my sketchbook, I could be in another world. And that world was full of rockets. Since I couldn't watch my shows, I started drawing.

NARRATIVE

Revise

Revise to improve your first draft. Revise your phase autobiography. Make sure your writing is focused, grabs your reader's interest, and holds it to the end.

Editing Checking Your Work

While a phase autobiography is not as formal as a report, it should still be free of errors in grammar, mechanics, and spelling.

Conventions

Once your autobiography sounds the way you want it to, check your grammar, mechanics, and spelling. Use the following checklist.

GRAMMAR

_____ **1.** Do I use correct forms of verbs (*My dad gave me,* not *My dad give me*)?

_____ **2.** Do my subjects and verbs agree in number (*We were living*, not *We was living*)?

_____ **3.** Do I use the right words *(do, due, dew)*?

MECHANICS

_____ **4.** Do I use correct end punctuation after each sentence?

_____ **5.** Do I use commas correctly?

_____ **6.** Do I use apostrophes with contractions *(I couldn't)*?

_____ **7.** Do I start all my sentences with capital letters?

_____ **8.** Do I capitalize all proper nouns (*Brooklyn*)?

SPELLING

_____ **9.** Have I spelled all my words correctly?

Edit

Edit your autobiography. Make sure your thoughts are clear and focused and that your sentences are linked. Carefully proofread your final copy.

Publishing Sharing Your Writing

A phase autobiography shouldn't be allowed to gather dust. It should be shared! This type of writing is perfect for sending to family and friends by mail or e-mail. It also makes an interesting addition to a family Web site. Magazines that accept student writing are also good places for a phase autobiography. Finally, this sort of writing should definitely be kept in a journal or portfolio to be read again in later years.

Publish

Share your phase autobiography. Find one way to share your phase autobiography with relatives or friends. (See page 129.)

Narrative Writing
Across the Curriculum

What is a kite? Paper, wood, string . . . but when you put those pieces together in the right way, the kite suddenly soars to the skies.

What is a narrative? People, events, places . . . but when you carefully build a narrative, it can soar to the sky. Sometimes a narrative soars so far and so fast, it carries you away with it.

For example, in social studies, writing about a cultural experience can carry you away. In math, learning-log entries can help you explore new concepts. In science, a story script can explain a topic you are studying. In any class, incident reports give you the opportunity to record events you have personally observed. The following chapter will lead you through these kinds of narrative writing.

What's Ahead

- **Social Studies:** Writing a Letter About a Cultural Experience
- **Math:** Writing a Learning-Log Entry
- **Science:** Writing a TV Script
- **Practical Writing:** Creating an Incident Report

TEKS 7.17B

Social Studies:
Writing a Letter About a Cultural Experience

Cultural experiences are fun and great opportunities to learn about the world. Museums are particularly interesting, and there are so many of them. The following personal letter, written by Lisa to her friend Juan, tells about her experience at an art museum. It contains an opinion, a complaint, and a request for information.

The **beginning** expresses an opinion.

Hi Juan,

I really enjoyed my first visit to the art museum. I think it's the best museum I've ever been in, and I've visited quite a few. I envy you getting to work at such a fun place and getting paid too! I loved the modern art the best, especially the sculptures. The museum gift shop was cool too. I bought some stationary for my mom there. She's going to love it.

The **middle** makes a complaint.

I just have one little complaint. There were too many people! Several gallery rooms were so crowded I could hardly avoid getting my feet stepped on. I was unable to spend very long looking at any one painting because of all these bodies pushing me forward. So much for going to the museum on a Saturday.

The **ending** requests information.

Could you tell me when's the best time to visit when there aren't so many people? I'd like to come back and see the art I missed the first time, but not if it's so crowded. Also, tell me what days and hours you are working there. I'd love to see you and maybe even get a personal tour.

Your friend,

Lisa

TEKS 7.17B
ELPS 3G

Writing Tips

Before you write . . .

- **Select a topic.**
  Write a letter about the cultural experience your teacher assigns or choose an experience that relates to something you are studying.
- **Take notes about what you experience.**
  Record specific details about what you liked and what you didn't like.

Sensory Chart

Subject:

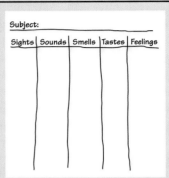

Sights	Sounds	Smells	Tastes	Feelings

During your writing . . .

- **Express an opinion.**
  Tell why you enjoyed or didn't enjoy the experience.
- **Register a complaint.**
  Give details about something you didn't like to a person who can do something about it.
- **Make a request.**
  Your request may refer to your complaint or something else involving the experience.

After you've written a first draft . . .

- **Revise your first draft.**
  Make sure that your personal letter is in the proper letter format, is interesting, and reflects your experience.
- **Check for accuracy.**
  Double-check your facts and details.
- **Edit for correctness.**
  Check for grammar, capitalization, punctuation, spelling, and correct letter format.

Try It Think about cultural events where you live: parades, festivals, concerts, and so on. Choose one event you enjoyed or would like to attend, and write a letter to a friend describing your experience. Include an opinion, complaint, and/or request.

Math: Writing a Learning-Log Entry

When you write in a learning log, you make a personal connection to the things you are learning in class. In his math class, Ethan wrote a learning-log entry based on his experience of building kites.

The **beginning** tells what is being studied.

The **middle** contains explanations and examples.

The **ending** relates the information to the student's experience.

Friday, September 24

Today in math class we learned about angles. Angles are created when two lines extend from a point. Three types of angles are vertical, complementary, and supplementary.

- Vertical angles are opposite each other. They share one point called a vertex.
- Complementary angles add up to 90°.
- Supplementary angles add up to 180°.

Angles can be found in places besides math books. For example, last summer when my brother and I made kites, the kites had all sorts of angles created by the wood frame. Now, by learning to recognize and measure different angles, the next kites I build will be even better!

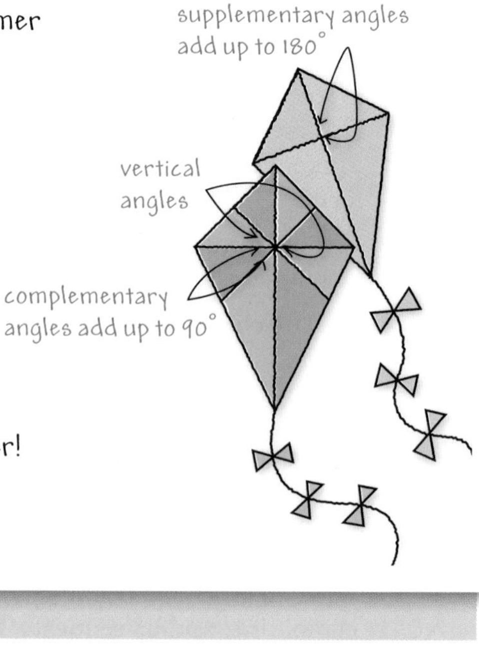

Writing Tips

Before you write . . .

- **Format your learning log.**
Set up your learning log so that you like the way it looks. Also, make sure to follow your teacher's guidelines.
- **Pay attention in class.**
Take notes to make sure you understand the material your teacher presents.

During your writing . . .

- **Record the date.**
Write the date of each learning-log entry.
- **Write down what you are learning.**
Record the most important facts.
- **Reflect on the information.**
Relate what you are learning to your own experiences.
- **Include sketches.**
Make sketches in your learning log if your teacher shows you a picture of something interesting. Also copy and label any important diagrams that help explain a concept.

After you've written a first draft . . .

- **Reread your work.**
Read your learning-log entries to review the material and decide if you need to add any details.
- **Use your learning log.**
Return to your learning log whenever you are asked to write a paper for that class. It will be full of excellent topics for writing assignments.

Try It Write a learning-log entry about something you recently learned in math class. Record the facts and include sketches or equations to explain concepts.

Science: Writing a TV Script

When you write a factual TV script, you are telling a story to make an idea clearer. This type of narrative writing is helpful for learning a scientific concept. In the sample below, a student used a classroom experience to help explain the different types of clouds.

The **beginning** sets the scene.

Characters: *Student, Tai; Teacher, Mr. Hynek*

Setting: *School courtyard*

Tai: Why are these clouds all feathery, Mr. Hynek? Shouldn't clouds be fluffy?

Mr. Hynek: Clouds have many different shapes. Remember the clouds yesterday?

Tai: They looked like a gray blanket. What were they?

The **middle** uses dialogue to explain the scientific ideas.

Mr. Hynek: They were stratus clouds, Tai. Since stratus clouds are low to the ground, they make everything look gray. Fog is a type of stratus cloud at ground level. Stratus clouds bring rain or drizzle.

Tai: They did yesterday! Which clouds are fluffy?

Mr. Hynek: Those are cumulus clouds. When they are small and fluffy, cumulus clouds usually mean fair weather. If they grow really tall, they can become thunderheads and bring rain or storms.

Tai: Today I see feathery clouds reaching across the sky. The sun is shining, and the sky is bright blue. It looks like good weather for today.

Mr. Hynek: Right, Tai. Cirrus clouds tend to be high in the sky. Sometimes the ends of cirrus clouds curl in thin streamers. Cirrus clouds usually mean fair weather.

The **ending** closes the scene.

Tai: Now when I look at the clouds, I see a lot more than just fluff!

Writing Tips

Before you write . . .

- **Select an interesting science topic.**
  Review the chapters you have recently studied in your science book. Select a topic that you think would interest your readers and make a good story.
- **Imagine ways to dramatize the topic.**
  Think in terms of a good story that will hold your readers' interest with good characters, an interesting setting, action, and natural dialogue.

During your writing . . .

- **Let the story tell itself.**
  Be open and imaginative, and have fun as you write.
- **Be clear and direct.**
  Explain the idea, concept, and important details as simply and clearly as possible.
- **Keep it conversational.**
  Write natural-sounding dialogue that your readers will enjoy.

After you've written a first draft . . .

- **Revise your first draft.**
  Make sure that your script is imaginative, conversational, easy to follow, and will sustain your readers' interest.
- **Check for accuracy.**
  Double-check your details and correct any factual errors.
- **Edit for correctness.**
  Check for grammar, punctuation, capitalization, sentence structure, and spelling errors.

Try It Search for a science topic that you would like to write a TV script about. Invent characters, situations, and dialogue that could help you explain the topic and interest your readers. Then write your script.

Practical Writing:
Creating an Incident Report

When you see an accident, you may be asked to write up an incident report telling just what you observed. It's important that you include everything you saw in a clear way. The following incident report was written by the student set director of a middle school play.

INCIDENT REPORT

The **beginning** names the student and gives the date.

Ronnette Williams
May 13, 2010

An accident happened today at 4:15 p.m. on the auditorium stage. I was there as student set director, and so were Ms. Davis and the following students: Randy Dover, Danielle Walters, Maylie Royce, and Sumey Lee.

The **middle** answers each of the 5 Ws: *who, what, where, when,* and *why.*

Here's what happened. We were moving the flats for *Phantom of the Country Opera* when one tipped over and fell on Randy Dover. Ms. Davis saw the flat fall, shouted a warning, and tried to catch it herself. The flat hit Randy's shoulder and knocked him down. Ms. Davis pulled the flat off Randy, and he scrambled out.

The **ending** tells the outcome of the incident.

Randy said he wasn't hurt, but Ms. Davis found a small scrape on his shoulder. She sent him to Nurse Greene. Randy was checked by the nurse, who treated his scrape and released him. Ms. Davis asked me to write up a report of what I saw. She also asked Randy to write a report.

ELPS 3H

Writing Tips

Before you write . . .

- **Follow a proper format.** Ask your teacher or school administrator if there is an incident report form you should fill out. If not, base your report on the sample on page 152.
- **Review the facts.** Jot down notes to yourself that answer the 5 Ws: *who, what, when, where,* and *why.*

5 Ws Chart

Subject:

Who?	What?	When?	Where?	Why?

During your writing . . .

- **Be objective.** Report what happened. Avoid blaming anyone or adding your own opinion.
- **Be honest.** Record what you witnessed. Don't tell half-truths or change events slightly to produce a certain outcome.
- **Be complete.** Provide all the information that teachers, advisors, or administrators would need.

After you've written a first draft . . .

- **Review your statements.** Make sure that your sentences are clear and complete. Check to see that you have answered all the 5 Ws.
- **Check for accuracy.** Double-check dates, times, facts, and details.
- **Edit for correctness.** Check grammar, punctuation, capitalization, and spelling.

Try It Write an incident report as if you had witnessed the following:

Who: Todd Chen
What: Hit his thumb with a hammer
When: At 4:30 p.m. on May 14, 2010
Where: In the wings of the auditorium stage
Why: Working on the set for *Phantom of the Country Opera*
Follow-up: Nurse Greene checked to make sure the thumb wasn't broken, and she washed and bandaged it, and sent Todd home.

Narrative Writing

Writing for the Texas Assessment

When you take state tests in Texas, you often have to write. The prompt tells you what to write about and gives some things to remember. Read the following prompt.

Prompt

> Write a composition about a special time you spent with friends doing outdoor activities.

Use the information below to help you write your composition.

REMEMBER THAT YOU SHOULD—

- ☐ write about a special time you spent with friends doing outdoor activities.
- ☐ include all important details about the event.
- ☐ make your story interesting with sensory words and natural dialogue.
- ☐ use correct sentences, grammar, punctuation, capitalization, and spelling.

Prewriting Select a Form

The prompt doesn't tell you what form of writing to use. How can you decide which one? Think about which genre best fits the meaning you want to convey to an audience.

Do you want to:

- describe the facts of what happened?
- give your audience a sense of what it was like to be there?
- explain the events that took place?
- share your personal experience?
- give information?
- persuade readers to try this activity for themselves?

Answering the questions above will help you decide on a form.

Ramiro wanted to share a personal experience. He decided the best form was a narrative because it allowed him to tell a story of a special time he spent with his friends.

Plan the Writing

Ramiro remembered what a great time he had on the first nice spring day with his friends. He decided to write about that day. To plan his draft, he used a time line. It helped him choose events and organize them.

Time Line

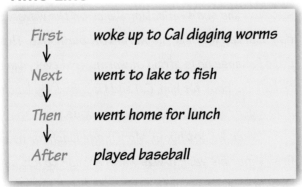

First ↓	woke up to Cal digging worms
Next ↓	went to lake to fish
Then ↓	went home for lunch
After	played baseball

Drafting Creating Your First Draft

Next, Ramiro used his time line to write his personal narrative. Read Ramiro's narrative below.

The **beginning** states the focus of the narrative (**underlined**).

Last Saturday was the first nice spring day this year. My friends and I spent the whole day together. We hadn't made any special plans, but we still had a fun-filled day.

I woke up just before 8:00 that morning because there was a scraping noise outside my bedroom window. Looking out, I saw my friend Cal digging a hole near our back fence. My other friend Beto was standing there watching, and his little sister Marcie, who follows Beto everywhere, was holding a can.

"What do you think you're doing?" I yelled from my window.

"Digging worms," said Cal. "Find your fishing stuff and get down here!"

By 8:30 we were on our way to the lake. The sun was already warming us up, and soon it was too hot for jackets, so we tied them around our waists. When we got to the lake, we settled down on a pier, tossed our lines in the water, and watched the sun's reflection dance on the waves. Soon the fish started nibbling the worms off our hooks. That annoyed Beto because he is afraid of worms, and every time Marcie had to bait his hook for him, Cal and I laughed. By lunchtime we had a stringer full of bluegills and rock bass.

Each **middle** paragraph tells about the activities and the characters involved in them.

When we got home, Mom made lunch for us, and for the first time this year, it was warm enough to eat outside at the picnic table. After lunch, we played cards for a while. We had to play Old Maid because Marcie doesn't know any other games,

Specific details are used to show why this day was special for the writer.

but it was fun to play it again because you can yell and act up like a little kid.

Pretty soon five or six other kids showed up looking for something to do. We decided to play baseball in the lot near the cemetery. A great thing happened during that game. I became the first one in the neighborhood to hit a home run over the cemetery fence. I came close a couple of times last year, so this was a turning point in my career. We'll play ball after supper every night this summer.

The **ending** paragraph reflects on the experience.

All in all, it was a great day. It's amazing that all a guy like me needs to have fun is a can of worms, a deck of cards, a baseball, and a few friends.

Respond to the reading. Answer the following questions about the sample response.

- ☐ **Focus and Coherence** (1) What is the focus of the writer's response?
- ☐ **Development of Ideas** (2) What are some of the details in the writing that flesh out the ideas?
- ☐ **Organization** (3) How is the response organized?
- ☐ **Voice** (4) Does the writer's voice come through in his word choice? Give examples.

Literature Connection: You can find a personal narrative in "It's Not About the Bike" by Lance Armstrong.

TEKS 7.14A

Writing Tips

Use the following tips as a guide when responding to a narrative writing prompt.

Before you write . . .

- **Understand the prompt.**
  Remember that a narrative prompt asks you to tell a story.
- **Plan your time wisely.**
  Spend several minutes planning before you start writing. Use a time line to help you put your ideas in order.

Time line

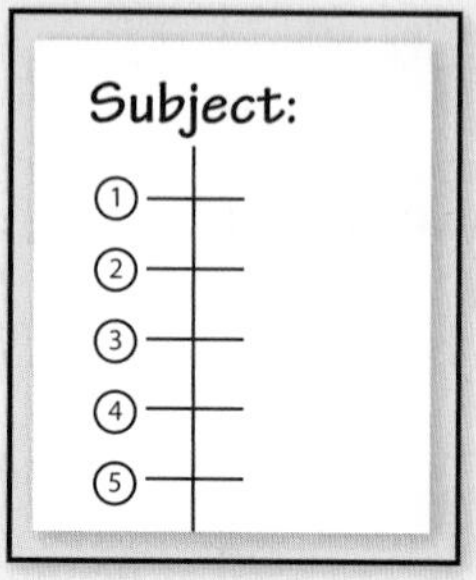

During your writing . . .

- **Decide on a focus for your narrative.**
  Use key words from the prompt as you write your focus statement.
- **Be selective.**
  Tell only the main events in your narrative.
- **End in a meaningful way.**
  Reflect on the importance of the narrative.

After you've written a first draft . . .

- **Check for completeness and correctness.**
  Present events in order. Delete any unneeded details and neatly correct any errors.

Plan and write a response. Respond to the prompt on page 154. Complete your writing within the time limit your teacher sets. Remember to select a form and use the tips above as you write.

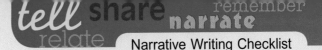

Narrative Writing in Review

Purpose: In narrative writing, you tell a story about something that has happened.

Topics: Narrate . . . an experience that taught you something,
a time of personal change, or
a memorable event.

Prewriting

Select a topic from your own life. Look through old photos or your journal to find a special occasion. Also, use sentence starters to get you thinking about possible topics. (See page **102**.)

Remember the details by writing freely and answering the 5 Ws. (See page **103**.)

Organize details about the people involved in this special time. List sensory details to use in describing the activity. Include dialogue that reveals the speaker's personality or that keeps the action moving. (See pages **104–106**.)

Drafting

In the beginning, grab the reader's attention by using interesting details or dialogue. (See page **109**.)

In the middle, tell the events of the story in time order. Establish your own voice to describe events, and use sensory details, dialogue, and action words to create a clear picture for the reader. (See pages **110–111**.)

In the ending, tell why the experience was important and how it taught you something. (See page **112**.)

Revising

Review the writing for focus and coherence, organization, development of ideas, and voice. (See pages **114–121**.)

Editing

Check your writing for conventions. Review punctuation of dialogue, and ask a friend to check the writing, too. (See pages **124–128**.)

Make a final copy and proofread it for errors before sharing it with other people. (See page **129**.)

Assessing

Use the scoring rubric to assess your finished writing. (See pages **48–49**.)

describe
define

ELPS 2C, 3E, 3G, 3H, 4C, 4G

TEXAS WRITE SOURCE Online
www.hmheducation.com/tx/writesource

Expository Writing

Writing Focus

- Expository Paragraph
- Comparison-Contrast Essay
- Cause-and-Effect Essay

Grammar Focus

- Subject-Verb Agreement
- Subordinating Conjunctions

Learning Language

Work with a partner. Read the meanings and share answers to the questions.

1. A **comparison** tells how things are alike.
   Make a comparison between two things in your classroom.
2. A **contrast** tells how two things are different.
   Make a contrast between two kinds of pets.
3. To **make your case** means to give strong reasons that support your opinion.
   What is an opinion you could make a case for?

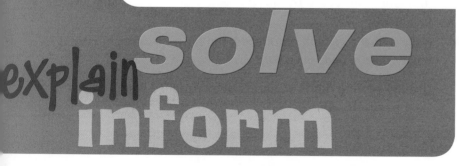

solve
explain
inform

Expository Writing

Expository Paragraph

What's the difference between a school bus driver and a cold? One knows the stops, and the other stops the nose!

All kidding aside, when you explain the similarities and differences between two things, you are comparing and contrasting them. Doing this helps you to understand each thing better. In an expository paragraph (a paragraph that *explains*), you can compare and contrast all sorts of things: soul music and R & B, science fiction and fantasy, or even tacos and pizza.

In this chapter you will write a comparison-contrast paragraph about two similar things. Maybe next time someone says, "What's the difference between . . . ?," you'll already know the answer!

Writing Guidelines

Subject: Two things to compare and contrast
Purpose: To explain
Form: Expository paragraph
Audience: Classmates

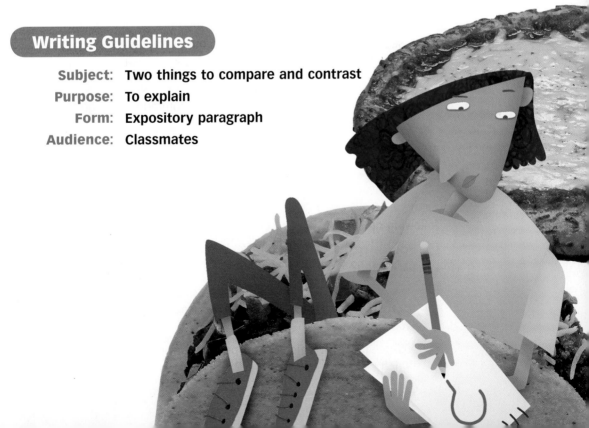

ELPS 3H, 4G

Expository Paragraph

The simplest form of expository writing is the expository paragraph. It usually starts with a **topic sentence**, which lets the reader know what the paragraph will be about. The **body** sentences give details that support the topic sentence, and the **closing sentence** ends the explanation. The paragraph below compares and contrasts a student's two favorite foods.

Topic Sentence

What'll It Be: Tacos or Pizza?

Tacos and pizza might seem totally different, but they actually have a lot in common. Even though tacos come from Mexico, and pizza comes from Italy, each food is an American favorite. Both are foods with a solid base you can pick up and eat. Tacos have a tortilla shell made from ground corn or flour. Pizzas are cooked on a crust that is basically a flat loaf of bread. Both foods are loaded with toppings. One way they are different is that taco fixings get cooked separately and then put together, but pizza ingredients get baked right along with the crust. Ingredients for both tacos and pizza include meats, cheeses, sauces, and vegetables. These foods have one more thing in common: They go fast when served!

Body

Closing Sentence

Respond to the reading. On your own paper, answer each of the following questions.

- ☐ **Focus and Coherence (1) What is the topic of the paragraph?**
- ☐ **Organization (2) Does the essay focus on one food at a time (subject by subject) or compare tacos and pizza together (point by point)?**
- ☐ **Voice (3) Is the voice of this paragraph formal or informal? Which words make it that way?**

TEKS 7.14A, 7.22A
ELPS 2I, 3E

Prewriting Selecting a Topic

The writer of the essay on page 162 that compares pizza and tacos started by brainstorming a list of things he was interested in. Then he wrote down something he could compare to each item. He shared his list with a partner. Together they discussed which topic would make the most interesting essay.

Topics List

Topics to Compare

~~Grandmother Garcia~~	~~Grandmother Foster~~
Skateboards	Scooters
~~Baseball~~	~~Softball~~
Tacos	Pizza

Prewrite

Make a list and select a topic. Using the list above as a guide, jot down a few topics or items that interest you. For each, write at least one thing that might make an interesting comparison and contrast. Consult with a partner, and then choose two items with enough similarities and differences to write a comparison-contrast paragraph.

Drafting Developing a Controlling Idea

Once you have two things to compare, it's time to develop a controlling idea, or thesis, for your paragraph. Express your controlling idea in a topic sentence that introduces your comparison-contrast essay.

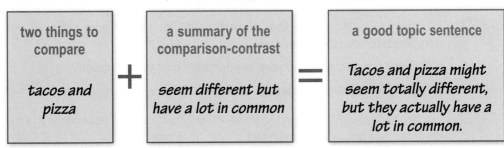

two things to compare	+	a summary of the comparison-contrast	=	a good topic sentence
tacos and pizza		*seem different but have a lot in common*		*Tacos and pizza might seem totally different, but they actually have a lot in common.*

Draft

Write your topic sentence. Using the example above as a model, write a topic sentence for your paragraph. You may need to try a few different versions to make sure this sentence says what you want it to say.

TEKS 7.14B
ELPS 5B

Drafting Creating Your First Draft

Now it's time to think about your two topics and write the first draft of your paragraph. The following suggestions can help you.

- Start with your topic sentence.
- Include your details point by point. Each idea should build on the next to create a coherent paragraph.
- Create a closing sentence that shows your interest in the topic.

Draft **Write your first draft.** Put the details in an order that makes the most sense and builds from one idea to the next.

Revising Improving Your Paragraph

Read back through your draft. Then check for *focus and coherence, organization, development of ideas,* and *voice* in your paragraph.

Revise **Review and improve your paragraph.** Think about the questions below as you work on your writing.

1. Is my topic sentence clear and interesting?
2. Have I organized my details point by point?
3. Do the details build upon the topic sentence?
4. Does my closing sentence show my interest in the topic?

Editing Checking for Conventions

Carefully edit your revised paragraph for *conventions.*

Edit **Edit your writing.** Use the following questions to help you check your paragraph for conventions.

1. Have I corrected any errors in punctuation or capitalization?
2. Have I checked my grammar and spelling?

Edit **Proofread your paragraph.** Make a neat, final copy of your comparison-contrast paragraph and proofread it one more time.

Expository Writing

Comparison-Contrast Essay

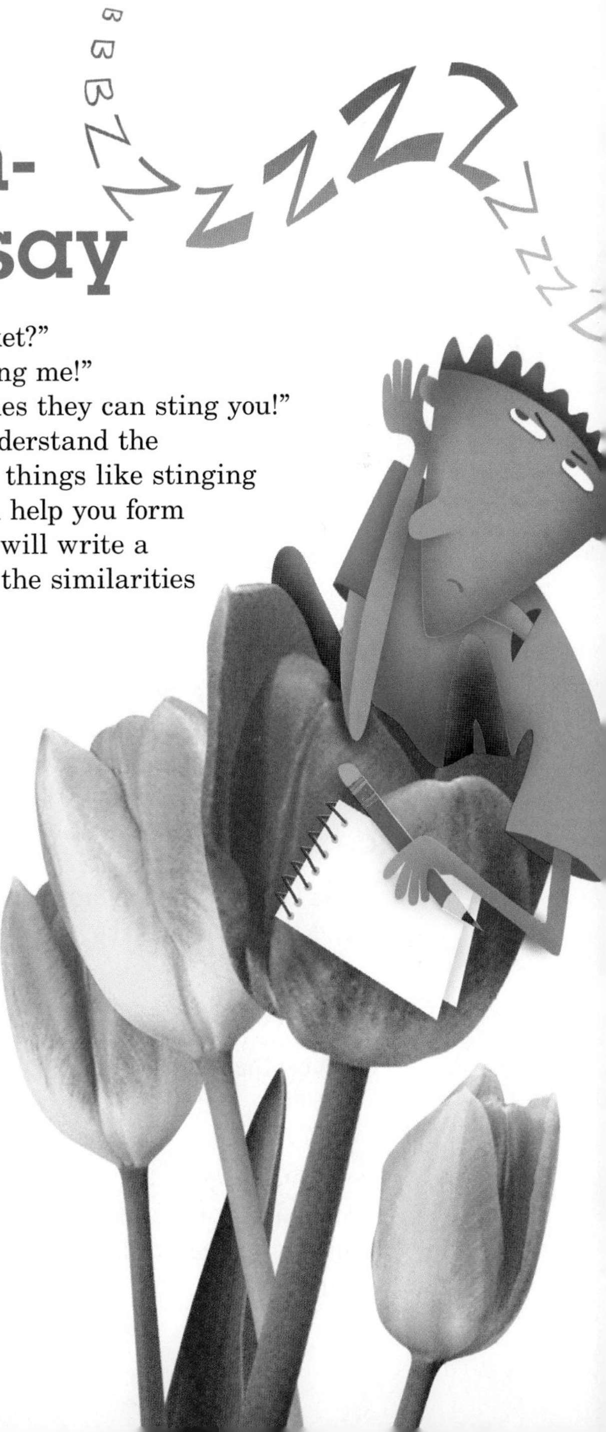

"What is that, a bee or a yellow jacket?"

"What's the difference? Both can sting me!"

"The big difference is how many times they can sting you!"

Sometimes it's very important to understand the similarities and differences between two things like stinging insects. A comparison-contrast essay can help you form this understanding. In this chapter, you will write a comparison-contrast essay that explains the similarities and differences between two animals.

Writing Guidelines

Subject: Two animals

Purpose: To explain similarities and differences

Form: Comparison-contrast essay

Audience: Classmates

Understanding Your Goal

Your goal in this unit is to write a well-organized expository essay that compares and contrasts two animals. The traits listed in the chart below will help you plan and write your essay. The scoring rubric on pages 48–49 will also help you. Refer to it often to improve your writing.

Traits of Comparison-Contrast Writing

Focus and Coherence

Include only details that will help your reader understand your comparison. Avoid unnecessary information that might distract your reader from the controlling idea.

Organization

Introduce your comparison in the beginning and provide a point-by-point comparison in the middle. Include a conclusion that reinforces your controlling idea.

Development of Ideas

Think through everything you include in your essay. Make sure your ideas are developed with interesting details to help your reader understand and appreciate them.

Voice

Use language that expresses your personality and individuality and shows enthusiasm for your subject.

Conventions

Follow the rules for grammar, capitalization, punctuation and spelling.

Literature Connection. You can read another example of expository writing in the article "What Do You Know About Sharks?" by Sharon Guynup.

Comparison-Contrast Essay

In the following essay, a student writer tells about two insects that look similar but are very different.

Beginning
The beginning introduces the two insects and gives a focus statement (**underlined**).

Middle
The first middle paragraph compares and contrasts the physical characteristics of the animals.

The second middle paragraph deals with the insects' diets.

What's the Buzz?

Gardens that overflow with vibrant flowers may also overflow with stinging insects. An experienced gardener knows that not all of these insects are created equal. Honeybees and yellow jackets (wasps), for example, may look similar, but they're really very different creatures.

At first glance, anybody could mistake a honeybee for a yellow jacket. Both are about an inch long, with black and yellow stripes on their abdomens. Also, both have a pair of wings that buzz as they fly. A closer look shows differences, though. First, honeybees are fuzzy, but yellow jackets have a smooth, hard skin. Second, honeybees have little pollen baskets on their legs, while yellow jackets have none. Third, each insect has a stinger, but a honeybee uses its stinger only as a last defense. It actually dies after it stings once. A yellow jacket can sting over and over and not die.

Honeybees and yellow jackets have completely different diets. Honeybees eat honey, of course. They make it out of flower nectar, which is a sweet liquid that flowers create. As honeybees go from flower to flower, they pollinate the plants. That's why people want as many honeybees around as possible. Yellow jackets, on the other hand, don't pollinate flowers. If a yellow jacket has to choose between a flower and a can of soda, it'll take the soda every time. Yellow jackets also like to eat garbage and even other insects. So, if a honeybee comes to your window box, it is there to visit the flowers. If a yellow jacket comes, it is probably planning to eat the dead flies in the windowsill.

Middle
The third paragraph explains their habitats.

Both insects build nests, but the two kinds of nests are really different. A honeybee's nest is a honeycomb made out of wax. Many of the little cells inside a honeycomb are full of honey, but others hold pupae, which are baby bees. Yellow jackets make their nests out of a paper-like substance that holds no honey. Another difference between the homes of bees and yellow jackets is their size. Beehives can be very large, with tens of thousands of bees. One queen rules a complicated society, with different jobs for male drones and female workers and guards. Yellow jackets' nests are usually smaller, with only a dozen or so insects and no complex organization.

Ending
The ending sums up the comparison and gives the reader something to think about.

Though honeybees and yellow jackets might seem the same, they are quite different. Honeybees are gentle helpers, but yellow jackets are mean scavengers. A neighbor summed it up pretty well: "In my garden, bees are guests, but yellow jackets are pests."

Respond to the reading. **Answer the following questions about the sample essay.**

- ☐ **Focus and Coherence** **(1) How does the writer capture your interest?**
- ☐ **Organization** **(2) How are the middle paragraphs organized?**
- ☐ **Development of Ideas** **(3) What two details in the essay are most interesting to you?**
- ☐ **Voice** **(4) What makes the writer sound knowledgeable?**

Go Online!

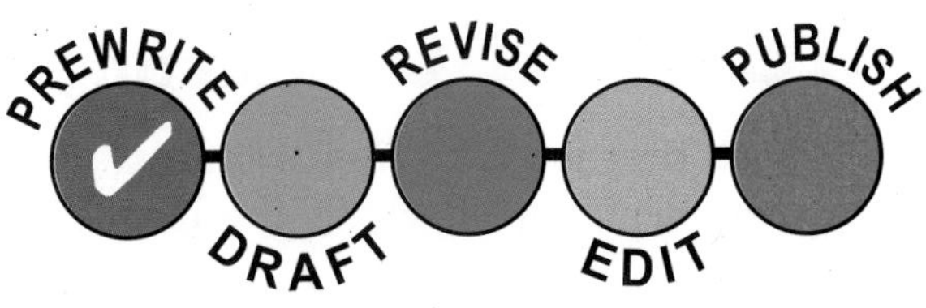

Prewriting

You may not have any idea what to write about yet. Don't worry. That's what prewriting is all about. It can help you select a topic, gather details, and organize them in the best way.

Keys to Effective Prewriting

1. *Select two subjects that could be made into an interesting comparison-contrast essay.*
2. *Gather details about each subject, making sure you have enough information for an essay.*
3. *Write a focus statement that names your controlling idea and sums up the similarities and differences.*
4. *Write topic sentences that tell what each body paragraph will be about.*
5. *Organize your details with a list or an outline.*

TEKS 7.14A, 7.22B

Prewriting Selecting a Topic

Your first job is to find two animals that you would like to compare and contrast. Begin by checking the list below to find out which animal groups interest you most.

birds	spiders	amphibians	sea creatures	mammals
fish	insects	reptiles	single-celled animals	primates

Using this list, Luc chose his favorite categories and listed them in a chart. Then he wrote pairs of animals he would enjoy comparing and contrasting.

Topics Chart

Birds	*Reptiles*	*Sea Creatures*
eagle and buzzard	*king cobra and rattler*	*white shark and dolphin* (circled)
hummingbird and finch	*anaconda and python*	*octopus and squid*
pigeon and falcon		*orca and blue whale*

Prewrite

Create your own chart. Use the example above as a model to create your own animal topics chart.

1. Choose three categories of animals you are interested in and list them across the top.
2. Under each category, write pairs of animals you would like to compare and contrast.
3. Circle the pair of animals that you want to write about.

Prewrite

Make a written research plan. Record ideas for obtaining information about the two animals you chose.

1. Decide what kinds of facts about the two animals you will use in your essay.
2. Write down key words that you can use in a search.
3. List possible sources (electronic, print, experts, etc.).

TEKS 7.23D
ELPS 4G, 5B

Understanding Plagiarism and Paraphrasing

Two important ideas to understand as you research your essay are plagiarism and paraphrasing.

The following sentence was found in a book about great white sharks:

> *The great white shark has developed the ability to keep its body temperature higher than the surrounding water, which allows it to hunt more successfully.*

Plagiarism

The following sentence was written by a student:

> *The white shark has the ability to keep its body temperature higher than the surrounding water. This allows it to hunt more successfully.*

Even though the writer has changed a few words, these sentences are unacceptable.

Plagiarism is copying or using another person's words or ideas without giving credit. Plagiarism is never acceptable in writing.

Paraphrasing

The following sentence was written by a student:

> *According to well-known shark expert Dr. Nancy Thurston, "The great white shark has developed the ability to keep its body temperature higher than the surrounding water." This ability permits the shark to hunt its prey more successfully, especially difficult-to-catch seals.*

Paraphrasing means restating another person's ideas using your own words. Paraphrasing is acceptable in writing as long as you explain that you are using another person's ideas. To show that you are paraphrasing, you can use quotation marks around the exact words. You can also refer to the person whose ideas you are using.

Try It Work with a partner to write paraphrases of these sentences.

1. The reputation of the great white shark as an "eating machine" is somewhat exaggerated.
2. The image of the great white shark as a monster of the deep was created for many people by the movie *Jaws*.
3. Great white sharks have been known on rare occasions to leap over boats, even knocking people into the water.

TEKS 7.14B, 7.17A
ELPS 5G

Prewriting Organizing Point by Point

Your comparison-contrast essay will be organized **point by point**. That means that you will discuss one point about both subjects before you move on to the next point.

Paragraphs in a Point-by-Point Essay

In point-by-point organization, each paragraph is about one main idea.

- The **first body paragraph** should discuss *physical characteristics* of both animals.
- The **second body paragraph** should discuss *diet.*
- The **third body paragraph** should discuss *habitat.*
- **Other body paragraphs** may deal with *behaviors, history,* or the animals' *future outlook.*

Details in a Point-by-Point Essay

Within each body paragraph, details are also arranged point by point. If the size of one animal is given, the size of the other is given next. That way, each detail can be separately compared or contrasted.

Try It In each example below, decide if the details are organized point by point. If not, jot down the details you would need to research to make the sentences follow point-by-point organization.

1. Dolphins grow to about 8 feet in length. Sharks, on the other hand, eat anything they find.
2. Both dolphins and sharks have dorsal fins and pectoral fins, but dolphins have a blowhole for breathing, while sharks use gills.
3. Sharks have rough skin, but dolphins are very smart.

Prewrite **Organize the facts for your paragraphs.** Make a two-column chart to record the information for the two animals you are comparing. Use the information above about the paragraphs. Make a point-by-point comparison for the topic of each paragraph. Record the data in the appropriate column for each animal.

TEKS 7.14A, 7.14B, 7.17A

Writing Topic Sentences

Now that you have gathered details and learned about point-by-point organization, you are ready to write topic sentences for your body paragraphs. Each topic sentence should sum up the paragraph's main idea (physical characteristics, diet, and so on) for both animals. (See pages 614–615 for more information about topic sentences.)

For his essay on white sharks and dolphins, Luc wrote a topic sentence for each main idea.

- **Topic sentence 1:** *(physical characteristics)* Both white sharks and dolphins have bodies that are perfect for life at sea.
- **Topic sentence 2:** *(diet)* Both of these great ocean hunters enjoy the same favorite foods.
- **Topic sentence 3:** *(habitat)* Even though both white sharks and dolphins live in warm ocean waters, they lead very different lives.

Prewrite

Write your topic sentences. Refer to the models above as you create your topic sentences.

1. **Review your research notes about your animals' physical characteristics. Sum up the animals' similarities and differences in your first topic sentence.**
2. **Now, review your notes about the animals' diet. Sum up the animals' similarities and differences in diet in your second topic sentence.**
3. **Repeat the process for each idea you want to include in your essay.**

Writing a Focus Statement

Your topic sentences can help you develop a focus (thesis) statement which sums up the similarities and differences. Your focus statement should be a general comparison from which you can add details to create a focused piece of writing.

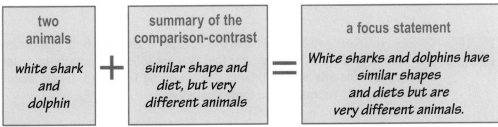

two animals		summary of the comparison-contrast		a focus statement
white shark and dolphin	+	*similar shape and diet, but very different animals*	=	*White sharks and dolphins have similar shapes and diets but are very different animals.*

Prewrite

Write your focus statement. Using the model above, write a focus statement for your comparison-contrast essay. Make sure your statement is a general starting point that can be built up with details.

TEKS 7.14B, 7.17A
ELPS 5G

Prewriting Organizing Your Ideas

Before you write your essay, you should create an organized list to plan your essay. The directions below can guide you.

Directions	Organized List
Write your focus (thesis) statement.	*White sharks and dolphins have similar shapes and diets but are very different animals.*
Write your first topic sentence.	*1. Both white sharks and dolphins have bodies that are perfect for life at sea.*
Compare your details.	*– same shape, different tail – sharks twice as big – same color, different texture*
Write your second topic sentence.	*2. Both of these great ocean hunters enjoy the same favorite foods.*
Compare your details.	*– both follow schools of fish – different teeth – dolphins picky; sharks not*
Write your third topic sentence.	*3. Even though both white sharks and dolphins live in warm ocean waters, they lead very different lives.*
Compare your details.	*– sharks loners; dolphins in pods – dolphins "talk"; sharks don't – both follow ships*

Prewrite

Create your organized list. Use the directions above to help you create your own organized list. Remember that you are following a point-by-point organization. Include topic sentences followed by facts and details about each animal that support these topic sentences.

TEKS 7.14C

Go Online!

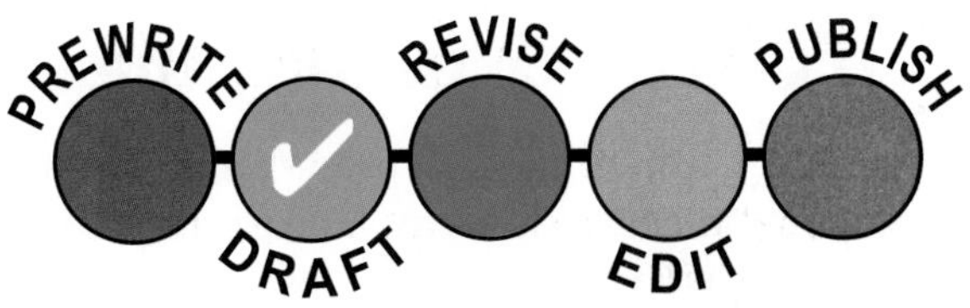

Drafting

Once you've finished your prewriting, it's time to write your first draft. You're ready to write a first draft when you know enough about your topic and have written a clear focus statement.

Keys to Effective Drafting

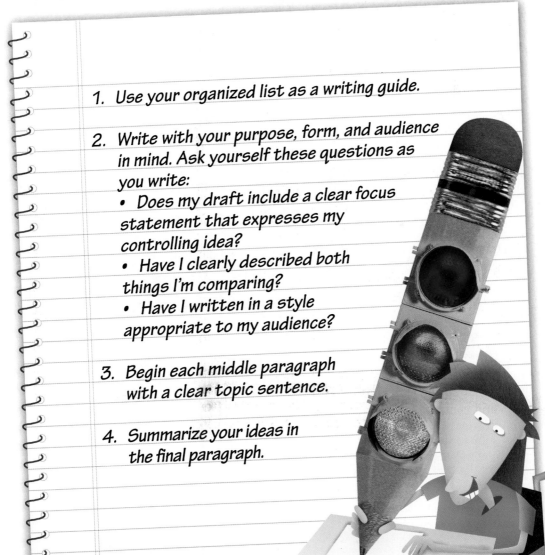

1. Use your organized list as a writing guide.
2. Write with your purpose, form, and audience in mind. Ask yourself these questions as you write:
   - Does my draft include a clear focus statement that expresses my controlling idea?
   - Have I clearly described both things I'm comparing?
   - Have I written in a style appropriate to my audience?
3. Begin each middle paragraph with a clear topic sentence.
4. Summarize your ideas in the final paragraph.

TEKS 7.14A, 7.17A(i)
ELPS 4C

Drafting Getting the Big Picture

After finishing your prewriting, you are ready to write a first draft of your comparison-contrast essay. The graphic below shows how the parts of your essay will fit together. (The examples are from the student essay on pages 177–180.)

Beginning

The **beginning** introduces the two animals and gives a focus statement.

Focus Statement

White sharks and dolphins have similar shapes and diets but are very different animals.

Middle

Each **middle paragraph** covers one main point of comparison.

Topic Sentences

Both white sharks and dolphins have bodies that are perfect for life at sea.

Both of these great ocean hunters enjoy the same favorite foods.

Even though both white sharks and dolphins live in warm ocean waters, they lead very different lives.

Ending

The **ending** thoughtfully sums up the comparison and contrast.

Closing Sentences

That's one final difference between sharks and dolphins. Dolphins are very curious and very friendly, so the swimmer can breathe easily—just like his friend, the dolphin.

TEKS 7.14A, 7.17A(i), 7.17A(ii), 7.17A(v)

Starting Your Essay

The first paragraph of your essay should grab your reader's attention and introduce your topic. Here are some strategies you can use to begin your first paragraph.

Beginning
Middle
Ending

- **Share an experience.**
  When I looked into the eyes of the dolphin at Sea World, I felt as though I had met a friend.
- **Give interesting information.**
  Swimmers may fear sharks, but sharks fear dolphins!
- **Create a dramatic scene.**
  A man paddles in the ocean, unaware that a large gray hunter is eyeing him.
- **Quote an authority.**
  "Meeting a shark face-to-face tends to focus one's attention," says shark expert Dr. Nancy Thurston.
- **Ask an intriguing question.**
  Would you know what to do if you met a shark in open water?

Beginning Paragraph

Luc begins his essay with a dramatic scene. Then he introduces the two animals he will compare by asking a question. Finally, he adds his focus statement.

The writer gets the reader's attention.

The focus statement is given (underlined).

A man paddles in the ocean, unaware that a large gray hunter is eyeing him. The creature suddenly swims toward him, and its dorsal fin breaks the surface. Is it a white shark or a dolphin? These creatures might look alike, but the difference between them could mean life or death. White sharks and dolphins have similar shapes and diets but are very different animals.

Draft **Write a beginning paragraph.** Write the opening of your comparison-contrast essay. Use one of the strategies above to get your reader's attention. Then add your focus statement.

EXPOSITORY

TEKS 7.14B, 7.17A(iii)
ELPS 4C

Drafting Developing the Middle Paragraphs

Remember to use your organized list and follow these tips.

- The **first middle paragraph** compares and contrasts the animals' *physical characteristics*.
- The **second middle paragraph** compares *diets*.
- The **third middle paragraph** compares *habitats*.
- **Other middle paragraphs** are optional and may cover such things as *behavior, history,* or *future outlook*.

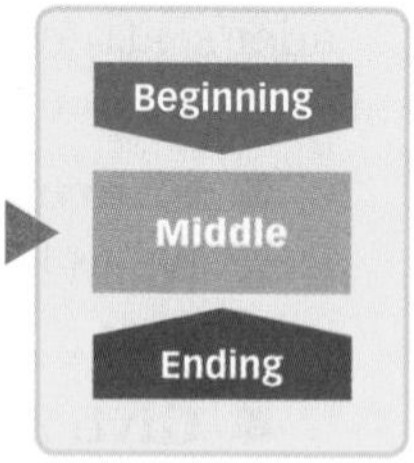

Using Comparison-Contrast Words

Certain words can help you make a comparison, while others create a contrast. (See pages 572–573 for additional transitions.)

Comparison

like	some	also
as	identical	both
alike	similar	each

Contrast

while	still	different
although	yet	however
whereas	but	even though

Middle Paragraphs

The topic sentence tells about physical characteristics (underlined).

The writer uses comparison-contrast words (in blue).

The closing sentence contains a final detail.

Both white sharks and dolphins have bodies that are perfect for life at sea. They have similar shapes, with long bodies, dorsal fins on their backs, pectoral fins on their bellies, and tails. The shark's tail is vertical, but the dolphin's tail is horizontal. On the whole, white sharks are bigger than dolphins. Most dolphins are no more than 8 feet long, but white sharks often grow to be 16 feet! Though sharks and dolphins have similar coloring, with gray backs and white bellies, their skin feels completely different. Sharkskin is like sandpaper because it is made up of millions of sharp scales. Dolphins have smooth, rubbery skin with blubber underneath. One other difference is that a shark has gills, since it breathes water

TEKS 7.14B, 7.17A(iii)
ELPS 5B

as other fish do. A dolphin, however, is a mammal, so it has a blowhole for breathing air.

Topic Sentence

Both of these great ocean hunters enjoy the same favorite food. They follow schools of fish and swim in to snatch them up. White sharks have rows of flat, triangular teeth, like knives. These teeth are made for cutting their food so they can swallow it in chunks. That's how sharks eat giant ocean tuna. Dolphin teeth are smaller and shaped like cones. They're perfect for biting into a fish or squid and holding on. Then dolphins swallow the food whole. Dolphins are picky eaters, unlike sharks, which also eat marine mammals like seals and otters. In fact, white sharks will eat just about anything, including license plates, tin cans, and even other sharks!

The writer covers details point by point.

Closing Sentence

Topic Sentence

Even though both white sharks and dolphins live in warm ocean waters, they lead very different lives. White sharks tend to cruise the oceans alone, but dolphins swim in pods, or schools, of between 10 and 500 creatures. Amazingly, dolphins have been seen in groups of more than 2,000! In their pods, dolphins make clicks and squeals for communication and echolocation, which is using sound to locate objects. Sharks don't make any sound except the crunch of bones! Both sharks and dolphins like to follow ships. Sharks follow them because someone might dump garbage out, but dolphins think it's fun to swim alongside them, leaping and playing.

The writer's voice shows genuine interest in the topic.

Closing Sentence

Draft

Write your middle paragraphs. Create the body of your comparison-contrast essay using your organized list as a guide.

TEKS 7.14C, 7.17A(i)

Writing Ending Your Essay

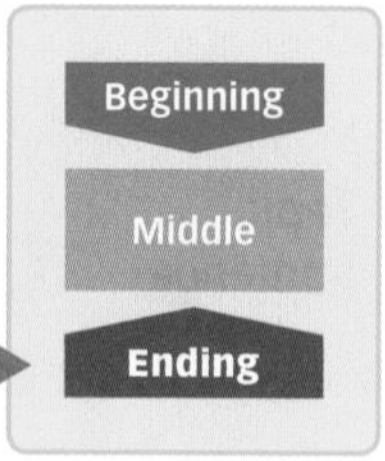

The ending of your essay should sum up the comparison and contrast and leave your reader with something to think about. Here are some effective strategies for ending your essay.

- **Add a new insight.**
  Perhaps the biggest difference between sharks and dolphins is that dolphins are smart, friendly mammals, but sharks are small-brained, cold-blooded fish.
- **Refer back to your beginning.**
  The gray dorsal fin comes out of the water—but is this a shark or a dolphin?
- **Quote your authority again.**
  As Dr. Nancy Thurston explains, "I've never met a person as interesting as a great white shark!"
- **Answer your intriguing question.**
  By the way, if you meet a shark in open water, smack it on the nose. That just might scare it away!

Ending Paragraph

The essay is summed up in a thoughtful way.

So whatever happened to the ocean swimmer? The gray dorsal fin comes out of the water—but is this a shark or a dolphin? The creature leaps over the swimmer and squeaks a greeting before diving again. That's one final difference between sharks and dolphins. Dolphins are very curious and very friendly, so the swimmer can breathe easily—just like his friend, the dolphin.

Draft **Write your ending.** Write the final paragraph of your essay. Try one of the strategies listed above to give the reader something to think about.

Draft **Rethink form, purpose, and audience.** Take another look at how well you've answered your questions of form, purpose, and audience. Is your essay still on target?

Go Online!

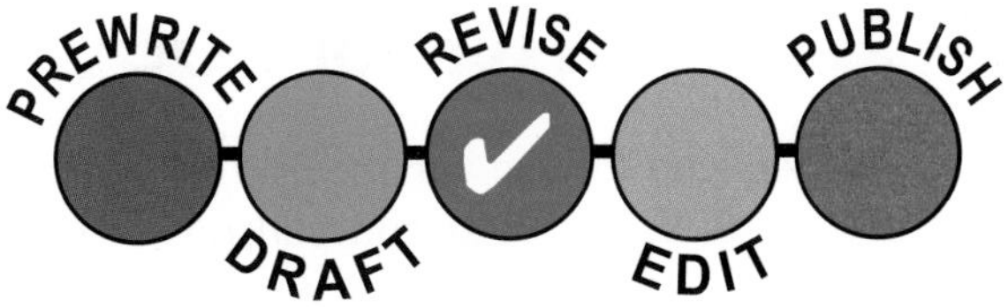

Revising

Now that you have written a draft, it's time to begin revising. You might add or remove details, shift sentences around, and refine your writing to make it clear and smooth.

Keys to Effective Revising

1. *Read through your entire draft to get a feeling of how well your essay works.*
2. *Make sure your focus statement clearly names the two things you compare and contrast.*
3. *Revise your paragraphs so that each one begins with a topic sentence, covers one main point, and includes only necessary details.*
4. *Make sure you sound knowledgeable and excited about your subject.*
5. *Check that your words and sentences make clear comparisons and contrasts.*

Texas Traits

Revising for Focus and Coherence

When you revise for *focus and coherence*, you make sure that you have written only about your controlling idea: the comparison between two things. All the details in your essay must relate to one of the items you're comparing, or to how they are alike or different. Don't include details that don't help the reader grasp your controlling idea.

You also need to make sure that your essay has no inconsistencies. You can't say one thing at the beginning and the opposite at the end.

How do I check for inconsistencies?

To check for inconsistencies, look for statements or ideas that contradict each other. Read the first and last paragraphs of this essay. Can you spot the inconsistency in the writer's essay?

> *Shark attacks are not nearly as common as many people believe. The image of the bloodthirsty demon of the deep is undeserved. Scientists tell us that sharks are hunters by nature. They are no more "evil" than a cat that catches a mouse or a robin that eats a worm.*

> *So beware next time you go to the beach. Blank, beady eyes may be watching you. A pale, ghostly killer may be silently stalking you, its innocent prey. Monstrous jaws may be waiting to make a meal of you!*

Revise

Check your essay. Read through your first draft or have a partner read it. Be sure your draft does not contain inconsistencies or unnecessary details.

TEKS 7.14C, 7.17A(v)
ELPS 3E

How can transitions help my comparison-contrast essay?

In a comparison-contrast essay, you move from point to point. But your essay has to be more than a list of ways two items are alike and different. You will need to connect your ideas, sentences, and paragraphs and avoid jumping from subject to subject. One way to help readers follow your ideas is to use transitions. Transitions are connecting words, such as *although* and *similarly,* that help the reader follow the movement of your ideas. They strengthen the internal coherence of your writing and make your points clearer.

Try It Read this passage from a student's comparison-contrast essay. Can you find places where she could use comparing and contrasting transitions?

Leopards and cheetahs are magnificent animals. Their habitats are different. Leopards spend much of their time in trees, where their spots mimic the patterns of light on leaves. Cheetahs blend perfectly into tall, dry grasses. The cheetah is the world's fastest land mammal and uses its speed to run down antelope, hare, and other small animals. The leopard uses its great strength to drag its kill up into trees. Cheetahs are found only in southern and eastern Africa. Leopards have a wider range and live in parts of Africa, central Asia, China, and India. Cheetahs and leopards are endangered.

Focus and Coherence
A transition makes this difference clearer.

Dolphins are picky eaters, unlike sharks, which also eat marine mammals like seals and otters.

(Original: *Dolphins are picky eaters. Sharks eat marine mammals like seals and otters.* — with inserted edits ", unlike" and "which also")

Revise **Add transitions.** Check your essay for comparison and contrast transitions. Have a partner suggest places where you could add transitions to make your essay clearer and easier to follow.

TEKS 7.25C

Texas Traits

Revising for Organization

When you revise your essay for *organization*, check to make sure you have done all of the following:

- presented your ideas in a format that makes sense for your topic and is easy for the reader to follow;
- covered all your details point by point;
- written paragraphs that have unity—that is, they are about one main idea; and
- connected ideas, sentences, and paragraphs with transition words.

How can I check for point-by-point organization?

One way to check your essay for point-by-point organization is to make a "hopscotch chart" for each middle paragraph. A chart like this can help you see if you covered each detail for both subjects. If you write about the body shape of the shark, you should also write about the body shape of the dolphin. (The hopscotch chart to the right was created by Luc to check the details in his first middle paragraph on page 178.)

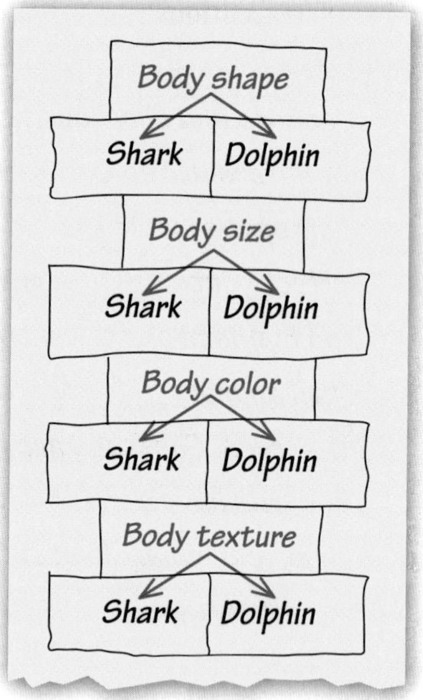

Revise

Create your own hopscotch chart. In the body of your paper, choose one of your middle paragraphs and graph the details in it using a hopscotch chart.

1. Write the first type of detail (for example, "Body shape") in a single box.
2. Draw double boxes below.
3. If you covered that detail for an animal, write its name in one of the double boxes.
4. Don't "hop" to the next single box until you have covered the detail for both animals.
5. Repeat the process for each detail in the paragraph.

Revise

Revise your details. If you forgot to cover one type of detail for a specific animal, revise your essay to include the detail.

Have I taken out any unnecessary details?

You'll know that your paragraphs have unity if each one deals with one main point. That one main point should be stated in your topic sentence. Each sentence in the paragraph should support that main point. You should have no sentences or unrelated details that do not support the main point.

Try It Read the following paragraph. Pay special attention to the main point stated in the topic sentence. Then indicate which details should be removed because they do not support the topic sentence.

Both lions and tigers are carnivores that hunt for their meat, though they go about it in different ways. Among lions, the lionesses are the best hunters. They stalk and bring down prey and then drag it back to the pride. Male lions are the ones with manes. Tigers, on the other hand, are solitary, so both males and females must know how to hunt. Tigers live in India, but lions live in Africa. Although lions and tigers have been known to attack humans, both great cats prefer hunting and eating wild game.

Organization
An unrelated detail is deleted.

Sharks eat marine mammals like seals and otters. ~~White sharks have many teeth.~~ In fact, white sharks will eat just about anything, including license plates, . . .

Revise **Check for unnecessary details.** Read through each paragraph, checking to see whether all the details support the main point in the topic sentence. Remove any details that do not.

TEKS 7.25B
ELPS 3H

Texas Traits Revising for Development of Ideas

To revise for *development of ideas*, make sure you have included evidence that explains your topic and interests your reader. If you have too little evidence, you won't be able to "make your case." If your evidence is poorly organized, it won't matter how strong it is. It will be too difficult for your readers to follow.

You should also make sure to include a balance of similarities and differences. Keep in mind that your essay both compares and contrasts. The quickest way to check for balance is to count the number of comparison words (similar, like, also) and contrast words (different, instead, but) you use.

How do I know if my details are interesting?

If your essay contains only details that everybody knows, the reader will be bored. Look for information that amazes, entertains, or informs.

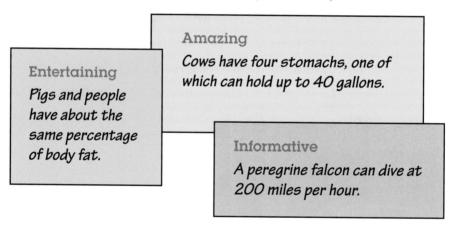

Amazing
Cows have four stomachs, one of which can hold up to 40 gallons.

Entertaining
Pigs and people have about the same percentage of body fat.

Informative
A peregrine falcon can dive at 200 miles per hour.

Try It Read the following details. For each, indicate whether you think the detail is interesting and why. Explain your thoughts to a partner.

1. A typical box turtle lives longer than a human being.
2. Dolphin brains are seven times larger than human brains.
3. Parrots have feathers of different colors.
4. As arthropods, crabs are giant spiders of the sea.
5. Dogs come in all shapes and sizes.

Revise **Review your details. Do you have several details that are amazing, entertaining, or informative? If not, check encyclopedias or the Internet to find a few more interesting details that you can use as evidence to support your main idea.**

TEKS 7.25B
ELPS 3H

Have I included relevant reasons that support my conclusion?

Your essay should have a conclusion that sums up your main point. A strong conclusion is based on the reasons you provide in the body of the essay. Make sure that you include enough relevant reasons to support your conclusion.

Try It Below are three pieces of evidence a student is planning to include in his comparison-contrast essay. What is a conclusion he could make based on the evidence?

- *Octopi and jellyfish both have large heads, or domes.*
- *A jellyfish does not have a true brain, but an octopus has a large brain.*
- *A jellyfish and an octopus have tentacles that surround a large mouth.*

Here is a conclusion another student plans to make at the end of her comparison-contrast essay. What kinds of evidence must she include to be able to make this conclusion?

Orangutans and chimpanzees may seem similar, but they have a number of striking differences.

Development of Ideas
An interesting detail helps balance comparisons and contrasts.

They have similar shapes, with long bodies, dorsal fins on their backs, pectoral fins on their bellies, and tails. ^ *The shark's tail is vertical, but the dolphin's tail is horizontal.*

On the whole, white sharks are bigger than dolphins. . . .

Revise **Check your conclusion.** Is your conclusion based on the evidence you provide in your essay? If not, you may need to add more relevant reasons—or change your conclusion.

ELPS 3E

Texas Traits

Revising for Voice

When you check your essay for *voice*, you want to make sure your writing sounds original and enthusiastic. The reader should be able to tell that you are interested in the topic you are writing about.

Is my voice original, or is it too predictable?

Your voice sounds predictable if you repeat the same sentence pattern over and over. Read the following paragraph. Notice how predictable the writing becomes.

> Both butterflies and moths come from larvae. Both insects go through metamorphosis. Butterflies create a chrysalis. Moths create a cocoon. Both insects turn into pupae. Butterflies come out with colorful wings. Moths come out with pale wings. Both insects let their wings dry. Butterflies fly off during the day. Moths fly off during the night.

The reason this voice sounds so predictable is that the writer uses just one pattern for his comparisons: "Both A and B do the same thing." He also uses just one pattern for his contrasts: "A does one thing. B does a different thing." Here are some other patterns that the writer should try.

Comparison

A and B are similar in that . . .
A does one thing, and B also . . .

B is like A because both . . .
Just as A does one thing,
B also . . .

Contrast

Even though A does one thing, B . . .
A and B are completely
different because . . .
Unlike A, B . . .
On the one hand, A . . .
On the other hand, B . . .

Try It Rewrite the predictable paragraph above. Use some of the comparison and contrast patterns shown above to make the voice sound original. Share your revised paragraph aloud with a partner.

Revise **Revise for voice.** Review your essay and look for places where your voice sounds too predictable. Try some of the patterns above to make your voice sound more original.

TEKS 7.14C

Is my point of view consistent?

Your point of view in an essay is the vantage point from which the subject is observed. For example, a comparison-contrast essay in the first-person point of view uses the words *I, me,* and *my.* The point of view is the writer's.

> My research told me that both chimpanzees and orangutans are fruit-eaters.

A comparison-contrast essay in the third-person point of view simply states actions, ideas, and descriptions without using words such as *I, me,* and *my.*

> Orangutans move around by swinging with their arms from trees, while chimpanzees walk using their fists for support.

Either point of view is fine, but make sure you are consistent. Don't switch from one point of view to another.

Try It Read this paragraph from a student's comparison-contrast essay. Does she use a consistent point of view? What revisions does she need to make? Explain your thoughts to a classmate.

> An octopus has large, sensitive eyes, but a jellyfish has no eyes at all. I wondered how they were able to move around, but found out that their heads are sensitive to light. This helps guide them through the water and find food.

Voice
Changes make the voice less predictable and more enthusiastic.

White sharks tend to cruise the oceans alone, but

dolphins swim in pods, or schools, of between 10 and 500

Amazingly, of more than 2,000!

creatures. Dolphins have been seen in groups. In their

pods, dolphins make clicks and . . .

Revise **Check your point of view.** Review your essay. Does your essay have a consistent point of view? Check to make sure you don't shift from one to another.

EXPOSITORY

Texas Traits

Revising Using a Checklist

Revise

Check your revising. On a piece of paper, write the numbers 1 to 8. If you can answer "yes" to a question, put a check mark after that number. If not, continue to work with that part of your essay.

Focus and Coherence

____ **1.** Do all the details support the main idea of my comparison-contrast essay?

____ **2.** Have I eliminated all inconsistencies and unnecessary details?

Organization

____ **3.** Have I covered all details in a point-by-point format?

____ **4.** Have I used transitions to tie my ideas, sentences, and paragraphs together?

____ **5.** Does each paragraph focus on one main idea which is expressed in the topic sentence?

Development of Ideas

____ **6.** Have I included enough relevant, interesting evidence to support my conclusion?

____ **7.** Does my essay contain a balance of similarities and differences?

Voice

____ **8.** Is my point of view consistent throughout the essay?

Revise

Make a clean copy. When you've finished revising, make a clean copy of your essay before you edit. This makes checking for conventions easier.

Go Online!

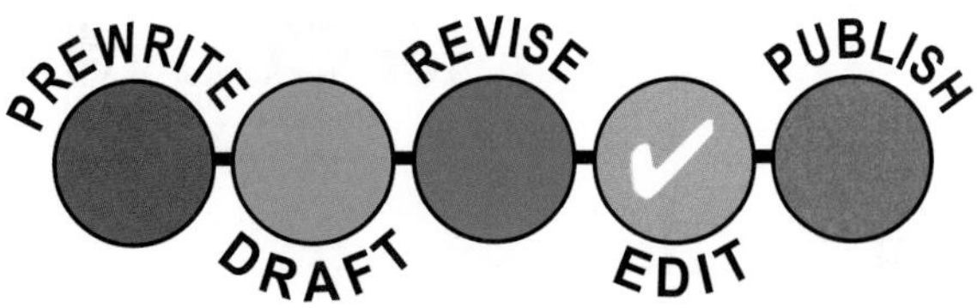

Editing

After you are done revising, your essay is ready for editing. As you edit, focus on conventions: grammar, mechanics, sentence structure, and spelling.

Keys to Effective Editing

1. *Use a dictionary, a thesaurus, and the "Proofreader's Guide" in the back of this book.*
2. *Check for any words or phrases that may be confusing to the reader.*
3. *Check your writing for correct grammar, punctuation, capitalization, and spelling. Ask someone else to check your writing for errors, too.*
4. *If you are using a computer, edit on a printed computer copy. Then enter your changes on the computer.*
5. *Use the editing and proofreading marks located inside the back cover of this book.*

TEKS 7.14D

Texas Traits Editing for Conventions

Grammar

How can I check subject-verb agreement?

Your subjects and verbs must agree in number. This can be tricky in comparison-contrast writing, because you often use compound subjects. The following rules will help you check for subject-verb agreement with compound subjects. (Also see pages **570–571**.)

If two singular subjects in a compound subject are joined by the word *and*, the verb should be plural.

An ant and an aphid form a partnership.

If the compound subject contains two singular subjects joined by the word *or* (or *nor*), the verb should be singular.

An ant or an aphid relies on its partner.

If the compound subject has a singular subject and a plural subject joined by *or* (or *nor*), the verb should agree with the subject closest to the verb.

Neither aphids nor the ant minds this partnership.

GRAMMAR Try It Read the following sentences. Decide which verb in parentheses makes the sentence have correct subject-verb agreement.

1. A flower and a bee (need, needs) each other.
2. Either Carmen or Daniel (write, writes) for the school newspaper.
3. A hamster or a gerbil (gnaw, gnaws) on wood.

Edit **Check your compound subjects.** **Read your essay, watching for places where you use compound subjects. Check to make sure the verb agrees in number with the compound subject. Then check for subject-verb agreement in all your sentences.**

TEKS 7.19A(vii)
ELPS 2C, 2I, 3D, 3G, 3H

How can subordinating conjunctions help me compare and contrast?

Subordinating conjunctions connect unequal ideas. These conjunctions are especially useful for creating strong contrasts. (Also see pages 792 and 794.)

Strong Contrasts

although, even though, where, though, even so, however, because

GRAMMAR Try IT In the paragraph below, find subordinating conjunctions that create strong contrasts. For each, indicate what is being contrasted.

Although seals are clever hunters, otters have developed an ingenious technique for opening oysters. Otters float on their backs and balance stones on their bellies. Even though this may look silly, the technique allows otters to crack oysters open by hitting them on the stones. Though seals are known for performing tricks, this oyster trick is one they'll never master because they have no hands.

Edit **Check your use of subordinating conjunctions. Read your essay and look for a sentence where you used a subordinating conjunction to create a strong contrast. If you don't find one, create a strong contrast by combining two short sentences using a subordinating conjunction.**

Learning Language

Using different kinds of sentences can make your writing more interesting. Decide on a topic that you and a partner are both interested in. First, you say a simple sentence about the topic. Then have your partner turn the sentence into a compound sentence using a word such as *and, but,* or *or*. Finally, you say a complex sentence using a word such as *because, since, after, although, when, that, who,* or *which*. Then switch roles. Here is an example:

you: **Cooking is a lot of fun. (simple sentence)**

your partner: **Cooking food is fun, but eating it is even better. (compound sentence)**

you: **Cooking, which I learned from my dad, is a great skill to have. (complex sentence)**

TEKS 7.14C

Sentence Structure

When you edit for *sentence structure*, you correct any errors in your sentences. You may also look at your sentence variety during this step.

Too many of the same kind of sentences can make your writing repetitive and boring. You can vary your sentence structure by writing compound and complex sentences, in addition to simple sentences.

Have I used a variety of sentences in my essay?

A simple sentence has one subject part and one verb part:

Dolphins breathe oxygen.
subject *verb*

A compound sentence consists of two or more simple sentences, joined by a conjunction or semicolon:

Sharks also breathe oxygen, but they get it from water.
subject *verb* *subject* *verb*

A complex sentence is a simple or compound sentence that contains a dependent clause. This kind of sentence usually contains a word such as *because, since, after, although, when, that, who,* or *which*:

Dolphins and sharks breathe oxygen, which comes from different sources.
simple sentence *dependent clause*

Try It Read each sentence. Tell if it is a simple, compound, or complex sentence.

1. Seals and sea otters are marine animals.
2. Sea otters are playful, which makes them favorites of people.
3. Seals hunt fish, but sea otters dive for oysters on the sea floor.
4. Sea otters lie on their backs, and then they crack open their oysters.
5. Anyone who has seen a seal on a rock will not forget it.

Edit **Check your sentence structure. Have you used simple, compound, and complex sentences in your essay? Make sure your essay includes a variety of each kind.**

Mechanics: Punctuation

When you edit for *mechanics,* you check for correct use of capitalization and punctuation. To edit your punctuation, look for correct use of periods, question marks, commas, and other punctuation marks.

Have I used commas correctly with introductory words, phrases, and clauses?

Whenever you start a sentence with an introductory word, phrase, or clause, you need to set it off with a comma.

First, otters float on their backs and hold a flat stone.

Holding the stone on their bellies, otters crack the oyster shell on the stone.

When they've finished eating the oyster, otters dive back down for another snack.

When the same word, phrase, or clause comes at the end of a sentence, don't set it off with a comma.

Otters dive back down for another snack when they've finished eating the oyster.

Try It Read each sentence. On your own paper, rewrite the sentences and correct the use of commas if necessary.

1. Although trained seals can perform tricks they can't crack open oysters on their bellies.
2. Sea otters are at risk, because their habitat is threatened.
3. Next we need to pack a lunch to eat on the boat.
4. The seal barked like a dog, when the trainer gave a signal.
5. After observing seals in the wild, I decided to become a biologist.

Edit **Check your punctuation.** Read through your draft. Have you correctly punctuated all introductory words, phrases, and clauses? Make necessary corrections.

Editing Using a Checklist

Edit **Check your editing.** On a piece of paper, write the numbers 1 to 8. If you can answer "yes" to a question, put a check mark after that number. If not, continue to edit for that convention.

Conventions

GRAMMAR

____ **1.** Do all my subjects and verbs agree in number?

____ **2.** Have I used subordinating conjunctions to connect unequal ideas?

MECHANICS

____ **3.** Have I set off introductory words with commas?

____ **4.** Have I set off introductory phrases with commas?

____ **5.** Have I set off introductory clauses with commas?

SENTENCE STRUCTURE

____ **6.** Have I included simple, compound, and complex sentences to vary my sentence structures?

SPELLING

____ **7.** Have I spelled all my words correctly?

____ **8.** Have I double-checked the words my spell-checker may have missed?

Creating a Title

- Sum up the comparison: **Hunters of the Deep**
- Name the two animals: **Wolf and German Shepherd**
- Be creative: **Guest or Pest?**

TEKS 7.14E

Go Online!

Publishing

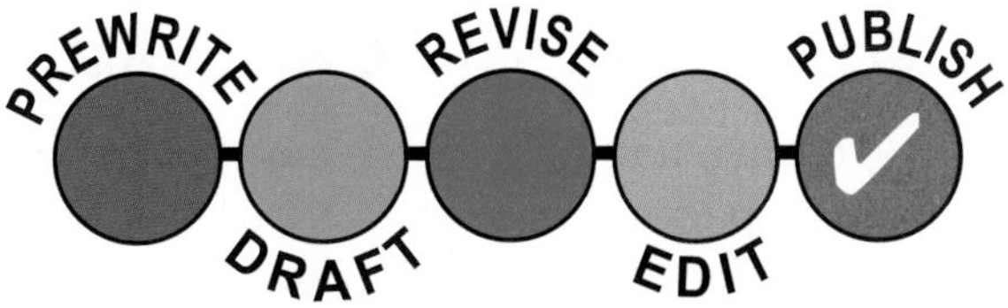

Sharing Your Essay

After writing, revising, and editing your comparison-contrast essay, make a neat final copy to share. Consider your audience and think about a format that would appeal to them. Suggestions are included below.

Publish **Make a final copy.** **Follow your teacher's instructions or use the guidelines below to format your essay. Create a clean final copy of your essay and carefully proofread it.**

Focus on Presentation

- **Use blue or black ink and write neatly.**
- **Write your name in the upper left corner of page 1.**
- **Skip a line and center your title; skip another line and start your writing.**
- **Indent every paragraph and leave a one-inch margin on all four sides.**
- **Write your last name and the page number in the upper right corner of every page after the first one.**

Create a Mini-Documentary

Turn your essay into a script for a wildlife documentary. Ask friends to help you act it out and film it. Use effects that will appeal to your audience.

Go Online!

Upload your comparison-contrast essay for others to read.

Illustrate Your Essay

Prepare an illustrated copy of your comparison-contrast essay for your classroom portfolio or e-portfolio. If possible, include diagrams of each animal.

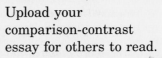

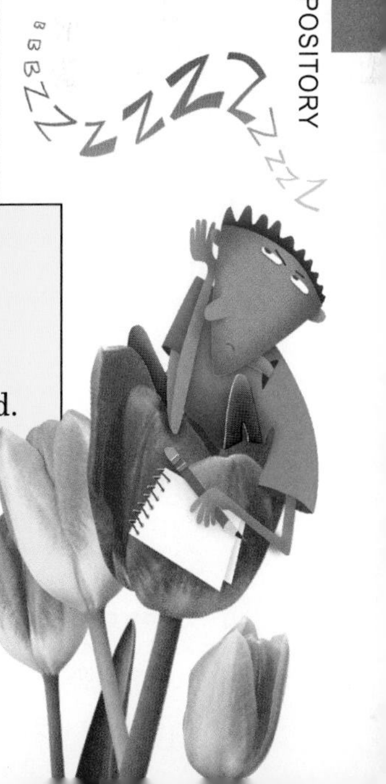

ELPS 4I, 4K

Evaluating an Expository Essay

To learn how to evaluate a comparison-contrast essay, you'll use the scoring rubric on pages 48–49 and the essays that follow. These essays are examples of writing for each score on the rubric.

Notice that this first essay received a score of 4. Read the description for a score of 4 on pages 48–49. Then read the essay. Use the same steps to study the other examples. Always remember to think about the overall quality of the writing.

Writing that fits a score of 4 is very strong.

4

The beginning grabs reader's interest.

The writer includes a strong focus statement.

Middle paragraphs make point-by-point comparisons.

You Big Ape!

Imagine that you're in the ape house at the zoo. In two side by side glass cages full of climbable trees, tire swings, and piles of fruits and vegetables, you see a big ape and a smaller ape—a gorilla and a chimpanzee. They're as alike as cousins, and yet you could never mistake one for the other. Gorillas and chimpanzees are similar in many ways, but the more you pay attention to them, the more differences you can see.

The similarities and differences show up first in the two apes' physical appearance. Both gorillas and chimps have typical apelike bodies with arms longer than their legs. Both are covered with thick black hair, and both walk on all fours but can stand for a little while. Here are some more similarities: Both walk on their knuckles, and both have hands with fingers and feet that can grasp objects. However, there's a big difference that anyone can see right away. Gorillas are much larger than chimpanzees, with male gorillas weighing about 450 pounds in the wild, which is about three times as much as male chimps. Which one would you rather meet in the forest? Let's find out.

In terms of behavior, these two forest apes differ in a surprising way: the huge gorilla is more peaceful than the small chimp. Chimps jump and holler, while gorillas are quiet; a chimpanzee is more likely to attack, while gorillas defend themselves basically by showing how big they are and bluffing by pounding their chests. Nevertheless, there are similarities in the ways chimps and gorillas live and behave. For example, both animals live in groups containing a dominant male, junior males, and females with children. At mealtimes, both kinds of ape eat mostly fruits and vegetables, but chimps sometimes hunt for meat, while gorillas do not. When it's time to sleep, chimps and gorillas both build nests in trees, although adult male gorillas sleep on the ground. All in all, both kinds of apes live in ways that are well adapted to the forest.

Paragraphs include topic sentences, body sentences, and closing sentences.

A major adaptation for both kinds of ape is their intelligence. Chimpanzees and gorillas might be the two animals that come closest to human beings in brain power. Chimpanzees are famous for their curiosity. They use tools, such as by digging for termites with small sticks. And while nether kind of ape can speak, both have been taught words by scientists. Koko the gorilla has an especially large vocabulary. It's no wonder humans like apes so much; they remind us of ourselves.

Information is presented in a meaningful format.

When you're looking at the chimp and the gorilla side by side in the zoo, you might ask yourself which one you like better. There's no right answer! Both of them are amazing animals with great physical and mental strength, and they're different enough from each other so that we can easily tell them apart.

Voice is confident and interested.

ELPS 4I, 4K

Writing that fits a score of 3 is strong.

3

The writer clearly identifies the topic.

Comparison format is not consistently point by point.

Sentence variety keeps the reader interested.

Frog or Toad?

A common question is, "What is the difference between frogs and toads?" It is hard to tell the difference if you are looking straight at a frog or a toad when you see one in your driveway at night. "Is that a frog or a toad?" you might ask. The answer is surprising. Even scientists do not always agree on what is a frog and what is a toad! Some experts say that toads are a type of frog. I will examine the similiarities and differences that make toads and frogs such a confusing pair.

To begin with, frogs and toads are both amphibians, which means they live both on land and in water, and they are both in an order called the Anura. When you look at a toad and a frog, you can easily see that they both have the same basic body type. They have short bodies, webbed feet, and powerful legs. That is true of both toads and frogs. However, there are some differences that are pretty well known to people.

One of the main differences is their skin. Frogs have smoother, moister skin, while toads have drier skin. Toads have thick skin, while frogs have thinner skin. Toads often have warty skin, but it is not true that touching a toad causes warts. That is just a supersition. A frog's moist skin is connected to the fact that frogs are more aquatic than toads are. That means that frogs spend more time in the water. Toads like to live in cooler, drier places, while frogs can also be found in the tropics.

ELPS 4I, 4K

Some errors are distracting.

The writer defines unfamiliar terms.

The frog's and toad's way of getting around is similar but different. As I mentioned, both creatures have powerful hind legs. However, frogs's legs are longer and are better for jumping, while toad's legs are shorter and toads spend much of their time walking rather than jumping. That probably has to do with living more on land, because if you're on land you might walk, but if you're in a pond you can hop from one lily pad to another.

There are more similiarities between toads and frogs. For example, both of them catch insects for food. And both of them lay thousand of eggs at a time, and the eggs are fertilized externally, which means outside the body. And both of them go through a tadpole stage and metamorphose (change) into an adult.

So are frogs and toads more alike or different? In my opinion, they are more alike. As a matter of fact there are exceptions to the rules, because there are some toads that have moist skin and some frogs that have warty skin, so that there really is no clear dividing line between the two. However, there is such a thing as a toad and such a thing as a frog, which is why we have two different words for them. The trouble is, we don't always know which is which.

ELPS 4I, 4K

Writing that fits a score of 2 is strong in some ways.

2

The writer's voice shows interest.

The writing lacks a clear focus statement.

Specific details are presented in sequence.

Many errors exist in spelling, mechanics, and sentence structure.

The ending does not create an organized essay.

Hawks and Vultures

I saw a bird soaring over the river the other day and I said "Look a hawk!" But my dad told me it wasn't a hawk. It was a vulture. I asked him how you can tell the difference. That was what got me interested in this topic.

First let's talk about the way they fly. Vultures are excellent at soaring and gliding, so they don't have to flap their wings much They just soar on the air current. So if you see something you think is a hawk and it soars for a long time without flapping its wings, it's probably a vulture.

Second, although both of them eat other animals, hawks are mostly hunters and vultures are mostly Scavingers. People usually think there's something bad about Scavingers, but actually their important, they get rid of dead animals. Vultures have a huge appitite so they get rid of a lot of dead bodies. Vultures aren't very strong which is one reason why they scavinge instead of hunt most of the time, or else just hunt small weak pray. Hawks are stronger and have keen eyes and sharp talons and beaks that let them spot their pray from far off and kill them.

There is no dout that hawks and vultures both have a place in Nature. The world would not be the same place without ether of them.

ELPS 4I, 4K

Writing that fits a score of 1 is weak.

1

There is no clearly focused introduction.

Many errors in spelling, grammar, and sentence structure are distracting.

Material is not organized in a coherent way.

Text stops without a conclusion.

Rats and Mice

People like mice and they don't like rats, that's the big difference. People don't like mice either a lot of the time but they realy hate rats. Which is because rats are biger and scary. They have big teeth and there bites are dangerus. Rats can carry disease. Like the Plag.

What's alike about rats and mice and what's different. Both are rodents. There are an amazeing number of rodents in the world. There is so many different kinds of rodents that I don't know what they all have in common such as chipmoncks gophers beavers and hampsters. Rats live all over the world. They travel in ships. They are very inteligent. They eat anything just like humans. They live near people, like in cities and they eat garbage and other human food. I read that there are as many rats as people. A mouse is smaller so people aren't as scared of them. Mice also live near people and in fields and they also eat anything they can get their little paws on. Mice and rats both spread disease. A mouse doesn't hurt you by coming up and biting like a rat but that's about all. It doesn't say if mice are as smart as rats.

My conclusion is, mice and rats are pretty much alike except rats are biger. Some people like mice and that's okay but I don't.

ELPS 5B, 5G

Evaluating and Reflecting on Your Writing

You've put a lot of time and effort into your comparison-contrast essay. Now take some time to score and think about your writing. On your own paper, finish each sentence starter below. To score your writing, refer to the scoring rubric on pages 48–49 and the examples you just read.

My Comparison-Contrast Essay

1. *The best score for my comparison-contrast essay is . . .*
2. *It's the best score because . . .*
3. *The best part of my comparison-contrast essay is . . .*
4. *The part that still needs work is . . .*
5. *The main thing I learned about writing a comparison-contrast essay is . . .*

Expository Writing

Cause-and-Effect Essay

Any big change can have many effects. For example, a dam on a river could destroy the habitat for certain animals, but could create new habitats for others. Put another way, a dam could be bad for some fish but good for the geese. Before people decide on a big change like building a dam, they should understand all the effects that the change will have.

In this chapter, you will write a cause-and-effect essay about a change in your school or community. As you write, you'll discover how one event can change the world around you in many ways.

Writing Guidelines

Subject: A change and its effects
Purpose: To explain
Form: Cause-and-effect essay
Audience: Classmates

Cause-and-Effect Essay

A cause-and-effect essay describes an event and what happens because of it. In the following essay, Rosalva writes about what happened when a dam was built on the river near her home.

Beginning

The cause is introduced, and the focus statement (**underlined**) sums up the effects.

Middle

Each middle paragraph explains one of the main effects.

Lower Forks Dam

After the big flood of 2001, Lower Forks built a dam on the Fox River. The dam stopped the flooding and created Fox Lake, but it had many other effects, too. Life in this town is completely different now. The dam changed the landscape and the lives of people and animals in Lower Forks.

First of all, the dam changed the landscape. When the dam was finished, water rose to swallow the riverbanks and the homes of animals that lived there. Trees along the south bank got flooded and died. A couple houses had to be torn down, too. One family even had their home hauled up the hillside. Still, Fox Lake was born. Cattails grew up among the dead trees, making a new wetland.

The dam changed the way people and animals use the water. People used to canoe from Upper Forks down to Kingston. After the dam was built, they stopped because of the long portage around the dam. Instead of canoes, the lake is full of motorboats and fishing boats. People catch different fish now, too. The river used to be full of catfish, but they're mostly gone, and the Department of Natural Resources stocks Fox Lake with walleye. Other new types of animals have shown up, too. Canada geese stop at Fox Lake when

ELPS 4G, 5G

Specific details make each effect clear.

they migrate. Cranes have moved in on the south side of the lake, and a family of otters lives among the cattails.

Every season in Lower Forks feels different because of the dam. Before, when the snow melted, the river was fast and deep. It often flooded. As summer came on, the river calmed down to run only about a foot deep. Now, spring rarely brings any flooding. After a long, dry summer, the riverbed below the dam is sometimes only inches deep. Every winter, Fox Lake freezes over, which the river seldom did.

Ending

The ending reflects thoughtfully on the cause and its effects.

After the 2001 flood, it was obvious that Lower Forks needed help. A dam on the Fox River got rid of the flooding, created Fox Lake, and made a new wetland habitat. Lower Forks used to be just a river town, but now it is also a lake town, and that fact affects everyone.

Respond to the reading. On your own paper, write answers to the following questions about the sample essay.

- ☐ **Focus and Coherence** (1) What is the cause explained in the essay? (2) What are several of the effects?
- ☐ **Organization** (3) How did the writer organize the effects?
- ☐ **Voice** (4) What words and phrases show the writer's knowledge of this topic?

TEKS 7.14A, 7.22A

Prewriting Selecting a Topic

Whether you live in a quiet town like Lower Forks or a bustling city like San Antonio, one change can cause many other changes. For this assignment, you'll need to find a change in your school or community that has had many effects. Rosalva chose to brainstorm changes with a few partners. Together, they narrowed down Rosalva's list and decided on a topic.

Brainstorming

removing all the parking meters from downtown
building the Lower Forks dam
switching from a junior high to a middle school
requiring kids to do volunteer service to graduate
offering healthy food choices in the school cafeteria

Prewrite **Select your topic.** **Brainstorm a list of changes in your school or community. Concentrate on changes that you know a lot about. After you've created a list, choose the topic you are most interested in.**

Gathering Details

Once you have selected a change (cause), it's time to think about the effects it has had. One easy way to think about effects is to use a Cause-Effect Chart. Rosalva used the following chart to gather details about her topic.

Cause-Effect Chart

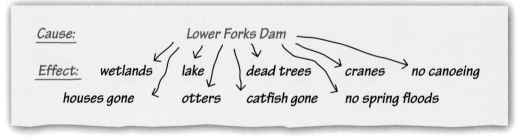

Cause: *Lower Forks Dam*

Effect: *wetlands*, *lake*, *dead trees*, *cranes*, *no canoeing*, *houses gone*, *otters*, *catfish gone*, *no spring floods*

Prewrite **Gather details.** **Create your own Cause-Effect Chart using the sample above as a guide. Write your cause at the top. Then write all the effects you can think of below it. Draw arrows to connect the cause to the effects.**

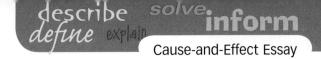

TEKS 7.14B, 7.17A(i), 7.17A(iii), 7.17A(v)

Grouping Details

Next, you need to organize the details you have gathered. Rosalva reviewed her Cause-Effect Chart and noticed that the effects fell into three categories. She also added details as she worked.

Grouping Chart

The landscape	*People and animals*	*How the seasons feel*
lake	*otters*	*no spring floods*
wetlands	*catfish gone*	*frozen lake in winter*
dead trees	*cranes*	*water low in summer*
homes gone	*no canoeing*	

Prewrite **Group your details.** **Review your Cause-Effect Chart. Notice how some details are related. Group your effects into categories.**

Writing an Introduction

In your cause-and-effect essay, each part has a different job. The opening paragraph introduces the cause. It also contains a focus statement that sums up the effects. But the introduction has to do more than just list the cause and effects. It has to grab the reader's attention. Here are some ways to do that in a cause-and-effect essay:

- Quote an authority.

  Mayor Cheng states, "The Lower Forks Dam means big changes."
- Ask an intriguing question.

  How would you like to have a lake right here in Lower Forks?
- Share an experience.

  My favorite memory is exploring the banks of the Fox River with my grandfather. Now those banks are gone.
- Give interesting information.

  The creation of Lower Forks Dam will change the economic future of Lower Forks. Many new jobs will be created to support the new dam.

Prewrite **Plan your introduction.** **Try a few different ways you could use to start your essay. Keep in mind the goal of really grabbing the reader's attention.**

TEKS 7.17A(i), 7.17A(iii)

Drafting Creating Your First Draft

Keep the following tips in mind as you write your first draft:

- **BEGINNING** Capture your reader's interest. Then write a focus statement that names the cause and lists or summarizes its effects.
- **MIDDLE** Create a separate paragraph for each effect. Begin each paragraph with a topic sentence and support it with facts and details.
- **ENDING** Write an ending that thoughtfully sums up your essay.

You may want to revisit your opening paragraph and find another quote from your authority, answer the intriguing question, or offer new insights into the shared experience or interesting information.

Draft **Write your first draft. Follow the tips above to create the first draft of your cause-and-effect essay. Be sure to include a strong conclusion.**

Revising Improving Your Writing

Think about these traits in your first draft before you revise your essay.

- ☐ **Focus and Coherence** Do all the details in my essay relate to either the cause or its effects? Is my essay free of inconsistencies? Are there any contradictions?
- ☐ **Organization** Does my beginning contain a clear focus statement? Is my ending consistent with the beginning?
- ☐ **Development of Ideas** Do I clearly name the cause? Do I include enough details for each effect? Are my ideas consistent throughout?

Revise **Revise your writing. Consider the questions above as you revise. Make any changes that will improve your essay.**

Editing Checking for Conventions

Once you finish revising your essay, edit it by focusing on *conventions.*

- ☐ **Conventions** Have I checked spelling, capitalization, and punctuation? Have I also checked for usage and grammar errors?

Edit **Edit your work. Edit your essay using the questions above. Have a trusted classmate edit your essay as well. Then make a final copy and proofread it.**

Expository Writing

Across the Curriculum

Because expository writing shares information, you will use it throughout your school day, in just about every class.

This chapter gives you several examples of expository writing for different classes—an informative letter written for social studies, directions for a math procedure, a definition of a scientific process, and an e-mail that requests information. Finally, you will practice responding to an expository prompt.

Whatever the class, sharing your knowledge with a reader is often the key to communication and learning.

What's Ahead

- **Social Studies:** Writing a Business Letter
- **Math:** Writing Explanations
- **Science:** Writing an Extended Definition
- **Practical Writing:** Writing an E-Mail Request

TEKS 7.17B

Social Studies:
Writing a Business Letter

Even though e-mail is fast and convenient, sometimes a letter is the most effective way to get the response you want. The following letter was written by a student who had a complaint about a product he purchased.

The letter follows the business letter format.

100 Crabtree Way
Big Spring, TX 79720
January 12, 2010

Dear Texas College Sports Products, Inc.:

The beginning reflects the writer's opinion.

I recently purchased a red sweatshirt with the logo of the Stockton College Fighting Prairie Dogs on the front. It was manufactured by your company. I liked the design, color, and fit of the sweatshirt very much. The graphic of the Fighting Prairie Dog is really cool.

The middle explains the complaint.

However, I found that after one washing, the colors on the Fighting Prairie Dog graphic faded drastically. It is now barely visible. The only parts that can still be seen are the eyes and front teeth.

The ending includes a request.

I feel that the materials or manufacturing of the Fighting Prairie Dog graphic are defective. Would you be willing to replace the sweatshirt with a better-quality graphic or refund my money? Could you also send me information on more Fighting Prairie Dog sportswear? Thank you very much.

Sincerely,

Richard Martinez

Writing Tips

Use the following tips as a guide when you are asked to write a business letter or letter of complaint.

Before you write . . .

- **Decide on a purpose.**
  Know what you want to happen as a result of your letter.
- **Review the facts.**
  Make a list that includes your complaint, details to support it, and to whom you should address your letter.

During your drafting . . .

- **Be specific.**
  Describe your complaint, including the circumstances, and what you are asking the reader of the letter to do.
- **Stay calm and courteous.**
  You may be upset about your complaint, but showing anger will not help you get what you want.

After you've written a first draft . . .

- **Double-check your tone.**
  Sounding reasonable and courteous is the best way to achieve your goal in writing a letter of complaint.
- **Check for correctness.**
  Read your letter, looking for errors. If possible, have someone else read it as well. Make sure your writing is free of errors in grammar, punctuation, capitalization, and spelling. Write or print a clean final copy.

Try It Write a letter of complaint. Use the letter on page 212 as a model of what to include and what tone to use.

ELPS 4C

Math: Writing Explanations

Once you can explain a math procedure to others, you know you have mastered it. Sharika wrote the following explanation to show how fractions are multiplied.

The **beginning** names the math procedure.

The **middle** explains the procedure.

The **ending** provides more advanced information.

Multiplying a Fraction by a Fraction

At first it might sound scary to multiply one fraction by another. But anyone who knows that $2 \times 4 = 8$ can multiply one fraction by another:

$$\frac{2}{1} \times \frac{4}{1} = \frac{8}{1}$$

What happened in the example above? The top numbers, or numerators, were multiplied together ($2 \times 4 = 8$), and so were the bottom numbers, or denominators ($1 \times 1 = 1$). The same technique works with other fractions.

$$\frac{1}{2} \times \frac{3}{4} = \frac{3}{8}$$

It might seem confusing that the product (3/8) is smaller than the two fractions that got multiplied. A way to make this less confusing is to replace the word "times" with the word "of." The equation above would read "one-half of three-quarters is three-eighths."

There's one last thing to do when multiplying fractions: Remember to reduce the product to its simplest form.

$$\frac{3}{8} \times \frac{2}{3} = \frac{6}{24} \text{ simplified to } \frac{1}{4}$$

Writing Tips

Before you write . . .

- **Select a topic.**
  If your teacher has not given you a topic, search for one in your notes or math textbook.
- **Study the procedure.**
  Review the procedure that you will be writing about. Make sure you understand it thoroughly and have considered different ways of explaining it.
- **Think of examples.**
  Pick examples that will help you to clarify your explanation. A simple example can work as well as a more complex one, as long as it allows you to show every step of the process.

During your writing . . .

- **Think of your audience.**
  Imagine that the reader knows nothing about the math procedure you are explaining. Guide the reader step by step.
- **Organize your thoughts.**
  Decide on an order for presenting the information. Think of how your teacher or textbook first introduced the idea to you.
- **Focus on one step at a time.**
  Present the steps of the procedure in order. Write sentences that explain what you are doing in each example.

After you've written a first draft . . .

- **Check for completeness.**
  Make sure that you have included all the information a reader needs to understand the concept.
- **Check for correctness.**
  Edit and proofread your work to eliminate errors in spelling, punctuation, and other conventions.

Try It Write directions for a procedure that you are learning in math class. Use examples and clear steps.

Science: Writing an Extended Definition

A definition of a science term or process can be complicated. An essay that defines a term and includes examples, explanations, and many details is called an *extended definition*. The following student essay is an extended definition of a natural process.

The **beginning** provides a basic definition of the term.

The **middle** provides examples and supporting details.

The **ending** gives the reader something to think about.

What Is Metamorphosis?

Some animals grow by changing from one form to another. This process is called metamorphosis. A creature that goes through metamorphosis has one form as an infant and a completely different form as an adult. Differences can include shape, size, diet, and even habitat. Animals such as amphibians, crustaceans, and insects go through metamorphosis.

One example of metamorphosis occurs in frogs. They begin life as tadpoles, which are small, legless animals with long tails. Tadpoles live completely in the water, like fish. As tadpoles mature into frogs, they grow legs and gradually lose their tails. Frogs cannot live underwater. Instead, they must breathe air.

Butterflies also go through an amazing metamorphosis. They start out in a larva stage, in which they are caterpillars with many short legs. In the pupa stage, caterpillars wrap themselves in a chrysalis (a cocoon) and become dormant, which is like a very deep sleep. While dormant, they do not eat or move around, but they do change. When the butterfly finally breaks out of its chrysalis, it has wings, a different body, and six long legs.

People grow up, but they don't go through metamorphosis. As a result, they won't roll out of bed one morning and discover they have grown wings!

TEKS 7.14E, 7.17A(iii)
ELPS 3E, 5G

Writing Tips

Before you write . . .

- **Do your research.**
  Make sure you thoroughly understand the term or process that you are going to define. Consult several sources if you have questions about a topic.
- **Organize your thoughts.**
  Write a statement that defines the term. Then plan how you will extend that definition with facts and examples.

Cluster

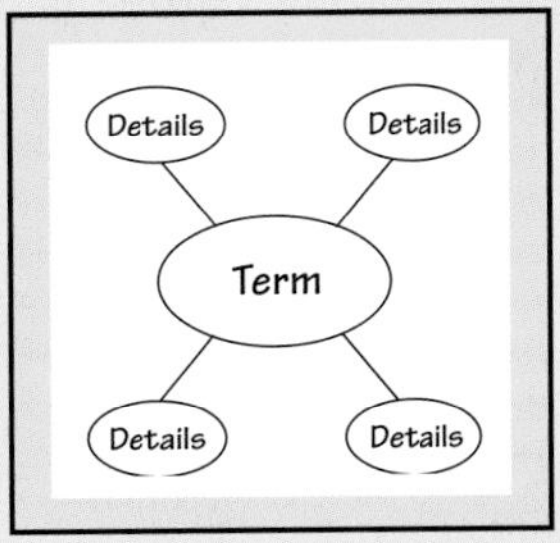

During your drafting . . .

- **Define your term.**
  Place your basic definition in the first paragraph.
- **Extend the definition.**
  Provide the reader with facts and examples that help explain the scientific term.
- **Use a comparison or a contrast.**
  Compare examples that fit the definition with those that don't.
- **Eliminate unnecessary information.**
  Make sure your definition does not include unnecessary details that could distract the reader from your main points.

After you've written a first draft . . .

- **Get feedback.**
  Ask a classmate to read your definition. Use the feedback to improve your coverage of the topic and clear up things that are unclear.
- **Proofread carefully.**
  Go over your essay to make sure that there are no mistakes in grammar, punctuation, capitalization, or spelling.

Try It Draft an extended definition of a scientific term related to nature or the environment. Then trade papers with a partner and offer suggestions for revising. Use the feedback to revise your draft.

Practical Writing:
Writing an E-Mail Request

E-mail allows quick communication between people across town—or across the world. The following e-mail message was sent by a student to request information from a businessperson she had met on a field trip.

The **heading** includes sending information and a subject line.

The **beginning** shares a greeting and the purpose of the e-mail.

The **middle** lists questions.

The **closing** politely completes the e-mail message.

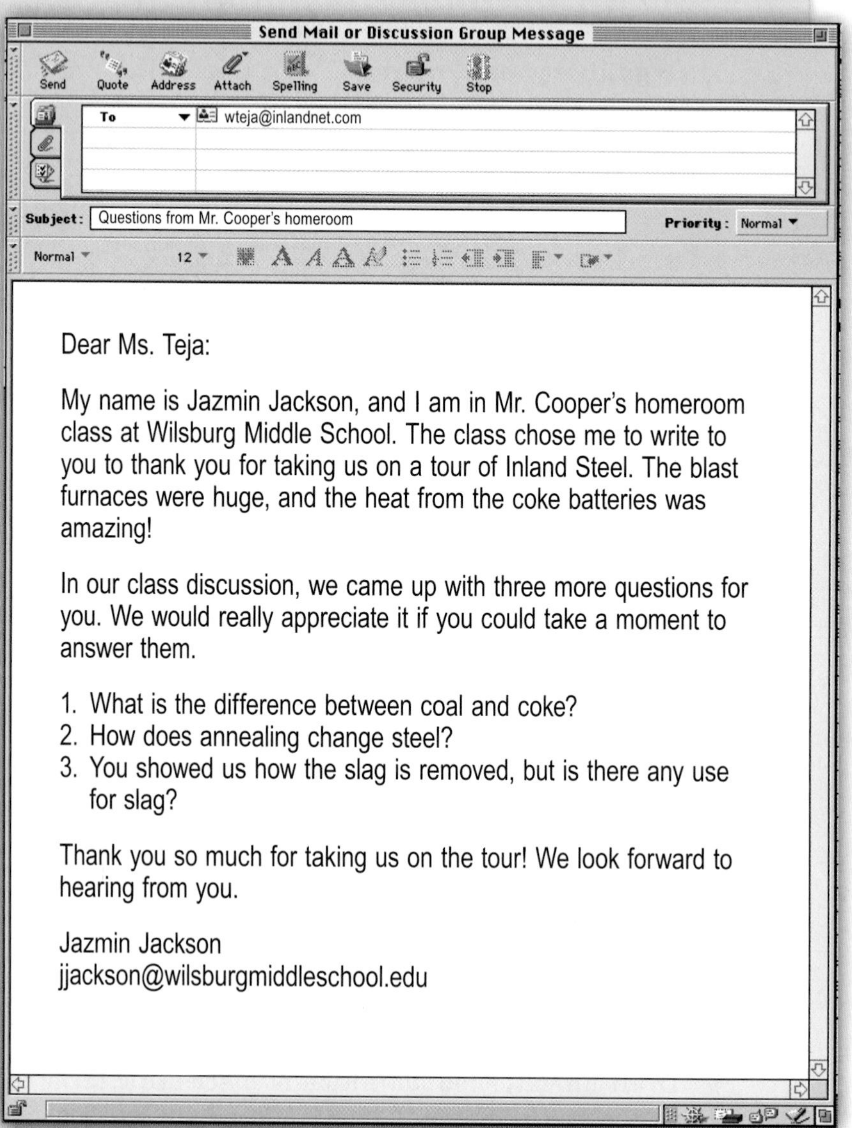

Dear Ms. Teja:

My name is Jazmin Jackson, and I am in Mr. Cooper's homeroom class at Wilsburg Middle School. The class chose me to write to you to thank you for taking us on a tour of Inland Steel. The blast furnaces were huge, and the heat from the coke batteries was amazing!

In our class discussion, we came up with three more questions for you. We would really appreciate it if you could take a moment to answer them.

1. What is the difference between coal and coke?
2. How does annealing change steel?
3. You showed us how the slag is removed, but is there any use for slag?

Thank you so much for taking us on the tour! We look forward to hearing from you.

Jazmin Jackson
jjackson@wilsburgmiddleschool.edu

Writing Tips

Before you write . . .

- **Know your goal.**
  Think about what information you need. Then write a few questions for the person.
- **Think about your reader.**
  Ask a reasonable number of questions that can be easily answered.

During your writing . . .

- **Fill in the heading.**
  Complete the e-mail's heading. Then type in a subject line that tells your reader the topic at a glance.
- **Greet your reader and state your purpose.**
  Identify yourself, be polite, and make sure your reason for writing is clear.
- **Give important facts.**
  Provide any details that the reader needs to understand your request.

After you've written a first draft . . .

- **Check your facts.**
  Double-check the information you include in your e-mail.
- **Tune up your questions.**
  Make sure you've asked only necessary questions and have worded them in the best way.
- **Proofread carefully.**
  Review your e-mail to make sure that there are no mistakes in grammar, mechanics, or spelling.

Try It Remember a field trip you really enjoyed. Think of three questions you would like to ask about the place that you visited. Write an e-mail to a person who works at the location and politely ask your questions.

Expository Writing

Writing for the Texas Assessment

When you take state tests in Texas, you often have to write. The prompt tells you what to write about and gives some things to remember. Read the following prompt.

Prompt

Write a composition about a change in your school or community and the effects it caused.

Use the information below to help you write your composition.

REMEMBER THAT YOU SHOULD—

- ☐ write about a change in your school or community and the effects it caused.
- ☐ make sure each sentence helps readers understand your composition.
- ☐ include specific details about your ideas to make sure readers fully understand what you have to say.
- ☐ use correct sentences, grammar, punctuation, capitalization, and spelling.

Prewriting Selecting a Form

The prompt doesn't tell you what form of writing to use. How can you decide which one? Think about which form best fits what you want to say.

Do you want to:

- compare two things?
- analyze a cause-and-effect relationship?
- explain an object?
- share a personal experience?
- give information?
- persuade someone to do something?

Answering these questions will help you decide on the best form for telling your audience about your topic.

Planning the Writing

Ana thought about how building the new shopping center on the outskirts of town had changed the way people shopped and used the downtown in her community. To plan her draft, Ana used a cause-and-effect chart. It helped her identify the change and its effects.

Cause-and-Effect Chart

Cause:	*Effect:*
new shopping center	*- stores close downtown* *- other stores will move to the new shopping center* *- fewer people come to downtown events* *- downtown festival may be cancelled* *- jobs may be lost in downtown stores and restaurants* *- traffic jams at new shopping center* *- cost for widening roads at new shopping center*

Drafting Writing the Cause-and-Effect Essay

Next, Ana used her chart to write her cause-and-effect essay. Read Ana's cause-and-effect essay.

The **beginning** states the controlling idea of the response (**underlined**) and uses key words from the prompt.

The **middle** paragraphs tell about the cause and analyze its effects, both good and bad.

Many people in our community were excited when the shopping center on the east side of town was built. Perhaps some had visions of new and interesting places to shop. Others may have hoped to find a job in the new stores and businesses in the shopping center. Few people seemed to be worried about the effects this change would have on our attractive and busy downtown shopping area. These effects are now becoming clear.

Most people would agree that a healthy and active downtown makes an important contribution to the quality of life in our community. A healthy, thriving downtown attracts people, who meet each other, eat, have fun, and spend money. This money supports their friends and neighbors who own the stores and businesses. But how has our community's quality of life been affected by the new shopping center?

The signs are not good. At least six stores and businesses have closed. Two have relocated to the new shopping center. A café and a restaurant sit empty. Empty windows stare out at the people who pass by. Yellowing signs in the windows state that the store is for rent. Shelves that used to hold items for sale collect dust. More importantly, the people who used to work in these stores no longer have their jobs. Some have been able to find new jobs. But not all. Other changes are also noticeable. Fewer shoppers come to downtown. Some of the stores that remain are no longer open in the evening. There is even a rumor that the monthly downtown festival will no longer be held.

The **middle** describes some positive effects of the change.

Most people would agree that not all of the changes brought by the new shopping center are negative. The shopping center has created new jobs. Parking is easier at the new center. But how long will it be before some of these stores also sit empty as the economy worsens? There are already frequent traffic jams at the shopping center entrance. The city has already talked about widening Adams Boulevard to ease traffic at the center.

The **concluding statement** summarizes the effects of the change and includes the writer's judgment about these effects.

Overall, has the new shopping center had a positive effect on our town? While it has brought both good and bad, I feel the balance is tipped toward the negative.

Respond to the reading. Answer the following questions to see how these traits were used in the sample response.

- ☐ **Focus and Coherence** (1) What is the topic of the response? (2) What key words in the prompt are used?
- ☐ **Organization** (3) How does Ana organize the events of her essay?
- ☐ **Voice** (4) What words and phrases show the writer's feelings?

Literature Connection: You can find an example of expository writing in the magazine article, "Like Black Smoke: The Black Death's Journey" by Diana Childress.

TEKS 7.14A

Writing Tips

Use the following tips as a guide when responding to an expository writing prompt.

Before you write . . .

- **Understand the prompt.**
  Remember that an expository prompt asks you to explain.
- **Plan your time wisely.**
  Spend several minutes planning before starting to write. Use a graphic organizer, such as a Venn diagram, to help you organize your ideas.

Venn Diagram

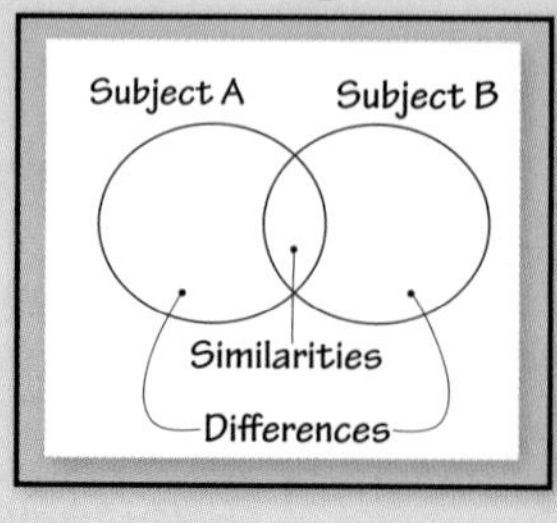

During your writing . . .

- **Decide on a focus for your essay.**
  Keep your main idea or purpose in mind as you write.
- **Be selective.**
  Use examples and explanations that directly support your focus.
- **End in a meaningful way.**
  Remind the reader about the importance of the topic.

After you've written a first draft . . .

- **Check for completeness and correctness.**
  Present your details in a logical order and correct errors in grammar, capitalization, punctuation, and spelling.

Plan and write a response. Respond to the prompt on page 220. Complete your writing within the period of time your teacher gives you. Remember to select an appropriate form and use the tips above as you write.

Expository Writing in Review

Purpose: In expository writing, you *explain something* to readers.

Topics: Explain . . . how to do or make something,
how things are similar or different,
the causes of something,
the kinds of something, or
the definition of something.

Prewriting

Select a topic that you know something about, or one that you want to learn about. (See page 170.)

Gather the important details and organize them according to time order, point-by-point, or in order of importance. (See pages 171–172 and 174.)

Write a focus statement, telling exactly what idea you plan to cover. (See page 173.)

Drafting

In the beginning, introduce your topic, say something interesting about it, and state your focus. (See page 177.)

In the middle, use clear topic sentences and specific details to support the focus. (See pages 178–179.)

In the ending, summarize your writing and make a final comment about the topic. (See page 180.)

Revising

Review the focus and coherence, organization, development and ideas, and voice. (See pages 182–189.)

Editing

Check your writing for conventions. Also have a trusted classmate edit your writing. (See pages 192–195.)

Make a final copy and proofread it for errors before sharing it. (See page 197.)

Assessing

Use the rubric to assess your finished writing. (See pages 48–49.)

persuade

argue

ELPS 2C, 3E, 4C, 4G

TEXAS WRITE SOURCE Online

www.hmheducation.com/tx/writesource

Persuasive Writing

Writing Focus

- **Persuasive Paragraph**
- **Problem-Solution Essay**
- **Editorial**

Grammar Focus

- **Prepositions and Prepositional Phrases**
- **Adjectival Clauses**

Learning Language

Work with a partner. Read the meanings and share answers to the questions.

1. If you convince people, you make them believe something.
   How would you convince someone that you liked sports?
2. You persuade by getting someone to think or act the way you want them to.
   Persuade a classmate to sit next to you.
3. To sum up means to tell the main points in a few words.
   Sum up what you did last night.

convince

reason

support

Persuasive Writing

Persuasive Paragraph

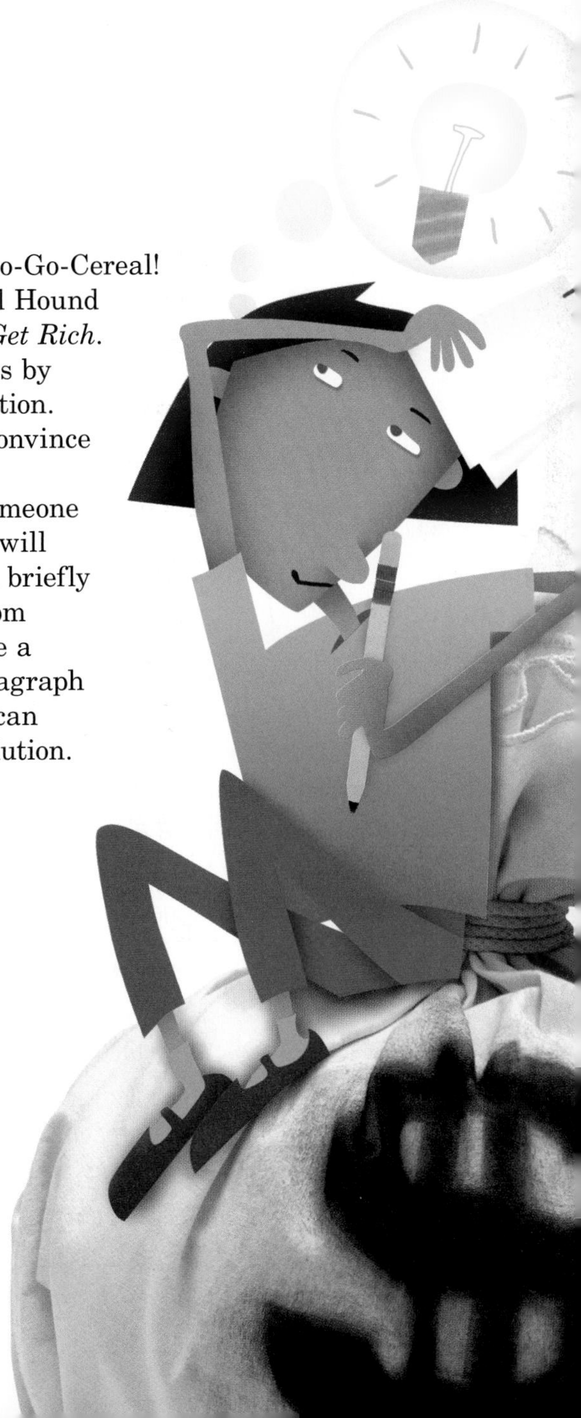

Are you too busy for breakfast? Try Go-Go-Cereal! Are you sick of unwanted e-mail? Try Mail Hound 3000! Need money? Send for *100 Ways to Get Rich.* Often, commercials try to persuade viewers by presenting a problem and proposing a solution. In 30 seconds, commercials like this can convince some viewers to buy a product or service.

Do you have the power to persuade someone in 30 seconds or less? In this chapter, you will write a persuasive paragraph. First, you'll briefly present a problem that you know about from personal experience. Then you will propose a solution to the problem. Think of your paragraph as a 30-second commercial and see if you can convince your reader to "buy into" your solution.

Writing Guidelines

Subject: A problem and a convincing solution
Purpose: To propose a solution
Form: Persuasive paragraph
Audience: Classmates, teachers, or parents

ELPS 4G, 5G

Persuasive Paragraph

A persuasive paragraph starts with a **topic sentence** that presents the problem. The **body** sentences explain the problem and convince the reader to agree with a proposed solution. The **closing sentence** sums up the solution. The persuasive paragraph below was written by Sarah, a student who wanted to convince her parents to change a family rule.

Topic Sentence

Body

Closing Sentence

Time Is Money

Some teenagers have a problem: They're bored and broke. They have too much time and too little money. The problem often stems from a family rule that forbids teenage siblings from working until they reach a certain age, usually 16 or older. Instead, they are supposed to focus on homework and grades. The fact that the teenagers remain bored and broke won't change until this type of rule is changed. Why alter it? Many teenagers make the A-B honor roll each semester and do their homework every night. A part-time job on the weekends would not stop them from completing their homework. Often, such a rule was made because an older sibling had grade problems once he or she started working. To be fair, however, each individual should have a chance to prove that he or she is responsible. All teenagers want to do is turn their extra time into a little extra money and feel that they have some control over their lives.

Respond to the reading. On your own paper, answer each of the following questions.

- ☐ **Focus and Coherence** (1) What problem does the writer present, and what solution does she propose?
- ☐ **Organization** (2) Where does the writer switch from talking about the problem to talking about the solution?
- ☐ **Voice** (3) What words or phrases show that the writer truly believes in the solution?

TEKS 7.14A, 7.18A
ELPS 5G

Prewriting Selecting a Topic

Your first step in writing a persuasive paragraph is to choose a problem to write about. For a paragraph, it's best to focus on a problem that you believe you can actually solve. Sarah used a cluster to think about possible topics.

Topics Cluster

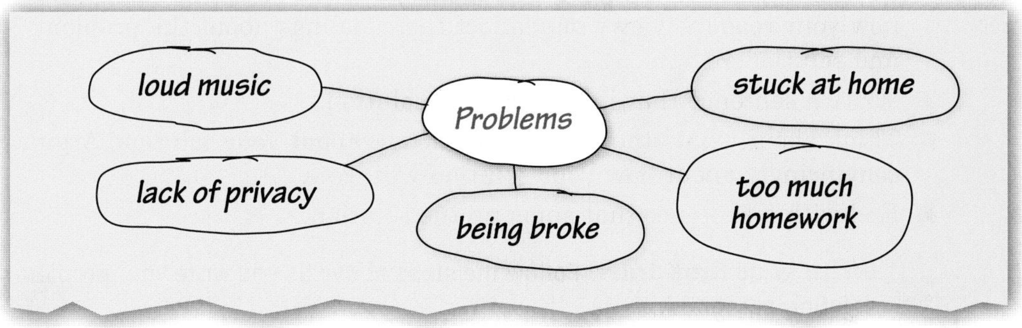

Prewrite **Create a cluster.** **Use the sample above as a guide to create your own cluster about problems you believe you can solve. Choose one problem to write about in a paragraph.**

Defining the Problem and Solution

Once you have selected a problem, present it in a topic sentence. Beneath it, write a few sentences about possible solutions, just as Sarah did below.

Problem-Solution Chart

Topic Sentence: *Some teenagers have a big problem: They're bored and broke.*

Solution 1: *Parents should raise the allowance.*

Solution 2: *Teenagers should find free things to do.*

Solution 3: *Parents should change the family rule about getting a job.* *

Prewrite **Create a problem-solution chart.** **Write a sentence that names the problem you will be writing about. Then write three or four more sentences that propose solutions. Put a star next to the best solution for your paragraph.**

TEKS 7.18B
ELPS 5G

Drafting Creating the First Draft

Once you have written a sentence about the problem and considered some possible solutions, you are ready to write your first draft. Follow these guidelines as you write.

- Start with your topic sentence, which tells about the problem.
- Provide details showing that the problem needs to be solved. Consider how your readers' views may affect their feelings about the problem and solution.
- Write a sentence that introduces the solution.
- Think about what other people may think about your solution. Argue convincingly about how your solution will work.
- End with a sentence that sums up the solution.

Draft **Write your first draft. Follow the steps above as you write your problem-solution paragraph.**

Revising Improving Your Writing

Read over your first draft. Consider how well you addressed *focus and coherence, organization, development of ideas,* and *voice* in your paragraph.

Revise **Revise your paragraph. Review and improve your paragraph as needed. Think about the following questions as you work on your writing.**

1. **Do I clearly present a problem and propose a solution?**
2. **Do I move logically from the problem to the solution?**
3. **Do I develop my ideas as I move from the problem to the solution?**
4. **Do I use words that sound natural and sincere?**

Editing Checking for Conventions

When you edit your paragraph, pay special attention to *conventions.*

Edit **Edit your paragraph. Use the following questions to guide your editing.**

1. **Do I use correct punctuation and capitalization?**
2. **Have I checked for mistakes in grammar and spelling?**

Edit **Proofread your paragraph. Before sharing your paragraph, make a final copy and proofread it one more time for errors.**

Persuasive Writing

Problem-Solution Essay

It's easy to see problems. Maybe your city has a problem with litter or noise pollution or traffic. Maybe your school needs a new gymnasium or more computers or better wheelchair access. Everyone can see problems, but people who see solutions can make a real difference in the world around them.

In this chapter, you will be writing a persuasive problem-solution essay. First, you'll need to convince the reader that the problem is serious. Then you must show that you have the best solution. With a well-written problem-solution essay, perhaps you can solve a problem in your school or community.

Writing Guidelines

Subject: A problem in your school or community

Purpose: To propose a solution

Form: Persuasive essay

Audience: Classmates and community members

Understanding Your Goal

Your goal in this chapter is to write a well-organized persuasive essay that proposes a solution to a problem. The traits listed in the chart below will help you plan and write your essay. The scoring rubric on pages 48–49 will also help you. Refer to it often to improve your writing.

Traits of Problem-Solution Writing

Focus and Coherence

Clearly explain the problem and offer the solution you think is the best. Consider the views of others but refocus them to your solution at the end.

Organization

Develop an essay with a clear opinion statement and well-organized paragraphs.

Development of Ideas

Build on your ideas to support why your solution is the best answer for solving the problem.

Voice

Sound confident and convincing about the problem and your solution.

Conventions

Check your writing for errors in grammar, punctuation, capitalization, and spelling.

Literature Connection. You can find another example of persuasive writing in the problem-solution essay "Homeless" by Anna Quindlen.

Problem-Solution Essay

A problem-solution essay is usually organized in two parts: (1) the writer convinces the reader that there is a problem, and (2) the writer persuades the reader to help with the solution. In the following essay, a student writes about a pollution problem at a local beach.

Beginning
The beginning introduces the problem and gives an opinion statement (**underlined**).

Waterfront Rescue

If people visited City Beach last summer, they probably noticed the mess. Litter was scattered across the picnic area, and cans and bottles were all over the beach. <u>The condition of City Beach has become a big community problem, and it won't be solved until everyone gets involved.</u>

Middle
The first middle paragraph convinces the reader that the problem is serious.

Mr. Sean Johnson of the city's maintenance department said the city can pay for just eight hours of work at the beach every week. This means that a worker comes to the park only one day each week. He or she empties the trash barrels but doesn't have time to gather all the trash left on the ground. When people leave their trash under the picnic tables or on the beach, it never gets picked up. Other people see how messy the area is, and they leave litter behind, too.

The second middle paragraph proposes a solution.

The big problem at City Beach needs a big solution. Students from Lakeview School could be part of that solution. They could form a committee to keep the beach cleaner next summer. They might even start a tradition, and the students from Lakeview could do this every year.

The other middle paragraphs persuade the reader to help solve the problem.

First, the committee would need to organize volunteers to spend Saturday morning at the beach just before it opens for the summer. Kids could wear protective gloves as they go around the park and pick up litter. They could put bottles and cans in recycling bins. Hot dogs, soda, and ice cream could be served to everyone who helps.

After the beach is cleaned up, the committee should add more garbage barrels and some "no littering" signs. Local organizations and businesses could sponsor the barrels. The signs could be bright and colorful, but they should also remind people that there is a fine for littering in the park.

Ending

The ending answers a possible counter-argument and calls the reader to action.

Some people might say it's not the job of Lakeview students to clean the beach, but if they make it their job, they can be the first ones to enjoy a clean beach. Also, once people see that the park is being cleaned, they may volunteer to help, too. Lakeview students should take charge of cleaning City Beach and make it attractive once again!

Respond to the reading. Answer the following questions about the sample essay.

- ☐ **Organization** **(1) Which paragraphs deal with the problem? (2) Which paragraphs deal with the solution?**
- ☐ **Development of Ideas** **(3) What details convince the reader to take the problem seriously? (4) What details persuade the reader to help solve the problem?**
- ☐ **Voice** **(5) What words or phrases make the voice of the writer persuasive?**

Go Online!

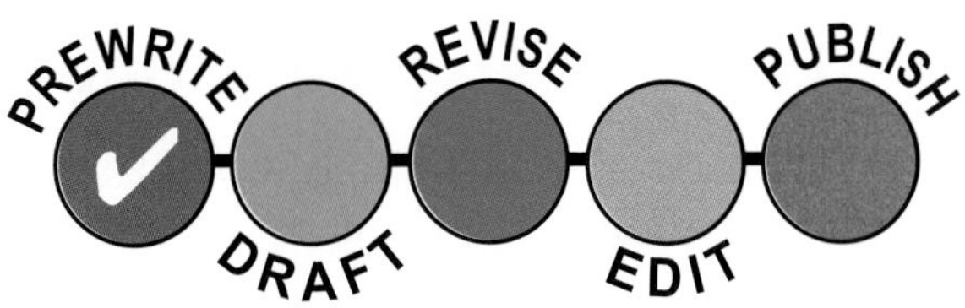

Prewriting

Before you begin to write, you'll need to select a topic, gather details, and organize your ideas. This process is called prewriting.

Keys to Effective Prewriting

1. Select a problem that you care about and that fits the assignment.
2. Choose the best option for a solution.
3. Gather details about the problem and the solution.
4. Write a clear opinion statement to guide you.
5. Think about the opinions of others and how to address them.
6. Create a list or an outline as a planning guide.

TEKS 7.14A

Prewriting Selecting a Problem

The first step in writing a problem-solution essay is to select a problem. A cluster can help you think of the problems all around you.

Topics Cluster

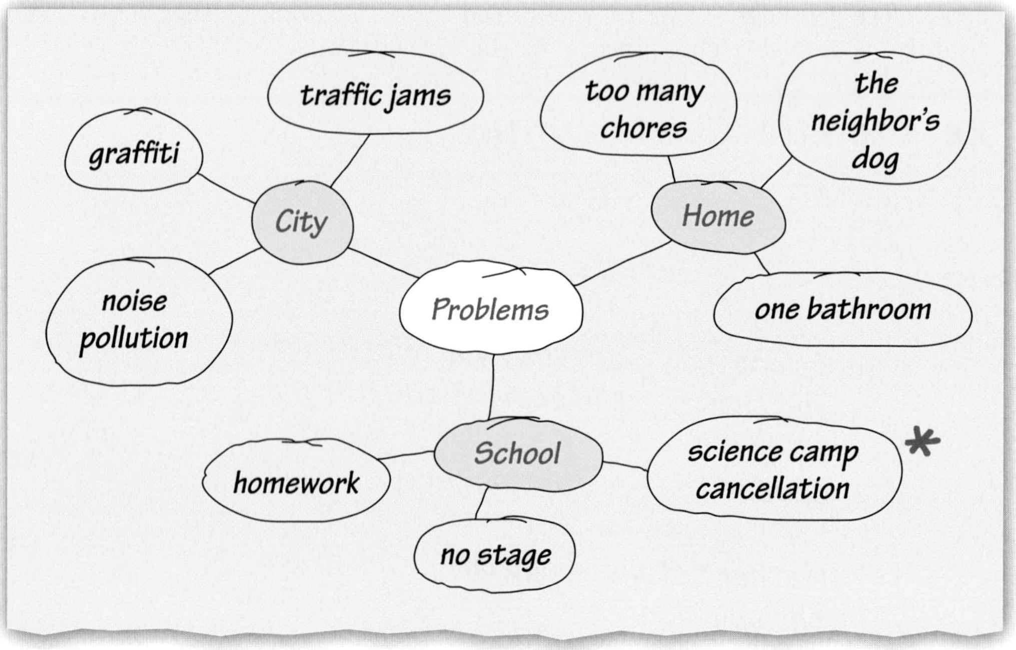

Prewrite **Create a cluster.** Use the cluster above as a guide for creating your own topics cluster. Then use the questions below to help choose the best topic.

1. Which problem do I know a lot about?
2. Which problem could I help solve?

Texas Traits

Focus on the Texas Traits

Focus and Coherence The best writing always begins with a strong focus that is maintained throughout the work. In this case, the focus of your essay is a problem that you can help solve. After you select your topic, you'll gather more details about the problem so that you can propose a realistic solution.

Gathering Details About the Problem

Your reader will have two questions: (1) why does the problem exist, and (2) why should it be solved? Think about and respond to what others think and to any concerns your reader may have. A chart like the one below can help you gather persuasive details such as examples, suggestions, and quotations.

Gathering Chart

Problem: The school board might cancel science camp.

Why does the problem exist?	*Why should the problem be solved?*
Camp costs $30 per student.	*Without science camp, we wouldn't get to do our outdoor projects.*
This year science camp would cost $3,000.	*–mini-steam engines*
The school budget has been cut.	*–solar panels*
Parents feel the money would be better spent on science books.	*Nature is the place to learn about nature.*
The economy has been bad.	*–rock and plant identification*
Teachers feel that everybody goes or nobody goes.	*–birds, animals, insects*
The school board believes it is a difficult expense to defend.	*Sixth graders want to save the camp, too.*

Prewrite

Gather answers. **Make your own chart like the one above. In one column, list reasons for the problem. In the other, list reasons why the problem should be solved. Work with a partner. Share your opinions of each other's work. Be sure you consider and respond to what other people may think and any concerns they may have.**

TEKS 7.18B
ELPS 5G

Prewriting Proposing a Solution

A problem can have many possible solutions. Use a sentence starter like the one below to make a list of as many solutions as you can think of.

Sentence Starter

Science camp will be canceled unless . . .

the economy gets better.

the school board cuts something else.

parents volunteer to run science camp at the school.

students figure out how to raise $3,000 per year. *

Prewrite **Write down solutions.** Use a sentence starter that states your problem and ends with a word such as "unless" or "until." Write as many solutions as you can. Which solution could you and your reader help bring about?

Gathering Details About the Solution

Now that you have chosen a solution, you need to think about your readers. Think about the concerns they may have and how to answer each concern. Use a chart like the one below to record your thoughts and plan your responses. You will also need to think about how to address possible counterarguments your readers may have.

Concerns	*Responses*
How would the money be handled?	*• Set up fund at a local bank. Make adult responsible for fund.*
How would student council be involved?	*• A student council member could assist the adult.*
How could kids raise money?	*• Possible jobs: bake sales, babysit, rake lawns, etc.*

Prewrite **Collect your details.** What concerns might your reader have about your solution? How will you address those concerns? What counterarguments might your reader have? How will you address those? Use the above chart as a model as you gather details.

Understanding Facts and Opinions

To convince your reader that the problem needs to be solved and that your solution will work, you need to use both facts and opinions. An opinion is a feeling or belief. A fact is a detail that can be proven true. Facts make great support for your opinions. Strong writing uses a balance of facts and opinions.

Opinion

Science camp should not be cut from the curriculum.

(This statement expresses a feeling and cannot be checked.)

Fact

Science camp is one of the proposed cuts in the school budget.

(This statement can be proven true.)

Try It Number a piece of paper from 1 to 8. Then decide if each statement below is a fact or an opinion. Write "O" for opinion and "F" for fact.

1. Rossman Middle School has the best band in the state.
2. Paula has a 4-point average.
3. The student council meets every third Tuesday before school.
4. Selling garden plants is always the best fundraiser.
5. Victor is the best player on the football team.
6. Victor is the tallest player on the football team.
7. Mr. Castillo has taught at this school longer than anyone else.
8. Math is the hardest subject in the curriculum.

Prewrite **Check for facts and opinions.** Look over your list of details. Count how many facts and how many opinions you have gathered. Be sure to include both kinds of statements in your writing. Also make sure that your opinions are supported by facts.

TEKS 7.18A, 7.18C
ELPS 3E, 5B

Prewriting Planning Your Essay

An opinion statement names the problem and proposes a solution.

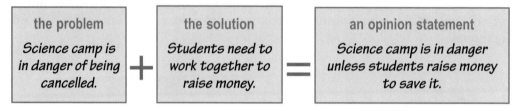

the problem		the solution		an opinion statement
Science camp is in danger of being cancelled.	+	*Students need to work together to raise money.*	=	*Science camp is in danger unless students raise money to save it.*

Prewrite **Write your opinion statement.** Using the statement above as a model, write your opinion statement. Share your opinion statement with a partner.

Organizing Your Essay

The directions below can help you create an organized list for your essay.

Directions	Organized List
Write your opinion statement.	*Science camp is in danger unless students raise money to save it.*
Summarize the problem.	*1. Without science camp, students will miss out on a unique learning experience.*
List facts and details.	*– rock identification* *– nature experiments*
Propose the solution.	*2. Science camp is for everybody, and it won't be saved unless everybody helps raise money.*
List facts and details.	*– "science camp" fund at bank* *– $3,000 per year needed*
Continue the solution.	*3. Students can raise money in many ways.*
List facts and details.	*– talent auction* *– bake sales*

Prewrite **Make an organized list.** To create your list, follow the "Directions" above. You will use this list as a guide when you write.

TEKS 7.14C

Go Online!

Drafting

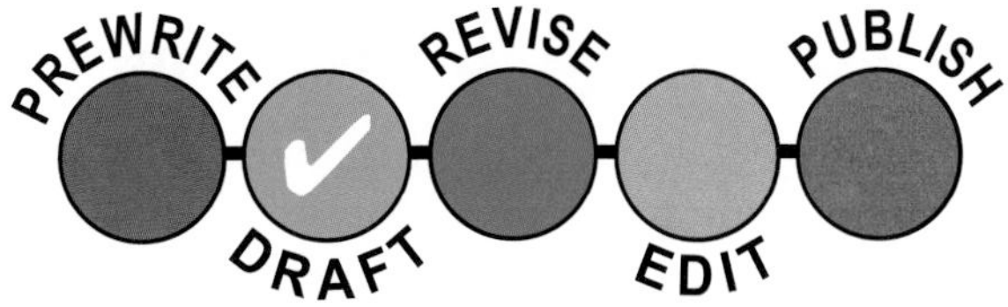

Once you finish creating a plan for your problem-solution essay, you are ready to put your ideas on paper.

Keys to Effective Drafting

1. *Use your organized list or an outline as a planning guide.*
2. *Write a clear opinion statement.*
3. *Write with your purpose, form, and audience in mind. Ask yourself these questions as you write:*
   - *Am I proposing a solution to a problem?*
   - *Do I consider my audience by addressing and answering concerns and counterarguments?*
4. *Use specific details to convince your reader that the problem is serious and your solution will work.*

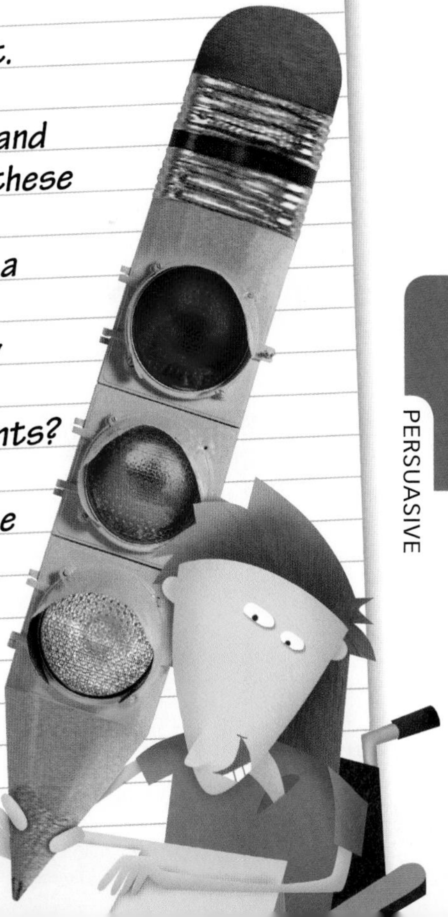

TEKS 7.14B
ELPS 4C

Drafting Getting the Big Picture

Now that you have finished prewriting, you are ready to create a first draft of your problem-solution essay. The graphic that follows shows how the parts of your essay will fit together. (The examples are from the student essay on pages 243–246.)

Beginning

The **beginning** introduces the problem and provides the opinion statement.

Opening Sentences

Science camp is in danger unless students raise money to save it.

Middle

The **first middle** paragraph summarizes the problem.

The **second middle** paragraph proposes a solution.

Other middle paragraphs contain details about the solution.

Topic Sentences

Without science camp, students will miss out on a unique learning experience.

Science camp is for everybody, and it won't be saved unless everybody helps raise money for it.

Students can raise money in many ways.

Ending

The **ending** answers a counterargument and gives a call to action.

Answer to a Counterargument

Some people say it's too much work to save science camp, but the fact is that if students all help out, they can reach the necessary goal. Science camp is a terrific tradition that deserves to be saved.

Call to Action

Tell Principal Jeffries that students are ready to save science camp.

TEKS 7.14B, 7.18A, 7.25D

Starting Your Essay

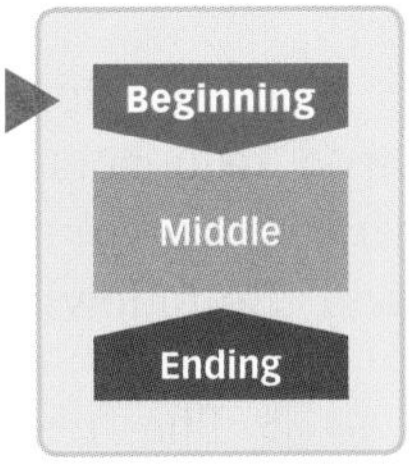

It's time to create your draft. The first paragraph of your persuasive essay gives the problem and your opinion statement. Here are some strategies for getting the reader's attention:

- **Ask a question:** What makes Wadsworth Middle School really special?
- **Quote someone:** "Nature is the best laboratory for learning about nature."
- **Share an experience:** When Lee Baker saw a crane at camp, he knew he wanted to study wildlife management.
- **Give background information:** The state cut money to schools this year, which means that Wadsworth Middle School might have to cancel science camp.

When using one of the above, use the strategy as a starting point on which to build your ideas. This will help create an organized essay.

Beginning Paragraph

The following essay captures the reader's attention by beginning with a quotation. The writer introduces the problem and gives an opinion statement.

A quotation gets the reader's attention.

The problem is introduced.

The opinion statement is given (underlined).

"Nature is the best laboratory for learning about nature." Ms. Jacobson says this whenever she talks about science camp. For 10 years, every seventh grader at Wadsworth Middle School has attended the three-day camp in May. Sixth graders spend a whole year looking forward to "their turn," and eighth graders wish they could go again. Now science camp might be cancelled because of budget cuts. Science camp is in danger unless students raise money to save it.

Draft

Draft an opening. Write the beginning paragraph of your problem-solution essay. Use a quotation or another strategy to get your reader's attention. Then introduce the problem and write your opinion statement.

TEKS 7.14B, 7.18C

Drafting Developing the Middle Part

After you have written your opening paragraph, you need to develop the middle part, or body, of your essay. As you write your middle paragraphs, use your organized list and the following tips.

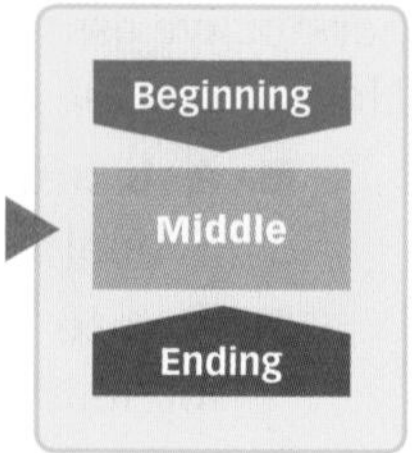

1. The **first middle paragraph** summarizes the problem.
2. The **second middle paragraph** proposes a solution.
3. The **other middle paragraphs** contain details that convince the reader your solution will work.

As you write, remember to include details that build upon the problem and the solution. These details should also offer support for your viewpoint on the issue. This will help you create a focused piece of writing. Leave out details that do not relate to the problem and solution.

Middle Paragraphs

The topic sentence summarizes the problem.

The body convinces the reader with details.

The closing sentence tells why the problem needs a solution.

Without science camp, students will miss out on a unique learning experience. In science class, students learn to identify rocks by picking them up out of a box. At science camp, they learn to identify rocks by finding them in cliff sides or riverbeds. Science camp also lets students experiment with different forms of energy. For example, students get to build miniature steam engines that are powered by campfires. They also make solar panels that heat camp water. These experiences would be tough to create in a classroom. Science camp helps students understand nature while it teaches them to work with each other.

TEKS 7.14B, 7.18C
ELPS 5G

Topic Sentence	Science camp is for everybody, and it won't be saved unless everybody helps raise money for it.
The second middle paragraph introduces a solution.	To get started, Principal Jeffries and the student council could set up a "science camp fund" at a local bank. One student and an adult could be responsible for keeping the account. Every year, science camp costs $3,000. That sounds expensive, but
Closing Sentence	if every student at Wadsworth raises just $10, the fund would be filled.
Topic Sentence	Students can raise money in many ways.
This middle paragraph offers details about the solution.	For example, they could hold a talent auction. By raking lawns, cleaning gutters, baby-sitting, or using other talents, students can meet the goal. They could also arrange a rummage sale, or they could hold a bake sale. Students could even ask local businesses to sponsor them.
Closing Sentence	If Wadsworth students all work together, they can easily raise the money.

Draft

Write your middle paragraphs. Build on the ideas in your prewriting plan to create middle paragraphs for your problem-solution essay. Make sure to include evidence that supports your viewpoint on the issue.

Drafting Tips

- **Follow the plan** in your organized list.
- **Use facts, examples, and quotations** to convince the reader to take the problem seriously and help solve it.
- **Avoid "fuzzy thinking."**
- **Use a convincing voice.**

TEKS 7.14C, 7.18B
ELPS 5G

Drafting Answering a Counterargument

In the ending, you should think about possible concerns your reader may have and answer a counterargument your reader could propose. Use the sentence frame below as a basic guide to answer a counterargument.

Beginning
Middle
Ending

Some people say ______________________,
(counterargument)
but the fact is ______________________.
(answer)

Draft **Consider counterarguments.** Think about the views and concerns your reader may have about your ideas. Using the guide above, write a counterargument that your reader might have and provide an answer.

Creating a Call to Action

A call to action is a command that tells the reader how to help solve the problem. The last sentence in the paragraph below includes a call to action.

Ending Paragraph

A counter-argument is answered.

A call to action asks the reader to help.

Some people say it's too much work to save science camp, but the fact is that if students all help out, they can reach the necessary goal. Science camp is a terrific tradition that deserves to be saved. Tell Principal Jeffries that students are ready to save science camp.

Draft **Write your ending.** Draft the final paragraph of your essay. Remember to summarize the problem and solution and call your reader to action.

Draft **Form a complete first draft.** Write a complete copy of your essay. Read the draft and think about how well you have addressed form, purpose, and audience. Note changes that you will make when revising.

Go Online!

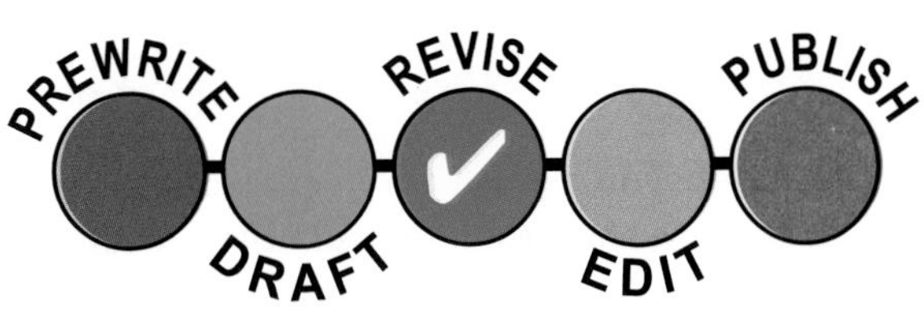

Revising

When you revise, you add or remove details, shift parts of the essay, and work on creating a more persuasive voice. You also check your essay for the traits of good writing.

Keys to Effective Revising

1. *Make sure you use the problem-solution form for your writing.*
2. *Use your opinion statement to clearly name the problem and then propose a solution.*
3. *Select the right words to address your purpose and audience.*
4. *Check that the details support your problem and solution.*
5. *Revise to include facts that will support your opinion statements.*
6. *Read through your entire draft to make sure that your essay works.*

TEKS 7.14C

Texas Traits

Revising for Focus and Coherence

When you revise for *focus and coherence,* check to make sure that you clearly state the problem and stay on topic as you present a solution. The words you use should also give focus to your essay by addressing your audience and purpose.

Do I focus on a clear problem and solution?

You can convince your reader that the problem is serious and that your solution will work when you make sure that your essay is well organized and flows smoothly. Strong writing has external coherence, which means that the major parts of your essay work well together. Check for external coherence by making sure that your introduction, body, and ending work well together.

Do my details help explain the problem and solution?

In a problem-solution essay, the details in your writing should provide clear answers to the following questions.

- Why does this problem exist?
- Why should the problem be solved?
- Who or what does this problem affect?
- Who can solve the problem?
- When does this problem need to be solved?

Try It Read the parts of a problem-solution essay below. On your own paper, put the parts in the order that they should appear in your essay.

1. Propose a solution.
2. Summarize the problem.
3. Introduce the problem.
4. Give details about the solution.

Revise **Review the form of your essay. Read your first draft. Check to see that the main parts of your essay are well-organized and flow. Use the questions above as a guide. If your essay does not clearly present the problem and then the solution, revise your writing to do so.**

Do my words fit my audience and purpose?

To be persuasive, focus on choosing the right words to address your audience and purpose. The right words will help you appeal to your audience and convince them to see things your way. The following examples show the importance of using words that fit your purpose and audience. Notice how much more persuasive the last statement is than the one that is too formal and the one that is too casual.

Too Formal

The student council should address this concern with the utmost speed.

Too Casual

The student council should hash out this deal A.S.A.P.

Just Right

The student council should discuss this problem right away.

Revise

Check for appropriate word choice. Read through your essay. Make sure your words help your audience to connect with your purpose. Replace any words that are too formal or too casual with words that are a better fit.

Focus and Coherence Word choice is changed to better fit the audience and purpose.

Without science camp, students will miss out on a ~~totally awesome~~ unique learning experience. In science class, students learn to identify rocks by picking them up out of a ~~stupid~~ box. At science camp, they learn to identify rocks by finding them in cliff . . .

TEKS 7.18C
ELPS 3G, 4G, 4K

Texas Traits

Revising for Organization

When you revise for *organization*, you check to make sure that your evidence is logically organized and that it supports your opinion. Each detail that you include should build on the ones before it while helping your reader better understand the problem you identified and the solution that you suggested.

Do I include strong topic sentences?

In the middle of your essay, you will need to summarize the problem and explain your solution. Including well-written, logical topic sentences for each paragraph will help readers follow your ideas and better understand your viewpoint.

A Good Topic Sentence. . .

- names the subject, and
- tells the focus or main point.

Try It Work with a partner to read the pairs of sentences below. Indicate which sentence in each is the better topic sentence.

1. Science camp is a unique learning experience for students.
   Students can find rocks and walk through streams.

2. Students work together to conduct experiments.
   At science camp, students learn not only about nature, but also about cooperation.

3. Student council can hold a bake sale.
   All students need to help raise money to keep science camp at our school.

Revise **Check your topic sentences. Read through your essay. Check to make sure that each paragraph contains a strong, clear topic sentence that supports your viewpoint. If not, rewrite a sentence to make it better or add a topic sentence.**

Are my details organized to support my viewpoint?

You will help readers understand your viewpoint by giving them logically-organized evidence that supports your position. Begin with your topic sentence, then present the details to support your point. Your goal is to get readers to follow your thinking so that you are better able to convince them to agree with you. Notice below how the details support the topic sentence and are in a logical order.

Topic Sentence

The band is in desperate need of new uniforms.

Detail Sentences

Membership has grown and we don't have enough uniforms for everyone.

The uniforms we do have are very small sizes.

Some students find their pants are two inches too short.

Try It Read the topic sentence below. Then choose which detail sentences support it. On your own paper, write a paragraph using the topic sentence and organizing the details you chose in logical order.

Topic Sentence: Band members could organize a concert to pay for part of the uniform cost.

1. We could ask permission to use the park pavilion for the show.
2. Red uniforms would be the best color choice.
3. Others could prepare an advertisement for the school newspaper.
4. Some band members could make posters to promote the event.
5. If each member sold 10 tickets, we should make a good profit.

Revise **Revise your paragraphs. Read each paragraph in your essay. Decide if your evidence is logically organized to support your viewpoint. If not, try moving sentences around so that they make more sense and better support your opinion.**

Texas Traits Revising for Development of Ideas

When you revise for *development of ideas,* you should check to make sure you have included both facts and opinions in your writing. You can also better develop your ideas by considering and addressing counterarguments.

Do I include facts to support my opinion?

In prewriting, you learned that opinions are someone's idea about something. They tell how a person thinks or feels. You also learned that facts share information that can be proven true. In your essay, be sure to use specific facts to support your opinions. Your readers will be more likely to agree with opinions that are based on facts.

Fact

The band uniforms should be replaced because they are torn and ripped.

Opinion

The band uniforms should be replaced because they look terrible.

Try It Read the following opinion statement and the detail sentences. Number your paper from 1 to 6. Write "F" if the detail sentence is a fact. Write "O" if the detail sentence is an opinion. Notice how the fact statements are more likely to help you convince your reader.

Opinion Statement: Brightwood Middle School should have a stage added to our auditorium.

1. The stage is higher so students can see and hear speakers.
2. Drama club is growing and hopes to present plays someday.
3. It is fun to watch a presentation when it is on a stage.
4. Building a stage at our school is the right thing to do.
5. The band director wants a safe place for instruments during concerts.
6. Everyone thinks a stage would make our school a better place.

Revise **Check your facts. Read your first draft. Identify which statements are facts and which are opinions. Make sure that you use clear, specific fact statements to support your opinions.**

Have I answered a reader counterargument?

You have answered a counterargument if you have considered how your reader may respond to your arguments for the proposed solution.

Reader's Concern

Some people say we don't need intramural sports,

Satisfying Answer

but intramural teams help students stay physically fit.

Try It Read the following answers to counterarguments. Indicate what is wrong with each: either the answer does not mention a concern, or the answer does not respond to the concern in a satisfying way.

1. Some people may think the crossing at Kane Street and Harper Avenue is safe, but those people are wrong.
2. The fact is that busywork wastes everybody's time.
3. Although most students like our school mascot, I don't.

Revise **Check for counterarguments.** Check to see that you have effectively answered a possible reader counterargument. Revise as needed.

Development of Ideas
An answer to a counterargument is improved.

Some people say it's too much work to save science camp, but the fact is that ~~those people have no idea what they're talking about~~ if students all help out, they can reach the necessary goal easily. Science. . .

Texas Traits

Revising for Voice

To revise for *voice*, check to make sure your writing sounds confident, enthusiastic, and persuasive. A strong, confident voice helps your reader believe in what you are saying.

How can my voice sound more confident?

One way to sound more confident is to make your point in the fewest words possible. Confident writing says a lot with a few words, and it is convincing. Writing that is not confident uses many words that say very little.

Not Confident

It might be a useful solution to the problem of too many cars in front of the school if the school could have a different place marked out for people to come to drop off or pick up students.

Confident

New parking rules could solve the traffic jams before and after school.

Try It Read the following sentences that lack a confident voice. On your own paper, rewrite each in as few words as you can. Share your revised sentences with a classmate.

1. The problem that there are some rooms that are warm and stuffy could be helped if there were some sort of policy about adjusting the thermostat.
2. If people would slow down when they are driving along the road with the bike route, then maybe it wouldn't be quite so tough for cyclists to use the route to get places.

Revise **Revise your voice. Read your essay and look for places where you could say the same thing using fewer words. Revise your writing to make it sound more confident.**

How can my voice sound more persuasive?

One way to make your voice sound more persuasive is to include a few suggestions. You should make sure the suggestions you offer match the audience you are trying to reach. There are two types of suggestions: mild and strong.

- **Mild Suggestion:** A mild suggestion uses a verb such as *may, could, would.* For example,

  The school district could ask parents for donations.

- **Strong Suggestion:** A strong suggestion uses a verb such as *should, ought,* or *must*. For example,

  The district must hold a fundraiser to pay for science camp.

Try It Read the following statements. Turn each one into a mild or strong suggestion using one of the verbs listed above.

1. It is up to students to help with recycling day.
2. It is important that classmates know that teasing isn't allowed.
3. Students don't report accidents to teachers.
4. Seventh graders help sixth graders learn new skills.
5. It is a good idea for students to walk home in pairs instead of alone.

Revise **Add suggestions. Check your essay. If the voice needs to be more persuasive in parts, add suggestions. Make sure your suggestions are appropriate for your audience.**

Voice
A statement is turned into a suggestion, and an important point is said in fewer words.

One student and an adult ~~are~~ could be responsible for keeping the account. ~~Taken on a yearly basis, the general expenses for science camp are round about in the range of $3,000 for the whole group of seventh graders who go.~~ Every year, science camp costs $3,000. That sounds expensive . . .

Texas Traits

Revising Using a Checklist

Revise

Check your revising. On a piece of paper, write the numbers 1 to 10. If you can answer "yes" to a question, put a check mark after that number. If not, continue to work with that part of your essay.

Focus and Coherence

____ **1.** Do I focus on a clear problem and solution?

____ **2.** Do the main parts of my essay flow smoothly?

____ **3.** Have I included persuasive details that will help my reader connect with my problem and solution?

Organization

____ **4.** Do I have clear topic sentences that show my viewpoint?

____ **5.** Have I organized my details in a way that makes sense?

Development of Ideas

____ **6.** Have I included facts and opinions in my essay?

____ **7.** Do I support my opinions with facts?

____ **8.** Have I answered a reader's possible counterargument?

Voice

____ **9.** Does my voice sound confident and persuasive?

____ **10.** Have I included suggestions that fit my audience?

Revise

Make a clean copy. When you've finished revising, make a clean copy before you edit. This makes checking for conventions easier.

Go Online!

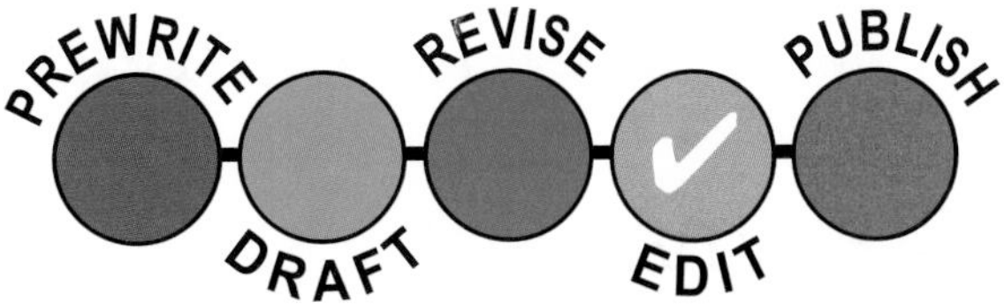

Editing

Once you are finished revising, you need to edit for grammar, punctuation, capitalization, and spelling. These rules are called *conventions.*

Keys to Effective Editing

1. *Use a dictionary, a thesaurus, and the "Proofreader's Guide" in the back of this book.*
2. *Check for correct usage of prepositions and prepositional phrases. Then check subject-verb agreement.*
3. *Make sure adjectival phrases are used correctly.*
4. *Check that compound and complex sentences are written correctly.*
5. *Make sure all words are spelled correctly.*
6. *Use the editing and proofreading marks inside the back cover of this book.*

TEKS 7.19A(v)

Texas Traits Editing for Conventions

Grammar

Do I use prepositions and prepositional phrases correctly?

A preposition is a word that shows position or direction and introduces a prepositional phrase. *On, in, from, behind,* and *of* are just a few prepositions. A prepositional phrase includes a preposition, the object of the preposition (a noun or pronoun), and the word that modifies the object.

The truck parked near the building.

In the sentence above, *near* is the preposition, *building* is the object, and *the* is the word that modifies the noun.

Edit **Check for prepositions and prepositional phrases. Identify any prepositions and prepositional phrases you have used in your writing. Make sure you have used them correctly.**

Do I have subject-verb agreement when I use prepositional phrases?

When using prepositional phrases in your writing, it is important to remember that your verbs need to agree in number with your subjects, rather than the objects of the prepositional phrases.

GRAMMAR Try It Tell which sentences below have correct subject-verb agreement.

1. Our safety glasses for the lab fits tightly.
2. The door under the stairs creaks.
3. Books with a cover stay protected.
4. That curtain over the windows blow in the breeze.

Edit **Check for subject-verb agreement. Review your essay. Check for subject-verb agreement when you use prepositional phrases.**

TEKS 7.19A(v)
ELPS 2I, 3D, 3E, 3H

Do I use adjectival clauses correctly?

Like an adjective, you use an adjectival clause to tell more about a noun. Adjectival clauses are dependent, meaning they can't stand alone. Instead they must be linked to a main clause.

An Adjectival Clause . . .

- has a noun and a verb;
- begins with a relative pronoun, such as *who, whom, whose, that,* or *which;*
- works like an adjective; and
- answers the questions *What kind? How many?* or *Which one?*

In the example sentences below, the adjectival clauses are in blue type.

People who ride bicycles **are very strong.**

The student whose homework I found **is thankful.**

Edit

Check your adjectival clauses. Make sure any adjectival clauses you have used follow the points listed above.

Learning Language

Many times, prepositions tell about the location of an item. A good way to remember prepositions is to think about the idea that most prepositions are anywhere "a mouse can go." In the examples below, the prepositions are in black type.

A mouse can go **up** a chimney.

A mouse can go **near** the sidewalk.

A mouse can go **under** the bed.

A mouse can go **down** a slide.

A mouse can go **around** the house.

Work with a partner. Tell your partner another place a mouse can go, using the sentences above as a model. Remember to use a preposition in your sentence. Have your partner tell the preposition that you used. Then switch roles and listen to your partner's sentences.

TEKS 7.14C, 7.19B
ELPS 3E

Sentence Structure

When you edit for *sentence structure,* you correct any errors in your sentences. Also, make sure you have correctly used compound and complex sentences.

Do I use compound and complex sentences correctly?

Using a variety of sentence types adds interest and balance to your writing.

Compound Sentence

A compound sentence is useful when you want to express two ideas that are equally important. It consists of two simple sentences that are usually joined by a comma and a coordinating conjunction such as *and, but, or, nor, so, for,* or *yet.*

The school will pay half the cost of the spring production, but the drama club will need to raise the rest of the money.

Complex Sentence

A complex sentence helps show the different kinds of connections between the ideas in your writing such as time, cause-effect, and comparison-contrast. It consists of a simple sentence plus a clause beginning with a subordinating conjunction such as *when, after, because,* or *as.*

The funding will be available when both groups reach an agreement.

Try It Work with a partner to tell whether each sentence is compound or complex.

1. Because the building is old, some restrooms aren't accessible.
2. The team needs new equipment, and the band needs uniforms.
3. Archery is offered as a summer class, but it is not a gym class.
4. Unless we act now, the marching band will be cut.

Edit **Check your sentences.** **Have you correctly used compound and complex sentences? If not, revise your sentences. If you don't have many complex and compound sentences, rewrite to add some.**

Spelling

When you edit for *spelling*, you read through your writing to make sure all words are spelled correctly. You can also use a computer program with spell check to help you.

Do I correctly spell all the words in my essay?

After you have revised your writing, you must check it for spelling errors. Here are some suggestions:

- Read your essay from the bottom up. Start with the last line and read to the first. This will force you to focus on each word.
- Circle words you are unsure of. You can go back and check them with a dictionary.
- Use a spell checker when you write with a computer.
- Learn basic spelling rules. These will help you when you write and when you edit.
- Ask a friend or classmate for help in catching errors.

Try It Rewrite the paragraph below on your own paper. Correct any spelling errors.

The band unifurms need to be replaced. We have many new membrs and not enough unifurms to fit them all. The unifurms we have are very small sizes. Some kids have pantes that are severil inches too short. The worst part is that many of the unifurms have teres and rips.

Edit **Check for spelling errors.** **Select one of the strategies above. Edit your writing for spelling errors. If you find some, correct them. Then write a clean copy of your essay.**

Conventions
The writer edited to create a complex sentence. Spelling errors were also corrected.

Science   and
Sceince camp helps students understand nature. It

teaches them to work with each other. Science camp is

for everybody. It won't be saved unless everybody helps

raise
rase money for it.

Editing Using a Checklist

Edit

Check your editing. On a piece of paper, write the numbers 1 to 9. If you can answer "yes" to a question, put a check mark after that number. If not, continue to edit for that convention.

Conventions

GRAMMAR

____ **1.** Have I correctly used prepositions and prepositional phrases in my writing?

____ **2.** Have I checked for subject-verb agreement when using a prepositional phrase?

____ **3.** Have I correctly used adjectival phrases in my writing?

MECHANICS

____ **4.** Did I correctly use punctuation and capitalization in my essay?

SENTENCE STRUCTURE

____ **5.** Have I used a variety of sentence types in my essay?

____ **6.** Have I used compound sentences correctly?

____ **7.** Have I used complex sentences correctly?

SPELLING

____ **8.** Have I spelled all words correctly?

____ **9.** Have I used at least one of the strategies to double-check my work?

Creating a Title

- Restate the call to action: **Stop the Bulldozers!**
- Write a slogan: **Science Camp for All**
- Be creative: **A Band on the Run**

TEKS 7.14E

Go Online!

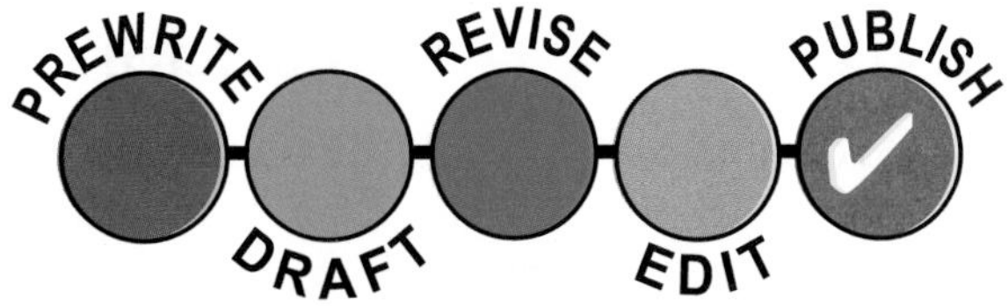

Publishing

Sharing Your Essay

After all your work to write, revise, and edit your problem-solution essay, you'll want to make a neat final copy to share. You may also want to publish and share your work with appropriate audiences, present your solution to a group, or advertise it with a poster.

Publish **Make a final copy.** **Follow your teacher's instructions or use the guidelines below. Create a clean final copy and carefully proofread it.**

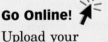

Focus on Presentation

- **Use blue or black ink and write neatly.**
- **Write your name in the upper left corner of page 1.**
- **Skip a line and center your title; skip another line and start your writing.**
- **Indent every paragraph and leave a one-inch margin on all four sides.**
- **Write your last name and the page number in the upper right corner of every page after the first one.**

Make an Oral Presentation

Decide what group could help your solution—your class, the student council, a student club, or some other group. Arrange to present your paper orally for this audience at their next meeting.

Go Online!

Upload your problem-solution essay for others to read.

Create a Poster

Develop a poster based on your essay. Decide on pictures and details to include. Create your poster and put it up where an appropriate audience can see it.

ELPS 4I, 4K

Evaluating a Persuasive Essay

To learn how to evaluate a persuasive essay, you'll use the scoring rubric on pages 48–49 and the essays that follow. These essays are examples of writing for each score on the rubric.

Notice that this first persuasive essay received a score of 4. Read the description for a score of 4 on pages 48–49. Then read the essay. Use the same steps to study the other examples. Always remember to think about the overall quality of the writing.

Writing that fits a score of 4 is very strong.

4

The reader is drawn in by a quotation.

The writer states a clear opinion.

The writer includes well-organized paragraphs.

The Give Me Twenty!

"Let's see those pushups! Come on! You can do it! Only two laps, let's go! Double time!"

That is the voice of Mr. Torres-Cepeda, our beloved gym teacher here at Redbud Middle School, trying to persuade us to try harder in gym class. He has a hard job, because lots of us don't want to exercise very much. According to experts, our nation's middle schoolers (and other young people) are out of shape and in danger of bad health, and we've got to get them to exercise more.

If you're not aware of this crisis, then the news stories about it will convince you. Doctors have done many studies of children's and teens' fitness, and the results are always pretty bad. In a study of fifth and seventh graders in 2009, half of the students failed a fitness test. Almost one-third of them were overweight. In another study, between 1999 and 2002, one-third of the teens were so physically unfit that they were out of breath after climbing stairs. They were at risk for heart disease. In the future, they will put more of a strain on our country's medical system. So physical fitness is not just a problem for people's health. It is also a problem for the economy.

Evidence is logically organized to support the author's viewpoint.

The writer considers and responds to views of others.

Something must be done to solve this problem and to get American kids on the physical fitness track. Some states have already made progress by giving students fitness tests every year. That way, schools and parents can find out whether their children are fit or not. However, keeping score doesn't mean you win the game! We need to take more action. Kids need to get up and walk more, run more, and play sports. In addition, we need to get more students involved in school sports. My solution is that every school should start a Physical Fitness Club and that students who partisipate in it should get extra credit on their report cards.

This would be an effective solution because many students would choose to do it for the extra credit, and they would discover that they really enjoyed the activity, and they would keep doing it. That would make exercise a part of their life.

Some people might say that kids already have too much school work. However, this wouldn't be like regular school work. It would be more like fun. The important thing is that students wouldn't be forced to do it, so the ones who did would really want to. Kids don't like being told what to do—have you ever noticed? My solution would not be ordering anyone around. If you think it's a good solution, contact me at school or at home and we can write a petition to give to the principal, Ms. Golden, to start a Physical Fitness Club. If Redbud Middle School does it, other schools will too, and our country's young people can start becoming fit.

ELPS 4I, 4K

Writing that fits a score of 3 is strong in most ways.

3

There are some errors in capitalization, spelling, and sentence structure.

The writer includes a clear opinion statement.

Speed Bumps for Safer Streets

My street, Fillmore ave., used to be a quiet, safe place for children to play, but it isn't anymore, at least not the way it used to be. When I was small, the only cars that went down this street were the ones belonging to people who lived here or were visiting, or delivery trucks and things like that. Now, however, if you watch the traffic go by, you'll see an endless string of cars from out of the nieghborhood. Where are they all going? Obviously they are going to the new shopping center. Everyone in town is going there. It's a great place with fancy restaurants, expensive clothes stores, and a movie theater. However, it has brought traffic problems to this peaceful nieghborhood. The city must do something to manage the traffic better!

What is the city supposed to do, you ask. It's not as if they can't do a thing, the way they pretend to. In fact I think the solution is obvious. The traffic isn't going to go away. So we have to make sure that the traffic slows down and that it stays on the main roads, not going way into the small streets where people have their houses. It's important for safety. To make sure this happens, I recommend that the city put speed bumps on Fillmore ave. and on the other streets where traffic is worse than it used to be. That would mean less cars would go down those streets and the cars that did would be going slower so they wouldn't be as dangerous.

This solution will work. How do I know? Because it works in other places. My aunt lives in Austin and in her neighborhood they put in speed bumps when some of the residence complained, because traffic was increasing there too for the same reason. With the speed bumps, people stopped turning onto her street, because the reason they turned onto that street was to find a short cut away from the main road, and if they had to slow down it wasn't a short cut.

Evidence is logically organized.

It's as simple as that. There may be other views and objections, however, I can answer them. Some readers will say that putting in speed bumps is too expensive. My reply is that saving lives is worth it. Even if just one preschooler's life is saved by not being run over, because of speed bumps being there, everyone would agree that's worth it. Also putting in speed bumps would cause some trouble for people who live on those streets, when the crews were there tearing up the street. However, that would only last for a short time, so it would be worth it too.

The writer answers objections confidently.

I am going to send an e-mail to the mayor and to the newspaper stating my solution, and I hope that people will support me. If you think this is a good idea, you should send e-mails to those places too, and they are more likely to do it.

The writer includes a call to action.

ELPS 4I, 4K

Writing that fits a score of 2 is strong in some ways.

2

Errors in spelling, usage, and sentence structure are distracting.

The writer has strong, interesting opinions.

A weak conclusion does not convince the reader.

Our School Needs Art Supplies

Our school needs more Art supplies. We have some, but not enough for all the students. Mrs. Toussaint tries really hard and she buys some of the Art supplies with her own money, which I don't think is fair. Every May we run out of crayons, markers, pads, paints, and brushes. We have enuogh easals. But paper and things to color with, they run out. Then what are we supposed to do in Art. Some people do there homework. Or Mrs. Toussaint brings in pictures of Art and we talk about it. I enjoy that. But were supposed to be learning to draw and paint, not look at stuff.

I have a solutian to this problem. The solutian is that we should have a funraiser. Do something after school to make money for Art supplies. It has to be something parents will attend because there the ones with the money! I asked myself what will parents come to and I had a couple of answers. One is a carnaval. But we already have a carnaval for the teams. So my other answer is we should have one of those auctions where parents come in and bid on items silently and the highest bid has to buy it. What will they bid on? They will bid on students' Art works. That way the auction supports Art. Parents will buy it because they love there kid's Art. Then Mrs. Toussaint will be able to afford more supplies. I hope you like this solutian because I think it is a good one.

ELPS 4I, 4K

Writing that fits a score of 1 is weak.

1

Many errors in spelling and grammar make the essay difficult to understand.

The paragraphs are not well organized.

The writer only provides weak evidence.

Too Many Clicks

Our school is full of clicks, everywere you go you run into it. You go to the lunchroom and you cant hardly find any place to sit every place is taken by some click. I used to belong to one but I don't any longer.

The clicks are so into fashin that's what bothers me. If you don't have just the right cloths they put you down. People can be so mean. Each click has its own look one is prepy one is goth etc. People have no individuallity. That wouldnt be so bad by itself but they have to go make other people feel bad so they can feel good about themselves. What can we do about it?

My solution is have school uniforms. Everybody has to wear the same thing every day. Nobody can critisize someone else just because they parents can't aford the best cloths.

They have done this in certin places and it worked. So I think it wold work here too.

The colors would be green and white because that's the colors of our school. Some people would not like to wear a uniform. They want to show off their cloths. That's they're problem. They wold have to do like everybody else.

Evaluating and Reflecting on Your Writing

You've put a lot of time and effort into your problem-solution essay. Now take some time to score and think about your writing. On your own paper, finish each sentence starter below. To score your writing, refer to the scoring rubric on pages 48–49 and the examples you just read.

My Problem-Solution Essay

1. *The best score for my problem-solution essay is . . .*
2. *It's the best score because . . .*
3. *The best part of my problem-solution essay is . . .*
4. *The part that still needs work is . . .*
5. *The main thing I learned about writing a problem-solution essay is . . .*
6. *In my next problem-solution essay, I would like to . . .*

Persuasive Writing

Creating an Editorial

Every major newspaper has an "Op/Ed" page, which is short for "Opinion/Editorial." An editorial is a short essay that gives a writer's opinion about a timely event or issue. Many times during the history of our country, editorials have paved the way for great changes.

In this chapter, you will be writing an editorial of your own. Perhaps your school is having a crisis over the food choices in the vending machines. Maybe some sports teams are arguing over who gets to use the gymnasium after school. In an editorial, you can give your opinion about the events happening around you.

Writing Guidelines

Subject: A school issue
Purpose: To persuade the reader
Form: Editorial
Audience: Classmates

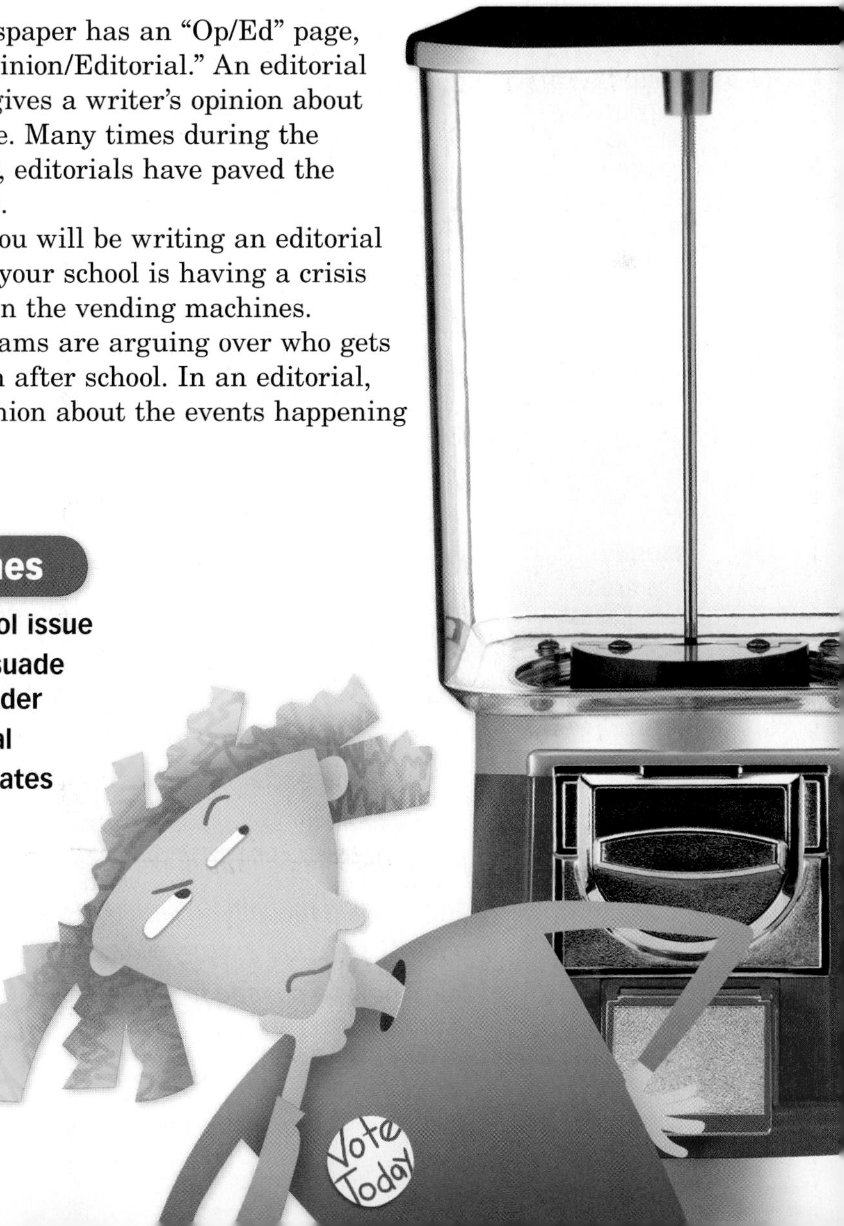

Editorial

An editorial expresses an opinion about a timely event. The editorial that follows was written by Hassan and published in his local newspaper.

Beginning
The issue is introduced, and the opinion statement is given (**underlined**).

Middle
The middle paragraphs support the writer's opinion.

Let the Kids Choose

A group of parents has asked the school board to remove the vending machines from Lincoln Middle School. They say that the soda and junk foods in the machines are creating bad eating habits among students. These parents are probably right, but removing vending machines won't solve the problem. <u>Lincoln Middle School should keep its vending machines so that students have more food choices, not fewer.</u>

A healthy diet is based on wise food choices. Removing the vending machines only removes the decisions students have to make about the foods they eat. The problem isn't the machines but what's in them. Machines that now hold only soda could just as easily hold juice, milk, and bottled water. Machines full of candy, cookies, and donuts could hold fruit snacks, nuts, and low-salt pretzels.

That doesn't mean that all the chips, cookies, donuts, and soda should be removed from the machines. If only healthy snacks are provided, students still won't learn anything about making smart choices. Instead, the vending machines should offer wholesome foods and other foods side by side. Then students will have to learn how to choose for themselves.

Ending

The opinion is summed up in a thoughtful way.

Healthy eating habits begin with wise food choices. Removing the vending machines won't help students learn anything about healthy food choices, but stocking those machines with a mix of foods will.

Bridgewood Gazette

OPINION/EDITORIAL

City Voices: Let the Kids Choose

A group of parents has asked the school board to remove the vending machines from Lincoln Middle School. They say that the soda and junk foods in the machines are creating bad eating habits among students. These parents are probably right, but removing vending machines won't solve the problem. Lincoln Middle School should keep its vending machines so that students have more food choices, not fewer.

A healthy diet is based on wise food choices. Removing the vending machines only removes the decisions students have to make about the foods they eat. The problem isn't the machines but what's in them. Machines that now hold only soda could just as easily hold juice, milk, and bottled water. Machines full of candy, cookies, and donuts could hold fruit snacks, nuts, and low-salt pretzels.

That doesn't mean that all the chips, cookies, donuts, and soda should be removed from the machines. If only healthy snacks are provided, students still won't learn anything about making smart choices. Instead, the vending machines should offer wholesome foods and other foods side by side. Then students will have to learn how to choose for themselves.

Healthy eating habits begin with wise food choices. Removing the vending machines won't help students learn anything about healthy food choices, but stocking those machines with a mix of foods will. by Hassan Nathan

Respond to the reading. On your own paper, write answers to the following questions about the editorial.

- ☐ **Organization** (1) What purpose does the ending serve?
- ☐ **Development of Ideas** (2) What is Hassan's opinion? (3) What details offer the strongest support? Name two.
- ☐ **Voice** (4) How would you describe the writer's voice? (5) What words make it sound that way?

TEKS 7.14A
ELPS 5G

Prewriting Selecting a Topic

An editorial gives an opinion about a current event or issue, so the best way to find a topic for an editorial is to focus on things happening around you. When Hassan received his assignment to write an editorial, he used sentence starters to make a list of all the current events he could think of.

Sentence Starters

At Lincoln Middle School,

the biggest problem is . . . the gym locker rooms are gross.
. . . that some homework is busywork.
the worst change is . . . removing the vending machines.
the one change I would make is . . . adding a study hall.
. . . starting school later!

Prewrite **Use sentence starters.** **Use the sentence starters above to think about issues or problems in your school. Finish each sentence with your opinion. Review your opinions and choose the one issue that will make the best editorial.**

Supporting Your Opinion

Now that you have selected an opinion, it's time to come up with reasons to support it. Hassan used a table diagram. The "tabletop" gives his opinion, and the "table legs" are reasons that support it.

Table Diagram

Opinion	*Lincoln Middle School should keep its vending machines.*		
Support	*students need the chance to choose good foods*	*the problem isn't the machines, but the junk food*	*machines should have all kinds of food in them*

Prewrite **Create a table diagram.** **Use the sample above as a guide to create your own table diagram. Write your opinion in the top box and your supporting reasons underneath. Come up with at least three reasons.**

Refining Your Opinion Statement

Now that you have selected an opinion and come up with reasons to support it, you are ready to write your opinion statement. An effective opinion statement gives your opinion and sums up the reasons for it.

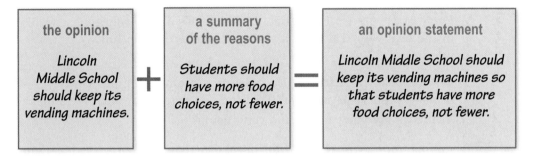

the opinion		a summary of the reasons		an opinion statement
Lincoln Middle School should keep its vending machines.	+	*Students should have more food choices, not fewer.*	=	*Lincoln Middle School should keep its vending machines so that students have more food choices, not fewer.*

Prewrite **Write an opinion statement. Create an opinion statement that combines your opinion with your reasons. Use the example above as a guide.**

Drafting Creating Your First Draft

As you write your editorial, make sure each part does its job.

- **Beginning paragraph:** Introduce your topic and give your opinion statement. Include some facts to support your opinion.
- **Middle paragraphs:** Present your reasons in a logical order or in order of importance. (See page 613 for help.)
- **Closing paragraph:** Reflect on your opinion and reasons and give your reader something to think about. Include facts that will help convince the reader that your opinion makes sense.

Draft **Write your first draft. Let your table diagram list and the tips above guide you as you write your editorial.**

tip Always think about your audience. In order to convince a reader to agree with you, avoid offending her or him. Therefore, don't blame or sharply criticize anyone in your editorial. Include facts to back up your ideas and opinions.

TEKS 7.14C, 7.17A(v)

Revising Improving Your Writing

Revise your first draft, focusing on the following traits of writing.

- ☐ **Focus and Coherence** Do I show internal coherence by logically moving from one point to another? Do I stay on topic?
- ☐ **Organization** Do I organize my sentences and paragraphs in the best way? Do I use a variety of transitions to link paragraphs?
- ☐ **Development of Ideas** Do I clearly state my opinion? Do I provide supporting reasons? Do I include details for each reason?
- ☐ **Voice** Is my voice polite and convincing?

Revise

Revise your editorial. Use the questions above to improve your writing.

Editing Checking for Conventions

Once you finish revising your editorial, polish it by focusing on *conventions.*

- ☐ **Conventions** Have I checked for errors in grammar, punctuation, capitalization, and spelling?

Edit

Edit your editorial. Check the conventions in your writing. Make a clean final draft and proofread it for any remaining errors.

Publishing Sharing Your Editorial

Because editorials share opinions about timely events or issues, this type of writing is made for publication. To find the right place to publish your editorial, ask yourself the following questions.

- Who is my audience? (Classmates? Parents? People in the community? People who belong to a specific organization?)
- What publication do these people read? (A local newspaper? A school paper or Web site? A PTO or PTA newsletter?)
- How can I submit my editorial to this publication? (What are the guidelines? How should I send in my writing?)

Publish

Publish your editorial. Use the questions above to help you find the right place to send your editorial for publication. Prepare your work according to the submission guidelines and send it in.

Persuasive Writing

Across the Curriculum

Some people think it's tough to be persuasive, but guinea pigs disagree. They use one sound to persuade their owners to feed them: "Reeeeeeeet!" They use another sound to persuade their owners to pet them: "Puuuuurrrrr!" Imagine that! With two simple sounds, a guinea pig can persuade people to do just what it wants. You can be just as persuasive as a guinea pig—both in and out of school—by using convincing words and ideas.

In this chapter, you will see how persuasive writing is used in many settings. For example, in social studies, you may write a campaign speech. In math, you may compile data into a persuasive graph. For science, you may write a proposal for a science fair project. And beyond the classroom, you may write a persuasive letter to convince someone to take action. Finally, you'll even learn how to be persuasive on a writing test.

What's Ahead

- **Social Studies:** Writing a Campaign Speech
- **Math:** Creating a Graph
- **Science:** Writing a Proposal
- **Practical Writing:** Drafting a Business Letter

Social Studies: Writing a Campaign Speech

In a democracy, leaders are chosen by a vote, and candidates give speeches to persuade people to vote for them. The following speech was written by a middle school student running for student council president.

The **beginning** grabs the listeners' attention and presents the main issue.

Elect Suzie Ruiz!

Have you, or any of your friends, had to serve a detention at Garfield Middle School this year? Do you know someone who had to eat lunch in the office? Many students have felt the effects of the new policies here at Garfield. I bet you have. Even though the ideas behind these rules are good, we want to make sure the new policies are fair to everyone. If you elect me president of the student council, I will work with Principal MacKekkin to change the way these policies are applied.

The **middle** provides reasons for the main issue.

I'm calling for a student court in which peers can advise the principal about a student who may have broken a rule. The student court can make sure all students receive reasonable punishments. It also can take the burden off Principal MacKekkin and the teachers of always being "the bad guys."

This paragraph lists the qualifications of the candidate.

My opponents promise that they will make life here at Garfield better, but they are not offering any real suggestions about how they will do it. I am. I have explained my idea of a student court. I also have plans for new fundraisers and other activities. I am well qualified to represent students from across the student body. I play clarinet in band, write for the school paper, and run track. I'm a good student. I'm a good listener.

The **ending** calls for listeners to vote.

So, if you want someone who will fight for student rights, elect Suzie Ruiz. Thank you for your time and for your votes!

TEKS 7.14C
ELPS 5G

Writing Tips

Before you write . . .

- **Decide on a main issue for your campaign speech.** Choose one main reason for your campaign. Make sure it is something students care about and can easily remember.
- **Organize your speech.** Think of an opening statement that will grab the listeners' attention. Plan the other points you will make and write down your qualifications.

During your writing . . .

- **Use details and examples.** Be specific about what you have to offer to voters and make your main reason a strong one.
- **Be concise.** Don't let your speech run on for very long. Make each sentence count and make sure each paragraph follows logically. Using short, simple sentences is a powerful way to present your campaign ideas.
- **Be dramatic.** Show that you feel strongly about representing your listeners.

After you've written a first draft . . .

- **Review your beginning and ending.** Make sure you get the listeners' attention and leave them with a memorable call for votes.
- **Read the speech aloud and check its length.** Smooth out any places where you trip over the words. Break up wordy sentences into shorter, more effective ones. Time your performance to make sure it fits within the time allowed.

Try It Imagine that you are running for student council. Write a short speech to convince your classmates to elect you. Use short, simple sentences appropriately to make your points.

Math: Creating a Graph

Statistics can be very persuasive, especially when they appear in a graph. The following report was written by a student who wanted to show the health risks of smoking.

The **beginning** introduces the topic.

Up in Smoke

What is in the cigarette smoke that makes it so harmful? Most people know that it contains two deadly substances: nicotine and tar. People may not also know that the cigarette smoke contains poison gases like carbon monoxide, ammonia, formaldehyde, and hydrogen cyanide.

The **middle** introduces the graph and provides statistics.

As the chart below shows, cigarette smoke kills both smokers and nonsmokers. Between 2000 and 2006, the number of Americans who died from secondhand smoke was more than 100 thousand. Among smokers, there were nearly half a million deaths per year. The message is clear: smoking kills smokers and nonsmokers alike.

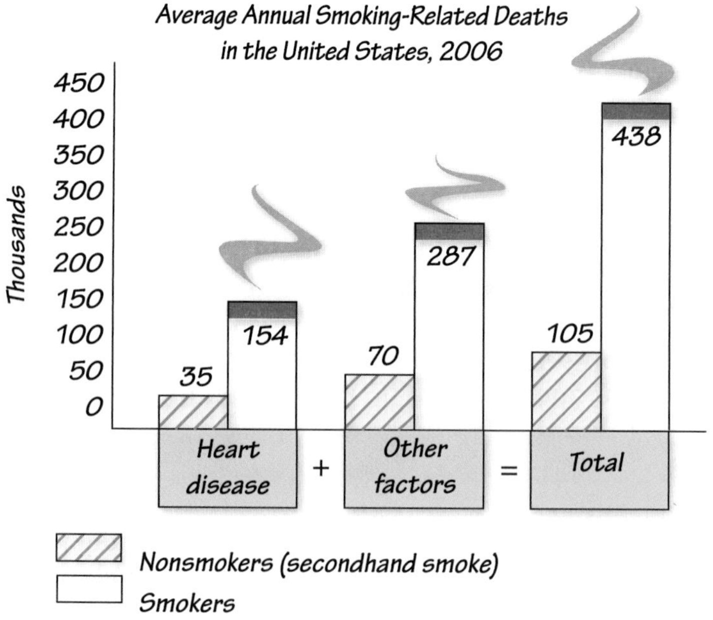

The **ending** gives the source of the information.

Source: American Heart Association

Writing Tips

Before you write . . .

- **Decide what you are trying to prove.**
  State your opinion in a simple sentence, such as "Smoking kills smokers and nonsmokers alike." Keep your focus in mind as you create your graph.
- **Research thoroughly.**
  Look at several well-respected sources. Find statistics that help you prove your opinion.
- **Plan your graph.**
  Decide how to make the information most persuasive. Consider different kinds of graphs, such as pie, line, or bar graphs. (See page 637.)

During your writing . . .

- **Quickly introduce your topic.**
  Give background information about your topic. Then write a few sentences that will help the reader understand what your graph shows.
- **Use colors and strong images.**
  Dress up your graph, but make sure that the reader will have no difficulty understanding exactly what you are trying to show.
- **Cite your sources.**
  List where you found the statistics for your graph.

After you've written a first draft . . .

- **Check your math.**
  Return to your sources to make sure your dates and numbers are correct.
- **Create a final version of your graph.**
  Make sure your graph is correct and clean. Proofread it a final time.

Try It Think of a health or fitness issue. Write an opinion that you think you can prove with a graph. Then research the topic to find the numbers you want. Finally, create a persuasive graph.

Science: Writing a Proposal

A well-written proposal can give you an advantage. In the proposal below, a student outlines a science fair project and asks his teacher for approval.

The **beginning** describes the project.

Traction and Four-Wheel Drive

Description: I'd like to test how well a motorized model truck climbs surfaces made of different materials and at different angles. I will create graphs to show how far and how fast the truck climbs in each situation.

The **middle** tells about the materials, the schedule, and the procedure.

Materials: I will use a radio-controlled four-wheel drive model truck, a plank, a protractor, a stopwatch, graph paper, and colored pencils. The different surface materials will include the following: water, aluminum foil, sandpaper, and loose sand.

Schedule: By March 2, I will have the materials collected and put together. By March 9, I will have run all my tests for different materials at different angles. By March 16, my display will be ready for the science fair.

Procedure:

- For each surface, the plank will be pitched at 10°, 20°, 30°, 40°, and 50°.
- First, I will test the plain wooden ramp at each pitch.
- Then I will repeat the experiment with the plank wet, with the plank coated with aluminum foil, coated with sandpaper, and finally coated with loose sand.
- I will create graphs displaying how far and how fast the truck climbed in each situation.

The **ending** focuses on the expected results.

Conclusion: I believe this experiment will show different levels of traction. Please let me know if this proposal is accepted. Any suggestions are welcome.

Writing Tips

Before you write . . .

- **Select a topic.**
  Find a science topic that interests you.
- **Plan your project.**
  Think of how to demonstrate or test your topic. What materials will you need?
- **Organize the proposal.**
  Follow the proposal format your teacher gives you or use the sample on page 282 as a guide. A graphic organizer such as a time line could help you plan your writing.

Time Line

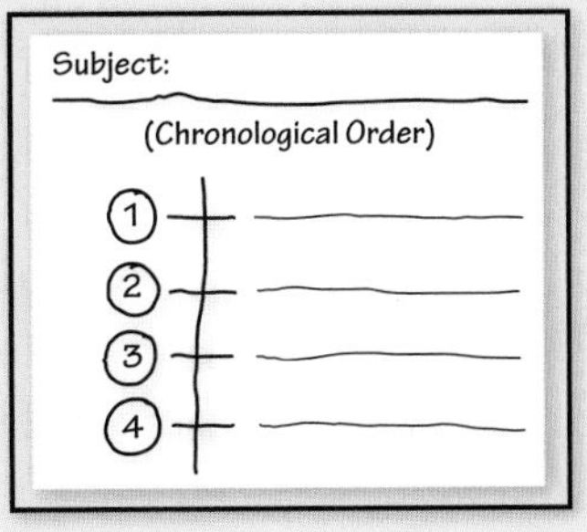

During your writing . . .

- **Be complete.**
  Give a quick overview of the project. Then list materials, provide a schedule, and talk about the procedure you will follow.
- **Be concise.**
  Get right to the point. Include only necessary information and important details.

After you've written a first draft . . .

- **Check for completeness.**
  Review your proposal as if you were the teacher and knew nothing about your idea. List any questions you might have. Then revise the proposal so that it answers those questions.
- **Edit your proposal.**
  Check your grammar, punctuation, capitalization, and spelling. Proofread your final copy.

Try It Imagine a science fair project you would be interested in doing. Using the tips above, write a proposal for it. Read your proposal aloud to a classmate.

TEKS 7.17B

Practical Writing: Drafting a Business Letter

In real-world situations, one of the best ways to get something done is to write a persuasive letter. The letter below was written by a student who wanted to convince a business owner to buy some guinea pigs from her.

The letter follows the correct format. (See pages 286–287.)

1212 Maple Park
San Antonio, TX 78230
March 24, 2010

Bruce Reynolds, Owner
Pet Project Pet Store
341 Jones Street
San Antonio, TX 78248

Dear Mr. Reynolds:

The **beginning** introduces the issue and shares an opinion.

Last year I bought two long-haired guinea pigs from your store. I think you have the best selection of small animals in the area. I tell that to everyone who wants a guinea pig.

The **body** of the letter expresses the writer's complaint and gives details about the problem.

An employee told me that I was buying two female guinea pigs. Unfortunately, that was not true. We now have five guinea pigs. I would like to sell the three babies and thought that you might buy them for your store. Our veterinarian confirms that all the babies are healthy females.

The **closing** includes a request for information along with details of how the reader can respond.

I would like to know if you are interested, or if you could help me find someone who would like them. You may call me at 555-9930 after 3:30 p.m. Thanks for your time.

Sincerely,

Jessica Botticini

Jessica Botticini

TEKS 7.17B
ELPS 5G

Writing Tips

Use the following tips as a guide when you are asked to write a persuasive letter.

Before you write . . .

- **Select a topic.**
  Think of an issue that concerns you.
- **Think about your opinion.**
  Consider some part of the issue that you have an opinion about.
- **Form your complaint.**
  Determine how you will express your problem or complaint.
- **Gather information.**
  Collect all the details you need in order to persuade your reader.

During your writing . . .

- **Give only important details.**
  Tell who you are and why you are writing. Be clear and businesslike.
- **Provide an easy response.**
  Give your reader an easy way to agree to help you, such as an enclosed postcard for reply.

After you've written a first draft . . .

- **Check for completeness.**
  Make sure you include all the information that the reader needs.
- **Check for correctness.**
  Proofread for errors in grammar, punctuation, capitalization, and spelling.

Try It Think of a problem in your school. Come up with an opinion and form a complaint. Then decide who you can ask for help and what they can do. Write a persuasive business letter to that person. (You may send the letter, or you may simply treat it as a school assignment.)

TEKS 7.17B
ELPS 5G

Parts of a Business Letter

1. The **heading** includes your address and the date. Write the heading at least one inch from the top of the page at the left-hand margin.

2. The **inside address** includes the name and address of the person or organization you are writing to.
   - If the person has a title, be sure to include it. (If the title is short, write it on the same line as the name. If the title is long, write it on the next line.)
   - If you are writing to an organization or a business—but not to a specific person—begin the inside address with the name of the organization or business.

3. The **salutation** is the greeting. Always put a colon after the salutation.
   - If you know the person's name, use it in your greeting.

     Dear Mr. Randahl:
   - If you don't know the name of the person who will read your letter, use a salutation like one of these:

     Dear Store Owner:
     Dear Sir or Madam:
     Dear Madison Soccer Club:

4. The **body** is the main part of your letter. In the body of the letter, you should express your complaint and provide details. This is also the place where you can propose a solution to the problem. Request any information that you hope to receive.

5. The **closing** comes after the body. Include a call to action along with all the information your reader will need to know in order to respond. Use *Yours truly* or *Sincerely* to close a business letter.

6. The **signature** ends the letter.

Try It Reflect on an issue that affects your community. Think of a person in the community, such as the mayor or a city council person, who may be able to help make a change about this issue. Draft a letter that includes your opinion, a complaint, and/or a request for information.

Business-Letter Format

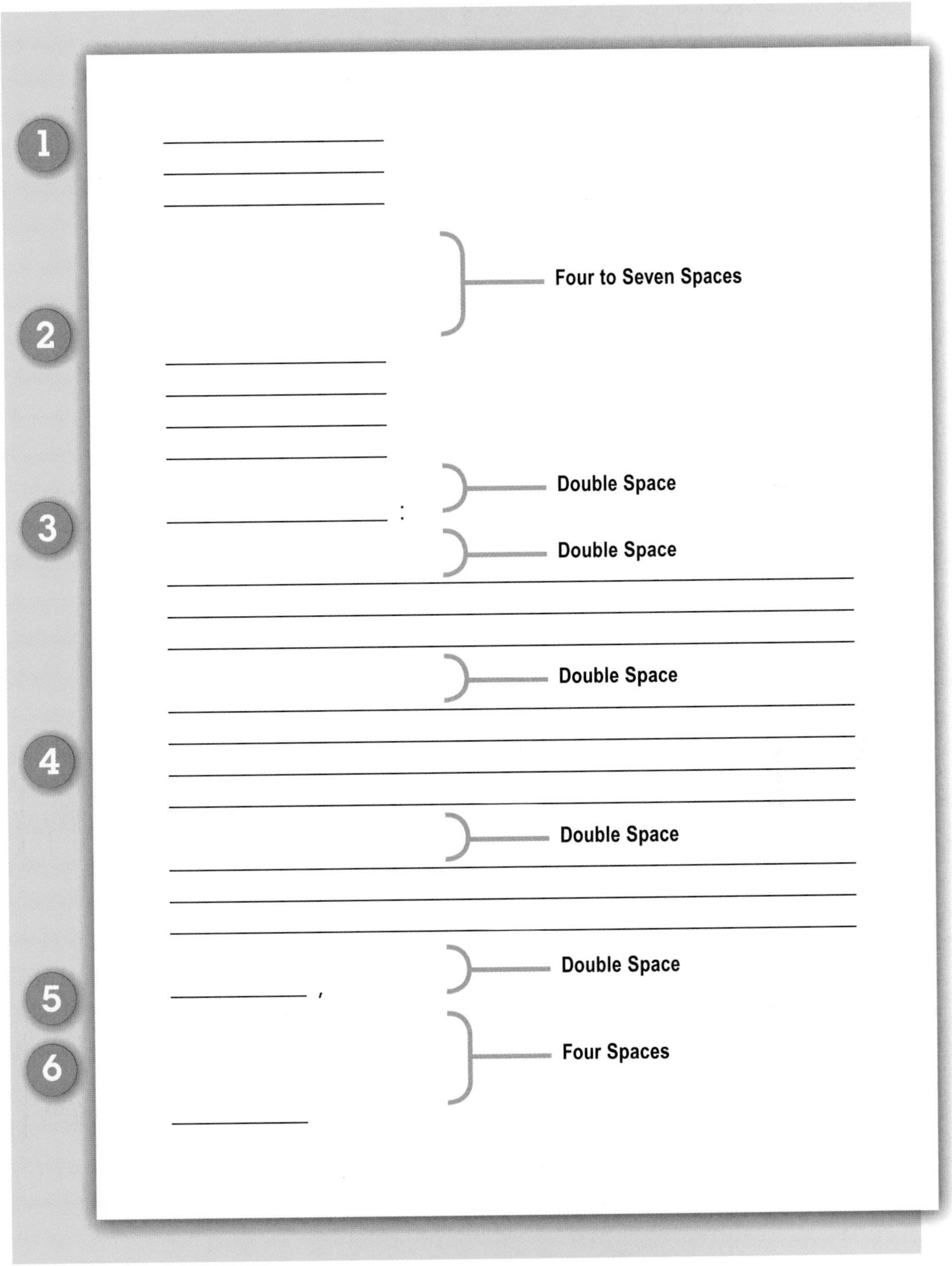

Persuasive Writing
Writing for the Texas Assessment

When you take state tests in Texas, you often have to write. The prompt tells you what to write about and gives some things to remember. Read the following prompt.

Prompt

Write an essay convincing someone of a way to improve learning at your school.

Use the information below to help you write your composition.

REMEMBER THAT YOU SHOULD—

- ☐ write to convince someone to improve learning.
- ☐ clearly state your position.
- ☐ include opinions that are supported by facts.
- ☐ organize your evidence in a way that makes sense and supports your viewpoint.
- ☐ use correct sentences, grammar, punctuation, capitalization, and spelling.

TEKS 7.14A

Prewriting Selecting a Topic

The prompt doesn't tell you what form of writing to use. How can you decide which one? Think about which form best fits what you want to say.

Do you want to:

- describe a person or place?
- offer a solution to a problem?
- explain an object?
- share a personal experience?
- give information?
- persuade someone to do something?

Answering these questions will help you decide on a form.

Clara wanted to persuade the school board in her school district. She decided the best form was a persuasive essay. This form will allow her to state her opinions and give facts to convince others to feel the same way.

Planning the Writing

To begin her response to the prompt, Clara decided on her opinion statement. Then she used a table diagram to plan her draft. It helped her identify facts that supported her position.

Learning would be improved if laptops were available for students to use.

Students who don't have a computer at home could use them for assignments.	*Everyone would be using the same format, which gives more time for instruction.*	*Laptops would help with computer literacy.*

Drafting Writing the Persuasive Essay

Next, Clara used her table diagram to write her persuasive essay. Read Clara's persuasive essay.

The **beginning** includes the opinion statement (**underlined**).

Each **middle** paragraph gives facts to support the opinion statement.

Improving student learning is a top priority for the school board. <u>There are many ideas on how to do this, but the best plan is to purchase laptop computers that students can check out of the media center.</u>

Students who don't have a computer at home could check out a laptop to do assignments. Papers, which were handwritten before, would look better done on a computer. All students would then have a chance to hand in work that will get them a good grade. Even students who already have a computer at home might need to use a school laptop because their brothers or sisters are always using the home computer.

School laptops would also end all those problems with different formats. It's so frustrating to get a disk from school that won't run on a home computer. It's worse to bring a disk from home and find out the school computer can't read the assignment. Learning is lost when the student and the teacher spend time figuring out how to fix the disk problem.

ELPS 4G, 5G

Finally, laptops would help with computer literacy. Students get to work in the media center only once a week right now, but that's just not enough time. More computers—especially ones that could be checked out—would help more students become computer literate.

The **ending** paragraph considers the views of others and responds to possible concerns or counter-arguments.

Buying laptops for the media center is something that will improve student learning. You may feel that it is risky to give kids such expensive equipment. A system can easily be set up to make sure that students learn how to carefully carry the laptops to and from school. Training can also be done so that they know how to use the laptops properly. Laptops will be an expense, but the problems they will solve make them worth the investment.

Respond to the reading. **Answer the following questions to see how the traits were used in Clara's response to the prompt.**

- ☐ **Focus and Coherence** **(1) What is the opinion in the essay? (2) What key words in the prompt does Clara use?**
- ☐ **Development of Ideas** **(3) What facts does Clara use to support her opinion?**
- ☐ **Voice** **(4) How would you describe Clara's voice in this essay (humorous, serious, angry)?**

Literature Connection: **Read another example of persuasive writing in the editorial titled "Do Professional Athletes Get Paid Too Much?" by Justin Hjelm.**

TEKS 7.14A
ELPS 5G

Writing Tips

Before you write . . .

- **Understand the prompt.**
  Remember that a persuasive prompt asks you to state and support an opinion. Decide on a form for your writing.
- **Plan your time.**
  Spend a few minutes planning before you start to write. Use a graphic organizer (table diagram) as a guide.

Table Diagram

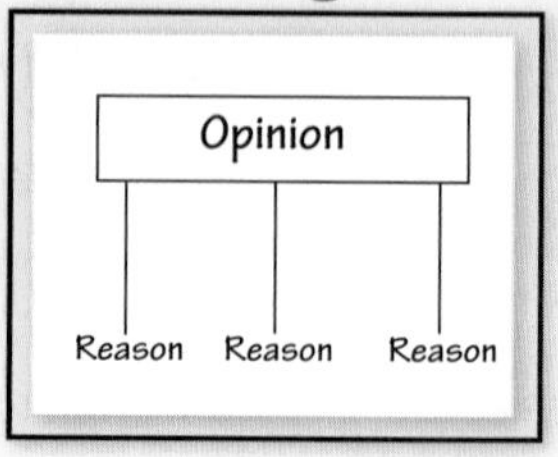

During your writing . . .

- **Form an opinion statement.**
  Think of an opinion that you can clearly support with facts.
- **Build your argument.**
  Think of reasons that support your opinion.
- **End effectively.**
  Tell readers what you would like to see happen.

After you've written a first draft . . .

- **Check for clear ideas.**
  Rewrite any ideas that sound confusing.
- **Check for conventions.**
  Correct errors in grammar, punctuation, capitalization, and spelling.

Plan and write a response. Respond to the prompt on page 288. Complete your writing within the period of time your teacher gives you. Remember to select an appropriate form and use the tips above as you write.

Persuasive Writing in Review

Purpose: In persuasive writing, you work to *convince* people to think the way you do about something.

Topics: Persuade readers . . . to agree with your opinion,
to take an action,
to support a cause, or
to solve a problem.

Prewriting

Select a topic that you care about, one that you can present confidently and that is appropriate for your audience. (See page 236.)

Gather details about your topic. (See page 237.)

Organize your ideas in a list or an outline. Put your opinion statement at the top, followed by topic sentences and supporting details. (See page 240.)

Drafting

In the beginning, give background information and clearly state your opinion. (See page 243.)

In the middle, write a paragraph for each main point. Use supporting facts and examples to persuade your reader. (See pages 244–245.)

In the ending, answer a counterargument, restate your opinion, and make a call to action. (See page 246.)

Revising

Review focus and coherence, organization, development of ideas, and voice. Make sure your reader will be able to follow your thinking. Use a confident, persuasive voice and a variety of sentences. (See pages 248–255.)

Editing

Check your writing for conventions. Ask a friend to edit the writing, too. (See pages 258–261.)

Make a final copy and proofread it for errors before sharing it with your audience. (See page 263.)

Assessing

Use the rubric as a guide to assess your finished writing. (See pages 48–49.)

experience

answer

ELPS 2C, 3E, 3G, 3H, 4G

TEXAS WRITE SOURCE Online

www.hmheducation.com/tx/writesource

Responding to Texts

Writing Focus

- **Response Paragraph**
- **Response to Literature**
- **Response to Expository Text**

Learning Language

Work with a partner. Read the meanings and share answers to the questions.

1. A response is a reaction to something or someone.
   What was your response to the last thing you read?
2. An expository text explains something in the real world.
   What expository text would you like to read?
3. Literature is imaginative or creative writing.
   What kind of literature do you most enjoy reading?
4. A team is a group of people who work together for a common goal.
   What teams do you belong to outside of school?

evaluate

REACT

preview

Responding to Texts

Response Paragraph

A typical jar of spaghetti sauce holds ten tomatoes, two stalks of celery, an onion, a green pepper, four cloves of garlic, and five other spices. How can one jar hold so much? All the ingredients in spaghetti sauce get boiled down until only the best parts remain.

A typical novel contains more than a thousand paragraphs about the main character. Even so, you can capture that same character in just one paragraph. All you need to do is "boil down" the information.

On the next page, you will read a sample paragraph about Moon Shadow, a boy who leaves China to find a new home in America. Then you will write a response paragraph of your own.

Writing Guidelines

Subject: An important character in a book or short story

Purpose: To carefully examine a character

Form: Response paragraph

Audience: Classmates

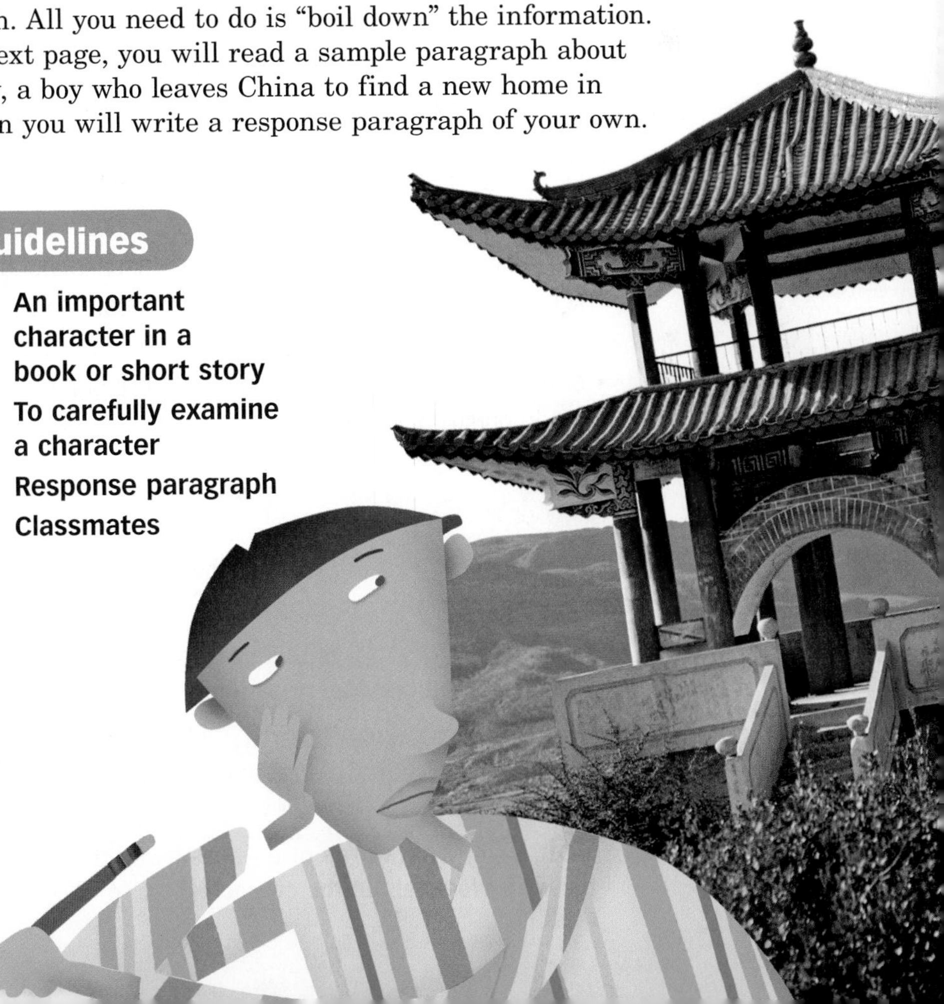

ELPS 4G

Response Paragraph

When you write a paragraph about something you've read, you may be asked to focus on one character. The **topic sentence** of your paragraph identifies the title, the author, and the character. The **body** sentences tell about the character, and the **closing sentence** tells how the character changed. In the following response, Keira writes about a character named Moon Shadow.

Topic Sentence

Body

Closing Sentence

Moon Shadow

In the book *Dragonwings* by Laurence Yep, a young Chinese boy named Moon Shadow learns how to live in America. Moon Shadow is eight years old when he leaves his mother and grandmother in China and sails to America to be with his father, Wind Rider. Together the two of them work long, hard days at a laundry in San Francisco. They send money back to China. At first, Moon Shadow is suspicious of Americans with their strange language. He knows that his long braid of hair makes him a target for neighborhood bullies. Moon Shadow also faces many frightening situations, including an earthquake, but he bravely keeps going. Later, he makes two American friends, Miss Whitlaw and Robin. They help him overcome his fears and learn the ways of his new country. He learns how important family and friends are in pursuing lifelong dreams.

Respond to the reading. On your own paper, answer each of the following questions.

- ☐ **Organization (1) Is this paragraph organized by time, by order of importance, or by logical order?**
- ☐ **Development of Ideas (2) What main problem does the character face? (3) What details about the problem does the writer include? Name two.**
- ☐ **Voice (4) What words or phrases near the end show how the writer feels about the character?**

TEKS 7.14A
ELPS 3E, 3H

Prewriting Selecting a Topic

Your first step in writing a response to literature is selecting a book or short story to write about. Keira began by listing books she had read. Then she wrote down the names and descriptions of characters that interested her.

Topics Chart

Books or Stories	Characters	Descriptions
Dragonwings	*Moon Shadow*	*young boy from China*
No More Dead Dogs	*Wallace Wallace*	*eighth-grade football hero*
"Flowers for Algernon"	*Charlie Gordon*	*a mentally challenged man*

Prewrite **Choose a book or short story. Make a chart like the one above. Circle the character that interests you most.**

Gathering Details About the Character

After you have chosen a character that you would like to write about, gather details about her or him. A cluster like the one below can help you.

Details Cluster

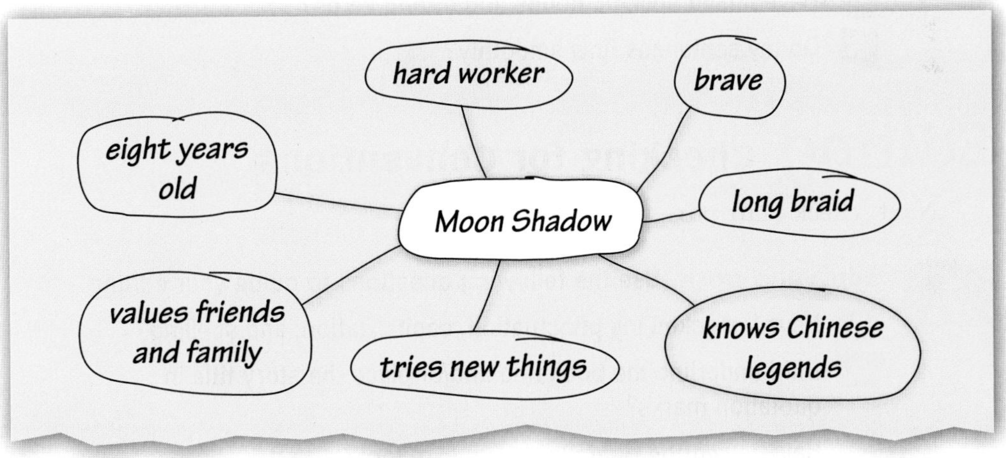

Prewrite **Create a cluster. First write the name of the character and circle it. Around the name, write details about the character's appearance, personality, hopes, and fears. Share one detail about your character with a partner.**

ELPS 5G

Drafting Creating Your First Draft

As you write your paragraph, make sure each part does its job.

- **Topic sentence:** Write a sentence that names the book or short story, its author, and the character that you will describe.
- **Body:** Write sentences that describe the character and the important things that happen to him or her in the story.
- **Closing sentence:** End with a sentence that tells how the character changes by the end of the story.

Draft

Write your first draft. Create a strong topic sentence, a body full of specific details, and a closing sentence that tells how the character changes.

Revising Improving Your Paragraph

Once you complete your first draft, it's time to revise your paragraph. Think about *focus and coherence, organization, development of ideas,* and *voice.*

Revise

Review your paragraph. Let the following questions guide your revision.

1. Have I written about one important character?
2. Are my sentences in the best order?
3. Does my voice show interest in the character and the story?
4. Have I used specific nouns and strong verbs?
5. Do my sentences flow smoothly?

Editing Checking for Conventions

Next, check your paragraphs for errors.

Edit

Edit your work. Use the following questions to guide your editing.

1. Have I checked my punctuation, capitalization, and spelling?
2. Did I underline the book title and/or place the story title in quotation marks?
3. Have I used the right words *(to, two, too)*?

Edit

Proofread your paragraph. After making a final copy of your paragraph, check it one more time for errors.

Responding to Texts

Response to Literature

Often the events in a story change the main character. For example, in this chapter you will read about Adam Zebrin, a boy whose life changes when he becomes fascinated with zebras. The way Adam changes gives clues to the theme of the story.

Writing about literature is a good way to connect characters and themes. In this chapter, you will write about a main character in a piece of literature and tell how the character contributes to the theme of the novel or story.

Writing Guidelines

Subject: A book or a story
Purpose: To interpret a story
Form: An essay
Audience: Classmates

Understanding Your Goal

What should you include in your response to literature? You should include a clear interpretation of the story's meaning, or theme. The chart below lists the key traits in a response to literature. You can use the rubric on pages 48–49 to assess your progress.

Traits of a Response to Literature

Focus and Coherence

Write a statement that explains the focus of your response and select details that support it.

Organization

Organize your response so that each sentence is logically linked to the next sentence.

Development of Ideas

As you write, build on ideas so that each sentence adds meaning to the sentences that come before it.

Voice

Use a voice that engages the reader and expresses your personal viewpoint.

Conventions

Correct any grammar, sentence structure, mechanics, or spelling errors.

Literature Connection. You can find an example of a response to literature in the book review titled "Serf on the Run" by Rebecca Barnhouse.

Response Essay

The novel *Esperanza Rising* tells the story of a group of migrant workers in California during the 1930s. A student who read the book wrote this interpretation of the story and its main character, Esperanza Ortega.

Beginning
The beginning introduces the book and states the focus (**underlined**).

Her Name Means Hope

Esperanza Rising, by Pam Muñoz Ryan, is the story of a Mexican girl who becomes a migrant worker in California. Making such a big move in life is never easy, but Esperanza must rise above even more problems than most immigrants do. In one year, she faces many difficulties that change her and make her a better person. Although she is only 14 years old when the story ends, it is clear that these challenges have taught Esperanza to be strong.

Middle
Each middle paragraph explains an important event in Esperanza's experience.

Migrants often come to the United States because they have been poor all of their lives, but that is not the case with Esperanza. She grows up on a big ranch in Mexico, and her family is rich and important. Esperanza spends her time going to school, learning to love the ranch, and being spoiled by "Papi," her father. Her main worry is what kind of dress she will wear to the next fancy party. When Papi dies the day before her 13th birthday, Esperanza and her mother find themselves without a home or a way to make money in Mexico. They decide to move to the United States.

In the beginning of their journey to California, Esperanza looks down on the other migrants. She is shocked by the living conditions in the migrant camps and believes that the other workers are not as intelligent as she is. Esperanza quickly learns that the peasants are smart, even smarter than she is in many ways. They know how to survive and support each other. She soon realizes that dignity and honor come from the way

ELPS 4G

Middle
This middle paragraph discusses a key event.

Ending
The ending paragraph summarizes the theme.

that someone lives life, not from family status.

Esperanza now faces the same problems that other Mexican immigrants do. She learns that immigrants have to deal with prejudice, poverty, and bosses who cheat them. Esperanza misses her old life. Still, like the other immigrants, she hopes that in America she will never run out of chances.

But Esperanza's problems soon get worse instead of better. Her mother is very sick and has to go to the hospital for many weeks, leaving Esperanza alone. Mama has always been a loving woman who faces her troubles with great strength, and Esperanza has always depended on her for support. Now Esperanza must be strong, and her mother's example helps her survive.

In the end, Esperanza learns to make the best of what she has. She has learned to love her new land and now realizes that worrying about dresses is not the most important thing. Esperanza, whose name means "hope" in Spanish, says, "Do not ever be afraid to start over." That's good advice for everyone.

Respond to the reading. Answer the following questions about the sample response to literature.

- ☐ **Organization** **(1) Are the middle paragraphs organized by time, by order of importance, or by some other logical order? (2) How is the theme stated in the book's ending?**
- ☐ **Development of Ideas** **(3) According to the second paragraph, what tragic experience does Esperanza go through? (4) How does Esperanza react to her difficulties?**
- ☐ **Voice** **(5) Find two sentences that show the writer's understanding of the story.**

Go Online!

Prewriting

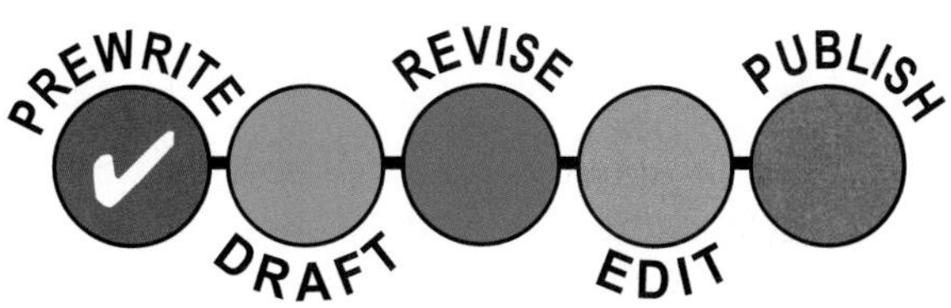

The writing process starts with prewriting. Begin by thinking about an interesting book or story you've read recently. Then gather details to include in your response and plan your paragraphs.

Keys to Effective Prewriting

1. *Select an interesting book or short story that you have read recently.*
2. *Identify the focus of the story and write a statement about it.*
3. *Gather details about the character and theme that support the focus.*
4. *Decide on your audience and the voice you will use to address it.*
5. *Decide on a pattern of organization for your middle paragraphs and write a topic sentence for each that expresses an idea.*

TEKS 7.14A

Prewriting Selecting a Topic

Think about books and stories that you have read recently. What main characters were the most interesting? What did these characters learn? A chart can help you think about main characters and what they learn.

Character Chart

Main Character	*What the Character Learns*
Crispin (from Crispin by Avi)	*Crispin learns that the most important things in life are friendships and courage—things nobody can take away.*
Adam Zebrin (from "Zebra" by Chaim Potok)	*Adam learns that art can help heal his body and his mind.*
Phoebe (from Walk Two Moons by Sharon Creech)	*Phoebe learns that every person she meets, no matter how odd, has value.*

Prewrite

Create a character chart. Use the chart above as a model and follow these directions.

1. **In the first column, list the main characters from books and stories you have read recently.**
2. **In the second column, write down what the character learns in the story.**
3. **Then choose one character to write about. Write one sentence telling why you chose this character.**

Texas Traits

Focus on the Texas Traits

Focus and Coherence The theme of a book or story is the overall message the story tells about life. One way to discover the theme in a book or story is to ask yourself what the main character learns through his or her experiences.

Gathering Details

Once you select a character, identify evidence from the text that teaches the character something about life (the theme). You will want to choose quotations from the text to support your response and illustrate key events that change the character in some way. A gathering chart can help you list key events.

Gathering Chart

Event 1	Event 2	Event 3
Adam runs into a car and is injured. - hurts his legs and left hand - can't run anymore - left hand doesn't heal well - feels like a loner because of his hand - friend calls him "gloomy life-form"	Adam gets drawing lessons from John Wilson. - surprised that John knows he is a loner - learns not to look directly at things he's drawing - finds out he is as good at drawing as he once was at running	Adam makes a helicopter sculpture from junk. - knows John lost an arm in Vietnam - gets so involved in making a helicopter that he uses left hand without thinking - begins to return to normal

Prewrite **Chart the key events.** **Create a chart like the one above. List key events that show important changes in the character. Under each event, list specific details and quotations that you might include in your response.**

Texas Traits

Focus on the Texas Traits

Voice Your interest in the character and the theme should come through in your essay. Engage the reader with details that show you care about this story.

TEKS 7.14A
ELPS 5G

Prewriting Writing a Focus Statement

Now that you have identified the main character and theme (what the main character learns), you are ready to write your focus statement.

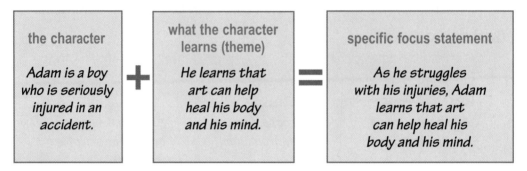

the character		what the character learns (theme)		specific focus statement
Adam is a boy who is seriously injured in an accident.	+	*He learns that art can help heal his body and his mind.*	=	*As he struggles with his injuries, Adam learns that art can help heal his body and his mind.*

Prewrite **Form a focus.** **Write a focus statement for your response using the statement above as a model.**

Planning the Middle Part of Your Essay

After you write a focus statement, the next step is to plan the middle paragraphs of your essay. Each middle paragraph should include a topic sentence and deal with one key event.

Below is the plan the writer of the sample essay made for the order of the key events. However, he later realized that he needed another event. He placed it between Events 2 and 3.

Event 1 – Adam's problems begin with his accident.

Event 2 – He decides to take art classes.

Event ~~3~~ 4 – He discovers he enjoys building rather than drawing.

Event 3 – Adam becomes good at drawing.

Prewrite **Plan your middle paragraphs.** **Review your gathering chart.**

1. **Decide on the best order for your events.**
2. **Add any events that you feel are necessary to explain your response.**
3. **Using your events, write a topic sentence for each of your middle paragraphs.**

TEKS 7.14C

Go Online!

Drafting

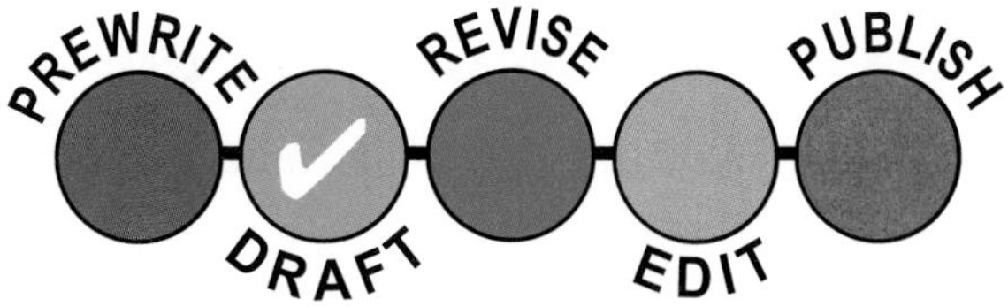

Now that you have done your prewriting, you need to write your essay. You can use your gathering chart, focus statement, and topic sentences as a guide.

Keys to Effective Drafting

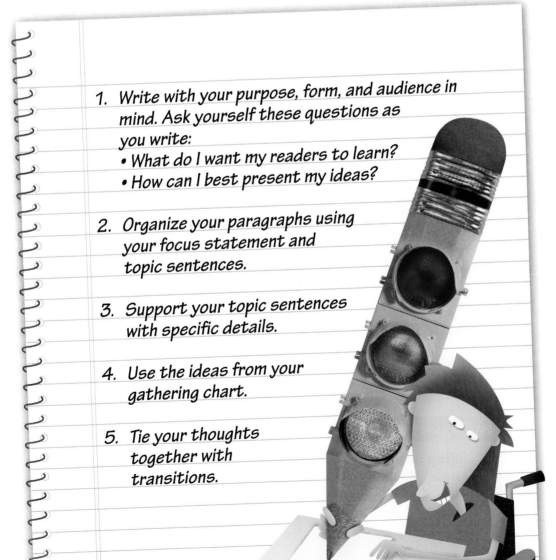

1. *Write with your purpose, form, and audience in mind. Ask yourself these questions as you write:*
   - *What do I want my readers to learn?*
   - *How can I best present my ideas?*
2. *Organize your paragraphs using your focus statement and topic sentences.*
3. *Support your topic sentences with specific details.*
4. *Use the ideas from your gathering chart.*
5. *Tie your thoughts together with transitions.*

Drafting Getting the Big Picture

The following chart shows how the three parts of a response to literature fit together. (The examples are from the essay on pages 309–312.) You're ready to write your response if you have . . .

- thought about your character and theme,
- written a clear focus statement, and
- planned your paragraphs.

Beginning

The **beginning** paragraph introduces an important character and states the focus of your interpretation.

Focus Statement

As he struggles with his injuries, Adam learns that art can help heal his body and his mind.

Middle

The **middle** paragraphs show the key events in the development of the story's theme.

Four Topic Sentences

Adam's problems start when he hits the car, injuring his legs and his left hand.

One day during the next spring, Adam's life begins to change.

The art class teaches Adam about drawing and about life.

At the end of the summer, Adam suddenly shifts his focus from drawing to building.

Ending

The **ending** paragraph explains and summarizes the theme.

Closing Sentences

In the same way, art trains Adam to think about what is around him rather than thinking only about himself.

TEKS 7.17C, 7.25D
ELPS 3E

Starting Your Interpretation

The beginning of a response to literature should introduce the focus of your essay and any important background information. Be sure that your opening includes . . .

- background about the character,
- the title and author of the work, and
- your focus statement.

Beginning
Middle
Ending

Beginning Paragraph

The beginning paragraph below starts with background information about the character and ends with the focus statement.

Background information begins the paragraph.

The last sentence forms the essay's focus (underlined).

In "Zebra" by Chaim Potok, Adam Zebrin sees a movie about zebras running in Africa. When he gets home, he runs around the neighborhood, trying to be as graceful as a zebra. Sometimes Adam runs so fast that he feels like he is flying. Racing along one day, he closes his eyes and seems to take off—right into the side of a car. As he struggles with his injuries, Adam learns that art can help heal his body and his mind.

Draft **Draft your beginning. Write the beginning paragraph of your essay. Include background information, the title and author, and your focus statement.**

Supporting Your Ideas

Citing evidence from a text is an effective way to support your ideas. A direct quotation should follow the idea that it supports.

1. **Find an example from the text that clearly supports an idea included in your background information.**
2. **Include the example word for word as it appears in the text, enclosed in quotation marks. Insert the quotation after the idea that it supports.**

Draft **Find evidence from the text. Look for quotations in the story or book that support your points. Share one of the quotations with a partner.**

Drafting Developing the Middle Part

Each middle paragraph tells about one key event in your interpretation of the story. Every middle paragraph should contain a topic sentence.

Beginning
Middle
Ending

Middle Paragraphs

The first paragraph below gives reasons for Adam's problems. The second covers another important event, and so on. Each topic sentence is underlined.

The first middle paragraph covers the first event, the accident.

Transitions (in blue) connect the events.

The second middle paragraph covers the start of Adam's recovery.

Adam's problems start when he hits the car, injuring his legs and his left hand. In a short time his legs recover, although he can't run anymore. His left hand doesn't heal as quickly, and it stays painful and stiff long after the accident. His hand makes him feel like he doesn't belong. Soon he becomes a loner, standing off on the side while everyone else plays. Finally, this inner conflict makes his only friend, Andrea, call him a "gloomy life-form."

One day during the next spring, Adam's life begins to change. He stands by himself near the playground when he notices a one-armed man coming toward him. The man pauses at a trash can, plucks something out, and places it in a plastic bag. When he gets to Adam, the man asks him for directions to the school office, and Adam tells him how to get there. It turns out that the one-armed man is John Wilson, a Vietnam veteran who plans to teach a summer art class. Adam and Andrea sign up for the class.

The third middle paragraph covers another step in Adam's recovery.

The art class teaches Adam about drawing and about life. John Wilson understands the problems Adam is experiencing. One day, John draws a picture of Adam and a zebra. The zebra seems to be moving mysteriously off the edge of the paper. Then John teaches Adam to draw, telling him not to look directly at the thing he is drawing. John instructs him to look at the space around the object. Adam takes the advice and discovers that he is as good at drawing as he once was at running. His left hand still hasn't healed, though.

The last middle paragraph covers the last stage in the recovery.

At the end of the summer, Adam suddenly shifts his focus from drawing to building. He builds a sculpture of a helicopter from some of the junk, mostly wire and paper, that John has collected from trash cans. As Adam builds the sculpture, he begins to use his left hand without thinking about it. Soon Adam's left hand recovers, and so does Adam. The conflict he has been having with himself slowly comes to an end.

Draft

Write the middle paragraphs of your essay. Use your gathering chart and the guidelines below.

1. Begin each middle paragraph with a topic sentence about the key event in the paragraph.
2. Add details that support the topic sentence. Refer to your gathering chart (page 305).
3. Connect your ideas with transitions to create a coherent piece of writing.

TEKS 7.14C

Drafting Ending Your Interpretation

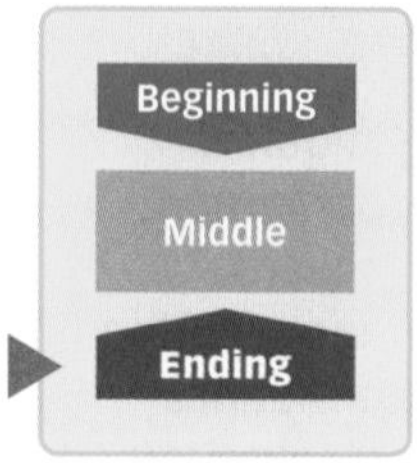

Your essay should focus on what the main character learns. This is the theme of the story. The following questions can help you summarize the theme.

- What does the main character learn from the key events?
- What did I learn from reading the book or story?

tip A theme is a general statement about life. As you interpret the theme of your book or story, remember to relate what the character learns to life in general.

Ending Paragraph

The ending paragraph below summarizes and further explains the theme by showing what Adam has learned.

The conclusion explains the theme (underlined).

John teaches Adam to pay attention to the space around an object. In the same way, art trains Adam to think about what is around him rather than thinking only about himself. Art gives him a new focus. Like many people, Adam has been trapped inside himself, but art helps him escape. Adam's days as a loner are over. In the end, Andrea playfully tells him, "You are becoming a pleasant life-form."

Draft **Draft your ending.** Write the last paragraph of your response. Be sure to sum up the theme by showing what the main character learned.

Draft **Form a complete first draft.** Make a complete copy of your essay. Think about how well you addressed your questions of audience, purpose, and form. Make adjustments as necessary. Write on every other line so that you have room for revising.

Go Online!

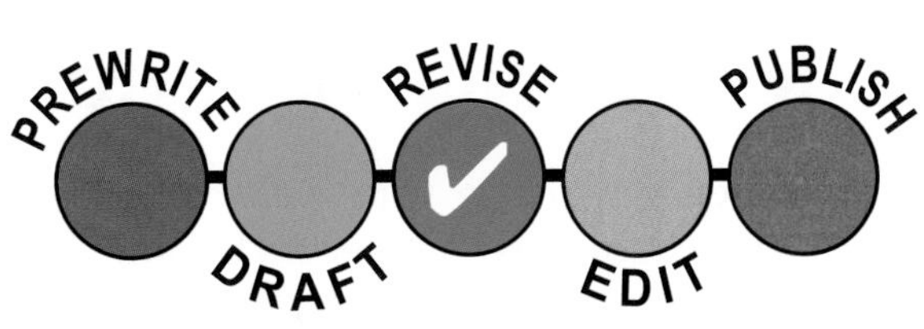

Revising

After you finish your first draft, you can begin revising. By reviewing focus and coherence, development of ideas, organization, and voice, you can make changes that will improve your writing.

Keys to Effective Revising

1. *Read your entire essay aloud.*
2. *Check your focus statement to make sure it expresses your purpose and topic.*
3. *Be sure that your details support the focus statement.*
4. *Check your voice for enthusiasm and interest that will engage the reader.*
5. *Use the editing and proofreading marks inside the back cover of this book.*

TEKS 7.14C

Texas Traits

Revising for Focus and Coherence

When you revise your writing for *focus and coherence,* check to be sure that every sentence supports the main idea or focus of the response. Each sentence in your response should build upon the sentences that came before it. This will help your reader understand the full picture you are trying to create with your writing.

How can I improve the internal coherence of my response?

Internal coherence means presenting your ideas in a logical sequence. Any detail that doesn't contribute to a reader's understanding only weakens the response's focus. The detail should be removed or replaced with another detail. Read the paragraph below and think about how the underlined sentence weakens the internal coherence of the sample response.

Esperanza's father died suddenly and unexpectedly. Her family had to deal with not only the loss of a loved one, but with the loss of their home as well. <u>There are many homeless people in our country today.</u> Esperanza was weak and desperate. Soon her mother got sick. Esperanza then discovered that she was much tougher than she had ever imagined.

Try It Read the paragraph below. Find the sentence that weakens the internal coherence and replace it with a new sentence.

The story "A Night in a Haunted House" is effective and truly frightening. Author Nancy Lo uses skillful description and action to create suspense and fear. The story is about three people who agree to spend a night in an old house, presumably haunted. I live in an old house that has a strange history. During the long night, they meet up with a mysterious stranger.

Revise **Revise for internal coherence.** **Look for details that support the focus of your response to literature. Are there any sentences that do not contribute and may distract the reader from your main focus? Are there any ideas that are not organized in a logical manner? If so, remove or replace them.**

How can I improve the external coherence of my response?

External coherence refers to how well your overall writing flows. Unlike such fiction forms as the short story or the novel, there is no plot or characters in an essay or response. Instead, ideas are presented and explained in a logical manner with support from details.

The following paragraphs were written by a student for a response essay. Notice how the beginning paragraph flows smoothly into the next paragraph.

> I enjoyed the novel *Riders on the Range,* about the life of a cowboy in the Old West. The details of the cattle drive that forms the heart of the book were precise and realistic. I could imagine myself back in that time and place. While fiction, this novel has the feel of the real West on every page.
>
> In creating the feel of the West, the author draws his reader in . . .

Revise

Revise for external coherence. **Read through your entire response. Do you have a clear introduction and conclusion to your response? Does the middle section present ideas and support from evidence in the text? If not, revise to strengthen the external coherence of your essay.**

Focus and Coherence
An extra sentence is deleted to make the focus stronger.

Running along one day, he closes his eyes and seems to take off—right into the side of a car. ~~There were lots of cars mentioned in the book.~~ As he has trouble with his injuries, Adam learns that art can help heal his body . . .

TEKS 7.14C, 7.17C

Texas Traits

Revising for Organization

When you revise for *organization*, make sure you have used a variety of transitions to connect your ideas. Also, check to see if your ending summarizes the theme. This will help your reader better understand the main idea of your response.

Do I use a variety of transitions?

When you respond to literature, you might use only transitions that show time: *First* one thing happened. *Then* another thing happened. *Afterward* a third thing happened. You can improve the organization of your essay by using some transitions that show other types of connections. Here are two types.

Importance	
For this reason	Truly
Especially	To emphasize
In fact	To repeat

Cause and Effect	
Because of	Therefore
As a result	Since
Due to	If . . . then

Try It Read the paragraph below. On your own paper, write down each underlined transition and indicate whether it shows *time, importance,* or *cause and effect.*

After Meg, Charles Wallace, and Calvin arrive on the planet, they notice strange behavior. Every girl jumps rope at the same time, and every boy bounces a ball in the same rhythm. In fact, when one boy gets out of rhythm, his mother fearfully pulls him from the street. Meg soon finds out that the ruler of the planet is IT. If IT can control people's lives so completely, then Meg knows she can't overpower IT. As a result, she chooses a weapon that IT can never defeat. . . .

Revise **Check the variety of your transitions.** Read your essay, looking for transitions. Do you use a variety, some to show time and others to show importance or cause and effect? If not, consider adding some new transitions.

TEKS 7.17C, 7.25A
ELPS 3E, 4G

Does my ending summarize the theme?

Showing what your character learned is often the best way to summarize the theme. Your summary should give your reader an insight about how the theme relates to life.

Try It Read the following ending. Work with a partner to find the sentences that indicate the character learns something from her experience.

> At the end of the novel, Sal and her father have returned to Bybanks, Kentucky. Gramps comes to live with them. His presence helps Sal remember what she has learned. She knows that after walking in other people's shoes, it's better to accept people than it is to judge them. Walking in another person's shoes helps us be better human beings.

Revise **Review your first draft.** Check to make sure that your ending summarizes the theme and relates it to life.

Organization
Changes help relate the theme to life.

Art gives him a new focus. [Like many people,] Adam has been trapped inside himself[,] [but art helps him escape. Adam's] ~~His~~ days as a loner are over. In the end, Andrea playfully tells him, "You are becoming a pleasant life-form."

RESPONSE

ELPS 3E

Texas Traits Revising for Development of Ideas

When you revise for *development of ideas,* check to make sure you have written a clear focus statement and included key events that support your focus. This will make your response more enjoyable and easier for the reader to understand.

Have I written a clear focus statement?

Your focus statement is clear if it names the main character and tells what the person learns (the theme). (See page 306.)

Clear Focus Statement

As Huckleberry and Jim travel the Mississippi, Huckleberry *(main character)* **learns that friendship is the most important thing in the world** *(the theme).*

Try It Read the following focus statements. Decide which statements clearly name the main character and tell what the person learns. If a focus statement is unclear, tell what is wrong with it.

1. In "Casey at the Bat," the "mighty Casey" learns that even big stars can't ignore the basics of baseball.
2. Branch Rickey is someone that few people know about.
3. In *Diary of a Young Girl*, Anne Frank is the main character.
4. Mrs. Luella Bates Washington Jones teaches a boy named Roger an important lesson about respect.
5. Mr. Pignati is an older man in *The Pigman*.

Revise **Review your focus statement. Make sure it names the main character and tells what she or he learns during the story. If your focus statement is unclear, revise it. Share your revised focus statement with a classmate.**

Have I included key events that support the focus?

Key events are those that affect the way a character acts, thinks, or feels. One way to check whether you have included only key events is to create a cause-effect chart.

Cause-Effect Chart

Key Event (Cause)	Change to the Character (Effect)
Esperanza's father dies.	*She is left poor and homeless.*
Esperanza has to deal with prejudice and injustice.	*She discovers that she is tougher than she thought.*
Esperanza's mom gets sick.	*She has to "grow up" quickly.*

Revise

Check your key events. **Make a chart like the one above. List key events and the ways they change the character. If any one of your body paragraphs doesn't show how the event changed your character, revise the paragraph to make the change clear.**

Development of Ideas
The focus statement is clarified.

Racing along one day, he closes his eyes and seems to take off—right into the side of a car. As he struggles with his injuries, Adam learns ~~to like art~~ that art can help heal his body and his mind.

Texas Traits

Revising for Voice

When revising your writing for *voice,* you think about how your writing "sounds" to your readers. You want to sound interested in the topic you are writing about so that your reader will be interested, too.

Does my voice show that I am interested in the character and theme?

Your voice will sound interested if you show that you really understand and care about the character and the theme. The voice in the first paragraph below is too flat. The writer does not sound interested.

Not Interested

Pony and Johnny go to an old church. That's where they hide. They read an old book. Pony recites a poem.

The voice in the next paragraph shows that the writer really cares about the situation in the novel.

Interested

Pony and Johnny cut their long "greaser" hair and hide out in an abandoned church in Windrixville. There's nothing to do but think about the terrible fight and Bob's death. To pass the time, they read *Gone with the Wind* to each other, and Pony recites "Nothing Gold Can Stay" by Robert Frost. Even then, Pony seems to know the poem is about his own life.

Revise

Check for an interested voice. Review your essay to see whether you sound interested in the character and the theme. Reading your writing out loud is a good way to get a feel for how your voice sounds. Revise any paragraphs that sound flat.

Do I use a variety of sentence structures in my response?

A variety of sentence structures keep your writing voice interesting and lively. It gives a rhythm to your response and holds your reader's interest. Short sentences can be combined into longer, more interesting sentences that flow. Below are two simple sentences from a student response.

The story ends with a terrible rainstorm.
The main character finds a way out of the storm to safety.

One way to combine these two simple sentences is to create a compound sentence.

The story ends with a terrible rainstorm, but the main character finds a way out of the storm to safety.

Another way to combine sentences is to create a complex sentence. This requires making more changes to the original sentences.

When a terrible rainstorm strikes at the story's end, the main character finds a way out of the storm to safety.

Try It Read the following response paragraph. Decide which sentences should be combined to form longer sentences or divided to form shorter sentences.

Author Ernest Hemingway tells the story of a boy. His name is Schatz. Schatz catches the flu and is afraid to fall asleep because he believes that he will never wake up again and die. I found this story truly memorable. It is memorable for its direct style. It is memorable for the strong feelings it creates in the reader.

Revise **Check the structure of your sentences.** Read your response aloud, listening for how your sentences affect voice. Revise to create simple, compound, and complex sentences.

TEKS 7.14E

Texas Traits

Revising Using a Checklist

Revise

Check your revising. On a piece of paper, write the numbers 1 to 9. If you can answer "yes" to a question, put a check mark after that number. If not, continue to work with that part of your essay.

Focus and Coherence

____ **1.** Do all of my details help the reader's understanding?

____ **2.** Do I need to cut any unnecessary sentences?

____ **3.** Does my writing flow as a whole?

Organization

____ **4.** Have I used a variety of transitions?

____ **5.** Does my ending summarize the theme?

Development of Ideas

____ **6.** Have I written a clear focus statement?

____ **7.** Have I included key events that support the focus?

Voice

____ **8.** Does my voice show interest in the character and the theme?

____ **9.** Do I use a variety of sentences to interest my reader?

Revise

Make a clean copy. Ask a classmate to read and respond to your writing. Make any needed revisions. Create a clean copy for editing.

Go Online!

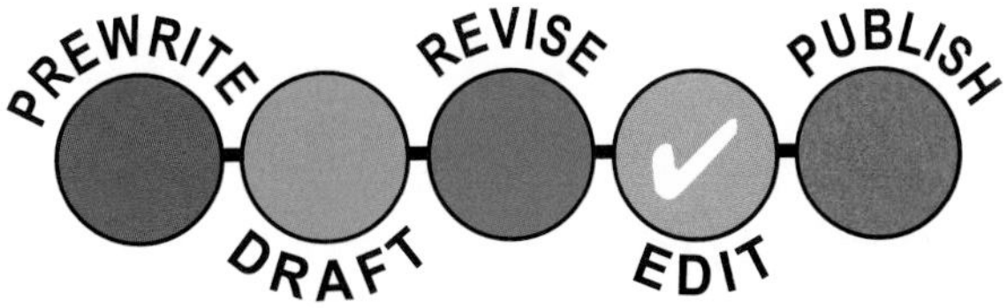

Editing

After you've finished revising your essay, it's time to edit for the following conventions: grammar, mechanics, sentence structure, and spelling.

Keys to Effective Editing

1. Make sure there are no errors in grammar, mechanics, and spelling.
2. Check for consistency in verb tenses.
3. Use a dictionary, a thesaurus, and the "Proofreader's Guide" in the back of this book.
4. If you use a computer, edit on a printed copy and enter your changes on the computer.
5. Use the editing and proofreading marks inside the back cover of this book.

TEKS 7.14D, 7.19C

Texas Traits Editing for Conventions

Grammar

Do I avoid shifts in verb tense?

When you write, make sure that your verb tenses are consistent. If you start telling about something in the present tense, don't shift to the past tense unless you have a good reason. (See page 543.)

Inconsistent Verb Tenses

Esperanza now faces the same problems that other Mexican immigrants do. She was shocked to learn that immigrants had to deal with prejudice, poverty, and bosses who cheat them.

Consistent Verb Tenses

Esperanza now faces the same problems that other Mexican immigrants do. She is shocked to learn that immigrants have to deal with prejudice, poverty, and bosses who cheat them.

GRAMMAR Try It

The following sentences should be written in the present tense. Correct any verbs that are not in present tense. The key verbs are in bold type.

1. Henry **did** not **have** any money, so he **is looking** for a job.
2. Tom **forgot** his old friends and **makes** new ones every month.
3. Before long, his new friends **learn** the same thing about him and **felt** the same way about him.
4. Willa Mae **continued** to take piano lessons even though they **are getting** more difficult.
5. Anne **writes** about her life in hiding and **dreamed** of a time when she and the others **can be** free.

Edit

Check your verbs. Make sure your response is written in the same verb tense throughout. If you find inconsistencies, correct them.

TEKS 7.19A(iii)
ELPS 2G, 3D, 3E, 3H, 4G, 4I

Do I use adjectival phrases correctly?

An adjectival phrase is a group of words that describes a noun or pronoun. It can begin with an adjective or sometimes an adverb. Like adjectives, adjectival phrases can add interesting details to your sentences and to your writing. Read the examples below.

The sea is blue.
The sea is a crystal clear shade of blue. (adjectival phrase)

The students are excited about the field trip.
The students are truly excited about the field trip. (adjectival phrase)

GRAMMAR Try It

Find the adjectival phrases in this paragraph.

The concert hall was filled with people. The pianist crossed the stage that was wide and spacious. She sat at the elegantly built grand piano. When she finished playing, the applause was loud and appreciative.

Edit

Edit for adjectival phrases. Make sure that your sentences containing adjectival phrases are clear.

Learning Language

Most of your writing will be in either present or past tense. It is important to make sure you use the same verb tense throughout your writing to help your reader understand. You can change a sentence from one tense to another by simply changing the verbs. Work with a partner to read the following sentences. Then discuss the differences.

Pedro plays quarterback on our school's football team.
Pedro played quarterback on our school's football team.

Now discuss with your partner how to change the following sentences into the verb tense shown in parentheses.

Soo Chen wants a little puppy. (past tense)
Lily and her brother learned about frogs at school. (present tense)
Danielle walks home from the bus stop. (past tense)

TEKS 7.19A(ii)

Sentence Structure

How do I combine short, choppy sentences?

One way to combine short sentences is to make one of the sentences into an appositive. An appositive is a group of words that follows a noun, renaming or explaining it. The following example shows how two short sentences are combined with an appositive. (See pages 574–576 for other ways to combine sentences.)

Two Short Sentences

Branch Rickey worked to integrate sports.
He was the general manager of the Dodgers in 1947.

Combined Sentence with Appositive

Branch Rickey, the general manager of the Dodgers in 1947, worked to integrate sports.

Try It Rewrite the following paragraph on your own paper, using appositives to make the four short sentences into two longer ones.

Jackie Robinson is an inspiration to many people. He was the first black player in the major leagues. In his book, Robinson gives much of the credit for his career to Branch Rickey. Rickey is an important man in professional sports.

Edit **Combine choppy sentences.** Read your essay. Look for sentences you could combine using an appositive.

Spelling

How do I edit my draft for spelling?

An important part of revision is reading over your writing to find spelling mistakes. Read every sentence and the words in it carefully. If you're not sure how to spell a word, consult a dictionary, thesaurus, or glossary in the back of your textbook.

Incorrect Pete was late for the fotball game.

Correct Pete was late for the football game.

A spell check on a computer will catch some, but not all, spelling errors. For example, if a word is misspelled but spells another word, the spell check will miss it. You should read over your writing to find other spelling mistakes. Watch out for words that sound the same but have different spellings and meanings.

Incorrect I wrote a letter to my pin pal.

Correct I wrote a letter to my pen pal.

Other times, you may write a word that sounds the same as the correct word, but is spelled differently and has a different meaning. The spell checker will not pick this up either.

Incorrect Are you coming to the fair to?

Correct Are you coming to the fair too?

Try It Rewrite the paragraph below on your own paper. Correct the eight spelling errors.

Maria attached the leesh to her dog's collar. Then they went outdores. Her dog snifed every tree and plant. Suddenly a cat crossed there path. The dog chazed after the cat, pulling poor Maria behind. The cat squeezed thru a fence and disapeared. The dog barked loudly for a minit and then turned around and walked home with Maria.

Edit **Edit for spelling.** Check your essay for misspelled words. Use a dictionary, thesaurus, or glossary to help you with the correct spelling. Remember that a spell checker on your computer will not find all misspelled words.

Editing Using a Checklist

Edit

Check your editing. On a piece of paper, write the numbers 1 to 10. If you can answer "yes" to a question, put a check mark after that number. If not, continue to edit for that convention.

Conventions

GRAMMAR

____ **1.** Do I use correct forms of verbs (*had come*, not *had came*)?
____ **2.** Do my subjects and verbs agree in number?
____ **3.** Do I use adjectival and other kinds of phrases correctly?

MECHANICS

____ **4.** Do I punctuate titles correctly?
____ **5.** Have I used punctuation between parts of complex and compound sentences?
____ **6.** Have I used quotation marks correctly to show evidence from the text?

SENTENCE STRUCTURE

____ **7.** Have I used appositives correctly?

SPELLING

____ **8.** Have I spelled all my words correctly?
____ **9.** Have I double-checked the words my spell-checker may have missed?
____ **10.** Have I consulted a dictionary when I am unsure of how to spell a word?

Creating a Title

- Use the title of the book or story: **Zebra**
- Refer to the character: **Adam's Recovery**
- Be creative: **Drawing on Inner Strength**

TEKS 7.14E

Go Online!

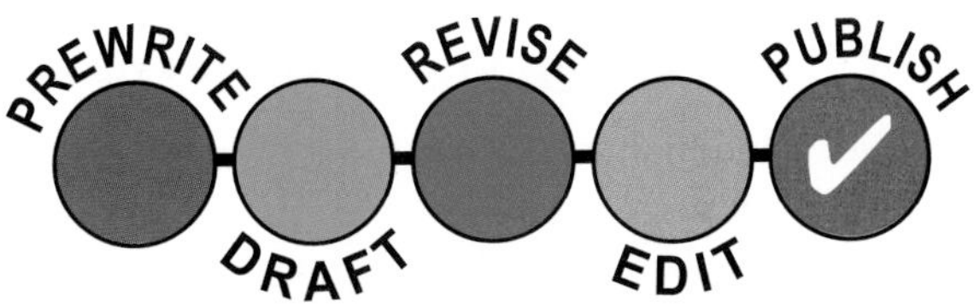

Publishing

Sharing Your Essay

After doing all of this work on your essay, you'll want to make it look good so that others can enjoy it. You may also decide to present your essay in some other form: a drawing, an introduction, or a submission to an online portfolio. (See the suggestions in the boxes below.)

Publish **Make a final copy. Follow your teacher's instructions or use the guidelines below to format your paper. Write a final copy of your essay and proofread it for errors.**

Focus on Presentation

- **Use blue or black ink and write neatly.**
- **Write your name in the upper left corner of page 1.**
- **Skip a line and center your title; skip another line and start your writing.**
- **Indent every paragraph and leave a one-inch margin on all four sides.**
- **Write your last name and the page number in the upper right corner of every page after the first one.**

Introduce It
Write a short introduction about your character and read it to the class. Try to convince your classmates to read the book or story by getting them interested in the character.

Go Online!
Upload your response essay for others to read.

Make a Drawing
Draw a picture of an important stage in your character's life. Post your essay and the illustration in your classroom.

ELPS 4I, 4K

Evaluating a Response to Literature

To learn how to evaluate a response to literature, you'll use the scoring rubric on pages 48–49 and the responses that follow. These responses are examples of writing for each score on the rubric.

Notice that this first response to literature received a score of 4. Read the description for a score of 4 on pages 48–49. Then read the response. Use the same steps to study the other examples. Always remember to think about the overall quality of the writing.

Writing that fits a score of 4 is very strong.

4

The first paragraph gives background information, title, author, and a focus statement.

Voice shows the writer's interest.

The Secret Freighter

In the novel The Secret Freighter, by Nathan Swartz, the freighter is secret because it is hiding a Jewish family and taking them from Europe to America to escape the Nazis. The Zemlinsky family comes from the city of Vienna in Austria. In the old days they were a happy family who owned a furniture repair shop and whose neighbors included Jews and Christians alike. When the Nazis take over, the Zemlinskys lose their shop and apartment and must flee for their lives. Despite many hardships, they escape, and in the process the main character, twelve-year-old Elise Zemlinsky, regains her faith in humanity.

The family's frightening adventures first take them overland through Europe, where they almost get captured several times. The family consists of Elise, her younger brother Felix, and their parents and grandparents. Escape is difficult because the grandparents and Felix cannot travel very fast. However, Papa Zemlinsky declares that they will not leave any of their loved ones behind. This is Elise's first glimpse of her father's true heroism. Although she is scared, she never loses her trust in him.

The Zemlinskys path takes them south from Austria into Italy across snowy mountains, where they have to hide from border patrols and suffer from hunger. In Italy, they try to get a boat, but they cannot, so they travel to France and Spain using false passports. Finally, they meet the captain of a freighter, who agrees to take them across the Atlantic. Unfortunately, the first mate is secretly a Nazi, and when a German U-boat stops the ship, the captain has to put the first mate under guard to keep him from betraying the Jewish family. Nevertheless, the freighter gets away safely. Although Elise's grandfather dies in a storm, the remaining Zemlinskys find a new home in New York, thanks to the captain and the many people who helped them earlier.

The sentences flow smoothly.

The story is shown through Elise's eyes (but in third person). As Elise encounters dangers, the reader sees her becoming more of a leader in the family, teaching Felix what to do when they hide and taking care of her grandmother. The reader also learns Elise's thoughts, as when she feels sorry for the first mate even though he is on the other side. "He was just confused," Elise thinks. "His leaders told him we were his enemies, and he didn't know better." Elise is a truly heroic young person who grows up in a terrible time. By sharing in her story, readers can understand how people can discover the best parts of themselves just when they think things are at their worst.

The writer provides evidence using quotations.

The ending explains the novel's theme.

ELPS 4I, 4K

Writing that fits a score of 3 is strong in most ways.

3

The writer includes an effective first paragraph and focus statement.

Some sentences should be combined.

Reggie Newcombe, Maasai Warrior

Reggie Newcombe, Maasai Warrior, by Susan Wellman is a great novel about a fourteen-year-old African-American boy who travels back in time and becomes a Maasai warrior in the days before the Europeans turned Africa into colonies. In it, Reggie is visiting Africa because his parents, they are both professors, are studying the history of Kenya. However, Reggie travels back in time and begins living among the Maasai, who herd cattle and are great warriors. He becomes a Maasai warrior too, but he shows the most courage when he shows his village that peace is better than war.

It all starts when Reggie meets the mysterious Dr. Lloyd. Dr. Lloyd doesn't know anything about modern times but knows a lot about the 22nd Century. It turns out that Dr. Lloyd is a time traveler from that century. He has gotten lost in time. He needs to fix his time machine in order to return home. Reggie stows away on the time machine and they go further back in time by mistake. The Maasai sieze Reggie and bring him to their village. They don't mean him any harm. They only want to find out about him. They let him live there, and Reggie becomes friends with a boy his age named Koyati. Koyati teaches Reggie about courage. Koyati's father has taught Koyati. Koyati will need courage to pass his initation.

The events are organized in time order.

The boys have to kill a lion with just their spears in order to become Maasai warriors. Reggie is very scared. However, he is able to do it with Koyati's help. Koyati doesn't tell anyone he helped, so Reggie becomes a warrior. He feels brave, but he still wonders what real courage is. He finds out when the other men try to make him join them in a war. Reggie refuses. They insult him. Finally he goes with them. However, he stays back. Then, when Koyati is going to be speared by an enemy, Reggie steps in and catches the spear on his shield. But he does not kill the other man. Everyone can see that Reggie is truly brave and that he was right to let the man go. The men from Reggie's village talk with the men they are fighting, and they agree to stop the war. It is all because of Reggie. A village elder says, "This is a new kind of courage. We have never heard of it before."

The writer includes a quotation from the text.

The ending explores the theme.

The last sentence does not belong.

Reggie Newcombe, Maasai Warrior is a great book because it tells an exciting story and shows warriors but also shows that there is a better way than fighting. Reggie is a really good main character because he goes through many changes. They are all interesting, and he turns into a warrior for peace. That is what I would like to be. By the way, Dr. Lloyd fixes the time machine and takes Reggie back to the present, so Reggie's parents never know he was gone.

Writing that fits a score of 2 is strong in some ways.

2

The response includes some run-on sentences.

Some sentences should be combined.

The writing lacks coherence.

The writer's voice shows real feeling.

The ending expands on the theme.

Magic Foot

This book is the story of Horacio Estes who grows up in poverty but grows up to be a soccer star. Its not a real story, he is fiction. In the book you see how he has to play soccer which they call football with an old ball that is falling apart when he is a young child. He and his friends play all the time but he is the best. This fiction book tells you to never give up. And if there is something you really want to do, try it.

Horacio keeps playing. He gains skills. Soon he is playing with older kids. When he's 13 he's playing with adults and beating them. He never gives up. People make fun of him because he cant aford a uniform. It bothers him. But he gets back at them by scoring goals they cant do anything about.

Soon he is a big soccer star. He led his team to a champinship and people always ask for his autograph but he is always generis. One day he gets shot in the leg by a crazy fan and he thinks its all over. His whole nation is upset. He comes back and leads them to another champinship. That's giving 210%.

I like this book because it told me what a real champin is like. Horacio is a real champin. He reminded me of some real life players but hes fictional. The message is never give up. If you give up you always lose. If you keep trying you have about a 50% chance of winning.

Writing that fits a score of 1 is weak.

1

Many errors in grammar, spelling, and mechanics distract the reader.

The response contains no focus statement.

There is little sense of organization.

The ending repeats the theme without expanding on it.

The Confidance Game by Deena Petrie

The story I read was the Confidance Game By Deena Petrie. It was about Dara this Cambodian American girl a gimnast. But she gets a bad score loses all her confidance. Its not fisical its mental. How she's going to compete again when she feels bad about herself. Then when she's practicing she sprans her ankle. That makes it worse. She tells herself to quit even tho everyone around her is saying no. Her parents and her coach try to tell her encourageing things but it doesn't work. She can't get her mind right.

Im not goin to tell you everything that happens in the story because you might want to read it yourself. The big thing that happens is she gets back her confidance. This woman who used to be a gymnast tells her "Confidance is everything. The ending is cool, you don't know whether she's goin to win. It's whatever you think. You now she has her confidance back and that's what is realy importent.

This book tells you that confidance is the most importent thing. There were some things I didn't like about it but the main idea is about confidance and I think that is definatly true.

ELPS 5B, 5G

Evaluating and Reflecting on Your Writing

You've put a lot of time and effort into your response. Now take some time to score and think about your writing. On your own paper, finish each sentence starter below. To score your writing, refer to the scoring rubric on pages 48–49 and the examples you just read.

My Response

1. *The best score for my response is . . .*
2. *It's the best score because . . .*
3. *The best part of my response is . . .*
4. *The part that still needs work is . . .*
5. *The main thing I learned about writing a response is . . .*

Responding to Texts

Response to Expository Text

Expository texts are written to explain something in the real world. They basically inform and describe in a variety of ways. Other forms of writing, such as poetry or stories, may make you feel and respond, but an expository text's purpose is to inform and entertain.

One way to respond to an expository text is to write a response that tells what the piece is about. It also expresses your reaction to it. In this chapter you will learn how to write a response to an expository text.

Writing Guidelines

Subject: An expository text you read
Purpose: To analyze and explain your response to the text
Form: A written response
Audience: Other people interested in the topic

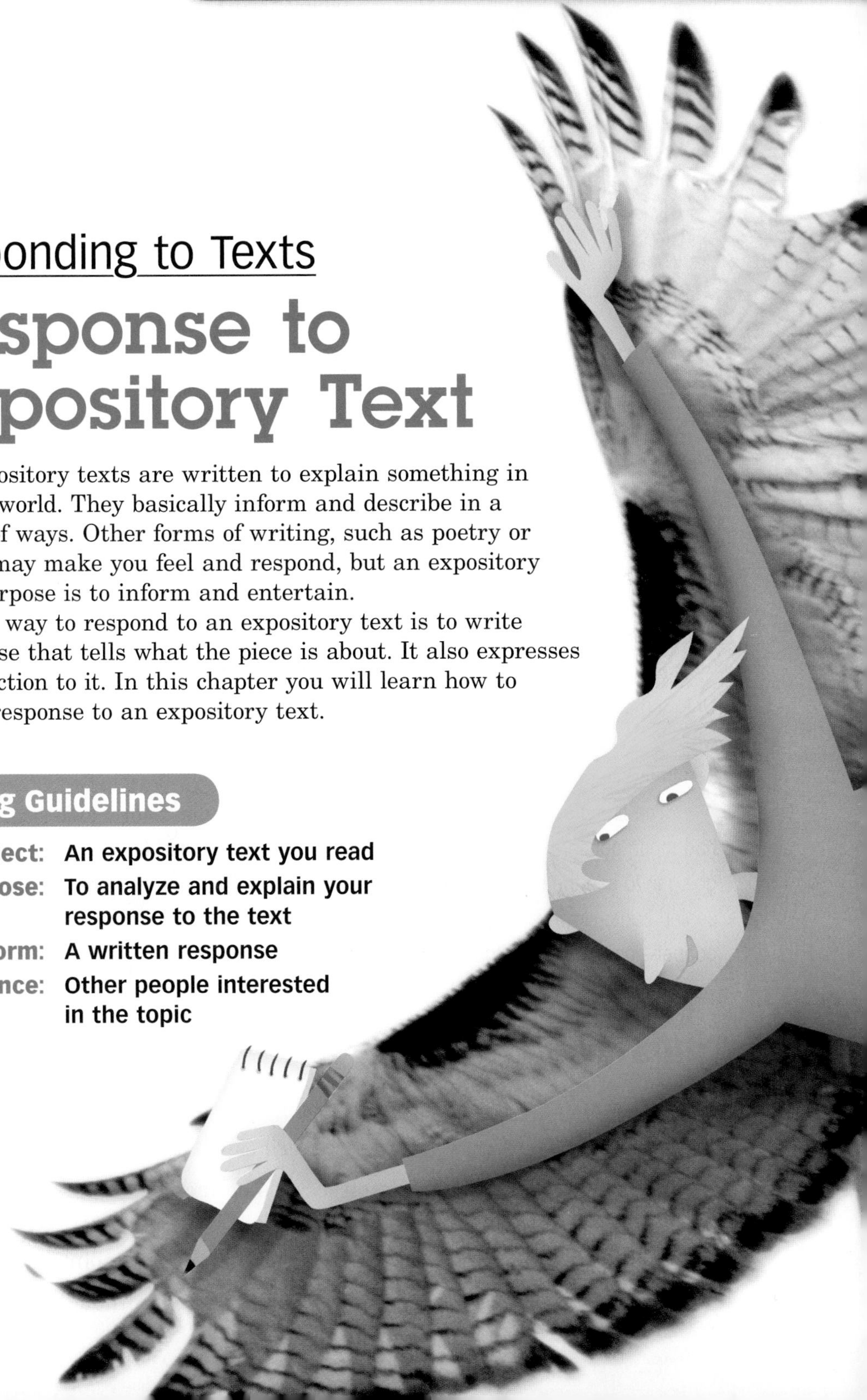

Response to Expository Text

For a class assignment, Teresha chose to write a response to the following essay about popcorn. You will find Teresha's response on the next page.

A Popular History of Popcorn

by Kenneth Rivera

Popcorn is one of the most popular snack foods around, but have you ever wondered who first thought of the great idea of popping kernels of corn? We don't know who that was, but among the first and best popcorn makers were the Native Americans. They not only ate popcorn, but actually wore it. Explorer Christopher Columbus and his men bought popcorn necklaces from the people they met in the New World.

The Pilgrims' first experience with popcorn may have taken place at the first Thanksgiving in 1621. It is said that the Native Americans who came to the feast brought several deerskin bags of popcorn to munch on.

By the late 1800s, Americans had developed a real love of popcorn. Unfortunately, many stores only sold unpopped popcorn in such large quantities that when it was stored, the popcorn lost its moisture. Moisture is what causes the corn to pop in the first place.

The first electric corn popper appeared in 1907. By the 1940s, movie theaters had made popcorn more popular than ever. People bought it at the snack bar before going in to see the show. Today, most people enjoy microwave popcorn that comes in sealed bags. However you like to pop it—in the microwave oven, on the stove, or in a popper—popcorn is still tops when it comes to snacks!

Writing the Response

When Teresha wrote her response to "A Popular History of Popcorn," she focused on the following elements of expository texts:

- **Meaning:** The first paragraph describes what the text is about.
- **Details:** The second paragraph focuses on factual details about the topic.
- **Voice:** The third paragraph shows the writer's viewpoint and attitude.
- **Thoughts:** The final paragraph tells what Teresha thought of the text.

Beginning
The beginning identifies the writer and tells what the essay is about.

Middle
The middle paragraphs focus on details and voice.

Ending
The ending reflects on the writer's thoughts of the essay.

A Response to "A Popular History of Popcorn"

Kenneth Rivera's essay "A Popular History of Popcorn," tells about popcorn in the past and present. It describes how Native Americans introduced popcorn to explorers and the Pilgrims and how the snack's popularity grew.

I thought the writer included some fascinating details about popcorn. For instance, Native Americans wore popcorn necklaces and stores once only sold unpopped corn in large bags.

Kenneth Rivera's style is light and entertaining. He starts his essay with a question that immediately grabs the reader's attention. He also writes with great enthusiasm. I like his ending, "popcorn is still tops when it comes to snacks!"

This essay was both informative and enjoyable to read. Now I know why popcorn is my favorite snack food!

Respond to the reading. Think about how Teresha uses the following traits in her review; then answer the questions that follow each trait.

- ☐ **Focus and Coherence** (1) What was the focus of each paragraph in Teresha's response?
- ☐ **Organization** (2) How did Teresha use details and quotations to support her response?
- ☐ **Voice** (3) How did Teresha's writing express her feelings about this essay?

Prewriting Understanding a Text

The first step to understanding an expository text is reading it. Teresha read the essay "A Popular History of Popcorn" several times. She saw that the structure of the writing was basically chronological, taking the reader through a history of popcorn in the Americas. She created a time line that showed when the events described happened.

	Columbus and men buy popcorn necklaces from Native Americans.
1621	*Pilgrims introduced to popcorn by Native Americans at first Thanksgiving*
Late 1800s	*Stores sell popcorn kernels in large quantities*
1907	*First electric corn popper sold*
1940s	*Movie theaters sell popcorn to patrons*
Today	*People enjoy microwave popcorn*

Prewrite **Choose an essay or article.** **Find an essay or article that is organized chronologically. Make a time line summarizing it.**

Analyzing the Qualities of a Text

Next, Teresha focused on information that goes beyond the details of the essay she read. She reread the essay and thought about the author's focus statement, organization, and voice. She also thought about own her reaction.

Focus Statement: Popcorn has been a popular snack food for a long time.

Author's Voice: light, entertaining, humorous

My Reaction: very positive, found essay informative and enjoyable

Prewrite **Identify the qualities of the text.** **Using Teresha's work as a model, reread your chosen article. List the author's focus statement, voice, and your reaction to the writing.**

Gathering Details

Teresha used a chart to help her gather details and quotations about the expository text she responded to—"A Popular History of Popcorn."

Gathering Chart

History	Details	Voice
• Native Americans • popular in movie theaters • microwave snack today	• once worn on necklaces • eaten at the first Thanksgiving • once sold only in large quantities	• enthusiastic • entertaining • a sense of humor • "popcorn is still tops when it comes to snacks!"

Prewrite **Create a gathering chart.** **Use the chart above as a guide to gather details and quotations from your chosen article or essay. Include appropriate column heads and fill in the information.**

Drafting Creating Your First Draft

With your chart in hand, you are ready to write the first draft of your response. Take it one paragraph at a time.

- **Beginning Paragraph** In your introductory paragraph, give the name of the essay or article and its author. Then summarize the main idea of the essay.
- **Middle Paragraphs** Use details from your gathering chart to write the middle paragraphs of your response. In the first middle paragraph, give details that made the essay interesting. In the second middle paragraph, focus on the writer's voice and how you responded to it. Use direct quotations from the text when possible to support your thoughts.
- **Ending Paragraph** In your last paragraph, write your conclusion, explaining your feelings about the essay, if you liked or disliked it, and why.

Draft **Create your first draft.** **Write the beginning, middle, and ending of your response essay. Follow the guidelines above.**

Revising Improving Your Writing

Once you finish the first draft of your response, set the draft aside for a while. Then return to your draft and revise it for the traits.

- ☐ **Focus and Coherence** Have I focused on the main idea of the essay? Have I cut out any extraneous information or inconsistencies?
- ☐ **Organization** Do I include a beginning, middle, and ending?
- ☐ **Development of Ideas** Do I give evidence from the text and actual quotations to support my ideas in depth?
- ☐ **Voice** Does my interest show? Is my response enjoyable to read?

Revise

Revise your response. Using the questions above as a guide, revise your work until it flows smoothly and is clear and interesting.

Editing Checking for Conventions

Now that you have revised your work, it's time to check it for any errors.

- ☐ **Conventions** Is my response free of errors in grammar, mechanics, and spelling?

Edit

Edit your response. Check your response carefully and correct any errors you find in grammar, capitalization, punctuation, or spelling.

Publishing Sharing Your Writing

Letting other people read your response encourages them to read and think about expository writing. Here are some ideas for publishing your response.

- Submit your response to the school paper.
- Post your response on a bulletin board where others can read it.
- Read your response to the class and answer questions about it.
- Send your response to the author (perhaps in care of the publisher). Let him or her know why you enjoyed the essay.

Publish

Share your opinion. Let other people see your response. Their reactions may give you new insights into the essay, and they may recommend other essays for you to read.

Responding to Texts
Across the Curriculum

Imagine that you are about to visit one of Texas' most colorful and historic cities. What museums and exciting historic sites would you visit? Imagine that you could travel to another planet. Where would you go? Mars, Neptune, or some undiscovered world? Literature and expository texts allow you to make these journeys.

This chapter shows you how you might respond to literary and expository texts in a number of classes. For example, you will learn how to respond to an article about visiting a city, and how to summarize a scientific article. The chapter will also help you prepare for a writing assessment.

What's Ahead

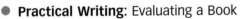

- **Social Studies:** Responding to an Article
- **Science:** Summarizing a Science Article
- **Practical Writing:** Evaluating a Book

Social Studies: Responding to an Article

Kara read the article "Ft. Worth—Where the West Begins" about some things to see and do in Fort Worth. She wrote this response about the article.

The **beginning** introduces the title of the article.

The **middle** shares important details from the article.

The **ending** tells how the writer responded to the article.

Ft. Worth—"Worth" a Look

I have never been to another city, but if I travel someday, I'm definitely going to visit Fort Worth. After reading "Ft. Worth—Where the West Begins," I feel I must see this place. The author points out a few of the city's cultural highlights, such as the National Cowgirl Museum and Hall of Fame and the Ft. Worth Museum of Science and History.

I liked some of the details the writer included. I never knew, for instance, that Sandra Day O'Connor grew up as a cowgirl on a ranch! I can just imagine her racing across the ranch on a horse. It's also fascinating to think there's an actual cattle drive every day at the Fort Worth stockyards.

I would have liked, however, if the writer had included other sites besides museums and historic places. I like to go to sports events and the theater, but he doesn't mention any of these. I would also like to know about the types of restaurants I should try on my visit to Fort Worth.

All in all, this was a good article that could have been better.

Writing Tips

Before you write . . .

- **Read the article carefully.**
  Read it once to get a feel for the material. Then reread the article paying more attention to the details.
- **Take notes.**
  Write down important ideas in the article and make note of details that you find particularly interesting.
- **Organize your thoughts.**
  Plan how you will structure your response. Think about how you will introduce your topic in the first paragraph and consider which facts and details you will use in the middle. Finally, decide on what your conclusion will be.

During your writing . . .

- **Find your voice.**
  Express your feelings and enthusiasm for your topic with well-chosen words and personal viewpoints. Engage your reader with an interesting style.
- **Chose details carefully.**
  Pick details that best support the main idea and will interest the reader.

After you've written a first draft . . .

- **Get feedback.**
  Ask one of your classmates or a family member to read your essay. See if the reader has any suggestions for revision.
- **Proofread carefully.**
  Go over your essay to make sure that there are no errors in grammar, mechanics, sentence structure, or spelling.

Try It Read a brief article that you find or one that your teacher hands out to you. Using the tips above, write a response to the article, including what you like or dislike about it. When you have finished, trade papers with a partner and revise based on his or her feedback.

Science: Summarizing a Science Article

A summary paragraph "boils down" the information in a longer piece of writing. The article on this page describes the excitement in the scientific community as new discoveries are made about the planet Mars. The paragraph is a student's summary of the article.

An Exciting New Era of Planetary Exploration

Mars, named for the Roman god of war, has always been an intriguing spark of color in the night sky. With its faint reddish hue and unusual brightness, it stands out among the field of stars. Mars is considered the most likely planet to have life forms. For thousands of years, humans have studied and pondered the Red Planet. Beginning with crude probes that reached the planet in the 1970s, scientists have progressed until we now have three satellites—two American and one from the European Union—in orbit around Mars.

By far the most detailed information on Mars has reached us through the Martian rover project. Two robots, named *Spirit* and *Opportunity*, were launched in 2003 and landed on the Red Planet early in 2004. Unlike some earlier probes, these robots landed perfectly and went to work studying the planetary surface. Their primary mission was to look for signs of water, and they recorded much data from each of the landing sites, which were on opposite sides of Mars.

Spirit landed in Gusev Crater, an area about the size of Connecticut. *Spirit* soon began to move around, dig in the sandy ground, and grind away at nearby rocks. On the other side of the planet, *Opportunity* rolled right into a small crater—a cosmic "hole in one." It went to work studying bedrock that was exposed when the crater was formed. Both rovers have added much new evidence to support the hypothesis that Mars was once a much wetter, warmer place than it is today. In 2007, *Spirit* took pictures of stones revealing an explosive past on Mars. Scientists hope the two vehicles will continue operating.

A Good Year for Mars

Topic Sentence

Body

Closing Sentence

Mars has been watched throughout history and is being closely studied today. It is the planet most likely to have life and was named for the Roman god of war. Humans have launched satellites that are in orbit around Mars. In 2004, two rovers, named Spirit and Opportunity, which found "by far the most detailed information" (Exciting) about Mars. The rovers landed on two different sides of the planet. Their main mission was to look for signs of water, and both rovers found evidence that water was once there. One set of pictures reveals significant past explosions. **Together, the rovers have sent much useful information back to Earth.**

Writing Tips

Before you write . . .

- **Read the article carefully.**
  Review the material to make sure you know it well. Use a dictionary to look up any words you don't understand.
- **Take notes.**
  Write down the main point of the article. Then make note of important details and quotations you will want to use in the summary.
- **Organize your thoughts.**
  Plan a good topic sentence to begin your paragraph. Then consider which facts you will use in the body. Finally, decide on a strong concluding sentence.

During your writing . . .

- **Stick to important facts.**
  Try to write a summary that is about one third the length of the original—or shorter. Focus on the main point of the article and the most important details to support the point.
- **Provide evidence from the text.**
  Support your points with facts from the article. You can include quotations to help the reader understand. If you use a direct quote from the article, enclose it in quotation marks.

After you've written a first draft . . .

- **Review your paragraph.**
  Make sure that you have captured the main point of the article. Check to see that you have included the most important details.
- **Proofread carefully.**
  Check your paragraph to make sure that there are no mistakes in grammar, capitalization, punctuation, or spelling.

Try It Read a brief article that you find in a newspaper or magazine. Using the tips above, write a single paragraph that summarizes the article. Include a quotation to provide evidence that supports the main idea.

TEKS 7.17B, 7.17C

Practical Writing: Evaluating a Book

A business letter provides an opportunity to communicate thoughts and feelings to business owners, government officials, and even publishers. The following letter was written by a student to a publisher in response to a book the publisher has released. It includes an opinion, a complaint, and a request for information.

April 7, 2011

David Milton, Publisher
Barney Books
100 Riverview Road
Dallas, TX 75201

Dear Mr. Milton:

I have just finished reading The History of Food by Camryn Sotelo. I found it thoroughly fascinating, informative, and delightful. I loved Ms. Sotelo's fun food facts, such as "The onion was likely named after a Latin word meaning *large pearl.*"

While I enjoyed the book, I wished there had been more illustrations showing the foods and facts. I think you missed an opportunity to make a good book even better for its readers.

Finally, I would like very much to contact Ms. Sotelo about making a presentation at our school. Could you please send me her address or e-mail or tell me how I can contact her? Thank you.

Sincerely,
Jon Nguyen

TEKS 7.17B, 7.17C
ELPS 5G

Writing Tips

Before you write . . .

- **Consider your purpose in writing the letter.**
  Decide on the focus of your business letter. Do you want to express an opinion, make a complaint, or request information?
- **Know your format.**
  Make sure you know how to format a business letter and how to structure the paragraphs, including an introduction, middle, and conclusion.

During your writing . . .

- **Be friendly.**
  Express your feelings in a straightforward and honest manner. Make any complaint without anger and in a positive fashion.
- **Use complete sentences.**
  Make sure your sentences are varied in structure and express your thoughts clearly and concisely.
- **Include quotations.**
  If you are writing about a book you have read, include direct quotations where possible to provide evidence of your opinion.

After you've written a first draft . . .

- **Check for format.**
  Make sure you have included the date, address, salutation, and closing with your signature under it.
- **Proofread carefully.**
  Review your letter and correct any mistakes in grammar, mechanics, and spelling before writing your final draft.

Try It Think of a book you have recently read. Then write a letter to the publisher expressing an opinion, registering a complaint, and/or requesting information.

Responding to Texts

Writing for Assessment

On some state and school tests, you may be asked to read a story and write a response to it. The next two pages give you an example of such a test. Read the directions, the story, and notice the student's underlining and comments (**in blue**). Then read the student's response on pages 352–353.

Response to Literature Prompt

Directions:

- Read the following story.
- As you read, make notes. (Your notes will not be graded.)
- After reading the story, write an essay. You have 40 minutes to read, plan, write, and proofread your work.

When you write, focus on the main characters in the story. Show your insight into how the characters change as they interact with each other. Use clear organization, and support your focus with examples from the text.

Acquiring the Taste

When Maria and Janelle became seventh graders, they thought they were pretty grown-up. They had graduated from Franklin Elementary and now attended Westmore Junior High. The old posters of cats and koalas had come down from their bedroom walls, and new posters of rock stars had gone up. Maria and Janelle decided they even needed to learn how to drink coffee. One Saturday morning, they met at Chiara's Coffee Shop and ordered cappuccinos.

"Bleck!" Maria said, letting the coffee dribble out of her mouth and back into the cup. "How can adults drink this stuff?"

Janelle laughed. "Cappuccino is an acquired taste." She took a sip and winced.

"If *acquired* means *awful*, I have to agree," Maria said. She took another taste. The stuff was bitter and burning. She gasped and started to choke.

Janelle leaned toward her and patted her back. "Maria, pull yourself together. Somebody's staring at us."

Maria looked across the coffee shop and saw an elderly lady sitting at another table. Her big brown eyes didn't blink as she stared at the two girls. The woman seemed to scowl.

Maria looked away and coughed into a napkin. "I wish she'd leave."

The woman pushed herself up with her stainless steel cane and shuffled away from the table. Instead of walking out the door, though, she walked to the counter and ordered. "A cappuccino and six biscotti."

"She must have worked up an appetite from all that staring," Maria whispered to Janelle, and they laughed quietly.

The woman turned around. In one hand, she held a tray with coffee and six slices of crunchy pastry. She stared at the girls. Then, ambling with her cane, the woman came right up to their table.

"Those cappuccinos are the best in the city," she said with a thick Italian accent. "But these biscotti are the best in the world. I should know. I brought this recipe with me from Rome."

The girls stared at her. Maria said, "You must be Chiara." *

"I must be," she said, pulling up a chair and sitting down. She lifted a piece of biscotti, dunked it into her coffee, and then raised it slowly to her mouth. "Here's how you learn to like cappuccino." She crunched on the pastry and slid the other biscotti toward the girls.

Each of them took a piece and dunked it into the coffee. Nervously, they bit in. The bitterness of the coffee somehow tasted right with the mild sweetness and crunch of the biscotti.

"Did you grow up in Rome?" Maria asked. "My great-grandma came from Italy."

"Yes. I even had children there—two daughters. * They were your age when we moved to America." As Chiara spoke, Maria could picture the places she described: the Colosseum, the Pantheon, and the fountains of Rome. The woman's voice carried Maria back 60 years, back to when Chiara had been her age. They connect.

Half an hour later, "the girls' coffee cups were empty, and their minds were full."

"Is there always biscotti?" Maria asked as she and Janelle got up to go. "I mean, every Saturday?"

Chiara said, "Sure. Always biscotti and cappuccino and stories."

"Then we'll be back," Maria pledged, and Janelle agreed. They'd acquired the taste. not just for coffee

Student Response

The following essay is a student's response to the story "Acquiring the Taste." Notice how the student uses details from the story to support the focus.

Beginning

The first paragraph states the focus of the essay.

The story "Acquiring the Taste" is about two seventh-grade girls who want to be grown-up. Maria and Janelle think that changing the posters on their walls and learning to drink coffee will make them more grown-up. These changes are just on the surface, though. When the girls meet a woman named Chiara, they find out that there's a lot more to growing up than just coffee.

Middle

The middle paragraphs support the focus with examples from the story.

Maria and Janelle go to Chiara's Coffee Shop because they feel like they need "to learn how to drink coffee." They order cappuccinos and get drinks that are bitter. Maria even starts to choke. The girls are acting pretty immature at this point.

Then Chiara comes to their table, gives them biscotti, and shows them how to dunk the pastry in their coffee. The sweet biscotti and the bitter coffee taste good together. Chiara also tells the girls stories about her life. She grew up in Rome and had daughters like Maria and Janelle before she moved to America. The girls like Chiara's stories more than they like the coffee.

In the end, "the girls' coffee cups were empty, and their minds were full."

Ending

The final paragraph explains how the characters have changed. It also discusses the overall meaning of the story.

By the end of the story, Maria and Janelle are more grown-up than when the story started. They've gone from having posters of rock stars in their bedrooms to actually meeting a person from Rome and learning about her life. The story "Acquiring the Taste" is about learning to like coffee, but it is also about developing an appreciation for the lives of other people and the stories they have to tell.

Respond to the reading. Answer the following questions about the sample prompt and student response.

- ☐ **Organization** (1) How did the underlining on pages 350–351 help the student organize the response?
- ☐ **Development of Ideas** (2) What is the focus of the student's response? (3) What changes in the characters does the student note?
- ☐ **Voice** (4) Is the student's voice objective or personal? What words tell you so?

Practice Writing Prompt

Draft

Practice a response to literature. Carefully read the directions to the practice writing prompt on the next two pages. Use about 10 minutes at the beginning to read the story, make notes, and plan your writing. Also leave time at the end to proofread your work.

Directions:

- Read the following story.
- As you read, make notes on your own paper.
- After reading the story, write an essay. You have 40 minutes to read, plan, write, and proofread your work.

When you write, focus on the main character. Show your insight into how he changes over the course of the story. Use clear organization, and support your focus with examples from the text.

The Mute King

From February through April, the school auditorium became Yan's second home. It wasn't that he liked drama. He hadn't even tried out for the spring production of *Once Upon a Mattress* because he was terrified of being onstage. Yan didn't like drama, but his girlfriend Kallie did. So he camped in the school auditorium every afternoon, his glossy black hair hanging over his face as he bent above algebra homework. Yan sat and worked, waiting for the times when Kallie came onstage and started to sing.

And could she sing! Kallie was playing Princess Winnifred the Woebegone, and whenever she came onstage, she owned the whole auditorium. Everybody stopped and just stared in amazement. Yan would lift his eyes from his algebra paper and let his pencil drop to the page and just soak in the sound of her voice. Those moments made all the waiting worthwhile. But the best moment of all was when play practice was done and Yan got to walk Kallie home.

"You should have tried out, you know," Kallie said to him one day as they strolled past the park.

Yan looked at her and shrugged. “You know I couldn’t talk in front of all those people.”

“I know, but you could’ve tried out for the part of the mute king,” Kallie shot back with a laugh.

Kallie hadn’t meant anything by it, but the comment stung Yan. The king in the play was under a spell that kept him from talking. Yan felt like he was under a spell, too. He knew this play as well as anybody. He’d watched it a hundred times. He could have recited the lines and sung every song. Instead, stage fright kept him where he was, in the seats instead of onstage. He was like the mute king, just waiting for his chance to speak.

Dress rehearsal came. Kallie looked great in her princess getup, and everybody buzzed with excitement. Still, by 3:15, the rehearsal hadn’t begun.

Suddenly, Kallie burst onstage and shuffled down the aisle. Behind her walked Mrs. Spejewski, who was in charge of music. Kallie approached Yan and pointed at him. “He can do it. He’s our only hope. He knows the whole play.”

“What? What?” Yan asked, standing up to protest.

“Our drummer Tony’s got the flu,” Mrs. Spejewski explained, “and Kallie says you know how to play drums.”

“Yeah, I do, but—”

“You’re hired,” Kallie said, grabbing Yan’s hand and pulling him toward the stage.

A moment later, Yan sat in the pit with the other musicians. He held drumsticks in his hand and stared at the printed music—but he knew every song by ear. Mrs. Spejewski lifted her baton, and the overture began. Yan played as if he’d always been behind those drums.

Out came the actors, and they sang, and Yan kept up the beat. Even when Kallie appeared to belt out her first solo, Yan didn’t give in to the old spell.

He smiled. At last, he had found his place in the play, and the mute king had found his voice.

Responding to Expository Texts

In this sample prompt and student response, the student responds to an expository text about the history of Texas. The writer includes information about the article's message and her feelings and thoughts about it.

Response to Expository Text Prompt

Directions:

- Read the following essay.
- As you read, make notes on your own paper.
- After reading the essay, write a response. You have 40 minutes to read, plan, write, and proofread your work.

Six Flags Over Texas

Texas is a big state in size and in history. Six flags have flown over Texas in its long past. Spanish exploration of what is now Texas began in 1519, and by 1682, when Spanish missionaries built the first two missions there, Spain's claim to Texas was secure.

French explorers first entered the region in 1685 and built a fort, but the Native Americans and the Spanish soon drove them out of Texas. For 140 years, Texas remained a Spanish colony. Then in 1821, Mexico declared its independence from Spain and made Texas part of its empire. Anglo-American settlers in Texas rebelled against Mexican rule and won their independence in 1836. For nine years Texas was an independent republic, proudly flying the Lone Star flag. But most Texans wanted to be part of the United States, and in 1845 Texas became the 28th state.

One more flag remained in the state's future. When Southern states seceded, or left, the Union over the issues of states' rights, Texas joined them in March 1861. It became part of the Southern Confederacy. A month later the Civil War broke out. After the war ended in April 1865, Texas rejoined the United States.

The six flags of Texas are a vivid symbol of a rich and glorious past.

Student Response

The following essay is a student's response to the article "Six Flags Over Texas."

Opening Paragraph: Identifies title and summarizes essay.

"Six Flags Over Texas" tells about Texas history under the six flags mentioned in the title. The Spanish were the first Europeans to explore and colonize Texas and were challenged for a short time by the French. Mexico ruled briefly, until the American settlers rebelled and gained their independence. Texas later became a part of the United States, leaving the Union to join the Southern Confederacy, which was defeated in the Civil War.

Middle Paragraphs: Describe details and author's voice.

There are lots of historical dates in this essay as the author swiftly moves through centuries of history. One date that stood out for me was 1836 when Texas gained its independence from Mexico. The Lone Star flag was a fitting symbol for the Republic of Texas.

The author writes with authority and seriousness about his subject. He obviously knows a lot about Texas history and shares it with the reader. He gets plenty of information into four paragraphs, and he does it skillfully.

Last Paragraph: Shows what writer likes and dislikes.

While I liked the essay and learned things about my home state that I didn't know, I wish the writer had included more facts about the different periods of Texas history. I also wish the essay had been longer to get more interesting details in. Basically, I liked what I read but wanted more.

Practice Writing Prompt

Draft

Practice a response to expository text. **Read the directions to the practice writing prompt on the next two pages. Use about 10 minutes at the beginning to read the story, make notes, and plan your writing. Also leave time at the end to proofread your work.** **Use the writing tips on page 359.**

Directions:

- Read the following essay.
- As you read, make notes on your own paper.
- After reading the essay, write a response. You have 40 minutes to read, plan, write, and proofread your work.

When you write, focus on the main idea. Use clear organization, and support your focus with examples from the text.

The Spanish Influence in Texas

How did Texas end up with so many cities with Spanish names, such as Amarillo and El Paso? Just about everywhere you go in Texas, you will see evidence of the Spanish influence in Texas. Many towns and cities were named during the exploration of Texas when Spanish conquistadors were traveling across the land.

Spanish explorer Don Juan de Oñate reached the area around El Paso in 1598. He called the area "El Paso del Norte," which means "The Pass of the North" in Spanish. Oñate's men then traveled on to New Mexico and established a colony for Spain.

Much later, in 1887, Amarillo was chosen for the site of a new town. It was probably named after the yellow soil in the area ("amarillo" means "yellow" in Spanish).

Next time you are traveling or simply looking at a map of Texas, keep your eye open for cities and towns that tell a story about the Spanish influence in the state. You may learn something new about Laredo, San Marcos, or Bandera.

Writing Tips

Before you write . . .

- **Read the essay carefully.**
  Review the material to make sure you know it well. Use a dictionary to look up any words you don't understand.
- **Take notes and write quotes.**
  Write down the focus of the essay. Then write down important details that support it. Note key quotations that can also be used to provide evidence of your thoughts.
- **Organize your thoughts.**
  Plan a topic sentence to begin each paragraph. Then consider which facts you will use in the body to support your ideas and develop them. Finally, think about a strong concluding sentence for the last paragraph.

During your writing . . .

- **Stick to the facts that support topic sentences.**
  Eliminate any facts or details that do not support the focus of your response or topic sentences. Make sure each sentence and paragraph links to the next one and builds on the previous ones.
- **Find a voice that engages.**
  Use your own words to paraphrase or summarize information. Let your words express your enthusiasm for your topic and sustain the reader's interest.

After you've written a first draft . . .

- **Review your draft.**
  Make sure that you have captured the focus and offered convincing and supporting details.
- **Proofread carefully.**
  Check your essay to make sure that there are no mistakes in grammar, mechanics, and spelling. Consult a dictionary if you need to.

imagine
entertain

ELPS 2C, 3E, 3G, 3H, 4G

TEXAS WRITE SOURCE Online
www.hmheducation.com/tx/writesource

Creative Writing

Writing Focus

- Story
- Poem

Learning Language

Work with a partner. Read the meanings and share answers to the questions.

1. A story is a work of **fiction**. It has made-up events and characters.
   What is your favorite work of fiction?
2. The **plot** of a story is the events that happen.
   Describe the plot of your favorite story.
3. A **decision** is when a person makes up their mind about something.
   Tell about a time when you made a big decision.
4. Students work together in **cooperative learning** groups.
   Explain why this activity is an example of cooperative learning.

show
create
discover

Creative Writing

Writing Stories

Have you ever seen a movie with amazing special effects but no story? What a disappointment! On the other hand, a movie with an amazing story may not need special effects.

What makes a story amazing or wonderful? Usually, it has *people* in a *place* where a *conflict* occurs. If readers or viewers care about the people and the conflict, they will care about the story.

In this chapter, you will read a sample story about a tough decision at a school dance. Then you will develop a decision story of your own to share.

Writing Guidelines

Subject: A decision
Purpose: To entertain
Form: Short story
Audience: Classmates

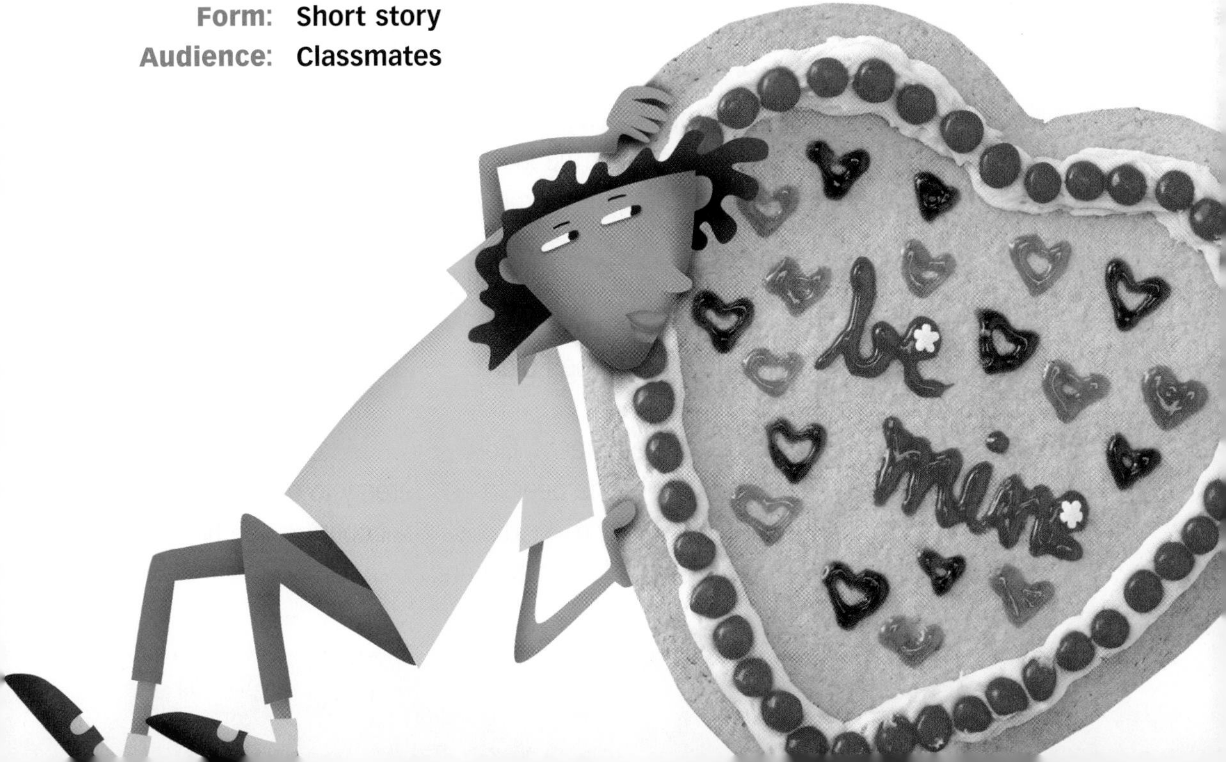

Short Story

One type of story is based on a tough decision that the main character must make. In the beginning, the character wonders what to do. Tension builds until he or she makes the decision, and the ending tells how that decision changes the character. The following story is about a girl named Celia who faces a tough decision at a school dance.

Beginning

The beginning introduces the characters, the setting, and the decision.

Just Keep Going . . .

"Why don't you take a break, Celia?" Shaundra shouted above the pounding beat of the dance music. "You've been serving punch all night. Aren't you going to dance?"

"No," Celia shot back. "I mean, sure. Of course I'm going to dance." She ran her thumb up the stack of party napkins. "But we've been really busy. People get thirsty, dancing."

"Yeah, and people who aren't dancing need something to do."

Celia watched the ice bob in the bowl. "Nobody's asked me."

"Girl, you think this is the '90s? You've got to do the asking." Shaundra took the ladle from Celia's hand and nodded across the gym. "Jeremy's been waiting for you all night."

Celia's eyes grew wide. "You better not have told him I like him!"

Rising Action

The rising action adds a conflict for the characters.

"Maybe I did. Maybe I didn't. If you don't ask him, you'll never know."

Drawing a deep breath, Celia clenched her fists beside her hips. How could she bear to ask Jeremy to dance? She stared out across the crowded basketball court to see him leaning against the folded bleachers.

Jeremy's hair was shaved short, and he wore a button-down shirt with khaki pants. He was more dressed up than Celia had ever seen him.

"Well," Shaundra said, "what's your decision?"

Celia began to walk. The first step was the hardest. She felt like she was teetering on a tightrope. The music pounded in her chest. Halfway there, she wondered if she should veer off to the restroom, but something inside her said, "Just keep going." Suddenly, she stood in front of Jeremy.

He looked up, saw her, and smiled. "What's up, Celia?" He was wearing cologne.

High Point

The high point is when the main character makes her decision.

Celia shrugged, and she couldn't think of a single thing to say. How was she going to get out of this one? Taking a deep breath, she blurted, "You don't want to dance, do you?"

Jeremy's smile grew broader. "Sure." They walked together out to the free-throw line. Then the beat stopped. Celia and Jeremy were left standing there, facing each other in dead silence. She wanted to sink into the floor. At last, the DJ started a slow song.

Ending

The ending suggests that the main character changes.

Jeremy murmured, "So, I guess Shaundra told you I like you."

Celia relaxed and smiled. "Maybe she did, and maybe she didn't."

Respond to the reading. Review the story and answer the following questions.

- ☐ **Organization** **(1) How does the writer build the suspense that leads up to Celia's decision?**
- ☐ **Development of Ideas** **(2) How are Celia and Shaundra different? (3) What decision is Celia struggling to make?**
- ☐ **Voice** **(4) What does the author do to keep your interest? List some phrases that are used for this purpose.**

TEKS 7.14A
ELPS 3E

Prewriting Selecting a Topic

A strong decision story starts with an interesting character. One way to create a character that readers will care about is to give the person one main strength and one main weakness. The strength makes the character admirable, and the weakness prepares the character for a tough decision. A table diagram like the one below can help.

Table Diagram

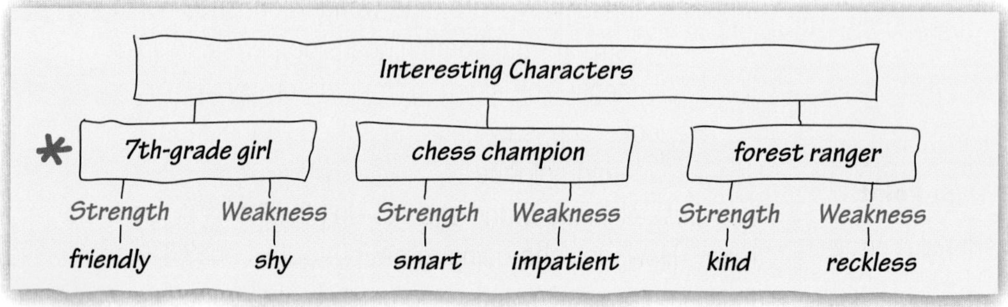

Prewrite **Create a table diagram.** List three characters you find interesting. Under each, list one strength to make your character likable and a weakness to challenge him or her. Choose one character to write about in a story.

Creating a Conflict

The difficult decision your character will face will create the conflict in your story. The writer of the sample story listed decisions that would be tough for her character.

Decisions List

Character weakness:

—Celia is shy.

Tough decisions:

—Whether to throw a surprise party for her best friend
—Whether to make friends with a new girl at school
—Whether to talk to a boy she likes

Prewrite **Choose a conflict.** Think about the character you chose and his or her weakness. List decisions that would be tough for the person to make. Choose one decision for your story. Share your decision with a partner.

Setting the Scene and Gathering Details

You have decided on the character and the conflict for your story. Now it's time to think about the place, or setting, where your story happens. Think of a specific, believable setting that would make the decision especially difficult.

For the main character of the sample story, the setting is a school dance. The author used a sensory chart to gather details about the setting.

Sensory Chart

Setting: School dance in a gymnasium

See	Hear	Smell	Taste	Touch/Feel
• punch bowl • khaki pants • shaved hair	• hip-hop • advice • awkward silence	• cologne • cookies	• punch • pretzels	• cold ice • pounding beat • dizzy • shaky

Prewrite **Set the scene.** **Choose a specific, believable setting for your story. Then use a sensory chart to gather details about the place. Try to come up with at least two details for each sense.**

Texas Traits

Focus on the Texas Traits

Organization

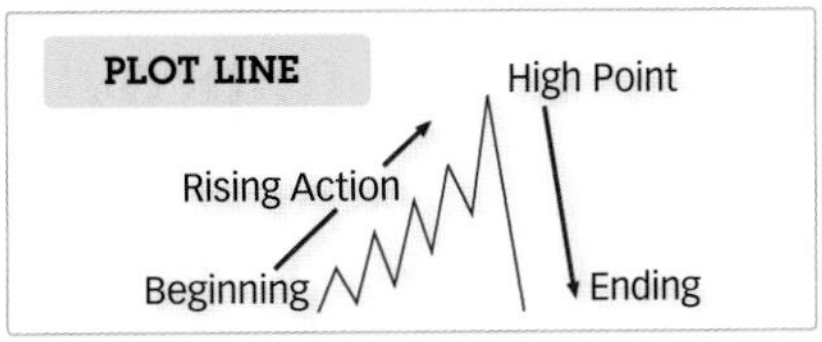

The actions that take place during a story make up the plot line. Each part of the plot plays an important role in the story.

- The **beginning** introduces the characters and setting.
- The **rising action** adds a conflict—a problem for the characters.
- The **high point** is the moment when the conflict is strongest, and a decision is made.
- The **ending** tells how the main character has changed.

TEKS 7.15A(i), 7.15A(ii), 7.15A(v)

Drafting Developing Your First Draft

Now that you have created a character, a conflict, and a setting, you are ready to write your story. As you write, use the following tips.

- **Create an engaging story line.** In your first sentence, focus on the character and the conflict so you immediately grab your reader's interest.

  Celia had watched Jeremy all evening at the dance, but he didn't seem to know she even existed.

- **Keep the action well-paced.** Have one event happen after another to hold the reader's interest and to keep your story moving forward.

  Celia began to walk. She felt like she was teetering on a tightrope. Soon she was standing next to Jeremy. He turned and looked directly at her.

- **Include dialogue that moves the action forward.** The dialogue the characters speak should be important to the story and sound natural.

  Jeremy murmured, "So, I guess Shaundra told you I like you."

  Celia relaxed and smiled. "Maybe she did, and maybe she didn't."

Draft

Write your first draft. Tell the story in a way that holds your reader's interest. Add to the plot with character, action, and dialogue. Remember to keep your reader guessing about what is going to happen next, but stay true to your characters and their decisions.

Revising Improving Your Writing

Once you complete your first draft, take a break. Later, you can return to your story and revise it by looking at the following traits.

- ☐ **Focus and Coherence** Have I made my main character's tough decision the focus of my story?
- ☐ **Organization** Do the events of the plot logically lead from one to another? Are the events clear?
- ☐ **Development of Ideas** Does the main idea or theme of my story come through with action, details, and dialogue?
- ☐ **Voice** Does my voice enhance the style of my story?

Revise

Revise your story. Use the questions above as a guide to revise. Read your story aloud to get a feeling about how your tone works.

Editing Checking for Conventions

After you finish revising your story, you should edit it for *conventions.*

- ☐ **Conventions** Have I checked my story for correct use of mechanics, such as capitalization and punctuation? Have I checked my grammar and spelling?

Edit

Edit your story. Use the questions above to guide your editing. When you finish, use the tips below to write a title. Then create a clean final copy and proofread it.

Creating a Title

Your title is your first opportunity to hook the reader and give some idea of what the story is about. A strong title will engage the reader, so make it memorable. Here are some tips for writing a strong title.

- Use a metaphor: **Teetering on a Tightrope**
- Borrow a line from the story: **Just Keep Going . . .**
- Be creative: **The Punch-Bowl Predicament**

Publishing Sharing Your Story

Stories are meant to be shared. Here are three publication ideas.

- **Recite your story.** Read your story out loud to the class or family members. If short enough, you may even recite your story from memory. Keep a dramatic tone in your voice to hold your listeners' interest. Use gestures and facial expressions where appropriate.
- **Create a skit.** Ask classmates to help you act out your story. Gather costumes and props. Perform your story for your class and have someone videotape it.
- **Submit your story.** Check the library for youth publications that accept stories. Format your work according to the submission guidelines and send your story in.

Publish

Present your story. Choose one of the ideas above or make up one of your own. Then share your story with the world.

Elements of Fiction

The following list includes many terms used to describe the elements or parts of literature. This information will help you discuss and write about the novels, poetry, essays, and other literary works you read.

Action: Everything that happens in a story

Antagonist: The person or force that works against the hero of the story (See *protagonist*.)

Character: A person or an animal in a story

Characterization: The way in which a writer develops a character, making him or her seem believable
Here are three methods:

- Sharing the character's thoughts, actions, and dialogue
- Describing his or her appearance
- Revealing what others in the story think or say about this character

Conflict: A problem or clash between two forces in a story
There are five basic conflicts:

- **Person Against Person** A problem between characters
- **Person Against Himself or Herself** A problem within a character's own mind
- **Person Against Society** A problem between a character and society, the law, or some tradition
- **Person Against Nature** A problem with some element of nature, such as a blizzard or a hurricane
- **Person Against Destiny** A problem or struggle that appears to be beyond a character's control

Dialogue: The words spoken between two or more characters

Foil: The character who acts as a villain or challenges the main character

Mood: The feeling or emotion a piece of literature or writing creates in a reader

Moral: The lesson a story teaches

Narrator: The person or character who actually tells the story, giving background information and filling in details between portions of dialogue

Plot: The action that makes up the story, following a plan called the plot line

Plot Line: The planned action or series of events in a story (The basic parts of the plot line are the beginning, the rising action, the high point, and the ending.)

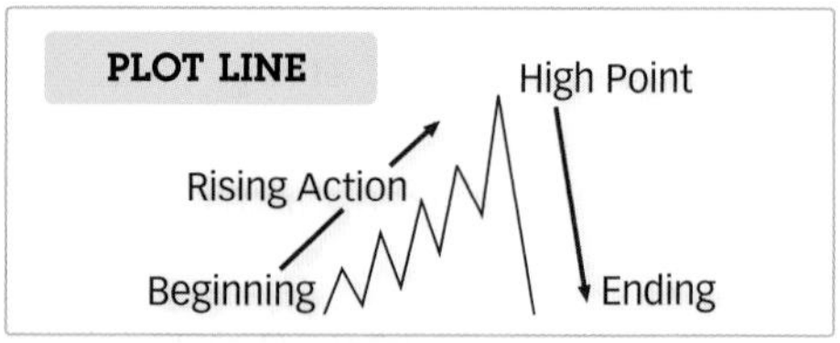

- The **beginning** introduces the characters and the setting.
- The **rising action** adds a conflict—a problem for the characters.
- The **high point** is the moment when the conflict is strongest.
- The **ending** tells how the main characters have changed.

TEKS 7.14C, 7.15A(iii), 7.15A(iv)
ELPS 3E, 5G

Point of View: The angle from which a story is told (The angle depends upon the narrator, or person telling the story.) The point of view should remain consistent throughout the story.

- **First-Person Point of View**
  This means that one of the characters is telling the story: "We're just friends—that's all—but that means everything to us."
- **Third-Person Point of View**
  In third person, someone from outside the story is telling it: "They're just friends—that's all—but that means everything to them."

Protagonist: The main character or hero in a story (See *antagonist.*)

Setting: The place and time period in which a story takes place. The setting should be specific and believable and relate to the characters in some way.

Theme: The message about life or human nature that is "hidden" in the story that the writer tells

Tone: The writer's attitude toward her or his subject (can be described by words like *angry* and *humorous*)

Total Effect: The overall influence or impact that a story has on a reader

Creating Setting and Character

Sensory details help to make a setting specific and real for the reader. Characters who are interesting and true to life also help strengthen your story. Imagine Celia and Jeremy went on a date to the movies after the dance. Look at the sensory chart below of what the setting might be like.

Sensory Chart

Setting: Movie theater during Celia and Jeremy's date

See	Hear	Smell	Taste	Touch/Feel
• bright images on screen	• murmuring voices in the darkness	• buttered popcorn	• fizzy soda	• hard back of seat

Try It Using details from the sensory chart above, write a paragraph describing a specific, believable setting. Include some details about the characters in the story. Make sure that your paragraph is written in a consistent point of view. Share your paragraph with a partner.

TEKS 7.15A(iv), 7.15A(v)
ELPS 3E

Character Development

You just finished writing a story about a character that makes a decision. Character development is central to any good story. Here are some things to keep in mind when you write about a character in your next story.

- **A character needs qualities.** Like people in real life, characters have personalities that make them who they are. Some of the character's qualities may be good and some bad. For example, a character may be hardworking, but unrealistic in his or her goals. This could get the person into trouble.
- **A character needs to want something.** Everyone has dreams, goals, things they want. A character without wants is uninteresting. A character who wants something—whether it be riches or a person to love—will take steps to get what they want. That will give you a good story line to write about.
- **A character needs to have an obstacle.** An obstacle of some sort—a rival for a loved one, for example—creates conflict, as the character tries to find a way to overcome the obstacle and get what he or she wants. The obstacle could be another person, an animal, or a force of nature (a storm perhaps). It could be a quality within the person himself that is preventing him from achieving his goal.
- **A character needs to change or grow.** No one stays the same in life. We are changing in many ways as we grow older. The character in your story must change too, as he or she faces a conflict and finds a way to succeed.

Other Ways to Develop Stories and Characters

- Foreshadowing is a technique used by writers to give the reader clues about what might occur later in the story. Using foreshadowing is one way to keep your audience interested in your characters.
- Flashback is another way to make your characters and story more engaging to the reader. In flashback, characters remember an event from the past. The current events in the story are interrupted by the character's memory.

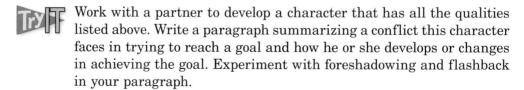

Try It Work with a partner to develop a character that has all the qualities listed above. Write a paragraph summarizing a conflict this character faces in trying to reach a goal and how he or she develops or changes in achieving the goal. Experiment with foreshadowing and flashback in your paragraph.

TEKS 7.15A(ii), 7.15A(iii), 7.15A(iv)
ELPS 5G

Now that you have spent time learning about the ways to create interesting characters and specific, believable settings, let's put it all together in a story of your own.

CREATIVE

Prewriting Selecting a Topic

Decide what kind of story you want to write. It might be a decision story, a science fiction story, or a story set in the past. Choose a main character that is interesting and will engage the reader. The following example tells about the main character of a decision story.

A girl must decide whether to try out for the class play or the cheerleading squad.

Prewrite **Face a decision. Think of a decision that your character might face. What qualities make your character interesting and engaging to the reader?**

Drafting Developing Your Story Line

To make your story line engaging, you want to keep the action well-paced and moving. Your character needs to face an obstacle in his or her journey to reach a goal. The example below shows a possible story line for the character.

The girl's best friend encourages her to become a cheerleader, but she is more interested in the play. What will she do?

Draft **Develop a story line. What actions will take place in your story? What obstacles will your character face? Write your paragraphs to explain the story line you have decided upon.**

Establishing a Strong Setting

Every story has a setting. To bring the setting to life for your readers, use sensory details that they can see, hear, taste, smell, or feel. Here is an example for our imagined story.

Bright posters advertising the two auditions and the sounds of girls cheering in the gym give the girl an uneasy feeling in her stomach as she tries to make her decision.

Draft **Create a setting. Think about the details that will bring your setting to life. Add sensory information to your draft so that your reader will see, hear, taste, smell, and feel your setting.**

TEKS 7.14D, 7.15A(v)
ELPS 3E, 4G

Revising Improving Your Writing

Once you complete your first draft, think about ways you can improve it.

☐ **Organization** Have I given the story a beginning, a middle, and an end? Is the conflict resolved in the ending in a way that satisfies?

☐ **Development of Ideas** Are my ideas fresh and original? Have I linked each idea and event to the next to keep the reader engaged?

☐ **Voice** Does my voice express my feelings about the characters and their conflicts? Have I used it and other literary strategies, such as dialogue, to enhance the tone and style of my story?

Revise

Revise your story. Read through your entire story. Then, use the questions above as a guide to revise.

Editing Checking Conventions

After revising your story, you should edit it for *conventions.*

☐ **Conventions** Have I used correct grammar and spelling? Have I used mechanics, such as punctuation in dialogue, correctly?

Edit

Edit your story. Use the questions above to guide your editing. Then create a clean final copy and proofread it.

Publishing Sharing Your Story

After the hard work of writing, it's fun to share your story with others. Here are three ways you can consider doing this.

- **Make a book of your story.** Neatly type your final draft and make a cover for it with the title and an illustration. Your teacher can display the storybooks on the bulletin board or on a reading table.
- **Read your story.** Read your story to the class. Engage your listeners by reading it with expression, especially the dialogue.
- **Act out your story.** Enlist your classmates to act out your story like a play. Create your own props and costumes. Put on your story play for family and friends.

Publish

Present your story. Choose one of the ideas above or make up one of your own. Then share your story.

Creative Writing

Writing Poems

"A poem begins with a lump in the throat," says Robert Frost, but that's not where poetry ends. Poetry doesn't tell readers what they should feel. It leads them to discover the feeling for themselves. Along the way, a poem also entertains them with carefully chosen words, phrases, and rhythms.

Most modern poems are written in free-verse style, which means they do not have to rhyme. In this chapter, you will write your own free-verse poem about a weather event. If all turns out well, people will be able to hear raindrops on their windows or feel the wind whirling around them when they read your poem.

Writing Guidelines

Subject: A type of weather
Purpose: To entertain
Form: Free-verse poem
Audience: Family and classmates

ELPS 4G, 5G

Free-Verse Poem

Traditional poems follow a strict pattern of rhythm and rhyme, but each free-verse poem creates its own form. Even so, when poets write free-verse poetry, they carefully consider each word and line. They want to make sure their poems sound good and create effective images (word pictures) in the reader's mind. Thanh wrote this free-verse poem to convey his feelings about lightning.

Lightning's Song

I am lightning!
I crackle and I boom,
"Look at me! Look at me!"
I branch across the sky,
like a giant, fiery tree!
I stalk across the earth
on legs of crackling flame.
I flash beneath the clouds,
brighter than the sun!
But when the sun returns,
the clouds carry me,
grumbling,
away.

Respond to the reading. Reflect on the traits in the free-verse poem above.

- ☐ **Organization** (1) Why are the lines of the poem staggered on the page?
- ☐ **Development of Ideas** (2) What sounds and sights does the writer include? List two of each.
- ☐ **Voice** (3) How does the author show the personality of the lightning?

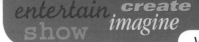

Prewriting Selecting a Topic

Like Thanh, you will be writing a poem about a memory of some type of weather. To generate possible topics, Thanh made a list of weather memories.

Listing

Weather Memories

- *Riding home in my uncle's car during a lightning storm*
- *Wind rattling the windows of our apartment*
- *My bare feet on hot sand at the beach*
- *Rain from one little cloud on a sunny day*
- *Wading through deep snow in the park*
- *Feeling fog's mist on my face on the way to school*

Prewrite **Make a list.** **Write the words "Weather Memories" as a heading on a blank piece of paper. Then start listing experiences you remember about weather until you have at least six memories. Select one as your topic.**

Gathering Details

Thanh created the following sensory chart to gather details about a lightning storm before writing his poem. These details helped him create effective images in his poem.

Sensory Chart

See	Hear	Smell	Taste	Touch/Feel
• bright flashes	• crackle	• dampness	• moist air	• mist or rain
• jagged lines	• rumble	• ozone		• heart thumping
• branching fingers	• boom			
• dark clouds				

He can also use figurative language, such as hyperbole, to create images. Hyperbole refers to the use of exaggeration. For example, the thunder might be described as an exploding bomb or lightning might turn the night into day.

Prewrite **Create a sensory chart.** **Gather sensory details about your own weather memory, using the chart above as a guide. Include specific details from the image in your mind. Include at least one example of hyperbole.**

TEKS 7.15B(i), 7.15B(ii), 7.15B(iii)

Prewriting Using Poetry Techniques

Poets play with the sounds of words. **Onomatopoeia** *(ŏn′ə-mat′ə-pē′ə)* is one example. It means using words that sound like the noises they name.

I crackle and I boom.

Sometimes poets use **personification** *(pər-sŏn′ə-fĭ-kā′shən)*, which means treating a nonhuman subject as if it were human. Thanh's lightning poem personifies lightning as a bold personality who speaks directly to the reader.

"Look at me! Look at me!"

Prewrite

Use special techniques. On your sensory chart, underline words that sound like noises. Circle words or details that could be used as personification.

Drafting Developing Your First Draft

The following tips will help you as you write your first draft.

- **Think** about the weather memory you have chosen. Scan your sensory chart again for details about it.
- **Recall** your feelings as you think about that memory.
- **Write** the first sentence or phrase that comes to mind. Don't worry about getting it perfect. Just get the words flowing.
- **Keep writing** until you run out of ideas and sensory details.
- **Try to create rhythm or a rhyme scheme.**

Shaping Poetry

Poets also play with the way words are placed on the page. **Line breaks,** for instance, help control the rhythm of a poem. In the following example, line breaks cause pauses that emphasize the word "grumbling" and represent the storm fading in the distance.

The clouds carry me,
    grumbling,
        away.

Draft

Write your first draft. Use the tips above to guide your writing. Experiment with onomatopoeia, personification, and shape using varying line breaks.

Revising Improving Your Poem

An expert gymnast makes a handstand look easy, even though it is not. A great poem may look simple, too, but it takes more than one draft to get there. Consider these traits when revising your poem.

- ☐ **Organization** Are my ideas in the best order? Do my line breaks and indents help the poem make sense? Do I use graphic elements, such as word position, to improve my poem's visual appeal?
- ☐ **Development of Ideas** Do I use sensory details? Does my poem convey my true thoughts and feelings?
- ☐ **Voice** Does my poem show my personality? Do I use creative poetic techniques like onomatopoeia, personification, and line breaks?

CREATIVE

Revise

Revise your poem. Using the questions above as a guide, keep revising until you are happy with your poem. Try different graphic elements, such as varying word position within the poem.

Editing Fine-Tuning Your Poem

Poems are shorter than most other types of writing, so every word and punctuation mark is important.

- ☐ **Conventions** Do my capitalization and punctuation make my poem clear? Do I avoid errors in spelling or grammar? Have I checked for any other errors that could distract the reader?

Edit

Edit your poem. Check your poem for conventions. Remember, poems sometimes break the rules for a reason, but never by accident.

Publishing Sharing Your Poem

When your poem is finished, share it with other people. Here are some good ways to do that. (See pages 57–64 for other publishing ideas.)

- **Post it.** Put it on a bulletin board, a Web site, or your refrigerator.
- **Submit it.** Send your poem to a contest or magazine.
- **Perform it.** Read your poem aloud to friends and family.

Publish

Publish your work. Poems are made to be shared. So make yours look its best, and then make it public.

TEKS 7.15B(i)

Writing a Parts of Speech Poem

Writing special forms of poetry can stretch your imagination. One simple form is a "parts of speech" poem. The examples below follow this pattern.

Each poem has five lines.

- **Line 1** is one article and one noun.
- **Line 2** is an adjective, a conjunction, and another adjective.
- **Line 3** is one verb, one conjunction, and one verb.
- **Line 4** is one adverb.
- **Line 5** is one article and one noun that completes the thought.

1 The wind
2 howling and sighing
3 shakes and rattles
4 rudely
5 the window

A snowflake
shy and hesitant
pauses and hovers
briefly
a butterfly

A puddle
dark and chill
splashes and soaks
thoroughly
a sock

Writing Tips

- **Select a topic.** Think of a weather-related noun that you would like to write a poem about.
- **Gather details.** Jot down details about the topic and choose a few to include in your poem.
- **Follow the form.** Review the pattern above and choose words to match it.

Draft

Create your parts of speech poem. Following the writing tips above, write your own parts of speech poem.

TEKS 7.15B(iii)

Writing Other Forms of Poetry

There are many additional forms of poetry. The following are three types of free-verse forms that work well for weather poems.

Concrete Poem

The words of a concrete poem are arranged in the shape of the subject. For example, Thanh's verse about lightning (see page 374) has a jagged shape like a lightning bolt. Here's a much shorter concrete poem:

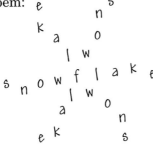

e s
n
k
a o
l w
s n o w f l a k e
l w
a o
n
e k s

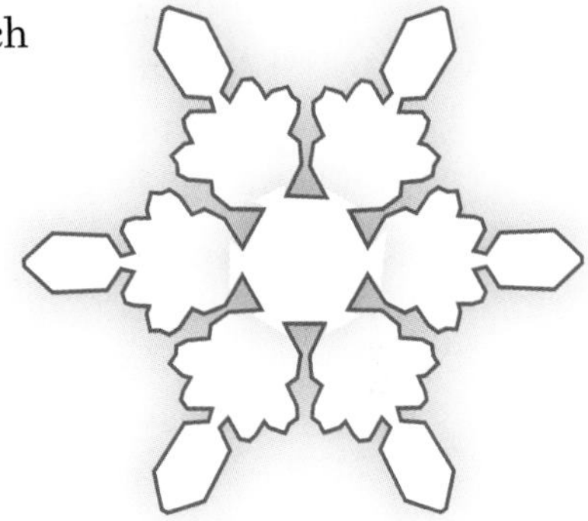

Acrostic Poem

In an acrostic poem, the first letter of each line together spell the subject. Sometimes acrostic poems are called "name poems."

See it glitter on the water's back!
Underneath, it glows through the belly of the wave.
Now it makes a rainbow in the spray.

5 Ws Poem

Each line in a 5 Ws poem answers *who? what? when? where?* and *why?*

My warmly bundled brother
steps down slowly
these frosty mornings
on frozen puddles
to hear the ice crack.

Draft **Write a poem.** Choose one of the three forms above and write your own weather poem. Remember to experiment with shape and word position.

TEKS 7.15B(i), 7.15B(ii)

Using Special Poetry Techniques

Poets use a variety of special techniques in their work. This page and the next define some of the most important ones.

Figures of Speech

- A **simile** *(sĭm´ə-lē)* compares two unlike things with the word *like* or *as*.

  Dry earth cracked
  like a jigsaw puzzle.

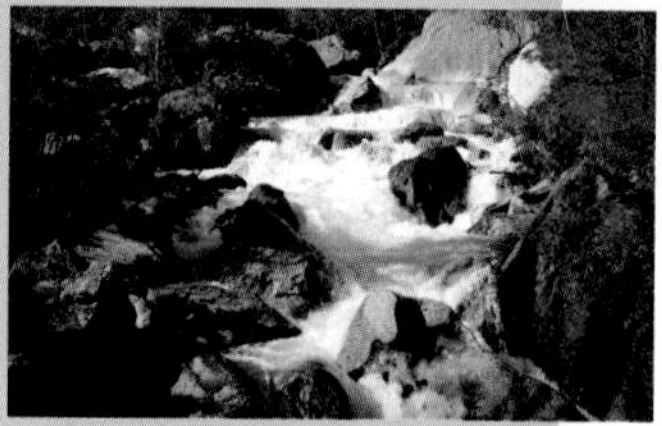

- A **metaphor** *(mĕt´ə-fôr)* compares two unlike things without using a comparison word (such as *like* or *as*), as in this line that uses a cattle stampede to represent a flooded river.

  The swollen river stampedes past.

- **Personification** *(pər-sŏn´ə-fĭ-kā´shən)* treats a nonhuman subject as if it were a person.

  Puddles beg me to stop and play.

- **Hyperbole** *(hī-pûr´bə-lē)* uses exaggeration for a special, often humorous, effect.

  A million degrees on the thermometer,
  and I still can't go swimming.

Sounds of Poetry

- **Alliteration** *(ə-lĭt´ə-rā´shən)* is the repetition of consonant sounds at the beginning of words.

  The wicked wind laughs long and loud.

- **Assonance** *(as´ə-nəns)* is the repetition of vowel sounds anywhere in words.

  Blustery autumn drums our door.

TEKS 7.15B(i), 7.15B(ii)

- **Consonance** *(kŏn′sə-nəns)* is the repetition of consonant sounds anywhere in words.

  Stark stones caressed by mist.

- **Line breaks** help to control the rhythm of a poem as it is read. Readers tend to pause slightly at the end of a line.

  We crest the rise and then
  plummet!

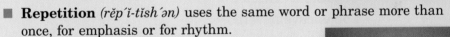

- **Onomatopoeia** *(ŏn′ə-mat′ə-pē′ə)* is the use of words that sound like what they name.

  Plop! Splat!
  Raindrops clap
  the roof and tap
  the skylight.

- **Repetition** *(rĕp′ĭ-tĭsh′ən)* uses the same word or phrase more than once, for emphasis or for rhythm.

  Hot today, so very.
  Hot as a coal stove.
  Hot as a steam iron.
  Hot as hot can be.

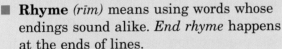

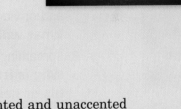

- **Rhyme** *(rīm)* means using words whose endings sound alike. *End rhyme* happens at the ends of lines.

  The dumpster lids are loaded down
  with white snow; in the street, it's brown.

  Internal rhyme happens within lines.

  Cold waves rolled beneath a gray sky.

- **Rhythm** *(rĭth′əm)* is the pattern of accented and unaccented syllables in a poem. The rhythm of free-verse poetry tends to flow naturally, like speaking. Traditional poetry follows a more regular pattern, as in the following example.

  Ăn éarthwŏrm wríggles áftĕr raín.

Try It Write your own example for two or more of the techniques explained on these two pages. Then expand at least one of your examples into a complete poem.

organize

NOTE

ELPS 2C, 2G, 2I, 3D, 3E, 4G

TEXAS WRITE SOURCE Online

www.hmheducation.com/tx/writesource

Research Writing

Writing Focus

- Research Report
- Multimedia Presentations

Grammar Focus

- Consistent tenses
- Conjunctive adverbs

Learning Language

Work with a partner. Read the meanings and orally share answers to the questions.

1. Research is the study of something to learn new facts.
   What topic would you choose to research?
2. A multimedia presentation uses pictures, charts, text, and/or video to give information about a topic.
   What will you use in your multimedia presentation?
3. Something that is consistent stays to one way of acting.
   Why is it important for a person to be consistent in his or her actions?

summarize

RESEARCH

cite

Research Writing
Building Skills

When your parents were your age, doing research meant using magazines and books. Nowadays, researchers can surf the Internet, explore CD-ROMs, check out documentaries on DVD, watch live Web casts, and even e-mail experts on the other side of the world! Of course, no report would be complete without magazines and books, but even these resources are easier to use than ever before.

In this chapter, you'll learn about research in today's world. You might even learn a few tips that you can pass on to your parents!

What's Ahead

- The Research Process
- Primary vs. Secondary Sources
- Evaluating Sources
- Using the Internet
- Using Reference Materials

TEKS 7.22A, 7.22B, 7.23A, 7.23B, 7.23C

The Research Process

Like any piece of writing, a research report requires completing steps in a writing process. Here are the steps involved in the research process.

1 Create a Research Plan

To begin your research report, you should use the following steps:

- Brainstorm ideas for topics. Think of as many topics that interest you as you can. Make a written list.
- Talk with your classmates and get their input about what topics are best for your research report.
- Decide upon a topic that is neither too narrow nor too broad for your report. If you like a topic, you may have to narrow it down or broaden it to fit your report.
- Write a major research question that you will answer about your topic. This question will guide your research.
- Plan to find and evaluate information from a wide variety of sources including reference books, periodicals, and Web sites.
- Create a written research plan for how you will find information about your topic.

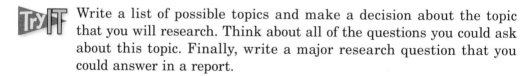

Try It Write a list of possible topics and make a decision about the topic that you will research. Think about all of the questions you could ask about this topic. Finally, write a major research question that you could answer in a report.

2 Gather Sources

Ask yourself these questions as you gather the sources needed for your research report:

- What print and electronic sources will I use for gathering information?
- What search strategies will help get the most out of each source?
- How will I categorize the information I find?
- What format will I follow to record bibliographic information about my sources?

TEKS 7.24A, 7.24B, 7.25A, 7.25B, 7.25C

3 Synthesize Information

When you synthesize information in your research, you combine facts and details to reach a conclusion. Here are some steps in this part of the research process:

- Narrow or broaden your research question if you think you need less or more information for your report.
- Ask yourself questions about each source you find. Is this source up to date? Is it a source that has authority on this topic? Is the main purpose of the source to provide objective information or does it have another purpose?
- Think about why one source might be more useful than another.

Try It Here are two topics for a research report you might write. Narrow the first topic into two smaller topics. Broaden the second topic into two larger topics.

National parks   Echo Canyon Trail at Enchanted Rock

4 Organize and Present Your Ideas

When you are satisfied with all the information you have collected, it is time to write your research report. Follow these steps to organize and present your research:

- Draw conclusions based on your research and how it relates to your research question.
- Paraphrase or summarize information that answers your question.
- Gather evidence that supports the main idea of your research.
- Give relevant reasons for your conclusion that will satisfy your reader.
- Present your findings in a meaningful format that will hold your reader's interest.

Try It Look back at the research question that you wrote earlier. Think about what you already know about your topic and draw a conclusion that might answer your research question.

TEKS 7.22B

Primary vs. Secondary Sources

Primary sources of information are original sources. They give you firsthand information. Secondary sources contain information that has been gathered by someone else. Most nonfiction books, newspapers, magazines, and Web sites are secondary sources.

Primary Sources

1
Visiting an animal shelter

2
Interviewing the manager of an animal shelter

3
Volunteering at an animal shelter

Secondary Sources

1
Visiting a Web site about an animal shelter

2
Reading an article about animal shelters

3
Watching a TV documentary about animal shelters

Types of Primary Sources

- **Diaries, Journals, and Letters** You can find these sorts of primary sources in libraries and museums.
- **Presentations** Historical sites, museums, guest speakers, and live demonstrations can give you firsthand information.
- **Interviews** You can interview an expert in person, by phone, by e-mail, or through the mail.
- **Surveys and Questionnaires** To gain information from many people at once, have them answer a list of questions. Then study the results.
- **Observation and Participation** You can observe a person, place, or thing or participate in an event yourself as a method of gathering firsthand information.

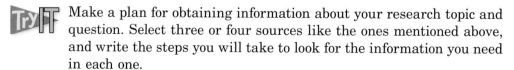

Try It Make a plan for obtaining information about your research topic and question. Select three or four sources like the ones mentioned above, and write the steps you will take to look for the information you need in each one.

TEKS 7.24B
ELPS 3E, 3H

Evaluating Sources

Before you use any information in your writing, you must decide on its usefulness and how it measures up to other sources. Ask yourself the following questions to help judge the value and trustworthiness of your sources.

Is the source a primary or a secondary source?

Firsthand facts are often more trustworthy than secondhand facts. However, many secondary sources can also be trustworthy.

Is the source an expert?

An expert is an authority on a certain subject. You may need to ask a teacher, parent, or librarian for help when deciding how experienced a particular expert is.

Is the information accurate?

Sources that are well respected are more likely to be accurate. For example, a large city newspaper is much more reliable than a supermarket tabloid.

Is the information complete?

If a source of information provides some facts about a subject, but you still have questions, find an additional source that is more useful.

Is the information current?

Take the most up-to-date information on a subject over an older source. Check for copyright dates of books and articles and for posting dates of online information.

Is the source biased?

A source is biased when it presents information that is one-sided. Some organizations, for example, have something to gain by using only some of the facts. Avoid such one-sided sources.

Try It Here are two magazine articles about UFOs: "My Twenty Years Investigating UFO Sightings" and "Scientists Debate the Existence of UFOs." Which one do you think is more reliable and valid? Discuss reasons for your answer with a partner.

TEKS 7.22B, 7.24B
ELPS 3H

Using the Internet

People all around the world publish information on the Internet. It is a great place to do research. By using the Internet, you can quickly find basic information in online encyclopedias or you can search for other sources. Just remember, information on the Internet comes from a variety of people and places, so you need to evaluate each source carefully. Is the author an expert on the topic? Is the site affiliated with an organization or university? Ask yourself questions like these to determine the reliability of Web sites.

Using a Browser

A browser is a program for exploring the Internet. A browser window has controls to help you travel the Internet from page to page. See the diagram below, which shows a browser window displaying a search site's page.

If you know the Web address of a page on the Internet, you can type it into the address bar and use your "Return" or "Enter" key to go there. By clicking the links on a page, you can go directly to related pages. The navigation arrows at the top of the browser window let you return to pages you have visited.

Try It Suppose that you have found a site that has the information you need for your research topic. Explain the steps you could take to determine the reliability and validity of the site.

Using a Search Site

A search site is like a computer catalog for the Internet. When you type a subject into the search box and use your "Return" or "Enter" key, the search site gives you a list of all the pages it knows that contain your subject. You can also explore subjects by clicking the index or directory headings.

Points to Remember

- **Use the Web carefully.**
  Look for sites that have *.edu, .org,* or *.gov* in the address. These are educational, nonprofit, or government Web sites and will offer the most reliable information. If you are not sure about a site, check with your teacher or librarian. Compare the sites to evaluate the information that each contains.

- **Use a search site.**
  A search site such as www.google.com or www.yahoo.com is like a computer catalog for the Internet. You can enter keywords to find Web pages about your subject.

- **Look for links.**
  Often, a Web page includes links to other pages dealing with your topic. Take advantage of these links.

- **Narrow your search.**
  The Web is huge and searches can get complicated. Use specific keywords and look at the descriptions with the search results. These descriptions will help you determine which sites might be more useful than others.

- **Know your school's Internet policy.**
  To avoid trouble, be sure to follow your school's Internet policy. Also follow any guidelines your parents may have set up for you.

Try It Benita is doing a research report about animal shelters. Her search located one site that is published by an animal safety magazine and another by a veterinarian. Which source do you think would be more useful for this topic? Give reasons for your choice.

Searching a Computer Catalog

Every computer catalog is a little different. Therefore, the first time you use a particular computer catalog, it's a good idea to check the instructions for using it or ask a librarian for help. With a computer catalog, you can find information on the same book in three ways:

1. If you know the book's **title**, enter the title.
2. If you know the book's **author**, enter the author's name. (When the library has more than one book by the same author, there will be more than one entry.)
3. Finally, if you know only the **subject** you want to learn about, enter either the subject or a keyword. (A *keyword* is a word or phrase that is related to the subject.)

If your subject is . . .	**your keywords might be . . .**
constructing kites,	kite design, kite history, kite festivals and exhibitions.

Computer Catalog Screen

Author: Hunt, Leslie L.
Title: 25 Kites That Fly
Published: Dover Publications, 2001
Subjects: Kites, kite design and construction, kite design and plans, kite exhibitions, kite festivals, kite folklore, kite history
STATUS: Available
CALL NUMBER: 629.133Hun
LOCATION: Nonfiction

Try It Create a computer catalog screen like the one above for a book you have read or one you are reading.

Finding Books

Each catalog entry for a book includes a **call number**. You can use this number to find the book you are looking for. Most libraries use the Dewey decimal classification system to arrange books. This system divides nonfiction books into 10 subject categories.

000–099	General Works	500–599	Sciences
100–199	Philosophy	600–699	Technology
200–299	Religion	700–799	Arts and Recreation
300–399	Social Sciences	800–899	Literature
400–499	Languages	900–999	History and Geography

Using Call Numbers

A call number often has a decimal in it, followed by the first letters of the author's name. (See the illustration below.) When searching for a book, look for the number and then for the alphabetized letters.

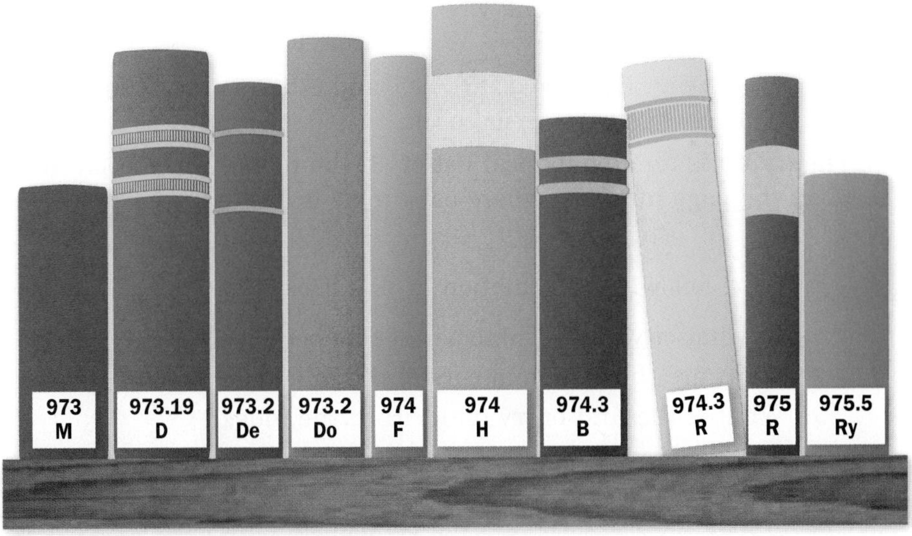

Try It Number your paper from 1 to 5. Place the following call numbers in order as you would find them on a library shelf.

347 Gil   793 Ka   822.82 Kam   636.7 B   546.44 C

TEKS 7.22B

Understanding the Parts of a Book

Understanding the parts of a nonfiction book can help you to use that book efficiently.

- The **title page** is usually the first page. It tells the title of the book, the author's name, the illustrator's name, and the publisher's name and city.
- The **copyright page** comes next. It tells the year the book was published. This can be important because some information in an old book may no longer be correct.
- A **preface**, a **foreword**, or an **introduction** may follow. It may tell what the book is about, why it was written, and how to use it.
- The **table of contents** shows how the book is organized. It gives the names and page numbers of the sections, chapters, and major topics.
- A **cross-reference** sends the reader to another page for more information.
- An **appendix** has extra information, such as maps, tables, and lists.
- A **glossary** explains special words used in the book. It's like a mini-dictionary.
- A **bibliography** lists books, articles, and other sources that the author used while writing the book.
- The **index** is an alphabetical list of all the topics in the book. It gives the page numbers where each topic is located.

Try It Find the following information in this book.

1. In what city is the publisher of this book located?
2. What are the page numbers of the table of contents?
3. What is the first entry under H in the index?

TEKS 7.22B

Using Reference Materials

The reference section in a library contains materials such as encyclopedias, atlases, and dictionaries.

Using Encyclopedias

An **encyclopedia** is a set of books, a CD, or a Web site with articles on almost every topic you can imagine. The topics are arranged alphabetically. The tips below can guide your use of encyclopedias.

- If the article is long, skim any subheadings to find specific information.
- Encyclopedia articles are written with the most basic information first, followed by more detailed information.
- At the end of an article, you may find a list of related topics. Use them to learn more about your topic.
- The index lists all the places in the encyclopedia where you will find more information about your topic. (See the sample below.) The index is usually in the back of the last volume of a printed set.

Encyclopedia Index

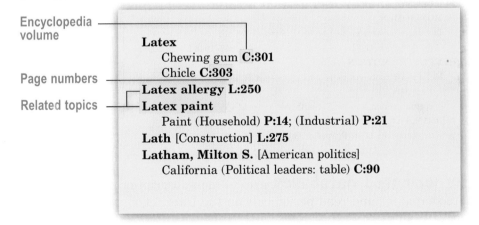

Encyclopedia volume
Page numbers
Related topics

Latex
Chewing gum **C:301**
Chicle **C:303**
Latex allergy L:250
Latex paint
Paint (Household) **P:14**; (Industrial) **P:21**
Lath [Construction] **L:275**
Latham, Milton S. [American politics]
California (Political leaders: table) **C:90**

Try It Using the index entries above, list the volume and page or pages where you might find the following information.

1. A description of chewing gum
2. An explanation of the difference between house paint and industrial paint
3. A list of political leaders of California

TEKS 7.22B
ELPS 5G

Finding Magazine Articles

Periodical guides are found in the reference section of the library and list magazine articles about many different topics.

- **Locate the right edition** of the *Readers' Guide to Periodical Literature* (or a similar guide). The latest edition will have the newest information, but you may need information from an older edition.
- **Look up your subject.** Subjects are listed alphabetically. If your subject is not listed, try another word related to it.
- **Write down the information** about the article. Include the name of the magazine, the issue date, the name of the article, and its page numbers.
- **Find the magazine.** Ask the librarian for help if necessary.

Readers' Guide Format

PEROXIDES — Subject Entry

Cosmetic and skin protective compositions. *Soap, Perfumery & Cosmetics* v77 no2 p57 F 2008. — Title of Article

See also — Cross-Reference

Hydrogen peroxide

PEROXISOMES

Treating a mystery malady. M. Egan. *Forbes* v173 no2 p38–39 F 2 2008. — Name, Volume, and Number of Magazine

Unloading dock. G. Chin. *Science* v303 no5666 p1947–1948 Mr 26 2008.

PERPETUAL MOTION

McKeon, 73, continues to be one for the ages. H. Bodley. *USA Today* Ja 16 2008. — Name of Author

Perpetual motion, almost. K. Smith. *Motor Trend* v56 no1 p24 Ja 2008. — Page Number/Date

PERRIN, PAT — Author Entry

What happened next? P. Perrin. *Appleseeds* v6 no6 p24–27 F 2008.

Internet-based databases are online subscription services that allow you to search for and read periodicals on the Internet.

Try It Arun did some preliminary research and found two magazine articles about the topic of perpetual motion, as shown above. His assignment is to use at least four different types of sources. What other steps could Arun take to locate more sources? Create a written research plan, describing other possible sources and how to locate them.

Keeping Track of Your Sources

As you research, keep track of your sources and notes so that you can cite them in your report. You need to write down the following information.

- **Encyclopedia:** Author's name (if listed). Entry title. Encyclopedia title. Edition (if given). Publication date. Type of source.
- **Book:** Author's name. Title. City: Publisher, Copyright date. Type of source.
- **Magazine:** Author's name. Article title. Magazine title, Date published. Page numbers. Type of source.
- **Internet:** Author's name (if listed). Page title. Site title. Date posted or copyright date (if listed). Type of source. Date found.

My Source Notes

Encyclopedia — *"Carbon dioxide." World View Encyclopedia. 21st ed. 2009. Print.*

Book — *Hudson, Allen. Carbon and Diamonds. New York: Marshall Science, 2006. Print.*

Article — *Hassan, H. "The properties of carbon dioxide." Geology Review, 16 Sept. 2009. Pages 36–39. Print.*

Internet — *American Geological Association. 19 Jan. 2008. Web. 30 April 2010.*

Try It Lisette is beginning her research for a report about electric cars. What steps could she use to find information about her topic? As Lisette finds information, what information will she need to record?

TEKS 7.23D, 7.25A
ELPS 3H

Avoiding Plagiarism

You must be careful to give credit for the facts and ideas you find in your research. Using other people's words and ideas without giving them credit is called plagiarism, and it is stealing. Here are two ways to avoid plagiarism.

- **Quote exact words:** When an author states something so perfectly that it makes sense to use those exact words, you may include them in quotation marks and give credit to the author.
- **Paraphrase:** However, it's usually best to put the ideas from a source in your own words. This is called paraphrasing. Remember, though, to give credit to the author of the idea.

Quoting Exact Words

How many people fought at the Alamo?

"On February 23, 1836, Santa Anna led his troops across the Rio Grande to the Alamo. Only about 200 men in the Texan Army were left to battle as many as 6,000 men in the Mexican Army."

Allende article
page 16

Paraphrasing

How many people fought at the Alamo?

Santa Anna and about 6,000 men arrived at the Alamo on February 23, 1836. Only 200 Texans were there to defend the Alamo.

Allende article
page 16

Try It Read the following passage from the article "Remember the Alamo" by Robert Allende. On a note card, quote the sentence that best sums up the passage. On another note card, paraphrase the entire passage. (Use the note cards above as a guide.) Explain why your paraphrase is not plagiarism.

The Texan Army was able to defend the Alamo for 13 days. On March 6, Santa Anna and his men forced their way into the Alamo through a hole in the outer wall. They defeated their opponents.

Although the Texan Army lost the battle at the Alamo, the fight became a symbol of heroism among the troops. At the Battle of San Jacinto, the troops shouted "Remember the Alamo!"

Taking Simple Notes

The notes for your research report should be easy to read and well organized and should cite the sources you used. Taking good notes will make the later steps in the writing process go smoothly.

Tia chose to write her report about Noah Webster. Below are her notes.

Details from source

History of Dictionaries
Earliest known—word list from Mesopotamia, dated from 600 B.C.
First English dictionary had only 3,000 words
Noah Webster published first American dictionary in 1828
(has never been out of print)
All About Books, pp. 56, 58

Bibliographic information

Webster called dictionary "An American Dictionary of the English Language"
Webster's dictionary changed greatly over years, many more words
Today "Webster" is substituted for "dictionary" by many people
Noah Webster - Dictionary Maker, pp. 48, 52

Tia combined details from two sources to draw her own conclusions.

We all use dictionaries. Do you know about the long and interesting history these special books have? The first dictionary was a simple word list created in Mesopotamia in 600 B.C. The first English dictionary had only 3,000 words in it. Noah Webster's An American Dictionary of the English Language appeared in 1828 and has never gone out of print. For many people today, the word "Webster" means "dictionary."

Try It Write a source for a simple note. Take the following book information and put it into the proper bibliographic format for a simple note.

The Great Blizzard of '88, by Erin Goldwyn, published in 1930 by The Information Press, pp. 14–17.

TEKS 7.22A
ELPS 3E

Gathering Details

A gathering grid can help you organize the information from your research. Such a grid can help you brainstorm ideas for writing your report, give form to your research, and let you share and connect thoughts with others who you share your grid with.

Gathering Grid

Francisco Coronado	Coronado—Great Explorer	Conquis-tadors of America	Weller article	Explorers' Web site
What is his background?	Born 1510 in Spain	Arrived in New World in 1535		Governor of New Galicia in Mexico
How was he great?	Led search for cities of gold north of Mexico			
What were his major deeds?	First European to explore much of Western U.S.	His men discovered the Grand Canyon.	Traveled as far east as Kansas	

Talking with your friends and classmates about possible topics for your research report may help you choose the most interesting topic. Your classmates will have different opinions and ideas about your topics. These ideas may show you a new aspect of the topics you brainstormed.

Try It Brainstorm a list of possible topics for a research report. Meet with a partner to discuss your ideas. Think about the opinions and ideas your partner shares.

Creating Note Cards

While a gathering grid is a great way to see all your research at one glance, sometimes you need more space for an answer. You can use note cards to keep track of longer answers and the details from your research.

When using note cards, number each card and write a question at the top. Then answer the question by writing a paraphrase (see page 396), a list, or a quotation. At the bottom, identify the source of the information (including a page number if appropriate).

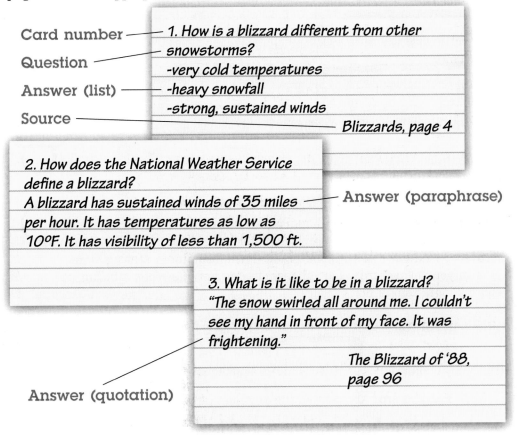

Card number — Question — Answer (list) — Source

1. How is a blizzard different from other snowstorms?
-very cold temperatures
-heavy snowfall
-strong, sustained winds
Blizzards, page 4

2. How does the National Weather Service define a blizzard?
A blizzard has sustained winds of 35 miles per hour. It has temperatures as low as 10°F. It has visibility of less than 1,500 ft.

Answer (paraphrase)

3. What is it like to be in a blizzard?
"The snow swirled all around me. I couldn't see my hand in front of my face. It was frightening."
The Blizzard of '88, page 96

Answer (quotation)

Try It Read the following sentences from an article about blizzards. On your own paper, paraphrase the author's words.

The Blizzard of 1888 is the most well-known snowstorm in American history. Most of the East Coast was isolated from the rest of the world, as telephone lines broke and roads were blocked.

TEKS 7.23C, 7.23D

Creating Bibliographic Information

Each fact on your note cards must have a source telling where you found it. When you write your research report you will need this information to include in your bibliography. Your bibliography will include the author's name, the title, the publisher and city, the publication year, page numbers, and the type of source.

In the case of a book, record all the following information about your source:

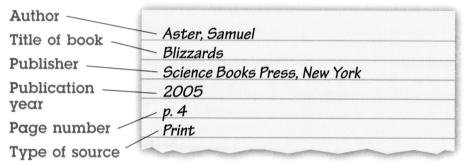

Paraphrasing and Plagiarism

As you learned earlier, plagiarism is the act of presenting someone else's ideas and words as your own. It is a form of cheating and will usually be discovered and earn you a poor grade. Paraphrasing is stating someone else's ideas in your own words. Paraphrasing is acceptable when writing a research report. Plagiarism is not.

Original Text: Mercury is the smallest of the eight planets in our solar system. Venus, the next planet, is smaller than Earth, and Mars, the fourth planet, is larger than Earth.

Plagiarism: Mercury is the smallest of the eight planets in our solar system.

Paraphrase: There are eight planets in the solar system, and Mercury is the smallest.

Try It Find a paragraph in a textbook or other nonfiction work. Paraphrase the information in the paragraph.

Research Writing

Research Report

History is full of stories of amazing people—whether leaders that helped develop our states and country or heroes who are still living today. We can learn a lot by finding out how these people grew throughout their lives, what obstacles they faced along the way, and how they overcame them. Their stories can inspire us to accomplish great things ourselves.

In this chapter, you will write a report about a person who interests you. You will use the research skills you learned about in "Building Skills" (pages 383–400) to uncover important information about this person. You will then compile the information in a research report to share with your classmates. Along the way, you're sure to learn a lot about your subject—and about yourself.

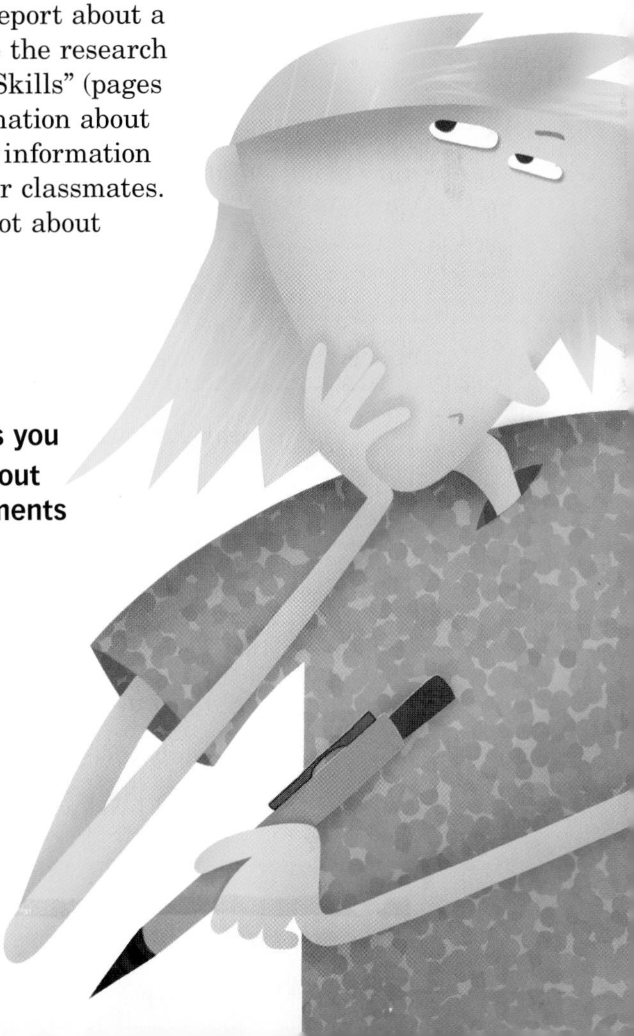

Writing Guidelines

Subject: A person who interests you
Purpose: To present research about a person's accomplishments
Form: Research report
Audience: Classmates

Research Report

Tina Trueba wrote this research report about an important figure in American history. Notice how the information in the report is organized. The side notes point out key features in the report.

↑ 1" ↓

← 1" →

The entire report is double-spaced.

Tina Trueba

Language Arts

May 4, 2010

An Independent Leader

Beginning

The opening shares an interesting fact to gain the reader's attention.

He was the only person to serve as governor of two different states. He was the only person to be both the governor of a state and the president of an independent nation. One of the largest cities in the United States is named after him. He was Sam Houston, and he is beloved by Texans as one of the founders of our state. Many factors made him a leader, such as being a good speaker. However, the most important factor may have been his independent spirit. Sam Houston was an outstanding leader because he made decisions based on what he thought was right.

The controlling idea identifies the topic (underlined).

Houston's Background

Born in 1793 in Virginia, Houston moved with his family to Tennessee as a child. At one point he ran away and lived with the Cherokee, who adopted him

↑ 1" ↓

Middle
The first middle paragraph gives background about the person.

Headings help the reader to understand the paper's organization.

Each of the middle paragraphs starts with a topic sentence that covers one main accomplishment.

Trueba 2

into their tribe. They gave him the name Kalanu, which means "Raven" (Brown 32).

As a young man, Houston entered law and politics in Tennessee. He rejoined the Cherokee for three years as a government agent, then moved to Texas. There, he commanded the army during the Texas Revolution and, in April 1836, won the Battle of San Jacinto and thus won the war. He was elected the first president of the Republic of Texas, and then governor and senator when Texas became a state. Throughout his experiences, Houston did what he thought was right, not what others thought he should do.

Houston's Accomplishments

Houston's actions in favor of Native Americans showed his strong sense of honor. Because of his experiences among the Cherokee, Houston became a lifelong supporter of Native American rights. He idolized the Cherokee chief, Oolooteka, whom he called his "Indian father" (Krantz). At the time, many European-Americans were prejudiced against Native Americans. In contrast, Houston took actions to help them. In 1817, the U.S. government moved the Cherokee from Tennessee to the Arkansas territory.

President Andrew Jackson put Houston in charge of the operation. Houston undoubtedly saved Cherokee lives by persuading them to move peacefully.

A source and page numbers are identified in parentheses.

In 1838, Houston tried to defend Native American rights by fighting, unsuccessfully, for a treaty that would preserve tribal lands (Brown 254–256). Then, as a U.S. Senator, Houston argued against the Kansas-Nebraska Bill because it took away Native American lands. "I am aware that in presenting myself as the advocate of the Indians and their rights . . . I shall stand very much alone," he said (356). Being alone did not change his stand. He was a pillar of strength.

The exact words of the author are given in quotation marks.

Houston's brave independence made him a hero in the Texas Revolution. In March 1836, the Alamo fell, and civilians were fleeing east to escape the Mexican army led by Santa Anna. Houston ordered his army to retreat. It was an unpopular move. He made a stand at the Brazos River, but after declaring, "I don't intend to leave the Brazos," he retreated farther east. The president of the revolutionary government wrote Houston a letter saying, "Sir, the enemy is laughing you to scorn . . . You must retreat no further" (200). Still, Houston kept retreating because he felt it was the right strategy. Then, on April 19, he stopped and

When the source is the same as the one before it, only the page number is listed in parentheses.

The writer's last name and page number appear on every page.

Trueba 4

prepared to face the enemy "though the odds are greatly against us" (204). Two days later, he attacked Santa Anna by surprise near the San Jacinto River, and won. By following his own judgment all the way, Houston had gained freedom for Texas.

As governor of Texas, Houston followed his conscience about an even larger struggle—the Civil War. Houston argued against Texas seceding from the Union because he foresaw that the South would lose. In February 1861, the people of Texas voted for secession, and in March, Governor Houston refused to sign an oath of loyalty to the Confederacy. As a result, he was removed from office.

Houston's Legacy

Ending The final paragraph sums up the report and tells the reader one last interesting fact.

After Houston was removed from office, he retired, and died peacefully two years later. His inspiring example lives on, not just because he was an important leader, but because he stood for doing the right thing. Texas Governor Rick Perry, in his 2003 State of the State Address, quoted Houston's motto, "Do right, and risk consequences." Sam Houston was born more than two centuries ago, but his spirit lives on in Texas.

ELPS 4G

Trueba 5

Works Cited

A separate page alphabetically lists sources cited in the report.

Brown, Marion. The Life and Times of Sam Houston. New York: Review Row, 1993. Print.

Fowler, M. “Do right.” Texas Review. 3 Feb. 2009, pages 8–10. Print.

Krantz, Mitchell. “Houston, Samuel.” Texas Tribune. Texas History Society. May 2008. Web. April 2010.

Perry, Rick. “State of the State Address.” Office of Governor Rick Perry. 11 Feb. 2003. Web. April 2010.

Respond to the reading. After you have finished reading the sample research report, answer the following questions about the traits of writing.

- ☐ **Focus and Coherence** (1) What is the main idea of the report? (2) What character trait is mentioned throughout the report?
- ☐ **Organization** (3) What is the main idea in each middle paragraph? Make a list.
- ☐ **Voice** (4) How does the use of quotations enhance the message of the report?

Go Online!

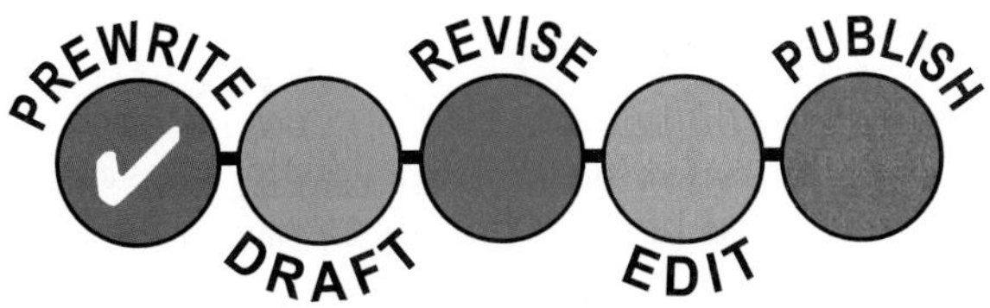

Prewriting

Prewriting is to writing what packing your gear is to traveling. The more prepared you are for the "journey," the more successful you will be. Keep the following points in mind as you prepare.

Keys to Effective Prewriting

1. *As a topic, choose an important person who interests you.*
2. *Make sure that there is enough and not too much to say about your topic. You need background information and at least three important ideas about the person.*
3. *Use a gathering grid to organize your research questions and answers. Use note cards for longer answers.*
4. *Be careful to credit your sources when paraphrasing ideas or quoting words. Avoid plagiarism.*
5. *Keep track of the publication details for all your sources and notes so you can use them in a works-cited page later.*

TEKS 7.14A, 7.22A
ELPS 3E, 3G

Prewriting Selecting a Topic

To find a topic, brainstorm a list of important people who interest you. Tina based her list on her answers to the following questions.

- What famous or historic people would I like to know more about?
- What events in history could I research? Who was involved?
- What interesting people does my social studies textbook mention?

Topics List

I'd like to know more about these people . . .

- *Sally Ride*
- *Teddy Roosevelt*
- *Davy Crockett*
- *Sam Houston*

I'd like to learn about the people involved in these events . . .

- *the battle of the Alamo*
- *the building of the Panama Canal*
- *the creation of comic books*

My textbook mentions these historical figures . . .

- *Sam Houston, 1793–1863, Texas leader*
- *Abraham Lincoln, 1809–1865, U.S. president*
- *Bill Pickett, 1870–1932, cowboy and rodeo pioneer*

Prewrite **Make your topics list. Brainstorm a list of at least five people whom you would like to learn more about.**

One way to decide on your topic is to discuss your ideas with your classmates. Sharing your thoughts may help you discover a new topic you want to look into.

Prewrite **Consult with your classmates. Share your list of possible topics with a partner. Discuss which topic you think is best. Consider your partner's thoughts.**

Sizing Up Your Topic

A good research report about an important person should include detailed information about the person's background and three or four major points about the person's accomplishments.

Tina decided to write about Sam Houston, a Texas leader she read about in her history textbook. Tina looked up her topic in an encyclopedia and wrote down the following notes.

Research Notes

Sam Houston

Background

- *Born in 1793 in Virginia and lived most of his life in Texas, which he led as both president and later governor when Texas joined the U.S.*

Major Accomplishments

- *He was famous as a soldier, war leader, and skilled political leader.*
- *He helped Texas win its independence from Mexico.*
- *He followed his conscience and took an unpopular position against secession at the time of the Civil War.*

Legacy

- *He helped to create the country and state of Texas.*
- *He remains a hero today for doing what he felt was right.*

From this information, Tina felt confident that she would be able to write a good research paper about Sam Houston.

Prewrite **Size up your topic.** Look up your chosen topic in an encyclopedia and on the Internet. List background information and the most important points about the person. Are there enough details to write a good research report?

Prewriting Writing a Research Question

A good way to begin your report is to write a question that will guide your research. As you look for information in your sources, you will try to answer your major research question. Your research question will give focus to your search and keep you on track.

Tina needs to ask herself what it is about Houston that she finds most interesting and wants to learn more about. The answer to her question will be the body of her research report. Here are some questions that Tina brainstormed:

- What did Houston do in the War of 1812?
- How did he help Texas win its freedom from Mexico?
- What role did he play in the conflict with the Cherokees?
- What made Sam Houston an outstanding leader?

Tina looked back at her questions and decided that the first three were too narrow to write a research report around. Her fourth question, *What made Sam Houston an outstanding leader?*, is a broader research question, so Tina decided to use it.

Tina reviewed the notes from her earlier research to see if she would be able to find information to answer her research question.

Question: What made Sam Houston an outstanding leader?

Possible Answer: His belief in always doing the right thing
Supporting Details: His support of the Cherokees, his stand against secession in Civil War

Possible Answer: His confidence in his own judgment
Supporting Detail: His victory at the battle of San Jacinto

Prewrite **Write a research question.** Think about the information you would like to know about your topic. Develop a major question that will guide your research.

Creating a Research Plan

The following steps will help you create a written plan that will make your final research report interesting, focused, and well researched.

1 Do preliminary research.

Explore a topic that interests you. Read about it in books, in magazine and newspaper articles, and on the Internet. Take notes and decide what most interests you about the topic based on your research.

2 Decide on your final topic.

Your original topic may have been too broad and now is the time to narrow it down. Maybe it was too narrow and you can broaden it. Perhaps your preliminary research led you in a new direction and you want to switch topics.

3 Ask questions.

What is a research question that you want answered about your topic? This question should be big enough to include interesting supporting details. It should be focused enough to lead to a meaningful conclusion about the topic. Eliminate questions that are too specific, uninteresting, or not general or meaningful enough.

4 Do additional research.

Now that you have your major research question, you need to go back and do more research, digging deeper to find the answers to the question that will form the focus of your report.

Below is part of Tina's research plan for her report on Sam Houston.

Research Question: What made Sam Houston an outstanding leader?

Possible Sources

- *visit Texas History Museum*
- *speeches by important Texas politicians*

Prewrite **Create a research plan.** Write up your research plan based on the steps above. Keep it clear and simple.

TEKS 7.17A, 7.23A, 7.23D
ELPS 3G

Prewriting Gathering Sources

Now that you have written your research plan, you are ready to gather sources of information about your topic. The following tips will help you choose the best sources for accurate and reliable information.

Use Search Strategies

Good search strategies will save you time. Here are some strategies to use as you look for information.

- **Encyclopedias:** Research guides and indexes, usually found in the last volumes of encyclopedias, can direct you to the best entry for finding information about your topic.
- **General books on your topic:** Indexes in the back of the book will point to the specific pages about any aspect of your topic.
- **The Internet:** Search engines will help you find Web sites about your topic, often listed in order of importance.
- **Magazines and newspapers:** *The Readers' Guide to Periodical Literature* lists may guide you in finding magazines and newspapers with information about your topic.

Prewrite **Follow your research plan.** Use your research plan and the strategies above to begin gathering sources about your topic.

Choose Valid and Reliable Sources

A source is valid and reliable if it consistently contains accurate information. Sources should be objective and written by authors who have a strong knowledge of the topic.

Prewrite **Check your sources.** Find at least three sources that may help answer your research question. Talk with a partner about why it is important that each source be valid and reliable.

Synthesize Ideas

When you use information from a variety of sources, it is important to blend that information together to form your own ideas. You can not simply record information and stick it together. You need to understand how all the details work together to answer your research question.

Prewrite **Synthesize information.** Use the information you have collected so far to begin forming your own understanding. This new conclusion will help you to answer your research question.

TEKS 7.22B, 7.23A, 7.23B

Finding and Evaluating Information

When you first begin your search for information, you may be overwhelmed by the amount of details you find. What strategies can you use to find the information you are really looking for?

Search Books and Magazines

To find more information in print materials, try the following strategies.

- Check an encyclopedia entry for related terms and topics.
- Look at the works cited in the sources you are using. You may find another book or article that contains specific information to add to your research report.
- Ask a librarian at the reference desk for help. Librarians are trained in special ways to search the library for the information you need.

Search the Internet

To find more information online, try the following strategies.

- Make your search terms more specific. Rather than searching for "Sam Houston," Tina narrowed her search by using the search terms "Sam Houston biography." This helped Tina find only sites that deal with Sam Houston's life.
- Avoid personal Web sites and pages. These are pages created by individuals who have an interest in the topic you are researching. The information may or may not be accurate and objective.

Sort Your Sources

As you collect information, sort it into categories. You may choose to sort your information by time period, importance, or some other factor about your research topic. This step will help you identify areas where you need more information. You may also discover a particular aspect of your topic that you want to focus on in your report.

Prewrite

Collect and sort information. Using the search strategies above, find several sources related to your topic. Sort this collected information into categories and look for areas where you need more information.

TEKS 7.23B, 7.23D
ELPS 3E, 3G, 3H

Prewriting Finding Strong Sources

A research report that uses valid and reliable sources is likely to be valid and reliable itself. Your reader will feel confident that the details in your report are accurate if you use appropriate sources.

A valid and reliable source comes from an expert, agency, or institution. An unreliable source comes from an unknown source with no authority.

Try It Work with a partner to identify each of the sources below as either valid and reliable or not. Why is it important to choose only the valid and reliable sources for your research? Discuss your thinking with your partner.

autobiography by person being researched
magazine article written by fan of person being researched
biography by political opponent of person being researched
university Web site
blog by amateur historian

Prewrite **Check your sources.** As you select sources for your research, make sure that they are valid and reliable.

Using Categories in Your Research

As you find interesting facts and details about your chosen topic, think about how that information fits with the other information you've found. By sorting your research findings into categories, you can see relationships between the facts and details.

As Monique researched her topic, she sorted facts and details using a web. Monique later used her web to organize her research report.

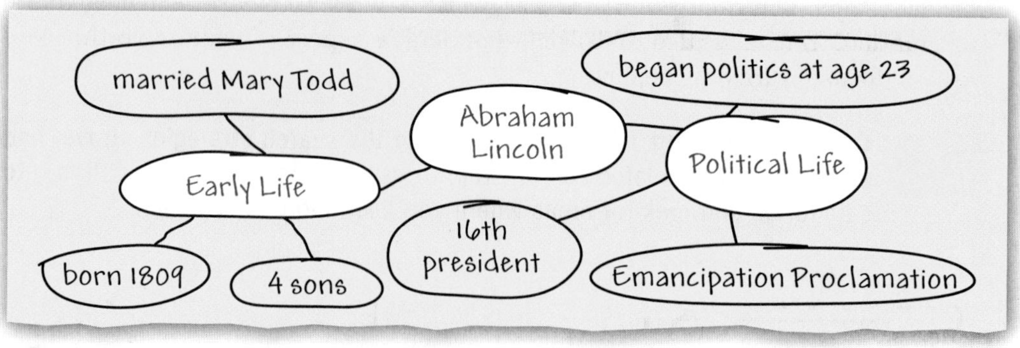

Prewrite **Categorize your findings.** Using a web or another graphic organizer, sort the information you've collected into categories. Look for new relationships that you hadn't noticed before.

TEKS 7.23A, 7.24B
ELPS 3E, 3H

Searching for More Information

Basic searches on the Internet or in the library may not turn up all the information you are looking for. You may need to use some more advanced ways to search for information.

One way to better define your search is by using the words AND, OR, or NOT in your search terms. These words can help you narrow down your search to find only the information that pertains to your topic. This technique can be used on an Internet search engine and in many library catalogs.

While using the Internet to research the history of basketball, Sean kept finding Web sites about the current basketball season. He decided to use the word AND to help narrow his search. His search term became "Basketball AND History."

Search Term: Basketball

Results:
- Schedule for 2010 Season
- MVPs for each team

Search Term: Basketball AND History

Results:
- Biography of Dr. James Naismith
- First rules of the game

Try It Work with a partner to brainstorm advanced search terms for each of the following topics. Explain why your search term is strong.

Acid Rain
Voting Rights
Organ Transplant
Colin Powell
The History of Automobiles
The Environment
Creation of the Internet
Albert Einstein

Now think about the types of sources you might find when searching for information about the above topics. Discuss with your partner why some sources may be more useful than others.

Prewrite **Refine your search. Try using the words AND, OR, and NOT to refine your search terms.**

TEKS 7.17A(iv), 7.23B
ELPS 3G

Prewriting Classifying Information

When you take notes on your research topic, it is helpful to sort information into categories. You may notice interesting information or draw new conclusions when you bring together information from various sources.

The examples below show how Tina placed information from two sources into categories.

> **Sam Houston was born in Virginia in 1793 and moved with his family to Tennessee when he was thirteen. He ran away two years later and joined the Cherokee in eastern Tennessee. They adopted him into their tribe. –from encyclopedia**

> **The Houstons lived in a frontier town in Tennessee, and Sam got a job as a clerk in a trader's store. He had his differences with his parents. He ran away to live with the Cherokees when he was fifteen. They adopted the young man into their tribe and gave him the name Kalanu, which means "Raven." –from book about Sam Houston**

Tina's Notes

Early Years
Born in Virginia in 1793
Moved with family to frontier town in Tennessee, age 13

Relations with Native Americans
Ran away to live with Cherokee
Adopted and named Kalanu, "Raven"

Prewrite **Sort your notes.** Think of two or three categories in which you can sort the information from your research. Share any new conclusions you've made with a partner.

Writing Your Focus Statement

After your research is done, you need to develop a focus statement or controlling idea to guide your writing. Your controlling idea serves as the focus for your report. Your focus statement should include an interesting topic and a special piece of information to emphasize about the topic.

Sample Focus Statements

Sam Houston, a 19th-century American soldier and statesman (an interesting topic), *helped Texas win its independence from Mexico* (the part to emphasize).

Robert Ballard, the man who found the Titanic (an interesting topic), *is both an ocean scientist and an explorer* (the part to emphasize).

Prewrite **Write your focus statement.** Review your research notes and write a statement that introduces your topic and shares a main point you want to emphasize.

Supporting Your Focus Statement

After you have developed a strong focus statement, you will need to collect evidence to support your point. Details from a variety of valid, reliable sources will make your research report interesting and informative.

Tina used her notes to find details that support her focus statement.

Sam Houston was an outstanding leader because he made decisions based on what he thought was right.
-opposed bill that would take away Native American lands
-retreated from Santa Anna's troops until he was ready to fight
-refused to sign oath of loyalty

Prewrite **Collect evidence.** Find details in your research notes that support the focus statement you have developed.

Prewriting Improving Your Focus

When you have done more research and thinking about your topic, you may find that you need to improve the focus of your research report and revise your major research question. You may need to narrow the research question because you have too much material to cover in a report. You may need to broaden the question because you have not found enough material to write your report.

Narrowing Your Research Question

Mai Ka chose U.S. President Roosevelt as the topic for her research report. Her research showed that Roosevelt had an active life as a ranch hand, explorer, writer, politician, big game hunter, and president. She created the following research question: What did Teddy Roosevelt achieve in his life?

After reading more about President Roosevelt, Mai Ka realized that this question covered too much ground. She began to look at particular parts of Roosevelt's life.

His concern for conservation
His participation in the Spanish-American War
His breaking up of big business trust funds
His helping to build the Panama Canal

Mai Ka still needed to find a focus. As she looked at the list she had written, she realized that three of the four were achieved in large part during his two terms as president. Mai Ka came up with two different questions:

What did Roosevelt achieve during his presidency?
Why is Roosevelt considered one of our greatest presidents?

Try It Look at the following research questions and revise them by narrowing the focus.

1. What is special about our national parks?
2. How did Thomas Edison come to invent the light bulb?

Broadening Your Research Question

Javier chose frontiersman Davy Crockett as his topic. Crockett, who came from Tennessee, traveled to Texas to fight at the Alamo. Javier came up with this major research question:

What did Davy Crockett do at the Alamo?

As Javier did further research about Davy Crockett, he learned that Crockett had many adventures as a frontiersman, author, and statesman before he came to the Alamo in the last year of his life. He jotted down some of these events.

- Fought in the Creek Indian War 1813–14
- Served in U.S. Congress from Tennessee for two terms, 1827–29 and 1832–34.
- Became a folk hero in his own lifetime and published his autobiography in 1834.

Javier wanted to find a research question that would touch on all these achievements in Crockett's life. This is the new, revised question he came up with:

Why was Davy Crockett a great American hero?

Ask yourself these questions as you improve the focus of your report:

- Is my research question broad enough to include everything I want to say about my topic?
- Is my research question narrow enough so that I find a clear focus for my ideas?
- Does my research question need clarifying to make it understandable both to myself and my readers?

Try It Broaden the following research questions to improve the focus of the intended research report.

1. What is unusual about the way a platypus has babies?
2. What happened when the first astronauts landed on the moon?

TEKS 7.14B
ELPS 3E

Prewriting Outlining Your Ideas

An outline is one way to organize your thinking and plan your report. You can use either a topic outline or a sentence outline to list the main ideas of your report. A **topic outline** lists ideas as words or phrases; a **sentence outline** lists them as full sentences.

Sentence Outline

Below is the first part of a sentence outline for Tina's report on pages **402–406**. Notice that the outline begins with the focus statement and then organizes ideas below it.

Focus statement	*FOCUS STATEMENT: Sam Houston was an outstanding leader because he made decisions based on what he thought was right.*
I. Topic Sentence (for second middle paragraph)	*I. Houston's actions in favor of Native Americans showed his strong sense of honor.*
A. B. C. Supporting Ideas	*A. He called Cherokee Chief Oolooteka his "Indian father."* *B. He saved many Cherokee lives by persuading them to move peacefully.* *C. As president of Texas, Houston tried to pass a treaty to preserve tribal lands from settlers.*
II. Topic Sentence (for third middle paragraph)	*II. In 1836, Houston's brave independence made him a hero in the Texas Revolution.*

Remember: In an outline, if you have a I, you must have at least a II. If you have an A, you must have at least a B.

Prewrite

Create your outline. Write a sentence outline for your report, using the details from your research. Consult with a partner to make sure that each topic sentence (I, II, III, . . .) supports the focus statement and that each detail (A, B, C, . . .) supports the topic sentence above it. Use your outline as a guide when you write the first draft of your report.

TEKS 7.22B, 7.24B
ELPS 3H

Evaluating the Validity of Sources

As you do your research, you will find a wide variety of sources. Before you use information from these sources, you will need to evaluate them for reliability and validity. Certain elements will help you to do this successfully.

- **Publication date.** Information is changing all the time. A more recent publication date doesn't mean the information in the work is necessarily better, but it is probably more up-to-date.
- **Language.** The word choices an author makes will tell you a lot about his or her expertise and attitude toward the subject. If, for example, the author gives strong opinions, he or she may be biased. A biased author affects the validity of a source.
- **Coverage.** A book that deals with many topics may not be as useful as one that deals only with the topic you are researching.
- **Point of view.** Point of view in a research source should be as objective as possible. For example, if the author has some connection to the topic, it can be both good and bad. He or she will have inside information many others won't have, but may also be biased either for or against the subject.

Try It Read the descriptions of sources below and decide which is a valid source for research and which is not. Explain your thinking to a partner.

Don Taylor's book *UFOs—Real or Science Fiction?,* published in 2005, offers a thorough look at unidentified flying objects (UFOs). As a research scientist, Taylor has interviewed many people who have reported seeing UFOs and offers a balanced view of this intriguing phenomenon.

Phil Racine's *The Inside Story on UFOs,* published in 1990, argues that UFOs exist and that the government is trying to cover up their existence. He describes in detail his own abduction by aliens in a UFO. Racine is a novelist and UFO enthusiast.

TEKS 7.23C, 7.25D

Citing Sources in Your Report

As you write, remember to give credit to the sources you quote directly or paraphrase in your report.

When You Have All the Information

- The most common type of credit (citation) lists the author's last name and the page number in parentheses.

  Two hundred people were evacuated from the hospital during the hurricane (Oliver 29).

- If you already name the author in your report, just include the page number in parentheses.

  Author Isla Hernandez explains . . . Vitamin D is an important vitamin for both men and women (120).

When Some Information Is Missing

- Some sources do not list an author. In those cases, use the title and page number. (If the title is long, use only the first word or two.)

  The Sahara Desert made it difficult for people in North Africa to communicate with people in South Africa ("History" 39).

- Some sources (especially Internet sites) do not use page numbers. In those cases, list just the author.

  The recycling program is crucial to making our community a responsible, Earth-friendly place to live (Linzer).

- If a source does not list the author or page number, use the title.

  People remember her as a great diplomat, a fierce war leader, and a strong ruler ("Kingdom").

Notice that in each of the examples above, the period comes after the parentheses that include the title or author credit.

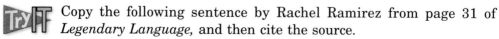

Try It Copy the following sentence by Rachel Ramirez from page 31 of *Legendary Language,* and then cite the source.

The President's words have proven to be one of the most influential speeches of all time.

TEKS 7.14C

Go Online!

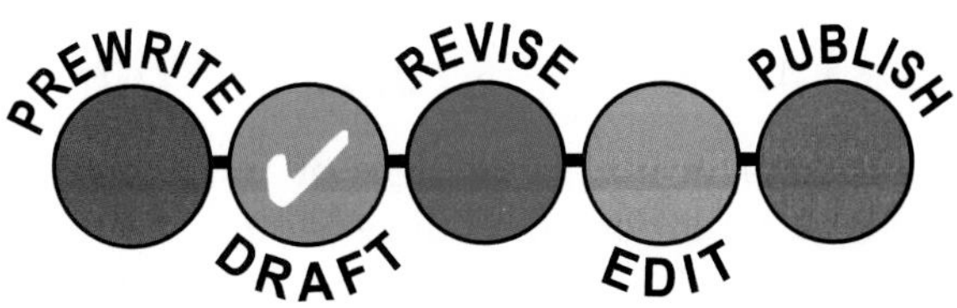

Drafting

With your research and planning finished, it's time to write the first draft of your report. This is your chance to share your information and thoughts with other people. As you write, keep the following points in mind.

Keys to Effective Drafting

1. *Write with your purpose, form, and audience in mind. Ask yourself these questions as you write:*
   - *Who will read your research report?*
   - *What is their purpose for reading it?*
2. *Use your first paragraph to grab your reader's attention, introduce your topic, and present your controlling idea.*
3. *Start each paragraph with a topic sentence.*
4. *In your ending paragraph, explain how the person has contributed to history.*
5. *Remember to cite the sources of any ideas you paraphrase or quote. List your sources alphabetically on a works-cited page.*

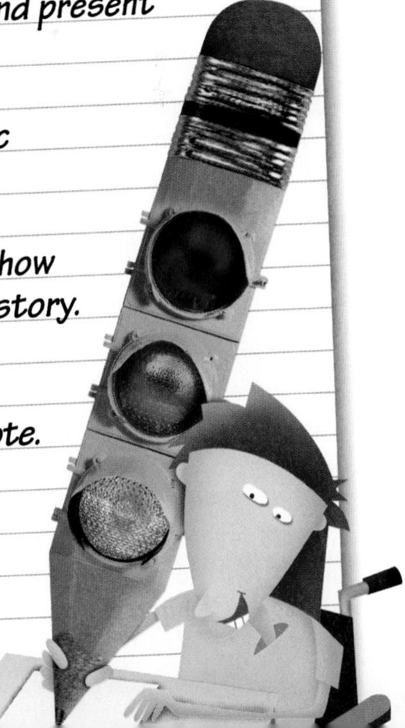

TEKS 7.14A, 7.17A(i), 7.17A(ii), 7.25D

Drafting Starting Your Research Report

The opening paragraph of your report should grab the reader's attention, introduce your topic, and contain a clear controlling idea. This is your focus statement. To start your opening paragraph, try one of the following approaches.

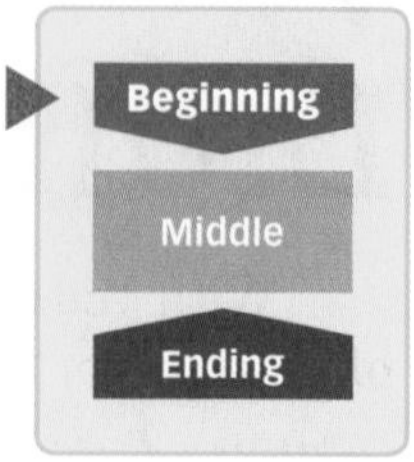

- **Start with an interesting fact.**
  Sam Houston was the only person to serve as governor of two different states.
- **Ask a question about your topic.**
  Why is Houston, a hero in the 1800s, still beloved by Texans today?
- **Start with a quotation that will grab your reader's attention.**
  "Do right, and risk consequences," was Sam Houston's motto.

Tina decided to begin her opening paragraph with an interesting fact.

Beginning Paragraph

The beginning paragraph starts with an interesting fact and ends with the focus statement (underlined).

He was the only person to serve as governor of two different states. He was the only person to be both the governor of a state and the president of an independent nation. One of the largest cities in the United States is named after him. He was Sam Houston, and he is beloved by Texans as one of the founders of our state. Many factors made him a leader, such as being a good speaker. However, the most important factor may have been his independent spirit. Sam Houston was an outstanding leader because he made decisions based on what he thought was right.

Write your opening paragraph. Use one of the strategies listed above to start your paragraph. After you grab the reader's attention, be sure to introduce your topic. End your paragraph with a clear focus statement.

TEKS 7.14B, 7.25D

Developing the Middle Part

Begin the middle part of your report with background information, starting with where and when your subject lived, and how that person became involved in her or his work. Then provide details that build on these ideas and create a focused report.

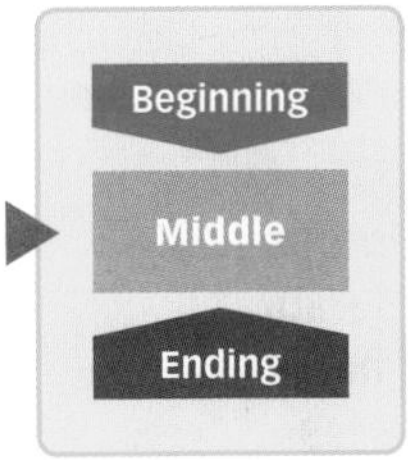

Each middle paragraph should include a topic sentence that covers one main idea. Support the topic sentence using facts, details, and quotations. Be sure to cite the source of any quotations you include.

Middle Paragraphs

This middle paragraph explains the subject's background and correctly cites a source.

All the details support the topic sentence (underlined).

Houston's Background

Born in 1793 in Virginia, Houston moved with his family to Tennessee as a child. At one point he ran away and lived with the Cherokee, who adopted him into their tribe. They gave him the name Kalanu, which means "Raven" (Brown 32).

As a young man, Houston entered law and politics in Tennessee. He rejoined the Cherokee for three years as a government agent, then moved to Texas. There, he commanded the army during the Texas Revolution and, in April 1836, won the Battle of San Jacinto and thus won the war. He was elected the first president of the Republic of Texas, and then governor and senator when Texas became a state. Throughout his experiences, Houston did what he thought was right, not what others thought he should do.

TEKS 7.25D

In this paragraph, the writer cites information from a source without interrupting her flow of ideas.

Houston's Accomplishments

Houston's actions in favor of Native Americans showed his strong sense of honor. Because of his experiences among the Cherokee, Houston became a lifelong supporter of Native American rights. He idolized the Cherokee chief, Oolooteka, whom he called his "Indian father" (Krantz). At the time, many European-Americans were prejudiced against Native Americans. In contrast, Houston took actions to help them. In 1817, the U.S. government moved the Cherokee from Tennessee to the Arkansas Territory. President Andrew Jackson put Houston in charge of the operation. Houston undoubtedly saved Cherokee lives by persuading them to move peacefully.

Tina used a quotation to help the reader understand Houston's character.

In 1838, Houston tried to defend Native American rights by fighting, unsuccessfully, for a treaty that would preserve tribal lands (Brown 254–256). Then, as a U.S. Senator, Houston argued against the Kansas-Nebraska Bill because it took away Native American lands. "I am aware that in presenting myself as the advocate of the Indians and their rights . . . I shall stand very much alone," he said (356). Being alone did not change his stand.

Houston's brave independence made him a hero in the Texas Revolution. In March 1836, the Alamo fell, and civilians were fleeing east to escape the Mexican army led

TEKS 7.14B, 7.25D

by Santa Anna. Houston ordered his army to retreat. It was an unpopular move. He made a stand at the Brazos River, but after declaring, "I don't intend to leave the Brazos," he retreated farther east. The president of the revolutionary government wrote Houston a letter saying, "Sir, the enemy is laughing you to scorn . . . You must retreat no further" (200). Still, Houston kept retreating because he felt it was the right strategy. Then, on April 19, he stopped and prepared to face the enemy "though the odds are greatly against us" (204). Two days later, he attacked Santa Anna by surprise near the San Jacinto River, and won. By following his own judgment all the way, Houston gained freedom for Texas.

As governor of Texas, Houston followed his conscience about an even larger struggle—the Civil War. Houston argued against Texas seceding from the Union because he foresaw that the South would lose. In February 1861, the people of Texas voted for secession, and in March, Governor Houston refused to sign an oath of loyalty to the Confederacy. As a result, he was removed from office.

The fourth middle paragraph builds on the idea that Houston does what he thinks is right despite what others think.

Draft **Write your middle paragraphs.** **Continue to support your controlling idea to develop a focused report.**

TEKS 7.14C, 7.17A(i), 7.25B

Drafting Ending Your Research Report

Your ending paragraph should bring your report to a thoughtful conclusion. Try one or more of the following ideas in your closing paragraph.

- Remind the reader about the overall point or focus of the report.
- Give relevant reasons for the conclusions that you have made.
- Explain the person's contribution to history.

Beginning

Middle

Ending

Ending Paragraph

The ending paragraph sums up the report and tells the reader one last interesting fact.

Houston's Legacy

After Houston was removed from office, he retired, and died peacefully two years later. His inspiring example lives on, not just because he was an important leader, but because he stood for doing the right thing. Texas Governor Rick Perry, in his 2003 State of the State Address, quoted Houston's motto, "Do right, and risk consequences." Sam Houston was born more than two centuries ago, but his spirit lives on in Texas.

Draft **Write your final paragraph.** Bring your research report to a close. Include a conclusion that is supported by relevant reasons.

Draft **Look over your report.** Read your report, focusing on how well you have addressed your questions of audience, purpose, and form. Note ideas for revisions.

Creating Your Works-Cited Page

A works-cited page should be included with your research report. This page lists all the sources you used in your research report. The following two pages show the proper format for common types of sources. Notice that the second line and additional lines for each source are indented.

Encyclopedia

Author (if available). Article title (in quotation marks). Title of the encyclopedia (underlined or in italics if typed). Edition (if available). Date published. Type of source.

"Samuel Houston." Columbia Encyclopedia. 7th ed. 2008. Print.

Books

Author or editor (last name first). Title (underlined or in italics if typed). City where the book was published: Publisher, copyright date. Type of source.

Brown, Marion. The Life and Times of Sam Houston. New York: Review Row, 1993. Print.

NOTE Include a state abbreviation (or country) after the city if needed for clarity.

Magazines

Author (last name first). Article title (in quotation marks). Title of the magazine (underlined or in italics if typed), Date (day, month, year): Page numbers of the article. Type of source.

Fowler, M. "Do right." Texas Review, 3 Feb. 2009: 8–12. Print.

TEKS 7.23C

Internet

Author (if available). Page title (if available, in quotation marks). Site title (underlined or in italics if typed). Name of sponsor (if available). Date published (if available). Type of source. Date found.

Krantz, Mitchell. "Houston, Samuel." Texas Tribune. Texas History Society. May 2008. Web. April 2010.

Draft

Format your sources. Check your report and your list of sources (from page 395) to see which sources you actually used. Then follow these directions.

1. Write your sources using the guidelines above and on the previous page. You can write them on a sheet of paper or on note cards.
2. Alphabetize your sources.
3. Create your works-cited page. (See the example below.)

Works Cited

Brown, Marion. The Life and Times of Sam Houston. New York: Review Row, 1993. Print.

Fowler, M. "Do right." Texas Review, 3 Feb. 2009: 8–10. Print.

Krantz, Mitchell. "Houston, Samuel." Texas Tribune. Texas History Society. May 2008. Web. April 2010.

Perry, Rick. "State of the State Address." Office of Governor Rick Perry. 11 Feb. 2003. Web. April 2010.

Go Online!

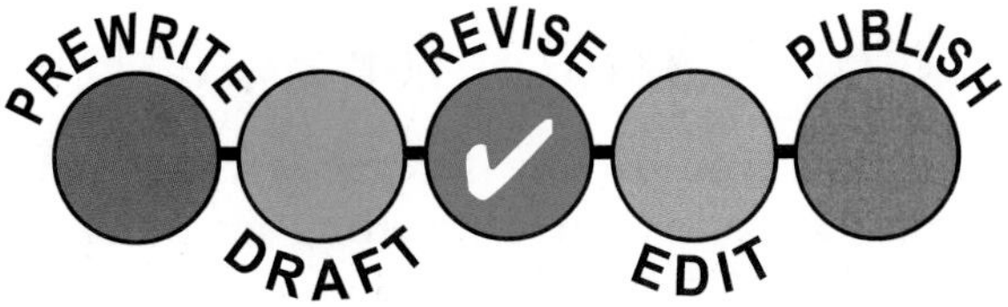

Revising

A good research report needs more than one draft. The first time through, you work mainly with organization and ideas. In the second draft, you fill in missing information, rearrange ideas for clarity, and polish your voice. Take the time to make your report as good as it can be.

Keys to Effective Revising

1. *Read your entire draft to get an overall sense of your report.*
2. *Review your controlling idea to be sure that it clearly states the main point you want to emphasize.*
3. *Check that you have enough evidence to support your focus statement.*
4. *Make sure your beginning draws readers in. Then check that your ending brings your report to an interesting close.*
5. *Make sure you sound knowledgeable and interested in the topic.*
6. *Check for inconsistencies in your paragraphs.*

TEKS 7.17A(iii), 7.25B
ELPS 3E

Texas Traits

Revising for Focus and Coherence

When you revise for *focus and coherence*, you make sure that all details relate to your controlling idea and that you have removed any details that do not.

Have I checked for inconsistencies?

In a research report, a detail that does not connect with the controlling idea may confuse your reader. If your reader can not follow the flow of ideas, he or she may lose interest in your report.

Try It Read this paragraph about poison ivy. Find details that are inconsistent with the main idea. Share your findings with a partner.

> The poison ivy plant is poisonous to touch, causing allergic reactions in many people. Other skin conditions are insect bites and reactions to lotions. The poison can also stay on clothes and affect a person up to one year after the clothes contacted the poison ivy. Certain laundry detergents could also cause reactions from clothes.

Revise **Check for consistency. Make sure each detail in your report tells about the topic you have selected. Delete any inconsistencies you find.**

Have I gathered evidence for the topic?

When revising, you may find places where information should be added to provide evidence of your conclusions. Look back at your research notes to find details that help your reader understand your conclusions.

A paragraph in Tina's draft dealt with Houston's relations with the Native Americans. Tina added the underlined detail to provide evidence of Houston helping the Cherokee.

> . . . In contrast, Houston took actions to help them. In 1817, the United States government moved the Cherokee from Tennessee to the Arkansas Territory. President Andrew Jackson put Houston in charge of the operation. <u>Houston undoubtedly saved many Cherokee lives by persuading them to move peacefully.</u>

Now the reader can clearly see how Tina made the conclusion about Houston helping the Cherokee.

Revise **Check for evidence. Make sure each conclusion you have made is supported by evidence. If you find a point that needs more support, look back at your research notes to find evidence.**

TEKS 7.17A(v), 7.25D
ELPS 3E

Have I used a variety of transitions?

A research report should read smoothly and hold the reader's interest. There must be a continuous flow of ideas, each idea leading logically to the next. One way to do this is to use a variety of transitions to link paragraphs.

One transition technique is to state the main idea at the end of a paragraph and then repeat the same idea in a different way at the start of the next paragraph.

> . . . Juan Seguin led his troops as they fought on the Texan side in the Battle of the Alamo. Although originally from Mexico, Seguin was fiercely loyal to Texas.
>
> Seguin later showed his continued loyalty to Texas as he served as Justice of the Peace in Bexar County . . .

Revise **Check your transitions.** **Review your draft. Make sure you have used a variety of transitions to link your ideas from paragraph to paragraph.**

Do the quotations I used flow with my ideas?

It is important to make sure that any quotations you include in your report do not interrupt your flow of ideas. Quotations should help support the points in your report, rather than distract the reader.

Try It Read the following paragraph from Monica's report. Then read the quotation Monica found in her research. Discuss with a partner how Monica could use the quotation in her writing without interrupting her flow of ideas.

> Obedience training is an important step in owning and caring for a dog. Many pet owners feel that having a trained dog allows them to feel in control of their pet in any situation. An obedient dog gives owners the confidence to take their dogs into many different environments.

> "Obedience training allowed me to have control in any situation."
> –Leann Duncan, pet owner

Revise **Check your quotations.** **Review your draft. Make sure that the quotations you have included add to your points and do not distract the reader.**

TEKS 7.25A

Texas Traits Revising for Organization

When you revise for *organization,* you check that all the facts and details in your research report are connected. The details in your report should also link back to the focus statement.

Do my conclusions relate to my focus statement?

The following is the focus statement for Tina's report on Sam Houston:

> Sam Houston was an outstanding leader because he made decisions based on what he thought was right.

The second paragraph of Tina's draft deals with Houston's early life and summarizes some of his achievements. Although it offers examples of his independent spirit, it never states this as a main idea. Tina decided to add this sentence which restates the focus statement in different words:

> Throughout his experiences, Houston did what he thought was right, not what others thought he should do.

As Tina reviewed the draft, she decided that each paragraph needed a topic sentence that related to the focus statement. Read these topic sentences.

> **Third paragraph:** Houston's action in favor of Native Americans showed his strong sense of honor.

> **Fourth paragraph:** In 1836, Houston's brave independence made him a hero in the Texas Revolution.

Each topic sentence draws a conclusion about a quality that is described by the events in the paragraph. These sentences also support the controlling idea that Houston was an outstanding leader because he did what he thought was right.

Revise

Revise paragraphs. Review your paragraphs to see if each has a clear topic sentence that is supported by the details and that relates to the focus statement. Revise as necessary.

How can I use headings to organize my report?

Headings that summarize sections of your report will help your reader better understand. The headings should be brief and give the reader an idea of what the section will be about.

D'Jon wrote his research report about the space program and NASA. He used the following headings to help his readers better understand the sections of his report.

Early Thinking about Space
The Space Race
First Human in Space
First Space Flight
Animals in Space
Current Developments

Try IT Read the descriptions of sections from Lily's research report about rocks and minerals. Think of an interesting heading for each section that will help the reader understand what the section will be about.

Different types of rocks: sedimentary, metamorphic, igneous
Locations where rocks are found
Uses for different rocks and minerals

Organization
Headings are added to help the reader's understanding.

Houston's Accomplishments
^
Houston's actions in favor of Native Americans showed his strong sense of honor. Because of his experiences among the Cherokee, Houston became a lifelong supporter of Native American rights.

Revise **Write headings.** Add headings to your research report. Make sure the headings briefly summarize the main ideas of each section.

TEKS 7.17A(v)
ELPS 3E

Revising for Development of Ideas

When you revise for the *development of ideas,* you look for ways to make your writing more interesting for your reader. One way to do this is to use rhetorical devices, such as hyperbole or alliteration. These techniques may improve the sound of your writing.

Can I use rhetorical devices to improve my writing?

Rhetorical devices can help your words become more powerful. Your reader may understand your points in a new and different way. Here are some rhetorical devices you can use.

- **Anaphora: the repetition of the same word or words at the beginning of successive sentences**

  She was the first African American congresswoman to come from the South. She was an advocate for minorities and the poor . . . She was Barbara Jordan.

- **Metanoia: qualifying a statement by recalling it and expressing it in a stronger way**

  William B. Travis was a great Texan; no, he was a great American.

- **Hyperbole: the exaggeration of something for emphasis or effect**

  The governor fearlessly stood up against the world for what he believed was right.

- **Alliteration: the repetition of the same sounds at the beginning of words**

  Poison ivy puts panic in minds of people.

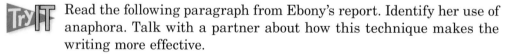

Try It Read the following paragraph from Ebony's report. Identify her use of anaphora. Talk with a partner about how this technique makes the writing more effective.

The people of Galveston will never forget the Hurricane of 1900. They remember the loss of lives. They remember the damage to the island. They remember that the seawall was built to protect them.

Revise **Use a rhetorical device.** Rewrite a sentence or paragraph from your research report using one or more of the rhetorical devices described above.

How can I use simile, metaphor, and personification as I revise?

To make your writing more interesting and engaging for the reader, you may choose to use similes, metaphors, or personification. Below are explanations of each of these rhetorical devices.

- **Simile: a comparison between two things that are different but that resemble each other in some way. Similes use the words *like* or *as*.**

  The sky was as black as coal when the clouds rolled in.

  Citizens fled like a herd of frightened cattle to escape the storm.

- **Metaphor: a comparison between two things that does not use *like* or *as***

  The highway was a river of cars as people evacuated.

  The rifle shots, distant thunder before the storm, could be heard a mile away.

- **Personification: representing animals or inanimate objects as having human characteristics**

  The thundercloud vented its anger with a flash of lightning.

  The car blinked its lights and roared ahead.

Development of Ideas
A metaphor is added to maintain the reader's interest.

"I am aware that in presenting myself as the advocate of the Indians and their rights . . . I shall stand very much alone," he said (356). Being alone did not change his stand. ^ *He was a pillar of strength.*

Revise **Try simile, metaphor, or personification.** Review your draft for places where you could use a simile, a metaphor, or personification.

TEKS 7.14E, 7.25A

Texas Traits

Revising for Voice

When you revise for *voice,* you check to make sure your writing "sounds" like you.

Research reports are mainly meant to provide information. While the voice can be friendly and interesting, it must also have some degree of authority so that readers know that the information is factual and can be trusted.

Is my personal voice heard in my report?

In her report, Tina used a voice that was informative, but not overly formal. To give her voice more authority, she included quotations from Houston and others.

Here are examples of Tina's voice and how the same text written by another writer might have been less effective.

Strong Voice: In 1836, Houston's brave independence made him a hero in the Texas Revolution.

Weak Voice: In 1836, Houston helped to win the Texas Revolution.

Strong Voice: After Houston was removed from office, he retired, and died peacefully two years later. However, his inspiring example lives on, not just because he was an important leader, but because he stood for doing the right thing.

Weak Voice: After Houston was removed from the governorship he retired, and later died. However, he lives on as an important leader.

Tina also asked her teacher to listen as she read her report aloud. Tina used her teacher's feedback to identify additional places she could improve her writing voice.

Revise

Check for voice. Review your draft to look for examples of strong and weak voice. Revise sentences or paragraphs to give your report a friendly but authoritative voice. Consider your focus statement as you work on the revisions. If possible, read your report aloud to your teacher and revise based on his or her feedback.

TEKS 7.17A(iv), 7.25A

Have I effectively paraphrased my sources?

When you paraphrase, you take facts and details from various sources and blend them together in your own voice.

In her research, Tina found the following information:

Texas seceded from the United States on February 1, 1861, and while he disagreed vehemently with this decision, Sam Houston did not fight it. "I love Texas too well to bring civil strife and bloodshed upon her . . ." he said. He was evicted from office on March 16, 1861 for refusing to take an oath of loyalty to the Confederacy.

Another source had this to say about what happened next:

President Lincoln, through an intermediary, offered to send 50,000 troops to prevent Texas' secession, but Houston turned down the offer. "Allow me to most respectfully decline any such assistance of the United States Government," he wrote to Lincoln. He knew that the war would bring enough violence to his beloved state, and he didn't want to make it worse.

Tina combined the details from these two sources and paraphrased the information. In this case, Tina was also able to simplify some information.

In February 1861, the people of Texas voted for secession, and in March, Governor Houston refused to sign an oath of loyalty to the Confederacy. As a result, he was removed from office. President Lincoln offered to send troops to keep Houston in office and to keep Texas from seceding, but once again, Houston followed his own idea of what was right. He refused the offer, because he did not want to trigger violence.

Revise

Paraphrase information. Read through your report, paying special attention to places where you have paraphrased. Make sure your paraphrased writing is effective. Revise as necessary.

Revising Using a Checklist

Revise **Check your revising.** On a piece of paper, write the numbers 1 to 9. If you can answer "yes" to a question, put a check mark next to that number. If not, continue to work with that part of your essay.

Focus and Coherence

_____ **1.** Have I included a strong focus statement?

_____ **2.** Have I included only relevant ideas with no inconsistencies?

_____ **3.** Do I need to add details to provide more support for my focus statement?

Organization

_____ **4.** Are all sentences in a paragraph linked and supportive of the focus statement?

_____ **5.** Does each paragraph transition logically to the next one?

Development of Ideas

_____ **6.** Have I developed my ideas in depth?

_____ **7.** Have I used rhetorical devices to add emphasis?

Voice

_____ **8.** Does my voice come through in information I've paraphrased?

_____ **9.** Does my voice show authority with the topic?

Revise **Make a clean copy.** When you've finished revising your report, make a clean copy before you begin to edit.

Go Online!

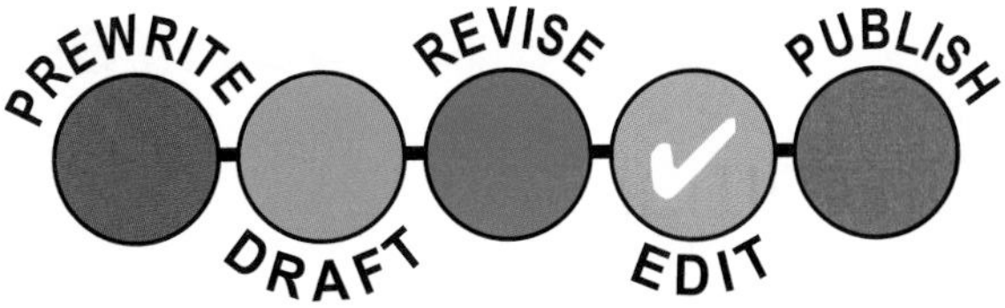

Editing

Once you have finished revising your report, edit your work for conventions like grammar, punctuation, capitalization, and spelling.

Keys to Effective Editing

1. *Use a dictionary, a thesaurus, your computer's spell-checker, and the "Proofreader's Guide" in the back of this book.*
2. *Read your research report out loud and listen for words or phrases that may be incorrect.*
3. *Look for errors in grammar, mechanics, sentence structure, and spelling.*
4. *Check that you have used quotation marks correctly.*
5. *If you use a computer, edit on a printed computer copy. Then enter your changes on the computer.*
6. *Use the editing and proofreading marks inside the back cover of this book.*

TEKS 7.14D, 7.19A(i), 7.19C

Texas Traits

Editing for Conventions

Grammar

When you edit for *grammar,* you make sure you use nouns, verbs, pronouns, adjectives, adverbs, and all other parts of speech correctly.

Have I used consistent tenses in my sentences?

When you edit your writing, look out for inconsistent verb tenses within the same sentence or from one sentence to another.

Incorrect Sam Houston *was* a friend to the Cherokee and *tries* to help them.

Correct Sam Houston *was* a friend to the Cherokee and *tried* to help them.

Incorrect Davy Crockett *makes* the long journey to the Alamo. He *wanted* to be a part of the fight for Texas independence.

Correct Davy Crockett *made* the long journey to the Alamo. He *wanted* to be a part of the fight for Texas independence.

Edit **Check for consistent tense. Read through your research report. Make sure the tenses in your sentences are consistent.**

Have I used progressive verbs correctly?

The progressive verb tense is used to show ongoing action. Below, you will see that progressive verbs can be used to express present, past, or future.

- *Present progressive* describes action happening at the same time the sentence is written.

  Dr. Mayer is researching the effects of sunshine on mood.

- *Past progressive* describes a past action that was happening at the same time as another event.

  Dr. Mayer was researching the effects of sunshine on mood while Dr. Rodriguez studied depression in rats.

- *Future progressive* describes a continuous action that will take place in the future.

  Dr. Mayer will be presenting his findings at a conference in May.

Edit **Check your progressive verbs. Make sure you have used present, past, and future progressive verbs correctly.**

TEKS 7.19A(iv)
ELPS 3C

Have I used conjunctive adverbs correctly?

A conjunctive adverb is an adverb that joins together two clauses in a sentence. Conjunctive adverbs help to make a logical connection between ideas.

John set the table and then made the salad.

We arrived late and consequently missed the first scene of the play.

Here are some common conjunctive adverbs:

also	besides	certainly	finally	instead
next	now	still	otherwise	therefore

GRAMMAR Try It Copy the following paragraph and underline the conjunctive adverbs.

Sleep is an important activity that indeed we all need. The ideal amount of sleep is eight hours a night; however, many people get by with far less. Too little sleep can impair your performance; furthermore, it can affect your health.

Edit **Use conjunctive adverbs. Edit your sentences to add conjunctive adverbs where they will make your writing stronger.**

Learning Language

Sometimes writing includes many short and choppy sentences. If all your sentences are too short, the reader may become bored and lose track of what you are trying to say. You can use conjunctive adverbs to combine some shorter sentences and make your writing flow better. With a partner, discuss how to combine the following sentence pairs using a conjunctive adverb.

1. We climbed the trail all day long. We reached the top of the mountain.
2. Gregory has to study for his test. He could get a bad grade on the test.

TEKS 7.17A(v)

Sentence Structure

When you edit for *sentence structure*, you correct errors in sentences. You can also make sure you have used a variety of sentence types to make your writing more interesting.

Have I used a variety of sentences?

A research report, like any piece of writing, needs variety to hold the reader's interest. Writing that has only one kind of sentence becomes boring to read. Try to use different kinds of sentences when you write.

Simple sentence: **Steven Spielberg is a famous filmmaker.**

Compound sentence: **Spielberg went to college in California, but he left school to pursue a career in film.**

Complex sentence: **After making short independent films for several years, Spielberg began to direct episodes of television series in his early twenties.**

Compound-complex sentence: **Spielberg's big break came in 1975, when he directed a film about a killer shark, and it became a box office smash.**

Try It Read the paragraph below from a research report on Steven Spielberg. Then rewrite it by combining sentences to create a variety of different kinds of sentences.

Steven Spielberg has been a top filmmaker for more than three decades. He directed his first adventure film in 1981. He has made three more films in that series since then. The latest one was released in 2008. Spielberg has made more serious films, too. He made a film about American soldiers in World War II. He also made a movie about the Holocaust. It earned seven Academy Awards.

Edit **Vary your sentences.** **Edit your sentences to include a variety of sentence types.**

Mechanics: Punctuation

Have I used commas correctly?

Commas are punctuation marks that are used to show items in a series or to separate parts of a sentence. Introductory words are examples of sentence parts that use commas.

No, I won't be able to go to the game.

Hey, what are you doing here?

Try IT Write one sentence with correct commas for each of the following introductory words: please, yes, oh.

Have I used colons and semicolons correctly?

Semicolons are punctuation marks that act like a combination of a comma and period. They create less of a pause than a period, but more of a pause than a comma does. Semicolons are useful for research reports and other nonfiction writing. They separate two sentence clauses while showing a relationship between the two.

Pigs are misunderstood animals; they are actually very clean and extremely smart.

They have a good reason for rolling in mud; it protects their skin from being burned by the sun.

Colons are punctuation marks that create a longer, more dramatic pause than a semicolon. They are mostly used as introductory devices.

- **Items in a list.** *We brought the following items on our camping trip: food, sleeping bags, and a change of clothes.*
- **Quotations that are long or formal.** *At the end of his speech, the president declared: ". . . someday years from now our children can tell their children that this was the time when we performed, in the words that are carved into this very chamber, 'something worthy to be remembered.'"*
- **Appositives that introduce a person or thing.** *My presentation is about a a great leader of our state: Lyndon B. Johnson.*

Edit **Check your punctuation.** Check your sentences for correct punctuation. Add, delete, or move commas, semicolons, and colons where needed.

Editing Using a Checklist

Edit

Check your editing. On a piece of paper, write the numbers 1 to 7. If you can answer "yes" to a question, put a check mark next to that number. If not, continue to work on that part of your research report.

Conventions

GRAMMAR

____ **1.** Do I keep tenses consistent within sentences and from sentence to sentence?

____ **2.** Do I use progressive verbs correctly?

____ **3.** Do I use conjunctive adverbs correctly?

MECHANICS

____ **4.** Do I use commas and other punctuation marks correctly in compound and complex sentences?

____ **5.** Do I use semicolons to separate two related clauses in a sentence?

____ **6.** Do I use colons before items in a list, before some quotations, and before introductory clauses?

SENTENCE STRUCTURE

____ **7.** Have I used a variety of simple, compound, complex, and compound-complex sentences?

Creating a Title

- Use strong, vivid words: **The Honor of Houston**
- Give the words rhythm: **Houston: Homegrown Hero**
- Be imaginative: **A Pillar of Strength**

Go Online!

Publishing

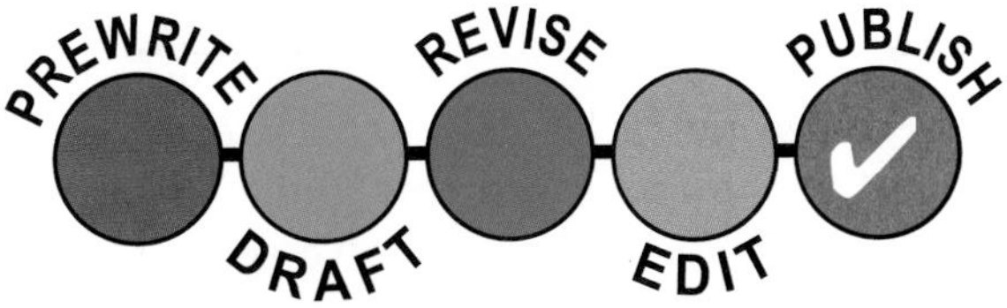

Sharing Your Report

After you have worked to write and improve your report, you'll want to make a neat-looking final copy to share. You may also decide to prepare your report as an electronic presentation, an online essay, or an illustrated report.

Publish **Make a final copy. Use the following guidelines to format your report. Create a clean final copy and carefully proofread it.**

Focus on Presentation

- **Use blue or black ink and double-space the entire paper.**
- **Write your name and the date in the upper left corner of page 1. Include any other information your teacher requires.**
- **Skip a line and center your title; skip another line and start your writing.**
- **Indent every paragraph and leave a one-inch margin on all four sides.**
- **For a research report, you should write your last name and the page number in the upper right corner of every page after page 1.**

Creating a Title Page

If your teacher requires a title page, follow his or her requirements. Usually you center the title one-third of the way down from the top of the page. Then go two-thirds of the way down and center your name, your teacher's name, the name of the class, and the date. Put each piece of information on a separate line.

An Independent Leader

Tina Trueba
Mr. Salazar
Language Arts
May 4, 2010

Go Online!
Upload your research report for others to read.

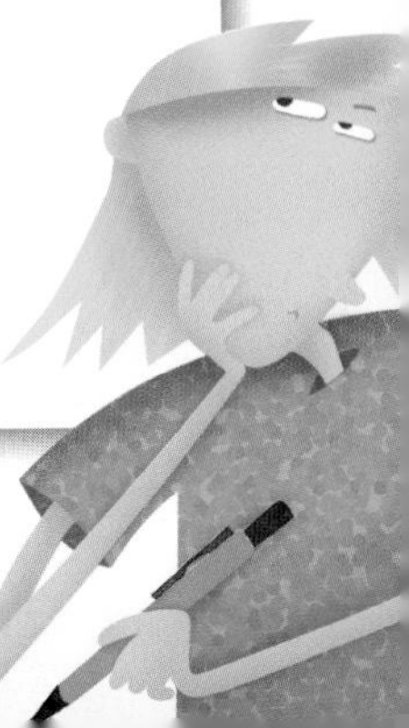

RESEARCH

Evaluating and Reflecting on Your Writing

You've put a lot of time and effort into your research report. Now take some time to score and think about your writing. On your own paper, finish each sentence starter below. To score your writing, refer to the scoring rubric on pages 48–49.

My Research Report

1. *The best score for my research report is . . .*

2. *It's the best score because . . .*

3. *The best part of my research report is . . .*

4. *The part that still needs work is . . .*

5. *The most important thing I learned about writing a research report is . . .*

Making Oral Presentations

"The world famous Flying Ling has just crawled into the loudspeaker. He gives the signal. The fuse is lit. This is one oral presentation that should start off with a bang . . . "

Luckily, when you make an oral presentation, you won't have to crawl into a loudspeaker, but you might feel like crawling under a rock. "Stage fright" happens to everyone. Careful preparation is the key to overcoming this feeling and creating an effective oral presentation. This chapter will lead you through the process. With a little work, your presentation will be a big hit!

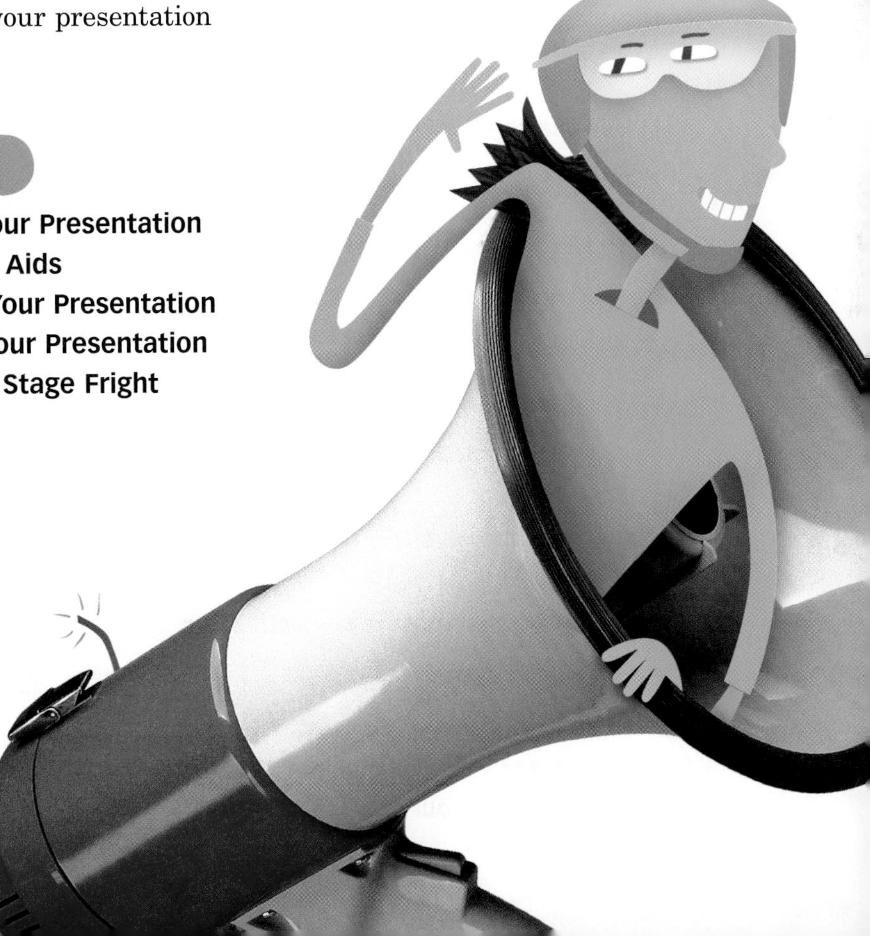

What's Ahead

- Preparing Your Presentation
- Using Visual Aids
- Organizing Your Presentation
- Delivering Your Presentation
- Overcoming Stage Fright

Preparing Your Presentation

Preparing a presentation from a research report is different than writing a speech from scratch. You already have a topic, you've gathered lots of information, and you know the type of speech you will make. Here are some tips to help you shape the information from your report into a good presentation.

- Grab your listeners' attention with an opening question or a surprising fact.
- Know how much time you have to give your presentation.
- Emphasize your most important points and cut unneeded information.
- Mark your paper for visual aids or gestures.

Using Your Research

Below are some notes (on white paper) that Tina wrote during her research. For her presentation, she will draw a conclusion that will interest her audience. Notice Tina's notes (on gold paper) for her presentation.

An Independent Leader

He was the only person to serve as governor of two different states. He was the only person to be both the governor of a state and the president of an independent nation. One of the largest cities in the United States is named after him. He was Sam Houston, and he is beloved by Texans as one of the founders of our state. Many factors made him a leader, such as being a good speaker. However, the

Here's a question for you: Who was the only American to serve as both the governor of a state and the president of an independent nation? The answer is Sam Houston. His name lives on all over our state—even as one of the largest cities in the United States. Houston deserves these honors. He was a great leader with an independent spirit. He made decisions based on what he thought was right.

Look back at your research notes. Decide if there is a new conclusion you want to share with your audience. Also, review your report for points you want to use in your presentation.

TEKS 7.14E, 7.25A

Using Visual Aids

To make your research report work orally, you will need to summarize your findings for your presentation. Visual aids are a good tool for paraphrasing and summarizing your research report for your audience. Visual aids should be informative, but also hold your audience's attention.

Visual aids like those listed below are informative and will hold your audience's interest.

Posters	show words, pictures, or both.
Photographs	help your audience "see" who or what you are talking about.
Charts	compare ideas or explain main points.
Transparencies	highlight key words, ideas, or graphics.
Maps	show specific places being discussed.

Here are some tips for preparing your visual aids.

1. **Bigger is better.** Be sure your visual aids can be seen by the people in the back row.
2. **Keep the wording simple.** Use labels that summarize your points.
3. **Make your visual aids eye-catching.** Colorful and attractive designs are the key.
4. **Ask for help.** Have a classmate or teacher look at your visual aids. Make adjustments based on feedback you receive.

Create visual aids. Decide on visual aids that will show your conclusions effectively. When you have made a draft of your visual aid, ask a classmate or teacher for feedback. Revise as needed.

TEKS 7.25B

Organizing Your Presentation

Now that you've written some notes and created visual aids, you're ready to organize your presentation. *Remember:* An informative presentation is meant to be listened to, not read. It must be simple, dramatic, and well organized. Use the following tips.

1. **Start strong.** Grab the audience's attention and keep it.
2. **Gather evidence to explain the topic.** Synthesize and summarize research in a logical order and use transitions to guide your audience from one idea to another.
3. **End even stronger.** Your ending should top your opening with something memorable.

Using Note Cards

Putting information on note cards is a simple and an effective way to organize your oral presentation. Don't use the same cards you used to write your research report. Instead, synthesize and boil down the facts and details from those cards into a concise organization. Keep important ideas but drop less important ones. Use supportive details, but just pick the strongest ones. Tina did this and gave her presentation using the new note cards as a guide.

Note-Card Guidelines

- Write out your entire introduction on the first note card.
- Use a separate card for each of the main ideas that follow.
- Number each card and write the main idea at the top. Add specific details for that idea underneath.
- Note your visual aids on appropriate cards, with instructions for what to do with each one.
- Write out your entire ending on the last note card.

Create your note cards. Look over Tina's note cards on the next page. Then create cards that synthesize information from your research report for each step in your presentation. Be sure to add notes to yourself about using visual aids. Also, write a memorable ending.

Organizing Your Note Cards

Tina created the note cards below to guide her oral presentation. She used the note cards as she presented to keep her presentation organized and on track. Notice that Tina numbered each note card in order to keep her presentation in the order that she planned.

1

Introduction

Here's a question for you: Who was the only American to serve as both the governor of a state and the president of an independent nation? The answer is Sam Houston. His name lives on all over our state—even as one of the largest cities in the United States. Houston deserves these honors. He was a great leader with an independent spirit. He made decisions based on what he thought was right.

2

Houston's Accomplishments

(Use photo visual aid.)

- *March 1836 Alamo fell.*
- *Civilians fled to escape Mexican army.*
- *Houston retreated.*

3

Ending

So, when you are out and about in the state of Texas, and you see the name Houston everywhere you look, remember what that name means to our state and to our country. Remember the man who stood firm on his beliefs. Remember . . .

TEKS 7.25C

Delivering Your Presentation

The format for an informative presentation is very different from that of a written report. Instead of reading your words on paper, your audience will listen to you deliver them orally. To plan the delivery of your presentation, follow these guidelines:

- **Deliver from your notes.** If you were to simply read your report, it would not be as interesting because it was meant to be read, not heard. In general, listeners can't process as much information as readers. Look at the main ideas in your notes and address them briefly.
- **Dramatize your facts.** Find more interesting, dramatic ways to state the facts included on your note cards. Ask rhetorical questions. Look for ways to add humor to your presentation.
- **Use visual aids to replace explanation.** Use pictures, charts, and other visual aids to make your point and "show" what is happening in your presentation so you don't have to "tell" so much.

Using Body Language and Voice

1. **Breathe deeply** and give yourself a moment to think about what you will say.
2. **Make eye contact,** but if looking at your audience is hard for you, look slightly above their heads.
3. **Use simple hand gestures,** such as pointing to a visual aid, to add emphasis and interest.
4. **Speak loudly and clearly** so the people in the back of the room can hear you. Speak at a relaxed pace and don't rush.

Practice and present. Using the tips above, practice delivering your presentation. If you practice in front of friends or family members, consider their suggestions.

Overcoming Stage Fright

If you think you're the only one who feels nervous speaking in front of a group, you're wrong. Everyone feels that way at one time or another. There are things that you can do to relax and reduce "stage fright."

1 Practice, practice, practice.

Preparation is the key. The more often you rehearse your presentation, the more relaxed you will be. Practicing in front of friends or family will also help you get used to having an audience.

2 Take a deep breath.

Arrange your notes. Look around before you begin. Don't rush into your presentation.

3 Focus.

Concentrate on what you are doing and on what comes next. Visualize the steps in your presentation.

Using a Checklist

Practice your presentation using the checklist below. If possible, video-record yourself so that you can see what you do well and what you can improve. Also consider having someone else watch your presentation and make suggestions.

____ **1.** I maintain eye contact with my audience instead of staring at my notes.

____ **2.** My voice is loud and clear.

____ **3.** My voice and appearance show that I am interested in my topic.

____ **4.** I speak at a natural pace (not too fast or too slow).

____ **5.** I avoid "stalling" words like *um, er,* and *like.*

____ **6.** My visual aids are large and easy to understand.

____ **7.** I make gestures for emphasis, and I point out my visual aids.

Presentation Tips

Before your presentation . . .

- **Get everything organized.**
  Put the main points of your presentation on note cards and make your visual aids.
- **Time your speech.**
  If it's too long or too short, adjust the length by adding or removing note cards.
- **Practice.**
  The more you remember without looking at your notes, the easier it will be to give the presentation.

During your presentation . . .

- **Project your voice.**
  Be sure everyone can hear you.
- **Speak clearly and slowly.**
  Don't rush through your presentation.
- **Maintain eye contact.**
  Make a connection with your audience.
- **Hold visual aids so that everyone can see them.**
  Point out the things that you are talking about.

After your presentation . . .

- **Answer questions.**
  Clarify any information that your audience asks about.
- **Make closing comments.**
  Summarize the audience's questions and concerns.

Practice and present. Have a final practice with a friend or someone at home. After you make your presentation in the classroom, listen for suggestions from your teacher and classmates. You can try out these ideas in your next presentation.

Research Writing

Multimedia Presentations

If you've just written your best report or essay ever, you may want to share it with a larger audience. To reach a larger audience, you may have to shift from being the writer to being the director. As director, you can write a multimedia presentation complete with special effects, which a wide range of viewers can enjoy.

There are several kinds of devices and software that you can use to produce multimedia presentations. Just add a little imagination, and you'll be connecting with your audience in a new, dynamic way.

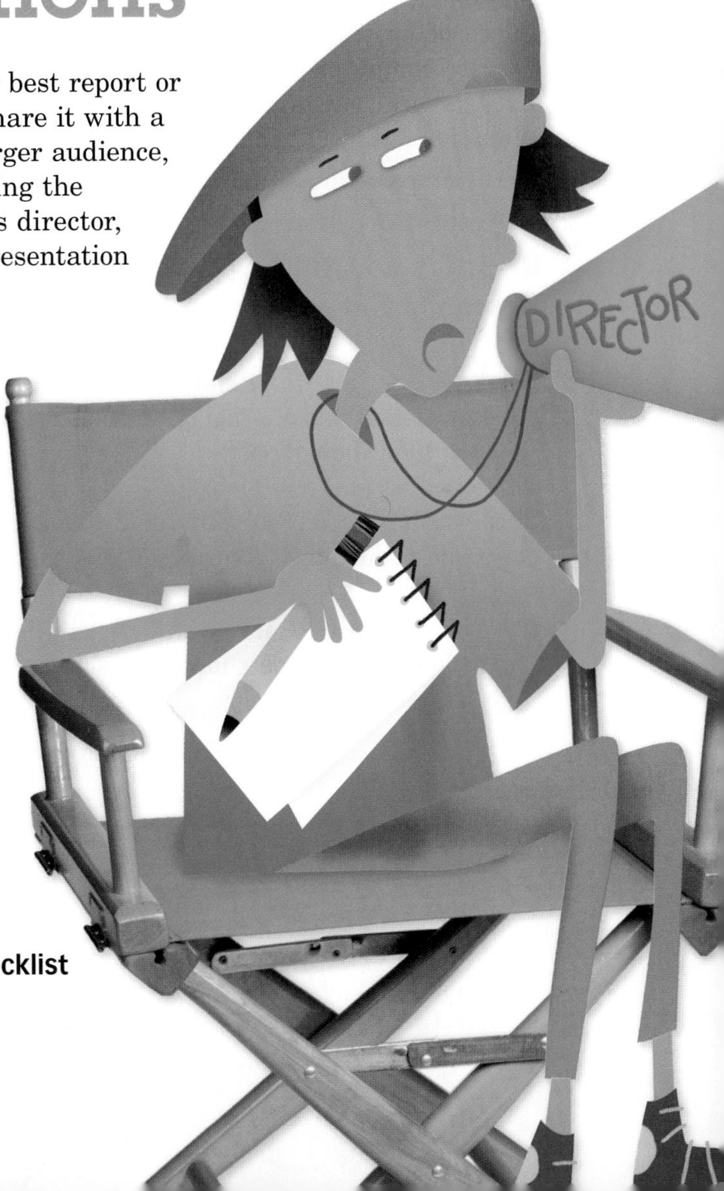

What's Ahead

- **Creating Slide Shows**
- **Creating Video Presentations**
- **Creating Web Pages**
- **Interactive Report Checklist**

TEKS 7.17D

Creating Slide Shows

With the help of a computer, you can design a slide show report that others can interact with. Your computer-generated slides will make your report clearer and more interesting.

Prewriting Selecting a Topic and Details

For your slide show report, you will want to use something you've already written that will interest both you and your audience. After you've chosen your piece of writing, summarize the main idea and state the conclusion. Then create computer-generated slides that express your ideas and details. Use text to share your main points. Include some of the following as you create your slides:

- **Pictures** such as photos or clip art
- **Animations** that show a process, tell a story, or make a transition
- **Videos** of something you've filmed yourself
- **Sounds and music** to use as background or to make a point

Prewrite **Select a topic.** **Refer to the writing projects that you have already completed. Find one that can be represented visually using text and graphics in a slide show format.**

Once you have selected your topic, begin planning the ideas that you will include in your slide show. Think of ideas that can be represented visually.

Prewrite **Think about main ideas.** **Make a list of the main ideas that you will include in the slide show. For each main idea, write down some possible pictures or photographs, animations, or music and sounds that you can use to represent the idea.**

Drafting Preparing the Slide Show

Before you create your slide show, you need to make a storyboard. A storyboard is a "map" of the slides you plan to use. Include one box in the storyboard for each main idea. Then add links from these boxes to additional information.

When you have finished planning your slides, it is time to create them. Use computer software to design the slides. Consider using bulleted lists and charts to summarize your ideas. Show the user how to get around in the report using easily recognized navigation buttons, such as arrows or the words "next" and "back."

Draft **Create a storyboard. Refer to your report and note cards to help you map out your storyboard. Include ideas for what your audience will see. Consider adding music and sound effects to enhance the visuals. This careful preparation will give you an idea of how the slides should look before you actually make them on the computer.**

Revising Improving Your Slide Show

The content of each slide should give a main point about your topic. Read back through your slides and make sure each conclusion you have made is relevant and important.

Since your audience is on their own in viewing this type of multimedia presentation, it's important to double-check to make sure that it works as it should. Have several friends or family members test it for you. Ask them to tell you if it is clear and interesting.

Revise **Get feedback. If your "testers" have good suggestions for making your slide show more meaningful, revise the text and design where necessary.**

Editing Checking for Conventions

Check the text on each slide for grammar, punctuation, capitalization, and spelling errors. Ask an adult or a classmate to check your slides, too.

Edit **Make corrections. After you've made corrections, go through the slide show once more to make sure it works well.**

TEKS 7.17D

Creating Video Presentations

A video can be an effective and exciting way to present information. Creating a video presentation requires planning and patience. Be prepared to plan every detail before the tape starts to roll.

Prewriting Choosing a Format

Unlike a written report or a slide show, a video could take many forms. Below are some choices that Tina considered for her video presentation about Sam Houston:

- **Create a Talk Show.** Tina could interview Sam Houston as if he were on a television talk show. She could incorporate much of the information from her research report in the dialogue of the interview as Houston talks about his life. Tina would play the interviewer and a classmate would play Sam Houston. If your topic isn't a person, you can interview an expert on the topic in your talk show video.
- **Make a Documentary.** Documentary films are very popular formats for nonfiction topics. Tina thought about making a documentary of Sam Houston's life, illustrated by still pictures and brief reenactments with her classmates of scenes from his life. Tina would provide the narration for the documentary.
- **Do a Teleplay.** Instead of doing brief snippets or reenactments from Houston's life, Tina could put his life into a teleplay that could be acted out by classmates. Each individual scene could be connected with brief narration. Tina could feel free to take some dramatic license as she created dialogue for Houston and other characters during the Cherokee removal, the Texas war for independence, and other events in his life.

Prewrite **Choose your video format. Decide what format best suits the topic you are working with for a video presentation.**

TEKS 7.14E, 7.17D, 7.25C

RESEARCH

Drafting Preparing the Video Presentation

Before you begin filming your video, you need a script—the dialogue for the talk show, the narration for the documentary, or the screenplay for the teleplay. Here are some tips for your draft.

- **Plan it out.** Break your video presentation into scenes. Each scene should deal with an event or an aspect of your topic. The scenes should be related and help the audience understand your topic.
- **Make it real.** Any video presentation will contain spoken words, whether in narration or dialogue between characters. This spoken language must be natural, engaging, and dramatic.
- **Include action.** Body language is important in a video, where the visual is recorded and not live. Make sure you write in stage directions telling your actors what to do.

Draft

Draft a script. Use the tips above and your chosen piece of writing to draft a script for your video presentation.

Revising Improving Your Video Presentation

Review the script, then read it aloud to a classmate or your teacher. Use feedback to make improvements to your script. Have a rehearsal. Assign parts and act it out. If possible, have everyone memorize their parts. Try to include, if necessary, costumes and props.

Revise

Get feedback. Use your classmate's or teacher's best suggestions to revise the text or any other aspect of your video presentation.

Editing Checking for Conventions

Edit your script for errors in grammar, sentence structure, mechanics, and spelling. Rehearse the presentation until you get it just right. You may wish to make a preliminary recording that you can watch and note places that need improvement.

Edit

Make your video. Incorporate all suggestions and improvements. Now record your presentation.

TEKS 7.17D, 7.25A

Creating Web Pages

Prewriting Setting up Your Web Page

To share your Web page presentation, you will need a Web site on which to upload your presentation. Speak with your teacher about options you may use. There are many software programs available to help you with the creation of the actual Web pages. Find out which programs are available at your school.

Follow these steps to plan your Web page presentation:

- **Summarize your research.** Once you have selected a previously written report, summarize your information into a more compact form for your audience. Stick with main ideas and keep only those details that best support the ideas.
- **Create an attractive design.** Web pages often use text features like magazines or newspapers. Think about how some information might work in a sidebar. Create a storyboard for each Web page you plan to make.
- **Think creatively.** Try something different. For example, you could make your Web page look like a newspaper, with headlines and articles about your topic.
- **Think visually.** Most Web pages have art to enhance their look and heighten reader interest. Decide on graphics that would balance or help explain your text.

Prewrite **Summarize your report. Using your written research report, condense and summarize text to fit on a Web page.**

TEKS 7.14E, 7.17D, 7.23D

Drafting Selecting Text and Art

Now you are ready to put your text and art onto your Web pages.

- **Cut and expand to fit.** If your text is too long for the page you have created, edit it to fit. If too short, be prepared to add more text, but only add pertinent facts, no "filler."
- **Balance your page.** Make sure you have balanced art with text. Too many graphics can draw the reader away from your information and hold less appeal.
- **Cite your sources.** Just as you did in a written report, you should cite the sources you used for your research. By citing valid and reliable sources, you are convincing your audience that the information on your Web page is accurate and relevant.

Draft

Draft your page. Put the text and art in place. Be sure to cite your sources.

Revising Improving Your Web Page

As you go over your work, ask yourself these questions:

- Is my Web page easy to read and follow?
- Do my graphics enhance the information?
- Is the page too cluttered? Does it need to be redesigned to make it cleaner and simpler?

Revise

Revise your page. Share your Web page with your teacher or another adult, and ask for feedback. Make further revisions, if necessary, from their suggestions.

Editing Checking for Conventions

As you edit, check your Web page presentation for correct use of grammar, mechanics, sentence structure, and spelling.

Edit

Edit your Web page. Make all necessary corrections to the text. Move, add, or delete graphics for visual appeal.

Samples of Multimedia Presentations

Multimedia presentations offer exciting and different formats for your research report. Tina decided to try each of the three formats presented on the previous pages. Here are Tina's notes for each type of presentation.

Computer-Generated Slide Show

Sound Effects: Sounds of men fighting in battle, horses running.
Slide 1: April 21, 1836—Sam Houston led surprise attack against Mexican army.

Slide 2: Battle of San Jacinto—Santa Anna's troops fight Houston's troops

my defeats Mexican army
n Jacinto River.

at San Jacinto, Texas
pendence.

Video Talk Show

Host: Welcome to Talk of the Town. Our guest tonight is the distinguished former governor of Texas Sam Houston. Thank you for being here, Governor.

Houston: The pleasure is all mine.
Host: Let's talk about your last

ys as governor. In
the people of Texas voted
m the Union, yet you
their will and refused to
yalty to the Southern
led to you being
ice. Why did you do that?

Web Page Newspaper

SENATOR HOUSTON OPPOSES BILL
1854—Today Texas senator Sam Houston denounced the Kansas-Nebraska Bill on the floor of the Senate. According to Houston, the bill would take away Native American lands unjustly, opening it up to white settlement. "I am aware that in presenting myself as the advocate of

d their rights . . . I shall
alone," the senator told
uston is one of only a few
rs to oppose the bill.

Interactive Report Checklist

Use the following checklist to make sure your multimedia presentation is the best it can be. If you answer all questions with a "yes," it's ready!

Focus and Coherence

____ **1.** Did I choose a strong report for my multimedia presentation?
____ **2.** Did I choose main ideas that best support the focus?
____ **3.** Does the evidence I present support my conclusions?

Organization

____ **4.** Did I introduce my topic clearly in the beginning?
____ **5.** Did I use an appropriate format to present my ideas?
____ **6.** Did I present a powerful and thoughtful ending?

Development of Ideas

____ **7.** Did I use enough details to support my focus?
____ **8.** Do all of my ideas build on one another and relate to the focus?

Voice

____ **9.** Does my voice fit well with the format I used?
____ **10.** Do my words and tone work for my audience?

Conventions

____ **11.** Is all text used in my presentation free of grammar, mechanics, and spelling errors?

LISTEN
respect

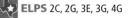

ELPS 2C, 2G, 3E, 3G, 4G

TEXAS WRITE SOURCE Online
www.hmheducation.com/tx/writesource

The Tools of Language

Learning Language

Work with a partner. Read the meanings and share answers to the questions.

1. Strategies are plans that help you achieve something.
   What are two strategies you can use to study for tests?
2. When you get feedback on your work, someone tells you how well you are doing.
   Give an example of feedback a teacher might give about your writing.
3. When things make sense, people can understand them.
   Why should your sentences make sense? Explain.

clarify speak
observe

Listening and Speaking

"Didn't you hear what I told you?"

"I'm sorry. I heard you, but I wasn't listening."

That statement shows the difference between hearing and listening. Simply hearing what your teachers, coaches, parents, and classmates say is not the same as listening to them. When you listen, you think about what you hear, and that's what makes listening an important learning skill.

Speaking well is also important. In fact, listening and speaking skills are so closely related that *good listeners* are likely to be *good speakers*. Improving these skills will make you more confident and successful in school—and beyond!

What's Ahead

- **Listening in Class**
- **Participating in a Group**
- **Speaking in Class**

ELPS 2D, 2G, 2H, 2I

Listening in Class

Listening takes more effort than hearing. Good listening habits include paying attention, staying focused, and thinking about the speaker's ideas. The following tips will help you become a better listener—in and out of school.

1. **Figure out your purpose for listening.** Is the speaker introducing a new idea, explaining a key example, or reviewing for a test?
2. **Listen carefully.** Think about what you hear. Use your mind to help you understand what your ears are hearing.
3. **Listen for the main ideas and take notes.** Writing down a speaker's main ideas will help you focus on what is essential. When you don't understand something you've heard, make a note to yourself or simply put a question mark in the margin of your notebook. Then, ask the speaker for clarification.
4. **Condense information.** Use lists, abbreviations, and phrases to keep information brief, organized, and easy to understand. Skip the small, unnecessary words such as articles and modifiers. Shorten some words—*intro* for introduction, *chap* for chapter, and so on.

Condense information. The next time you take notes in class, practice condensing or summarizing information. Use lists and abbreviations. Avoid unnecessary wording. The example below can guide you.

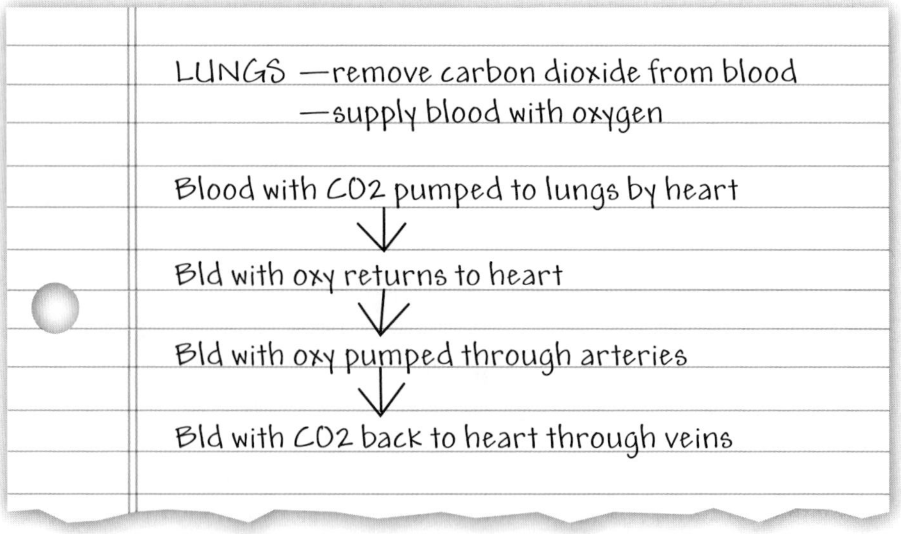
LUNGS —remove carbon dioxide from blood
—supply blood with oxygen
Blood with CO2 pumped to lungs by heart
Bld with oxy returns to heart
Bld with oxy pumped through arteries
Bld with CO2 back to heart through veins

ELPS 2I, 3E, 3H

A Closer Look at Listening and Speaking

Improving your listening and speaking skills will help you become a better learner. Good listeners and good speakers follow these basic guidelines.

Good Listeners . . .

- think about what the speaker is saying.
- pay attention to the speaker's tone of voice, gestures, and facial expressions.
- interrupt only when necessary to ask questions.

Good Speakers . . .

- speak loudly and clearly.
- maintain eye contact with their listeners.
- emphasize their main ideas by changing the tone and volume of their voice.

Try It Focus on speaking and listening skills by trying this activity. One person in your class will be the speaker, and the rest will be listeners. Each listener will need a full sheet of paper and a pencil or pen. The speaker will read the following instructions.

1. Write your name at the top of your paper.
2. Fold your paper in half.
3. Draw a star in the middle of your paper.
4. Tear off the corner of your paper.
   All listeners now compare their papers. Are they all the same? If they are not, discuss these two questions:
   - What information did the speaker leave out?
   - What questions did the listeners have about the directions?

ELPS 2I, 3E, 5G

Participating in a Group

When you participate in a group, you work together with others. That means you need to (1) listen to what the other members of the group say, (2) add to their thoughts, and (3) ask for their comments about your ideas. By following some basic guidelines and tips, you will be able to work smoothly within a group.

Guidelines for Group Discussion

- **Select a group leader.** This person makes sure that the group stays focused and that everyone gets a chance to participate. Rather than selecting the same person for all of the group work, try having each member take a turn as the group leader.
- **Select a recorder.** The recorder takes notes on the meetings and keeps a list of important decisions.
- **Agree on a goal or focus.** Be sure that everyone agrees on what the group is supposed to accomplish.

Group Discussion Tips

- **Listen carefully** when someone else is speaking.
- **Share your ideas** with the group.
- **Be respectful at all times,** especially when you disagree with someone's ideas. ("I understand your point, but I think . . . ")
- **Stick to the topic** and keep your goal in mind.

Try It What would you do if . . . ? Imagine yourself in the situations below. Keeping in mind the guidelines and tips above, write a few sentences explaining what you would do in each case.

Situation 1

You are assigned to be part of an English class discussion group, but everyone in the group talks all at once. What should you do?

Situation 2

You are the leader of a discussion group. One group member keeps criticizing other members when they try to give their opinions. What should you do?

Group Skills

It's a pleasure to work in a group when the members respect each other, because the group will get more done. A few specific skills will improve a group's effectiveness: observing, cooperating, encouraging, and clarifying.

Observe the speaker by . . .

- watching body language, including facial expressions, gestures, and posture.
- listening to the tone of voice—excited, nervous, or shy.

Cooperate by . . .

- staying positive and waiting your turn.
- being respectful when you disagree.

Encourage others by . . .

- complimenting them on their ideas.
- asking them for their opinions.

Clarify by . . .

- asking if there are any questions you can answer.
- restating a speaker's idea to be sure you understand it.

Try It Observe, cooperate, encourage, and clarify. Read the situations and questions below and discuss your answers with a classmate.

1. When Jim speaks, he talks too fast and looks out the window.
   What impression will Jim's listeners get from the way he speaks?
2. Juana is shy about speaking in the group.
   What can group members do to encourage Juana to participate?
3. Yolanda notices that group members sometimes seem confused about what she is saying.
   What should Yolanda do when listeners appear to be puzzled?

ELPS 3G

Speaking in Class

Speaking in class is sometimes like playing a sport—it's a team effort. You can only speak effectively in the classroom or have a good discussion when the group is working well together. These basic strategies will help you and your classmates become better speakers.

Before you speak . . .

- listen and take notes.
- think about what others are saying.
- wait until it's your turn to speak.
- plan how you can add something positive to the discussion.

When you speak . . .

- speak loudly and clearly.
- stick to the topic.
- avoid repeating what's already been said.
- support your ideas with examples.
- look at others in the group or class.

Play "Twenty-Question Who Am I?" In your group or class, select one person to play the part of the mystery guest. The mystery guest is a famous person whose identity everyone else has to guess by asking "yes" or "no" questions. As you play this game, practice using the strategies listed above.

1. Each player takes a turn asking one question until someone guesses who the famous person is.
2. The player who guesses correctly becomes the next mystery guest.
3. If no one guesses correctly within 20 questions, the mystery guest reveals his or her identity and becomes a new famous person.

Learning Language

When it comes to writing, there are many new words and ideas to learn. *The writing process, the traits of writing, prewriting, drafting,* and *revising* are just a few of them.

If you play soccer, you know that there is a vocabulary, or certain group of words, related to this sport. Without words such as *offsides, goal, header,* and *throw-in,* you would have a hard time playing this game.

The vocabulary related to writing works in the same way. Without knowing the meaning of *prewriting, drafting,* and *revising,* you would have a hard time writing a strong story or report. This chapter will help you learn all about the language of writing so you can do your best work!

What's Ahead

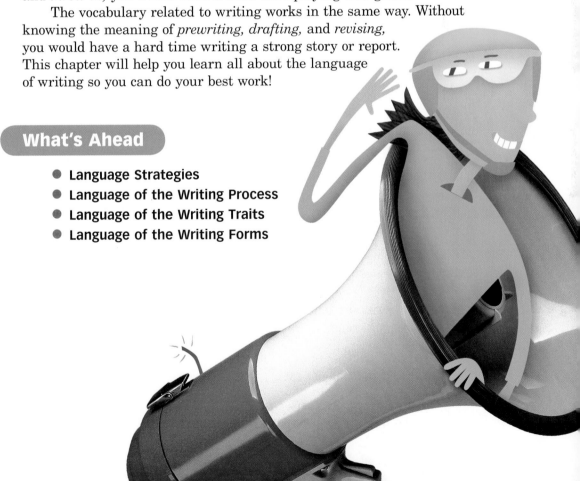

- **Language Strategies**
- **Language of the Writing Process**
- **Language of the Writing Traits**
- **Language of the Writing Forms**

ELPS 2C, 2D, 2G, 2H, 3D

Language Strategies

You hear new words in conversation every day. Here are some strategies to help you understand, remember, and use the new language you hear.

Listen for Language Patterns

In a language pattern, a word or phrase is repeated. Paying attention to the repeated word or phrase helps you understand its meaning.

You hear: Marcos **lives in** a house.
You hear: Anna **lives in** an apartment.
You can say: My family **lives in** a house.

Try It: Turn to a partner. Say two more sentences that include the phrase *lives in.*

Talk Around the Problem Word

If you don't know a word, use familiar words instead. Then ask someone to tell you the word.

You can say: In gym class, we ran slowly around the track. What is that kind of running called? (Jogging)

Try It: The next time you don't know the correct word to use, talk around it. Then ask a friend to tell you the word.

Use Academic Language

Your teachers may use unfamiliar words in class. Repeating the words will help you remember them.

You hear: Your assignment is to answer the questions.
You repeat: assignment

Try It: Listen in class and repeat words you think you may not remember. Then try using them in different sentences.

Ask "Did I say that correctly?"

If you are unsure whether you've used language correctly, ask a classmate or a teacher.

You can say: The car stops with the foot press. Did I say that correctly?

Try It When you don't know the correct name for something, use the word or phrase you think is correct. Then ask if you've used language correctly.

Teach a Friend

To remember new words, use them to teach someone you know, such as a friend, family member, or classmate.

You hear: Earth orbits, or moves around, the Sun.
You can say: The Moon orbits Earth.

Try It Explain something to a classmate, using a new word you have learned. Help your classmate understand the new word, too.

Take Notes or Draw a Picture

Write new words in a notebook. Add information or your own drawings and graphic organizers to remember how to say them and their meanings. When taking notes in class, listen for the main ideas and be alert for such signal words as *most important* and *for example.*

You hear: Parallel lines go in the same direction and never meet.
What you do: Write *parallel lines* and draw a picture of them.

You hear: The cerebrum and cerebellum have different functions.
What you do: Be prepared to list those functions under one of the main parts—*cerebrum* or *cerebellum.*

Try It Keep a vocabulary notebook. The next time you hear a word you want to remember, write or draw it in your notebook.

ELPS 4C

Language of the Writing Process

Read each of the terms. Then read about what they mean.

Prewrite

The first step of the writing process is to prewrite, or plan your writing. You determine your purpose, audience, genre, and topic. Then you generate ideas and develop a focus statement, or main idea.

When you are learning about writing, sometimes the purpose and audience are given to you. Sometimes the genre is given to you, too. You learn many ways to generate ideas, such as brainstorming. You also learn ways to plan and arrange your ideas.

Draft

When you draft, you do the actual writing. As you draft, you build on your prewriting ideas, keeping in mind your focus statement. You categorize ideas into paragraphs as you go. You also connect your ideas to the focus statement so that your audience can follow what you are saying.

Revise

Next, it is time to read your draft and revise it, or make changes. When you revise, you should concentrate on the ideas in your writing. You judge whether the ideas are right for the purpose, audience, and genre. You make ideas clear and connect them to each other for your audience. Don't be afraid to create several drafts. Remember that drafting is part of the process!

Edit

When you edit, you look for and correct mistakes in grammar, sentence structure, capitalization, punctuation, and spelling. The result is your final draft.

Publish

To publish, you get feedback from others (for example, your classmates or teacher) and make any last changes. Then you make a neat final copy and present it to your audience.

ELPS 2C, 2I, 3A, 3E, 4C

Vocabulary: Writing Process

audience	**draft**	**edit**
mechanics	**prewrite**	**publish**
punctuation	**purpose**	**revise**
focus statement		

1. **Say the word.** Listen and read along as your teacher reads each word aloud. Practice pronouncing each word.

2. **Discover the meaning.** With a partner, make a three-column chart. List the vocabulary words in the first column, the meanings in the second column, and an example sentence in the third. Start with the words you already know. With your partner, discuss what you think the other words mean.

3. **Learn more.** Listen as your teacher explains the meaning of each word. Work with your partner to add new information to your chart.

4. **Show your understanding.** Use your notebook to answer the questions below.
   - What should you do first—publish or edit?
   - How might your writing change if your audience is a friend rather than a teacher?
   - What is something you might change when you revise your writing?
   - What is something you might change when you edit your writing?

5. **Write it, show it.** In your notebook, add notes and drawings to help you remember what the words mean. Use a web to show how the vocabulary words connect to each other.

ELPS 2I, 3D, 3E

The Writing Process in Action

You've learned the language of the writing process. Now it's time to see the process in action! First your teacher will show you how to do each step of the writing process. Then you will write together, using the following questions. As you write together, your teacher will ask you to do things. These questions are called *requests*. Be sure to respond to your teacher's requests.

Prewrite

1. Decide on a topic. For example, select an interesting event that has happened recently in your school or town.
2. Who is your audience for this piece of writing?
3. What genre, or form, will you use to write?
4. What would you like to say about the event?

Draft

1. How can you sort your ideas into categories?
2. How can you organize those ideas into paragraphs that support your topic?

The Writing Process in Action

These pages from the first unit in your book show the writing process in action.

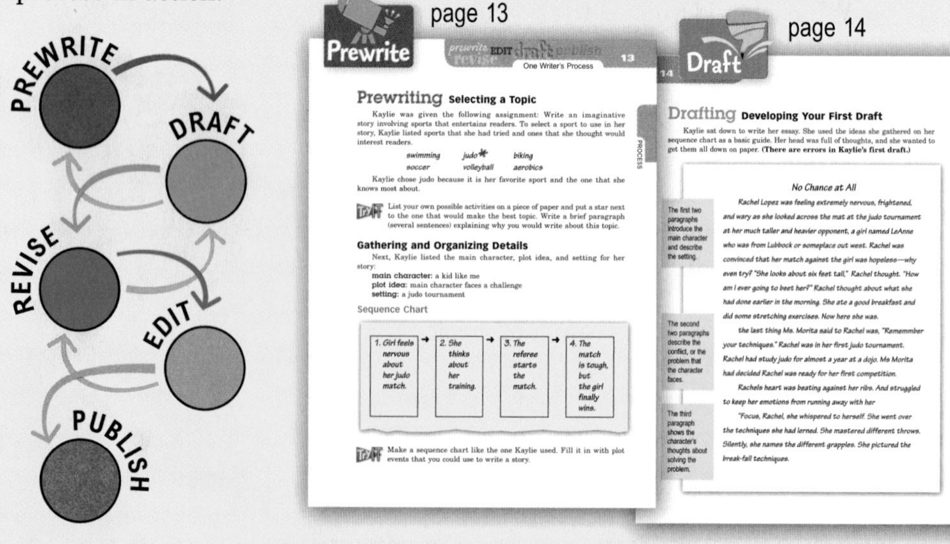

ELPS 2G, 3D, 3E, 3G

Revise

1. Is everything you included important to your focus statement?
2. Are there any sentences you should add or take out?
3. Does each sentence and paragraph build on the ones before?
4. Did you choose the right words for your audience?

Edit

1. Did you follow all the rules of grammar and mechanics?
2. Are the sentences put together correctly?
3. Are all the words spelled correctly?

Publish

1. Have you used the feedback you received?
2. Is your writing neat and easy to read?

Turn and Talk

Talk to a classmate about which step is most important. Listen to his or her ideas.

Example: The most important step is ________.

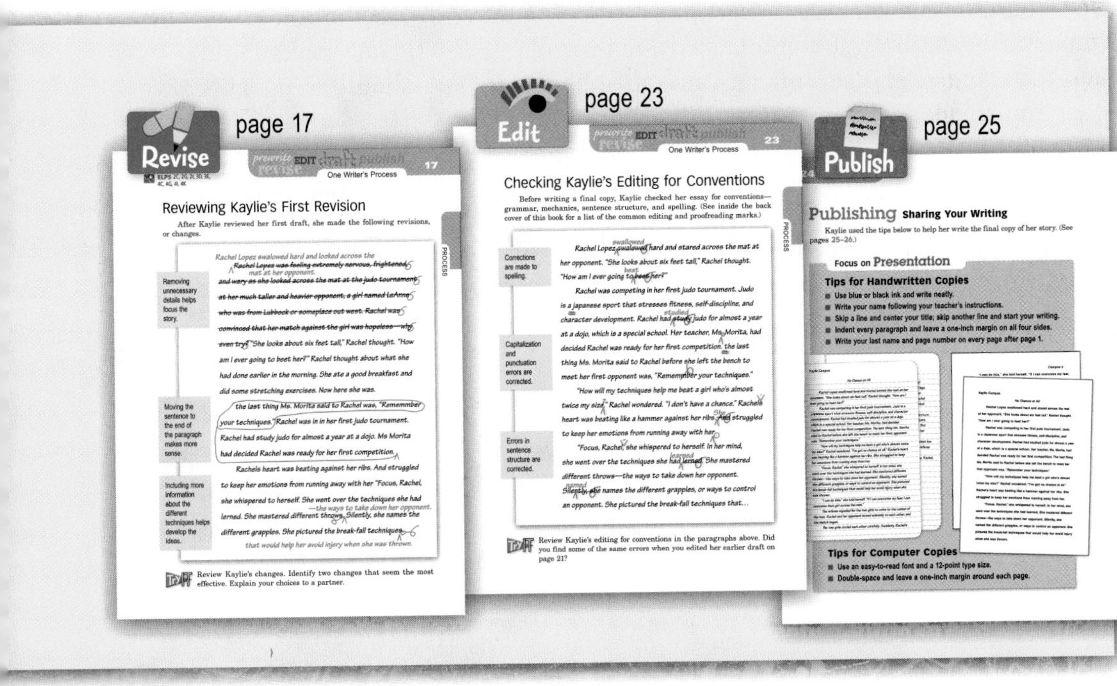

ELPS 4C

Language of the Writing Traits

Read each of these terms. Then read about what they mean.

Focus and Coherence

If your writing has focus, all the ideas connect to the focus statement. Writing that has coherence has ideas that connect to each other. Focus and coherence make ideas clear and easy to follow.

Organization

Your ideas should be organized, or arranged in a way that makes your writing easy to follow from beginning to end. Each sentence should logically follow the one that comes before it. In the same way, each paragraph should build on the ones before. All sentences should add to the readers' understanding of the main idea.

Development of Ideas

You must develop your ideas in depth. Include interesting and important details that come from your own ideas. Each sentence should add meaning to the sentence that comes before it. You should support your main ideas with important details.

Voice

Your writing voice should show the way you think and feel, and it should reflect your personality. It should also keep the reader interested all the way through.

Conventions

Conventions include the rules of grammar, sentence structure, mechanics, and spelling. Why are conventions so important? Writing that is free of errors is easier to read and understand.

ELPS 2C, 2G, 2H, 2I, 3D, 4C, 4G

Vocabulary: Writing Traits

coherence	**conventions**	**depth**
development	**focus**	**organization**
voice		

1. **Say the word.** Listen and read along as your teacher reads each word aloud. Practice pronouncing each word.
2. **Discover the meaning.** Use this book to find more information about the vocabulary words. Compare your findings with those of a partner. Write your discoveries in your vocabulary notebook.
3. **Learn more.** Listen as your teacher explains the meaning of each word. Work with your partner to restate the meanings and add the new information to your vocabulary notebook.
4. **Show your understanding.** Use your notebook to answer the questions below.
   - Why is it important for your writing to have focus and coherence?
   - What might happen if your writing isn't organized?
   - What are some ways to develop ideas about a trip to a museum?
5. **Write it, show it.** In your notebook, add any last notes or drawings to help you remember what the words mean. Use a chart or other graphic organizer to add example sentences for each vocabulary word.

ELPS 3E, 3G, 3H

Language of Descriptive Writing

The purpose of a descriptive essay is to describe a person, place, thing, event, or how to do something. Usually, descriptive essays follow a basic organization. A beginning paragraph identifies the topic and grabs the reader's interest. The middle paragraphs describe the topic with details, and the ending paragraph provides a conclusion of the description.

Descriptive Essay Organization

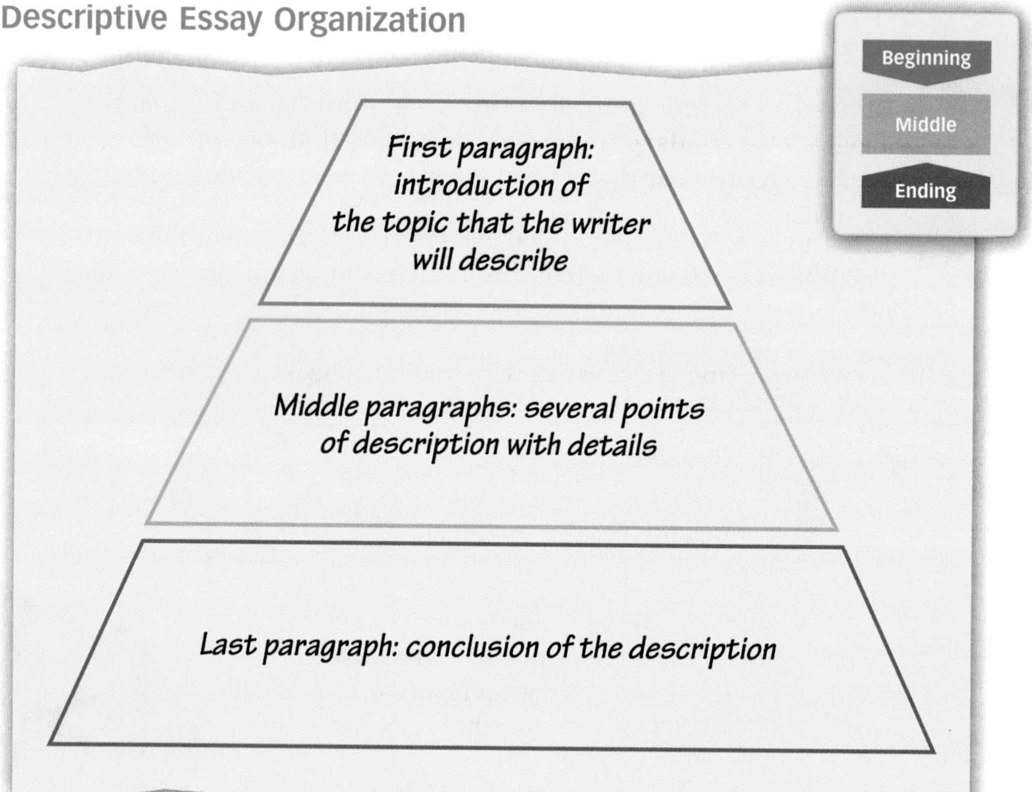
Beginning
Middle
Ending
First paragraph: introduction of the topic that the writer will describe
Middle paragraphs: several points of description with details
Last paragraph: conclusion of the description

Turn and Talk

Explain to a partner why the middle part of the graphic organizer is so important in a descriptive essay.

The middle part of the graphic organizer ________________.

Vocabulary: Descriptive Writing

describe	**familiar topic**	**order of location**
senses	**sensory detail**	**vivid detail**

1. **Say the word.** Listen and read along as your teacher reads the words aloud. Then repeat each word.

2. **Discover the meaning.** Work with a partner to find the meanings of the vocabulary words. Use the writing model on pages 76–77 to figure out what the words mean. Make notes about what you think.

3. **Learn more.** Listen as your teacher explains the meaning of each word. Work with your partner to find examples of these words in the writing model on pages 76–77. Make changes to your notes about the vocabulary words.

4. **Show your understanding.** Use your notebook to answer the questions below. Listen to directions from your teacher. When following directions, listen for action words such as *write* and signal words such as *next.* These words tell you what to do and when.
   - What is the purpose of a descriptive essay?
   - What vivid details would you use to describe your school? Why?
   - What is another familiar topic you could describe?

5. **Write it, show it.** In your notebook, write or draw examples of words to help you remember their meanings.

ELPS 2G, 2I, 3E, 3G, 4C, 5B

Reading the Descriptive Model

What Do You Know?

Next you will read a model descriptive essay about a student's locker at school. What do you know about lockers? Do you use one at school? Is it messy or organized? What do you keep in it? Describe what students keep in a locker.

Build Background

Lockers often line the hallways of a school. Lockers are where students can keep their personal items. Some students throw everything they need for school in their lockers. Others like to keep their lockers organized. Some students personalize their lockers with pictures, stickers, magnets, and other decorative and special items.

Listening

Listen as your teacher or a classmate reads aloud *My Home Away from Home.* As you listen, make notes about words that appeal to the senses. Share your notes with a classmate. Tell each other your answers to the questions below.

1. What words tell you that the description is organized by location?
2. How do you know the writer's locker is messy?
3. How do you think the writer feels about his locker?

Key Location Words

around	below	in the middle
inside of	in the back	on the top
near	underneath	under

Look at the phrases and words in the box. They are location words that the writer uses to describe his locker. You will see these words when you read the writing model. With a partner, use these words to describe a place in your classroom. Then, use the words to write sentences about your discussion.

ELPS 4G, 4I

Read Along

Now it's your turn to read. Read along as your teacher or classmate reads pages 76–77 aloud. As you read, think about details that describe location.

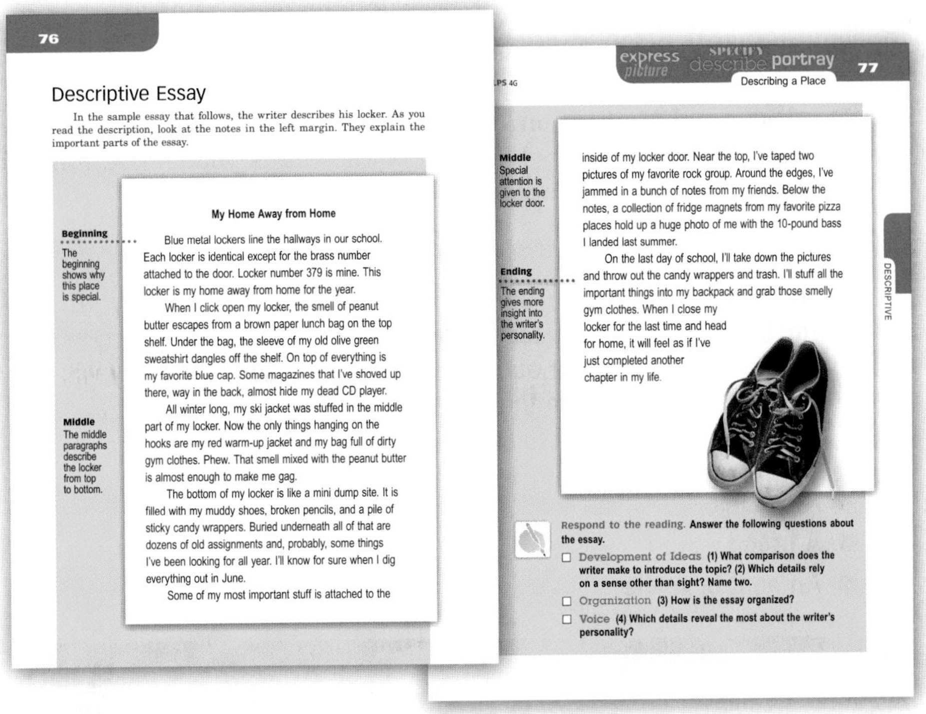
76

Descriptive Essay

In the sample essay that follows, the writer describes his locker. As you read the description, look at the notes in the left margin. They explain the important parts of the essay.

My Home Away from Home

Beginning The beginning shows why this place is special.

Blue metal lockers line the hallways in our school. Each locker is identical except for the brass number attached to the door. Locker number 379 is mine. This locker is my home away from home for the year.

When I click open my locker, the smell of peanut butter escapes from a brown paper lunch bag on the top shelf. Under the bag, the sleeve of my old olive green sweatshirt dangles off the shelf. On top of everything is my favorite blue cap. Some magazines that I've shoved up there, way in the back, almost hide my dead CD player.

Middle The middle paragraphs describe the locker from top to bottom.

All winter long, my ski jacket was stuffed in the middle part of my locker. Now the only things hanging on the hooks are my red warm-up jacket and my bag full of dirty gym clothes. Phew. That smell mixed with the peanut butter is almost enough to make me gag.

The bottom of my locker is like a mini dump site. It is filled with my muddy shoes, broken pencils, and a pile of sticky candy wrappers. Buried underneath all of that are dozens of old assignments and, probably, some things I've been looking for all year. I'll know for sure when I dig everything out in June.

Some of my most important stuff is attached to the

express picture SPECIFY describe portray 77
Describing a Place

ELPS 4G

Middle Special attention is given to the locker door.

inside of my locker door. Near the top, I've taped two pictures of my favorite rock group. Around the edges, I've jammed in a bunch of notes from my friends. Below the notes, a collection of fridge magnets from my favorite pizza places hold up a huge photo of me with the 10-pound bass I landed last summer.

Ending The ending gives more insight into the writer's personality.

On the last day of school, I'll take down the pictures and throw out the candy wrappers and trash. I'll stuff all the important things into my backpack and grab those smelly gym clothes. When I close my locker for the last time and head for home, it will feel as if I've just completed another chapter in my life.

Respond to the reading. Answer the following questions about the essay.

- ☐ Development of Ideas (1) What comparison does the writer make to introduce the topic? (2) Which details rely on a sense other than sight? Name two.
- ☐ Organization (3) How is the essay organized?
- ☐ Voice (4) Which details reveal the most about the writer's personality?

DESCRIPTIVE

After Reading

Copy the following chart on a sheet of paper and fill it in with the items the writer describes by location. Use your chart to summarize the writing model with a partner.

Location	Items
Top of Locker	
Middle	
Bottom	
Door	

LANGUAGE

ELPS 3G, 3H

Oral Language: Descriptive Writing

The person or people who will listen to you or read your writing are called the audience. When you speak or write to describe, it is important to use sensory details so that your audience can picture what you are describing in their minds.

Try It Read about the situation below. Then choose two audiences from the list. With a partner, discuss how the words you choose might be different for each audience.

Situation

You went on a roller coaster with some friends. It was scary and fun. Describe the roller coaster and your ride on it. Use plenty of details so that when your audience hears the description, they will see the roller coaster ride in their minds.

Audiences

- **A teacher**
- **A friend**
- **An aunt or uncle**

ELPS 2G, 2H, 3E, 3G, 3H

Effective Talk

When you answer a question, you might use a few words, a sentence, or a few sentences to explain your ideas. Descriptions include details that help readers see things in their minds. When you use more details to describe something, your reader will have a clearer picture of what you are describing.

Read the question and answers below. In the first box, there is only a word. In the second box, there are a few words that answer the question. The third answer contains more detail and does a better job answering the question.

What is your new house like?

big

big and blue

My new house is slate blue, is two stories tall, and has six rooms. The windows are large and let in a lot of sunlight. There is a basketball hoop in the driveway, and there is a big garage where we keep our bicycles.

Try It Choose a question to talk about with a partner. First make notes about details that would give your partner more information about your ideas. Then use your notes to describe your ideas to your partner.

Here are some ideas to get you started.

1. How would you describe your school cafeteria?
2. Think of a person you admire. How would you describe him or her?
3. Think about a place where you enjoy spending time. How would you describe it to someone who has never been there?

ELPS 3E, 3G, 3H

Language of Narrative Writing

A personal narrative is writing that tells about a real experience in the narrator's life. Narratives usually include a beginning paragraph, middle paragraphs, and an ending paragraph. The beginning introduces the story and usually gives some background. The middle paragraphs tell about the experience in chronological order, or time order. An ending paragraph concludes the story.

Personal Narrative Organization

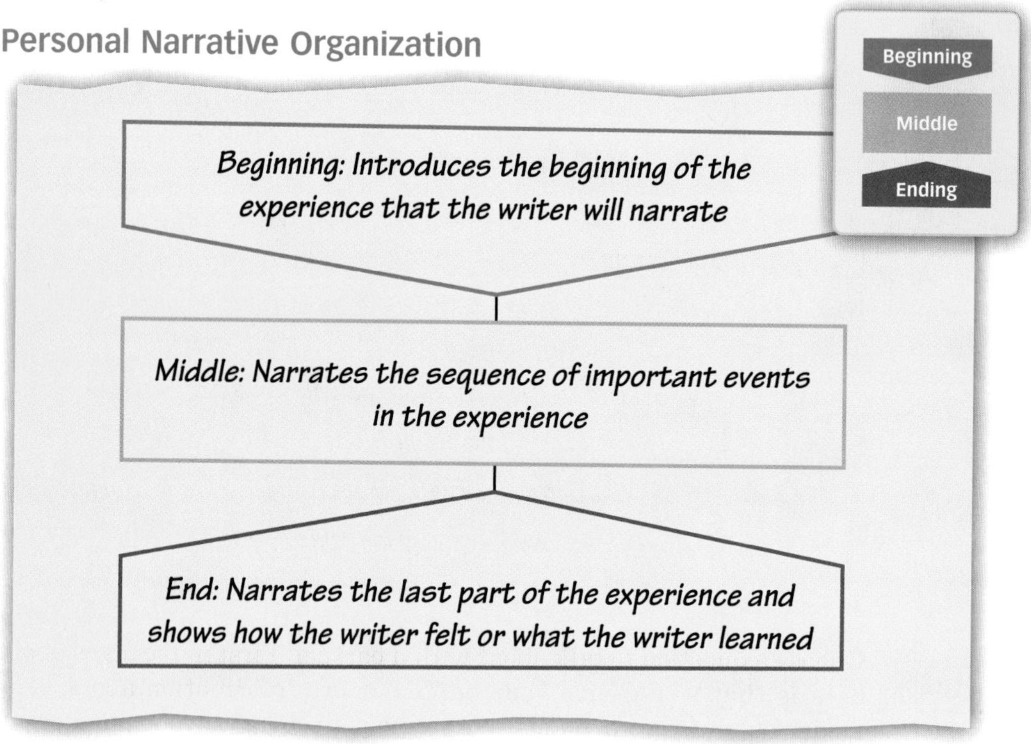
Beginning
Middle
Ending
Beginning: Introduces the beginning of the experience that the writer will narrate
Middle: Narrates the sequence of important events in the experience
End: Narrates the last part of the experience and shows how the writer felt or what the writer learned

Turn and Talk

Talk with a partner about the organization of a personal narrative.

A personal narrative begins ________________.

ELPS 2C, 2D, 2G, 2H, 2I, 4C, 4G

Vocabulary: Narrative Writing

action	background	experience
chronological order	dialogue	personality
narrative	narrator	

1. **Say the word.** Listen as your teacher reads the words aloud. Then repeat each word.

2. **Discover the meaning.** You will find some words in the yellow box next to the writing model on pages **99–100**. Also use the writing model to help. Make note cards with meanings and examples.

3. **Learn more.** Listen as your teacher explains the meaning of each word. Work with your partner to correct or revise your note cards.

4. **Show your understanding.** Use your notebook to answer the questions below.
   - Why is it important to give the reader some background information?
   - If a narrative is in chronological order, which scene comes at the beginning?
   - Why should a writer show the characters' personalities?

5. **Write it, show it.** In your notebook, add pictures or examples to help you remember what each word means. For the word *personality,* you could write words that describe different people's personalities.

ELPS 2G, 2I, 3E, 3G, 4C

Reading the Narrative Model

What Do You Know?

Next you will read a sample personal narrative about the writer's first day at a new school. How did you feel on your first day at middle school? Have you been in a similar new situation? What happened? How did you feel? Why? Describe the experience to a partner.

Build Background

Many people worry about being in new situations. They want to fit in and they want others to like them, but they're not sure that this will happen. They worry about their appearance, their clothes, and their behavior. Usually, people learn that it's best to just be themselves. When you don't worry, your confidence shows.

Listening

Listen as your teacher or a classmate reads aloud *Home Team or Visitor?* As you listen, make notes about words that appeal to the senses. Share your notes with a classmate. Tell each other your answers to the questions below.

1. What are two things the writer says that show he is nervous?
2. Why does the writer "breathe a sigh of relief?"
3. What lesson does the writer learn from this experience?

Key Expressions

all eyes were glued on me	**away from all those eyes**
center of attention	**feel my face getting hot**
heart kicked against my ribs	

Look at the expressions in the box. You will see these phrases when you read the model narrative. The writer used these phrases to help the reader picture the experience. Use the words to tell a partner about a time when you were nervous in a new situation.

Read Along

Now it's your turn to read. Turn to page 99–100. Read the personal narrative writing model as your teacher or a classmate reads it aloud.

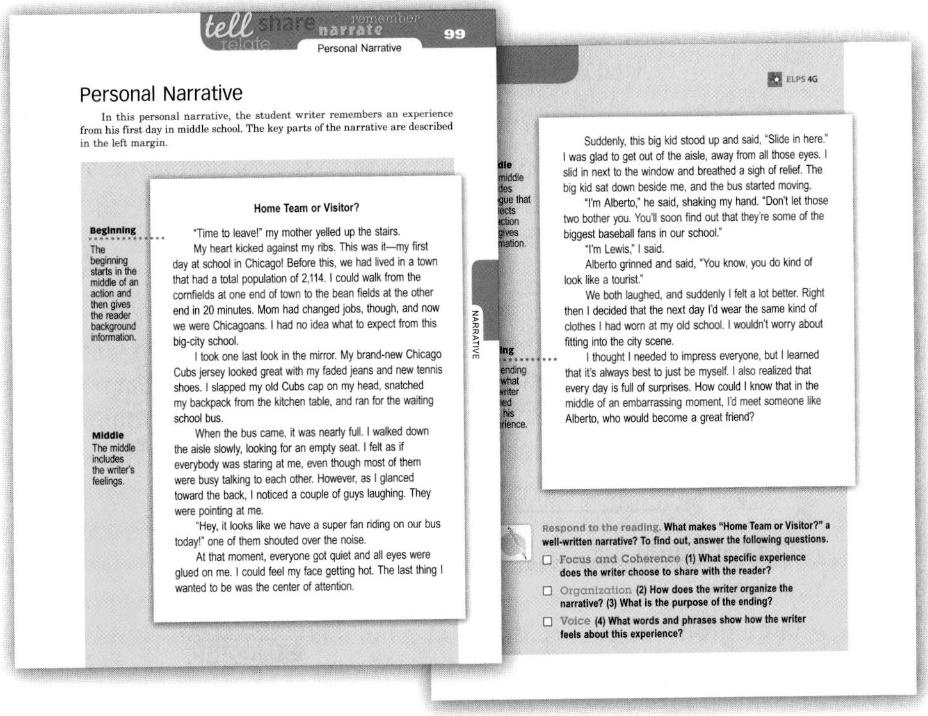
99 Personal Narrative

Personal Narrative

In this personal narrative, the student writer remembers an experience from his first day in middle school. The key parts of the narrative are described in the left margin.

Beginning The beginning starts in the middle of an action and then gives the reader background information.

Middle The middle includes the writer's feelings.

Home Team or Visitor?

"Time to leave!" my mother yelled up the stairs.

My heart kicked against my ribs. This was it—my first day at school in Chicago! Before this, we had lived in a town that had a total population of 2,114. I could walk from the cornfields at one end of town to the bean fields at the other end in 20 minutes. Mom had changed jobs, though, and now we were Chicagoans. I had no idea what to expect from this big-city school.

I took one last look in the mirror. My brand-new Chicago Cubs jersey looked great with my faded jeans and new tennis shoes. I slapped my old Cubs cap on my head, snatched my backpack from the kitchen table, and ran for the waiting school bus.

When the bus came, it was nearly full. I walked down the aisle slowly, looking for an empty seat. I felt as if everybody was staring at me, even though most of them were busy talking to each other. However, as I glanced toward the back, I noticed a couple of guys laughing. They were pointing at me.

"Hey, it looks like we have a super fan riding on our bus today!" one of them shouted over the noise.

At that moment, everyone got quiet and all eyes were glued on me. I could feel my face getting hot. The last thing I wanted to be was the center of attention.

NARRATIVE

ELPS 4G

Suddenly, this big kid stood up and said, "Slide in here." I was glad to get out of the aisle, away from all those eyes. I slid in next to the window and breathed a sigh of relief. The big kid sat down beside me, and the bus started moving.

"I'm Alberto," he said, shaking my hand. "Don't let those two bother you. You'll soon find out that they're some of the biggest baseball fans in our school."

"I'm Lewis," I said.

Alberto grinned and said, "You know, you do kind of look like a tourist."

We both laughed, and suddenly I felt a lot better. Right then I decided that the next day I'd wear the same kind of clothes I had worn at my old school. I wouldn't worry about fitting into the city scene.

I thought I needed to impress everyone, but I learned that it's always best to just be myself. I also realized that every day is full of surprises. How could I know that in the middle of an embarrassing moment, I'd meet someone like Alberto, who would become a great friend?

Respond to the reading. **What makes "Home Team or Visitor?" a well-written narrative? To find out, answer the following questions.**

- ☐ Focus and Coherence **(1) What specific experience does the writer choose to share with the reader?**
- ☐ Organization **(2) How does the writer organize the narrative? (3) What is the purpose of the ending?**
- ☐ Voice **(4) What words and phrases show how the writer feels about this experience?**

After Reading

Copy the following chart on a piece of paper and fill it in with the events the writer tells about. Use your chart to summarize the writing model with a partner.

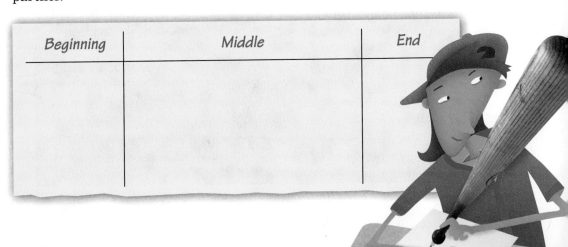

Beginning	Middle	End

ELPS 2G, 3E, 3G, 3H

Oral Language: Narrative Writing

Without an audience, there would be no one to hear your thoughts and feelings. That's why you need to pay attention to your listeners and readers when you speak and write. You should present your ideas in a way that will appeal to your audience. Use a tone and format that will hold your readers' and listeners' interest.

Try It Read about the situation below. Then choose two audiences from the list. With a partner, discuss how you might use a different format or style to address each audience.

Situation

You've just come home from a vacation with your family. It was the first time you had ever visited that place. You had a great time! You saw thrilling sights, met interesting people, and ate tasty foods. You'll always remember this vacation. Tell your audience about it.

Audiences

- **Your best friend**
- **Your class**
- **A large group of your relatives at a holiday**

ELPS 2G, 3E, 3G, 3H

Effective Talk

When you tell about an event, you sometimes summarize the experience using a few words and sentences. Narratives tell about experiences by including details that show how the writer feels. When you use more details to show feelings, your reader will have a better understanding of your experience.

Read the question and the answers below. In the first box, there is only a one-word answer. In the other boxes, the writer includes more details. The last box shows the most details.

How did you feel on your first day at a new school?

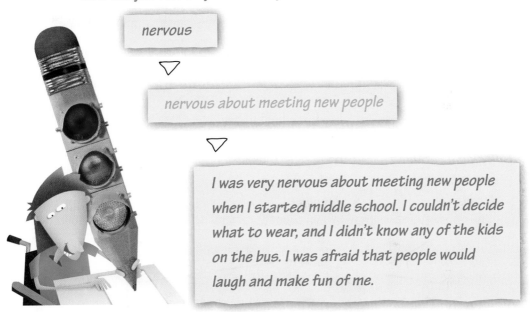

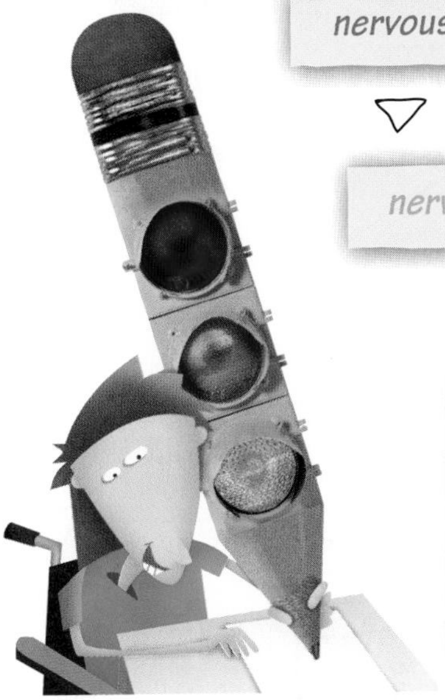

nervous

▽

nervous about meeting new people

▽

I was very nervous about meeting new people when I started middle school. I couldn't decide what to wear, and I didn't know any of the kids on the bus. I was afraid that people would laugh and make fun of me.

Try It Choose a question that you would like to talk about with a partner. Make notes about the time order of events and about details that could make your story entertaining. Then use your notes to describe your experiences to your partner.

Here are some ideas to get you started.

1. Have you had an interesting experience with an animal? Tell what happened.
2. Where have you traveled or gone on vacation? Tell what happened on your trip.

ELPS 3G, 3H

Language of Expository Writing

Expository writing is writing that explains information to the writer's audience. This type of writing might explain one subject, or it might compare two subjects. Most often, expository essays have the same basic organization: an introduction and controlling idea, supporting details, and a conclusion.

Expository Essay Organization

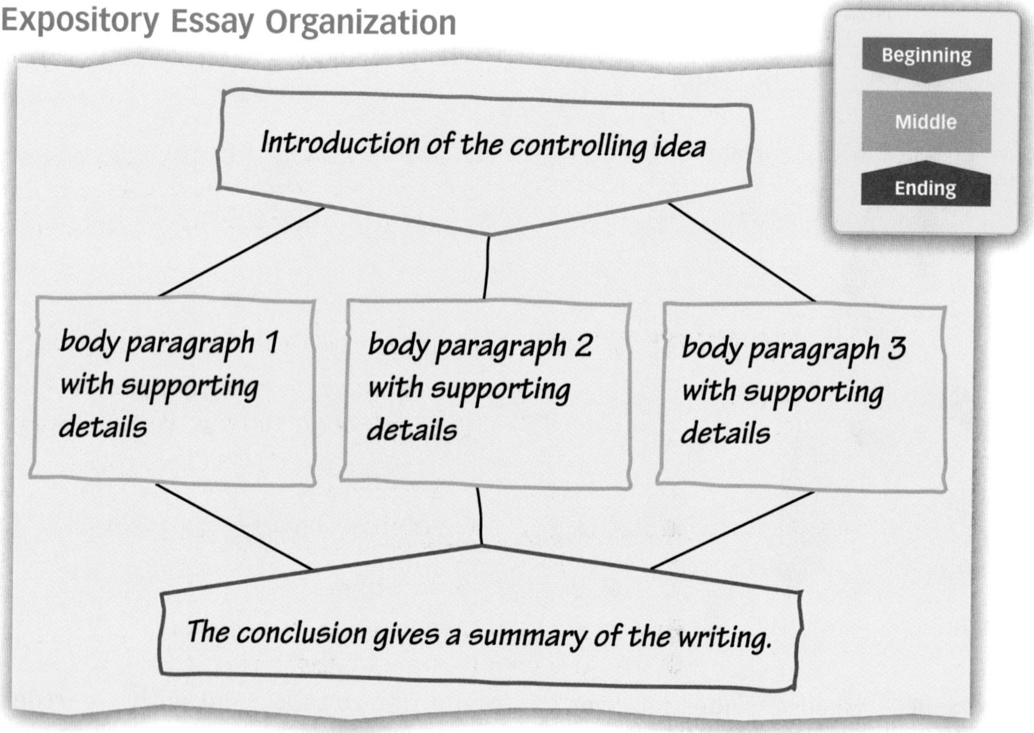

Turn and Talk

Talk with a partner about one important part of the graphic organizer.

The graphic organizer shows that ________________.

ELPS 2C, 2G, 2H, 2I, 3A, 4C

Vocabulary: Expository Writing

body paragraph	**compare**	**conclusion**
contrast	**expository**	**introduction**
subject	**supporting detail**	

1. **Say the word.** Listen and read along as your teacher reads the words aloud. Practice pronouncing each word.

2. **Discover the meaning.** Work with a partner to find some of the vocabulary words in the yellow box next to the writing model on pages 167–168. Write notes about what you think the words mean.

3. **Learn more.** Listen as your teacher explains the meaning of each word. Work with your partner to find examples of these words in the writing sample on pages 167–168.

4. **Show your understanding.** Use your notebook to answer the questions below. Your teacher will give you directions. When following directions, listen for action words such as *write* and signal words such as *next*. These words tell you what to do and when to do it.
   - Would you start your writing with a body paragraph or an introduction? Why?
   - What do a subject and an introduction have in common?
   - Can an expository essay contain opinions? Why or why not?

5. **Write it, show it.** Draw pictures to help you remember what each word means. You may wish to add synonyms, or words that mean the same thing. For example, near *conclusion* you could write *ending*.

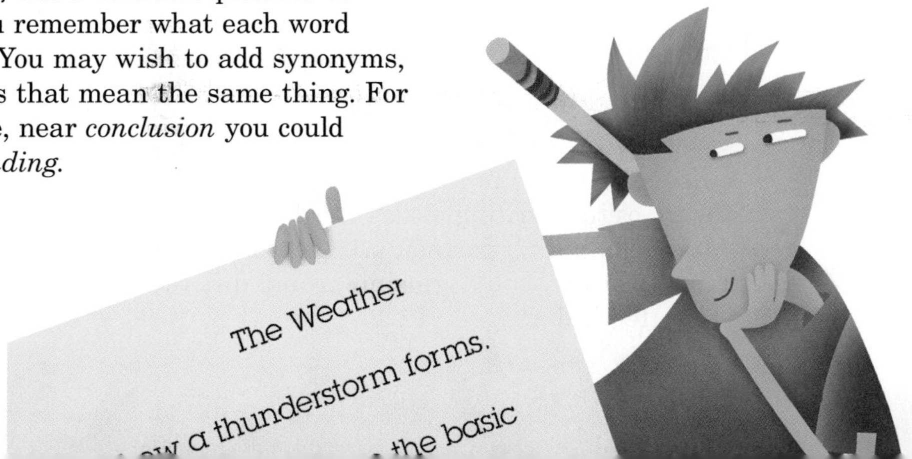

ELPS 2G, 2H, 2I, 3E, 3G, 4C

Reading the Expository Model

What Do You Know?

Next you will read *What's the Buzz?,* a sample expository essay, on pages 167–168. What do you know about honeybees and yellow jackets? Have you ever seen a honeybee or a yellow jacket? Describe what you saw.

Build Background

Honeybees and yellow jackets are flying insects with two pairs of wings. Honeybees eat nectar and pollen from flowers. They help plants reproduce. Yellow jackets eat insects and meat. Yellow jackets are aggressive and may sting a person several times. A honeybee will rarely sting unless it is threatened.

Listening

Listen as your teacher or a classmate reads *What's the Buzz?* aloud. As you listen, make a note about the controlling idea. A controlling idea is the main idea that a writer wants to emphasize. Writers include important details, or specific pieces of information, to support the controlling idea. For example, the writer uses signal words like those in the box below to tell the reader a comparison is being made. Listen for those words. Then be prepared to answer the questions below.

1. What is the writer's controlling idea?
2. How does the writer compare and contrast the insects' appearance?
3. What does the quotation from the neighbor mean?

Key Compare-Contrast Words

also	both	but
comparing	contrasting	different
like	same	similar

Look at the words in the box. You will see some of these words when you read the expository writing model. Read them several times so you can quickly recognize them. With a partner, use the words to talk about how two places in your school or community are similar and different. Then decide which place you like better and why.

Read Along

Now it's your turn to read. Read along as you teacher or a classmate reads pages **167–168** aloud. As you read, think about the main idea and details.

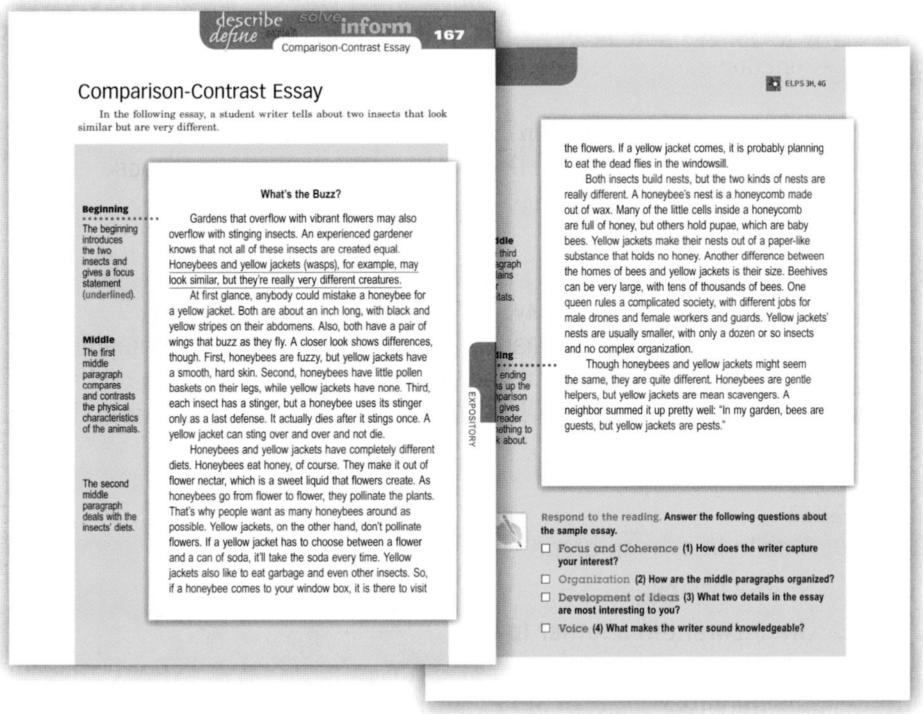
describe solve inform define explain 167
Comparison-Contrast Essay

Comparison-Contrast Essay

In the following essay, a student writer tells about two insects that look similar but are very different.

Beginning
The beginning introduces the two insects and gives a focus statement (underlined).

What's the Buzz?

Gardens that overflow with vibrant flowers may also overflow with stinging insects. An experienced gardener knows that not all of these insects are created equal. Honeybees and yellow jackets (wasps), for example, may look similar, but they're really very different creatures.

Middle
The first middle paragraph compares and contrasts the physical characteristics of the animals.

At first glance, anybody could mistake a honeybee for a yellow jacket. Both are about an inch long, with black and yellow stripes on their abdomens. Also, both have a pair of wings that buzz as they fly. A closer look shows differences, though. First, honeybees are fuzzy, but yellow jackets have a smooth, hard skin. Second, honeybees have little pollen baskets on their legs, while yellow jackets have none. Third, each insect has a stinger, but a honeybee uses its stinger only as a last defense. It actually dies after it stings once. A yellow jacket can sting over and over and not die.

The second middle paragraph deals with the insects' diets.

Honeybees and yellow jackets have completely different diets. Honeybees eat honey, of course. They make it out of flower nectar, which is a sweet liquid that flowers create. As honeybees go from flower to flower, they pollinate the plants. That's why people want as many honeybees around as possible. Yellow jackets, on the other hand, don't pollinate flowers. If a yellow jacket has to choose between a flower and a can of soda, it'll take the soda every time. Yellow jackets also like to eat garbage and even other insects. So, if a honeybee comes to your window box, it is there to visit

EXPOSITORY

ELPS 3H, 4G

the flowers. If a yellow jacket comes, it is probably planning to eat the dead flies in the windowsill.

Both insects build nests, but the two kinds of nests are really different. A honeybee's nest is a honeycomb made out of wax. Many of the little cells inside a honeycomb are full of honey, but others hold pupae, which are baby bees. Yellow jackets make their nests out of a paper-like substance that holds no honey. Another difference between the homes of bees and yellow jackets is their size. Beehives can be very large, with tens of thousands of bees. One queen rules a complicated society, with different jobs for male drones and female workers and guards. Yellow jackets' nests are usually smaller, with only a dozen or so insects and no complex organization.

Though honeybees and yellow jackets might seem the same, they are quite different. Honeybees are gentle helpers, but yellow jackets are mean scavengers. A neighbor summed it up pretty well: "In my garden, bees are guests, but yellow jackets are pests."

Respond to the reading. **Answer the following questions about the sample essay.**

- ☐ Focus and Coherence **(1) How does the writer capture your interest?**
- ☐ Organization **(2) How are the middle paragraphs organized?**
- ☐ Development of Ideas **(3) What two details in the essay are most interesting to you?**
- ☐ Voice **(4) What makes the writer sound knowledgeable?**

After Reading

Copy the following chart on a sheet of paper and fill it in with a partner. Use your chart to summarize the writing model or to respond to your partner's questions about it.

	Similarities	Differences
Appearance		
Diet		
Habitat		

ELPS 3G, 3H

Oral Language: Expository Writing

The person or people who will listen to you or read your writing are called the audience. When you speak or write, it is important to choose just the right words that will reach your audience. In writing, the tone, or the way you write, will be different for each audience.

Try It Read about the situation below. Then choose two audiences from the list. With a partner, discuss how the words you choose might be different for each audience.

Situation

Your school will soon have a new outdoor eating area, a track, and new soccer and baseball fields. The student government discussed where they thought each of these new features should be built, and what they will look like. You will explain how these new features will look.

Audiences

- **A child in second grade**
- **School principal**
- **Grandparent in another town**

Effective Talk

When you answer a question, you might use a few words, a sentence, or a few sentences to explain your ideas. Explanations include details that help people understand. When you use more details to tell about something, the other person will have a better understanding.

Read the question and answers below. In the first box, there are only three words. In the second box, there is a short sentence that answers the question. The third answer contains more detail and does a better job answering the question.

How is the new soccer field different from the old one?

in the back

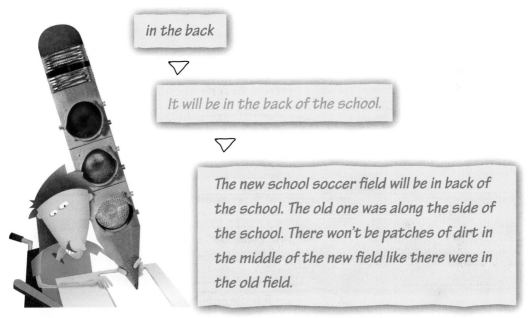

It will be in the back of the school.

The new school soccer field will be in back of the school. The old one was along the side of the school. There won't be patches of dirt in the middle of the new field like there were in the old field.

Try It Choose a question to talk about with a partner. Write two or three ideas to explain your answer to your partner. Next, add details that will help you explain your ideas to your partner. Finally, use your notes as you and your partner discuss your answers to the questions.

Here are some ideas to get you started.

1. How are you and your brother or sister alike? How are you different?
2. How are elementary school and middle school alike and different?

ELPS 2H, 3E, 3G, 3H

Language of Persuasive Writing

A persuasive essay is writing that tries to convince others to believe something. A persuasive essay might try to convince the reader to take action or it might present a solution to a problem. Most persuasive essays follow a similar organization. A beginning paragraph introduces an issue and gives the writer's opinion. Details to support the opinion are included in the middle paragraphs. The ending paragraph summarizes the opinion and makes a powerful statement.

Persuasive Essay Organization

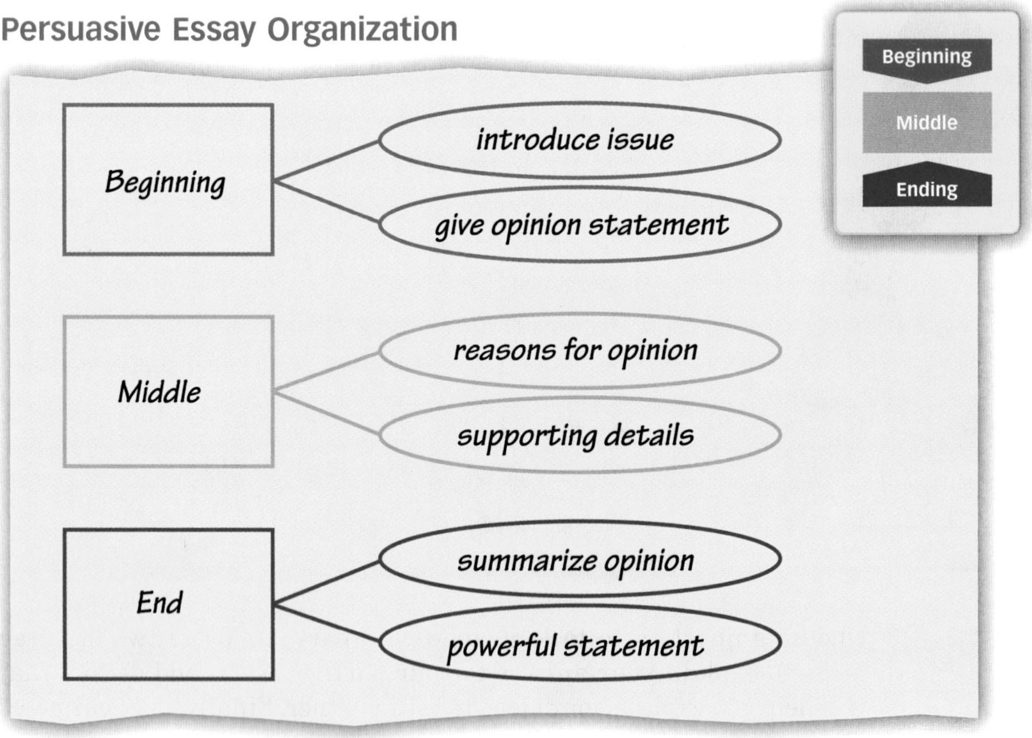

Turn and Talk

Talk with a partner about an opinion that you have.

I believe that ______________.

Vocabulary: Persuasive Writing

call to action	**convince**	**opinion**
counterargument	**persuasive**	**propose**
quotation	**solution**	

1. **Say the word.** Listen as your teacher reads the words aloud. Then repeat each word.

2. **Discover the meaning.** Work with a partner. Look for some of the vocabulary words in the yellow box next to the writing model on pages 233–234. Discuss the meanings with your partner and write notes about them.

3. **Learn more.** Listen as your teacher explains the meaning of each word. Work with your partner to correct or add to your notes about word meaning.

4. **Show your understanding.** Use your notebook to answer the questions below.
   - Why might someone write a persuasive essay?
   - How can you convince readers that a problem needs to be solved?
   - Why is a call to action an effective way to end a persuasive essay?

5. **Write it, show it.** In your notebook, add examples or simple definitions to help you remember what each word means.

ELPS 2G, 2I, 3G

Reading the Persuasive Model

What Do You Know?

Next you will read a sample persuasive essay about a pollution problem at a beach. What is pollution? What kinds of problems does pollution cause? How can the problems be solved? Give your ideas about this situation.

Build Background

Litter is trash that has not been thrown away properly. Litter in public places creates many problems. It is unhealthy and costly. It takes time and money for workers to pick it all up. Buying garbage cans and getting rid of the public's trash also costs money.

Listening

Listen as your teacher or a classmate reads aloud *Waterfront Rescue.* As you listen, pay attention to the problem, the proposed solution, and the call to action. Be prepared to answer the questions below.

1. How does the writer present the seriousness of the problem?
2. What solution does the writer propose?
3. What is the writer's call to action?

Key Words

business	**committee**	**community**
condition	**organize**	**solved**
sponsor	**volunteer**	

Look at the words in the box. You will see these words when you read the persuasive essay writing model. Think about a problem in your own community. Use the words to talk about the problem and possible solutions.

Read Along

Now it's your turn to read. Turn to pages 233–234. Read the writing model as your teacher or a classmate reads it aloud.

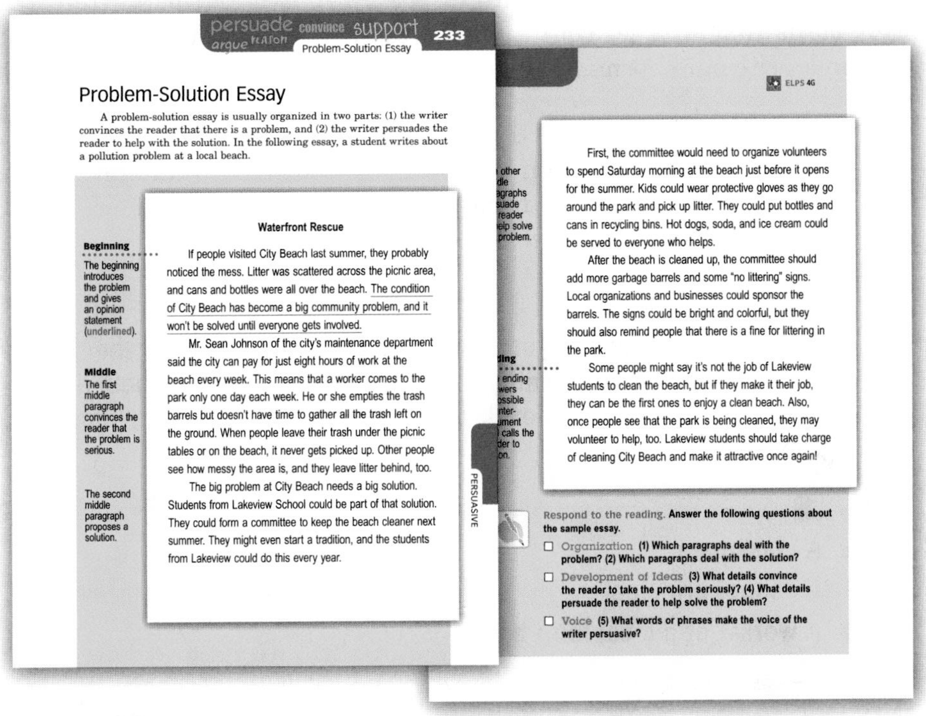
persuade convince support argue reason 233 Problem-Solution Essay

Problem-Solution Essay

A problem-solution essay is usually organized in two parts: (1) the writer convinces the reader that there is a problem, and (2) the writer persuades the reader to help with the solution. In the following essay, a student writes about a pollution problem at a local beach.

Beginning
The beginning introduces the problem and gives an opinion statement (underlined).

Middle
The first middle paragraph convinces the reader that the problem is serious.

The second middle paragraph proposes a solution.

Waterfront Rescue

If people visited City Beach last summer, they probably noticed the mess. Litter was scattered across the picnic area, and cans and bottles were all over the beach. The condition of City Beach has become a big community problem, and it won't be solved until everyone gets involved.

Mr. Sean Johnson of the city's maintenance department said the city can pay for just eight hours of work at the beach every week. This means that a worker comes to the park only one day each week. He or she empties the trash barrels but doesn't have time to gather all the trash left on the ground. When people leave their trash under the picnic tables or on the beach, it never gets picked up. Other people see how messy the area is, and they leave litter behind, too.

The big problem at City Beach needs a big solution. Students from Lakeview School could be part of that solution. They could form a committee to keep the beach cleaner next summer. They might even start a tradition, and the students from Lakeview could do this every year.

PERSUASIVE

ELPS 4G

...other ...dle ...graphs ...suade ...reader ...elp solve ...problem.

...ding ...ending ...wers ...ossible ...nter- ...ument ...calls the ...der to ...on.

First, the committee would need to organize volunteers to spend Saturday morning at the beach just before it opens for the summer. Kids could wear protective gloves as they go around the park and pick up litter. They could put bottles and cans in recycling bins. Hot dogs, soda, and ice cream could be served to everyone who helps.

After the beach is cleaned up, the committee should add more garbage barrels and some "no littering" signs. Local organizations and businesses could sponsor the barrels. The signs could be bright and colorful, but they should also remind people that there is a fine for littering in the park.

Some people might say it's not the job of Lakeview students to clean the beach, but if they make it their job, they can be the first ones to enjoy a clean beach. Also, once people see that the park is being cleaned, they may volunteer to help, too. Lakeview students should take charge of cleaning City Beach and make it attractive once again!

Respond to the reading. **Answer the following questions about the sample essay.**

- ☐ Organization **(1) Which paragraphs deal with the problem? (2) Which paragraphs deal with the solution?**
- ☐ Development of Ideas **(3) What details convince the reader to take the problem seriously? (4) What details persuade the reader to help solve the problem?**
- ☐ Voice **(5) What words or phrases make the voice of the writer persuasive?**

After Reading

Copy the following chart on a piece of paper and fill it in with information from the persuasive essay. Use your chart to summarize the writing model with a partner.

	Information from Essay
Problem	
Opinion	
Statement	
Solution	
Call to Action	

ELPS 3E, 3G, 3H, 3I

Oral Language: Persuasive Writing

The audience for a persuasive writing piece is the people you are trying to convince. When you speak or write to persuade, it is important to choose powerful words that will get your audience to agree with you. You may want to speak and write more formally to adults and more informally to people your own age.

Try It Read about the situation below. Then choose two audiences from the list. With a partner, discuss how the words you choose might be different for each audience.

Situation

The local food bank in your community is low on food for the needy and is looking for donations. You feel your school can help by having a food drive. You will explain the problem, propose a solution, and provide a call to action.

Audiences

- **A classmate**
- **A school principal**
- **A worker at a local food bank**

ELPS 2G, 2H, 2I, 3G, 3H

Effective Talk

When you answer a question, you can reply with only a few words or you can add more detail to your response. If your answer is short, it does not tell the listener much about your feelings or ideas. If you give an answer with details, it shows that you have thought hard about the question.

Read the question and answers below. In the first box, there is a phrase. In the second box, there is a sentence that answers the question. The third answer contains more detail and does a better job answering the question.

Why should you support the local food bank?

to help the needy

We should support the local food bank because they don't have enough food to help the needy.

The local food bank doesn't have enough food to help the needy. We can support them by having a food drive at school. People could donate cans and bags of food to the food bank.

Try It Choose a question to talk about with a partner. Write two or three ideas for answering the question. Next, add details that will help your partner understand your ideas. Finally, use your notes as you and your partner discuss your answers to the questions.

Here are some ideas to get you started.

1. What is a problem at your school that students can help solve? How can they help?
2. What is a problem in your community that your school can help solve? What can your school do?

ELPS 3E, 3G, 3H

Language of Response Writing

When you write a response to a text, you tell about something you read, such as a story or article. You use it to connect characters and themes. Your essay shows that you understand what you just read. In the first paragraph, you say what the text is about. In the middle paragraphs, you explain about the important events and describe the characters. In the ending paragraph, you summarize the theme or main idea.

Response to Texts Organization

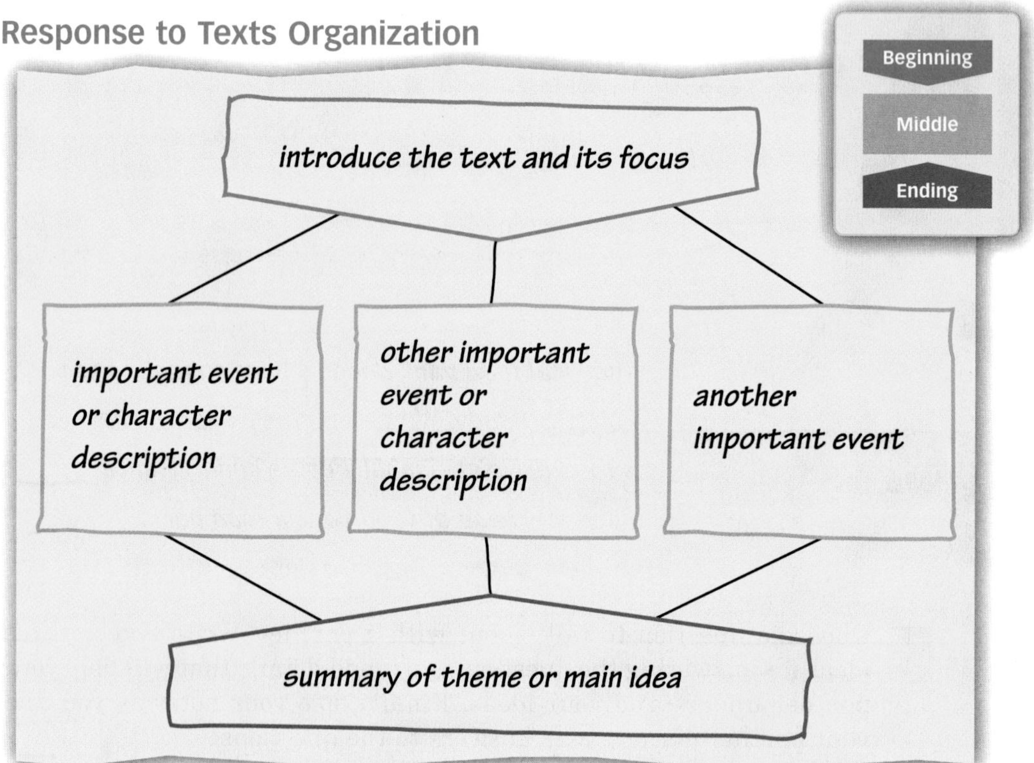

Turn and Talk

Talk with a partner about how to organize a response essay.

The response essay is organized____________________.

Vocabulary: Response Writing

characters	**details**	**focus**
events	**experience**	**interpretation**
summary	**theme**	

1. **Say the word.** Listen as your teacher reads the words aloud. Then repeat each word.

2. **Discover the meaning.** Work with a partner. Choose some of the vocabulary words in the yellow box next to the writing model on pages 301–302. Talk about the words you know and write notes about what you think the words mean.

3. **Learn more.** Listen as your teacher explains the meaning of each word. Check the notes you wrote and correct them. Then write meanings for the other words you learned. Work with your partner to find examples of these words in the writing sample on pages 301–302.

4. **Show your understanding.** Write answers to the questions below in your notebook.
   - Why is it important to know the focus of the text when you write a response essay?
   - Where in the essay does the writer summarize the theme or main idea? Why?

5. **Write it, show it.** Write some sentences about a favorite story in your notebook. Label different parts of your writing with some of the vocabulary words you just learned. Add notes about the other vocabulary words to help you remember and understand them.

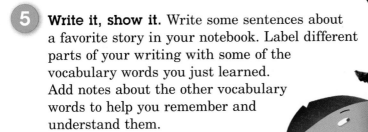

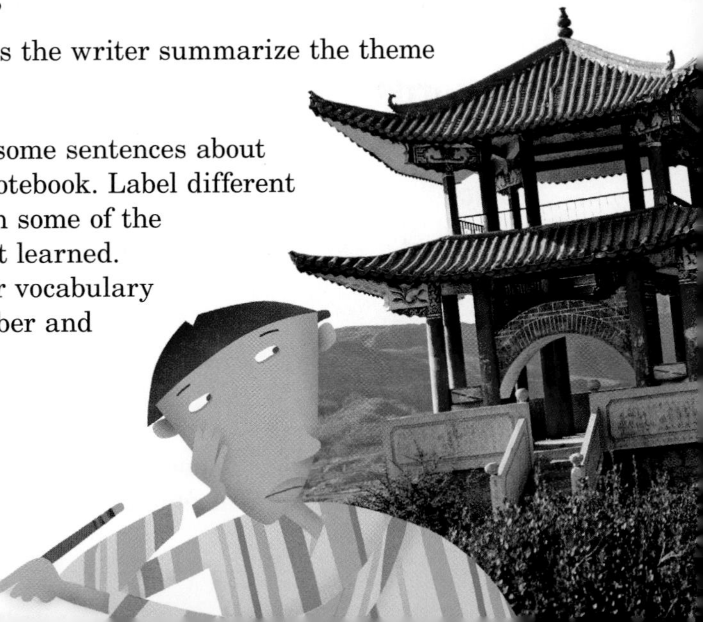

ELPS 2G, 2I, 4C

Reading the Response Model

What Do You Know?

Next you will read *Her Name Means Hope,* a response essay on pages **301–302**, about a girl who migrates, or moves, from Mexico to work in California. Have you ever moved to a faraway place? What does it feel like when you visit a new place?

Build Background

Since the United States became a country in 1776, immigrants, or people who come from other parts of the world, have moved here. Some immigrants and many United States citizens work as migrant farm workers. There are many of these jobs, and the skills can be learned quickly. The workers often move as the seasons change and new crops are planted and grow. Because of this, it is often difficult for their children to go to school every day.

Listening

Listen as your teacher or a classmate reads *Her Name Means Hope* aloud. As you listen, write notes about the problems the main character experiences. Think about what the theme of the story might be. Be ready to answer these questions:

1. How is Esperanza different from other migrant workers?
2. What are some of the problems immigrants have in the United States?
3. What is the theme of the story?

Key Words

advice	dignity	immigrant
intelligent	journey	migrant worker
poverty	survive	

Look at the words in the box. You will see these words when you read the writing model. Write a sentence for each word. Share your sentences with a partner. Discuss how your understanding of each word is either the same as or different from as your partner's understanding.

ELPS 4G, 4I

Read Along

Now it's your turn to read. Turn to page 301–302. Read the writing model as your teacher or a classmate reads it aloud. Think about how the paragraphs work together.

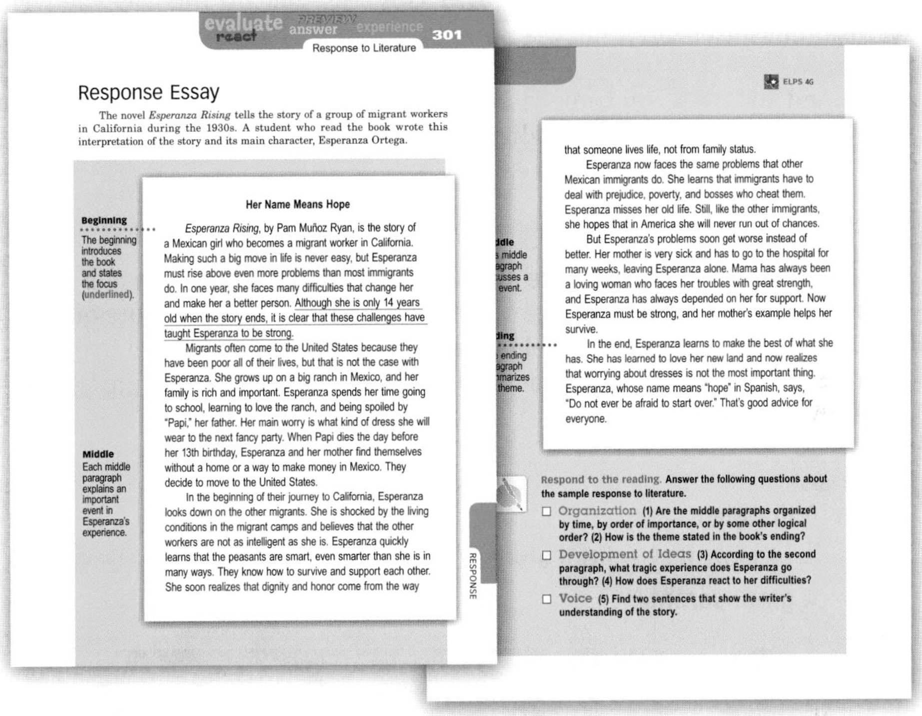
evaluate react answer experience 301
Response to Literature

Response Essay

The novel *Esperanza Rising* tells the story of a group of migrant workers in California during the 1930s. A student who read the book wrote this interpretation of the story and its main character, Esperanza Ortega.

Beginning The beginning introduces the book and states the focus (underlined).

Her Name Means Hope

Esperanza Rising, by Pam Muñoz Ryan, is the story of a Mexican girl who becomes a migrant worker in California. Making such a big move in life is never easy, but Esperanza must rise above even more problems than most immigrants do. In one year, she faces many difficulties that change her and make her a better person. Although she is only 14 years old when the story ends, it is clear that these challenges have taught Esperanza to be strong.

Middle Each middle paragraph explains an important event in Esperanza's experience.

Migrants often come to the United States because they have been poor all of their lives, but that is not the case with Esperanza. She grows up on a big ranch in Mexico, and her family is rich and important. Esperanza spends her time going to school, learning to love the ranch, and being spoiled by "Papi," her father. Her main worry is what kind of dress she will wear to the next fancy party. When Papi dies the day before her 13th birthday, Esperanza and her mother find themselves without a home or a way to make money in Mexico. They decide to move to the United States.

In the beginning of their journey to California, Esperanza looks down on the other migrants. She is shocked by the living conditions in the migrant camps and believes that the other workers are not as intelligent as she is. Esperanza quickly learns that the peasants are smart, even smarter than she is in many ways. They know how to survive and support each other. She soon realizes that dignity and honor come from the way

RESPONSE

ELPS 4G

that someone lives life, not from family status.

Esperanza now faces the same problems that other Mexican immigrants do. She learns that immigrants have to deal with prejudice, poverty, and bosses who cheat them. Esperanza misses her old life. Still, like the other immigrants, she hopes that in America she will never run out of chances.

But Esperanza's problems soon get worse instead of better. Her mother is very sick and has to go to the hospital for many weeks, leaving Esperanza alone. Mama has always been a loving woman who faces her troubles with great strength, and Esperanza has always depended on her for support. Now Esperanza must be strong, and her mother's example helps her survive.

In the end, Esperanza learns to make the best of what she has. She has learned to love her new land and now realizes that worrying about dresses is not the most important thing. Esperanza, whose name means "hope" in Spanish, says, "Do not ever be afraid to start over." That's good advice for everyone.

Respond to the reading. **Answer the following questions about the sample response to literature.**

- ☐ Organization **(1) Are the middle paragraphs organized by time, by order of importance, or by some other logical order? (2) How is the theme stated in the book's ending?**
- ☐ Development of Ideas **(3) According to the second paragraph, what tragic experience does Esperanza go through? (4) How does Esperanza react to her difficulties?**
- ☐ Voice **(5) Find two sentences that show the writer's understanding of the story.**

After Reading

Copy the following chart on a piece of paper and fill it with the answers to these questions. What is Esperanza like? How did she change when she came to the United States? Discuss your ideas with a partner.

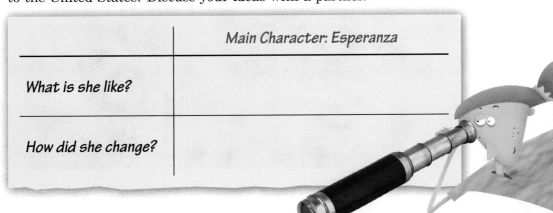

	Main Character: Esperanza
What is she like?	
How did she change?	

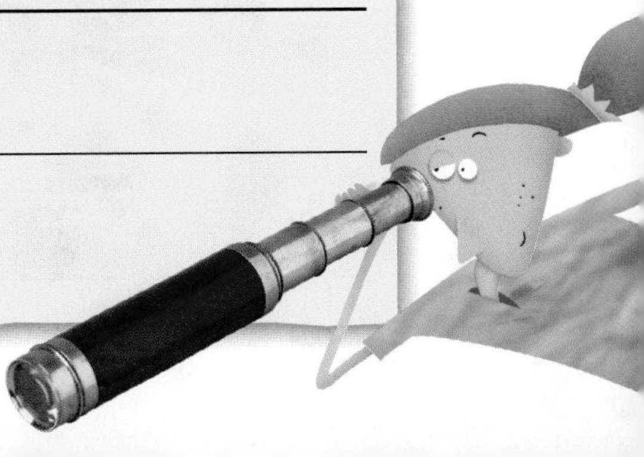

LANGUAGE

ELPS 3H

Oral Language: Response Writing

The person or people who will listen to you or read your writing are called the audience. When you speak or write, it is important to choose just the right words that will reach your audience. In writing, the tone, or the way you write, will be different for each audience.

Try It Read about the situation below. Then choose two audiences from the list. With a partner, discuss how the words you choose might be different for each audience.

Situation

You read a story you like about a boy named Barry who wants to learn to paint. A girl at school agrees to help him. Barry's picture gets displayed at school. Barry helps the girl play baseball. This is a book about what happens when people help each other. You will explain why you liked the book.

Audiences

- **A librarian**
- **An elementary school student**
- **A grandparent**

ELPS 2G, 3G, 3H

Effective Talk

When you answer a question, you might use one word, a few words, a sentence, or a few sentences to help explain your ideas. Explanations include details about the main ideas you are presenting. When you use more details to tell about something, the reader will have a better understanding of what you are trying to say.

Read the question and the answers below. In the first box, there are only two words. In the second box, a sentence answers the question. The third box contains more details and gives the reader a better idea of what the story is about.

What is the theme of the book?

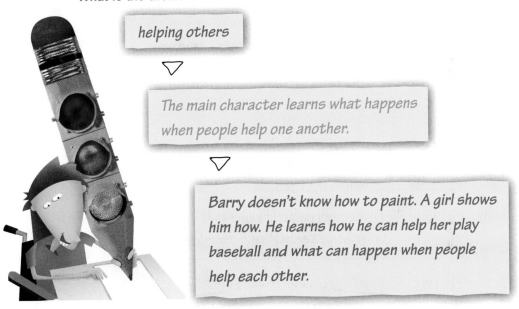

helping others

The main character learns what happens when people help one another.

Barry doesn't know how to paint. A girl shows him how. He learns how he can help her play baseball and what can happen when people help each other.

Try It Think of new questions your partner might ask you about a story that you have read. Write notes about details that would help to answer these questions for your partner. Use your notes to describe your questions and answers to your partner. Here are some ideas to get you started.

1. What traits does the main character have that make me like or dislike him or her?
2. What is the most important event in this book?

ELPS 3G, 3H

Language of Creative Writing

Creative writing is writing that tells a story. In some stories, the main character experiences a conflict and has to make a difficult decision. The story gets more interesting until the character makes his or her decision. The ending tells how the character changes.

Creative Writing Organization

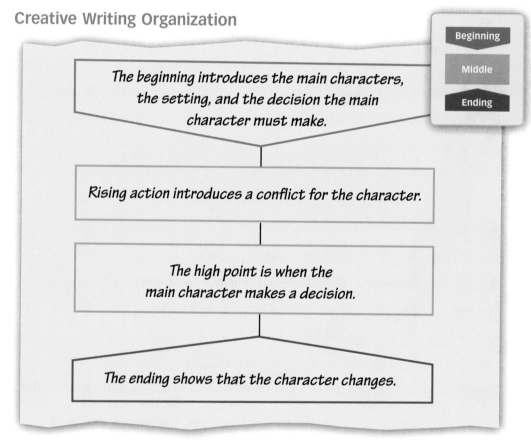

Beginning

Middle

Ending

The beginning introduces the main characters, the setting, and the decision the main character must make.

Rising action introduces a conflict for the character.

The high point is when the main character makes a decision.

The ending shows that the character changes.

Turn and Talk

Talk with a partner about why the graphic organizer helps writers to create an interesting story.

The graphic organizer helps ______________.

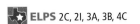

Vocabulary: Creative Writing

conclusion	**conflict**	**high point**
rising action	**setting**	**tension**
tough decision		

1. **Say the word.** Listen and read along as your teacher reads the words aloud. Notice the words that end in *-ion* and how they sound. Practice pronouncing each word.

2. **Discover the meaning.** Work with a partner. Choose some of the vocabulary words in the yellow box next to the writing model on pages **362–363**. Talk about the words you know. Write notes about what you think the words mean.

3. **Learn more.** Listen as your teacher explains the meaning of each word. Work with your partner to find examples of these words in the writing sample. Write notes about other new words.

4. **Show your understanding.** Write answers to the questions below in your notebook. Your teacher will give you directions.
   - What are some ways you can introduce characters and settings?
   - How can you find the rising action in a story?
   - Does the main character always learn something and make changes? Why or why not?

5. **Write it, show it.** Write short sentences in your notebook to help you remember what the words mean. Try to connect the meanings by using more than one vocabulary word in a sentence.

ELPS 2G, 2I, 3G

Reading the Creative Writing Model

What Do You Know?

Next you will read *Just Keep Going . . .* , a short story about a girl who made a difficult decision at a school dance. Do you like to dance? Would you ask someone to dance?

Build Background

Some schools have dances for students. Volunteers help decorate the gym, set up, and serve the food. In the past, people took dates to dances. Most of the time, boys asked girls to be their dates. Girls almost never asked boys. Now many people go without dates. They go with a friend or a group of friends. If people have dates, the girls will ask boys to go as often as boys ask the girls.

Listening

Listen as your teacher or a classmate reads *Just Keep Going . . .* aloud. As you listen, take notes about the decision, the rising action, and the high point of the plot. Be ready to discuss the questions below with a partner.

1. What is the setting of the story?
2. What are the main events?
3. Why does Celia smile at the end of the story?

Key Words

bleachers	button-down shirt	clenched
cologne	deep breath	khaki pants
ladle	pounding beat	slow music
sink into the floor	teetering on a tightrope	

Look at the words and phrases in the box above. You will find these words when you read the short story writing model. The writer used these words and phrases to create a vivid image of the setting and action. With a partner, use the words to talk about people at a school dance or party. Talk about what they are wearing, what they might do, and how they feel. Describe people who are shy and those who are outgoing.

ELPS 4G, 4I

Read Along

Now it's your turn to read. Turn to page 362–363. Read the writing model as your teacher or a classmate reads it aloud.

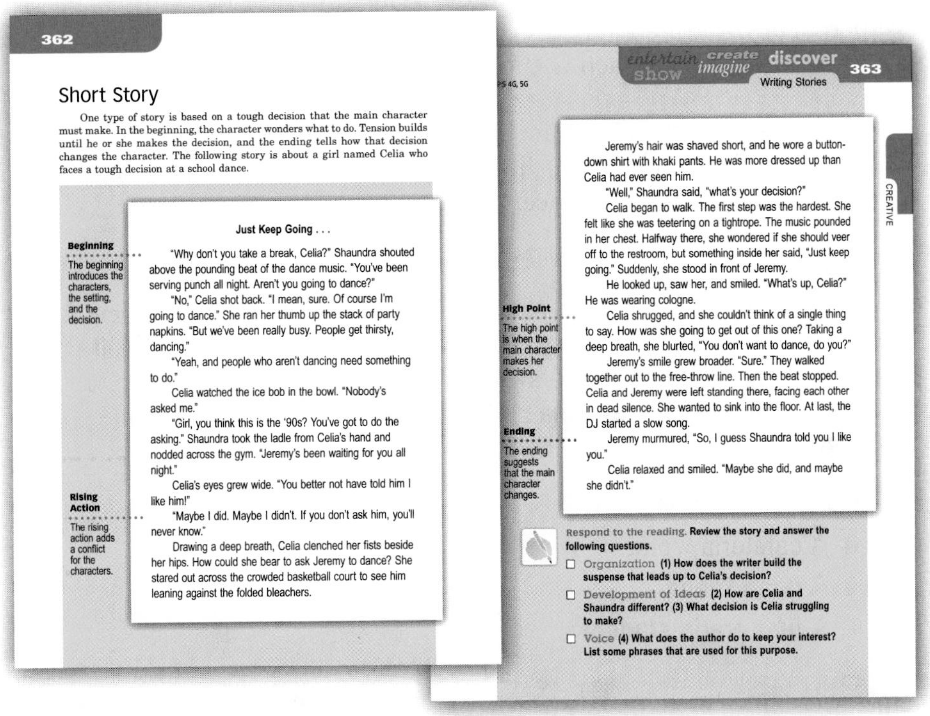
362

Short Story

One type of story is based on a tough decision that the main character must make. In the beginning, the character wonders what to do. Tension builds until he or she makes the decision, and the ending tells how that decision changes the character. The following story is about a girl named Celia who faces a tough decision at a school dance.

Beginning
The beginning introduces the characters, the setting, and the decision.

Rising Action
The rising action adds a conflict for the characters.

Just Keep Going . . .

"Why don't you take a break, Celia?" Shaundra shouted above the pounding beat of the dance music. "You've been serving punch all night. Aren't you going to dance?"

"No," Celia shot back. "I mean, sure. Of course I'm going to dance." She ran her thumb up the stack of party napkins. "But we've been really busy. People get thirsty, dancing."

"Yeah, and people who aren't dancing need something to do."

Celia watched the ice bob in the bowl. "Nobody's asked me."

"Girl, you think this is the '90s? You've got to do the asking." Shaundra took the ladle from Celia's hand and nodded across the gym. "Jeremy's been waiting for you all night."

Celia's eyes grew wide. "You better not have told him I like him!"

"Maybe I did. Maybe I didn't. If you don't ask him, you'll never know."

Drawing a deep breath, Celia clenched her fists beside her hips. How could she bear to ask Jeremy to dance? She stared out across the crowded basketball court to see him leaning against the folded bleachers.

entertain create imagine discover show 363
Writing Stories
CREATIVE

Jeremy's hair was shaved short, and he wore a button-down shirt with khaki pants. He was more dressed up than Celia had ever seen him.

"Well," Shaundra said, "what's your decision?"

Celia began to walk. The first step was the hardest. She felt like she was teetering on a tightrope. The music pounded in her chest. Halfway there, she wondered if she should veer off to the restroom, but something inside her said, "Just keep going." Suddenly, she stood in front of Jeremy.

He looked up, saw her, and smiled. "What's up, Celia?" He was wearing cologne.

Celia shrugged, and she couldn't think of a single thing to say. How was she going to get out of this one? Taking a deep breath, she blurted, "You don't want to dance, do you?"

Jeremy's smile grew broader. "Sure." They walked together out to the free-throw line. Then the beat stopped. Celia and Jeremy were left standing there, facing each other in dead silence. She wanted to sink into the floor. At last, the DJ started a slow song.

Jeremy murmured, "So, I guess Shaundra told you I like you."

Celia relaxed and smiled. "Maybe she did, and maybe she didn't."

High Point
The high point is when the main character makes her decision.

Ending
The ending suggests that the main character changes.

Respond to the reading. Review the story and answer the following questions.
Organization (1) How does the writer build the suspense that leads up to Celia's decision?
Development of Ideas (2) How are Celia and Shaundra different? (3) What decision is Celia struggling to make?
Voice (4) What does the author do to keep your interest? List some phrases that are used for this purpose.

After Reading

Copy the following chart on your own paper. Fill in the chart with sensory details from the story writing model. Talk with a partner about how these details helped you understand the writing model.

See	Smell	Hear	Taste	Touch/Feel

LANGUAGE

ELPS 3H, 3G, 3I

Oral Language: Creative Writing

When you write a short story, you want to entertain your audience. When you speak or write to entertain, it is important to choose just words that will keep your readers' and listeners' interest. In writing, the tone, or the way you write, will be different for each audience.

Try It Read about the situation below. Then choose two audiences from the list. With a partner, discuss how the words you choose might be different for each audience.

Situation

Regina just moved to a new city. She is lonely. She is in a new school and doesn't know anyone. She meets a girl in class and talks to her. They like many of the same things. The girl invites Regina to eat with her at lunch. She makes many new friends. You will retell the story.

Audiences

- **A cafeteria worker**
- **A good friend**
- **A first grade student**

Effective Talk

When you answer a question, you might use a phrase, a complete sentence, or many sentences. Summaries include important ideas that help readers understand what they are reading. When you use more details to summarize or retell a story, the reader will have a better understanding.

Read the question and the answers below. In the first box, there are only two words. In the second box, a sentence answers the question. The third box contains more detail and does more to answer the question.

What happens when the character moves to a new city?

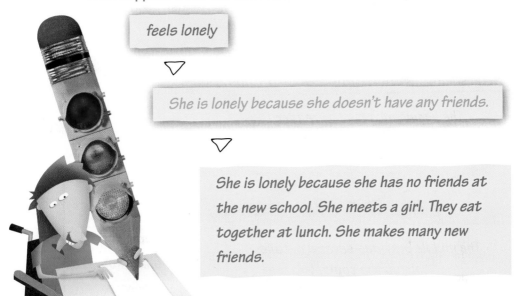

feels lonely

She is lonely because she doesn't have any friends.

She is lonely because she has no friends at the new school. She meets a girl. They eat together at lunch. She makes many new friends.

Try It Choose a new question that you would like to talk about with a partner. First make notes about details that would give your partner more information about your ideas. Then use your notes to describe your ideas to your partner.

Here are some ideas to get you started.

1. What would you do if you went to a party and didn't know anyone?
2. How would you get a friend to go with you to a place where you didn't want to go alone?

ELPS 3E, 3G, 3H

Language of Research Writing

When you write a research report, you share what you learned in your investigation of a topic. Your research topic may be assigned, or you may choose to write about something you like. In the beginning of most research writing, you explain why you are writing the paper. This explanation is called the controlling idea. The middle paragraphs provide details about the topic. The ending sums up the writing and often gives the reader another interesting fact. Sources are listed on a separate sheet of paper.

Research Report Organization

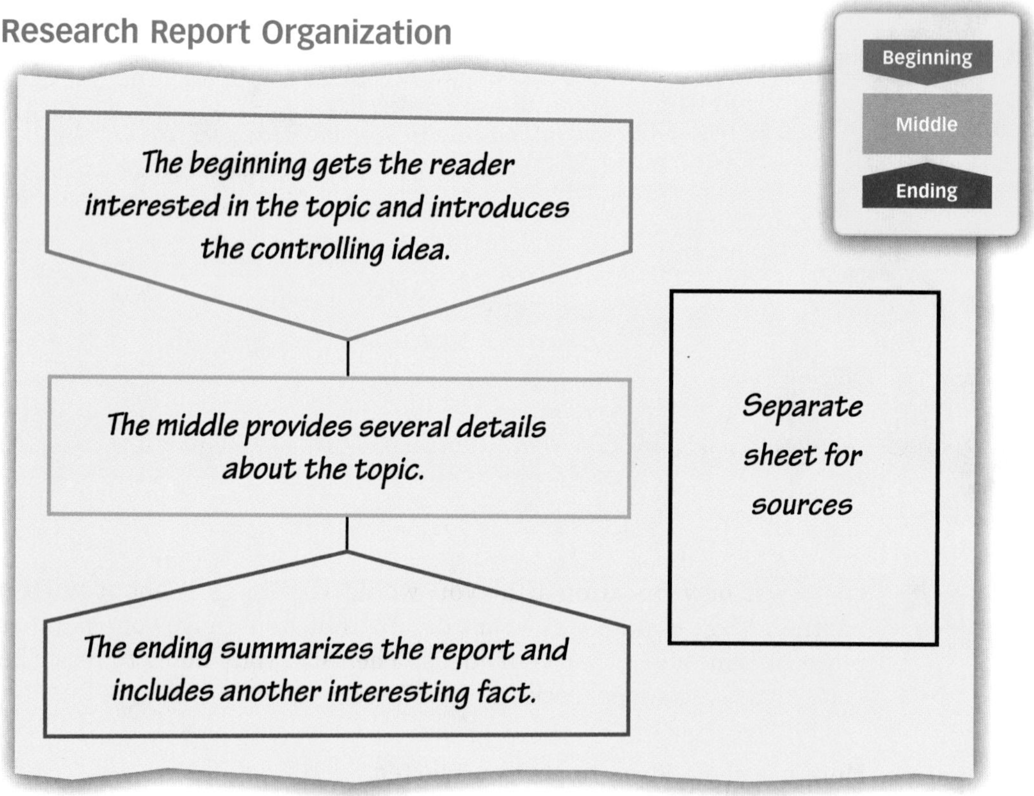
Beginning
Middle
Ending
The beginning gets the reader interested in the topic and introduces the controlling idea.
The middle provides several details about the topic.
The ending summarizes the report and includes another interesting fact.
Separate sheet for sources

Turn and Talk

Talk with a partner about each part of the graphic organizer.

The beginning________________. The middle________________.
The ending________________.

ELPS 2C, 2I, 3B, 4C

Vocabulary: Research Writing

background	**quotations**	**sources cited**
reader's attention	**research**	**topic sentence**
sums up	**controlling idea**	

1. **Say the word.** Listen and read along as your teacher reads the words or phrases aloud. Then repeat each word or phrase.

2. **Discover the meaning.** Work with a partner. Choose some of the vocabulary words or phrases in the boxes next to the writing model on pages 402–406. Talk about the words or phrases you know. Write notes about what you think the words or phrases mean.

3. **Learn more.** Listen as your teacher explains the meaning of each word or phrase. Work with your partner to check and correct your earlier notes. Find examples of these words or phrases in the writing sample on pages 402–406.

4. **Show your understanding.** Answer the questions below in your notebook. Your teacher will give you directions.
   - How can you begin a report to gain the reader's attention?
   - What is the purpose of the controlling idea?
   - Why do you use quotations? What punctuation do you use to show quotations?

5. **Write it, show it.** In your vocabulary notebook, add notes or drawings to help you remember what each word or phrase means. For example, you can draw an outline of a research paper and label the parts, such as controlling idea, to show where each one appears. Then include examples of words you cannot draw.

ELPS 2G, 2I, 4C

Reading the Research Report Model

What Do You Know?

Next you will read a research report about a man who was a leader in Texas over 100 years ago. Who are some leaders that you know about? Where and when did they live? What makes a person a good leader?

Build Background

Texas was a country before it became a part of the United States in 1845. During this time, both the United States and Texas had many problems. Wars were fought, there was slavery in some states, and many people were forced to leave their homes. Southern states even decided to form their own country. At this time, both Texas and the United States needed strong leaders to make difficult decisions.

Listening

Listen as your teacher or a classmate reads *An Independent Leader* aloud. As you listen, make a note about the controlling idea, or the main idea the writer wants to emphasize. Writers include important details, specific pieces of information, to support the controlling idea. For example, the writer uses words like those in the box to give more information. Listen for these words. Be ready to answer the questions below.

1. In what ways did Sam Houston serve as a leader?
2. How did Sam Houston help other people?
3. Why is Sam Houston such an important part of Texas history?

Key Words

beloved	**conscience**	**founders**
independent	**loyalty**	**seceding**
spirit	**survive**	

Look at the words in the box. You will see these words when you read the writing model. With a partner, use the words to talk about how leaders should be able to help people. Discuss what you think leaders should do where you live.

ELPS 4G, 4I

Read Along

Now it's your turn to read. Turn to pages 402–406. Read the writing model as your teacher or a classmate reads it aloud.

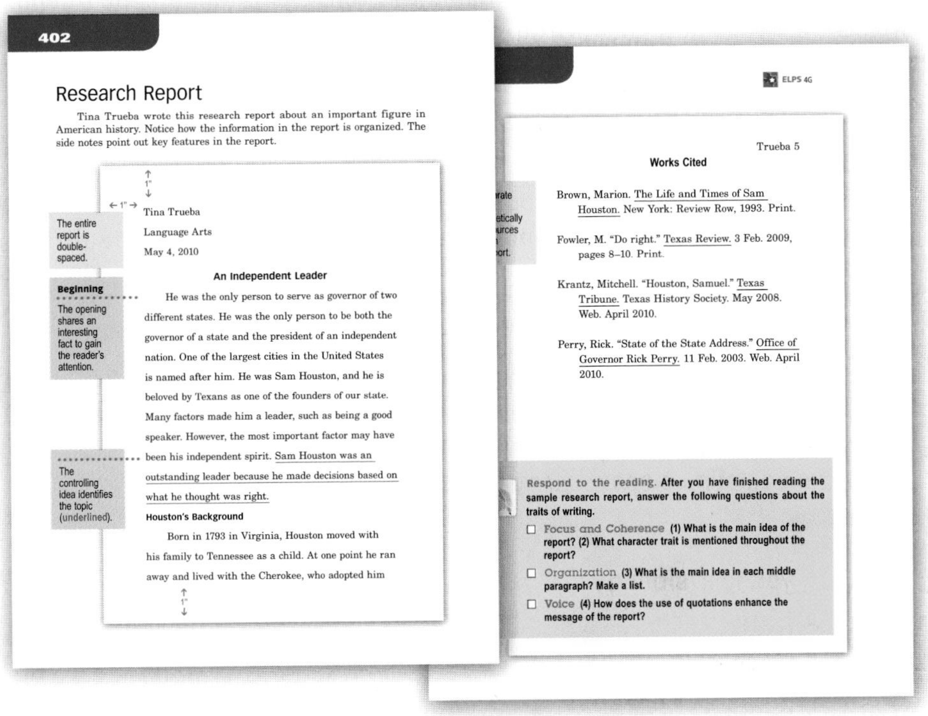
402

Research Report

Tina Trueba wrote this research report about an important figure in American history. Notice how the information in the report is organized. The side notes point out key features in the report.

The entire report is double-spaced.

Tina Trueba
Language Arts
May 4, 2010

An Independent Leader

Beginning
The opening shares an interesting fact to gain the reader's attention.

He was the only person to serve as governor of two different states. He was the only person to be both the governor of a state and the president of an independent nation. One of the largest cities in the United States is named after him. He was Sam Houston, and he is beloved by Texans as one of the founders of our state. Many factors made him a leader, such as being a good speaker. However, the most important factor may have been his independent spirit. Sam Houston was an outstanding leader because he made decisions based on what he thought was right.

The controlling idea identifies the topic (underlined).

Houston's Background

Born in 1793 in Virginia, Houston moved with his family to Tennessee as a child. At one point he ran away and lived with the Cherokee, who adopted him

ELPS 4G

Trueba 5

Works Cited

Brown, Marion. The Life and Times of Sam Houston. New York: Review Row, 1993. Print.

Fowler, M. "Do right." Texas Review. 3 Feb. 2009, pages 8–10. Print.

Krantz, Mitchell. "Houston, Samuel." Texas Tribune. Texas History Society. May 2008. Web. April 2010.

Perry, Rick. "State of the State Address." Office of Governor Rick Perry. 11 Feb. 2003. Web. April 2010.

Respond to the reading. After you have finished reading the sample research report, answer the following questions about the traits of writing.

- ☐ Focus and Coherence (1) What is the main idea of the report? (2) What character trait is mentioned throughout the report?
- ☐ Organization (3) What is the main idea in each middle paragraph? Make a list.
- ☐ Voice (4) How does the use of quotations enhance the message of the report?

After Reading

Copy the following chart on your own paper. Fill in the chart with details you learned about Sam Houston. Discuss your details with a partner. Decide which detail you think is most important.

	Sam Houston
Background	
Accomplishments	
Legacy	

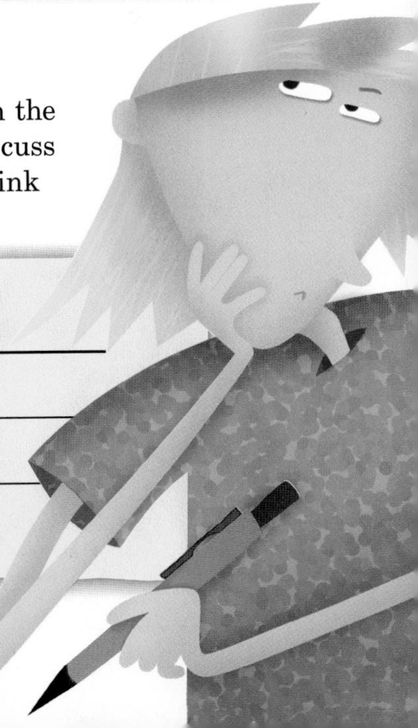

LANGUAGE

ELPS 3G, 3H, 3I

Oral Language: Research Writing

When writing a research report, you need to explain your topic to the audience. When you speak or write about the topic, it is important to choose just words that your audience will understand. Depending upon your audience, your writing might be formal or informal.

Try It Read about the research topic below. Then choose two audiences from the list. Think about what each audience would be interested in knowing about your topic if you had to retell it. With a partner, discuss how the words and examples you choose might be different for each audience.

Topic

Europe is a very interesting place to explore. It is a continent with many countries that are close together. The people in Europe speak different languages. Because the countries are so close, the people sometimes speak many languages.

Audiences

- **A younger sibling**
- **A pilot**
- **A teacher**

ELPS 2G, 2H, 2I, 3G, 3H

Effective Talk

When you answer a question, you might use one word, a few words, a sentence, or a few sentences. Explanations include details to help readers understand. When you use more details to tell about something, your reader will have a better understanding.

Read the question and the answers below. In the first box, there are only two words. In the second box, a sentence answers the question. The third box contains more detail and does more to answer the question.

How would you describe Europe?

interesting place

Europe is an interesting place to explore.

Europe is an interesting continent to explore. The countries are very close to each other. Because of this, the people often speak different languages.

Try It Choose a place in the world you would like to learn more about and talk about it with a partner. Think of questions you would like to ask about that place. Write two or three ideas for answering the questions. Add details that will help your partner understand what you are talking about. Use your notes as you discuss your answers.

Here are some ideas to get you started.

1. Is there a country you have read about that you would like to visit? How would you describe that country?
2. What are some languages you would like to speak? Where are they spoken?

Using Reference Materials

Reference materials are important tools for writers. These materials provide useful and reliable facts and information. For example, you might use an encyclopedia and an almanac to do research for a report. Most libraries have a range of reference books. Many references can also be found online, but you must be careful to evaluate the reliability and accuracy of online reference materials.

A dictionary and thesaurus can help you spell and understand words. If you use these reference materials often, your vocabulary will grow, and your writing and speaking skills will improve.

What's Ahead

- Checking a Dictionary
- Using a Thesaurus

TEKS 7.21

Checking a Dictionary

A dictionary is the most reliable source for learning the meanings of words. It offers the following aids and information.

- **Guide words** are located at the top of every page. They show the first and last entry words on a page, so you can tell whether the word you're looking up is listed on that page.
- **Entry words** are the words that are defined on the dictionary page. They are listed in alphabetical order for easy searching.
- **Parts of speech** labels tell you the different ways a word can be used. For example, the word *Carboniferous* can be used as a noun or as an adjective.
- **Syllable divisions** show where you can divide a word into syllables.
- **Spelling and capitalization** (if appropriate) are given for every entry word. If an entry is capitalized, capitalize it in your writing, too.
- **Spelling of verb forms** is shown. Watch for irregular forms of verbs because the spelling can be a whole new word.
- **Illustrations** are often provided to make a definition clearer.
- **Accent marks** show which syllable or syllables should be stressed when you say a word.
- **Pronunciations** are special spellings of a word to help you say the word correctly.
- **Pronunciation keys** give symbols to help you pronounce the entry word correctly.
- **Etymology** gives the history of a word [in brackets]. Knowing a little about a word's history can make the definition easier to remember.

Remember: Each word may have several definitions. It's important to read all of the meanings to determine if you're using the word accurately.

Try It Open a dictionary to any page and find the following information.

1. Write down the guide words on that page.
2. Find a multisyllable word and write it out by syllables. Jot down the word's part of speech. (There may be more than one.)
3. Find an entry that includes spelling of verb forms and write them down.

Dictionary Page

Guide words
Entry word
Part of speech
Syllable division
Spelling and capitalization
Spelling of verb forms
Illustration
Accent marks
Pronunciation
Pronunciation key
Etymology

carbon dioxide | carburetor 150

carbon dioxide *n.* A colorless or odorless gas that does not burn, composed of carbon and oxygen in the proportion CO_2 and present in the atmosphere or formed when any fuel containing carbon is burned. It is exhaled from an animal's lungs during respiration and is used by plants in photosynthesis. Carbon dioxide is used in refrigeration, in fire extinguishers, and in carbonated drinks.

carbonic acid *n.* A weak acid having the formula H_2CO_3. It exists only in solution and decomposes readily into carbon dioxide and water.

car·bon·if·er·ous (kär′bə-**nĭf**′ər-əs) *adj.* Producing or containing carbon or coal.

Carboniferous *n.* The geologic time comprising the Mississippian (or Lower Carboniferous) and Pennsylvanian (or Upper Carboniferous) Periods of the Paleozoic Era, from about 360 to 286 million years ago. During the Carboniferous, widespread swamps formed in which plant remains accumulated and later hardened into coal. See table at **geologic time.—Carboniferous** *adj.*

car·bon·ize (**kär**′bə-nīz′) *tr. v.* **car·bon·ized, car·bon·iz·ing, car·bon·iz·es 1.** To change an organic compound into carbon by heating. **2.** To treat, coat, or combine with carbon.—**car′bon·i·za′tion** (kär′be-nī-zā′shən) *n.*

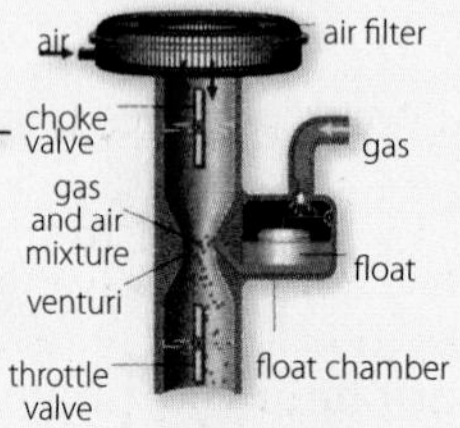

carburetor
cross section of a carburetor

carbon monoxide *n.* A colorless odorless gas that is extremely poisonous and has the formula CO. Carbon monoxide is formed when carbon or a compound that contains carbon burns incompletely. It is present in the exhaust gases of automobile engines.

carbon paper *n.* A paper coated on one side with a dark coloring matter, placed between two sheets of blank paper so that the bottom sheet will receive a copy of what is typed or written on the top sheet.

carbon tet·ra·chlor·ide (tĕt′rə-**klôr**′īd′) *n.* A colorless poisonous liquid that is composed of carbon and chlorine, has the formula CCl_4, and does not burn although it vaporizes easily. It is used in fire extinguishers and as a dry-cleaning fluid.

Car·bo·run·dum (kär′bə-**rŭn**′dəm) A trademark for an abrasive made of silicon carbide, used to cut, grind, and polish.

car·bun·cle (**kär**′bŭng′kəl) *n.* **1.** A painful inflammation in the tissue under the skin that is somewhat like a boil but releases pus from several openings. **2.** A deep-red garnet.

car·bu·re·tor (**kär**′bə-rā′tər *or* **kär**′byə-rā′tər) *n.* A device in a gasoline engine that vaporizes the gasoline with air to form an explosive mixture. [First written down in 1866 in English, from *carburet*, carbide, from Latin *carbō*, carbon.]

ă	pat	ôr	core
ā	pay	oi	boy
âr	care	ou	out
ä	father	ŏŏ	took
ĕ	pet	ŏŏr	lure
ē	be	ōō	boot
ĭ	pit	ŭ	cut
ī	bite	ûr	urge
îr	pier	th	thin
ŏ	pot	*th*	this
ō	toe	zh	vision
ô	paw	ə	about

Using a Thesaurus

A thesaurus is a useful reference tool for writers. It contains words and their synonyms, or words with similar meanings. A thesaurus will help you find alternate words, rather than repeating the same words over and over.

In most cases, a thesaurus will have the following features:

- **Entry words** are the words you are looking for in the thesaurus. They are listed in alphabetical order for easy searching.
- **Key words** are the words for which synonyms are listed. Sometimes, the entry word you are looking up is not a key word. For example, under the entry word *acquaintance,* the thesaurus may list "See *friend.*" You would then find the entry word *friend* to see the synonyms for *acquaintance.*
- **Synonyms** are words that have the same meaning as the key word.
- **Parts of speech** labels tell you the different ways a word can be used.
- **Pronunciations** are special spellings of a word to help you say the word correctly.
- **Antonyms** are words that have an opposite meaning as the key word you are looking up. For example, under the key word *friend,* a thesaurus may list *enemy* as an antonym.
- **Related words** are words that are similar to your key word in meaning, but may not be an exact synonym. For example, *individual* may be listed as a related words under the key word *friend.*

Below you will see a sample thesaurus entry for the key word *distract.*

distract (v.) bewilder, disturb, mislead, puzzle
Antonyms clarify, explain
Related Words put off, upset

Try It Use a thesaurus to find a new word to replace each word or phrase in italics. Write the new word. Then say the sentence with the new word to a partner.

1. Conor was feeling *worried* about the upcoming math test.
2. What does this symbol *mean?*
3. Don't *tire* yourself *out* lifting those boxes.

compare vary

ELPS 2C, 3D, 3E, 3G, 3H, 4C

Basic Grammar and Writing

Learning Language

Work with a partner. Read the meanings and share answers to the questions.

1. There are eight parts of speech writers use in their writing. They include nouns, adjectives, verbs, adverbs, pronouns, interjections, prepositions, and conjunctions.
   Which of these parts of speech do you think are most important in your writing? Why?
2. Nouns are words that name people, places, things, or ideas.
   What is an example of each of these kinds of nouns?
3. A paragraph is made up of several sentences. There is a main idea that is supported by each sentence.
   Write a paragraph by starting with a main idea and adding two sentences that support this main idea.

MODIFY CONNECT choose

Working with Words

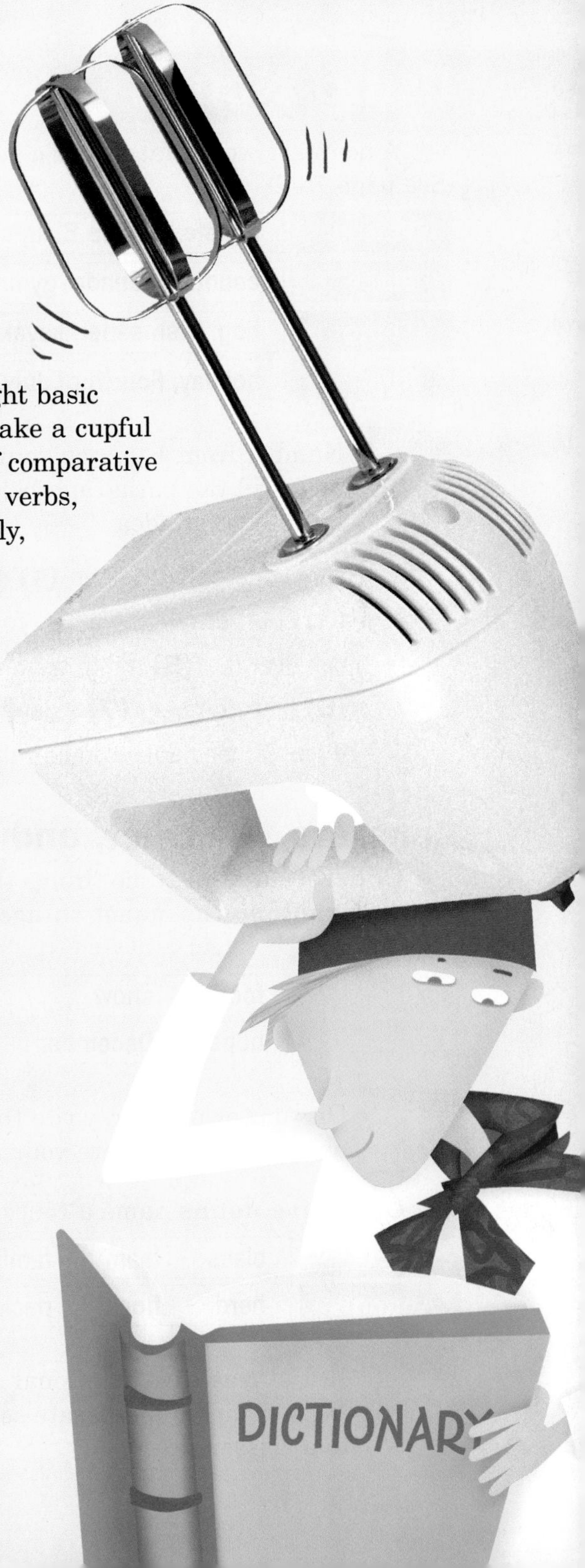

Writing is like cooking. You have eight basic ingredients, called the parts of speech. Take a cupful of specific nouns and add a tablespoon of comparative adjectives. Then blend in a pint of action verbs, seasoned with superlative adverbs. Finally, mix in the pronouns, interjections, prepositions, and conjunctions, and you'll be cooking with words!

This section provides some basic information about each part of speech and answers the question,

"How can I use words effectively in my own writing?"

What's Ahead

- **Using Nouns**
- **Using Pronouns**
- **Choosing Verbs**
- **Describing with Adjectives**
- **Describing with Adverbs**
- **Connecting with Prepositions**
- **Writing with Phrases**
- **Connecting with Conjunctions**

ELPS 3E

Using Nouns

A noun is a word that names a person, place, thing, or idea in your writing. (See page 754.)

Person	athlete, Bonnie Blair, students, President Taft
Place	country, Canada, gymnasium, Tampa, middle school
Thing	dog, Irish setter, kayaks, stopwatch
Idea	holiday, Fourth of July, strength, freedom

GRAMMAR Try It Number from 1 to 9 on your own paper. For each of the 9 underlined nouns in the paragraph below, write whether it is a person, a place, a thing, or an idea.

Volleyball is a team **(1)** sport. Team **(2)** members play on a **(3)** court divided by a net. To start, the **(4)** players on team A serve the ball over the **(5)** net to team B. Players on team B can hit the ball three **(6)** times on their **(7)** side of the net before returning the ball to team A. If team B isn't able to return the **(8)** ball, team A scores a **(9)** point.

Concrete, Abstract, and Collective Nouns

Concrete nouns name things that can be seen or touched.

Abstract nouns name things you can think about but cannot see or touch.

Concrete	food	snow	storm	heart
Abstract	hope	December	fear	love

GRAMMAR Try It On your own paper, write three more concrete nouns and three more abstract nouns. Share your nouns with a partner.

Collective nouns name a collection of people, animals, or things.

People	class	team	family	troop	crew
Animals	herd	flock	pack	pod	school

GRAMMAR Try It List at least five additional collective nouns of your own. Use each of these nouns in a separate sentence. Read one of your sentences aloud to a classmate.

TEKS 7.20A
ELPS 5G

Proper and Common Nouns

Proper nouns name specific people, places, things, or ideas. Proper nouns are always capitalized. A **common noun** is any noun that is not a proper noun.

	Person	Place	Thing	Idea
Common	catcher	stadium	bat	league
Proper	Rachel	Yankee Stadium	Louisville Slugger	American League

Common nouns — The man toured the stadium on the holiday.
Proper nouns — Randy Williams toured Yankee Stadium on Labor Day.

GRAMMAR Try It Make a chart like the one above. Add four more common and four more proper nouns. Be sure to capitalize the proper nouns.

General and Specific Nouns

When you use specific nouns in your writing, you give the reader a clear picture of people, places, things, and ideas. The following chart shows the difference between **general nouns** and **specific nouns**.

General	tennis player	tournament	court	principle
Specific	Roger Federer	U.S. Open	tennis court	fairness

GRAMMAR Try It Read the facts below about Pete Sampras. Then write a brief paragraph about him, using as many specific nouns as possible.

Full Name:	Pete Sampras
Born:	August 12, 1971
Birthplace:	Washington, D.C.
Family:	wife Bridgette Wilson, children Christian and Ryan
Occupation:	retired tennis player
Accomplishments:	has won 14 of tennis's Grand Slam titles (second highest number to date); ranked World No. 1 for a record 286 weeks

ELPS 3E

What can I do with nouns in my writing?

Show Possession

You can make your writing more specific by naming who (or what) possesses something. See the guidelines below. (Also see 664.4 and 666.1.)

Forming the Singular Possessive

- Add an apostrophe and an *s* to a singular noun: **Pat's ball.**
- For multi-syllable nouns ending in an *s* or a *z* sound, the possessive may be formed in two ways: **Cletus' glove** or **Cletus's glove.**

Forming the Plural Possessive

- Add an apostrophe for most plural nouns ending in *s*: **the boys' bats.**
- Add an apostrophe and an *s* for plural nouns not ending in *s*: **the men's lockers.**

GRAMMAR Try It List five singular nouns in one column and five plural nouns in another column. (Include at least one or two singular nouns that end in an *s* or a *z* sound.) Then exchange papers with a classmate and write a sentence for each noun, using the possessive form of the word. Discuss the results with your partner.

Rename the Subject

Whenever you use a noun after a linking verb *(am, is, are, was, were, be, been, being)*, the noun renames the subject and is called a **predicate noun**.

Dad was a pitcher for his high school team, but he was never a catcher.

GRAMMAR Try It List the 10 predicate nouns in the paragraph below.

Gita is not just any soccer player; she is the best scorer in the league. When she was a young girl, her mother was the coach of the local soccer team. Gita often tagged along with her mother to the matches. She must have been a keen observer because she learned very quickly when she started playing. Although her teammates were good players, Gita was a standout. She has been a top-rated player for the last three years. Gita has also been an excellent role model for youngsters, and someday she may be an excellent coach.

TEKS 7.19A(v)
ELPS 3E, 5B

Make the Meaning of the Verb Complete

Some sentences are not complete with just a subject and a verb.

Reggie threw. (*What* did Reggie throw?)

Nell trusts. (*Whom* does Nell trust?)

When you use a transitive verb like "threw" or "trusts" in a sentence, you need to include a **direct object** to make the meaning of the verb complete. The direct object is a noun (or pronoun) that answers the question *what* or *whom.*

Reggie threw the football. **Nell trusts her teammates.**

To add further information, you might include a noun (or pronoun) that answers the question *to whom* or *for whom*. This type of noun is called an **indirect object**. In order for a sentence to have an indirect object, it must also have a direct object.

Wayne tossed Raj the ball. (Wayne tossed the ball *to Raj.*)

I made my sister a pom-pom. (I made a pom-pom *for my sister.*)

GRAMMAR Try It Write the direct object in each of the following sentences. If there is an indirect object as well, write it and underline it.

Example: Tennis can give you a strong body.
body, you

1. This sport burns calories, too.
2. Aunt Sheryl gave me a racquet.
3. I play tennis regularly.
4. Yesterday, I sent Ruth a powerful serve.

Add Specific Information

Another kind of object noun is the **object of a preposition** (see 756.7). A **prepositional phrase** begins with a preposition and ends with an object. You can use prepositional phrases to add specific information to sentences. The object of each prepositional phrase below is highlighted in blue. (Also see pages 554–555.)

I do some stretches before a game of tennis.

I also drink lots of water during a game.

GRAMMAR Try It Write a brief sports-related paragraph that includes five prepositional phrases. Underline the object of each prepositional phrase. Choose from these prepositions: *over, under, before, after, during,* and *against.* (See page 790 for more.) Read your paragraph aloud to a partner.

TEKS 7.19C
ELPS 5B

Using Pronouns

A pronoun is a word used in place of a noun. The noun replaced, or referred to, by the pronoun is called the pronoun's **antecedent**. The arrows below point to each pronoun's antecedent. (Also see 758.1.)

The volleyball team was determined, so it won the match.

Coach Johnson said that she never saw a team work so hard.

The **personal pronouns** listed below are the most common pronouns used by writers. (For a complete list of personal pronouns, see page 762.)

Personal Pronouns

I	you	he	she	it	we	they
me		him	her		us	them

Person and Number of a Pronoun

Pronouns show "person" and "number" in writing. The following chart shows which pronouns are used for the three different persons *(first, second, third)* and the two different numbers *(singular or plural).*

		Singular	Plural
First Person	(The person speaking)	I called.	We called.
Second Person	(The person spoken to)	You called.	You called.
Third Person	(The person spoken about)	He called. She called. It called.	They called.

GRAMMAR Try It Number your paper from 1 to 4. Write sentences that use the pronouns described below as subjects.

Example: first-person singular pronoun *(I)*
I want to join the basketball team.

1. third-person singular pronoun
2. third-person plural pronoun
3. second-person singular pronoun
4. first-person plural pronoun

Indefinite Pronouns

An **indefinite pronoun** refers to people or things that are not named or known. The chart below lists which indefinite pronouns are singular, which are plural, and which can be singular or plural.

Indefinite Pronouns

Singular				Plural	Singular or Plural
another	either	nobody	someone	both	all
anybody	everybody	no one	something	few	any
anyone	everyone	nothing		many	most
anything	everything	one		several	none
each	neither	somebody			

When you use a singular indefinite pronoun as a subject, the verbs and the other pronouns that refer to the subject all must be singular. If the indefinite pronoun is plural, the verbs and other pronouns must all be plural.

Singular

Everybody does her or his stretches before practice.

Plural

Several of the boys do their sit-ups after warming up.

Singular or Plural

Most of the time is spent on drills. (singular)
Most of the players are looking forward to the match. (plural)

Learning Language

Pronouns are useful because you can use them to replace nouns. Repeating nouns over and over can be distracting to your reader. In the example sentences below, the noun and pronoun are in blue type.

Arun lives in my building. Arun says Arun loves basketball.
Arun lives in my building. He says he loves basketball.

Working with a partner, rewrite the sentences below using pronouns in place of the nouns in blue type.

Diana walks to school. Diana goes through the park.
This present is for Yvette. I hope Yvette likes it.
Pao left earlier. Pao will spend two hours at Pao's soccer practice.

ELPS 5B, 5G

How can I use pronouns properly?

Avoid Repetition

You can use pronouns in your writing to avoid repeating the same nouns over and over again. (See pages 758–766.) Read the sample paragraph below. How many times did the writer use "Lance Armstrong"?

Without Pronouns

Lance Armstrong, a champion cyclist, was born in 1971. Lance Armstrong's competitive nature led Lance Armstrong to win the Iron Kids Triathlon when Lance Armstrong was only 13 years old. Armstrong became a member of the United States Olympic Team in 1992. Despite getting cancer at age 25, Lance Armstrong went on to win the Tour de France seven times by 2005.

Now read the revised sample below. The writer has replaced some of the nouns with pronouns. Which pronouns refer to Lance Armstrong?

With Pronouns

Lance Armstrong, a champion cyclist, was born in 1971. His competitive nature led him to win the Iron Kids Triathlon when he was only 13 years old. Armstrong became a member of the United States Olympic Team in 1992. Despite getting cancer at age 25, he went on to win the Tour de France seven times by 2005.

GRAMMAR Try It

On a separate sheet of paper, write a paragraph of at least five sentences describing your favorite sport, game, or activity. Use each of the pronouns from the following list once. Be sure you use each pronoun with the correct singular or plural antecedent. When you have finished, share your paragraph aloud with a partner.

Example: Every tennis player has <u>his</u> own way of serving the ball.

his	its	their	he	them	her	they	it

TEKS 7.19C
ELPS 5B

Avoid Agreement Problems

You can make your writing clear by using pronouns properly. You must use pronouns that agree with their antecedents. (An **antecedent** is the noun or pronoun that a pronoun replaces or refers to.) Pronouns must agree with their antecedents in number, person, and gender. (See **764.1–764.4**.)

When Mom and Dad go golfing, they usually rent a golf cart.

Uncle Carl didn't know how to golf, so Dad taught him.

Agreement in Number

The **number** of a pronoun is either singular or plural. The pronoun must match the antecedent in number.

- A singular pronoun refers to a singular antecedent.

Dad has had his own golf clubs since he was 18 years old.

- A plural pronoun refers to a plural antecedent.

All of the woods have their own protective covers.

GRAMMAR Try It

Using correct antecedents is important when writing your own sentences. Read the example sentences below (the pronouns are shown in black). Then, use each pronoun in the box below to write your own sentences. Read your sentences aloud to a partner. Have your partner identify the antecedent in each of your sentences.

Examples:

Dad plays golf whenever **he** gets a chance.

Golfers try to keep **their** scores as low as possible.

The pitted surface of a golf ball helps **it** fly smoothly.

his	its	their	he	them	her	they	it

Agreement in Person

When you use pronouns, you must choose either first, second, or third **person** pronouns. If you start a sentence with one "person," don't shift to another "person" later in the sentence.

Pronoun shift: **I have learned a lot about Babe, and with all that knowledge you can write an interesting report.**

Correct: **I have learned a lot about Babe, and with all that knowledge I can write an interesting report.**

GRAMMAR Try It

For each sentence below, change the underlined pronoun so it doesn't cause a shift in person.

1. We are studying famous athletes in their social studies class.
2. If golfers knew how many sports Babe shined in, you would be amazed.
3. She was an incredible athlete, and we won 13 straight golf tournaments in 1946.
4. Babe won 82 golf tournaments in all, and you became famous on both sides of the Atlantic.
5. Babe qualified for five Olympic events in 1932, but, as a woman, you could compete in only three.

Agreement in Gender

The **gender** of a pronoun *(her, his, its)* must be the same as the gender of its antecedent. Pronouns can be feminine (female), masculine (male), or neutral (neither male nor female).

Babe Didrikson's father required his children to take part in a sport.

Babe Didrikson excelled in nearly every sport she tried.

GRAMMAR Try It

Number your paper from 1 to 5. Correct each underlined pronoun so that it agrees with its antecedent in gender.

Babe challenged some old-fashioned ideas about his role in sports. Although best known for golf, she did not limit himself to that sport. He played basketball, tennis, and softball. Its participation in the 1932 Olympics led to three medals in track and field. The Associated Press named him Athlete of the Year six times.

What else should I know about pronouns?

Make Your References Clear

When you use a pronoun, don't confuse your reader by making its antecedent unclear. Make sure that the word your pronoun refers to is obvious; it should plainly refer to only one noun.

Confusing Pronoun Reference

Ancient Egyptian drawings show some people playing handball. They were found in tombs.

(Which noun—*drawings* or *people*—does the pronoun *they* refer to?)

There are two ways to fix this error. The first way is to reword the sentences to clarify your meaning.

In ancient Egyptian tombs, drawings were found. They show some people playing handball.

The second way to fix the error is to reword the sentences without using a pronoun.

Ancient Egyptian drawings show some people playing handball. The drawings were found in tombs. (or)

Ancient Egyptian drawings found in tombs show some people playing handball.

GRAMMAR Try It

Correctly rewrite the passage below that contains confusing pronoun references. (There are five.)

People played many games long before they were included in the Olympics. Field hockey, for example, is one of the oldest competitive sports in the world. It began with the ancient civilizations of Egypt, Greece, and Rome.

Today, players use field hockey rules that were developed in the mid-1800s in England. They say that there are 11 people per team. Each team tries to advance the ball down the field to the other team's goal cage. Players can hit it only with the flat side of their sticks. Players can shoot at the goal only from within the "striking circle," which extends 16 feet from the goal.

Now, every four years, field hockey teams vie for the World Cup. When the 2002 World Cup competition was held in Perth, Australia, more people became aware of it. In fact, field hockey has gained in popularity every year.

Choosing Verbs

Writers must constantly make choices, and one of their most important choices is which verb to use to express their thoughts clearly.

Action Verbs

An **action verb** tells what the subject is doing. Action verbs help bring your writing to life.

A luge zooms down ice-covered canals.
Lugers race at high speeds through the frozen canals.

Linking Verbs

A **linking verb** connects (links) a subject to a noun or an adjective in the predicate.

Common Linking Verbs

Forms of "be"	be is	are was	were am	been being		
Other linking verbs	appear seem	become smell	feel sound	grow taste	look	remain

A luge is a type of sled.
(The linking verb *is* connects the subject *luge* to the noun *type*. *Type* is a **predicate noun**.)

The rider must be brave.
(The linking verb *be* connects the subject *rider* to the adjective *brave*. *Brave* is a **predicate adjective**.)

GRAMMAR Try It

For the sentences below, write the subject, the linking verb, and the predicate noun or predicate adjective that follows the verb. (One of the sentences does not include a linking verb.)

One kind of luge track is natural, following the contours of a snowy mountain. The other kind (used in the Olympics) is a frozen ice canal built for speed. The luger lies on the luge, faceup and feetfirst. During a run, she or he remains still to increase speed. Obviously, speed is very important. The luger with the fastest run becomes the leader in a competition.

Helping Verbs

The simple predicate may include a **helping verb** plus the main verb. The helping verb makes the verb more specific.

Valerie will **attempt a luge run.**
(The helping verb *will* helps express future tense.)

She may **need special clothing.** (*May* helps express a possibility.)

The track, which was destroyed, had been **built for the 1984 Olympics in Sarajevo.** (*Had been* helps express past perfect tense and passive voice.)

GRAMMAR Try It Select a helping verb from the following list to complete each sentence in the paragraph below. One helping verb will be used twice.

would	**does**	**will**	**could**	**should**

I **(1)** ______ like to ride a luge, but Mom **(2)** ______ not think that's a good idea. Dad thinks that I **(3)** ______ learn more about luges first. Are there any luge schools that I **(4)** ______ attend? I **(5)** ______ research that on the Internet, and perhaps I **(6)** ______ find an instructor nearby.

Irregular Verbs

Most verbs in the English language are regular. A writer adds *ed* to regular verbs to show a past action. A writer can also use *has, have,* or *had* with the past participle to make other verb tenses. **Irregular verbs** do not follow the *ed* rule. Instead of adding *ed* to show past tense, the word might change. (See the list of irregular verbs on page 772.)

Present	I speak.	She runs.
Past	Yesterday I spoke.	Yesterday she ran.
Past Participle	I have spoken.	She has run.

GRAMMAR Try It On your own paper, write five sentences using the irregular verbs listed below. Share your best sentence with a partner.

1. took
2. make
3. has seen
4. went
5. ride

How can I use verbs effectively?

Show Powerful Action

You can use **action verbs** to show the reader exactly what is happening (or has happened).

Ordinary Action Verbs

Vashon shot the basketball through the hoop.

Dave got the rebound and ran up the court.

Powerful Action Verbs

Vashon flipped the basketball through the hoop.

Dave grabbed the rebound and dashed up the court.

Try to avoid using linking verbs *(is, are, was, were)* too much. Often, a stronger (action) verb can be made from another word in the same sentence.

Kristy is a good basketball player. (linking verb)

Kristy plays basketball well.
(The action verb *plays* is made from the word *player.*)

Create Active Voice

A verb is in the **active voice** if the subject in the sentence is doing the action. (See page 776.) A verb is passive if the subject is not doing the action. Try to use active verbs as much as possible because they make your writing sound more direct and action packed.

The ball was passed from Kristy to Tamika. (passive)

Kristy passed the ball to Tamika. (active)

GRAMMAR Try It Rewrite each of the following sentences so that the verb is in the active voice rather than the passive voice.

Example: A basket was made by Will.
Will made a basket.

1. Thirteen points were scored by Yao in the first half.
2. A layup was attempted by me, but I missed the basket.
3. Most of the fouls were called by one referee.
4. A zone defense was played by the opposing team.
5. Basketball games at my school are attended by many people.

TEKS 7.19C
ELPS 5G

Show When Something Happens

You can use different verb tenses to "tell time" in sentences. The three **simple tenses** are *present, past,* and *future*. (See page 770.)

At times, you might need to use different tenses in the same sentence to show that one action happened before another action.

The Harlem Globetrotters is a basketball team that began in the 1920s.

Both a present tense verb and a past tense verb appear in the sentence, and it makes sense. However, you need to avoid a shift in verb tense if it is unnecessary.

Shift in tense:

They tour the country and played any team that will take them on.
(The verb tense shifts from *present* to *past*, confusing the reader.)

Corrected:

They tour the country and play any team that will take them on.

GRAMMAR Try It

For each blank in the sentences below, write a verb that is the same tense as the first verb in the sentence.

1. When the Globetrotters play another team for the first time, their opponents ________ surprised.
2. Early on, the Globetrotters recruited players from many places, and they ________ a long time to play together as a team.
3. One cannot deny the skill of these team members; they ________ superior athletes.
4. The Globetrotters will play at the arena next week, and I ______ there.

GRAMMAR Try It

Write a friendly letter to a favorite sports figure or other famous person you admire. Include at least six sentences in the body of your letter. Use *present, past,* and *future* tenses to describe some achievement of the person you are writing to, and make sure your sentences are consistent in tense. Also use correct letter format, including a salutation and a closing. When you have finished, share your letter aloud with the class.

TEKS 7.19A(i)
ELPS 5G

How else can I use verbs?

Show Special Types of Action

You need **perfect tense verbs** to express certain types of action. (See page **774** in the "Proofreader's Guide.") There are three perfect tenses.

play, played	Singular	Plural
Present perfect tense states an action that *began in the past but continues or is completed in the present.*		
Present perfect (use *has* or *have* + past participle)	I have played. You have played. He or she has played.	We have played. You have played. They have played.
Past perfect tense states an action that *began in the past and was completed in the past.*		
Past perfect (use *had* + past participle)	I had played. You had played. He or she had played.	We had played. You had played. They had played.
Future perfect tense states an action that *will begin in the future and will be completed by a specific time in the future.*		
Future perfect (use *will have* + past participle)	I will have played. You will have played. He or she will have played.	We will have played. You will have played. They will have played.

GRAMMAR Try It

Identify the tense of each underlined verb in the following paragraphs. The first one has been done for you.

1. past perfect

At the end of last summer, our local bowling alley **(1)** had burned down. Since then our bowling league **(2)** has moved to another bowling alley across town. I hope the owners of the old alley **(3)** will have rebuilt our bowling alley by the start of the next season. We **(4)** have missed bowling there.

GRAMMAR Try It

Write a paragraph of at least four sentences explaining an achievement you accomplished in the past. Use the *present perfect, past perfect*, and *future perfect* tenses at least once in your paragraph's sentences. When you have finished, share your paragraph with a partner. If he or she points out any errors in your use of tense, make the corrections.

TEKS 7.19A(i)
ELPS 3E

Form Verbals

Verbals are words that are made from verbs but are used as other parts of speech. Verbals are used as nouns, adjectives, and adverbs, and they are often used in phrases. (See 780.2–780.4.)

Gerunds

A **gerund** is a verb form that ends in *ing* and is used as a noun.

Bowling is an enjoyable activity.
(The gerund *bowling* acts as a subject noun.)

You should try bowling in our league.
(The gerund phrase *bowling in our league* acts as a direct object.)

Participles

A **participle** is a verb form used as an adjective. A participle ends in *ing* or *ed*.

Regina had a bowling party on her birthday.
(The participle *bowling* describes what kind of party; *bowling* acts as an adjective.)

A ball spinning down the next alley hit the pocket perfectly.
(The participial phrase acts as an adjective describing *ball*.)

Infinitives

An **infinitive** is a verb with "to" before it. An infinitive can be used as a noun, an adjective, or an adverb.

My goal for today is to get three strikes.
(The infinitive phrase *to get three strikes* acts as a predicate noun.)

Our plan to go bowling is still a "go."
(*To go bowling* acts as an adjective modifying the noun *plan*.)

Please watch me carefully to evaluate my form.
(*To evaluate my form* acts as an adverb modifying the verb *watch*.)

GRAMMAR Try It

Write a sentence for each of the verbals listed below. Share your sentences with a partner.

1. knocking down the pins *(gerund phrase)*
2. to earn a good score *(infinitive phrase)*
3. spinning *(participle)*
4. taking a few long strides *(participial phrase)*
5. to make a spare *(infinitive phrase)*

Describing with Adjectives

Adjectives are words that describe or modify nouns or pronouns. Sensory adjectives help the reader see, hear, feel, smell, and taste what writers are describing. (Also see pages 782 and 784.)

Without Adjectives

Leroy dived into the water. He swam along the lane markers to the end of the pool. His coach held up a stopwatch.

With Adjectives

Leroy dived into the cold, blue water. He swam along the red, white, and blue lane markers to the end of the Olympic-sized pool. His cheering coach held up an oversized stopwatch.

Adjectives answer three questions: *what kind? how many (much)?* or *which one? Remember:* Proper adjectives can be made from proper nouns (England, *English;* Italy, *Italian*) and are capitalized.

What Kind?	French **bread**	sour **lemon**	black **cat**
How Many (Much)?	two **puppies**	few **friends**	some **milk**
Which One?	this **chair**	these **students**	those **caps**

GRAMMAR Try It

For each blank in the sentences below, write an adjective of the type called for in parentheses.

1. There are *(how many?)* students on the swim team.
2. Marla just got a *(what kind?)* swimsuit.
3. She has swum on the team for *(how many?)* years.
4. Marla always swallowed *(how much?)* water during practice.
5. Last year, she injured her *(which one?)* elbow during a race.
6. During the conference meet, Marla's relay team won a *(what kind?)* medal.
7. Altogether, Marla won *(how many?)* medals during the meet.
8. The *(which one?)* meet was the highlight of last season.
9. This year's *(what kind?)* swim team will be as good as last year's.
10. Marla accepts *(how much?)* responsibility for her performances.

Comparative and Superlative Forms

You can use comparative adjectives to compare two things. For most one-syllable adjectives, add *er* to make the **comparative form**. To compare three or more things, add *est* to make the **superlative form**.

Positive	Comparative	Superlative
large	larger	largest

Comparative: **A volleyball is larger than a baseball.**
Superlative: **The largest ball in professional team sports is a basketball.**

Add *er* and *est* to some two-syllable words and use *more* or *most* (or *less* or *least*) with others. Always use *more* or *most* with three-syllable adjectives.

Positive	Comparative	Superlative
joyful	more joyful	most joyful

Comparative: **Swimming is a more strenuous sport than golf is.**
Superlative: **I think that gymnastics is the most strenuous of all sports.**

NOTE Some adjectives use completely different words to express comparison—for example, *bad, worse, worst.* (See 784.6.)

GRAMMAR Try It

Write the positive, comparative, or superlative form of the underlined adjective to fill in the blanks in each of the following sentences.

1. You will see some fast balls in baseball, but a golf ball hit from a tee is a ____________ ball. The ____________ of all balls in sports is a jai-alai ball.
2. The soccer practices are ____________, but the games are more difficult than the practices are. I had the ____________ of all my games when I was sick.
3. Student athletes do some amazing feats. Of course, professional athletes can do things that are ____________ than what the students can do. However, participants in extreme sports can do the ____________ feats of all.
4. While Angela is a ____________ runner, Lee is a better runner, and Takeisha is the ____________ runner of all.
5. For a few players, spiking a volleyball is easy. For many other players, serving is ____________ than spiking the ball. Then there are those who find setting up the ____________ part of the game.

TEKS 7.14C
ELPS 5G

How can I strengthen my writing with adjectives?

Use Sensory Details

Writers use adjectives to help create **sensory details**. Sensory details help readers create vivid images in their minds by using all their senses. Note how the sensory adjectives help create vivid images and add effective details in the following paragraph.

> **The sweet aroma of fresh-mown grass floated off the baseball diamond. Bright white lines had been carefully painted on it. The buzzing crowd waited in anticipation. Food and drink vendors began hawking their mouth-watering treats as the first blaring notes of "The Star-Spangled Banner" tumbled out of the band's shiny instruments.**

Try It Find a copy of a story you wrote earlier in the year. Reread your writing and look for places where adjectives could be used to create more vivid images. Rewrite one paragraph of your story, focusing on using adjectives to create sensory details.

Form Extra-Strength Modifiers

Compound adjectives are made of two or more words. Some are spelled as one word; others are hyphenated. (Use a dictionary to check spelling.)

> **Some baseball fields feature man-made grass.**

GRAMMAR Try It For each of the following sentences, write a compound adjective to fill in the blank. Make your compound adjectives by combining words from the following list. (All of them should be hyphenated.)

front	high	filled	row	flying	third	fan	base

Example: We entered the noisy, ___________ stadium just as the game started.
fan-filled

1. Our tickets were for ___________ seats.
2. Santiago hit a ___________ ball toward the bleachers.
3. The ___________ umpire shouted, "Foul ball!"

Include Adjectives in the Predicate

Most adjectives are placed before the nouns they describe. A **predicate adjective** comes after a linking verb and describes the noun or pronoun before it.

The worn mitt is ancient, and it smells musty.

Darnell remains confident about the mitt's supposed "luck."

GRAMMAR Try It Write a predicate adjective to fill in each blank in the paragraph below. The linking verbs are underlined.

When Mom dropped me off at baseball practice, I was **(1)** ______ . Our opening game was only three days away. The whole team seemed **(2)** ______ . Our fielders were **(3)** ______ , and some of the batters were really **(4)** ______ . Carl, our main pitcher, looked **(5)** ______ . We didn't know how the other team would play, but we felt **(6)** ______ . We couldn't wait!

GRAMMAR Try It Write a brief paragraph describing a personal experience related to your favorite sport. In your paragraph, use at least five linking verbs, such as *become, feel, seem, appear,* and *sound,* that link to predicate adjectives.

Be General or Specific

You can use **indefinite adjectives**, such as *few, many, more,* and *some,* to give the reader approximate information. (*Approximate* means "general" rather than "specific.")

Some neighborhood kids picked teams for baseball.

Gina and Sandy decided to play another game.

A **demonstrative adjective** points to a specific noun. The demonstrative adjectives are *this, that, these,* and *those.*

Those kids over there want to play, too.

I want to use this bat when it's my turn.

Note that both indefinite and demonstrative adjectives must come before the nouns they modify. If they appear alone, they are pronouns.

GRAMMAR Try It Write two sentences that use indefinite adjectives and two that use demonstrative adjectives. Exchange papers with a classmate and underline each other's indefinite and demonstrative adjectives.

Describing with Adverbs

Adverbs describe or modify verbs, adjectives, or other adverbs. You can use adverbs to answer *how? when? where?* or *how much?* (See pages **786** and **788**.)

How?	gracefully	**Deena did a back flip gracefully on the beam.**
When?	yesterday	**She was in the semifinals yesterday.**
Where?	indoors	**The events were all held indoors.**
How Much?	barely	**Mark barely met the time limit on his routine.**

GRAMMAR Try It

For each of the following paragraphs, write the adverbs you find. (The number of adverbs in each paragraph is shown in parentheses.)

I. I went with Darla to a gymnastics competition today. She told me about the men who perform gymnastic routines on a pommel horse. These athletes must practice regularly. The most basic skills are extremely difficult to master because only the hands can touch the horse. The athlete spends most of the time carefully balancing on one arm as his free hand reaches to begin the next skill. There are no stops or pauses allowed. At the end of his routine, the gymnast's dismount is a landing without any steps or hops afterward. That's a challenge! (5)

II. Although Darla really liked the uneven bars when she started gymnastics, her favorite event now has become the balance beam. She fearlessly leaps, jumps, and does handsprings on a four-foot-high, four-inch-wide beam! The hard ground lies below. Her dance moves are expertly completed. Of course, she is very flexible, but she must concentrate totally for the 90 seconds of her routine. (7)

Comparative and Superlative Adverbs

You can use adverbs to compare two things. The **comparative form** of an adverb compares two people, places, things, or ideas. The **superlative form** of an adverb compares three or more people, places, things, or ideas.

tip For most one-syllable adverbs, add *er* to make the comparative form and *est* to make the superlative form.

Positive	Comparative	Superlative
soon	sooner	soonest

While you add *er* and *est* to some two-syllable adverbs, you need to use *more* or *most* (or *less* or *least*) with others. Always use *more* or *most* with adverbs of three or more syllables.

Positive	quickly	importantly
Comparative	more quickly	more importantly
Superlative	most quickly	most importantly

Comparative: I ran faster than my guard did.
Ed plays basketball more frequently than I do.

Superlative: Kayla ran fastest of all and grabbed the jump ball.
Of all of us, Ed plays basketball most frequently.

tip Make sure that you write a complete comparison: *I ran faster than my guard did* rather than *I ran faster than my guard.*

GRAMMAR Try It In each sentence below, change the adverb (underlined) twice: first to compare two things and then to compare three (or more) things. Reword the sentences as needed. Share your sentences with a partner.

Example: Delia quickly put on her uniform.
I put my uniform on more quickly than Delia did.
Of the three of us, Beryl put hers on most quickly.

1. She would be on the soccer field soon.
2. Rolando kicked the ball powerfully.
3. Joe skillfully set up his teammates.

How can I use adverbs effectively?

Describe Actions

You can make your writing more descriptive by using adverbs. Since they can appear just about anywhere in a sentence, experiment to find the best place to include them. *Remember:* Changing an adverb's location may slightly change the meaning of the sentence.

Greg smoothly rowed his kayak through the water.

Greg rowed his kayak smoothly through the water.

Greg rowed his kayak through the water smoothly.

Smoothly, Greg rowed his kayak through the water.

GRAMMAR Try It

Rewrite the following sentences, placing the adverb (in parentheses) where you think it fits best.

1. I decided to try kayaking myself. *(finally)*
2. I will have to practice. *(definitely)*
3. I don't want to go where the current is fast. *(really)*
4. A kayak has a low probability of capsizing. *(surprisingly)*
5. Kayakers should learn how to flip themselves back up again if they do capsize. *(actually)*

Add Emphasis

You can stress the importance of something with adverbs. Generally, use adverbs of degree (those that answer *how much?*) for this job. (See 786.4.)

We paddled extremely fast in the river rapids.

Rapids can be awfully dangerous.

Try It

Write a short paragraph about this picture that shows kayakers in calm water. Use a few adverbs to add emphasis.

Express Frequency

With adverbs, you can describe how often something happens or how often something is done in a certain way. Adverbs that tell how often include *often, sometimes, usually, occasionally, always,* and so on.

Dwight has always enjoyed track-and-field events.
He is rarely disappointed in the athletes' performances.

GRAMMAR Try It

Use three of the following "how often" adverbs in sentences about your attitude toward a specific sport.

regularly	**never**	**occasionally**	**always**	**seldom**	**frequently**

When you use a negative adverb such as *hardly, barely,* or *scarcely* in a sentence, avoid using another negative term *(no, not, neither)* to express the same idea. Using two negative words together results in a **double negative**, which is an error.

I can't hardly fit this skateboard in my backpack.

To correct a double negative, remove one of the negative terms:

I can't fit this skateboard in my backpack.
I can hardly fit this skateboard in my backpack.

Be Precise

With adverbs, you can tell the readers exactly when *(then, yesterday, now, right away)* or where *(here, there, nearby, inside)* something happens.

Leila then invited me to jump on her trampoline.
"Will you stay close while I jump?" I asked.

GRAMMAR Try It

For each blank, write an adverb that tells "when" or "where."

When I went to Leila's house **(1)** _______, I saw her trampoline. Other families who lived **(2)** _______ also had trampolines. I asked Leila if we could try out her trampoline **(3)** _______. **(4)** _______ we jumped for a long time. Leila's friend next door called to us. "Come **(5)** _______ and jump on our trampoline, too!" she said.

Connecting with Prepositions

A preposition is a word (or words) that show how one word or idea is related to another. A preposition is the first word of a prepositional phrase, a phrase that acts as an adjective or an adverb in a sentence. (See page 790 for a complete list of prepositions.)

The Astrodome is located in Houston, Texas.
(The preposition *in* shows the relationship between the verb *is located* and the object *Houston, Texas.* The prepositional phrase acts as an adverb telling "where.")

When the panels in the roof were painted, the grass died.
(The preposition *in* shows the relationship between the noun *panels* and the object *roof.* The prepositional phrase acts as an adjective telling "which ones.")

Preposition or Adverb?

If a word that sometimes is used as a preposition appears alone in a sentence, that word is probably an adverb, not a preposition.

Two students lagged behind the group.
(*Behind the group* is a prepositional phrase.)

Two students lagged behind, so we waited.
(*Behind* is an adverb that modifies the verb *lagged.*)

"To" as a Preposition or Part of an Infinitive Phrase

If the words that follow *to* do not include the object of the preposition (a noun or pronoun), then *to* is not a preposition. When a verb or verb phrase follows *to*, *to* is considered an infinitive, a kind of verbal. (See page 545.)

We are going to the stadium.
(*To the stadium* is a prepositional phrase.)

We are going to watch a football game.
(*To watch* is an infinitive.)

GRAMMAR Try It

Write four sentences about a place where people play a sport. Use the word *around* as a preposition in one sentence and as an adverb in another. Use the word *to* as a preposition in one sentence and as part of an infinitive in another.

TEKS 7.19A(v)

How can I use prepositional phrases?

Add Information

You can use a prepositional phrase as an adjective to describe either a noun or a pronoun. Adjectives answer *what kind? how many?* or *which one?* Notice the prepositions *on* and *for* in the following sentences. Each preposition begins a prepositional phrase.

Which one?

The Major League Baseball park on Chicago's north side, **Wrigley Field, is a**

Which kind?

stadium just for baseball.

GRAMMAR Try It

Write a prepositional phrase that could modify each of the subjects below. Your phrases should answer *what kind? how many?* or *which one?* Use a variety of prepositions to introduce your prepositional phrases.

Example: the players
the players on our team

1. the most exciting game
2. the sports arena
3. that camera
4. the referee

Check Subject-Verb Agreement

When using prepositional phrases, you must be careful to have correct subject-verb agreement in your sentences. When a prepositional phrase is placed between the subject and the verb in a sentence, subject-verb agreement can become confusing. In the sentences below, notice the subjects and verbs in blue.

Incorrect: The umbrella **with many colors** keep **me dry.**
(The verb *keep* agrees in number with the object *colors.*)
Correct: The umbrella **with many colors** keeps **me dry.**
(The subject *umbrella* **agrees in number with the verb** *keeps.***)**

GRAMMAR Try It

On a piece of paper, write the following paragraph, correcting subject-verb agreement. Be sure that subjects and verbs agree.

The baseball team with new players need to buy new uniforms. The old uniforms with the eagle mascot is falling apart. The players on the other team laughs at The Mighty Eagles' uniforms. Something must be done soon!

TEKS 7.19A(iii)
ELPS 5G

Writing with Phrases

Using phrases in your writing will allow you to add more information and details to support your ideas. An adjectival phrase is a group of words that acts as an adjective in a sentence, modifying a noun or pronoun. An adverbial phrase is a group of words that acts as an adverb in a sentence, modifying a verb or adverb.

How can I use adjectival phrases?

Add Information

You can use an adjectival phrase as an adjective to modify a noun or pronoun by telling *what kind? how many?* or *which one?* In the example sentences below, the adjectival phrases are in blue type. The arrows point from the adjectival phrase to the noun that is being described.

The student in the middle of the row **raised his hand.** *(Which one?)*

The dog with the brown eyes **wagged his shaggy tail.** *(What kind?)*

The shadow of the two airplanes **crossed over the field.** *(How many?)*

GRAMMAR Try It

Identify the adjectival phrase in each sentence. Some have more than one phrase. Then work with a partner to decide which noun or pronoun is being described.

1. We read the letter from Aunt Susan.
2. I bought the milk at the store around the corner.
3. Did you see the new film by my favorite director?
4. Juan bought the bike with the fancy seat in the store.
5. He is the one in the blue jacket.
6. The boots of the three children from next door are here.

GRAMMAR Try It

On a piece of paper, write a paragraph that describes a special event, such as a music concert, play, or sports game. Include at least one adjectival phrase in each sentence that answers the questions *which one? what kind?* or *how many?*

How can I use adverbial phrases?

Describe

You can use an adverbial phrase to describe a verb or adverb by answering the questions *where? when?* or *in what way?* In the example sentences below, the adverbial phrases are in blue type. The arrows point from the adverbial phrase to the verb or adverb that is being described.

The swimmer swam across the lake. *(Where?)*

The outdoor concert began early in the evening. *(When?)*

The senator spoke with great eloquence. *(In what way?)*

GRAMMAR Try It

Copy each sentence on your own paper. Underline the adverbial phrase in each sentence. Some have more than one phrase. Then draw an arrow from the phrase to the verb or adverb it describes.

1. Sam awoke before dawn.
2. Margarita danced across the floor in a carefree way.
3. The driver drove the empty bus to the parking lot.
4. The painters arrived at nine on the dot.
5. Judge Garcia listened to the lawyer from his bench with great patience.
6. The salesperson went from door to door.

GRAMMAR Try It

Find a story or essay that you wrote earlier this year. Read through your writing. Look for places where adverbial phrases would help the reader understand your ideas. Choose a paragraph to rewrite, using adverbial phrases to better describe verbs and/or adverbs. Read your revised paragraph aloud to the class.

TEKS 7.19A(vii)
ELPS 3E

Connecting with Conjunctions

Conjunctions connect words, groups of words, and sentences. There are three kinds of conjunctions: *coordinating, subordinating,* and *correlative*. The following sentences show some of the ways to use conjunctions. (See page **792** for a list of common conjunctions.)

Coordinating Conjunctions

Connect Words

Should I play basketball or volleyball this winter?

I am good at dribbling and shooting the ball.

Connect Compound Subjects and Predicates

All the coaches and current team members attend tryouts.

The coaches will test our skills and make the final decisions.

Connect Sentences

I hope I make the team, but I am not worried about it.

The team has practice every day, and that's a big commitment.

Subordinating Conjunctions

Connect Dependent Clauses to Independent Clauses

Players remain on the team as long as their grades are satisfactory.

When the team goes to the playoffs, students seem to have more school spirit.

Correlative Conjunctions

Connect Noun Phrases and Verb Phrases

Our team neither wins all the time nor loses all the time.

Being part of a team can help you improve not only your physical abilities but also your mental skills.

GRAMMAR Try It

Choose three of the sentences above to use as models. Write three sentences of your own imitating the three you've chosen. (Make sure to use your own words.) Underline the conjunctions you use. Read your sentences aloud to a partner.

How can I use conjunctions?

Connect a Series of Ideas

You can use a conjunction to connect a series of three or more words or phrases in a row. Place commas between the words or phrases and place a conjunction before the final item.

Blind athletes compete in skiing, swimming, and football.
(The conjunction *and* connects three nouns.)

They also ride bikes, lift weights, or shoot targets.
(The conjunction *or* connects three verb phrases.)

GRAMMAR Try It Copy the following sentence beginnings. Include a series of three or more ideas to finish each one. Read your favorite sentence aloud to a partner.

1. My favorite sports are . . .
2. I admire how the players . . .
3. A few sports I'd like to try include . . .

Expand Sentences with Coordinating Conjunctions

You can use **coordinating conjunctions** *(and, but, or, nor, for, so, yet)* to make compound subjects and predicates and to write compound sentences.

Blind individuals and visually impaired people are able to participate in sports, but they don't always have the necessary equipment.
(The conjunction *and* creates a compound subject, and *but* creates a compound sentence.)

GRAMMAR Try It For each blank below, write a coordinating conjunction. Tell whether it connects a compound subject, a compound predicate, or a compound sentence.

An athlete may be blind, **(1)** _______ that doesn't mean he or she is less talented than any other athlete. In fact, some blind athletes have competed against sighted individuals **(2)** _______ won medals. The International Blind Sports Association conducts sports programs for blind people, **(3)** _______ it changes negative ideas about them in the process. The organization wants to spread its message, **(4)** _______ it runs public service campaigns. A blind person **(5)** _______ a sighted individual can be a successful athlete.

TEKS 7.19A(vii), 7.19B
ELPS 3E, 5B

Expand Sentences with Subordinating Conjunctions

You can use a **subordinating conjunction** to connect a dependent clause to another sentence. A dependent clause (one that *cannot* stand alone as a sentence) must be connected to an independent clause (one that *can* stand alone as a sentence). This type of sentence is known as a **compound-complex sentence.** In the expanded sentences below, the dependent clauses are underlined, and the subordinating conjunctions are in blue.

> **Although martial arts teach self-defense, they also provide benefits to the body, mind, and spirit. Students improve themselves as they make progress in these three areas.**

GRAMMAR Try It

Use each of the following subordinating conjunctions to write your own compound-complex sentences: *until, because, when, since, even though*. Try to use each conjunction in a separate sentence. Share your favorite sentence with a partner.

Show a Relationship

You can use **correlative conjunctions** to show a relationship between two words, phrases, or clauses. Correlative conjunctions are always used in pairs: *both/and, not only/but also, neither/nor, either/or, whether/or.*

> **While performing martial arts, people use not only their bodies, but also their minds.**
>
> **Both tai chi and jujitsu are forms of martial art.**

GRAMMAR Try It

For each of the blanks in the sentences below, write the correlative conjunctions that make the most sense. (More than one answer may be correct.)

1. The martial arts stress ________ aggression ________ domination.
2. Practicing martial arts can help improve ________ your health ________ your self-esteem.
3. A bow to an instructor can express ________ gratitude ________ respect.

Building Effective Sentences

Imagine eating the same thing every day, at every meal. Eventually, you would dislike even the cheesiest pizza or the most scrumptious ice cream. People just naturally like variety.

The same is true with writing. A story with one long sentence after another, or one short sentence after another, would soon become boring. Sometimes a short sentence expresses feeling in a way that a long sentence cannot, and a long sentence does a better job of explaining a complicated idea. One key to clear writing is sentence variety.

What's Ahead

You will learn about . . .

- **writing complete sentences.**
- **fixing sentence problems.**
- **improving your sentence style.**
- **combining sentences.**
- **adding variety to your sentences.**
- **using different types of sentences.**
- **expanding and modeling sentences.**

Writing Complete Sentences

A sentence is a group of words that forms a complete thought. Writers use complete sentences in order to communicate clearly. The following group of words does not form a complete thought:

live | of | types | reefs | coral | many | in | animals

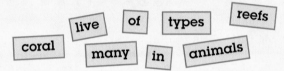

The jumble of words above does not make sense. When these same words are rearranged into a sentence, however, they do make sense. They communicate a clear, complete thought:

many | types | of | animals | live | in | coral | reefs

GRAMMAR Try It On your own paper, unscramble the word groups below to create complete sentences. (See the helpful clues in parentheses.) Remember to capitalize and punctuate each sentence correctly.

Example: in corals clear live shallow water *(equal adjectives)*
Corals live in clear, shallow water.

1. they simple creatures without are eyes *(pronoun subject)*
2. tiny animals corals the in eat floating ocean *(prepositional phrase)*
3. form limestone reefs huge of coral ridges under water *(appositive)*
4. fish sharks and eat seals *(compound direct objects)*
5. some hundreds grow very slowly for corals and live of years *(compound verb)*
6. the Reef is about Barrier 1,250 Great long miles *(prepositional phrase)*
7. shrimp and on live fish coral reefs *(compound subject)*
8. purple can red be yellow coral green or *(a series)*
9. pollution can and hurt garbage coral oil *(appositive)*

Write NOW **Write three sentences about the animals living on a coral reef. On another sheet, mix up the words and leave out punctuation and capitalization. Ask a classmate to rearrange the words so they form complete sentences.**

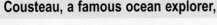

Basic Parts of a Sentence

Every sentence has two basic parts: a complete subject (which tells who or what is doing something) and a complete predicate (which tells what the subject is doing).

Complete Subject	Complete Predicate
Who or what did something?	*What did the subject do?*
Jacques Cousteau and Emile Gagnan	**invented modern scuba gear.**
Cousteau, a famous ocean explorer,	**was also a film producer.**

GRAMMAR Try It Divide a piece of paper into two columns. For each of the sentences below, write the complete subject in the left column and write the complete predicate in the right column.

In the following sentences, the words that come before the verb are the *complete subject*. The verb and all the words that follow it are the *complete predicate*.

Example: People have always explored under the sea.
People | have always explored under the sea.

1. The first piece of diving equipment was a snorkel made of a hollow reed.
2. The ancient Greeks used diving bells to walk underwater.
3. The English astronomer Edmond Halley discovered a comet and invented a diving bell.
4. Scuba stands for self-contained underwater breathing apparatus.
5. Diving suits with heavy helmets appeared for the first time in the 1800s.
6. Harry Houdini, the famous magician, invented a diving suit.
7. Plastic or rubber swim fins help a diver swim through the water.
8. The first team of women divers to live underwater for weeks was led by Sylvia Earle.
9. Earle, who spent more than 6,000 hours underwater, continues to work on saving oceans.

ELPS 2C, 3C

Subjects and Predicates

Every sentence has a subject and a predicate. A simple subject consists of the subject without the words that modify it. A simple predicate is the verb without the words that modify it or complete the thought. In the sentences below, the **simple subjects** are orange and the **simple predicates** are blue.

Complete Subject	Complete Predicate
Octopuses	have the most complex brain of all invertebrates.
Their acute sense of touch	also aids in their survival.

A compound subject includes two or more subjects that share the same predicate (or predicates). A compound predicate includes two or more predicates that share the same subject (or subjects).

Complete Subject	Complete Predicate
Lobsters and crabs	scatter and hide from preying octopuses.

Learning Language

A compound subject of singulars joined by the words *or* or *nor* must have a singular verb in the predicate.

Either Hank **or** Javier **is studying** marine animals.

Neither Jermaine **nor** his sister **is visiting** the aquarium.

A compound subject of plurals joined by *or* or *nor* must have a plural verb in the predicate.

Either the parents **or** the teachers **are going** on the field trip.

Neither students **nor** their siblings **are going** by themselves.

Work with a partner to write a pair of sentences using *or* or *nor* with singular compound subjects. Write another pair with plural compound subjects.

How can I make sure my sentences are complete?

Check Your Subjects and Predicates

Incomplete thoughts are called fragments. Fragments may be missing a subject, a predicate, or both. Study the fragments below. Then read the complete sentences made from them. Notice that a subject, a predicate, or both have been added to make the corrections.

Fragment	Sentence
Are lurking in Monterey Bay.	Strange creatures **are lurking in Monterey Bay.** (A subject is added.)
Battery-powered robots deep to gather data.	**Battery-powered robots** dive **deep to gather data.** (A simple predicate is added.)
Part of a $10 million study of the ocean's climate.	Underwater robots are **part of a $10 million study of the ocean's climate.** (A subject and a simple predicate are added.)

GRAMMAR Try It

Number your paper from 1 to 5. Read each group of words below. If the group of words is a complete sentence, write "C" next to the number. If it is a fragment, write "F" and tell if you need to add a subject, a predicate, or both to make it a complete sentence.

Example: Can operate for days or weeks on lithium flashlight batteries.
F–subject

1. They can gather ocean data cheaper than research ships can.
2. According to scientist Francisco Chavez, "We to predict undersea weather."
3. Can affect surface weather, shoreline recreation, and fishing.
4. Monterey Bay once the largest sardine fishery in the world.
5. Scientists think many sardines may have died because of a change in underwater weather.

Write NOW

Correct any fragments above by adding the missing parts to form complete sentences. Exchange papers with a classmate and check each other's sentences.

Edit Your Writing Carefully

A sentence must express a complete thought. A sentence fragment does not do this even though it may look like a sentence with a capital letter and end punctuation. Reading a sentence out loud, however, can help a writer figure out whether a sentence is expressing a complete thought.

In the example below, the writer found and underlined a number of fragments. Then she turned the fragments into complete sentences by adding information to finish each thought.

Some Fragments	All Sentences
Before a newly hatched lobster looks like a real lobster. The newborn must shed its shell three times. When baby lobsters are 15 days old. They live within three feet of the surface of the ocean. Called "bugs" during this stage.	**Before a newly hatched lobster looks like a real lobster, the newborn must shed its shell three times. When baby lobsters are 15 days old, they live within three feet of the surface of the ocean. They are called "bugs" during this stage.**

GRAMMAR Try It Read the following paragraph and check for fragments. Then, on your own paper, tell how many fragments you found. Rewrite the paragraph, correcting each of the fragments.

Before lobsters become a favorite food of many people. The animals begin life as tiny creatures swimming near the surface of the ocean. When the baby lobsters are about a month old. They begin looking for a hiding place on the ocean's floor. After they settle into this spot or find another safe habitat. They spend their first year hiding in small tunnels. Because they have so many enemies. The young lobsters usually eat just the food that floats through their little tunnels.

***Write* NOW** **Write a short paragraph about lobsters or another sea creature you know about. Have a classmate check your writing for fragments.**

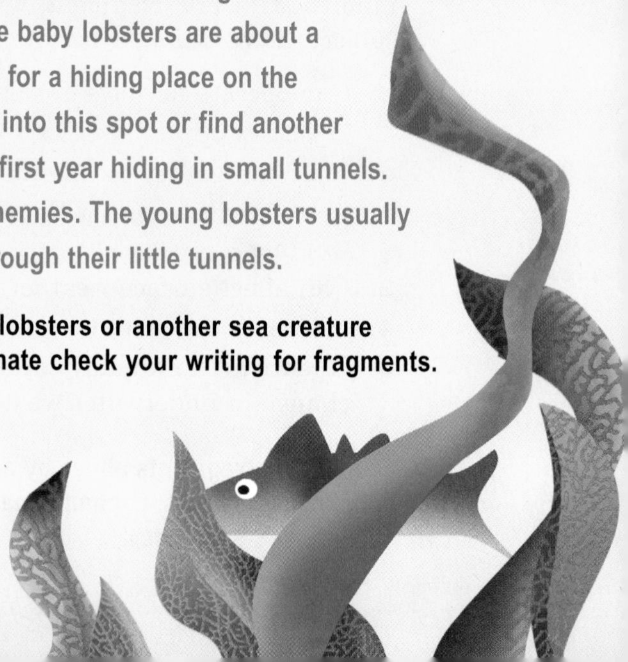

Move Misplaced Modifiers

A misplaced modifier can make a sentence very confusing. You can avoid this problem by making sure that modifiers are placed next to the words they modify. This is especially important when using descriptive phrases.

Misplaced Modifiers	Corrected Sentences
Looking like a balloon with fins, the predator lets the puffer fish escape. (It sounds as though the predator looks like a balloon.)	**Looking like a balloon with fins, the puffer fish escapes from the predator.** (or) **The puffer fish, looking like a balloon with fins, escapes from the predator.** (Move the word being modified closer to its modifying phrase.)
We set out to observe fish in a glass-bottom boat. (It sounds like the fish are in a glass-bottom boat.)	**We set out in a glass-bottom boat to observe fish.** (or) **To observe fish, we set out in a glass-bottom boat.**

GRAMMAR Try It

Rewrite each of the sentences below so that the proper word is modified.

Example: Hiding in deep sea grasses, you can find the puffer fish.
You can find the puffer fish hiding in deep sea grasses.

1. Camouflaged by the seaweed, predators can't always see the fish.
2. Prized for superb flavor, many people want a puffer fish for dinner.
3. Although it is tasty, poison makes the puffer fish dangerous to eat.
4. When properly trained, puffer fish can be prepared by careful chefs.
5. Swimming in an aquarium, I saw a puffer fish and its cousin, a porcupine fish.

Write NOW

Using the facts below, write two sentences containing misplaced modifiers. (Hint: Separate your modifying phrase from the thing it is describing.) Then exchange sentences with a classmate and correct each other's work. Read the corrected sentence back to your partner.

A Porcupine Fish

– normally swims around with spikes lying flat
– when threatened, spikes stick out and body inflates
– inflates by taking in tiny gulps of water
– sends a jet spray into sand, looking for mollusks

Fixing Sentence Problems

Avoid Run-On Sentences

Sometimes you may accidentally write a run-on sentence by putting together two or more sentences. One type of run-on is called a *comma splice,* in which the sentences are connected with a comma only. Another type of run-on has no punctuation at all.

One way to fix run-on sentences is to add a comma and a coordinating conjunction (*and, so, or, for, but, yet,* and *nor*). Another way is to connect the two sentences with a semicolon.

Run-On Sentence	Corrected Sentences
Manta rays are similar to sharks they both have skeletons made of cartilage.	**Manta rays are similar to sharks, for they both have skeletons made of cartilage.**
	Manta rays are similar to sharks; they both have skeletons made of cartilage.

GRAMMAR Try It

On your own paper, correct the run-on sentences below by adding a comma and a coordinating conjunction.

Example: Manta rays live in warm oceans these fish have fins that look like giant wings.

Manta rays live in warm oceans, and these fish have fins that look like giant wings.

1. These huge creatures look ferocious they are really quite gentle.
2. Mantas use their wings to "fly" through the water they look like great floating triangles.
3. Manta rays that weigh more than 3,000 pounds can leap out of the water they can also gracefully avoid divers underwater.
4. Manta rays do not have a stinging barb they do not have sharp teeth.
5. These unique fish often swim near the surface they sometimes swim in deeper lagoon water, too.

Write NOW **Now rewrite each run-on sentence above, correcting each with a semicolon.**

TEKS 7.19A(vii)

Eliminate Rambling Sentences

A rambling sentence occurs when you use too many *ands* to combine your ideas. You can eliminate rambling sentences by checking for extra *ands*. Here are two ways to correct the same rambling sentence.

Rambling Sentences	Corrected Sentences
The number of North Atlantic right whales has been reduced by heavy whaling and only about 300 whales are left and efforts to increase their numbers are starting to bring results.	**The number of North Atlantic right whales has been reduced by heavy whaling; therefore, only about 300 whales are left. Efforts to increase their numbers are starting to bring results.** (Replace the first *and* with a semicolon and a conjunctive adverb to connect two related thoughts. Drop the second *and* to make two sentences.)
	The number of North Atlantic right whales has been reduced by heavy whaling. There are only about 300 whales left, although efforts to increase their numbers are starting to bring results. (Drop the first *and* to make two sentences. Combine thoughts by using a subordinating conjunction to create a subordinate clause.)

tip Some *ands* are needed in sentences to connect compound subjects, compound predicates, items in a list, and so on.

GRAMMAR Try It Correct the following rambling sentences on your own paper. Try using a subordinating conjunction where possible. (See **794.1**.)

1. Right whales were prized by whalers and they were easy to hunt and the whales were almost hunted to extinction and then, 100 years ago, laws were made to protect them.
2. Female whales give birth and they nurse their babies, called calves, for 13 months, sometimes carrying them on their backs, and then the mothers keep the babies close to them for another year and a female may have a calf every three to five years.
3. The northern right whale was almost extinct and the species is now making a comeback and scientists are finding that more babies are being born each year and last year 14 whale calves were born and that was the most calves born in one year recently.

ELPS 3E

What can I do to write clear sentences?

Make Subjects and Verbs Agree

Writers must be careful to make the subjects and verbs in each of their sentences agree. That means a singular subject needs a singular verb, and a plural subject needs a plural verb. (Also see 778.1.) Indefinite pronouns used as subjects can be tricky because some of them can be singular or plural. (See the chart on page 535.)

Singular or Plural Subjects

A verb must agree with its subject in number.

- If a subject is singular, the verb must be singular, too.
  A pod is a group of dolphins.
- If a subject is plural, the verb must be plural.
  Bottleneck dolphins live in pods.

  Don't forget that most nouns ending in *s* or *es* are plural, and most verbs ending in *s* are singular.
- If an indefinite pronoun is singular, its verb must be singular, too.
  Nobody wants to be left behind for the dolphin tour.
- If an indefinite pronoun is plural, its verb must be plural also.
  Many like watching the playful dolphins.

GRAMMAR Try It Number your paper from 1 to 6. For each of these sentences, write the form of the verb (or verbs) that agrees with its subject.

Example: Bottlenose dolphins sometimes swims with whales.
swim

1. Like humans, both is mammals.
2. A dolphin are not a porpoise.
3. Dolphins hunts and plays together.
4. Everybody know that dolphins does not chew their food.
5. Using its tail, a dolphin often flip a fish out of the water and then eat it.
6. Dolphins fears sharks.

Write **NOW** **Write one sentence using the subject "dolphins" and another using the subject "all." Make sure your subjects and verbs agree. Share your sentences with a partner.**

Compound Subjects Connected by "And"

A compound subject connected by the word *and* usually needs a plural verb.

Our guide and our chaperones take us on a tour.

Compound Subjects Connected by "Or"

A compound subject connected by the word *or* needs a verb that agrees in number with the subject nearest to the verb.

Tour guides or the boat's captain talks about the dolphins.
(*Captain,* the subject nearer the verb, is singular, so the singular verb *talks* is used.)

GRAMMAR Try It Number your paper from 1 to 8. Write the correct verb choice for each of these sentences.

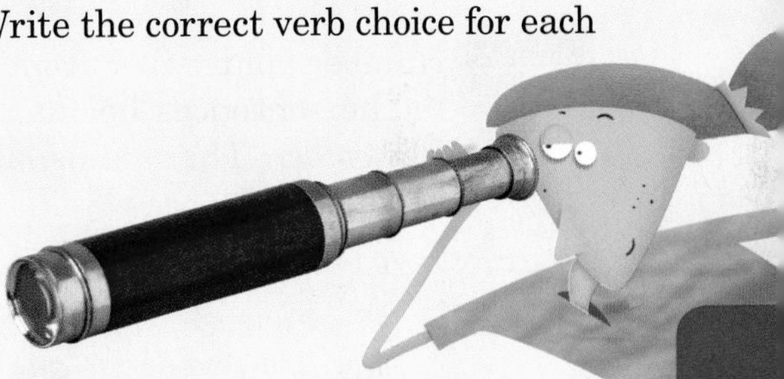

Example: Manatees and a dolphin pod *(is, are)* fun to watch.
are

1. Large tours or small private boats *(let, lets)* people view dolphins in harbor areas.
2. A telescope and an observation deck *(offer, offers)* clear views of the marine life.
3. Passengers or a crew member *(report, reports)* interesting sights.
4. Electronic games and cell phones *(is, are)* not affected by the ship's magnetic navigation equipment.
5. Either a dolphin or manatees *(like, likes)* to swim in a boat's wake.
6. Sometimes, dark skies or rain *(spoil, spoils)* the outings.
7. My brothers and Mom *(enjoy, enjoys)* boat rides more than I do.
8. Dockside shopkeepers and restaurant owners *(wait, waits)* impatiently for the tour to be over.

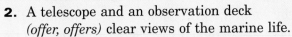

Write NOW **Rewrite sentence 5 above so that a singular verb is correct. Rewrite sentence 6 so that a plural verb is correct. (Do not add or change anything—except the word order.)**

What should I do to avoid nonstandard sentences?

Avoid Double Negatives

Two negative words used together in the same sentence form a double negative *(not no, barely nothing, not never)*. Double negatives also happen if you use contractions ending in *n't* with a negative word *(can't hardly, didn't never)*. Your writing will not be accurate if you use double negatives.

Negative Words

nothing nowhere never not barely hardly nobody none no

Negative Contractions

don't can't won't shouldn't wouldn't couldn't didn't hadn't

GRAMMAR Try It

Number your paper from 1 to 5. List the double negatives you find in the sentences below and then correctly rewrite each sentence. *Remember:* There is usually more than one way to correct a double negative.

Example: My family never has no time to go to the ocean.
never has no
My family never has any time to go to the ocean.

1. Just yesterday, Dad said, "I can't hardly find time to watch TV."
2. I wonder why we aren't going nowhere for a vacation this year.
3. Maybe it's because Mom and Dad don't barely get any time off.
4. Or maybe it's because my brother and I wouldn't hardly want to miss any baseball games.
5. I don't want nothing to keep us from taking an ocean-side vacation.

Avoid Using "Of" for "Have"

Do not use "of" in a sentence when you mean "have." When *have* is said quickly it can sound like *of.*

Incorrect: We could of gone to the beach together.

Corrected: *We could have gone to the beach together.*
We could've gone to the beach together.

Write NOW

Write four sentences. Use double negatives in two. In the others use "of" when you really mean "have." Exchange papers with a classmate, rewrite each other's sentences correctly, and then check each other's work.

Improving Your Sentence Style

There are a number of ways to add variety to your sentences and improve your writing style. Here are four of the most common ways.

1. **Combine short sentences.**
2. **Use different types of sentences.**
3. **Expand sentences by adding words and phrases.**
4. **Model sentences of other writers.**

What happens when too many sentences in a paragraph are the same length or follow the same pattern? Read the following paragraph to find out.

Little Variety

Eelgrass is a flowering saltwater plant. It grows along the coasts of the Atlantic, Pacific, and Indian Oceans. Eelgrass helps the environment in two ways. It uses photosynthesis and puts oxygen into our water and air. Many fish and marine animals live at least part of their lives in eelgrass. Eelgrass is home to crustaceans, sea stars, clams, and young salmon.

Using different types of sentences would keep this paragraph from sounding choppy. Read the following version, which has a better variety of sentences.

Good Variety

Eelgrass, a flowering saltwater plant, grows along the coasts of the Atlantic, Pacific, and Indian Oceans. Eelgrass helps the environment in two ways. First, through photosynthesis, eelgrass puts oxygen into our water and air. Second, eelgrass is "home" to many fish and marine animals. Crustaceans, sea stars, clams, and young salmon live at least part of their lives in eelgrass.

Try It Read the paragraph below. Then, on your own paper, rewrite the paragraph by creating more sentence variety.

Eelgrass along the Atlantic coast was almost destroyed during the hot weather in 1930–1931. The water temperature rose. The eelgrass died out. Fish and animals that lived in the eelgrass died. Then the fishing industry ran into trouble. There were fewer fish. This made a bad economy worse. It took nearly 20 years for the eelgrass to grow back. Today, boat engines destroy eelgrass. Coastal construction and oil spills also kill eelgrass. People need to protect this valuable plant.

How can I make my sentences flow smoothly?

Writers often combine sentences to help writing flow more smoothly. Too many short sentences can make writing sound choppy. Combining some sentences will add variety to your writing and improve your overall writing style.

Combine with Phrases

Short Sentences	Combined Sentences
Combining Using Two or More Phrases	
Seals don't have hands. Seals have short front flippers.	**Seals have short front flippers instead of hands.**
Combining Using an Appositive Phrase	
Elephant seals sometimes weigh more than 5,000 pounds. Elephant seals are the largest seal species.	**Elephant seals, the largest seal species, sometimes weigh more than 5,000 pounds.**
Combining Using a Prepositional Phrase	
Seals are able to stay submerged at great depths. Seals can do this for long periods of time.	**For long periods of time, seals are able to stay submerged at great depths.**

GRAMMAR Try It Combine each of the following sets of sentences by using the method given in parentheses.

1. Seals can lift their bodies off the ground. Seals do this with their flippers. *(prepositional phrase)*
2. Sea lions can swim at the top speed of 25 mph. Sea lions are the fastest seals. *(appositive phrase)*
3. Antarctic seals eat krill. These are tiny shrimp-like creatures. *(appositive phrase)*
4. Baby harp seals are born with white fur. The white fur is a natural camouflage. *(appositive phrase)*
5. The stout-bodied walrus is a unique-looking mammal. It has wrinkled skin and long tusks. *(prepositional phrase)*

Write **NOW** **Write a pair of sentences for a classmate to combine. Model your sentences after one of the sentence pairs above.**

TEKS 7.19C

Combine with a Series of Words

You can combine sentences using a series of words, phrases, or clauses. When using a series, you must make sure that your sentences use parallel words or phrases. Parallel sentence structure means using the same pattern of words to show that each item in the series is equally important.

Combining with a Series

Short Sentences	*Combined Using a Series of Words*
Moray eels eat shrimp and small fish. They also enjoy crabs and octopuses.	**Moray eels eat** shrimp, small fish, crabs, **and** octopuses.
Short Sentences	*Combined Using a Series of Phrases*
Eels make good aquarium pets if they have plenty of room to swim. They also need a place to hide. They need plenty of food to eat, too.	**Eels make good aquarium pets if they have** plenty of room to swim, plenty of places to hide, **and** plenty of food to eat.

GRAMMAR Try It Using a series of parallel words or phrases, combine each of the following groups of sentences. (You must change some words to make the sentences work.)

Example: Moray eels are related to American eels and conger eels. Worm eels and wolf eels are also related to moray eels.

American, conger, worm, and wolf eels are all related to moray eels.

1. Eels have long, thin bodies. They have snake-like heads. All eels also have large mouths.
2. Some moray eels can weigh up to 100 pounds. Some can grow to 10 feet long. They can look like prehistoric monsters.
3. Moray eels live in caves. They live in coral reefs. Some also live in shallow waters.
4. Would you like to keep an eel for a pet? How about seeing an eel in the wild? And what would you think of eating "eel surprise" for dinner?

Write NOW **Write one sentence about another animal in which you use one or more words and one or more phrases in a series. Make sure that your sentences are parallel.**

TEKS 7.19A(vi)
ELPS 3E

Combine with Relative Pronouns

You can combine two short sentences by using a relative pronoun to make a complex sentence. A complex sentence contains one independent, or main, clause and one dependent clause. (See 750.2–750.3 for more information.)

Relative pronouns include words such as *who, which, that, whose, whom,* and so on.

Combining with Relative Pronouns

Two Short Sentences	*Combined Using a Relative Pronoun*
The Bay of Fundy has the world's highest tides. The bay is in Nova Scotia.	**The Bay of Fundy, which is in Nova Scotia, has the world's highest tides.** or **The Bay of Fundy, which has the world's highest tides, is in Nova Scotia.**

GRAMMAR Try It

Combine each set of sentences below by using the relative pronoun in parentheses. (A dependent clause beginning with the relative pronoun "which" is always set off by commas.)

Example: At high tide, the water rises as much as 53 feet. This is as high as a four-story building. *(which)*

At high tide, the water rises as much as 53 feet, which is as high as a four-story building.

1. Many people love exploring tidal pools. These people enjoy viewing sea creatures close-up. *(who)*
2. Tide-pool creatures can survive the varying temperatures of water and air. These temperatures may be as hot as 86 degrees Fahrenheit in summer or –22 degrees Fahrenheit in winter. *(which)*
3. Many animals and plants thrive in tidal zones. These animals and plants need constant moisture. *(that)*
4. At around mid-tide, you can hear what is called the "voice of the moon." This "voice" is actually the roar of the tidal currents. *(which)*

Write NOW

Write freely for 5 minutes about a water-related experience. Afterward, underline any sentences containing relative pronouns. Also find two shorter sentences in your writing that you can combine using a relative pronoun. Share your sentences with a partner.

TEKS 7.14C
ELPS 3E

What can I do to add variety to my writing?

Writers use different types of sentences to add variety to their writing and make it sound interesting. The three common types of sentences are **simple**, **compound**, and **complex**. By learning to write these three types of sentences effectively, you can create sentence variety in your writing.

Write Simple Sentences

A **simple sentence** is one independent clause. (An independent clause is a group of words that can stand alone as one sentence.) A simple sentence may contain a single or compound subject and a single or compound predicate.

Simple Sentence = One Independent Clause

Single Subject with a Single Predicate

Icebergs are a hazard to shipping.

Single Subject with a Compound Predicate

Usually ships avoid icebergs but sometimes collide with one.

Compound Subject with a Single Predicate

"Growlers" and "bergy bits" are two names for small Arctic icebergs.

GRAMMAR Try It Write the paragraph below on your own paper. In each sentence, underline the simple subject once and the simple predicate twice. (*Remember:* Watch for compound subjects and verbs.)

Icebergs come from glaciers and float in the ocean. Antarctic icebergs are the largest type of iceberg. Antarctic icebergs and Arctic icebergs have only a small portion showing above the water. Most of an iceberg remains below the water. Tall castle bergs and pinnacle icebergs are found in the Arctic. Huge tabular icebergs with vertical sides and flat tops form in the Antarctic.

Write NOW **Write three simple sentences about something in nature that interests you. Exchange with a partner. Revise your partner's sentences so that the first sentence contains a single subject and predicate, the second one a compound subject, and the third one a compound predicate. Read the revised sentences aloud to a partner.**

TEKS 7.14C

Create Compound Sentences

A **compound sentence** is made up of two or more simple sentences (independent clauses) joined by a comma and a coordinating conjunction (*and, for, but, or, so, nor,* and *yet*) or by a semicolon.

Compound Sentence = Two Independent Clauses

Pacific manta rays are the largest in the ray family, and some of them have wingspans of 20 feet. (A comma and the conjunction *and* join the two independent clauses.)

Mobilla rays are smaller than the Pacific rays; Mobilla rays seem to enjoy swimming with and being touched by humans. (Here, the two independent clauses are joined by a semicolon.)

GRAMMAR Try It

On your own paper, join the following sets of independent clauses (simple sentences) using either a semicolon or a comma and a coordinating conjunction.

Example: Stingrays are known as "birds" of the sea. Manta rays are called the "gigantic birds" of the sea.

Stingrays are known as "birds" of the sea, but manta rays are called the "gigantic birds" of the sea.

1. Manta rays sometimes swim in tropical waters close to shore. They really prefer to roam in the open sea.
2. A manta ray is one of the gentlest creatures in the sea. For many years, the manta ray was known as a "devil fish."
3. Growths on either side of the manta's head look like horns. These "horns" help the ray to herd plankton into its mouth.
4. Female rays give birth to one or two babies at a time. Each "pup" may weigh as much as 25 pounds.
5. Baby manta rays learn to avoid predators. The babies spend much of their time on the sea floor, flapping their fins to throw sand over their bodies.

Write NOW

Choose a piece of writing that you wrote earlier this year. Read through your writing to make sure you have used compound sentences correctly. Revise your writing by combining some simple sentences into compound sentences.

TEKS 7.14C, 7.17A(v), 7.19B
ELPS 3E

Develop Complex Sentences

A main or independent clause has its own subject and verb and is a complete sentence. A subordinate or dependent clause cannot stand alone. When you join a subordinate clause to a main clause, it's a **complex sentence**. Complex sentences may contain relative pronouns *(that, which, who)* and subordinating conjunctions *(after, although, because, before, until, when, while)*.

Complex Sentence =

A Dependent Clause	+	**An Independent Clause**
Because the *Atlantis* is equipped for research,		**it carries a submersible called *Alvin*.**
An Independent Clause	+	**A Dependent Clause**
***Alvin* is a white and orange sub**		**that is used to explore underwater mountains.**

GRAMMAR Try It

Number your paper from 1 to 3. Then write the dependent clause in each of the following complex sentences.

Example: Because scientists were exploring undersea mountains south of Kodiak Island in Alaska, *National Geographic Today* sent a reporter along on the expedition.

Because scientists were exploring undersea mountains south of Kodiak Island in Alaska

1. Alvin is launched by a giant A-frame, which first lifts the sub off of *Atlantis'* deck and then sets the sub into the water.
2. When the sub is cut loose, it falls below the ocean's surface and starts to descend into the darkness.
3. *Alvin* maneuvers around on the sea floor and gathers crabs and coral until the engine runs out of power and has to resurface.

Write NOW

Locate an essay you wrote earlier this year. Find places where complex sentences would add variety to your writing. Revise your essay and share your revisions with a partner.

Use Questions and Commands

Writers use a variety of sentences to make statements, ask questions, give commands, or show strong emotion. See the chart below.

Kinds of Sentences

Declarative .	Makes a statement about a person, a place, a thing, or an idea	**An adult loggerhead sea turtle weighs 200 to 350 pounds.**	This is the most common kind of sentence.
Interrogative ?	Asks a question	**Do you know where they nest?**	A question gets the reader's attention.
Imperative .	Gives a command	**Find out what a loggerhead looks like.**	Commands often appear in dialogue or directions.
Exclamatory !	Shows strong emotion or feeling	**Wow, its head is 10 inches wide!**	Use these sentences for occasional emphasis.

Learning Language

When speaking, your voice should go up slightly at the end of a question. This helps the person you are talking to know that you are asking for an answer.

With a partner, practice saying the following questions aloud. Read them once with no emphasis at the end, then read them again with your voice going up slightly at the end. Talk about the difference you hear.

Are you going with us on the aquarium field trip?
Which sea animal are you most interested in?
What have you learned about loggerhead turtles?

Write NOW **Write four sentences—one of each kind—about a sea creature you find interesting.**

TEKS 7.19A(v)
ELPS 3E

What can I do to add details to my sentences?

Expand with Prepositional Phrases

Writers use prepositional phrases to add details and information to their sentences. The chart below shows how this is done. Prepositional phrases function as adjectives or adverbs. *Remember:* A prepositional phrase includes a preposition, the object of a preposition, and the modifiers of the object. (See page 790 for a list of prepositions.)

Prepositional Phrase	Use in a Sentence
Some fish have beaklike mouths of fused teeth.	The phrase acts as an **adjective** to describe the noun *mouths*.
Parrot fish live on coral reefs.	The phrase acts as an **adverb** to modify the verb *live*.

- Prepositional phrases used as adjectives answer the questions *How many? Which one? What kind?*
- Prepositional phrases used as adverbs answer the questions *When? How? How often? How long? Where? How much?*

GRAMMAR Try It Write the prepositional phrases that you find in the following sentences. (There are 10 phrases in sentences 1 through 5.)

Example: Parrot fish can be a variety of colors and patterns.
of colors and patterns

1. These fish swim between coral formations.
2. Their beaklike teeth scrape algae-covered coral from the reef.
3. After swallowing pieces of algae-covered coral, the parrot fish spits out the bits of coral.
4. At night, parrot fish sleep along the bottom of the reef.
5. Some types of parrot fish bury themselves in the sand until morning.

Write Now **Use one or two prepositional phrases to add information to each of the sentences below. Share your best sentence with a partner.**

1 **City aquariums have huge tanks of water.**

2 **One of my favorite tanks contains freshwater fish.**

3 **A new exhibit presents tropical fish.**

TEKS 7.19A(i)
ELPS 3E

Expand with Participial Phrases

Writers sometimes make their sentences more interesting by adding participial phrases. A participial phrase includes a participle and its modifiers. (A participle is a verb form usually ending in *ed* or *ing*.) A participial phrase serves as an adjective in a sentence.

Participial Phrases

Sea horses have a body encased in hard armor.
(This participial phrase modifies the noun *body*.)

Drifting from one coral to another, sea horses are beautiful to watch.
(This participial phrase modifies the noun *sea horses*.)

GRAMMAR Try It

Write the participial phrase in each of the following sentences. Also identify the noun that it modifies.

Example: Adapting their color to their surroundings, some sea horses depend on camouflage for protection.

adapting their color to their surroundings, sea horses

1. Reaching the length of 10 inches, sea horses swim slowly among seaweed.
2. Depending on the size of its brooding pouch, a sea horse hatches between 10 and 100 eggs.
3. The bottom of a large aquarium or reef tank covered in a layer of sand is a good home for sea horses.
4. A sea horse likes certain types of structures, including colorful coral branches.
5. An adult sea horse maintained in good health may live more than three years.

Write NOW

Write a brief paragraph about the sand dollar or another interesting sea creature. Include at least two participial phrases in your writing. Read your paragraph aloud to a classmate.

A Sand Dollar

– missing its cover of little spines when washed up on a beach
– related to sea lilies and starfish
– pores, or little holes, used to move seawater for movement
– lives on top or just beneath the surface of sandy areas
– eats organic particles
– no real predators
– when alive, often found with other sand dollars

How can I make my sentences more interesting?

Model Sentences

You can learn a great deal about writing by studying the sentences of other writers. When you come across sentences that you like, practice writing some of your own that use the same pattern. This process is called *modeling.*

Professional Models	Student Models
I walked along the sandy beach, inhaling the smell of salty surf and dried seaweed.	I ate at the carnival, devouring the huge sour pickles and salty French fries.
Manatees have blimpy bodies, giant beaver tails, and rubbery faces bristling with whiskers. —*Muse*	My tabby cat has a fat tummy, huge tiger paws, and soft fur marked by dark orange stripes.

Guidelines for Modeling

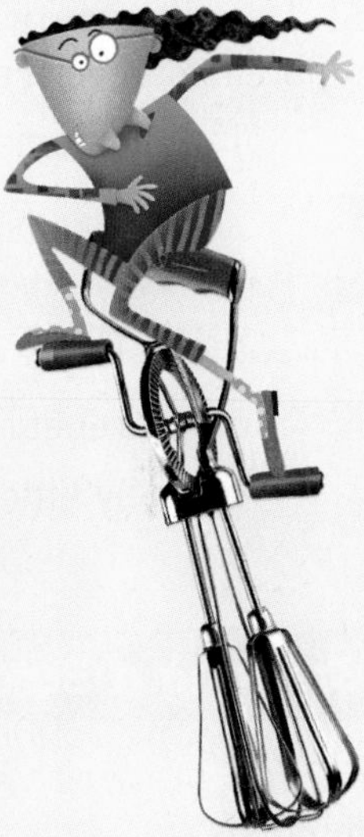

- Find a sentence or a short passage that you like and write it down.
- Think of a topic for your practice writing.
- Follow the pattern of the sentence or passage as you write about your own subject. (You do not have to follow the model exactly.)
- Build each sentence one part at a time and check your work when you are finished. (Take your time.)
- Review your work and change any parts that seem confusing or unclear.
- Share your new sentences with your classmates.
- Find other sentences to model and keep practicing.

Write NOW On your own paper, model the following sentences. *Remember:* You do not have to follow the model sentence exactly.

1. The sun was dropping into the dark ocean, but I kept wandering down the beach.
2. Ocean waves pounded the beach, washing away Tegan's sand castle.
3. I wanted to dive into the water, swim out to the nearest island, and hide away for a day or two.

TEKS 7.19C
ELPS 3E

Develop a Sentence Style

Modeling sentences can help you make your writing more exciting, lively, and appealing. The following writing techniques will also help you improve your style.

Varying Sentence Beginnings

To add variety to the common subject-verb pattern, try beginning a sentence with a phrase or a dependent clause.

In his hand he held a whip.

—*Black Stallion* by Walter Farley

As winter drew on, Mollie became more and more troublesome.

—*Animal Farm* by George Orwell

Moving Adjectives

Usually, you write adjectives before the nouns they modify. You can also emphasize adjectives by placing them after the nouns.

I would come in from a day of progging for crab, sweating and filthy.

—*Jacob Have I Loved* by Katherine Paterson

Repeating a Word

You can repeat a word to emphasize a particular idea or feeling.

Little by little, the wind died down.

—*The Count of Monte Cristo* by Alexandre Dumas

Creating a Balanced Sentence

You can write a sentence that uses parallel words, phrases, or clauses for emphasis.

The wind in our ears drove us crazy and pushed us on.

—*Rogues to Riches* by Rob King

Write **NOW** **Study the sample sentences above. Then write your own sentences that follow each sample pattern. Share your sentences with your classmates.**

Constructing Strong Paragraphs

One thing that can help you gain control of your writing is learning to write a good paragraph. Think of the paragraph as an important building block for all of your writing. If you can create strong, well-organized paragraphs, you can also create effective essays, book reviews, and reports.

A paragraph is made up of a group of sentences focused on one topic. Each sentence should add something to the overall picture. A paragraph can be developed to explain a process, share an opinion, describe something, or tell a story.

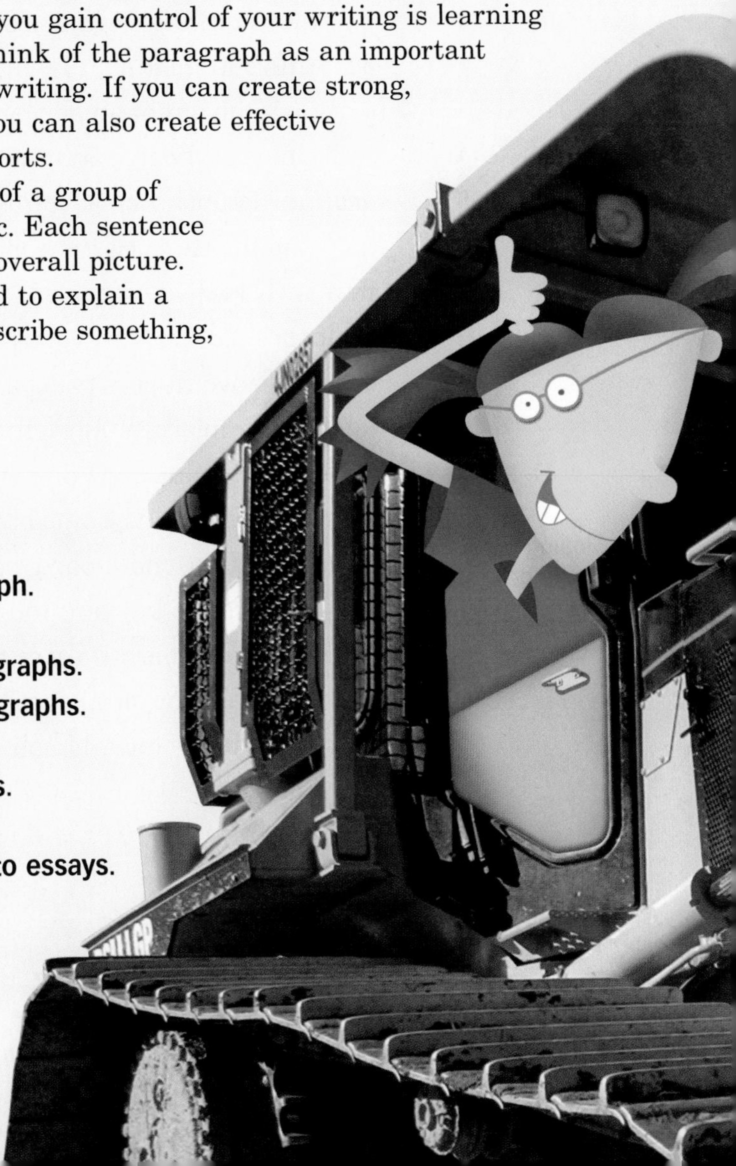

What's Ahead

You will learn about . . .

- **the parts of a paragraph.**
- **types of paragraphs.**
- **writing effective paragraphs.**
- **adding details to paragraphs.**
- **gathering details.**
- **organizing your details.**
- **refining your details.**
- **turning paragraphs into essays.**
- **using a checklist.**

The Parts of a Paragraph

Most paragraphs have three main parts: a topic sentence, a body, and a closing sentence. Paragraphs usually begin with a **topic sentence** that tells what the paragraph is about. The sentences in the **body** share details about the topic, and the **closing sentence** brings the paragraph to a close.

Topic Sentence

Body

Closing Sentence

Adventure Sports

Many outdoor enthusiasts are looking for more adventure in their sports. Why else would a sane person jump out of an airplane, do some acrobatic tricks on a skyboard, and then parachute to the ground? People seek adventure by water, too. They navigate the same rivers and shoot the same rapids that early Native Americans, fur traders, and explorers did. They travel by canoe, kayak, or raft. On land, adventurers backpack and camp in the wilderness, in areas where they might meet bears, moose, and mountain lions. After climbing mountains, some outdoor enthusiasts ski, snowboard, or even bike down to the bottom. Today, an adventure sport is out there for just about anyone, and more sports are being invented all the time.

Respond to the reading. How many types of adventure sports are mentioned? What do they all have in common?

A Closer Look at the Parts

The Topic Sentence

The topic sentence tells the reader what a paragraph is going to be about. A good topic sentence (1) names the topic and (2) states a specific detail or a feeling about it. Here is a simple guide for writing a topic sentence.

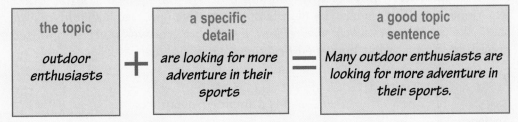

the topic		a specific detail		a good topic sentence
outdoor enthusiasts	+	*are looking for more adventure in their sports*	=	*Many outdoor enthusiasts are looking for more adventure in their sports.*

The topic sentence is usually the first sentence in a paragraph, although sometimes it comes later. It guides the direction of the sentences in the rest of the paragraph.

Many outdoor enthusiasts are looking for more adventure in their sports.

The Body

The sentences in the body of the paragraph include the details needed to understand the topic.

- **Use specific details to make your paragraph interesting.**
  The specific details below are shown in red.

  People seek adventure by water, too. They navigate the same rivers and shoot the same rapids that early Native Americans, fur traders, and explorers did.

- **Organize your sentences in the best possible order.**
  Five common ways to organize sentences are chronological (time) order, order of location, order of importance, comparison, and logical order. (See page 613.)

The Closing Sentence

The closing sentence comes after all the details in the body. It will often restate the topic, give the reader something to think about, or provide a transition into a following paragraph.

Today, an adventure sport is out there for just about anyone, and more sports are being invented all the time.

ELPS 5G

Types of Paragraphs

There are four basic types of paragraphs: *narrative, descriptive, expository,* and *persuasive*. Each type requires a different way of thinking and planning.

Write Narrative Paragraphs

In a **narrative paragraph**, you share a personal story or an important experience with the reader. The details in a narrative paragraph should answer the 5 Ws (*who? what? when? where?* and *why?*). A narrative is often organized according to time (what happened *first, next, then, finally*).

My Camping Adventure

Topic Sentence

Camping in the wilderness can be a real adventure, especially if you have a close encounter with a bear.

Body

One night while camping, my mom, dad, and younger sister were sound asleep in the tent, but I was wide-awake. Suddenly, I heard snorting noises coming from our campsite. I crept to the door and peered out cautiously. By the light of the moon, I saw a big brown bear munching on a bag of our marshmallows. I wanted to shout a warning, but I was so scared that I couldn't get out one sound. As I crawled across the tent to wake my dad, I must have bumped my sister. She sat up and screamed. Her scream startled me, and I yelled, "It's a bear!" Our shouts must have scared the bear because when we opened the tent, there was no bear.

Closing Sentence

My family said I must have been dreaming about a bear, but they couldn't explain how that bag of marshmallows disappeared.

Respond to the reading. Find the key word repeated in the topic sentence and the closing sentence. Does this paragraph answer the 5 Ws?

Draft

Write your own paragraph. Write a paragraph that tells about a memorable experience you've had. Include the 5 Ws and any details that are needed.

Develop Descriptive Paragraphs

When you write a **descriptive paragraph**, you give a detailed picture of a person, a place, an object, or an event. Descriptive paragraphs include many sensory details (sight, sound, smell, taste, touch).

Topic Sentence

Body

Closing Sentence

Rainbow Rock

Rainbow Rock, a huge man-made wall, helps people learn rock-climbing techniques. Rainbow Rock rises 30 feet above the ground and is covered with purple, green, and red climbing paths. Each path contains a variety of odd-shaped footholds, rough outcroppings, and challenging overhangs. The purple path offers a low-key climbing experience that just about anybody can scratch and scramble up. The green path is more advanced and ends with a very tricky, smooth overhang right at the top. The difficult red path has tiny, slippery toeholds that are only about one inch in diameter. It almost takes a mountain goat to maneuver on this path. If someone missteps and falls, a harness snaps into action and catches the climber. He or she is left groaning and swinging in midair. Rainbow Rock may be just an artificial training ground, but it provides a real test of a rock climber's balance, strength, and courage.

Respond to the reading. Which of the five senses are covered in the paragraph? Which two or three details are especially descriptive?

Draft

Write your own paragraph. Write a paragraph that describes a place. Use lots of sights, sounds, and other sensory details in your description.

TEKS 7.19A(viii)
ELPS 5G

Construct Expository Paragraphs

In an **expository paragraph**, you share information. You can explain a subject, give directions, or show how to do something. Transition words like *first, next, then,* and *finally* are often used in expository writing.

Topic Sentence

Body

Closing Sentence

Snowboarding

Today, snowboarding is one of the most popular and exciting winter sports in America. While people have been skiing and ice-skating for centuries, snowboarding has been around for only about 40 years. In 1998, snowboarding became an Olympic sport in Nagano, Japan. By the year 2000, 7.2 million snowboarders, also known as "shredders," were hitting the slopes. Now, both children and adults seem to love snowboarding. Freestyle snowboarders do all sorts of jumps and tricks. These people use a soft boot and a fairly short board. On the other hand, Alpine snowboarders focus on carving turns down the slopes and on racing. Their boots are hard, and their boards are longer and narrower. Snowboarding will probably continue to take the winter sports scene by storm.

Respond to the reading. List the transitions used between sentences in the paragraph above. (See pages 634–635 for a list of transitions.)

Draft

Write an expository paragraph. Write a paragraph that explains a sport that you know very well. Be sure to use transitions to connect your ideas.

Build Persuasive Paragraphs

In a **persuasive paragraph**, you share your opinion (or strong feeling) about a topic. To be persuasive, you must include plenty of reasons, facts, and details to support your opinion. Persuasive writing is usually organized by order of importance or by logical order (as in the paragraph below).

Face the High Ropes Course Challenge

Topic Sentence

The high ropes course is waiting to help young people build confidence and group cooperation. It's also a lot of fun. Many courses, indoor and outdoor, are available in camps, clubs, and schools across America. Some may think that climbing the high ropes is dangerous, but it isn't. Safety ropes and harnesses are carefully managed by course experts and members of each group to give lots of support. When someone attempts to cross a suspended log or move by rope across an expanse that seems scary, teammates will encourage the climber. Even if someone cannot complete the course, he or she will feel supported and know the accomplishment of having faced the challenge. Why not join a group this summer and experience the true team spirit and the confidence that a high ropes course offers?

Body

Closing Sentence

Respond to the reading. What is the writer's opinion in the paragraph? Name reasons that support her opinion. When is the most important reason given?

Draft

Write an opinion paragraph. Write an opinion about an outdoor activity. Include at least three strong reasons that support your opinion. Read your paragraph aloud to a partner.

Writing Effective Paragraphs

Use the following general guidelines when you write paragraphs.

Prewriting Selecting a Topic and Details

- Select a specific topic.
- Collect facts, examples, and details about your topic.
- Write a topic sentence that states what your paragraph is going to be about. (See page 587 for help.)
- Decide on the best way to arrange your details.

Drafting Creating the First Draft

- Start your paragraph with the topic sentence.
- Write sentences in the body that support your topic. Use the details you collected as a guide.
- Connect your ideas and sentences with transitions.
- End with a sentence that restates your topic, leaves the reader with a final thought, or (in an essay) leads into the next paragraph.

Revising Improving Your Writing

- Add information if you need to say more about your topic.
- Move sentences that aren't in the correct order.
- Delete sentences that do not support the topic.
- Rewrite any sentences that are not clear.

Editing Checking for Conventions

- Check the revised version of your writing for grammar, mechanics, and spelling errors.
- Then write a neat final copy and proofread it.

tip When you write a paragraph, remember that readers want . . .

- original ideas. *(They want to learn something new and interesting.)*
- personality. *(They want to hear the writer's voice.)*

How can I find interesting details?

Every paragraph needs good supporting details. Here are several types of details you can use in expository and persuasive paragraphs: facts, explanations, definitions, reasons, examples, and comparisons. You might get these details from personal knowledge and memories or from other sources of information.

Use Personal Details

For narrative and descriptive writing, personal details can add interest. Personal details may include sensory, memory, and reflective details.

- **Sensory details** are things that you see, hear, smell, taste, and touch. (These details are important in descriptive paragraphs.)
  He or she is left groaning and swinging in midair.
- **Memory details** are things you remember from experience. (These details are important in narrative paragraphs.)
  Her scream startled me, and I yelled, "It's a bear!"
- **Reflective details** are things you think about or hope for. (These details are often used in narrative and descriptive paragraphs.)
  Rainbow Rock may be just an artificial training ground, but it provides a real test of a rock climber's balance, strength, and courage.

Use Other Sources of Details

To collect details from other sources, use the following tips.

1. **Talk with someone you know.** Parents, neighbors, friends, or teachers may know a lot about your topic.
2. **Write for information.** If you think a museum, a business, or a government office has information you need, send for it.
3. **Read about your topic.** Gather details from books, magazines, and newspapers.
4. **Use the Internet.** The quickest source of information is the Internet. Remember to check Internet sources carefully for reliability. (See page 387.)

TEKS 7.17A(iii)
ELPS 5G

How do I know what kinds of details to gather?

Here are tips that will help you collect the right kinds of details when you write paragraphs about people, places, objects, and events, and when you write definitions.

Writing About a Person

When writing about or describing a person, make sure you collect plenty of information. The following guidelines will help.

Observe ■ If possible, carefully watch the person. Maybe the person laughs in a special way or wears a certain type of clothing.

Interview ■ Talk with your subject. Write down words and phrases that the person uses.

Research ■ Use whatever sources are necessary—books, articles, the Internet—to find out more about this person.

Compare ■ Can your subject be compared to some other person?

Describe ■ List any physical characteristics and personality traits.

Writing About a Place

When describing or writing about a place, use details that help the reader understand why the place is important to you.

Observe ■ Study the place you plan to write about. Use photos, postcards, or videos if you can't observe the place in person.

Remember ■ Think of a story (or an anecdote) about this place.

Describe ■ Include the sights, sounds, and smells of the place.

Compare ■ Compare your place to other places.

Writing About an Object

When writing about an object, tell your reader what kind of object it is, what it looks like, how it is used, and why this object is important to you.

Observe ■ Think about these questions: How is it used? Who uses it? How does it work? What does the object look like?

Research ■ Learn about the object. Try to find out when it was first made and used. Ask other people about it.

Define ■ What class or category does this object fit into? (See "Writing a Definition" on the next page.)

Remember ■ Recall interesting stories about this object.

TEKS 7.17A(iii)
ELPS 5G

Writing About an Event

When writing about or describing an event, focus on the important actions or on one interesting part. Also include sensory details and answer the 5 Ws. The following guidelines will help.

Observe ■ Study the event carefully. What sights, sounds, tastes, and smells come to mind? Listen to what people around you are saying.

Remember ■ When you write about something that has happened to you, recall as many details connected with the event as you can.

List ■ Answer the *who? what? when? where?* and *why?* questions for facts about the event.

Investigate ■ Read about the event and ask other people what they know about it.

Evaluate ■ Decide why the event is important to you.

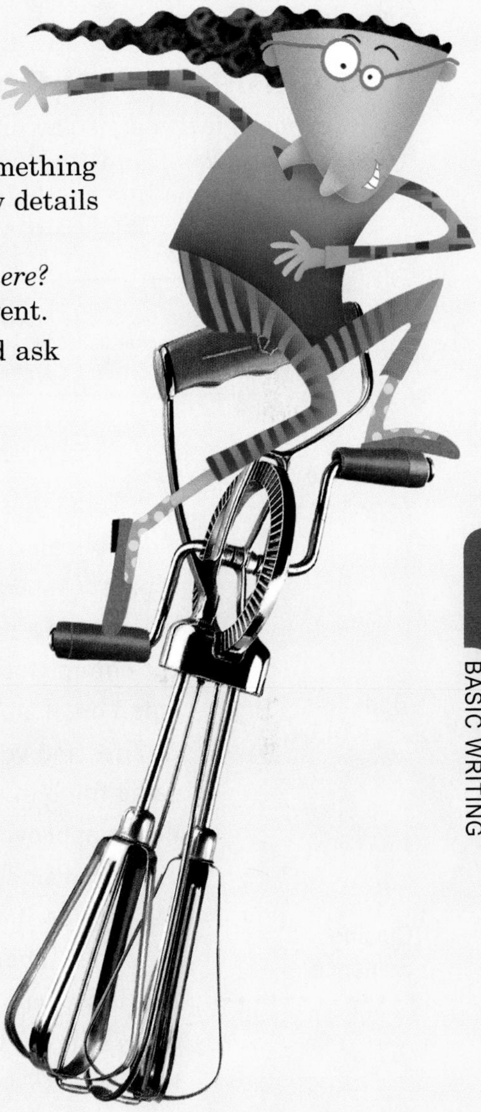

Writing a Definition

When you write a definition, you need to think about three things.

- First put the **term** you are defining *(coyote)* into a **class** or category of similar things *(wild member of the dog family).*
- Then list special **characteristics** that make this individual different from others in that class *(like a wolf, only smaller).*

Term—*A coyote*

Class—*is a wild member of the dog family and is*

Characteristic—*like a wolf, only smaller.*

Draft **Think about a topic you are interested in.** Where might you find facts about your topic? Use appropriate resources to identify and develop facts about your topic as well as details that support your topic.

What can I do to organize my details effectively?

After you've gathered your details, you need to organize them in the best possible way. You can organize a paragraph by *time, location, importance, comparison,* or *logical order.* Graphic organizers can help you keep your details in order.

Use Chronological Order

Chronological means "according to time." Transition words and phrases (*first, second, then,* and *finally*) are often used in narrative and expository paragraphs. A time line can help you organize your details.

Bill-to-Law Time Line

Bill introduced by senator in Senate	Goes to committee for study	Voted on by Senate (passed)	Voted on by House (passed)	Goes to president to sign into law	If vetoed, back to House and Senate (needs 2/3 vote each)

Making a Law

Topic Sentence

Turning a bill into a law at the federal level is a complicated process. First, a senator or House representative introduces a bill, or potential law. Then the bill goes to a committee for study. After studying the bill, the committee recommends that the bill be changed or voted on. If a bill is introduced in the Senate, all senators discuss and vote on it. Next, the representatives do the same thing in the House. When both the Senate and the House approve it, the bill goes to the president. If the president signs the bill, it finally becomes a law. However, the president can veto the bill, but even with a veto, the bill can still become a law if two-thirds of the Senate and the House vote in favor of it. Because of this process, many bills get blocked, detoured, or totally changed along the way.

Body

Closing Sentence

Respond to the reading. How are steps in making a law shown in the time line (or chart)? How are they given in the paragraph?

Use Order of Location

Often, you can organize descriptive details by order of location. For example, a description may move from left to right, from top to bottom, or from one direction (north) to another (south). Words or phrases like *next to, before, above, below, east, west, north,* and *south* may be used to show location. A drawing or map can help you organize your details.

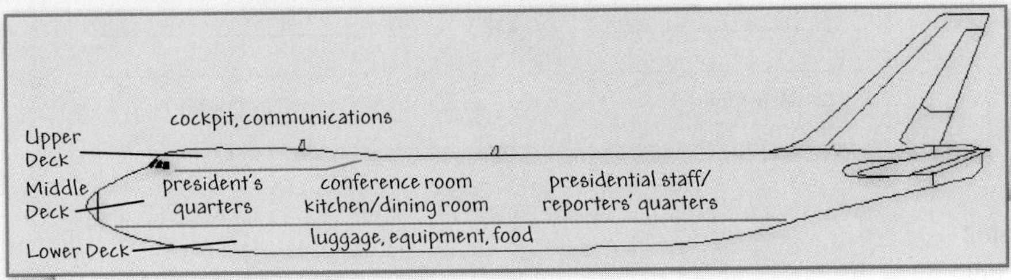

The President's Plane

Topic Sentence

Air Force One, the president's plane, is a 747 jet with many special features. The lower level holds luggage, ultra-modern electronic equipment, and enough food for 100 people to eat 20 meals each. The 747's middle deck, which looks more like a hotel than an airplane, has the most sections. The president's quarters, at the front of the plane, include an office, an exercise room, and a bedroom. A large conference room and a kitchen make up the center section. The conference room doubles as a dining room. At the rear of the plane, the president's staff and the television and print reporters have work and rest areas. On the upper deck is the cockpit and a very sophisticated communications room. Air Force One has been modified in other ways, too, but that information is considered top secret.

Body

Closing Sentence

Respond to the reading. With what part of *Air Force One* does the description begin? Where does it end?

Use Order of Importance

Persuasive and expository paragraphs are often organized by order of importance—from *most* to *least* important, or from *least* to *most* important.

Most important		Least important
1. ________		3. ________
2. ________	or	2. ________
3. ________		1. ________
Least important		Most important

Topic Sentence

Body

Closing Sentence

Presidential Powers

The president of the United States is the nation's most powerful leader. The president's most important duty is to "preserve, protect, and defend the Constitution of the United States." The Constitution serves as the blueprint for governing this country and for safeguarding the rights and freedoms of its citizens. Serving as commander in chief of the armed forces is probably the president's second-most important duty. In this role, the president can deploy troops to protect the country and its people. In times of national emergency, Congress can give the president even more control over the armed forces. The president can also appoint judges and make treaties, but he cannot make any laws. Only Congress has that power. Finally, as head of the executive branch, the president is in charge of 4 million employees. This might be the president's least-favorite job! All in all, the job of being president carries a lot of responsibility.

Respond to the reading. **How are the details organized in this paragraph? On your own paper, list them in reverse order (most to least or least to most). Which order works better?**

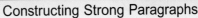

TEKS 7.14B
ELPS 3E, 5G

Use Comparison-Contrast Order

Expository paragraphs are often organized by comparison-contrast order, which shows how two subjects are both alike and different. A Venn diagram can be used to show differences (**A** and **B**) and similarities (**C**).

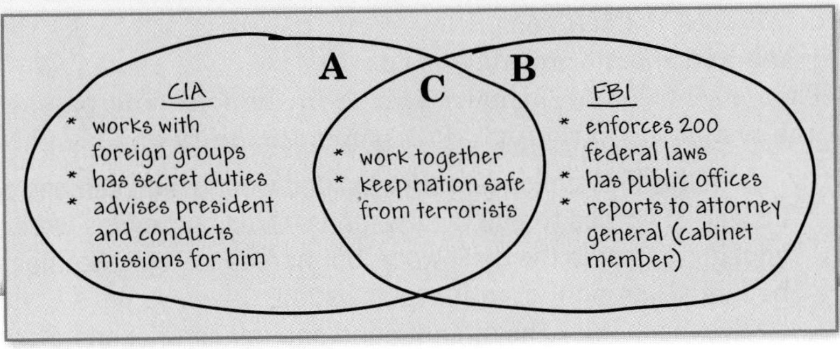

Spy vs. Spy

Topic Sentence

The Central Intelligence Agency (CIA) and the Federal Bureau of Investigation (FBI) help protect the United States. Although they share a goal and sometimes work together, the two groups are very different. The CIA's job is to collect information about foreign groups that may harm the United States. The CIA also works with the FBI to watch for spies or terrorists in the United States. Not only does the FBI hunt for spies, but it also enforces more than 200 federal laws. CIA agents depend on secrecy to do their duties, while FBI agents work in offices across the country and do not hide their identities. The CIA advises the president and conducts special missions ordered by the president. The FBI reports to the attorney general, who is a member of the president's cabinet. Despite their differences, these two groups help keep the nation safe.

Body

Closing Sentence

Respond to the reading. Find two body sentences that include contrasting details. What words show the contrast?

Draft

Write a paragraph. Choose two teams, groups, or organizations to compare. Use a Venn diagram to list the details. Then write your paragraph. Read your paragraph aloud to a partner.

TEKS 7.17A(iii)

How can I be sure all my details work well?

Create Unity in Your Writing

In a well-written paragraph, each detail tells something about the topic. If a detail does not tell something about the topic, it breaks the *unity* of the paragraph and should probably be cut.

The detail (sentence) shown in blue in the following passage does not fit with the rest of the paragraph. It disrupts the unity and should be cut.

> **In the 1800s, pioneers who headed west used oxen and mules instead of horses to pull their wagons. Oxen and mules were strong enough to handle the daily work, but horses weren't. So the pioneers bought six or eight oxen for each wagon.** Cowboys used horses to drive cattle herds. **The strength and endurance of oxen helped settlers cross the Rocky Mountains.**

Try It In the paragraph below, find three details (sentences) that do not support the topic sentence. Then read the paragraph aloud without those sentences. How does cutting those details affect the paragraph's unity?

> A "prairie schooner" was a type of covered wagon used by pioneers. It was about four feet wide and ten feet long. That's much smaller than my bedroom at home. With the cover on, a prairie schooner stood about ten feet tall. The wagon box was made of hardwood and was about three feet deep. The pioneers made the wagon box watertight by using tar. People also used tar to patch a leaky roof. A watertight prairie schooner could float across slow-moving rivers. The side boards were slanted outward so that river water didn't come in under the edges of the cover. River water has bacteria in it. The wagon box was packed tight with everything the pioneers planned to take to their new home.

Look at your paragraph. **Study the comparison-contrast paragraph you wrote (page 599). Do all your details support your topic? Would the unity of your paragraph be improved if you cut a detail or two?**

Develop Coherence from Start to Finish

An effective paragraph reads smoothly and clearly. When all the details in a paragraph are tied together well, the paragraph has *coherence* and is easy for the reader to follow. One way to make your writing smooth and coherent is to use transitions.

Try It Number your paper from 1 to 6. Use the transitions in black to help tie the paragraph below together. (Use each transition only once.) When you finish, read the paragraph. Does it read smoothly? If not, switch some transitions.

first	**in addition to**	**besides**	**although**
then	**also**	**second**	**finally**

There are several simple ways in which kids can help the environment. ________ (1), they can recycle things like plastic, glass, cans, newspapers, and magazines. ________ (2), they can pick up trash on school grounds and playgrounds. ________ (3) they can clean up their own yards. ________ (4) it takes some work, kids can plant trees. ________ (5) looking nice, trees help the environment by producing oxygen, by removing pollution from the air, and by providing food and shelter for birds. ________ (6), kids can help even more by giving Planet Earth a voice. They can speak up and remind other people to take care of the environment, too.

Read your paragraph. Read your comparison-contrast paragraph from page 599. Underline any parts that don't flow smoothly. Then use transitions to make the writing smoother. (See pages 634–635.)

TEKS 7.17A(v), 7.19A(viii)

How can I turn my paragraphs into essays?

Use an Essay Plan

Turning a group of paragraphs into an essay is not simply a matter of placing one after another. To begin with, each paragraph needs to be well written and well organized. Here are some additional tips to follow.

1 Plan the organization.

Organize your essay in a way that fits your topic—chronological order, order of importance, logical order, order of location, and so on.

2 State the topic and focus in the first paragraph.

Begin with an interesting fact or example to catch the reader's attention. Then tell what your essay is about in a focus statement, which includes the topic and a main idea or feeling about it.

3 Develop your writing idea in the middle paragraphs.

Use each paragraph in the body of your essay to explain and support one part of your focus statement. Each paragraph must have a topic sentence, which deals with one part of the focus, followed with supporting details.

4 Finish with a strong ending.

The final paragraph is usually a review of the main points in the essay. Your ending may emphasize the importance of the topic or may leave the reader with something to think about.

5 Use transition words or phrases to improve coherence.

Transition words and phrases show the relationship between ideas in each paragraph. They can do this by showing relationships with time (*before, during, finally*) and with contrast (*however, but, yet*). Other transition words and phrases show a result (*therefore, as a result, so*) or point out an addition (*and, also, furthermore*).

Write NOW

Write a short essay on a topic that interests you. Use transitions to link paragraphs and show the coherence of your ideas. Try to use two or more of the different kinds of transitions including time, contrast, result, and addition.

How do I know if I have a strong paragraph?

Use a Paragraph Checklist

You'll know that you have a strong paragraph if it gives the reader complete information on a specific topic. One sentence should identify the topic, and the other sentences should support it. Use the checklist below to help you plan and write effective paragraphs.

Focus and Coherence

____ **1.** Do I focus on an interesting topic sentence?

____ **2.** Does each sentence support the topic sentence?

Organization

____ **3.** Is my topic sentence clear?

____ **4.** Does each sentence logically lead to the next one?

Development of Ideas

____ **5.** Have I developed my controlling idea in depth?

____ **6.** Does each sentence add meaning to the ones before it?

Voice

____ **7.** Does my voice show interest and knowledge of my topic?

____ **8.** Does my voice engage the reader and establish a meaningful connection?

Conventions

____ **9.** Are my words well chosen and concise?

____ **10.** Have I used a variety of sentences to make my paragraph appealing to read?

____ **11.** Do I use correct grammar, mechanics, and spelling?

improve
support

ELPS 2C, 2I, 3D, 3E, 4G

A Writer's Resource

Learning Language

Work with a partner. Read the meanings and share answers to the questions.

1. A **topic** is a subject that you choose to write about in an essay or report.
   What are three topics that interest you enough to write about?
2. A **strategy** is a step or set of steps that help you reach a goal.
   What strategy might you use to choose a topic to write about?
3. When something **expands**, it becomes larger.
   What can you do to expand your knowledge of writing?

organize
REFERENCE
select

A Writer's Resource

If you're like most students, you often have questions when you are in the middle of a writing assignment. If a question pops up when you're in class, you can ask your teacher or a classmate. If, however, a question pops up when you're not in class, you need to find another source to ask or check.

This "Writer's Resource" chapter can be a great source for answering many of your questions, like "How can I find the best topics to write about?" or "How can I make my voice more expressive?" or "What can I do to make my final copy look better?"

What's Ahead

You will learn how to . . .

- find topics and get started.
- collect and organize details.
- write terrific topic sentences.
- use new forms.
- create a voice.
- improve your writing style.
- expand your vocabulary.
- write more effective sentences.
- connect sentences and paragraphs.
- improve your final copy.
- set up practical writing.

TEKS 7.14A

How can I find the best topics to write about?

Try a Topic-Selecting Strategy

A distinguished writer once said, "There are few experiences quite so satisfactory as getting a good writing idea." This may be overstating it a little, but getting a good writing idea is certainly an important step in the writing process. Let's say, for example, you are asked to write a report about a topic you have studied in a science unit. Your job would be to select a "good writing idea," a specific topic, to write about.

General Subject Area: bacteria
Specific Writing Topic: fighting harmful bacteria

The following strategies will help you select effective, specific topics that you can feel good about.

Journal Writing Write on a regular basis in a personal journal, recording your thoughts and experiences. Review your entries from time to time and underline ideas that you would like to write more about later.

Clustering Begin a cluster (also called a web) with a key word or phrase. Select a general term or an idea that is related to your writing assignment. Then cluster related words around the key word, as in the model below.

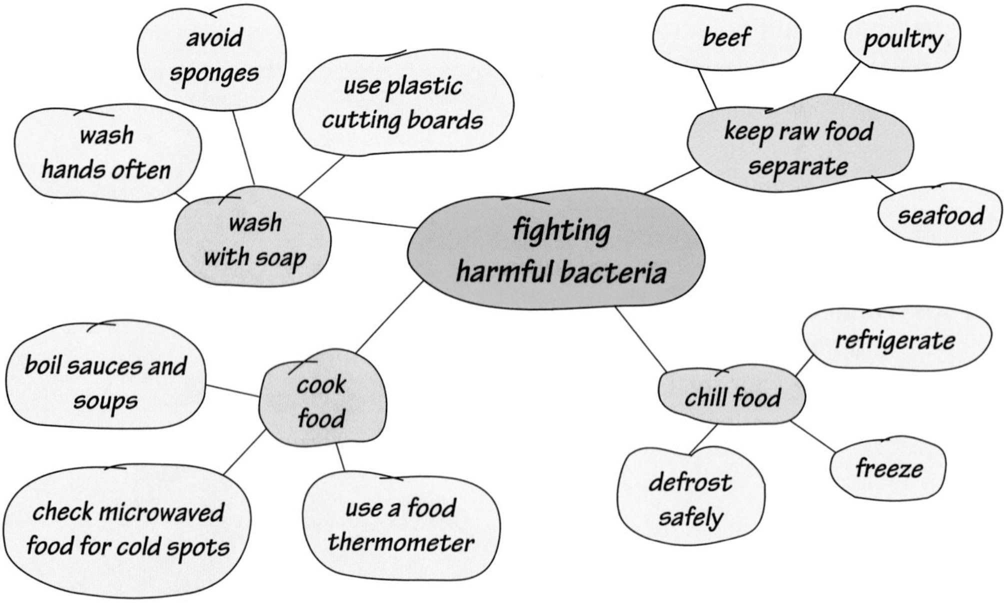

Listing List ideas as they come to mind when you think about your assignment. Keep your list going as long as you can. Then look for words in your list that you feel would make good writing topics.

Freewriting Write nonstop for 5 to 10 minutes to discover some possible writing ideas. Begin writing with a particular idea in mind (one related to the writing assignment). Underline the ideas that might work as topics for your assignment.

Sentence Completion Complete a sentence starter in as many ways as you can. Try to word your sentence so that it leads you to a topic you can use for a particular writing assignment.

Reading is . . .
Journal entries help me . . .
Painting can be . . .
Last year my writing . . .
I think it would be fun . . .
I would not mind . . .
My friend is . . .
I wish my parents . . .
I like to share . . .
My favorite animal . . .
My part-time job . . .

Review the "Basics of Life" List

The words listed below name many of the categories or groups of things that most people need in order to live a full life. The list provides an endless variety of possibilities for topics. Consider the first category, *work/occupation*. You could write about . . .

- the occupation of a friend or a family member,
- what you think your all-time favorite occupation would be, or
- why your work is rewarding.

work/occupation	senses	rules/laws
clothing	machines	tools/utensils
housing	intelligence	heat/fuel
food	history/records	natural resources
communication	agriculture	personality/identity
exercise	land/property	recreation/hobby
education	community	trade/money
family	science	literature/books
friends	plants/vegetation	health/medicine
purpose/goals	freedom/rights	art/music
love	energy	faith/religion

What can I do to get started?

Use a List of Writing Topics

The writing prompts listed below and the sample topics listed on the next page provide plenty of starting points for writing assignments.

Writing Prompts

Every day is full of experiences that make you think. You do things that you feel good about. You hear things that make you angry. You wonder how different things work. You're reminded of a past experience. These common, everyday thoughts can make excellent prompts for writing.

Describe (Descriptive)

The perfect bedroom
My favorite store
A parrot, a guinea pig, a ferret
Newborn lambs, calves, chickens
Stalking cats, galloping horses
Pioneer days, wagon-train life
Life in ancient Egypt, Greece, or Rome
Solar or lunar eclipses, rainbows
Meteor showers, hailstorms, sun dogs

Tell Your Story (Narrative)

My biggest surprise
Learning a lesson
Learning something amazing, surprising
Visiting a special place
Overcoming a challenge
A sudden or a big change

Compare-Contrast (Expository)

A shark and a manta ray
A llama and a camel
Soccer and football
Breakfast on Monday/breakfast on Sunday
Two seasons
Two months
Living in a city/small town
Yourself and a relative

Problem-Solution (Expository)

School rule about clothing
Being late to school
Keeping my cat off my bed
Keeping my brother out of my room
Getting to soccer practice
Convincing the city council we need a teen center
Getting my homework done on time

Editorial (Persuasive)

Individual sports in school
More field trips for students
An environment-friendly idea
Ways to help your community
Supporting a worthwhile cause
Putting an end to something unfair

Respond to . . . (Response to Texts)

A book that changed your thinking
A character you identify with
A poem that expressed a feeling
The biography of someone you admire

Research (Report)

Aquifers, oil wells, salt mines
Hot springs, mud slides, droughts
Deserts, tide pools, glaciers

Sample Topics

You come across many people, places, experiences, and things every day that could be topics for writing. A number of possible topics are listed below for descriptive, narrative, expository, and persuasive writing.

Descriptive

People: teacher, relative, classmate, coach, neighbor, bus driver, hero, someone you spend time with, someone you admire, brothers and sisters, someone with a special talent, someone from history

Places: hangout, garage, room, rooftop, historical place, zoo, park, hallway, barn, bayou, lake, cupboard, yard, empty lot, alley, valley, campsite, river, city street

Things: billboard, poster, video game, cell phone, bus, boat, gift, drawing, rainbow, doll, junk drawer, flood, mascot, movie

Animals: dolphin, elephant, snake, armadillo, eagle, deer, toad, spoonbill, squirrel, pigeon, pet, coyote, catfish, octopus, beaver, turtle

Narrative

A time I . . . did something mean, embarrassed myself or someone else, acted without thinking

A time someone . . . said the wrong thing, discovered an unexpected friend, made the wrong decision

Expository

Comparison-Contrast . . . Two friends, two places, two jobs, two teachers, two pets, two types of transportation, a house cat and a lion, a lake and the ocean

The causes of . . . sunburn, acne, hiccups, tornadoes, rust, computer viruses, arguments, success, failure, frostbite

Kinds of . . . crowds, friends, commercials, dreams, neighbors, pain, clouds, joy, stereos, heroes, chores, homework, frustration

Definition of . . . a good time, a conservative, "soul," a grandmother, loyalty, one type of music, advice, courage, hope, strength, fun, freedom, pride

Persuasive

School: homework, school government, hot/cold classrooms, lunchroom vending machines, closed-campus lunches, crowded hallways, crowded library/computer lab

Environment: beautifying a neighborhood, cleaning up a local park, petitioning for cleaner air, volunteering at the library

Home: too many chores, pet troubles, changing a curfew, getting enough computer time, sharing a bathroom/bedroom

TEKS 7.14B

How can I collect details for my writing?

Try Graphic Organizers

Graphic organizers can help you gather and organize your details for writing. Clustering is one method. (See page 606.) These two pages list other useful organizers.

Cause-Effect Organizer

Use to collect and organize details for cause-effect essays.

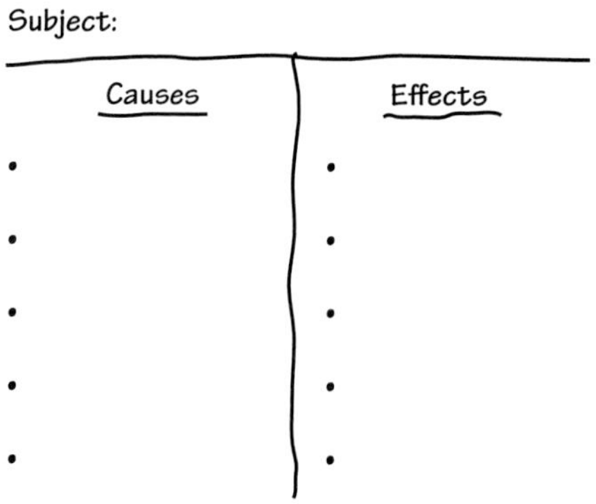

Problem-Solution Web

Use to map out problem-solution essays.

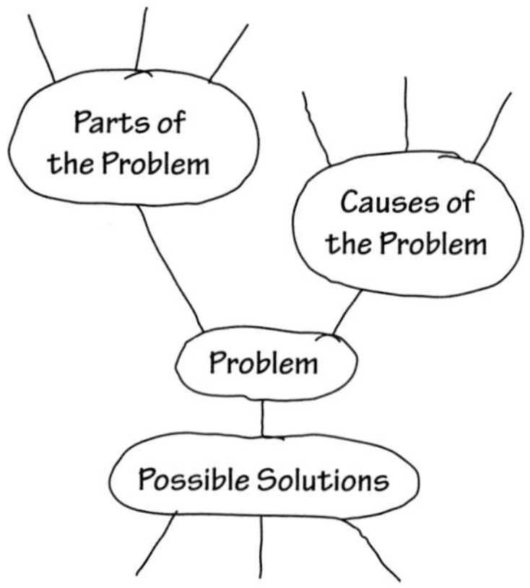

Time Line (Step-by-Step)

Use to collect details for personal narratives and how-to essays.

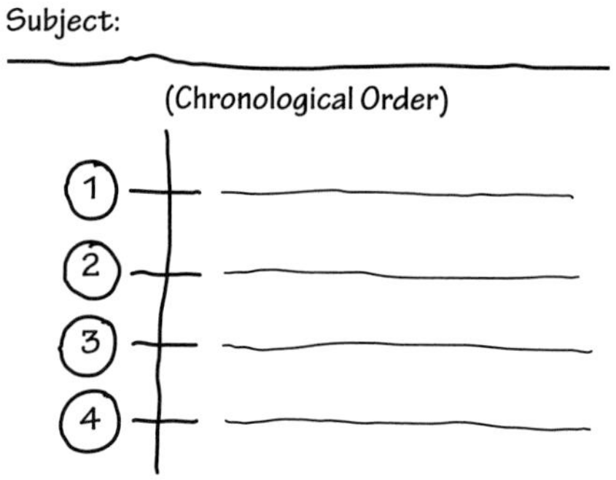

Action-Sensory Chart

Use to collect details for descriptive and narrative essays or for stories.

Topic:		
	Action Details	Sensory Details
Beginning		
Middle		
Ending		

Venn Diagram

Use to collect details to compare and contrast two subjects.

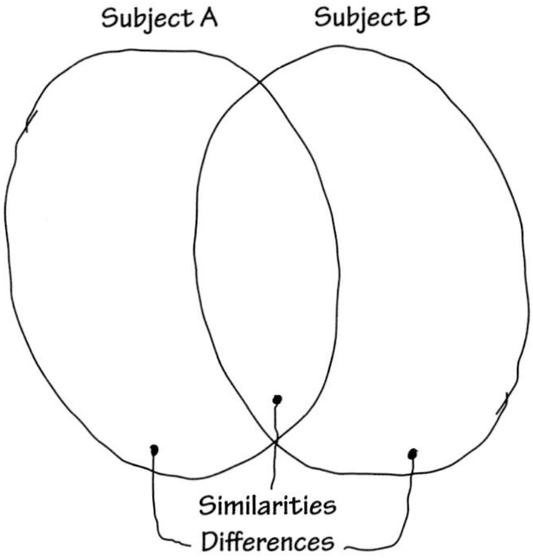

5 Ws Chart

Use to collect the *Who? What? When? Where?* and *Why?* details for personal narratives and news stories.

Subject:

Who?	What?	When?	Where?	Why?

Sensory Chart

Use to collect details for descriptive essays and observation reports.

Subject:

Sights	Sounds	Smells	Tastes	Feelings

Process Chain (5 Step)

Use to collect details for science-related writing, such as how a process or cycle works.

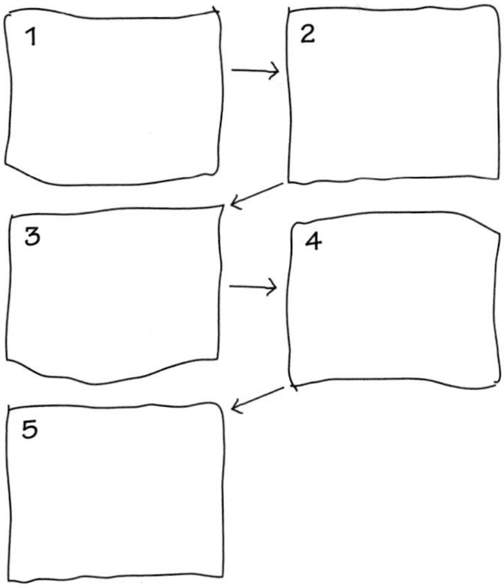

What can I do to organize my details better?

Make Lists and Outlines

List Your Details

You can use a variety of ways to organize details as you prepare to write an essay or a report. For most writing, you can make a simple list.

Sam Houston's background
- *born in 1793, Virginia*
- *lived with the Cherokee as a young man*
- *served in War of 1812*
- *helped win the Texas Revolution against Mexico*
- *died in 1863*

Strong leader
- *won the Battle of San Jacinto*
- *elected first president of republic of Texas*
- *elected governor and senator when Texas became state*

Man of conscience
- *defended rights of Native Americans when unpopular*
- *refused to sign oath of loyalty to Confederacy and removed*

Outline Your Information

After gathering facts and details, select two or three main points that best support your focus. Write an outline to organize your information.

I. Sam Houston lived from 1793 to 1863 and helped establish Texas as a republic and a state.
   A. He moved with his family to Tennessee as a child.
   B. He ran away from home and lived with the Cherokee.
   C. He entered law and politics in Tennessee.
   D. Houston served as a government agent to the Cherokee before moving to Texas.

II. Houston showed leadership ability and a strong sense of honor in his dealings with and for the Native Americans.
   A. . . .
   B. . . .

Use Patterns of Organization

- **Chronological (Time) Order** or **Step-by-Step** You can arrange your details in the order in which they happen (*first, then, next,* and so on). Use these patterns for narratives, history reports, directions, and explaining a process. (See page 596.)

  With a groan, I pulled on my heavy backpack and headed off barefoot up the giant sand hills at Sleeping Bear Dunes. At first, I thought this hike would be easy. Then, about halfway up, I began huffing and puffing . . .

- **Order of Location** You can arrange details in the order in which they are located (*above, below, beside,* and so on). Use order of location for descriptions, explanations, and directions. (See page 597.)

  Some of my most important stuff is attached to the inside of my locker door. Near the top, I've taped two pictures of my favorite rock group. Around the edges, I've jammed in a bunch of notes from my friends. Below the notes, a collection of fridge magnets from my favorite pizza places hold up a . . .

- **Order of Importance** You can arrange details from the most important to the least—or from the least important to the most. Persuasive and expository essays are often organized this way. (See page 596.)

  The president of the United States is the nation's most powerful leader. The president's most important duty is to "preserve, protect, and defend the Constitution of the United States." . . . Serving as commander in chief of the armed forces is probably the president's second-most important duty. . . .

- **Comparison-Contrast** You can write about two or more subjects by showing how they are alike and how they are different. Compare each subject separately or compare both, point by point, as in the example below. (See page 597.)

  Tacos and pizza might seem totally different, but they actually have a lot in common. Even though tacos come from Mexico, and pizza comes from Italy, each food is an American favorite. . . . Tacos have a tortilla shell made from ground corn or flour. Pizzas are cooked on a crust that is basically a . . .

- **Logical Order** You can organize information in a way that makes sense. Begin with a main idea followed by details, or start with details and lead up to the main point.

  As the chart below shows, you don't even have to be a smoker to die from cigarette smoke. Between 1995 and 2000, the number of Americans who died from secondhand smoke was more than a hundred thousand. Among smokers, there were nearly half a million deaths per year. The message is . . .

How can I write terrific topic sentences?

Try Eight Special Strategies

Writing a good topic sentence is a key to writing a great paragraph. A good topic sentence names the topic and states a specific feeling about it. Use the following strategies the next time you need to write a terrific topic sentence. (Also see page 587.)

Use a Number

Topic sentences can use number words to tell what the paragraph will be about.

Books come in a variety **of sizes.**

Mary Anne loves her job for a number **of reasons.**

Number Words		
two	couple	a pair
few	three	a number
several	four	many
a variety	five	a list

Create a List

A topic sentence can list the things the paragraph will talk about.

Mars has a faint reddish hue **and** unusual brightness**.**

In the next chapter, more rockets blasted off**,** ripped through the clouds**, and** tried to reach new galaxies**.**

Start with *To* and a Verb

A topic sentence that starts with "to" and a verb helps the reader know why the information in the paragraph is important.

To analyze **a character in a novel, you need to look at how he or she changes.**

To understand **the rules of basketball, listen to your coach.**

Use Word Pairs

Conjunctions that come in pairs can help organize a topic sentence.

Our car needs not only **new tires** but also **new brakes.**

Your teacher can be both **your mentor** and **your instructor.**

Word Pairs
if . . . then
either . . . or
not only . . . but also
both . . . and
whether . . . or
as . . . so

Join Two Ideas

A topic sentence can combine two equal ideas by using a comma and a coordinating conjunction: *and, but, or, for, so, nor, yet.*

A kite is fun to fly, and a boomerang is fun to throw.

A lot of bacteria are useful, but some bacteria cause illness.

Use a "Why-What" Word

A "why-what" word is a subordinating conjunction that shows how ideas are connected.

Because all of the students love astronomy, the teacher scheduled a trip to a planetarium.

When you have a cold, be careful not to spread germs.

"Why-What" Words	
so that	once
before	since
until	whenever
because	while
if	as long as
as	after
in order that	when

Use a "Yes, But" Word

A "yes, but" word is a subordinating conjunction that tells how two ideas are different.

Even though our choir is small, we have gotten great reviews.

Friends help each other instead of turning away.

"Yes, But" Words
however
instead of
although
even though
even if
unless
whether
whereas

Quote an Expert

Sometimes the best way to start a paragraph is to quote someone who knows about your topic.

Michael Jordan once said, "You have to expect things of yourself before you can do them."

Amelia Earhart put it best: "It is far easier to start something than to finish it."

What other forms can I use for my writing?

Try These Forms of Writing

Finding the right *form* for your writing is just as important as finding the right topic. When you are selecting a form, be sure to ask yourself who you're writing for (your audience) and why you're writing (your purpose).

Anecdote	A brief story that makes a point
Autobiography	A writer's story of her or his own life
Biography	A writer's story of some other person's life
Book review	A brief essay giving a response or an opinion about a book (See pages 299–336.)
Character sketch	Writing that describes a specific character in a story
Composition	A longer piece of writing, such as a story or an essay
Descriptive writing	Writing that uses details to help the reader clearly imagine a certain person, place, thing, or idea (See pages 71–91.)
Editorial	Newspaper letters or articles giving an opinion
Essay	A piece of writing in which ideas are presented, explained, argued, or described in an interesting way
Expository writing	Writing that explains by presenting the steps, the causes, or the kinds of something (See pages 161–225.)
Fable	A short story that often uses talking animals as the main characters and teaches a lesson or moral
Fantasy	A story set in an imaginary world in which the characters usually have supernatural powers or abilities
Freewriting	Writing whatever comes to mind about any topic
Historical fiction	A made-up story based on something real in history in which fact is mixed with fiction
Myth	A traditional story intended to explain a mystery of nature, religion, or culture
Narrative	Writing that relates an event, an experience, or a story (See pages 93–159.)

Novel A book-length story with several characters and a well-developed plot

Personal narrative Writing that shares an event or experience from the writer's personal life (See pages 97–136.)

Persuasive writing Writing that is meant to persuade the reader to agree with the writer about someone or something (See pages 227–293.)

Play A form that uses dialogue to tell a story and is meant to be performed in front of an audience

Poem Writing that uses rhythm, rhyme, and imagery (See pages 373–381.)

Proposal Writing that includes specific information about an idea or a project that is being considered for approval

Research report An essay that shares information on a topic that has been researched well and organized carefully (See pages 401–448.)

Response to literature Writing that is a summary or a reaction to something the writer has read (novel, short story, poem, article, and so on)

Science fiction Writing based on real or imaginary science and often set in the future

Short story A short piece of literature with only a few characters and one problem or conflict (See pages 361–372.)

Summary Writing that presents only the most important ideas from a longer piece of writing

Tall tale A humorous, exaggerated story (often based on the life of a real person) about a character who does impossible things

Tragedy Literature in which the hero is destroyed because of some serious flaw or defect in his or her character

How can I create a voice in my writing?

You can create your writing voice by using dialogue and by *showing* instead of *telling*.

Use Dialogue

Each person you write about has a unique way of saying things, and well-written dialogue lets the reader *hear* the speaker's personality and thoughts. For example, notice how the message below can be spoken in several different ways.

Message: Your new car is impressive.
Speaker 1: **"Whoa, Dad! Cool new wheels!"**
Speaker 2: **"Nice coupe, Bill. I've always been a sedan man myself."**
Speaker 3: **"Such a fancy car, Son! Hope you didn't spend too much."**

Each of these speakers delivers the same message in a unique way. The dialogue tells as much about the speaker as it does about the topic.

One way to improve your dialogue is to think about the speaker and her or his personality. Look at the three personality webs below and try to decide which one is *Speaker 1, Speaker 2,* or *Speaker 3* from above. How does the dialogue show their personalities?

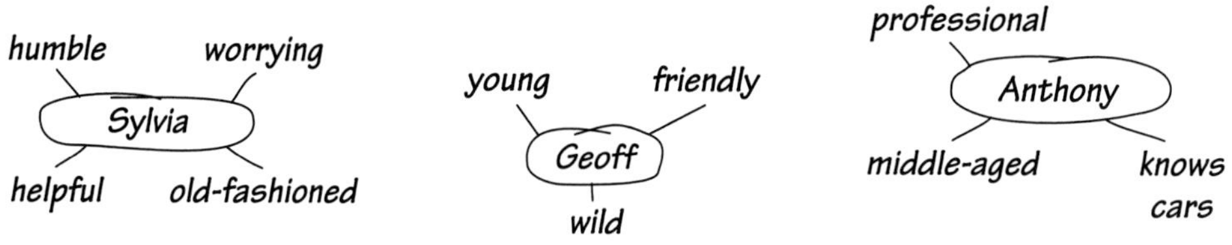

Tips for Punctuating Dialogue

- Indent every time a different person speaks.
- Put the exact words of a speaker in quotation marks.
- Set off the quoted words from the rest of the sentence by using a comma.
- At the end of quoted words, put a period or comma inside the quotation marks.

For more information and examples on how to punctuate dialogue, see 650.1, 658.1, and 660.1 in the "Proofreader's Guide."

Show, Don't Tell

The old saying "Seeing is believing" is especially true in writing. Writing that *tells* the reader something is not as strong as writing that *shows* the reader something, allowing him or her to decide how to feel about it. Notice the difference between the two paragraphs below.

Telling: **I rode on the roller coaster. It was frightening but fun.**

Showing: **As the roller coaster topped the first big hill, I could see my mom down below. She looked so small. Then the coaster began to surge down the hill. My hands went up, my heart jumped into my throat, and I let out a sound that was half laugh and half scream.**

The first paragraph simply *tells* the reader that the roller coaster ride was "frightening but fun." The second paragraph *shows* just how "frightening but fun" it really was.

Key Strategies for Showing

Next time you realize your writing is telling rather than showing, try one of these strategies.

- **Add sensory details.** Include sights, sounds, smells, tastes, and touch sensations. That way, the reader can "experience" the event.

  Telling: **The sandwich was difficult to eat.**

  Showing: **The cucumbers slipped out first. I squeezed the Kaiser roll together more tightly. But a tomato was soon hanging out and dripping. Next came a slice of onion. I carefully rebuilt the sandwich. Again, the cucumber was the first to escape.**

- **Explain body language.** Write about facial expressions and the way people stand, gesture, and move.

  Telling: **Sharissa was upset with me.**

  Showing: **Sharissa glared at me, tapped her foot, pursed her lips, and snorted.**

- **Use dialogue.** Let the people in your writing speak for themselves.

  Telling: **Dr. Mike told me I had a broken bone.**

  Showing: **"You won't have to take the garbage out or do other chores until your broken bone heals," said Dr. Mike.**

What can I do to improve my writing style?

Learn Some Writing Techniques

Writers put special effects into their stories and essays in different ways. Look over the following writing techniques and then experiment with some of them in your own writing.

Analogy A comparison of similar objects to help clarify one of the objects

Personal journals are like photograph albums. They both share personal details and tell a story.

Anecdote A brief story used to illustrate or make a point

Abe Lincoln walked two miles to return several pennies he had overcharged a customer. (This anecdote shows Lincoln's honesty.)

Exaggeration An overstatement or a stretching of the truth used to make a point or paint a clearer picture (See *overstatement.*)

After getting home from summer camp, I slept for a month.

Foreshadowing Hints or clues that a writer uses to suggest what will happen next in a story

Halfway home, Sarah wondered whether she had locked her locker.

Irony A technique that uses a word or phrase to mean the opposite of its normal meaning

Marshall just loves cleaning his room.

Local color The use of details that are common in a certain place or local area (A story taking place on a seacoast would contain details about the water and the life and people near it.)

Everybody wore flannel shirts to the Friday fish fry.

Metaphor A figure of speech that compares two things without using the word *like* or *as* (See page 380.)

In our community, high school football is king.

Overstatement An exaggeration or a stretching of the truth (See *exaggeration.*)

When he saw my grades, my dad hit the roof.

Parallelism Repeating similar words, phrases, or sentences to give writing rhythm (See page 584.)

We will swim in the ocean, lie on the beach, and sleep under the stars.

Personification A figure of speech in which a nonhuman thing (an idea, object, or animal) is given human characteristics (See page 380.)

Rosie's old car coughs and wheezes on cold days.

Pun A phrase that uses words in a way that gives them a humorous effect

The lumberjack logged on to the site to order new boots.

Sarcasm The use of praise to make fun of or "put down" someone or something (The expression is not sincere and is actually intended to mean the opposite thing.)

Micah's a real gourmet; he loves peanut butter and jelly sandwiches. (A *gourmet* is a "lover of fine foods.")

Sensory details Specific details that help the reader see, feel, smell, taste, and/or hear what is being described (See page 488.)

As Lamont took his driver's test, his heart thumped, his hands went cold, and his face began to sweat.

Simile A figure of speech that compares two things using the word *like* or *as* (See page 548.)

Faye's little brother darts around like a water bug.
Yesterday the lake was as smooth as glass.

Slang Informal words or phrases used by particular groups of people when they talk to each other

chill out   hang loose   totally awesome

Symbol An object that is used to stand for an idea

The American flag is a symbol of the United States. The stars stand for the 50 states, and the stripes stand for the 13 original U.S. colonies.

Understatement Very calm language (the opposite of exaggeration) used to bring special attention to an object or an idea

These hot red peppers may make your mouth tingle a bit.

How can I expand my writing vocabulary?

Study Writing Terms

This glossary includes terms used to describe the parts of the writing process. It also includes terms that explain special ways of stating an idea.

Antonym A word that means the opposite of another word: *happy* and *sad; large* and *small* (See page 625.)

Audience The people who read or hear what has been written

Body The main or middle part in a piece of writing that comes between the *beginning* and the *ending* and includes the main points

Brainstorming Collecting ideas by thinking freely about all the possibilities

Closing The ending or final part in a piece of writing (In a paragraph, the closing is the last sentence. In an essay or a report, the closing is the final paragraph.)

Coherence Tying ideas together in your writing (See page 601.)

Connotation The "feeling" a word suggests (See page 80.)

Denotation The dictionary meaning of a word

Dialogue Written conversation between two or more people

Figurative language Special comparisons, often called figures of speech, that make your writing more creative (See page 380.)

Focus statement The statement that tells what specific part of a topic is written about in an essay

Form A type of writing or the way a piece of writing is put together (See pages 616–617.)

Grammar The structure of language; the rules and guidelines that you follow in order to speak and write acceptably

Jargon The special language of a certain group, occupation, or field

Computer jargon: byte digital upload

Journal A notebook for writing down thoughts, experiences, ideas, and information

Limiting the subject Taking a general subject and narrowing it down to a specific topic

General subject → Specific topic
sports → golf → golf skills → putting

Modifiers Words, phrases, or clauses that describe another word

Our black **cat** slowly **stretched and** then **leaped** onto the wicker chair. (Without the blue modifiers, all we know is that a "cat stretched and leaped.")

Point of view The angle from which a story is told (See page 369.)

Purpose The specific reason that a person has for writing

to describe   to narrate   to persuade   to explain

Style How an author writes (choice of words and sentences)

Supporting details Facts or ideas used to tell a story, explain a topic, describe something, or prove a point

Synonym A word that means the same thing as another word (*dog* and *canine*) (See page 625.)

Theme The main point, message, or lesson in a piece of writing

Thesis statement A statement that gives the main idea of an essay (See *focus statement.*)

Tone A writer's attitude toward her or his subject

serious   humorous   sarcastic

Topic The specific subject of a piece of writing

Topic sentence The sentence that contains the main idea of a paragraph (See page 587.)

Blue jeans are a popular piece of American clothing.

Transition A word or phrase that connects or ties two ideas together smoothly (See pages 634–635.)

also   however   lastly   later   next

Usage The way in which people use language (*Standard usage* generally follows the rules of good grammar. Most of the writing you do in school will require standard usage.)

Voice A writer's unique, personal tone or feeling that comes across in a piece of writing

How can I mark changes in my writing?

Use the symbols below to show where and how your writing needs to be changed. Your teachers may also use these symbols to point out errors in your writing.

Symbols	Meaning	Example	Corrected Example
≡	**Capitalize a letter.**	Jack London wrote *Call of the wild.*	Jack London wrote *Call of the Wild.*
/	**Make a capital letter lowercase.**	Buck is the hard-working sled dog in the Novel.	Buck is the hard-working sled dog in the novel.
⊙	**Insert (add) a period.**	He started out in California His home . . .	He started out in California. His home . . .
(oval) or *sp.*	**Correct spelling.**	Dave, the wheeler dog, nipped and snarlled at Buck.	Dave, the wheeler dog, nipped and snarled at Buck.
(delete mark)	**Delete (take out) or replace.**	Buck he had a strong will to live.	Buck had a strong will to live.
∧	**Insert here.**	He would not be *defeated* by his life of toil.	He would not be defeated by his life of toil.
∧ ∧ ∧ (with , : ;)	**Insert a comma, a colon, or a semicolon.**	If Buck hadn't been strong he would have died.	If Buck hadn't been strong, he would have died.
∨ ∨ ∨ (with ' " ")	**Insert an apostrophe or quotation marks.**	Spitz was Bucks main threat.	Spitz was Buck's main threat.
? ! (over ∧ ∧)	**Insert a question mark or an exclamation point.**	Who would win the battle It took a long time to find out.	Who would win the battle? It took a long time to find out.
¶	**Start a new paragraph.**	After their fight, Buck truly became the lead sled dog. ¶Another important character . . .	After their fight, Buck truly became the lead sled dog. Another important character . . .
∿	**Switch words or letters.**	Jack London wrote also *Sea Wolf.*	Jack London also wrote *Sea Wolf.*

What can I do to increase my vocabulary skills?

Use Context

When you come across a word you don't know, you can often figure out its meaning from the other words in the sentence. The other words form a familiar context, or setting, for the unfamiliar word. Looking closely at the surrounding words will give you clues to the meaning of the new word.

When you come to a word you don't know . . .

- **Look for a synonym**—a word or words that have the same meaning as the unknown word.

  Sara had an ominous feeling when she woke up, but the feeling was less threatening when she saw she was in her own room.
  (An *ominous* feeling is a threatening one.)

- **Look for an antonym**—a word that has the opposite meaning as the unknown word.

  Boniface had always been quite heavy, but he looked gaunt when he returned from the hospital.
  (*Gaunt* is the opposite of *heavy.*)

- **Look for a comparison or contrast.**

  Riding a mountain bike in a remote area is my idea of a great day. I wonder why some people like to ride motorcycles on busy six-lane highways.
  (A *remote* area is out of the way, in contrast to a *busy* area.)

- **Look for a definition or description.**

  Manatees, large aquatic mammals (sometimes called sea cows), can be found in the warm coastal waters of Florida.
  (An *aquatic* mammal is one that lives in the water.)

- **Look for words that appear in a series.**

  The campers spotted blue jays, chickadees, and indigo buntings on Saturday morning.
  (An *indigo bunting,* like a *blue jay* or *chickadee,* is a bird.)

- **Look for a cause and effect relationship.**

  The amount of traffic at 6th and Main doubled last year, so crossing lights were placed at that corner to avert an accident.
  (*Avert* means "to prevent.")

How can I build my vocabulary across the curriculum?

On the next several pages, you will find many of the most common prefixes, suffixes, and roots in the English language. Learning these word parts can help you increase your writing vocabulary.

Learn About Prefixes

A **prefix** is a word part that is added before a word to change the meaning of the word. For example, when the prefix *un* is added to the word *fair (unfair)*, it changes the word's meaning from "fair" to "not fair."

ambi *[both]*
- **ambidextrous** (skilled with both hands)

anti *[against]*
- **antifreeze** (a liquid that works against freezing)
- **antiwar** (against wars and fighting)

astro *[star]*
- **astronaut** (person who travels among the stars)
- **astronomy** (study of the stars)

auto *[self]*
- **autobiography** (writing that is about yourself)

bi *[two]*
- **bilingual** (using or speaking two languages)
- **biped** (having two feet)

circum *[in a circle, around]*
- **circumference** (the line or distance around a circle)
- **circumnavigate** (to sail around)

co *[together, with]*
- **cooperate** (to work together)
- **coordinate** (to put things together)

ex *[out]*
- **exhale** (to breathe out)
- **exit** (the act of going out)

fore *[before, in front of]*
- **foremost** (in the first place, before everyone or everything else)
- **foretell** (to tell or show beforehand)

hemi *[half]*
- **hemisphere** (half of a sphere or globe)

hyper *[over]*
- **hyperactive** (overactive)

im *[not, opposite of]*
- **impatient** (not patient)
- **impossible** (not possible)

in *[not, opposite of]*
- **inactive** (not active)
- **incomplete** (not complete)

inter *[between, among]*
- **international** (between or among nations)
- **interplanetary** (between the planets)

macro *[large]*
- **macrocosm** (the entire universe)

mal *[bad, poor]*
- **malnutrition** (poor nutrition)

micro *[small]*
- **microscope** (an instrument used to see very small things)

mono *[one]*
monolingual (using or speaking only one language)

non *[not, opposite of]*
nonfat (without the normal fat content)
nonfiction (based on facts; not made-up)

over *[too much, extra]*
overeat (to eat too much)
overtime (extra time; time beyond regular hours)

poly *[many]*
polygon (a figure or shape with three or more sides)
polysyllable (a word with more than three syllables)

post *[after]*
postscript (a note added at the end of a letter, after the signature)
postwar (after a war)

pre *[before]*
pregame (activities that occur before a game)
preheat (to heat before using)

re *[again, back]*
repay (to pay back)
rewrite (to write again or revise)

semi *[half, partly]*
semicircle (half a circle)
semiconscious (half conscious; not fully conscious)

sub *[under, below]*
submarine (a boat that can operate underwater)
submerge (to put underwater)

trans *[across, over; change]*
transcontinental (across a continent)
transform (to change from one form to another)

tri *[three]*
triangle (a figure that has three sides and three angles)
tricycle (a three-wheeled vehicle)

un *[not]*
uncomfortable (not comfortable)
unhappy (not happy; sad)

under *[below, beneath]*
underage (below or less than the usual or required age)
undersea (beneath the surface of the sea)

uni *[one]*
unicycle (a one-wheeled vehicle)
unisex (a single style that is worn by both males and females)

Numerical Prefixes

deci *[tenth of a part]*
decimal system (a number system based on units of 10)

centi *[hundredth of a part]*
centimeter (a unit of length equal to 1/100 meter)

milli *[thousandth of a part]*
millimeter (a unit of length equal to 1/1000 meter)

micro *[millionth of a part]*
micrometer (one-millionth of a meter)

deca, dec *[ten]*
decade (a period of 10 years)
decathlon (a contest with 10 events)

hecto, hect *[one hundred]*
hectare (a metric unit of land equal to 100 ares)

kilo *[one thousand]*
kilogram (a unit of mass equal to 1,000 grams)

mega *[one million]*
megabit (one million bits)

Study Suffixes

A **suffix** is a word part that is added after a word. Sometimes a suffix will tell you what part of speech a word is. For example, many adverbs end in the suffix *ly*.

able *[able, can do]*
agreeable (able or willing to agree)
doable (can be done)

al *[of, like]*
magical (like magic)
optical (of the eye)

ed *[past tense]*
called (past tense of call)
learned (past tense of learn)

ess *[female]*
lioness (a female lion)

ful *[full of]*
helpful (giving help; full of help)

ic *[like, having to do with]*
symbolic (having to do with symbols)

ily *[in some manner]*
happily (in a happy manner)

ish *[somewhat like or near]*
childish (somewhat like a child)

ism *[characteristic of]*
heroism (characteristic of a hero)

less *[without]*
careless (without care)

ly *[in some manner]*
calmly (in a calm manner)

ology *[study, science]*
biology (the study of living things)

s *[more than one]*
books (more than one book)

ward *[in the direction of]*
westward (in the direction of west)

y *[containing, full of]*
salty (containing salt)

Comparing Suffixes

er *[comparing two things]*
faster, later, neater, stronger

est *[comparing more than two]*
fastest, latest, neatest, strongest

Noun-Forming Suffixes

er *[one who]*
painter (one who paints)

ing *[the result of]*
painting (the result of a painter's work)

ion *[act of, state of]*
perfection (the state of being perfect)

ist *[one who]*
violinist (one who plays the violin)

ment *[act of, result of]*
amendment (the result of amending, or changing)
improvement (the result of improving)

ness *[state of]*
goodness (the state of being good)

or *[one who]*
actor (one who acts)

Understand Roots

A **root** is a word or word base from which other words are made by adding a prefix or a suffix. Knowing the common roots can help you figure out the meaning of difficult words.

aster *[star]*
asterisk (starlike symbol [*])
asteroid (resembling a star)

aud *[hear, listen]*
audible (can be heard)
auditorium (a place to listen to speeches and performances)

bibl *[book]*
Bible (sacred book of Christianity)
bibliography (list of books)

bio *[life]*
biography (book about a person's life)
biology (the study of life)

chrome *[color]*
monochrome (having one color)
polychrome (having many colors)

chron *[time]*
chronological (in time order)
synchronize (to make happen at the same time)

cide *[the killing of; killer]*
homicide (the killing of one person by another person)
pesticide (pest [bug] killer)

cise *[cut]*
incision (a thin, clean cut)
incisors (the teeth that cut or tear food)
precise (cut exactly right)

cord, cor *[heart]*
cordial (heartfelt)
coronary (relating to the heart)

corp *[body]*
corporation (a legal body; business)
corpse (a dead human body)

cycl, cyclo *[wheel, circular]*
bicycle (a vehicle with two wheels)
cyclone (a very strong circular wind)

dem *[people]*
democracy (ruled by the people)
epidemic (affecting many people at the same time)

dent, dont *[tooth]*
dentures (false teeth)
orthodontist (dentist who straightens teeth)

derm *[skin]*
dermatology (the study of skin)
epidermis (outer layer of skin)

fac, fact *[do, make]*
factory (a place where people make things)
manufacture (to make by hand or machine)

fin *[end]*
final (the last of something)
infinite (having no end)

flex *[bend]*
flexible (able to bend)
reflex (bending or springing back)

flu *[flowing]*
fluent (flowing smoothly or easily)
fluid (waterlike, flowing substance)

forc, fort *[strong]*
forceful (full of strength or power)
fortify (to make strong)

fract, frag *[break]*
fracture (to break)
fragment (a piece broken from the whole)

Learn More Roots

gen *[birth, produce]*
congenital (existing at birth)
genetics (the study of inborn traits)

geo *[of the earth]*
geography (the study of places on the earth)
geology (the study of the earth's physical features)

graph *[write]*
autograph (writing one's name)
graphology (the study of handwriting)

homo *[same]*
homogeneous (of the same birth or kind)
homogenize (to blend into a uniform mixture)

hydr *[water]*
dehydrate (to take the water out of)
hydrophobia (the fear of water)

ject *[throw]*
eject (to throw out)
project (to throw forward)

log, logo *[word, thought, speech]*
dialogue (speech between two people)
logic (thinking or reasoning)

luc, lum *[light]*
illuminate (to light up)
translucent (letting light come through)

magn *[great]*
magnificent (great)
magnify (to make bigger or greater)

man *[hand]*
manicure (to fix the hands)
manual (done by hand)

mania *[insanity]*
kleptomania (abnormal desire to steal)
maniac (an insane person)

mar *[sea, pool]*
marine (of or found in the sea)
mariner (sailor)

mega *[large]*
megalith (large stone)
megaphone (large horn used to make voices louder)

meter *[measure]*
kilometer (a thousand meters)
voltmeter (device to measure volts)

mit, miss *[send]*
emit (to send out; give off)
transmission (sending over)

multi *[many, much]*
multicultural (of or including many cultures)
multiped (an animal with many feet)

numer *[number]*
innumerable (too many to count)
numerous (large in number)

omni *[all, completely]*
omnipresent (present everywhere at the same time)
omnivorous (eating all kinds of food)

onym *[name]*
anonymous (without a name)
pseudonym (false name)

ped *[foot]*
pedal (lever worked by the foot)
pedestrian (one who travels by foot)

phil *[love]*
Philadelphia (city of brotherly love)
philosophy (the love of wisdom)

phobia *[fear]*
acrophobia (a fear of high places)
agoraphobia (a fear of public, open places)

phon *[sound]*
phonics (related to sounds)
symphony (sounds made together)

photo *[light]*
photo-essay (a story told mainly with photographs)
photograph (picture made using light rays)

pop *[people]*
population (number of people in an area)
populous (full of people)

port *[carry]*
export (to carry out)
portable (able to be carried)

psych *[mind, soul]*
psychiatry (the study of the mind)
psychology (science of mind and behavior)

sci *[know]*
conscious (being aware)
omniscient (knowing everything)

scope *[instrument for viewing]*
kaleidoscope (instrument for viewing patterns and shapes)
periscope (instrument used to see above the water)

scrib, script *[write]*
manuscript (something written by hand)
scribble (to write quickly)

spec *[look]*
inspect (to look at carefully)
specimen (an example to look at)

spir *[breath]*
expire (to breathe out; die)
inspire (to breathe into; give life to)

tele *[over a long distance; far]*
telephone (machine used to speak to people over a distance)
telescope (machine used to see things that are very far away)

tempo *[time]*
contemporary (from the current time period)
temporary (lasting for a short time)

tend, tens *[stretch, strain]*
extend (to stretch and make longer)
tension (stretching something tight)

terra *[earth]*
terrain (the earth or ground)
terrestrial (relating to the earth)

therm *[heat]*
thermal (related to heat)
thermostat (a device for controlling heat)

tom *[cut]*
anatomy (the science of cutting apart plants and animals for study)
atom (a particle that cannot be cut or divided)

tract *[draw, pull]*
traction (the act of pulling)
tractor (a machine for pulling)

typ *[print]*
prototype (the first printing or model)
typo (a printing error)

vac *[empty]*
vacant (empty)
vacuum (an empty space)

vid, vis *[see]*
supervise (to oversee or watch over)
videotape (record on tape for viewing)

vor *[eat]*
carnivorous (flesh-eating)
herbivorous (plant-eating)

zoo *[animal or animals]*
zoo (a place where animals are kept)
zoology (the study of animal life)

What can I do to write more effective sentences?

Study Sentence Patterns

Sentences in the English language follow the basic patterns below. Use a variety of patterns to add interest to your writing. (Also see page 633.)

1 Subject + Action Verb

S AV
Wanda skateboards. (Some action verbs, like *skateboards,* are intransitive. This means that they *do not need* a direct object to express a complete thought. See 778.3.)

2 Subject + Action Verb + Direct Object

S AV DO
Jerome completed a wood carving at camp. (Some action verbs, like *completed*, are transitive. This means that they *need* a direct object to express a complete thought. See 778.2.)

3 Subject + Action Verb + Indirect Object + Direct Object

S AV IO DO
Nick's girlfriend gave him a watch.

4 Subject + Action Verb + Direct Object + Object Complement

S AV DO OC
The committee voted Jayne the best actor.

5 Subject + Linking Verb + Predicate Noun

S LV PN
Elephants are huge animals.

6 Subject + Linking Verb + Predicate Adjective

S LV PA
He is funny.

In the patterns above, the subject comes before the verb. In the patterns below, the subject (called a *delayed subject*) comes after the verb.

7 LV S PN
Is Larisa a poet? (A question)

8 LV S
There was a meeting. (A sentence beginning with *there* or *here*)

Practice Sentence Diagramming

Diagramming sentences can help you understand how the different parts of a sentence fit together. Here are the most common diagrams.

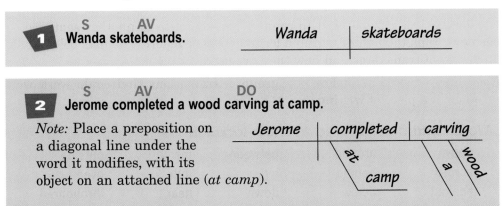

1 S AV
Wanda skateboards.

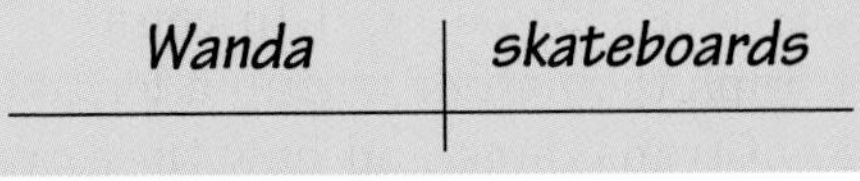

2 S AV DO
Jerome completed a wood carving at camp.

Note: Place a preposition on a diagonal line under the word it modifies, with its object on an attached line (*at camp*).

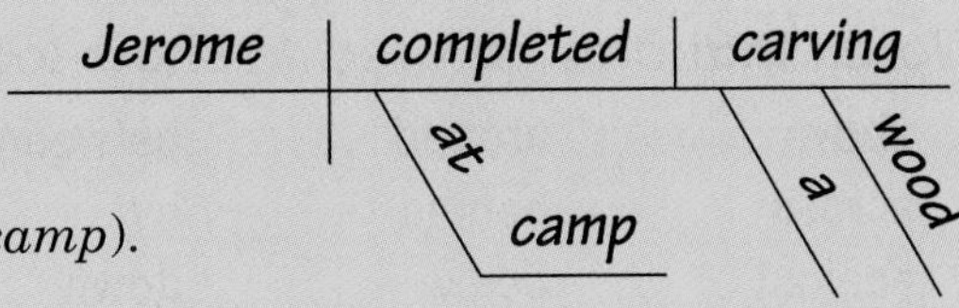

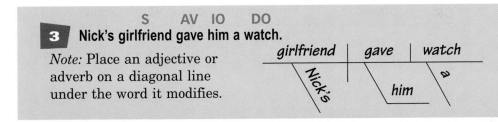

3 S AV IO DO
Nick's girlfriend gave him a watch.

Note: Place an adjective or adverb on a diagonal line under the word it modifies.

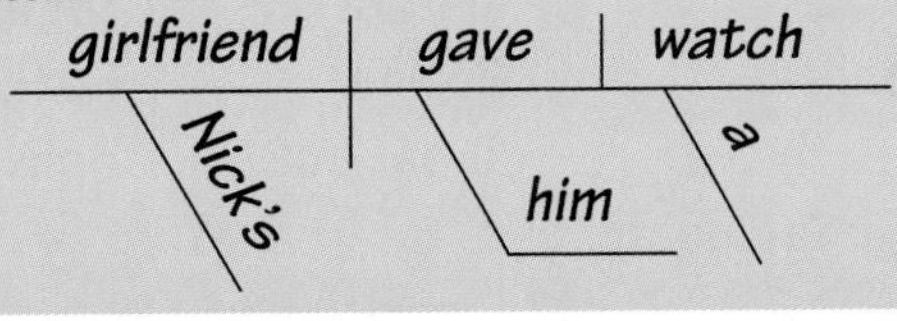

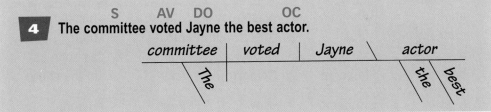

4 S AV DO OC
The committee voted Jayne the best actor.

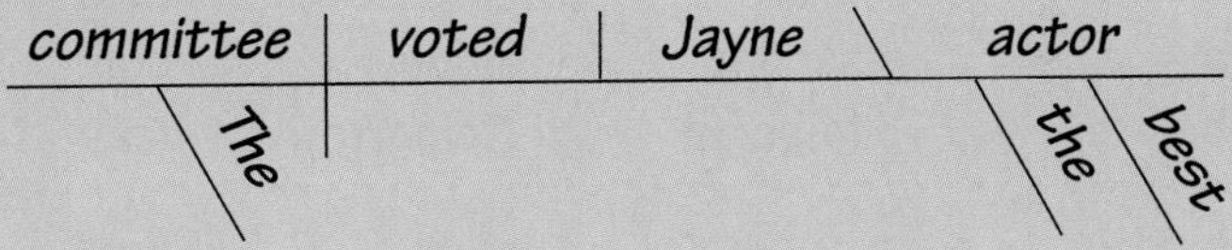

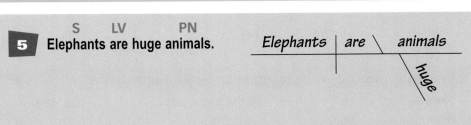

5 S LV PN
Elephants are huge animals.

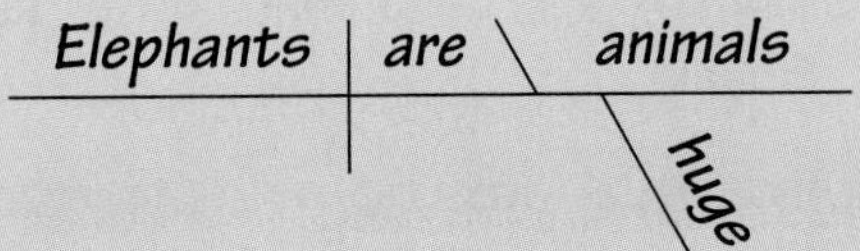

6 S LV PA
He is funny.

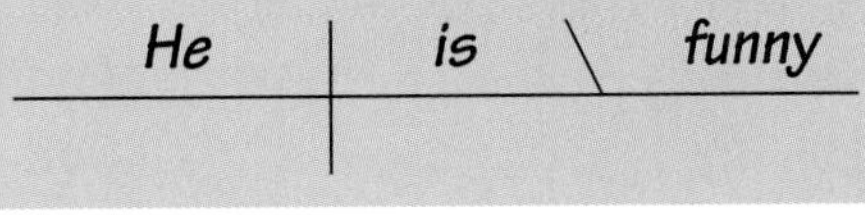

How can I connect my sentences and paragraphs?

Use Transitions

Transitions can be used to connect one sentence to another sentence or one paragraph to another within a longer essay or report. The lists below show a number of transitions and how they are used.

Note: Each colored list below is a group of transitions that could work well together in a piece of writing.

Words that can be used to show location

above	around	between	inside	outside
across	behind	by	into	over
against	below	down	near	throughout
along	beneath	in back of	next to	to the right
among	beside	in front of	on top of	under

Above	In front of	On top of
Below	Beside	Next to
To the left	In back of	Beneath
To the right		

Words that can be used to show time

about	during	yesterday	until	finally
after	first	meanwhile	next	then
at	second	today	soon	as soon as
before	to begin	tomorrow	later	in the end

First	To begin	Now	First	Before
Second	To continue	Soon	Then	During
Third	To conclude	Later	Next	After
Finally			In the end	

Words that can be used to compare two things

likewise	as	in the same way	one way
like	also	similarly	both

In the same way	One way
Also	Another way
Similarly	Both

Words that can be used to contrast things (show differences)

but	still	although	on the other hand
however	yet	otherwise	even though

On the other hand	Although
Even though	Yet
Still	Nevertheless

Words that can be used to emphasize a point

again	truly	especially	for this reason
to repeat	in fact	to emphasize	

For this reason	Truly
Especially	To emphasize
In fact	To repeat

Words that can be used to conclude or summarize

finally	as a result	to sum up	in conclusion
lastly	therefore	all in all	because

Therefore	As a result	To sum it up
Because	All in all	Because
In conclusion	Finally	Finally

Words that can be used to add information

again	another	for instance	for example
also	and	moreover	additionally
as well	besides	along with	other
	next	finally	in addition

For example	For instance	Next	Another
Additionally	Besides	Moreover	Along with
Finally	Next	Also	As well

Words that can be used to clarify

in other words	for instance	that is	for example

For instance	For example
In other words	Equally important

What can I do to make my final copy look better?

Add Graphics to Your Writing

You can add information and interest to essays and reports by using diagrams, tables, and graphs.

Diagrams are drawings that show the parts of something.

Picture diagrams show how something is put together. A diagram may leave out some parts to show only the parts you need to learn.

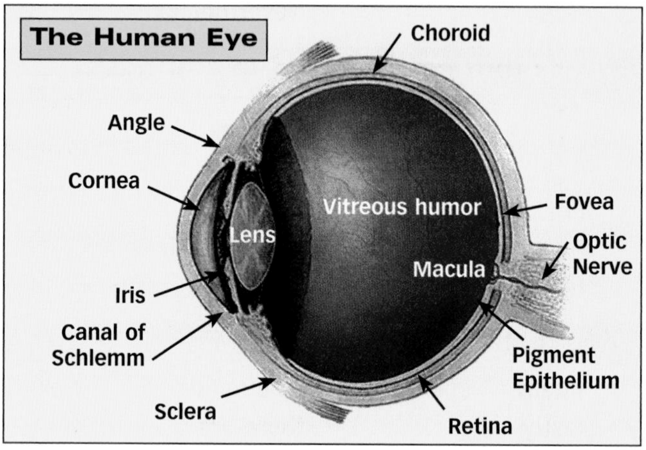

Line diagrams show something you can't really see. Instead of objects, line diagrams show ideas and relationships. This diagram shows how the Germanic languages are related to one another.

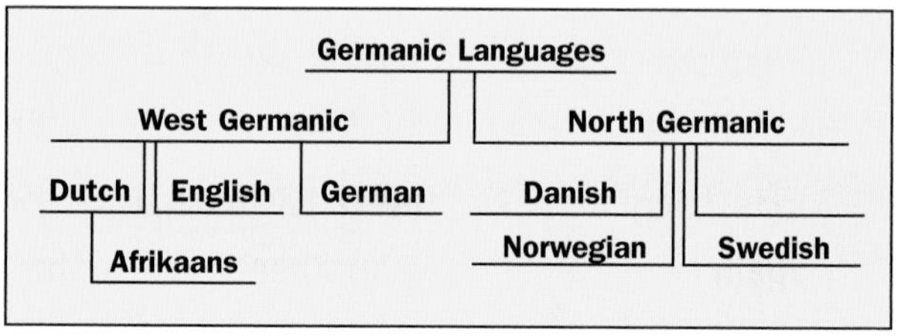

Tables are another form of diagram. Tables have two parts: rows and columns. Rows go across and show one kind of information or data. Columns go up and down and show a different kind of data.

To read a table, find where a row and a column meet. In the table below, to compare the size of Canada and the United States, find where the first row meets the first and third columns. Canada is slightly larger than the United States.

Comparing Countries

	Canada	Mexico	United States
Size (Sq. Miles)	3.85 million	759,000	3.8 million
Type of Government	Parliamentary	Republic	Republic
Voting Age	18	18	18
Literacy	99%	87%	98%

Graphs are pictures of information. **Bar graphs** show how things compare to one another. The bars on a bar graph may be vertical or horizontal. (*Vertical* means "up and down." *Horizontal* means "from side to side.") Sometimes the bars on graphs are called *columns*. The part that shows numbers is called the *scale*.

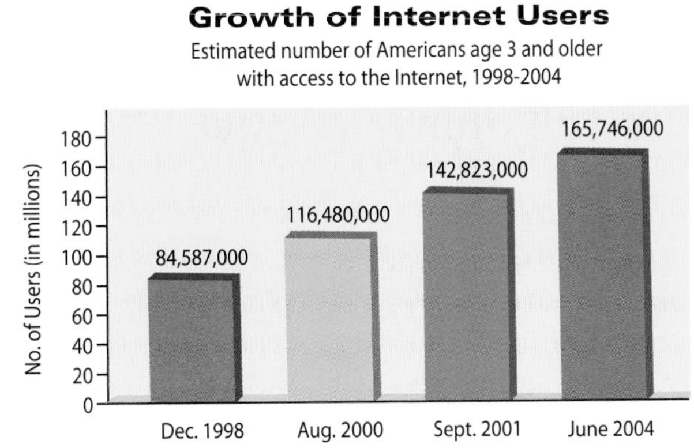

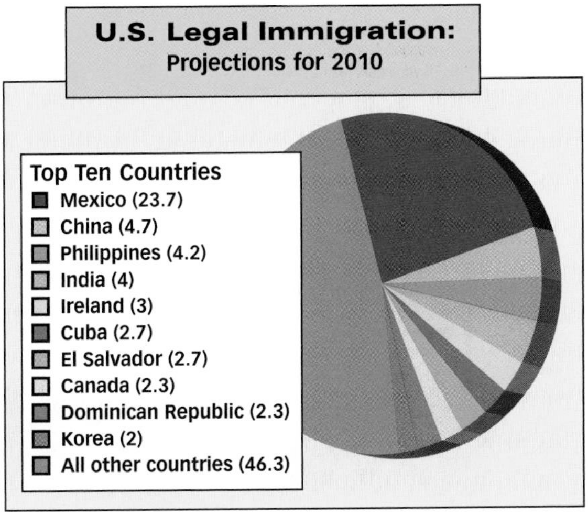

Pie graphs show how all the parts of something add up to make the whole. A pie graph often shows percentages. (A percentage is the part of a whole stated in hundredths: 35% = 35/100.) It's called a pie graph because it is usually in the shape of a pie or circle.

A pie graph begins with the largest segment at the top and moves clockwise around the circle by size. (Notice the example at the left.)

Line graphs show how something changes as time goes by. A line graph always begins with an L-shaped grid. One axis of the grid shows passing time; the other axis shows numbers.

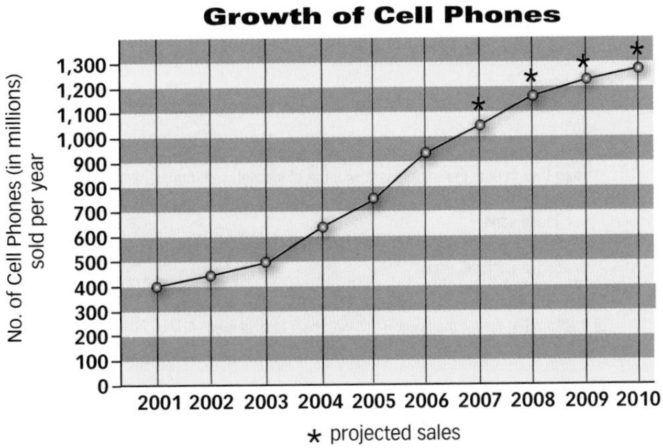

RESOURCE

How should I set up my practical writing?

Use the Proper Format

E-Mail Messages

E-mail allows quick communication between people across town or across the world. The heading includes the address and a subject line. The body should be set up in letter format.

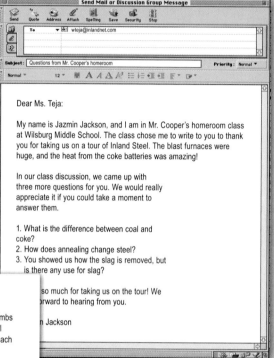

Send Mail or Discussion Group Message

Send Quote Address Attach Spelling Save Security Stop

To wteja@inlandnet.com

Subject: Questions from Mr. Cooper's homeroom Priority: Normal

Dear Ms. Teja:

My name is Jazmin Jackson, and I am in Mr. Cooper's homeroom class at Wilsburg Middle School. The class chose me to write to you to thank you for taking us on a tour of Inland Steel. The blast furnaces were huge, and the heat from the coke batteries was amazing!

In our class discussion, we came up with three more questions for you. We would really appreciate it if you could take a moment to answer them.

1. What is the difference between coal and coke?
2. How does annealing change steel?
3. You showed us how the slag is removed, but is there any use for slag?

so much for taking us on the tour! We rward to hearing from you.

n Jackson

Traction and Four-Wheel Drive

Description: I'd like to test how well a motorized model truck climbs surfaces made of different materials and at different angles. I will create graphs to show how far and how fast the truck climbs in each situation.

Materials: I will use a radio-controlled four-wheel drive model truck, a plank, a protractor, a stopwatch, graph paper, and colored pencils. The different surface materials will include the following: water, aluminum foil, sandpaper, and loose sand.

Schedule: By March 2, I will have the materials collected and assembled. By March 9, I will have performed all my tests for different materials at different angles. By March 16, the total display will be ready for the science fair.

Procedure:

- For each surface, the plank will be pitched at 10°, 20°, 30°, 40°, and 50°.
- First, I will test the plain wooden ramp at each pitch.
- Then I will repeat the experiment with the plank wet, with the plank coated with aluminum foil, coated with sandpaper, and finally coated with loose sand.
- I will create graphs displaying how far and how fast the truck climbed in each situation.

Conclusion: I believe this experiment will show different levels of traction. Please let me know if this proposal is accepted. Any suggestions are welcome.

Proposals

A proposal is a detailed plan for doing a project, solving a problem, or meeting a need.

Follow Guidelines

Business Letters

A letter is a written message sent through the mail. Letters follow a set format, including important contact information, a salutation (greeting), a body, and a closing signature.

1212 Maple Park
San Antonio, TX 78230
March 24, 2010

Bruce Reynolds, Owner
Pet Project Pet Store
341 Jones Street
San Antonio, TX 78248

Dear Mr. Reynolds:

Last year I bought two long-haired guinea pigs from your store. I think you have the best selection of small animals in the area. I tell that to everyone who wants a guinea pig. An employee told me that I was buying two female guinea pigs. Unfortunately, that was not true. We now have five guinea pigs. I would like to sell the three babies and thought that you might buy them for your store. Our veterinarian confirms that all the babies are healthy females.
I would like to know if you are interested, or if you could help me find someone who would like them. You may call me at 555-9770 after 3:30 p.m. Thanks for your time.

Sincerely,

Jessica Botticini
Jessica Botticini

Envelope Addresses

Place the return address in the upper left corner, the destination address in the center, and the correct postage in the upper right corner.

JESSICA BOTTICINI
1212 MAPLE PK
SAN ANTONIO, TX 78230

BRUCE REYNOLDS
PET PROJECT PET STORE
341 JONES ST
SAN ANTONIO, TX 78248

U.S. Postal Service Guidelines

1. Capitalize everything and leave out ALL punctuation.
2. Use the list of common address abbreviations at 690.1. Use numerals rather than words for numbered streets and avenues (9TH AVE NE, 3RD ST SW).
3. If you know the ZIP + 4 code, use it.

 capitalize **SPELL** punctuate

ELPS 2C, 3D, 3E, 3G

Proofreader's Guide

Learning Language

Work with a partner. Read the meanings and share answers to the questions.

1. **Mechanics** include punctuation and capitalization.
   Why is editing for mechanics important to a writer who is going to share his or her work with others?
2. **Commas** show a pause or a change in thought.
   Where do you find commas most useful in writing?
3. Cooperative learning can help students by **facilitating** the learning process.
   Does facilitating something make it easier or harder?
4. When you **improve** something, you make it better.
   Tell about one thing you could improve at school.

improve edit

ELPS 4C

Editing for Mechanics

Periods

Use a **period** to end a sentence. Also use a period after initials, after abbreviations, and as a decimal point.

641.1 At the End of Sentences

Use a period to end a sentence that makes a statement or a request. Also use a period for a mild command, one that does not need an exclamation point. (See page 580.)

The Southern Ocean surrounds Antarctica. (statement)

Please point out the world's largest ocean on a map. (request)

Do not use a laser pointer. (mild command)

NOTE It is not necessary to place a period after a statement that has parentheses around it if it is part of another sentence.

The Southern Ocean is the fourth-largest ocean (it is larger than the Atlantic).

641.2 After Initials

Place a period after an initial.

J. K. Rowling (author)

Colin L. Powell (politician)

641.3 After Abbreviations

Place a period after each part of an abbreviation. Do not use periods with acronyms or initialisms. (See page 692.)

Abbreviations: **Mr. Mrs. Ms. Dr. B.C.E. C.E.**

Acronyms: **AIDS NASA**

Initialisms: **NBC FBI**

NOTE When an abbreviation is the last word in a sentence, use only one period at the end of the sentence.

My grandfather's full name is William Ryan James Koenig, Jr.

641.4 As Decimal Points

Use a period to separate dollars and cents and as a decimal point.

The price of a loaf of bread was $1.54 in 1992.

That price was only 35 cents, or 77.3 percent less, in 1972.

ELPS 4C

Question Marks

A **question mark** is used after an interrogative sentence and also to show doubt about the correctness of a fact or figure. (See page 580.)

642.1
At the End of Direct Questions

Use a question mark at the end of a direct question (an interrogative sentence).

Is a vegan a person who eats only vegetables?

642.2
At the End of Indirect Questions

No question mark is used after an indirect question. (An indirect question tells about a question you or someone else asked.)

Because I do not eat meat, I'm often asked if I am a vegetarian.

I asked the doctor if going meatless is harmful to my health.

642.3
To Show Doubt

Place a question mark within parentheses to show that you are unsure that a fact or figure is correct.

By the year 2020 (?) the number of vegetarians in the United States may approach 15 percent of the population.

Exclamation Points

An **exclamation point** may be placed after a word, a phrase, or a sentence to show emotion. (The exclamation point should not be overused.)

642.4
To Express Strong Feelings

Use an exclamation point to show excitement or strong feeling.

Yeah! Wow! Oh my!

Surprise! You've won the million-dollar sweepstakes!

Caution: Never use more than one exclamation point in writing assignments.

Incorrect: **Don't ever do that to me again!!!**

Correct: **Don't ever do that to me again!**

ELPS 3E

Practice

End Punctuation

For each numbered sentence below, write the last word in the sentence and the correct end punctuation after it.

Example: The blue whale is the largest animal that has ever lived
lived.

(1) Whales may look like fish and swim like fish, but did you know that whales are really mammals **(2)** Just like other mammals, they have a heart with four chambers, they are warm-blooded, and they give birth to live young **(3)** They even have some hair

(4) Whales travel in small groups called pods **(5)** They communicate with each other using a series of clicks and whistles **(6)** The sounds are just remarkable **(7)** People think of them as songs and have even recorded them **(8)** Have you heard any of these recordings

(9) Gentle and friendly, many whale species seem to trust people **(10)** Scientists say that whales are very intelligent and that their vision and hearing are excellent **(11)** Would you believe that whales can live for quite a long time **(12)** Just imagine: Some large whales have probably lived for more than 100 years

Next Step: Based on the reading above, write two sentences about whales: one should be a question you would like to ask, and one should be an emotional personal comment. Use the correct end punctuation for each. Share your best sentence with a partner.

ELPS 4C

Commas

Use a **comma** to indicate a pause or a change in thought. This helps to keep words and ideas from running together so that the writing is easier to read. For a writer, no other form of punctuation is more important to understand than the comma.

644.1 Between Items in a Series

Use commas between words, phrases, or clauses in a series. (A series contains at least three items.) (See page 575.)

Chinese, English, and Hindi are the three most widely used languages in the world. (words)

Being comfortable with technology, working well with others, and knowing another language are important skills for today's workers. (phrases)

My dad works in a factory, my mom works in an office, and I work in school. (clauses)

644.2 To Keep Numbers Clear

Use commas to separate the digits in a number in order to distinguish hundreds, thousands, millions, and so on.

More than 104,000 people live in Kingston, the capital of Jamaica.

The population of the entire country of Liechtenstein is only 29,000.

NOTE Commas are not used in years.

The world population was 6.1 billion by 2003.

644.3 In Dates and Addresses

Use commas to set off items in an address and items in a date.

On August 28, 1963, Martin Luther King, Jr., gave his famous "I Have a Dream" speech.

The address of the King Center is 449 Auburn Avenue NE, Atlanta, Georgia 30312.

NOTE No comma is placed between the state and ZIP code. Also, when only the month and year are given, no comma is needed.

In January 2029 we will celebrate the 100th anniversary of Reverend King's birth.

Practice

Commas 1

- Between Items in a Series
- To Keep Numbers Clear
- In Dates and Addresses

For each sentence below, write the series, date, address, or number that should include a comma. Add the commas.

Example: The Civil War was caused by differences in opinion about slavery economics and politics.
slavery, economics, and politics

1. The war officially began on April 12 1861 when Confederate troops fired upon Fort Sumter, South Carolina.
2. Today Fort Sumter is a national monument at 1214 Middle Street Sullivan's Island South Carolina 29482.
3. South Carolina left the Union, and Virginia Arkansas Tennessee and North Carolina soon followed.
4. More than 13000 Union soldiers and 10000 Confederates lost their lives during the Battle of Shiloh.
5. Three other major battles of the war were fought at Wilderness Spotsylvania and Cold Harbor.
6. After four years of fighting, the war officially ended with the Confederates' surrender on April 9 1865 in Appomattox Virginia.
7. The final death toll of the Civil War was more than 620000 soldiers from both the North and the South.
8. You can learn about the Civil War by reading government papers diaries and letters written during that time period.
9. You can read records of soldiers who fought in the Civil War at the National Archives 700 Pennsylvania Avenue Washington DC 20408.

Commas . . .

646.1 To Set Off Nonrestrictive Phrases and Clauses

Use commas to set off nonrestrictive phrases and clauses—those not necessary to the basic meaning of the sentence.

People get drinking water from surface water or groundwater, which makes up only 1 percent of the earth's water supply. (The clause *which makes up only 1 percent of the earth's water supply* is additional information; it is nonrestrictive—not required. If the clause were left out, the meaning of the sentence would remain clear.)

Restrictive phrases or clauses—those that are needed in the sentence—restrict or limit the meaning of the sentence; they are not set off with commas.

Groundwater that is free from harmful pollutants is rare. (The clause *that is free from harmful pollutants* is restrictive; it is needed to complete the meaning of the basic sentence and is not set off with commas.)

646.2 To Set Off Titles or Initials

Use commas to set off a title, a name, or initials that follow a person's last name. (Use only one period if an initial comes at the end of a sentence.)

Melanie Prokat, M.D., is our family's doctor. However, she is listed in the phone book only as Prokat, M.

NOTE Although commas are not necessary to set off "Jr." and "Sr." after a name, they may be used as long as a comma is used both before and after the abbreviation.

646.3 To Set Off Interruptions

Use commas to set off a word, phrase, or clause that interrupts the main thought of a sentence. These interruptions usually can be identified through the following tests:

1. You can leave them out of a sentence without changing its meaning.
2. You can place them other places in the sentence without changing its meaning.

Our school, as we all know, is becoming overcrowded again. (clause)

The gym, not the cafeteria, was expanded a while ago. (phrase)

My history class, for example, has 42 students in it. (phrase)

There are, indeed, about 1,000 people in my school. (word)

The building, however, has room for only 850 students. (word)

Practice

Commas 2

- To Set Off Nonrestrictive Phrases and Clauses
- To Set Off Titles or Initials
- To Set Off Interruptions

For each of the following sentences, write the information that should be set off with a comma. Include the word before the information and add the commas.

Example: The ferret which is a cousin of the weasel can make a good pet.
ferret, which is a cousin of the weasel,

1. Ferrets once only wild animals of the Great Plains are now a common tame breed.
2. Victoria Patterson D.V.M. claims they are as smart and loving as dogs and cats.
3. John Carpenter M.D. says he has never had to treat a ferret bite.
4. Ferrets need toys to keep them busy—old socks for instance.
5. Any pet as you know needs a lot of care.
6. Ferrets are known for their active and curious nature which sometimes gets them into trouble.
7. Ferrets on the loose will for example dig in your houseplant dirt.
8. They will "steal" small things and hide them in or under the furniture which could be annoying.
9. Ferrets which are like cats in some ways can be trained to use a litter box.

Next Step: Write two sentences about your favorite pet. Include a nonrestrictive phrase or clause in one and an interruption in the other. Use commas to correctly set off these items. Share your best sentence with a partner.

ELPS 4C

Commas . . .

648.1 To Set Off Appositives

Commas set off an appositive from the rest of the sentence. An appositive is a word or phrase that identifies or renames a noun or pronoun.

The capital of Cyprus, Nicosia, has a population of almost 643,000. (Nicosia renames *capital of Cyprus,* so the word is set off with commas.)

Cyprus, an island in the Mediterranean Sea, is about half the size of Connecticut. (*An island in the Mediterranean Sea* identifies *Cyprus,* so the phrase is set off with commas.)

Do not use commas with appositives that are necessary to the basic meaning of the sentence.

The Mediterranean island Cyprus is about half the size of Connecticut. (*Cyprus* is not set off because it is needed to make the sentence clear.)

648.2 To Separate Equal Adjectives

Use commas to separate two or more adjectives that equally modify the same noun.

Comfortable, efficient cars are becoming more important to drivers. (*Comfortable* and *efficient* are separated by a comma because they modify *cars* equally.)

Some automobiles run on clean, renewable sources of energy. (*Clean* and *renewable* are separated by a comma because they modify *sources* equally.)

Conventional gasoline engines emit a lot of pollution. (*Conventional* and *gasoline* do not modify *engines* equally; therefore, no comma separates the two.)

Use these tests to help you decide if adjectives modify equally:

1. Switch the order of the adjectives; if the sentence is clear, the adjectives modify equally.

   Yes: **Efficient, comfortable cars are becoming more important to drivers.**

   No: **Gasoline conventional engines emit a lot of pollution.**

2. Put the word *and* between the adjectives; if the sentence is clear, use a comma when *and* is taken out.

   Yes: **Comfortable and efficient cars are becoming more important to drivers.**

   No: **Conventional and gasoline engines emit a lot of pollution.**

Practice

Commas 3

To Set Off Appositives

For each sentence below, write the appositive phrase as well as the noun it renames. Set off the appositive with commas.

Example: Reginald Fessenden a Scotsman living in Canada made the first voice broadcast on radio in 1906.
Reginald Fessenden, a Scotsman living in Canada,

1. Edwin Armstrong developed FM radio a signal offering clearer sound than AM radio.
2. Lee DeForest the "father of radio" used some of Armstrong's and some of Fessenden's ideas.
3. David Sarnoff another radio pioneer later moved into television, forming NBC.
4. Many other inventors people from all over the world added to the growth of radio.

To Separate Equal Adjectives

For each sentence below, write the adjectives that need commas between them. Add the commas.

Example: Lee DeForest was a vain determined inventor.
vain, determined

1. In the wild crazy years of the 1920s, radios become very popular.
2. During the Depression, even poor jobless people had radios to brighten their lives.
3. Soon, companies were designing radios with beautiful stylish cabinets.
4. A huge powerful radio was often the main piece of furniture in a living room.
5. Now the demand is for smaller lighter radios.

TEKS 7.20B(i)
ELPS 4C

Commas . . .

650.1 To Set Off Dialogue

Use commas to set off the exact words of a speaker from the rest of the sentence. (Also see page 618.)

The firefighter said, "When we cannot successfully put out a fire, we try to keep it from spreading."

"When we cannot successfully put out a fire, we try to keep it from spreading," the firefighter said.

NOTE Do not use a comma or quotation marks for indirect quotations. The words *if* and *that* often signal dialogue that is being reported rather than quoted.

The firefighter said that when they cannot successfully put out a fire, they try to keep it from spreading. (These are not the speaker's exact words.)

650.2 In Direct Address

Use commas to separate a noun of direct address from the rest of the sentence. (A noun of direct address is a noun that names a person spoken to in the sentence.)

Hanae, did you know that an interior decorator can change wallpaper and fabrics on a computer screen?

Sure, Jack, and an architect can use a computer to see how light will fall in different parts of a building.

650.3 To Set Off Interjections

Use commas to separate an interjection or a weak exclamation from the rest of the sentence.

No kidding, you mean that one teacher has to manage a class of 42 pupils? (weak exclamation)

Uh-huh, and that teacher has other classes that size. (interjection)

650.4 To Set Off Explanatory Phrases

Use commas to separate an explanatory phrase from the rest of the sentence.

English, the language computers speak worldwide, is also the most widely used language in science and medicine.

More than 750 million people, about an eighth of the world's population, speak English as a foreign language.

Practice

Commas 4

- To Set Off Dialogue
- In Direct Address
- To Set Off Interjections
- To Set Off Explanatory Phrases

For each of the following sentences, write the word or words that should be set off with a comma. Add the commas.

Example: Jenni let's go see a movie.
Jenni,

1. Hey do you want to go see a movie with us?
2. I answered "It depends on what movie."
3. Today's movies especially the computer-animated films are pretty amazing.
4. The earliest films lasting no more than 10 minutes were just brief looks at sports or fashions of the early 1900s.
5. Wow it cost a whole nickel to see one of those movies!
6. Did you know Curtis that movies were silent until 1927?
7. Music usually played on a piano often accompanied films, but they were still called "silent" movies.
8. In the first movie with sound, Al Jolson said "Wait a minute. You ain't heard nothin' yet!"

Learning Language **A noun of direct address does not always need to be a person's name. It could refer to a group of people and also requires a comma.**

Ladies and gentlemen, welcome to our show.

Work with a partner to think of other groups you might address. Write a few sentences, placing commas in the correct place.

TEKS 7.20B(i)
ELPS 4C

Commas . . .

652.1 To Separate Introductory Clauses and Phrases

Use a comma to separate an adverb clause or a long phrase from the independent clause that follows it.

If every automobile in the country were a light shade of red, we'd live in a pink-car nation. (adverb clause)

According to some experts, solar-powered cars will soon be common. (long modifying phrase)

652.2 In Compound Sentences

Use a comma between two independent clauses that are joined by a coordinating conjunction (such as *and, but, or, nor, for, so,* and *yet*), forming a compound sentence. An independent clause expresses a complete thought and can stand alone as a sentence. (Also see page 578.)

Many students enjoy working on computers, so teachers are finding new ways to use them in the classroom.

Computers can be valuable in education, but many schools cannot afford enough of them.

Avoid Comma Splices: A comma splice results when two independent clauses are "spliced" together with only a comma—and no conjunction. (See page 568.)

TEKS 7.20B(i)
ELPS 3E

Practice

Commas 5

- To Separate Introductory Clauses and Phrases
- In Compound Sentences

For each sentence below, write the word that should be followed by a comma. Add the comma.

Example: Often considered a Canadian sport hockey has also grown in popularity in the United States.
sport,

1. To be a good hockey player a person must be an excellent skater and a superb athlete.
2. Hockey players have a lot of gear but their most important pieces of equipment are their skates.
3. Since the skates must be kept clean and sharp every team has an equipment manager to sharpen the skates.
4. Although a skate appears to have one sharp blade each skate actually has two blades along a hollow center.
5. A deeper hollow means two sharp blades and that can mean faster skating.
6. Because they move from side to side a lot goalies prefer the control a flatter blade gives.
7. Regular skating dulls blades but they can be dulled even more quickly by crashing against another skater's blades.
8. The quality of the ice affects skating so stadiums take care to maintain their rinks.
9. While "fast ice" is hard and slick "slow ice" is soft and rough.

Next Step: Write four sentences about your favorite winter sport. Include two sentences with introductory clauses or phrases and two compound sentences. Place commas correctly. Read your best sentence aloud to a classmate.

TEKS 7.20B(ii)
ELPS 4C

Semicolons

Use a **semicolon** to suggest a stronger pause than a comma indicates. A semicolon may also serve in place of a period.

654.1 To Join Two Independent Clauses

In a compound sentence, use a semicolon to join two independent clauses that are not connected with a coordinating conjunction. (See 792.1.)

The United States has more computers than any other country; its residents own more than 164 million of them.

654.2 With Conjunctive Adverbs

A semicolon is also used to join two independent clauses when the clauses are connected by a conjunctive adverb (such as *as a result, for example, however, therefore,* and *instead*). (See 788.1.)

Japan is next on that list; however, the Japanese have only 50 million computers.

You might think that the billion people of China own a lot of computers; instead, the smaller country of Germany has twice as many computers as China.

654.3 To Separate Groups That Contain Commas

Use a semicolon between groups of words in a series when one or more of the groups already contain commas.

Many of our community's residents separate their garbage into bins for newspapers, cardboard, and junk mail; glass, metal, and plastic; and nonrecyclable trash.

Practice

Semicolons

For each of the following sentences, write the words on either side of the needed semicolons and insert the semicolons.

Example: Animation has become very popular however, artists actually began animating cartoons in the early 1900s.

popular; however

1. The first cartoons were hand drawn frame by frame as a result, each cartoon took a long time to create.
2. Winsor McCay took his time making his cartoons his five-minute cartoon *Gertie the Dinosaur* took more than a year to make.
3. Early cartoons created by individual artists took a lot of time their quality was very high compared to some later cartoons.
4. Some of the most well-known names in animation include Walt Disney, who led the way Max Fleischer, who thought up Popeye and Walter Lantz, the creator of Woody Woodpecker.
5. Computer-generated animation is now fairly common it can make animation look very real.
6. Computer-animated movies include Disney's *Toy Story, A Bug's Life,* and *Finding Nemo* Dreamworks' *Shrek, Antz,* and *Spirit: Stallion of the Cimarron* and Columbia Tri-Star's *Final Fantasy: The Spirits Within.*
7. Lately, *anime* has caught on in this country it is a Japanese style of animation.
8. Animated movies used to be made for children today, they are just as likely to be aimed at the parents, too.

Next Step: Write two independent clauses (sentences) about a cartoon you like and join them with a semicolon.

TEKS 7.20B(ii)
ELPS 4C

Colons

A **colon** may be used to introduce a list or an important point. Colons are also used in business letters and between the numbers in time.

656.1
To Introduce Lists

Use a colon to introduce a list. The colon usually comes after words describing the subject of the list (as in the first example below) or after summary words, such as *the following* or *these things*. Do not use a colon after a verb or preposition.

Certain items are still difficult to recycle: foam cups, car tires, and toxic chemicals.

To conserve water, you should do the following three things: fix drippy faucets, install a low-flow showerhead, and turn the water off while brushing your teeth.

Incorrect: To conserve water, you should: install a low-flow showerhead, turn the water off while brushing your teeth, and fix drippy faucets.

656.2
To Introduce Sentences

A colon may be used to introduce a sentence, a question, or a quotation.

This is why air pollution is bad: We are sacrificing our health and the health of all other life on the planet.

Answer this question for me: Why aren't more people concerned about global warming?

Joaquin shared this with us: "Iceland is the world's leader in the use of renewable energy."

656.3
After Salutations

A colon may be used after the salutation of a business letter.

Dear Ms. Manners: Dear Dr. Warmle: Dear Professor Potter:
Dear Captain Elliot: Dear Senator:

656.4
For Emphasis

Use a colon to emphasize a word or phrase.

The newest alternative energy is also the most common element on earth: hydrogen.

Here's one thing that can help save energy: a programmable thermostat.

656.5
Between Numbers in Time

Use a colon between the parts of a number that indicate time.

My thermostat automatically sets my heat to 60 degrees between 11:00 p.m. and 6:00 a.m.

Practice

Colons

The following letter needs colons placed correctly. Write the line number and the words or numbers that need colons. Then add the colons.

1 March 9, 2010

2 JoAnne White Cloud
3 1315 Wells Road
4 Colfax, WA 99201

5 Dear Ms. White Cloud
6 The Colfax Junior Heritage Club would like you to be the
7 guest speaker at our next meeting on April 6. During the last three
8 months, we have been studying the goals of the Spokane Tribe
9 independence, honesty, and tradition. These goals have inspired
10 many of us with Native American roots.
11 We meet in the large lecture hall at the community center.
12 The meeting will begin at 730 p.m. and end at about 900 p.m.
13 Here is our plan for the evening a short business meeting, your
14 presentation, time for questions, and refreshments.
15 Let me add one final thought Our club's goal is "peace through
16 understanding," and your visit could help us all to learn more about
17 our common history. I hope you will be able to join us in April.

18 Sincerely,

19 Carolyn Mose

Next Step: Write a note to a friend. Ask him or her to meet you at a certain time and place. Include colons after the salutation, between numbers in a time, and to introduce a list.

ELPS 4C

Quotation Marks

Quotation marks are used in a number of ways:

- to set off the exact words of a speaker,
- to punctuate material quoted from another source,
- to punctuate words used in a special way, and
- to punctuate certain titles.

658.1
To Set Off a Speaker's Exact Words

Place quotation marks before and after a speaker's words in dialogue. Only the exact words of the speaker are placed within quotation marks.

> **Marla said, "I've decided to become a firefighter."**
>
> **"A firefighter," said Juan, "can help people in many ways."**

658.2
For Quotations Within Quotations

Use single quotation marks to punctuate a quotation within a quotation.

> **Sung Kim asked, "Did Marla just say, 'I've decided to become a firefighter'?"**

When titles occur within a quotation, use single quotation marks to punctuate those that require quotation marks.

> **Juan said, "Springsteen's song 'The Rising' really inspired her."**

658.3
To Set Off Quoted Material

When quoting material from another source, place quotation marks before and after the source's exact words.

> **In her book *Living the Life You Deserve,* Tess Spyeder explains, "Choose a job you'll enjoy doing day after day over one that will fatten your bank account."**

658.4
To Set Off Long Quoted Material

If more than one paragraph is quoted from a single source, quotation marks are placed before each paragraph and at the end of the last paragraph.

Quotations that are more than four lines are usually set off from the rest of the paper by indenting each line 10 spaces from the left. Quotations that are set off in this way require no quotation marks either before or after the quoted material.

Practice

Quotation Marks 1

- To Set Off a Speaker's Exact Words
- For Quotations Within Quotations

For each of the following sentences, write the first and last word of each quotation or title, adding the correct quotation marks. Use ellipses as shown.

Example: Bettina said, My science project, which I will call Communicating with Your Pet, is a sure winner.
"My . . . 'Communicating . . . Pet,' . . . winner."

1. I don't know, I said. Are you sure Ms. Lazarus knows about your plans?
2. Sure. She even said, That's a wonderful idea, Bettina stated.
3. I said, That's not what I would have said. I would have told you that it's a crazy idea.
4. Then I asked, What are you going to do for scientific research? We're supposed to show our research for this project, you know.
5. Bettina replied, I'm going to keep track of how my dog, Moose, communicates with me when he wants something. I will record all my information in a chart.
6. Do you think Moose will cooperate? I asked.
7. I already asked him, Bettina replied, and he said, Go for it!
8. Bettina, you are incredible, I said.
9. Woof! Moose joined in from his spot under the table.

Next Step: Write a short conversation you might have with your pet or the pet of a friend. Use quotation marks correctly.

ELPS 4C

Quotation Marks . . .

660.1
Placement of Punctuation

Always place periods and commas inside quotation marks.

"I don't know," said Lac.

Lac said, "I don't know."

Place an exclamation point or a question mark inside the quotation marks when it punctuates the quotation.

Ms. Wiley asked, "Can you actually tour the Smithsonian on the Internet?"

Place it outside when it punctuates the main sentence.

Did I hear you say, "Now we can tour the Smithsonian on the Internet"?

Place semicolons or colons outside quotation marks.

First, I will read the article "Sonny's Blues"; then I will read "The Star Café" in my favorite music magazine.

660.2
For Special Words

Quotation marks also may be used (1) to set apart a word that is being discussed, (2) to indicate that a word is slang, or (3) to point out that a word or phrase is being used in a special way.

1. **Renny uses the word "like" entirely too much.**
2. **Man, your car is really "phat."**
3. **Aunt Lulu, an editor at a weekly magazine, says she has "issues."**

660.3
To Punctuate Titles

Use quotation marks to punctuate titles of songs, poems, short stories, lectures, episodes of radio or television programs, chapters of books, and articles found in magazines, newspapers, or encyclopedias. (Also see 662.3.)

"21 Questions" (song)
"The Reed Flute's Song" (poem)
"Old Man at the Bridge" (short story)
"Birthday Boys" (a television episode)
"The Foolish and the Weak" (a chapter in a book)
"Science Careers Today" (lecture)
"Teen Rescues Stranded Dolphin" (newspaper article)

NOTE When you punctuate a title, capitalize the first word, last word, and every word in between—except for articles *(a, an, the)*, short prepositions *(at, to, with,* and so on), and coordinating conjunctions *(and, but, or)*. (See 682.2.)

ELPS 5G

Practice

Quotation Marks 2

- Placement of Punctuation
- To Punctuate Titles

Copy the following sentences and properly place quotation marks, commas, and end punctuation.

Example: We're going on vacation next week Dan said to Chicago

"We're going on vacation next week," Dan said, "to Chicago."

1. He began singing lines from the song My Kind of Town
2. What do you know about Chicago I asked
3. Dan said, I know that Carl Sandburg wrote poems, such as Clark Street Bridge and Skyscraper, about Chicago
4. I know they have an elevated train system he added and it can get you just about anywhere in the city
5. Oprah Winfrey's show is taped there, so Mom wants to get tickets She loved the episode Bargain Shopping with Oprah he said
6. You just said Mom wants to get tickets But what about you What do you want to see I asked
7. I want to see Buckingham Fountain, the Sears Tower, and Navy Pier Dan said
8. Are you going to go shopping for some souvenirs on Michigan Avenue I teased
9. Oh, yeah Dan winked

Next Step: What would be your dream vacation? Write a brief discussion you might have with a friend, explaining your dream vacation. Punctuate it correctly with quotation marks and properly placed commas and end punctuation.

ELPS 4C

Italics and Underlining

Italics is slightly slanted type. In this sentence, the word *happiness* is typed in italics. In handwritten material, each word or letter that should be in italics is **underlined**. (See an example on page 429.)

662.1 In Printed Material

Print words in italics when you are using a computer.

In *Tuck Everlasting,* the author explores what it would be like to live forever.

662.2 In Handwritten Material

Underline words that should be italicized when you are writing by hand.

In <u>Tuck Everlasting</u>, the author explores what it would be like to live forever.

662.3 In Titles

Italicize (or underline) the titles of books, plays, book-length poems, magazines, newspapers, radio and television programs, movies, videos, cassettes, CD's, and the names of aircraft and ships.

Walk Two Moons (book)
Fairies and Dragons (movie)
The Young and the Hopeless (CD)
Columbia (space shuttle)
Teen People (magazine)
Everwood (TV program)
U.S.S. *Arizona* (ship)
Daily Herald (newspaper)

Exception: Do not italicize or put quotation marks around your own title at the top of your written work.

A Day Without Water (personal writing: do not italicize)

662.4 For Scientific and Foreign Words

Italicize (or underline) scientific and foreign words that are not commonly used in everyday English.

***Spinacia oleracea* is the scientific term for spinach.**

Many store owners who can help Spanish-speaking customers display an *Hablamos Español* sign in their windows.

662.5 For Special Uses

Italicize (or underline) a number, letter, or word that is being discussed or used in a special way. (Sometimes quotation marks are used for this same reason.)

Matt's hat has a bright red *A* on it.

Practice

Italics and Underlining

For each of the following sentences, write the word or words that should be italicized and underline them.

Example: Ancient Greek drama grew from dithyrambs, choral songs honoring the god Dionysus.
dithyrambs

1. One book about early drama in ancient Greece is I Came, I Saw, I Applauded.
2. Plays were acted out on a stage called a skene, the source of our modern words scene and scenery.
3. The book Ancient Greek Drama explains the interesting special effects used back then.
4. One of the most famous writers of Greek theater was Sophocles, who wrote the two plays Oedipus Rex and Antigone.
5. Another Greek writer, Homer, wrote a book-length poem called The Odyssey.
6. A recent article in the New York Times said that all modern drama stems from the early Greek tragedies.
7. Obviously confused, Ted thought the '60s movie Zorba the Greek was based on a 2,000-year-old play.
8. He had missed the day the class watched the video Ancient Greece: A Journey Back in Time.
9. Ted thinks he can prove his point if he brings in Imiskoubria 2030, a CD of Greek hip-hop he found at a resale shop.

Next Step: What special words are used in a hobby or an activity that you enjoy? Write a brief paragraph explaining the activity, correctly underlining the special words.

ELPS 4C

Apostrophes

Use **apostrophes** to form contractions, to form certain plurals, or to show possession.

664.1 In Contractions

Use an apostrophe to form a contraction, showing that one or more letters have been left out of a word.

Common Contractions

can't (cannot)	**couldn't** (could not)	**didn't** (did not)
doesn't (does not)	**don't** (do not)	**hasn't** (has not)
haven't (have not)	**isn't** (is not)	**I'll** (I will)
I'd (I would)	**I'm** (I am)	**I've** (I have)
they'll (they will)	**they'd** (they would)	**they've** (they have)
they're (they are)	**you're** (you are)	**wouldn't** (would not)
you'll (you will)	**you'd** (you would)	**you've** (you have)

664.2 In Place of Omitted Letters or Numbers

Use an apostrophe to show that one or more digits have been left out of a number, or that one or more letters have been left out of a word to show a special pronunciation.

class of '99 (*19* is left out)

g'bye (the letters *ood* are left out of *good-bye*)

NOTE Letters and numbers should not be omitted in most writing assignments; however, they may be omitted in dialogue to make it sound like real people are talking.

664.3 To Form Some Plurals

Use an apostrophe and *s* to form the plural of a letter, a sign, a number, or a word being discussed as a word.

A's +'s 8's *to*'s

Don't use too many *and*'s in your writing.

664.4 To Form Singular Possessives

To form the possessive of a singular noun, add an apostrophe and *s*.

the game's directions **Dr. Mill's theory**
Ross's bike **Roz's hair**

NOTE When a singular noun with more than one syllable ends with an *s* or *z* sound, the possessive may be formed by adding just an apostrophe.

Texas' oil (or) **Texas's oil** **Carlos' mother** (or) **Carlos's mother**

Practice

Apostrophes 1

- In Contractions
- In Place of Omitted Letters or Numbers
- To Form Singular Possessives

For each numbered sentence below, correctly write the words or numbers that need an apostrophe.

Example: Uncle Pauls farm isnt the kind you might imagine.
Paul's isn't

(1) Its a tree farm in Vermont, and Uncle Paul "grows" maple syrup! **(2)** A maple trees sap looks clear and is slightly sweet. **(3)** The common brown color and maple flavor happen when its boiled.

(4) "Sugarin season" lasts four to six weeks, from February to April. **(5)** It doesnt seem to me that hanging a bucket on a tree is hard work. **(6)** "But ysee," says Uncle Paul, "theres a lot more to it than that. **(7)** Horse-drawn sleds have to carry the syrup buckets because the maple forests arent open or level enough for tractors. **(8)** Also, a sleds runners dont damage the tree roots like a tractors wheels would. **(9)** Then we cook the collected sap until its a thick syrup."

(10) I couldnt believe that it takes 40 gallons of sap to make one gallon of syrup! **(11)** Each states maple tree sap has its own taste, so Massachusetts syrup doesnt taste the same as Vermonts. **(12)** Of course, you havent tasted the best until youve tried Uncle Pauls syrup.

Next Step: Explain the process for something you like to do. Include contractions and singular possessives. Properly place the apostrophes for each.

ELPS 4C

Apostrophes . . .

666.1 To Form Plural Possessives

The possessive form of plural nouns ending in *s* is usually made by adding just an apostrophe.

students' homework **teachers' lounge**

For plural nouns not ending in *s*, an apostrophe and *s* must be added.

children's book **people's opinions**

Remember: The word immediately before the apostrophe is the owner.

student's project (*student* is the owner)
students' project (*students* are the owners)

666.2 To Show Shared Possession

When possession is shared by more than one noun, add an apostrophe and *s* to the last noun in the series.

Uncle Reggie, Aunt Rosie, and my mom's garden
(All three own the garden.)

Uncle Reggie's, Aunt Rosie's, and my mom's gardens
(Each person owns a garden.)

666.3 To Form Possessives with Compound Nouns

The possessive of a compound noun is formed by placing the possessive ending after the last word.

her sister-in-law's hip-hop music (singular)
her sisters-in-law's tastes in music (plural)
the secretary of state's husband (singular)
the secretaries of state's husbands (plural)

666.4 To Form Possessives with Indefinite Pronouns

The possessive of an indefinite pronoun is formed by adding an apostrophe and *s*.

no one's **anyone's** **somebody's**

NOTE In pronouns that use *else*, add an apostrophe and *s* to the second word.

somebody else's **anyone else's**

666.5 To Express Time or Amount

Use an apostrophe with an adjective that is part of an expression indicating time (month, day, hour) or amount.

In today's Spanish class, we talked about going to Spain.
My father lost more than an hour's work when that thunderstorm knocked out our power.
I bought a couple dollars' worth of grapes at the store.

Practice

Apostrophes 2

- To Form Plural Possessives
- To Show Shared Possession
- To Form Possessives with Compound Nouns and Indefinite Pronouns
- To Express Time or Amount

For each of the following sentences, correctly write the word or words that need an apostrophe.

Example: Everyones schedule is upset when a blackout occurs.
everyone's

1. The eastern United States and Canadas worst blackout happened August 14, 2003.
2. Many people lost several hours work on their computers.
3. Annes, Jeremys, and Geoffs baseball games were canceled because of darkness.
4. My sister-in-laws candle store was very busy that night.
5. Nora, Kiki, and Sandys school had a generator, so people gathered there for the night.
6. It was anyones guess as to when the power would be restored.
7. Surprisingly, people didn't panic at the nights unusual darkness.
8. Peoples attention turned to skies unusually bright with stars.
9. Next door, the Wagners house was lit with some oil lamps.
10. Their childrens voices could be heard through the open windows.
11. Articles in the next days newspapers indicated how widespread the blackout was.
12. One editor in chiefs column asked why the blackout happened.
13. The electric companies reports blamed it on Ohio power lines that short-circuited.

TEKS 7.20B(ii)
ELPS 4C

Hyphens

Use a **hyphen** to divide words at the end of a line and to form compound words. Also use a hyphen between the numbers in a fraction and to join numbers that indicate the life span of an individual, the scores of a game, and so on.

668.1 To Divide Words

Use a hyphen to divide a word when you run out of room at the end of a line. A word may be divided only between syllables. Here are some additional guidelines:

- Never divide a one-syllable word: *raised, through.*
- Avoid dividing a word of five letters or fewer: *paper, study.*
- Never divide a one-letter syllable from the rest of the word: *omit-ted,* **not** *o-mitted.*
- Never divide abbreviations or contractions: *NASA, wouldn't.*
- Never divide the last word in more than two lines in a row or the last word in a paragraph.
- When a vowel is a syllable by itself, divide the word after the vowel: *epi-sode,* **not** *ep-isode.*

NOTE Refer to a dictionary if you're not sure how to divide a word.

668.2 In Compound Words

A hyphen is used in some compound words, including numbers from twenty-one to ninety-nine.

about-face **warm-up** **time-out**
down-to-earth **ice-skating** **high-rise**
thirty-three **seventy-five**

668.3 To Create New Words

A hyphen is often used to form new words beginning with the prefixes *self, ex, all,* and *great*. A hyphen is also used with suffixes such as *elect* and *free*.

self-cleaning **ex-employer** **all-natural** **mayor-elect**
self-esteem **ex-president** **great-aunt** **germ-free**

668.4 Between Numbers in a Fraction

Use a hyphen between the numbers in a fraction. Do not, however, use a hyphen between the numerator and denominator when one or both are already hyphenated.

four-tenths **five-sixteenths** **seven thirty-seconds (7/32)**

TEKS 7.20B(ii)
ELPS 3E

Practice

Hyphens 1

- To Divide Words
- In Compound Words
- To Create New Words

For each of the following sentences, correctly write the words that are incorrectly hyphenated or that should be hyphenated but are not.

1. My dad and his brother in law often go golfing together.
2. Thirty eight people bought lemonade from our stand.
3. Our troop's ex scoutmaster visited our last scout meeting.
4. Although Eileen is an excellent athlete, sometimes she does-n't have the right attitude.
5. Marta is taking a course in self defense at the community center.
6. Joan put a spoonful of fat free dressing on her salad.
7. People could not believe that Arnold Schwarzenegger was the governor elect of California.
8. Rex's speed in the mile run was an all time high for any student at Greenville Junior High.
9. Luke couldn't believe what a low price he paid when he bou-ght some kneepads for football.
10. Aaron's little sister begged him to take her on the merry go round.
11. Once we complete our essays, the teacher hands out some forms for self assessment.
12. Uncle Walter bought some souvenirs for us at the airport's duty free shop.

Next Step: Write two sentences in which you use some of the hyphenated words from the facing page. Share your sentences with a partner.

TEKS 7.20B(ii)
ELPS 4C

Hyphens . . .

670.1
To Form Adjectives

Use a hyphen to join two or more words that work together to form a single-thought adjective before a noun. Generally, hyphenate any compound adjective that might be misread if it is not hyphenated—use common sense. (See page 548.)

smiley-face sticker   dress-up clothes   fresh-breeze scent

Use the tests below to determine if a hyphen is needed.

1. When a compound adjective is made of a noun plus an adjective, it should be hyphenated.

   microwave-safe cookware   book-smart student

2. When a compound adjective is made of a noun plus a participle (*ing* or *ed* form of a verb), it should be hyphenated.

   bone-chilling story   vitamin-enriched cereal

3. Hyphenate a compound adjective that is a phrase (includes conjunctions or prepositions).

   heat-and-serve meals   refrigerator-to-oven dishes

Do *not* hyphenate compound adjectives in these instances:

1. When words forming the adjective come after the noun, do not hyphenate.

   This cookware is microwave safe.
   The cereal was vitamin enriched.

2. If the first of the two words ends in *ly,* do not hyphenate.

   newly designed computer   rarely seen species

3. Do not use a hyphen when a number or letter is the final part of a one-thought adjective.

   grade A milk   level 6 textbook

670.2
To Join Letters to Words

Use a hyphen to join a capital letter to a noun or participle.

U-turn   Y-axis   T-bar   A-frame

PG-rated movie   X-ray

670.3
To Avoid Confusion

Use a hyphen with prefixes or suffixes to avoid confusion or awkward spelling.

Re-collect (not recollect) **the reports we handed back last week.**

It has a shell-like (not shelllike) **texture.**

Practice

Hyphens 2

- To Form Adjectives
- To Join Letters to Words
- To Avoid Confusion

For each of the following sentences, correctly write the words that should be hyphenated.

Example: Cholesterol can be an artery clogging substance.
artery-clogging

1. Lyndeen pointed to some geese flying south in a V formation.
2. The chameleon had escaped from its cage, and the hard to spot creature was not found for days.
3. The patient complained of hearing belllike sounds all the time.
4. Dashiel used several C clamps to hold the pieces of wood together while the glue dried.
5. The souvenir that Alex showed the class was a miniature recreation of a famous sculpture in Paris.
6. Grandpa likes to have a soft boiled egg for breakfast.
7. I am going to use a stain covering paint in my bedroom.
8. Mary Anne grew up on a 2,000 acre farm in North Dakota.
9. As she took apart the kitchen faucet, Mom hoped that simply replacing the O ring would fix the leak.
10. The majority of shark species are not man eating fish.

Next Step: Write two sentences in which you use hyphenated adjectives. (Check the rules on the facing page to make sure your adjectives actually need hyphens.)

ELPS 4C

Dashes

The **dash** can be used to show a sudden break in a sentence, to emphasize a word or clause, and to show that someone's speech is being interrupted. There is no space before or after a dash.

672.1
To Indicate a Sudden Break

A dash can be used to show a sudden break in a sentence.

The three of us came down with colds, lost our voices, and missed the football game—all because we had practiced in the rain.

672.2
For Emphasis

A dash may be used to emphasize or explain a word, a series of words, a phrase, or a clause.

Vitamins and minerals—important dietary supplements—can improve your diet.

The benefits of vitamin A—better vision and a stronger immune system—are well known.

672.3
To Indicate Interrupted Speech

Use a dash to show that someone's speech is being interrupted by another person.

Well—yes, I understand—no, I remember—oh—okay, thank you.

Parentheses

Parentheses are used around words that are included in a sentence to add information or to help make an idea clearer.

672.4
To Add Information

Use parentheses when adding information or clarifying an idea.

Cures for diseases (from arthritis to cancer) may be found in plants in the rain forest.

Only about 10 percent (27,000) of the plant species in the world have been studied.

Practice

Dashes

Rewrite the sentences below, adding dashes where appropriate.

Example: Gingivitis that is, swollen gums is a common disease.
Gingivitis—that is, swollen gums—is a common disease.

1. I was going to I mean I *am* going to take the subway.
2. Only one thing will get Winifred to leave that island a hurricane.
3. Excuse me yes, I know that have you but I okay.
4. People's donations will fund this research research that could save many lives.
5. Danielle, be sure to bundle up it's below zero out there.

Parentheses

Write the parts of the sentences below that should be enclosed in parentheses. Add the parentheses.

Example: Randall got a majority 62% of the votes in the class election.
(62%)

1. Derek acting totally unlike himself yelled at his friend.
2. Genny wore her new shirt the sparkly blue one to the dance.
3. Oliver's mom my aunt will drive us to the theater.
4. John's constant itching led him to make an appointment with a dermatologist a skin doctor.
5. Three northeastern states Maine, New Hampshire, and Vermont had ice storms yesterday.

ELPS 4C

Ellipses

Use an **ellipsis** (three periods) to show a pause in dialogue or to show that words or sentences have been left out. Leave one space before, after, and between each period.

674.1 To Show Pauses

Use an ellipsis to show a pause in dialogue.

> **"My report," said Reggie, "is on . . . ah . . . cars of the future. One place that I . . . uh . . . checked on the Internet said that cars would someday run on sunshine."**

674.2 To Show Omitted Words

Use an ellipsis to show that one or more words have been left out of a quotation. Read this statement about hibernation.

> **Some animals, such as the chipmunk and the woodchuck, hibernate in winter. During this time, the animal's heart beats very slowly—only a few times per minute. Its body cools down so much that it nearly freezes, and this is called going into torpor.**

Here's how you would type part of the above quotation, leaving out some of the words. If the words left out are at the end of a sentence, use a period followed by three dots.

> **Some animals . . . hibernate in winter. During this time, the animal's heart beats very slowly . . . and this is called going into torpor.**

Practice

Ellipses

To Show Omitted Words

Read each of the following passages. Decide what the important parts are and rewrite each paragraph, leaving some of the words out. Use ellipses to show where you've left words out.

Passage A:

Spanish explorers of the late sixteenth century brought horses with them to North America. At first, the Native Americans thought the horses were big dogs. Then the Pueblo Indians learned to manage herds of horses. In a short time, horses became very important to other tribes, as well. Men riding horses were able to follow bison, which the people depended upon for food and shelter. Horses also became valuable for trading. As a result, tribes such as the Lakota and Crow grew and prospered.

Passage B:

Winter storms can be quite dangerous, and many people don't realize it. Icy roads lead to traffic accidents, or people become trapped in their cars during a blizzard. A storm may knock out power and leave homes without heat. People who remain outside risk injury due to exposure. Hypothermia, which results when body temperature falls below 90 degrees, and frostbite can result in permanent damage to a person's body. In addition, the heart is stressed by cold temperatures; add shoveling snow to that stress, and the heart can fail. The best way to avoid these dangers is to know the risks and be prepared with cold-weather supplies.

Next Step: Write a brief conversation between two friends discussing a recent storm. Use ellipses to show pauses in the dialogue.

TEKS 7.20A

Capitalization

676.1 Proper Nouns and Adjectives

Capitalize all proper nouns and all proper adjectives. A proper noun is the name of a particular person, place, thing, or idea. A proper adjective is an adjective formed from a proper noun.

Common Noun: **country, president, continent**

Proper Noun: **Canada, Andrew Jackson, Asia**

Proper Adjective: **Canadian, Jacksonian, Asian**

676.2 Names of People

Capitalize the names of people and also the initials or abbreviations that stand for those names.

Samuel L. Jackson **Aung San Suu Kyi**

Mary Sanchez-Gomez

676.3 Titles Used with Names

Capitalize titles used with names of persons; also capitalize abbreviations standing for those titles.

President Mohammed Hosni Mubarak **Dr. Linda Trout**

Governor Michael Easley **Rev. Jim Zavaski**

Senator John McCain

676.4 Words Used as Names

Capitalize words such as *mother, father, aunt,* and *uncle* when these words are used as names.

Uncle Marius **started to sit on the couch.** (*Uncle* is a name; the speaker calls this person "Uncle Marius.")

Then Uncle **stopped in midair.** (*Uncle* is used as a name.)

"So, Mom**, what are you doing here?" I asked.** (*Mom* is used as a name.)

Words such as *aunt, uncle, mom, dad, grandma,* and *grandpa* are usually not capitalized if they come after a possessive pronoun (my, his, our).

My aunt **had just called him.** (The word *aunt* describes this person but is not used as a name.)

Then my dad **and** mom **walked into the room.** (The words *dad* and *mom* are not used as names in this sentence.)

Practice

Capitalization 1

- Proper Nouns and Adjectives
- Names of People
- Titles Used with Names
- Words Used as Names

For each of the following sentences, correctly write the words that should be capitalized but are not.

Example: Yesterday grandpa told me he'd never seen the american capital.
Grandpa, American

1. A nickname people often use when talking about the united states government is uncle sam.
2. A congressperson from new york, senator hillary clinton, is married to a former president.
3. From 1993 to 2009, the two men who held the highest office in the country were president william clinton and president george w. bush.
4. In england and canada, queen elizabeth II has reigned since the 1950s.
5. Canada's governor general Michaëlle Jean represents the queen, who is the country's head of state.
6. After the 2006 election, prime minister Stephen Harper became the head of the canadian government.
7. Uncle Richard, who is mom's brother, lives in montreal, quebec.
8. One summer, grandma and I visited him.
9. Uncle Rich introduced mom to a friend of his, dr. sylvia hill, and they keep in touch with e-mail.

Next Step: Write two or three sentences that include the name of a person, a title used with a name, and a word used as a person's name. Also include a proper adjective. Use correct capitalization.

TEKS 7.20A

Capitalization . . .

678.1
School Subjects

Capitalize the name of a specific educational course, but not the name of a general subject. (Exception—the names of all languages are proper nouns and are always capitalized: *French, English, Hindi, German, Latin.*)

> **Roberto is studying accounting at the technical college.**
> (Because *accounting* is a general subject, it is not capitalized.)
>
> **He likes the professor who teaches Accounting Principles.**
> (The specific course name is capitalized.)

678.2
Official Names

Capitalize the names of businesses and the official names of their products. (These are called trade names.) Do not, however, capitalize a general word like "toothpaste" when it follows the trade name.

Old Navy	**Best Buy**	**Microsoft**	**Kodak**
Sony Playstation	**Tombstone pizza**	**Mudd jeans**	

678.3
Races, Languages, Nationalities, Religions

Capitalize the names of languages, races, nationalities, and religions, as well as the proper adjectives formed from them.

Arab	**Spanish**	**Judaism**	**Catholicism**
African art	**Irish linen**	**Swedish meatballs**	

678.4
Days, Months, Holidays

Capitalize the names of days of the week, months of the year, and special holidays.

Thursday	**Friday**	**Saturday**
July	**August**	**September**
Arbor Day	**Independence Day**	

Do not capitalize the names of seasons.

> **winter, spring, summer, fall (autumn)**

678.5
Historical Events

Capitalize the names of historical events, documents, and periods of time.

World War II	**the Bill of Rights**	**the Magna Carta**
the Middle Ages	**the Paleozoic Era**	

TEKS 7.20A

Practice

Capitalization 2

- School Subjects
- Official Names
- Races, Languages, Nationalities, Religions
- Days, Months, Holidays
- Historical Events

For each of the following sentences, correctly write any word that is incorrectly capitalized.

Example: Sue had lunch at Burger king last thursday.
King, Thursday

1. At the catholic church that Ramón's family attends, the priests speak spanish.
2. More than a million soldiers fought the battle of the bulge in Europe during World war II.
3. Cassandra's first class of the day is fundamentals of music.
4. After that, she has Science, math, gym, and english.
5. The handlin Museum has a new exhibit of african art.
6. Independence day falls on the first sunday of july this year.
7. My favorite sandwich is made with Skippy Peanut Butter.
8. During the period of time called the renaissance, people made many advances in Art, Literature, and Science.
9. Shabbat, a day of rest and prayer in the jewish religion, begins on friday evening and ends saturday evening.

Next Step: Write a sentence that tells your favorite brand of soda. Write another sentence about a holiday you enjoy. Capitalize words correctly.

TEKS 7.20A

Capitalization . . .

680.1 Geographic Names

Capitalize the following geographic names.

Planets and heavenly bodies. . . . . **Venus, Jupiter, Milky Way**

Lowercase the word "earth" except when used as the proper name of our planet, especially when mentioned with other planet names.

What on earth are you doing here?

Sam has traveled across the face of the earth several times.

Jupiter's diameter is 11 times larger than Earth's.

The four inner planets are Mercury, Venus, Earth, and Mars.

Continents . . . . **Europe, Asia, South America, Australia, Africa**
Countries . . . .**Morocco, Haiti, Greece, Chile, United Arab Emirates**
States. . . . . .**New Mexico, Alabama, West Virginia, Delaware, Iowa**
Provinces . . . . **Alberta, British Columbia, Quebec, Ontario**
Counties. . . . .**Sioux County, Kandiyohi County, Wade County**
Cities . . . .**Montreal, Baton Rouge, Albuquerque, Portland**
Bodies of water . . . .**Delaware Bay, Chickamunga Lake, Indian Ocean, Gulf of Mexico, Skunk Creek**
Landforms . . . . **Appalachian Mountains, Bitterroot Range**
Public areas. . . . .**Tiananmen Square, Sequoia National Forest, Mount Rushmore, Open Space Park, Vietnam Memorial**
Roads and highways . . . .**New Jersey Turnpike, Interstate 80, Central Avenue, Chisholm Trail, Mutt's Road**
Buildings . . .**Pentagon, Paske High School, Empire State Building**
Monuments . . . . **Eiffel Tower, Statue of Liberty**

680.2 Particular Sections of the Country

Capitalize words that indicate particular sections of the country. Also capitalize proper adjectives formed from names of specific sections of a country.

Having grown up on the hectic East Coast, I find life in the South to be refreshing.

Here in Georgia, Southern hospitality is a way of life.

Words that simply indicate a direction are not capitalized; nor are adjectives that are formed from words that simply indicate direction.

The town where I live, located east of Memphis, is typical of others found in western Tennessee.

TEKS 7.20A

Practice

Capitalization 3

- Geographic Names
- Particular Sections of the Country

Write the answer to each of the following questions.

Example: What is the name of the country located just south of the United States?
Mexico

1. What are the two continents not listed on the facing page?
2. Which four planets are closest to the sun?
3. What section of the country is famous for cowboys?
4. If you flew from New York to London, England, what body of water would you fly over?
5. What is the name of a mountain range in Colorado?
6. Which state is completely surrounded by an ocean, and what ocean is it?
7. What is the large, centrally located park in New York City?
8. What are two European countries?
9. Which city is the second largest in the United States?

Learning Language **Not only are buildings capitalized, but also rooms within buildings that have a number, name, or letter attached to them.**

Room 33 the Taylor Room Conference Room A

Work with a partner to list places around your school or community that should be capitalized.

TEKS 7.20A

Capitalization . . .

682.1
First Words

Capitalize the first word of every sentence and the first word in a direct quotation.

> **In many families, pets are treated like people, according to an article in the *Kansas City Star*.** (sentence)
>
> **Marty Becker, coauthor of *Chicken Soup for the Pet Lover's Soul*, reports, "Seven out of ten people let their pets sleep on the bed."** (direct quotation)
>
> **"I get my 15 minutes of fame," he says, "every time I come home."** (Notice that *every* is not capitalized because it does not begin a new sentence.)
>
> **"It's like being treated like a rock star," says Becker. "Now I have to tell you that feels pretty good."**

Do not capitalize the first word in an indirect quotation.

> **Becker says that in the last 10 years, pets have moved out of kennels and basements and into living rooms and bedrooms.** (indirect quotation)

682.2
Titles

Capitalize the first word of a title, the last word, and every word in between except articles *(a, an, the)*, short prepositions, and coordinating conjunctions. Follow this rule for titles of books, newspapers, magazines, poems, plays, songs, articles, movies, works of art, pictures, stories, and essays. (See 660.3.)

> ***Locked in Time*** (book)
>
> ***Boston Globe*** (newspaper)
>
> ***Dog Fancy*** (magazine)
>
> **"Roses Are Red"** (poem)
>
> ***The Phantom of the Opera*** (play)
>
> ***Daddy Day Care*** (movie)
>
> **"Intuition"** (song)
>
> **Mona Lisa** (work of art)

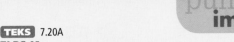

TEKS 7.20A
ELPS 3E

Practice

Capitalization 4

- First Words
- Titles

For each of the following sentences, correctly write any word that is incorrectly capitalized.

Example: Kai bought four tickets to the play *the Phantom Of the Opera.*
The, of

1. He said, "as long as I can get the tickets I want, I really don't mind waiting in line."
2. The *New York times* had a fantastic review of the play in an article called "Phantom appears; Here to stay."
3. Shar read the poem "the Road not Taken" by Robert Frost.
4. "That poem," said Shar, "Really makes me think."
5. it is one of his best-known poems.
6. Danté enjoys the electronic magazine *EEK!: Environmental education for Kids.*
7. "I learned about the careers of park rangers," he said, "And wildlife biologists."
8. after we saw the movie *The Cat In The Hat*, Bruce got a hat just like the cat's.
9. He said that It made him look cool.

Next Step: Write a sentence for each of the following: a name of a book, a song, and a movie. Make sure you capitalize correctly. Share your sentences with a partner.

TEKS 7.20A

Capitalization . . .

684.1 Abbreviations

Capitalize abbreviations of titles and organizations.

Dr. (Doctor) **M.D.** (Doctor of Medicine)
Mr. (Mister) **UPS** (United Parcel Service)
SADD (Students Against Destructive Decisions)

684.2 Organizations

Capitalize the name of an organization, an association, or a team.

New York State Historical Society **the Red Cross**
General Motors Corporation **the Miami Dolphins**
Republicans **the Democratic Party**

684.3 Letters

Capitalize the letters used to indicate form or shape.

T-shirt **U-turn** **A-frame** **T-ball**

Capitalize	Do Not Capitalize
American	**un-American**
January, February	**winter, spring**
Missouri and Ohio Rivers	**the rivers Missouri and Ohio**
The South is humid in summer.	**Turn south at the stop sign.**
Duluth Middle School	**a Duluth middle school**
Governor Bob Taft	**Bob Taft, our governor**
President Luiz Lula Da Silva	**Luiz Lula Da Silva, Brazil's president**
Nissan Altima	**a Nissan automobile**
The planet Earth is egg shaped.	**The earth on Grandpa's farm is rich.**
I'm taking World Cultures.	**I'm taking social studies.**

Practice

Capitalization 5

- Abbreviations
- Organizations
- Letters

Capitalize the words that need to be capitalized in the following sentences.

Example: The construction crew carefully lowered the i-beam onto the foundation.
I-beam

1. The green bay packers won the first two Super Bowls.
2. Our substitute teacher, ms. Lukas, will complete her m.a. degree this spring.
3. After I fell off the bleachers and broke my arm, mr. Stevenson took me to see dr. Bell at the clinic.
4. One of the largest ships in the United States Navy is the u.s.s. *Enterprise*.
5. Over the years, the smithsonian institution has become a world-famous museum.
6. The city council passed a new ordinance outlawing u-turns on Davis Avenue.
7. Most politicians seek public office as either a republican, a democrat, or an independent.
8. Did you see the new a-frame picnic shelter in Franklin Park?
9. The Northwest High School panthers' football games are broadcast on radio station kyxx.
10. Engineers at General motors corporation changed the angle of the b-pillar on their new sedan.
11. On the last day of school, the entire seventh-grade science class wore t-shirts with the words "mr. Kall is the coolest."

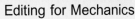

Plurals

686.1 Most Nouns

The **plurals** of most nouns are formed by adding *s* to the singular.

cheerleader — **cheerleaders** wheel — **wheels**
bubble — **bubbles**

686.2 Nouns Ending in *ch, sh, s, x,* and *z*

The plural form of nouns ending in *ch, sh, s, x,* and *z* is made by adding *es* to the singular.

lunch — **lunches** dish — **dishes** mess — **messes**
buzz — **buzzes** fox — **foxes**

686.3 Nouns Ending in *o*

The plurals of nouns ending in *o* with a vowel just before the *o* are formed by adding *s*.

radio — **radios** studio — **studios** rodeo — **rodeos**

The plurals of most nouns ending in *o* with a consonant just before the *o* are formed by adding *es*.

echo — **echoes** hero — **heroes** tomato — **tomatoes**

Exceptions: Musical terms and words of Spanish origin always form plurals by adding *s*.

alto — **altos** banjo — **banjos** taco — **tacos**
solo — **solos** piano — **pianos** burro — **burros**

686.4 Nouns Ending in *ful*

The plurals of nouns that end with *ful* are formed by adding an *s* at the end of the word.

three platefuls **six tankfuls** **four cupfuls** **five pailfuls**

686.5 Nouns Ending in *f* or *fe*

The plurals of nouns that end in *f* or *fe* are formed in one of two ways: If the final *f* sound is still heard in the plural form of the word, simply add *s*; if the final sound is a *v* sound, change the *f* to *ve* and add *s*.

roof — roofs **chief — chiefs** **belief — beliefs**
(plural ends with *f* sound)

wife — wives **loaf — loaves** **leaf — leaves**
(plural ends with *v* sound)

ELPS 3E

Grammar Practice

Plurals 1

- **Nouns Ending in *ch, sh, s, x,* and *z***
- **Nouns Ending in *o, ful, f,* or *fe***

For each of the following sentences, write the plural form of the underlined word or words.

Example: The class collected five box of books for the book drive.
boxes

1. Before the final bell rang, eight bus lined up in front of the school.
2. Several coral reef form a natural barrier for the chain of island off the South American coast.
3. Farmer in Idaho have a history of raising huge potato.
4. Jill likes two spoonful of sugar in her tea.
5. Clear the ash out of the fireplace before building a new fire.
6. Our school's music teacher wants 10 more soprano in the choir.
7. We saw 30 calf during our field trip to the Pell dairy farm.
8. Salid and Jerry decided to rent three video for the weekend.
9. After eating just one jalapeño pepper, Frank needed five mouthful of milk to cool his tongue.
10. Diego loves to play the bongo.
11. The drawing board in Mom's office faces a row of four window.
12. She enjoys watching the leaf change every fall.
13. Zack packed three lunch for the family's day of hiking.

Next Step: Write three sentences using the plurals of *radio, capful,* and *life*. Read your sentences aloud to a classmate.

Plurals . . .

688.1
Nouns Ending in *y*

The plurals of common nouns that end in *y* with a consonant letter just before the *y* are formed by changing the *y* to *i* and adding *es*.

fly — **flies** baby — **babies** cavity — **cavities**

The plurals of common nouns that end in *y* with a vowel before the *y* are formed by adding only *s*.

key — **keys** holiday — **holidays** attorney — **attorneys**

The plurals of proper nouns ending in *y* are formed by adding *s*.

There are three Circuit Citys in our metro area.

688.2
Compound Nouns

The plurals of some compound nouns are formed by adding *s* or *es* to the main word in the compound.

brothers-in-law **maids of honor** **secretaries of state**

688.3
Plurals That Do Not Change

The plurals of some words are the same in singular and plural form.

deer **sheep** **trout** **aircraft**

688.4
Irregular Spelling

Some words (including many foreign words) form a plural by taking on an irregular spelling; others are now acceptable with the commonly used *s* or *es* ending.

child — **children** woman — **women** man — **men**
goose — **geese** mouse — **mice** ox — **oxen**
tooth — **teeth** octopus — **octopuses** or **octopi**
index — **indexes** or **indices**

688.5
Adding an *'s*

The plurals of letters, figures, symbols, and words discussed as words are sometimes formed by adding an apostrophe and an *s*.

Dr. Walters has two Ph.D.'s.

My dad's license plate has three *2's* between two *B's*.

You've got too many *but's* and *so's* in that sentence.

For information on forming plural possessives, see **666.1**.

Grammar Practice

Plurals 2

- Nouns Ending in *y*
- Compound Nouns
- Plurals That Do Not Change
- Irregular Spelling
- Adding an *'s*

For each of the following sentences, write the correct form of any underlined plural that is not correct. If an underlined plural is correct, write "C."

Example: Aaron's mother said one of her sister-in-laws worked in a circus for three years.
sisters-in-law

1. The circus announcer shouted out, "Ladys and gentlemans, welcome to the finest show on earth!"
2. For the next five days, people entered the Fair Wing Circus Grounds through several archwaies set up near the roads.
3. Flags full of Fs and Ws flew above the tents.
4. Elaine expected to see elephants, but she did not expect to see mooses!
5. Faleena wondered if there were many mouses running around the circus grounds that might scare the elephants.
6. When a little girl saw the lion's sharp tooths, she started to cry.
7. The three clowns with donkies were so funny!
8. We could see the acrobats doing their warm-ups before climbing the ladder.
9. After the evening's performance, both Jane and Camille wrote in their diarys.

Abbreviations

690.1 Abbreviations

An **abbreviation** is the shortened form of a word or phrase. The following abbreviations are always acceptable in any kind of writing:

Mr. **Mrs.** **Ms.** **Dr.** **a.m., p.m.** (A.M., P.M.)

B.C.E. (before the Common Era) **C.E.** (Common Era)

B.A. **M.A.** **Ph.D.** **M.D.** **Sr.** **Jr.**

Caution: Do not abbreviate the names of states, countries, months, days, or units of measure in formal writing. Also, do not use signs or symbols (%, &) in place of words.

Common Abbreviations

AC alternating current
a.m. ante meridiem
ASAP as soon as possible
COD cash on delivery
DA district attorney
DC direct current
etc. and so forth
F Fahrenheit
FM frequency modulation
GNP gross national product
i.e. that is (Latin id est)
kg kilogram
km kilometer
kW kilowatt
l liter
lb. pound
m meter
M.D. doctor of medicine
mfg. manufacturing
mpg miles per gallon
mph miles per hour
oz. ounce
pd. paid
pg. (or p.) page
p.m. post meridiem
ppd. postpaid, prepaid
qt. quart
R.S.V.P. please reply
tbs., tbsp. tablespoon
tsp. teaspoon
vol. volume
vs. versus
yd. yard

Address Abbreviations

	Standard	Postal
Avenue	Ave.	AVE
Boulevard	Blvd.	BLVD
Court	Ct.	CT
Drive	Dr.	DR
East	E.	E
Heights	Hts.	HTS
Highway	Hwy.	HWY
Lake	L.	LK
Lane	Ln.	LN
North	N.	N
Park	Pk.	PK
Parkway	Pky.	PKY
Place	Pl.	PL
Plaza	Plaza	PLZ
Road	Rd.	RD
Route	Rt.	RTE
South	S.	S
Square	Sq.	SQ
Station	Sta.	STA
Street	St.	ST
Terrace	Ter.	TER
Turnpike	Tpke.	TPKE
West	W.	W

Grammar Practice

Abbreviations 1

Write out the words that the abbreviations in the following sentences stand for.

Example: The field is 50 m wide, not 50 yd. wide.
meters, yards

1. There are 16 oz. in a lb.
2. The article is on pg. 345 of vol. 2.
3. This item is COD, so the bill must be pd. when you get it.
4. The DA needs an M.D. ASAP!
5. TicTec is a mfg. company located near the Virginia Tpke.
6. If this car gets 32 mpg, how far will it go on a qt. of gas?

Write the standard abbreviations of the following addresses.

Example: 2103 East Fremont Court
2103 E. Fremont Ct.

1. 7828 West Greentree Road
2. 697 Samson Highway
3. 992A Ryan Avenue
4. 5 South Elm Lane
5. 1218 North Adobe Terrace
6. 22223 Maple Parkway
7. 250 High Street

Next Step: Create an imaginary address for a place you would like to live some day.

Abbreviations . . .

692.1 Acronyms

An **acronym** is an abbreviation that can be pronounced as a word. It does not require periods.

WHO — World Health Organization **ROM** — read-only memory

FAQ — frequently asked question

692.2 Initialisms

An **initialism** is similar to an acronym except that it cannot be pronounced as a word; the initials are pronounced individually.

PBS — Public Broadcasting Service

BLM — Bureau of Land Management

WNBA — Women's National Basketball Association

Common Acronyms and Initialisms

CETA	Comprehensive Employment and Training Act
CIA	Central Intelligence Agency
FAA	Federal Aviation Administration
FBI	Federal Bureau of Investigation
FCC	Federal Communications Commission
FDA	Food and Drug Administration
FDIC	Federal Deposit Insurance Corporation
FHA	Federal Housing Administration
FTC	Federal Trade Commission
HTML	Hypertext Markup Language
IRS	Internal Revenue Service
MADD	Mothers Against Drunk Driving
NAFTA	North American Free Trade Agreement
NASA	National Aeronautics and Space Administration
NATO	North Atlantic Treaty Organization
OEO	Office of Economic Opportunity
OEP	Office of Emergency Preparedness
ORV	off-road vehicle
OSHA	Occupational Safety and Health Administration
PAC	political action committee
PIN	personal identification number
PSA	public service announcement
ROTC	Reserve Officers' Training Corps
SADD	Students Against Destructive Decisions
SSA	Social Security Administration
SUV	sport-utility vehicle
SWAT	special weapons and tactics
TDD	telecommunications device for the deaf
TMJ	temporomandibular joint
TVA	Tennessee Valley Authority
VA	Veterans Administration
VISTA	Volunteers in Service to America
WAC	Women's Army Corps
WAVES	Women Accepted for Volunteer Emergency Service

Grammar Practice

Abbreviations 2

- Acronyms
- Initialisms

In each sentence below, write what the abbreviation stands for. (Be careful; some abbreviations can stand for more than one thing!) Choose from the list at the bottom of the page.

Example: Rachel's family makes a yearly donation to CARE.
Cooperative for American Relief to Everywhere

1. The newest model of this car has an ABS.
2. Grandma always writes "P.S. I love you" at the end of the letters that she sends to me.
3. Is this toothpaste approved by the ADA?
4. Jake's car stereo has AFT.
5. The awards program begins at seven o'clock CST.
6. Mom said that she has to get some cash from the ATM.
7. The HVAC technician came to our house to fix the furnace.
8. I used to go to PS 106 in Far Rockaway, New York.
9. Each of the math instructors is a member of the AFT.

American Dental Association
American Federation of Teachers
antilock braking system
automatic fine tuning
automatic teller machine
Central Standard Time
Cooperative for American Relief to Everywhere
heating, ventilation, and air conditioning
postscript
public school

Next Step: Use your imagination to write what these acronyms might stand for: *COMB, SMED,* and *TRIK.*

Numbers

694.1
Numbers Under 10

Numbers from one to nine are usually written as words; all numbers 10 and over are usually written as numerals.

two seven nine 10 25 106

694.2
Numerals Only

Use numerals to express any of the following forms:

money	**$2.39**
decimals	**26.2**
percentages	**8 percent**
chapters	**chapter 7**
pages	**pages 287–289**
time (with "a.m." or "p.m.")	**4:30 p.m.**
telephone numbers	**1-800-555-1212**
dates	**44 B.C.E.; July 6, 1942**
identification numbers	**Highway 36**
addresses	**2125 Cairn Road**
ZIP codes	**60004**
statistics	**a vote of 23 to 4**

When abbreviations and symbols are used (for instance, in science or math), always use numerals with them.

12° C 7% 33 kg 9 cm 55 mph

694.3
Very Large Numbers

You may use a combination of numerals and words for very large numbers.

Of the 17 million residents of the three Midwestern states, only 1.3 million are blondes.

You may spell out a large number that can be written as two words. If more than two words are needed, use the numeral.

More than nine thousand people attended the concert.

About 3,500 people missed the opening act.

Grammar Practice

Numbers 1

- Numbers Under 10
- Numerals Only
- Very Large Numbers

If a number in the sentences below is written incorrectly, write the correct form. Otherwise, write "correct."

Example: Yesterday morning at five-fifteen, Mom's cell phone rang once and stopped.
5:15

1. My family has 2 phone numbers: one for the regular telephone and one for the cell phone.
2. The cell phone number, 555-989-9889, is easy to remember.
3. Since we got the cell phone, our other phone bill has gone down nine percent.
4. Some businesses have ten or more phone numbers.
5. Alpha International, a company at Ten-Twenty Visible Lane, has 66 phone numbers.
6. Area codes were introduced in the United States about fifty years ago, when there were 87 of them.
7. As of June First, 1999, there were 215 area codes in use.
8. Each area code has almost eight million phone numbers.
9. With one point three billion phone numbers currently available, when will the United States run out of phone numbers?
10. In the United States, people make 30 million long-distance calls a day.
11. They make 1.5 billion local calls, which is a twenty-five percent increase since 1990.

Next Step: Write a sentence about the number of times you talk on the phone in a week. Write another sentence that includes the page numbers of the pages you're looking at.

Numbers . . .

696.1
Comparing Numbers

If you are comparing two or more numbers in a sentence, write all of them the same way: as numerals or as words.

Students from 9 to 14 years old are invited.

Students from nine to fourteen years old are invited.

696.2
Numbers in Compound Modifiers

A compound modifier may include a numeral.

The floorboards come in 10-foot lengths.

When a number comes before a compound modifier that includes a numeral, use words instead of numerals.

We need eleven 10-foot lengths to finish the floor.

Ms. Brown must grade twenty 12-page reports.

696.3
Sentence Beginnings

Use words, not numerals, to begin a sentence.

Nine students had turned in their homework. Fourteen students said they were unable to finish the assignment.

696.4
Time and Money

When time or money is expressed with a symbol, use numerals. When either is expressed with words, spell out the number.

6:00 a.m. (or) **six o'clock**

$25 (or) **twenty-five dollars**

SCHOOL DAZE
Jerry, haven't you finished your paper yet?
No, it's not due until three o'clock, and Mrs. Wright told me to add a few new twists and wrinkles.

Grammar Practice

Numbers 2

- Comparing Numbers
- Numbers in Compound Modifiers
- Sentence Beginnings
- Time and Money

For each of the following sentences, write the correct form of the number, word, or phrase that is incorrect.

Example: There were 18 15-pound babies at the audition for the diaper commercial.
eighteen

1. 12 of the babies were less than a year old.
2. Those selected would be paid 500 dollars for their "work."
3. The director said, "Will the people sitting in rows eight through 15 please stand up?"
4. 25 people stood up.
5. "Go to soundstage B at 10 o'clock," she said.
6. "The audition should be over by two p.m.," she added.
7. After almost 20 10-minute auditions, the director had to make a decision.
8. She whispered, "I can't decide between Baby Six and Baby 11."
9. 16 of the babies were sent home, and the two remaining babies were in the commercial together.

Next Step: Write a sentence comparing your age and the age of a baby you know. In another sentence, tell how much money you might get to baby-sit that baby.

TEKS 7.21

Improving Spelling

698.1
i before e

Write *i* before *e* except after *c*, or when sounded like *a* as in *neighbor* and *weigh*.

Some Exceptions to the Rule: *counterfeit, either, financier, foreign, height, heir, leisure, neither, science, seize, sheik, species, their, weird.*

698.2
Silent e

If a word ends with a silent *e*, drop the *e* before adding a suffix that begins with a vowel. There are exceptions, for example, *knowledgeable* and *changeable*.

state—stating—statement
like—liking—likeness
use—using—useful
nine—ninety—nineteen

NOTE You do not drop the *e* when the suffix begins with a consonant. Exceptions include *truly, argument,* and *ninth*.

698.3
Words Ending in y

When *y* is the last letter in a word and the *y* comes just after a consonant, change the *y* to *i* before adding any suffix except those beginning with *i*.

fry—fries—frying
hurry—hurried—hurrying
lady—ladies
happy—happiness
beauty—beautiful

When forming the plural of a word that ends with a *y* that comes just after a vowel, add *s*.

toy—toys **play—plays** **monkey—monkeys**

698.4
Consonant Endings

When a one-syllable word ends in a consonant *(bat)* preceded by one vowel *(bat)*, double the final consonant before adding a suffix that begins with a vowel *(batting)*.

sum—summary **god—goddess**

When a multisyllable word ends in a consonant preceded by one vowel *(control)*, the accent is on the last syllable *(contról)*, and the suffix begins with a vowel *(ing)*—the same rule holds true: double the final consonant *(controlling)*.

prefer—preferred **begin—beginning**

TEKS 7.21
ELPS 3E

Practice

Spelling 1

- *i* before *e*
- Silent *e*

For each of the following sentences, write the correct choice from each set of words in parentheses.

Example: Our *(nieghbor, neighbor)* Esteban bought his *(nineth, ninth)* wrench yesterday; soon he'll have a complete set.
neighbor, ninth

1. The *(cheif, chief)* reason he buys these tools is that he likes *(useing, using)* them for home-improvement projects.
2. Manuel, Esteban's seventh-grade son, is *(hopeful, hopful)* he will own his father's tools someday.
3. A tool *(reveiw, review)* in *Popular Mechanics* magazine rated his father's new scroll saw first out of 20 models.
4. Manuel and Esteban showed some of the tools to Mrs. Gomez, who shares *(thier, their)* enthusiasm for home improvement.
5. She likes to watch that *(fameous, famous)* TV show about fixing up old houses.
6. Mrs. Gomez was impressed with the *(variety, vareity)* of tools and asked Manuel to lend her a saw.
7. Using his best *(judgement, judgment)*, Manuel said he would have to ask his father if she could borrow the scroll saw.
8. After practicing for a while, Mrs. Gomez successfully cut a difficult design out of a *(peice, piece)* of oak.
9. She could not *(believe, beleive)* how smoothly the saw worked.
10. With great *(excitment, excitement)*, she ordered the same scroll saw for herself.

Next Step: Add a suffix to *arrive, care,* and *true*; then use each word in a sentence. Share your sentences with a partner.

TEKS 7.21

Practice

Spelling 2

- Words Ending in *y*
- Consonant Endings

For each sentence below, write the correct spelling of any underlined word that is misspelled.

Example: The boys bought three bags of frys for lunch.
fries

1. Mrs. Bock enjoys going to each of the six librarys in our city.
2. When the hurricane occured, it seemed that people were running everywhere.
3. Relief workers knew the food supplies would be greeted with happyness by the storm victims.
4. Samuel's father keeps busy repairing antique toies at his shop and shipping them back to their owners.
5. Workers' salaries could be droping since business is slow.
6. February's blizzard buryed Springfield under two feet of snow—even more in the valleys.
7. Students must stay within the school's boundaries during school dayes.
8. Phil trys to walk two miles every evening, and last week, he saw several rabbits hoping all over the city park.
9. Ms. Stanton needs three students to help her buy groceries for the retreat that our class is planing.
10. We beged the teacher to give us more time to write our essays.
11. The journies of Lewis and Clark led them through beautiful and dangerous territorys.
12. All the canaries took off at once, flaping their yellow wings.

Next Step: Write sentences using the plurals of the following words: *memory, chimney,* and *city*.

Yellow Pages Guide to Improved Spelling

Be patient. Becoming a good speller takes time.

Check your spelling by using a dictionary or list of commonly misspelled words (like the list that follows). And, remember, don't rely too much on computer spell-checkers.

Learn the correct pronunciation of each word you are trying to spell. Knowing the correct pronunciation of a word will help you remember how it's spelled.

Look up the meaning of each word as you are checking the dictionary for pronunciation. (Knowing how to spell a word is of little use if you don't know what it means.)

Practice spelling the word before you close the dictionary. Look away from the page and try to see the word in your mind's eye. Write the word on a piece of paper. Check the spelling in the dictionary and repeat the process until you are able to spell the word correctly.

Keep a list of the words that you misspell.

Write often. As noted educator Frank Smith said, "There is little point in learning to spell if you have little intention of writing."

A

abbreviate
aboard
about
above
absence
absent
absolute (ly)
abundance
accelerate
accident
accidental (ly)
accompany
accomplice
accomplish
according
account
accurate
accustom (ed)
ache
achieve (ment)
acre
across
actual
adapt
addition (al)
address
adequate
adjust (ment)
admire
adventure
advertise (ment)
advertising
afraid
after
afternoon
afterward
again
against
agreeable
agree (ment)
ah
aid
airy
aisle
alarm
alcohol
alike
alive
alley
allowance
all right
almost
already
although
altogether
aluminum
always
amateur
ambulance
amendment
among
amount
analyze
ancient
angel
anger
angle
angry
animal

anniversary
announce
annoyance
annual
anonymous
another
answer
Antarctic
anticipate
anxiety
anxious
anybody
anyhow
anyone
anything
anyway
anywhere
apartment
apiece
apologize
apparent (ly)
appeal
appearance
appetite
appliance
application
appointment
appreciate
approach
appropriate
approval
approximate
architect
Arctic
aren't
argument
arithmetic
around
arouse
arrange (ment)
arrival
article
artificial

asleep
assassin
assign (ment)
assistance
associate
association
assume
athlete
athletic
attach
attack (ed)
attempt
attendance
attention
attitude
attorney
attractive
audience
August
author
authority
automobile
autumn
available
avenue
average
awful (ly)
awkward

B

baggage
baking
balance
balloon
ballot
banana
bandage
bankrupt
barber
bargain
barrel

basement
basis
basket
battery
beautiful
beauty
because
become
becoming
before
began
beggar
beginning
behave
behavior
being
belief
believe
belong
beneath
benefit (ed)
between
bicycle
biscuit
blackboard
blanket
blizzard
bother
bottle
bottom
bough
bought
bounce
boundary
breakfast
breast
breath (n.)
breathe (v.)
breeze
bridge
brief
bright
brilliant

brother
brought
bruise
bubble
bucket
buckle
budget
building
bulletin
buoyant
bureau
burglar
bury
business
busy
button

C

cabbage
cafeteria
calendar
campaign
canal
cancel (ed)
candidate
candle
canister
cannon
cannot
canoe
can't
canyon
capacity
captain
carburetor
cardboard
career
careful
careless
carpenter
carriage

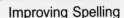

carrot
cashier
casserole
casualty
catalog
catastrophe
catcher
caterpillar
catsup
ceiling
celebration
cemetery
census
century
certain (ly)
certificate
challenge
champion
changeable
character (istic)
chief
children
chimney
chocolate
choice
chorus
circumstance
citizen
civilization
classmates
classroom
climate
climb
closet
clothing
coach
cocoa
cocoon
coffee
collar
college
colonel
color

colossal
column
comedy
coming
commercial
commission
commit
commitment
committed
committee
communicate
community
company
comparison
competition
competitive (ly)
complain
complete (ly)
complexion
compromise
conceive
concerning
concert
concession
concrete
condemn
condition
conductor
conference
confidence
congratulate
connect
conscience
conscious
conservative
constitution
continue
continuous
control
controversy
convenience
convince
coolly

cooperate
corporation
correspond
cough
couldn't
counter
counterfeit
country
county
courage
courageous
court
courteous
courtesy
cousin
coverage
cozy
cracker
cranky
crawl
creditor
cried
criticize
cruel
crumb
crumble
cupboard
curiosity
curious
current
custom
customer
cylinder

D

daily
dairy
damage
danger (ous)
daughter
dealt

deceive
decided
decision
declaration
decorate
defense
definite (ly)
definition
delicious
dependent
depot
describe
description
desert
deserve
design
desirable
despair
dessert
deteriorate
determine
develop (ment)
device (n.)
devise (v.)
diamond
diaphragm
diary
dictionary
difference
different
difficulty
dining
diploma
director
disagreeable
disappear
disappoint
disapprove
disastrous
discipline
discover
discuss
discussion

TEKS 7.21

disease
dissatisfied
distinguish
distribute
divide
divine
divisible
division
doctor
doesn't
dollar
dormitory
doubt
dough
dual
duplicate

E

eager (ly)
economy
edge
edition
efficiency
eight
eighth
either
elaborate
electricity
elephant
eligible
ellipse
embarrass
emergency
emphasize
employee
employment
enclose
encourage
engineer
enormous
enough
entertain
enthusiastic
entirely
entrance
envelop (v.)
envelope (n.)
environment
equipment
equipped
equivalent
escape
especially
essential
establish
every
evidence
exaggerate
exceed
excellent
except
exceptional (ly)
excite
exercise
exhaust (ed)
exhibition
existence
expect
expensive
experience
explain
explanation
expression
extension
extinct
extraordinary
extreme (ly)

F

facilities
familiar
family
famous
fascinate
fashion
fatigue (d)
faucet
favorite
feature
February
federal
fertile
field
fierce
fiery
fifty
finally
financial (ly)
foliage
forcible
foreign
forfeit
formal (ly)
former (ly)
forth
fortunate
forty
forward
fountain
fourth
fragile
freight
friend (ly)
frighten
fulfill
fundamental
further
furthermore

G

gadget
gauge
generally
generous
genius
gentle
genuine
geography
ghetto
ghost
gnaw
government
governor
graduation
grammar
grateful
grease
grief
grocery
grudge
gruesome
guarantee
guard
guardian
guess
guidance
guide
guilty
gymnasium

H

hammer
handkerchief
handle (d)
handsome
haphazard
happen
happiness
harass
hastily
having
hazardous
headache
height

hemorrhage
hesitate
history
hoarse
holiday
honor
hoping
hopping
horrible
hospital
humorous
hurriedly
hydraulic
hygiene
hymn

I

icicle
identical
illegible
illiterate
illustrate
imaginary
imaginative
imagine
imitation
immediate (ly)
immense
immigrant
immortal
impatient
importance
impossible
improvement
inconvenience
incredible
indefinitely
independence
independent
individual
industrial
inferior
infinite
inflammable
influential
initial
initiation
innocence
innocent
installation
instance
instead
insurance
intelligence
intention
interested
interesting
interfere
interpret
interrupt
interview
investigate
invitation
irrigate
island
issue

J

jealous (y)
jewelry
journal
journey
judgment
juicy

K

kitchen
knew
knife
knives
knock
knowledge
knuckles

L

label
laboratory
ladies
language
laugh
laundry
lawyer
league
lecture
legal
legible
legislature
leisure
length
liable
library
license
lieutenant
lightning
likable
likely
liquid
listen
literature
living
loaves
loneliness
loose
lose
loser
losing
lovable
lovely

M

machinery
magazine
magnificent
maintain
majority
making
manual
manufacture
marriage
material
mathematics
maximum
mayor
meant
measure
medicine
medium
message
mileage
miniature
minimum
minute
mirror
miscellaneous
mischievous
miserable
missile
misspell
moisture
molecule
monotonous
monument
mortgage
mountain
muscle
musician
mysterious

TEKS 7.21

N

naive
natural (ly)
necessary
negotiate
neighbor (hood)
neither
nickel
niece
nineteen
nineteenth
ninety
ninth
noisy
noticeable
nuclear
nuisance

O

obedience
obey
obstacle
occasion
occasional (ly)
occur
occurred
offense
official
often
omission
omitted
operate
opinion
opponent
opportunity
opposite
ordinarily
original
outrageous

P

package
paid
pamphlet
paradise
paragraph
parallel
paralyze
parentheses
partial
participant
participate
particular (ly)
pasture
patience
peculiar
people
perhaps
permanent
perpendicular
persistent
personal (ly)
personnel
perspiration
persuade
phase
physician
piece
pitcher
planned
plateau
playwright
pleasant
pleasure
pneumonia
politician
possess
possible
practical (ly)
prairie
precede
precious
precise (ly)
precision
preferable
preferred
prejudice
preparation
presence
previous
primitive
principal
principle
prisoner
privilege
probably
procedure
proceed
professor
prominent
pronounce
pronunciation
protein
psychology
pumpkin
pure

Q

quarter
questionnaire
quiet
quite
quotient

R

raise
realize
really
receipt
receive
received
recipe
recognize
recommend
reign
relieve
religious
remember
repetition
representative
reservoir
resistance
respectfully
responsibility
restaurant
review
rhyme
rhythm
ridiculous
route

S

safety
salad
salary
sandwich
satisfactory
Saturday
scene
scenery
schedule
science
scissors
scream
screen
season
secretary
seize
sensible
sentence
separate
several

TEKS 7.21

sheriff
shining
similar
since
sincere (ly)
skiing
sleigh
soldier
souvenir
spaghetti
specific
sphere
sprinkle
squeeze
squirrel
statue
stature
statute
stomach
stopped
straight
strength
stretched
studying
subtle
succeed
success
sufficient
summarize
supplement
suppose
surely
surprise
syllable
sympathy
symptom

T

tariff
technique
temperature
temporary
terrible
territory
thankful
theater
their
there
therefore
thief
thorough (ly)
though
throughout
tired
tobacco
together
tomorrow
tongue
touch
tournament
toward
tragedy
treasurer
tried
tries
trouble
truly
Tuesday
typical

U

unconscious
unfortunate (ly)
unique
university
unnecessary
until
usable
useful
using
usual (ly)
utensil

V

vacation
vacuum
valuable
variety
various
vegetable
vehicle
very
vicinity
view
villain
violence
visible
visitor
voice
volume
voluntary
volunteer

W

wander
wasn't
weather
Wednesday
weigh
weird
welcome
welfare
whale
where
whether
which
whole
wholly
whose
width
women
worthwhile
wouldn't
wreckage
writing
written

Y

yellow
yesterday
yield

ELPS 5B

Using the Right Word

708.1
a, an

A is used before words that begin with a consonant sound; *an* is used before words that begin with any vowel sound except long "u."

a heap, a cat, an idol, an elephant, an honor, a historian, an umbrella, a unicorn

708.2
accept, except

The verb *accept* means "to receive"; the preposition *except* means "other than."

Melissa graciously accepted defeat. (verb)

All the boys except Zach were here. (preposition)

708.3
affect, effect

Affect is almost always a verb; it means "to influence." *Effect* can be a verb, but it is most often used as a noun that means "the result."

How does population growth affect us?

What are the effects of population growth?

708.4
allowed, aloud

The verb *allowed* means "permitted" or "let happen"; *aloud* is an adverb that means "in a normal voice."

We aren't allowed to read aloud in the library.

708.5
allusion, illusion

An *allusion* is a brief reference to or hint of something (person, place, thing, or idea). An *illusion* is a false impression or idea.

The Great Dontini, a magician, made an allusion to Houdini as he created the illusion of sawing his assistant in half.

708.6
a lot

A lot is not one word, but two; it is a general descriptive phrase meaning "plenty." (It should be avoided in formal writing.)

708.7
all right

All right is not one word, but two; it is a phrase meaning "satisfactory" or "okay." (Please note, the following *are* spelled correctly: *always, altogether, already, almost.*)

ELPS 3E, 5B

Grammar Practice

Using the Right Word 1

- **accept, except; affect, effect; allowed, aloud; a lot**

For each of the following sentences, write the correct choice from each set of words in parentheses.

Example: When Josie reads her writing *(allowed, aloud)*, she hears the mistakes she needs to fix.
aloud

1. Sari's gentle touch and her soft voice had a calming *(affect, effect)* on the frightened collie.
2. Everyone at the school assembly stood and cheered when Franklin went forward to *(accept, except)* the community service award.
3. The use of pocket calculators is not *(allowed, aloud)* during the final exam.
4. That quiz won't *(affect, effect)* my grade *(a lot, alot)*.
5. Marlyn put all the wood *(accept, except)* the heaviest piece in his pickup truck.
6. Oil spills around the world *(affect, effect)* future generations of wildlife.
7. Greta volunteers at a senior center, reading the residents' mail *(allowed, aloud)* for them.
8. "Please *(accept, except)* our late report," we begged Mr. Potter.
9. Matthew's little brother is not *(allowed, aloud)* to cross the street unless his mom or dad is there.
10. Troy was upset when everyone *(accept, except)* him was able to walk to the playground.
11. The rule can have a bad *(affect, effect)* on him, it seems.

Next Step: Read about "a lot" on the opposite page. Think of a type of writing where you might use this phrase, and write two sentences using it. Share your sentences with a partner.

ELPS 5B

710.1
already, all ready

Already is an adverb that tells when. *All ready* is a phrase meaning "completely ready."

We have already eaten breakfast; now we are all ready for school.

710.2
altogether, all together

Altogether is always an adverb meaning "completely." *All together* is used to describe people or things that are gathered in one place at one time.

Ms. Monces held her baton in the air and said, "Okay, class, all together now: sing!"

Unfortunately, there was altogether too much street noise for us to hear her.

710.3
among, between

Among is used when speaking of more than two persons or things. *Between* is used when speaking of only two.

The three friends talked among themselves as they tried to choose between trumpet or trombone lessons.

710.4
amount, number

Amount is used to describe things that you cannot count. *Number* is used when you can actually count the persons or things.

The amount of interest in playing the tuba is shown by the number of kids learning to play the instrument.

710.5
annual, biannual, semiannual, biennial, perennial

An *annual* event happens once every year. A *biannual* (or *semiannual*) event happens twice a year. A *biennial* event happens once every two years. A *perennial* event happens year after year.

The annual PTA rummage sale is so successful that it will now be a semiannual event.

The neighbor has some wonderful perennial flowers.

710.6
ant, aunt

An *ant* is an insect. An *aunt* is a female relative (the sister of a person's mother or father).

My aunt is an entomologist, a scientist who studies ants and other insects.

710.7
ascent, assent

Ascent is the act of rising or climbing; *assent* is agreement.

After the group's ascent of five flights of stairs to the meeting room, plans for elevator repairs met with quick assent.

ELPS 3E, 5B

Grammar Practice

Using the Right Word 2

- **already, all ready; altogether, all together; among, between; amount, number; ascent, assent**

For each of the following sentences, write the word "correct" if the underlined word is used correctly. If it is incorrect, write the right word.

Example: The amount of professional football teams has grown over the last 30 years.
number

1. In a "draft," the teams choose new players from between the hundreds who want to join the NFL.
2. A team might think it already has the best players possible.
3. In that case, it is altogether possible they will be the champions.
4. When the team is altogether in the locker room, the coach encourages the players to do their best.
5. A good running back can dash between two defenders and avoid being tackled.
6. A quarterback needs the ascent of all the players to make a successful play.
7. Some players are on the field for a greater amount of time than other players.
8. On the day of the game, professionals must be already to play.
9. If they play well, their team's ascent in the rankings may mean a trip to the Super Bowl.

Next Step: Show that you understand the words *between* and *assent* by using them in a sentence. Then write another sentence using the words *amount* and *already*. Read your sentences aloud to a classmate.

ELPS 5B

712.1
bare, bear

The adjective *bare* means "naked." A *bear* is a large, heavy animal with shaggy hair.

Despite his bare feet, the man chased the polar bear across the snow.

The verb *bear* means "to put up with" or "to carry."

Dwayne could not bear another of his older brother's lectures.

712.2
base, bass

Base is the foundation or the lower part of something. *Bass* (pronounced like "base") is a deep sound or tone.

The stereo speakers are on a base so solid that even the loudest bass tones don't rattle it.

Bass (rhymes with "mass") is a fish.

Jim hooked a record-setting bass, but it got away . . . so he says.

712.3
beat, beet

The verb *beat* means "to strike, to defeat," and the noun *beat* is a musical term for rhythm or tempo. A *beet* is a carrot-like vegetable (often red).

The beat of the drum in the marching band encouraged the fans to cheer on the team. After they beat West High's team four games to one, many team members were as red as a beet.

712.4
berth, birth

Berth is a space or compartment. *Birth* is the process of being born.

We pulled aside the curtain in our train berth to view the birth of a new day outside our window.

712.5
beside, besides

Beside means "by the side of." *Besides* means "in addition to."

Besides a flashlight, Kedar likes to keep his pet boa beside his bed at night.

712.6
billed, build

Billed means either "to be given a bill" or "to have a beak." The verb *build* means "to construct."

We asked the carpenter to build us a birdhouse. She billed us for time and materials.

712.7
blew, blue

Blew is the past tense of "blow." *Blue* is a color and is also used to mean "feeling low in spirits."

As the wind blew out the candles in the dark blue room, I felt more blue than ever.

Grammar Practice

Using the Right Word 3

- **bare, bear; base, bass; berth, birth; beside, besides; billed, build**

For each of the following sentences, write the correct choice from each set of words in parentheses.

Example: In rural areas, families *(billed, build)* small shelters so that students who have to wait for the bus can stay out of the cold wind.
build

1. Julian claims that even on a cold, windy day, his *(bare, bear)* hands stay very warm.
2. *(Beside, Besides)* the strong north winds, last year's big storm brought a great deal of snow.
3. In only an hour, the snow completely covered the flagpole's stone *(base, bass)*.
4. A small tree *(beside, besides)* the library was bent over by the weight of the snow.
5. During that storm, Jake wore a hat that looked like it was made out of *(bare, bear)* fur.
6. Rena knew that the rumbling *(base, bass)* sound she heard meant a snowplow was coming down the street.
7. An ambulance with a woman about to give *(berth, birth)* was able to get through to the hospital.
8. My dad, who has a plow on his truck, *(billed, build)* his customers for plowing their driveways.
9. A passenger traveling through the storm by train was very happy to be in a comfortable *(berth, birth)*.
10. Incredibly, the storm didn't bother the people who were ice fishing for fresh *(base, bass)*.

Next Step: Write two sentences for the two different meanings of the word *bass*. Share your sentences with a partner.

ELPS 5B

714.1
board, bored

A *board* is a piece of wood. *Board* also means "a group or council that helps run an organization."

The school board approved the purchase of 50 pine boards for the woodworking classes.

Bored means "to become weary or tired of something." It can also mean "made a hole by drilling."

Dulé bored a hole in the ice and dropped in a fishing line. Waiting and waiting for a bite bored him.

714.2
borrow, lend

Borrow means "to *receive* for temporary use." *Lend* means "to *give* for temporary use."

I asked Mom, "May I borrow $15 for a CD?"

She said, "I can lend you $15 until next Friday."

714.3
brake, break

A *brake* is a device used to stop a vehicle. The verb *break* means "to split, crack, or destroy"; as a noun, *break* means "gap or interruption."

After the brake on my bike failed, I took a break to fix it so I wouldn't break a bone.

714.4
bring, take

Use *bring* when the action is moving toward the speaker; use *take* when the action is moving away from the speaker.

Grandpa asked me to take the garbage out and bring him today's paper.

714.5
by, buy, bye

By is a preposition meaning "near" or "not later than." *Buy* is a verb meaning "to purchase."

By tomorrow I hope to buy tickets for the final match of the tournament.

Bye is the position of being automatically advanced to the next tournament round without playing.

Our soccer team received a bye because of our winning record.

714.6
can, may

Can means "able to," while *may* means "permitted to."

"Can I go to the library?"

(This actually means "Are my mind and body strong enough to get me there?")

"May I go?"

(This means "Do I have your permission to go?")

Grammar Practice

Using the Right Word 4

- **board, bored; borrow, lend; brake, break; bring, take; by, buy, bye**

For each of the following sentences, write a word from the list above to fill in the blank. Use each word once.

Example: Students who enjoy working with tools almost never complain about being __________ in shop class.
bored

1. Protective glasses are required for a student driving a nail into a __________.
2. Lucinda said, "Mr. Johnson, I will need to __________ my uncle's band saw to cut this wood."
3. Brenda __________ five evenly spaced holes into the top of the trunk she is building.
4. The emergency __________ on the high-speed drill quickly stops its motor.
5. Mr. Johnson asked Lyle to __________ the extra plywood sheet back to the storage room.
6. Esai, the football team's quarterback, was able to finish his project because the team had a __________ last weekend.
7. Curtis said he could not afford to __________ the wood he wanted for his project.
8. As Lawrence walked __________ the pile of lumber, it fell over and hit his left leg.
9. Mr. Johnson asked the school nurse to __________ an ice bag to the classroom.
10. Lawrence was glad he didn't __________ his leg in the accident, but he did require crutches for a few days.
11. Angela said her family had some crutches that they could __________ to Lawrence.

716.1
canvas, canvass

Canvas is a heavy cloth; *canvass* means "ask people for votes or opinions."

Our old canvas tent leaks.

Someone with a clipboard is canvassing the neighborhood.

716.2
capital, capitol

Capital can be either a noun, referring to a city or to money, or an adjective, meaning "major or important." *Capitol* is used only when talking about a building.

The capitol building is in the capital city for a capital (major) **reason: The city government contributed the capital** (money) **for the building project.**

716.3
cell, sell

Cell means "a small room" or "a small unit of life basic to all plants and animals." *Sell* is a verb meaning "to give up for a price."

Today we looked at a human skin cell under a microscope.

Let's sell those old bicycles at the rummage sale.

716.4
cent, sent, scent

Cent (1/100 of a dollar) is a coin; *sent* is the past tense of the verb "send"; *scent* is an odor or a smell.

After our car hit a skunk, we sent our friends a postcard that said, "One cent doesn't go far, but skunk scent seems to last forever."

716.5
chord, cord

Chord may mean "an emotion or a feeling," but it is more often used to mean "the sound of three or more musical tones played at the same time." A *cord* is a string or rope.

The band struck a chord at the exact moment the mayor pulled the cord on the drape covering the new statue.

716.6
chose, choose

Chose (chōz) is the past tense of the verb *choose* (cho͞oz).

This afternoon Mom chose tacos and hot sauce; this evening she will choose an antacid.

716.7
coarse, course

Coarse means "rough or crude." *Course* means "a path" or "a class or series of studies."

In our cooking course, we learned to use coarse salt and freshly ground pepper in salads.

ELPS 5B

Grammar Practice

Using the Right Word 5

■ **capital, capitol; cell, sell; cent, sent, scent; chose, choose; coarse, course**

For each of the following sentences, write the correct choice from each set of words in parentheses.

Example: Last month, the entire seventh-grade class went to our state's *(capital, capitol)* city to watch a debate.
capital

1. Ben began sanding the *(coarse, course)* wood on the old desk.
2. Every student in science class gets a chance to look through a microscope at a single skin *(cell, sell)*.
3. After looking carefully at each toy, Darien *(chose, choose)* the model car kit.
4. Will opened the door and immediately smelled the *(cent, sent, scent)* of a burning candle.
5. Ms. Jur said that José, Cana, Fran, and Carmen could *(chose, choose)* the next film for the class to watch.
6. Senators from every state meet regularly in the *(Capital, Capitol)* building in Washington, D.C.
7. Julian will *(cell, sell)* candy for the school's fund-raiser.
8. The art class students picked the best drawings of the city and *(cent, sent, scent)* them to the mayor's office.
9. Teachers of each *(coarse, course)* expect that students will complete homework assignments on time.
10. Julio saw that the "sale" price of the CD was $9.99, which was only one *(cent, sent, scent)* less than its regular price of $10.

Next Step: Using the pairs of words in this exercise, write two sentences that offer a choice (as in the sentences above). Exchange papers with a partner and pick the right words for each other's sentences.

ELPS 5B

718.1
complement, compliment

Complement means "to complete or go with." *Compliment* is an expression of admiration or praise.

Aunt Athena said, "Your cheese sauce really complements this cauliflower!"

"Thank you for the compliment," I replied.

718.2
continual, continuous

Continual refers to something that happens again and again; *continuous* refers to something that doesn't stop happening.

Sunlight hits Peoria, Iowa, on a continual basis; but sunlight hits the earth continuously.

718.3
counsel, council

When used as a noun, *counsel* means "advice"; when used as a verb, *counsel* means "to advise." *Council* refers to a group that advises.

The student council asked for counsel from its trusted adviser.

718.4
creak, creek

A *creak* is a squeaking sound; a *creek* is a stream.

I heard a creak from the old dock under my feet as I fished in the creek.

718.5
cymbal, symbol

A *cymbal* is a metal instrument shaped like a plate. A *symbol* is something (usually visible) that stands for or represents another thing or idea (usually invisible).

The damaged cymbal lying on the stage was a symbol of the band's final concert.

718.6
dear, deer

Dear means "loved or valued"; *deer* are animals.

My dear, old great-grandmother leaves corn and salt licks in her yard to attract deer.

718.7
desert, dessert

A *desert* is a barren wilderness. *Dessert* is a food served at the end of a meal.

In the desert, cold water is more inviting than even the richest dessert.

The verb *desert* means "to abandon"; the noun *desert* (pronounced like the verb) means "deserving reward or punishment."

A spy who deserts his country will receive his just deserts if he is caught.

ELPS 3E, 5B

Grammar Practice

Using the Right Word 6

- **complements, compliments; counsel, council; creak, creek; cymbal, symbol; desert, dessert**

For each sentence below, write a word from the list above to fill in the blank.

Example: I would offer this ________ to any visitor to my city: Visit Becker Park.
counsel

1. Although my city is located in the ________, Becker Park is full of green trees and colorful flowers.
2. What I like most about the park is the little _______ that runs through it.
3. I like to hear the ________ of the boards when I walk on the bridge over the water.
4. Every six months, the city ________ organizes a day for volunteers to pick up trash and work in the gardens.
5. Last time, the cleanup day followed a parade, and someone found a ________ from the marching band!
6. The volunteer work ________ the work done by city employees.
7. On the day of the cleanup, each participant receives a T-shirt with a huge oak tree on the back, a _______ of Becker Park.
8. A local restaurant offers free coffee and ________ to the volunteers.
9. The city newspaper always ________ the volunteers' work in the next day's issue.

Next Step: Write two sentences that show your understanding of the words *complement* and *compliment*. Read your sentences aloud to a classmate.

ELPS 5B

720.1
die, dye

Die (dying) means "to stop living." *Dye* (dyeing) is used to change the color of something.

The young girl hoped that her sick goldfish wouldn't die.
My sister dyes her hair with coloring that washes out.

720.2
faint, feign, feint

Faint means "feeble, without strength" or "to fall unconscious." *Feign* is a verb that means "to pretend or make up." *Feint* is a noun that means "a move or an activity that is pretended in order to divert attention."

The actors feigned a sword duel. One man staggered and fell in a feint. The audience gave faint applause.

720.3
farther, further

Farther is used when you are writing about a physical distance. *Further* means "additional."

Alaska reaches farther north than Iceland. For further information, check your local library.

720.4
fewer, less

Fewer refers to the number of separate units; *less* refers to bulk quantity.

I may have less money than you have, but I have fewer worries.

720.5
fir, fur

Fir refers to a type of evergreen tree; *fur* is animal hair.

The Douglas fir tree is named after a Scottish botanist.

An arctic fox has white fur in the winter.

720.6
flair, flare

Flair means "a natural talent" or "style"; *flare* means "to light up quickly" or "burst out" (or an object that does so).

Jenrette has a flair for remaining calm when other people's tempers flare.

720.7
for, four

The preposition *for* means "because of" or "directed to"; *four* is the number 4.

Mary had grilled steaks and chicken for the party, but the dog had stolen one of the four steaks.

ELPS 3E, 5B

Grammar Practice

Using the Right Word 7

- **farther, further; fewer, less; fir, fur; flair, flare; for, four**

For each of the following sentences, write the correct choice from each set of words in parentheses.

Example: Native Americans of the 1700s had a *(flair, flare)* for traveling through deep forests.
flair

1. Today, experienced hikers take compass readings before hiking *(farther, further)* than they've ever been in an unknown forest.
2. They don't want to meet a bear, whose dark, thick *(fir, fur)* can camouflage it in a deep, shadowy forest.
3. Forests in northern Minnesota usually have *(fewer, less)* oak trees than forests in the southern part of the state.
4. Birch, elm, maple, and ash are *(for, four)* common types of trees in Minnesota.
5. In the fall, the brilliant colors of these trees really add *(flair, flare)* to the woods.
6. A *(fir, fur)* is a pine tree with soft, flat needles.
7. Studies show that young trees have *(fewer, less)* resistance to forest fires than old trees.
8. In a forest fire, a burning tree can look like a giant *(flair, flare)*.
9. Scientists seek *(farther, further)* information about forests in order to preserve them.
10. College scholarships are available *(for, four)* those who wish to study forestry.
11. Unfortunately, there are *(fewer, less)* forests worldwide than ever before.

Next Step: Write two sentences about trees to show your understanding of *fewer* and *less*. Share your sentences with a partner.

ELPS 5B

722.1
good, well

Good is an adjective; *well* is nearly always an adverb.

The strange flying machines flew well. (The adverb *well* modifies *flew*.)

They looked good as they flew overhead. (The adjective *good* modifies *they*.)

When used in writing about health, *well* is an adjective.

The pilots did not feel well, however, after the long, hard race.

722.2
hare, hair

A *hare* is an animal similar to a rabbit; *hair* refers to the growth covering the head and body of mammals and human beings.

When a hare darted out in front of our car, the hair on my head stood up.

722.3
heal, heel

Heal means "to mend or restore to health." *Heel* is the back part of a human foot.

I got a blister on my heel from wearing my new shoes. It won't heal unless I wear my old ones.

722.4
hear, here

You *hear* sounds with your ears. *Here* is the opposite of *there* and means "nearby."

722.5
heard, herd

Heard is the past tense of the verb "to hear"; *herd* is a group of animals.

The herd of grazing sheep raised their heads when they heard the collie barking in the distance.

722.6
heir, air

An *heir* is a person who inherits something; *air* is what we breathe.

Will the next generation be heir to terminally polluted air?

722.7
hole, whole

A *hole* is a cavity or hollow place. *Whole* means "entire or complete."

The hole in the ozone layer is a serious problem requiring the attention of the whole world.

722.8
immigrate, emigrate

Immigrate means "to come into a new country or area." *Emigrate* means "to go out of one country to live in another."

Martin Ulferts immigrated to this country in 1882. He was only three years old when he emigrated from Germany.

ELPS 3E, 5B

Grammar Practice

Using the Right Word 8

- good, well; heal, heel; heard, herd; heir, air; hole, whole

For each of the following sentences, write a word from the list above to fill in the blank.

Example: Exercise is __________ for a person's health.
good

1. It can help someone who's out of shape feel ______ again.
2. Some runners say they can get more ______ in their lungs if they run with their mouths open.
3. My _____________ family exercises at least three times a week.
4. We warm up slowly because we know that a pulled muscle takes a long time to ________.
5. Since Lora injured her ________, she is not participating for a while.
6. Exercising when you feel severe pain is usually not a ________ idea.
7. Shea dropped the barbells and put a ________ in the floor.
8. While hiking near his cousin's farm, Denzel ________ some rustling noises.
9. Then he saw a __________ of deer.
10. The team played __________ and won the game.
11. They have a ________ chance of making the play-offs.
12. A person who inherits property is called an ________.
13. Raymond might inherit a ________ bunch of old baseball cards from his grandpa.

Next Step: Write two sentences—one using the word *well* as an adjective and another using the word as an adverb. Read your sentences aloud to a classmate.

ELPS 5B

724.1
imply, infer

Imply means "to suggest indirectly"; *infer* means "to draw a conclusion from facts."

"Since you have to work, may I infer that you won't come to my party?" Guy asked.

"No, I only meant to imply that I would be late," Rochelle responded.

724.2
it's, its

It's is the contraction of "it is." *Its* is the possessive form of "it."

It's a fact that a minnow's teeth are in its throat.

724.3
knew, new

Knew is the past tense of the verb "know." *New* means "recent or modern."

If I knew how to fix it, I would not need a new one!

724.4
know, no

Know means "to recognize or understand." *No* means "the opposite of yes."

Phil, do you know Cheri?

No, I've never met her.

724.5
later, latter

Later means "after a period of time." *Latter* refers to the second of two things mentioned.

The band arrived later and set up the speakers and the lights. The latter made the stage look like a carnival ride.

724.6
lay, lie

Lay means "to place." (*Lay* is a transitive verb; that means it needs a word to complete the meaning.) *Lie* means "to recline." (*Lie* is an intransitive verb.)

Lay your sleeping bag on the floor before you lie down on it. (*Lay* needs the word *bag* to complete its meaning.)

724.7
lead, led

Lead (lēd) is a present tense verb meaning "to guide." The past tense of the verb is *led* (lĕd). The noun *lead* (lĕd) is the metal.

Guides planned to lead the settlers to safe quarters. Instead, they led them into a winter storm.

Peeling paint in old houses may contain lead.

724.8
learn, teach

Learn means "to get information"; *teach* means "to give information."

I want to learn how to sew. Will you teach me?

Grammar Practice

Using the Right Word 9

■ it's, its; lay, lie; lead, led; learn, teach

For each sentence below, write the word "correct" if the underlined word is used correctly. If it is incorrect, write the right word.

Example: Our science teacher said, "Its no secret that I love to challenge students to do their best."
It's

1. A good teacher will learn students more than just school subjects.
2. Classroom visitors usually just lie their coats over the back of a chair.
3. Hahn was selected to lead the students on the field trip through the state forest.
4. I will teach you how to make a sound with your thumbs, your mouth, and a piece of grass.
5. The winner of the race lead all the other runners from the beginning.
6. It's not a very exciting race when that happens.
7. Some paints made before 1978 contain led, which is dangerous if young children eat it.
8. After Shawn saw the museum exhibit, he decided to learn more about spiders.
9. The wolf spider has it's eyes arranged so it can see in all directions at once.
10. This spider will lay very still as it waits for its prey.
11. The female spider lays her eggs in a sac that she carries around with her.

Next Step: *Its* and *it's* can be challenging words to use correctly. Write two sentences that show you understand their meanings.

ELPS 5B

726.1 leave, let

Leave means "fail to take along." *Let* means "allow."

Rozi wanted to leave her boots at home, but Jorge wouldn't let her.

726.2 like, as

Like is a preposition meaning "similar to"; *as* is a conjunction meaning "to the same degree" or "while." *Like* usually introduces a phrase; *as* usually introduces a clause.

The glider floated like a bird. The glider floated as the pilot had hoped it would.

As we circled the airfield, we saw maintenance carts moving like ants below us.

726.3 loose, lose, loss

Loose (lüs) means "free or untied"; *lose* (lo͞oz) means "to misplace or fail to win"; *loss* (lôs) means "something lost."

These jeans are too loose in the waist since my recent weight loss. I still want to lose a few more pounds.

726.4 made, maid

Made is the past tense of "make," which means to "create," "prepare," or "put in order." A *maid* is a female servant; *maid* is also used to describe an unmarried girl or young woman.

The hotel maid asked if our beds needed to be made.

Grandma made a chocolate cake for dessert.

A maid strolled in the garden before the concert.

726.5 mail, male

Mail refers to letters or packages handled by the postal service. *Male* refers to the masculine sex.

My little brother likes getting junk mail.

The male sea horse, not the female, takes care of the fertilized eggs.

726.6 main, mane

Main refers to the most important part. *Mane* is the long hair growing from the top or sides of the neck of certain animals, such as the horse, lion, and so on.

The main thing we noticed about the magician's tamed lion was its luxurious mane.

726.7 meat, meet

Meat is food or flesh; *meet* means "to come upon or encounter."

I'd like you to meet the butcher who sells the leanest meat in town.

ELPS 3E, 5B

Grammar Practice

Using the Right Word 10

■ **leave, let; like, as; made, maid; mail, male**

For each of the following sentences, write a word from the list above to fill in the blank. Words may be used more than once.

Example: The new post office looks ________ a bank building.
like

1. Some postal workers deliver the ________ while driving a car.
2. On her delivery route, Charlene ________ 120 stops.
3. ________ the snow fell faster, she knew she would not complete her deliveries by 4:00 p.m.
4. The abbreviation "Mr." on a letter refers to a ________.
5. If no one is home, the carrier will ________ a notice about a package.
6. Since Mrs. Wong's young son was eager to put stamps on her letters, she ________ him do it.
7. The hotel ________ found several letters a guest had forgotten on the windowsill.
8. She couldn't just ________ them there, so she dropped them in a mailbox.
9. Kian happily read a letter from his grandmother ________ he walked upstairs to his room.
10. The Pony Express ________ history in the 1800s.
11. In those days, the postal service did not ________ women deliver letters.
12. Fortunately, it's not ________ that today.

Next Step: Write two sentences about getting mail. Use the words *like* and *as*. Share your sentences with a partner.

ELPS 5B

728.1
medal, metal, meddle, mettle

A *medal* is an award. *Metal* is an element like iron or gold. *Meddle* means "to interfere." *Mettle*, a noun, refers to quality of character.

Grandpa's friend received a medal for showing his mettle in battle. Grandma, who loves to meddle in others' business, asked if the award was a precious metal.

728.2
miner, minor

A *miner* digs in the ground for valuable ore. A *minor* is a person who is not legally an adult. *Minor* means "of no great importance" when used as an adjective.

The use of minors as miners is no minor problem.

728.3
moral, morale

Moral relates to what is right or wrong or to the lesson to be drawn from a story. *Morale* refers to a person's attitude or mental condition.

The moral of this story is "Everybody loves a winner."

After the unexpected win at football, morale was high throughout the town.

728.4
morning, mourning

Morning refers to the first part of the day (before noon); *mourning* means "showing sorrow."

Abby was mourning her test grades all morning.

728.5
oar, or, ore

An *oar* is a paddle used in rowing or steering a boat. *Or* is a conjunction indicating choice. *Ore* refers to a mineral made up of several different kinds of material, as in iron ore.

Either use one oar to push us away from the dock, or start the boat's motor.

Silver-copper ore is smelted and refined to extract each metal.

728.6
pain, pane

Pain is the feeling of being hurt. A *pane* is a section or part of something.

Dad looked like he was in pain when he found out we broke a pane of glass in the neighbor's front door.

728.7
pair, pare, pear

A *pair* is a couple (two); *pare* is a verb meaning "to peel"; *pear* is the fruit.

A pair of doves nested in the pear tree.

Please pare the apples for the pie.

ELPS 3E, 5B

Grammar Practice

Using the Right Word 11

- **medal, metal, meddle, mettle; miner, minor; moral, morale; pair, pare, pear**

For each of the following sentences, write the correct choice from each set of words in parentheses.

Example: Gold is used in electrical circuits because it is a *(metal, mettle)* that does not weaken with time.
metal

1. A *(pair, pare, pear)* of contact points is needed to make a simple on/off electrical switch.
2. An electrician will *(pair, pare, pear)* two inches of insulation from a wire before working with it.
3. A line worker shows *(meddle, mettle)* when she or he climbs a tower and begins working on high-voltage power lines.
4. After installing a new outlet, the electrician turned to the *(miner, minor)* problem of replacing a burned-out lightbulb.
5. The employees of Western Hills Electric Power won a *(medal, meddle)* for resource conservation.
6. Many people consider conservation of natural resources to be a *(moral, morale)* issue.
7. A coal *(miner, minor)* rides in a special cage that drops deep into the earth.
8. These workers dig for *(metal, mettle)* ore.
9. As long as working conditions and income are good, the *(moral, morale)* in the mine is good.
10. Thomas decided that he would no longer *(medal, meddle)* in matters that were really his sister's concern.
11. Try an apple or a *(pair, pare, pear)* as an afternoon snack.

Next Step: Write a sentence for each of the following: *medal, meddle, metal, mettle*. Share your best sentence with a partner.

730.1
past, passed

Passed is always a verb; it is the past tense of *pass*. *Past* can be used as a noun, as an adjective, or as a preposition.

A motorcycle passed my dad's 'Vette. (verb)

The old man won't forget the past. (noun)

I'm sorry, but I'd rather not talk about my past life. (adjective)

Old Blue walked right past the cat and never saw it. (preposition)

730.2
peace, piece

Peace means "harmony, or freedom from war." A *piece* is a part or fragment of something.

In order to keep peace among the triplets, each one had to have an identical piece of cake.

730.3
peak, peek, pique

A *peak* is a "high point" or a "pointed end." *Peek* means "brief look." *Pique*, as a verb, means "to excite by challenging"; as a noun, it means "a feeling of resentment."

Just a peek at Pike's Peak in the Rocky Mountains can pique a mountain climber's curiosity.

In a pique, she marched away from her giggling sisters.

730.4
personal, personnel

Personal means "private." *Personnel* are people working at a job.

Some thoughts are too personal to share.

The personnel manager will be hiring more workers.

730.5
plain, plane

A *plain* is an area of land that is flat or level; it also means "clearly seen or clearly understood" and "ordinary."

It's plain to see why the early settlers had trouble crossing the Great Plains.

Plane means "a flat, level surface" (as in geometry); it is also a tool used to smooth the surface of wood.

When I saw that the door wasn't a perfect plane, I used a plane to make it smooth.

730.6
pore, pour, poor

A *pore* is an opening in the skin. *Pour* means "to cause a flow or stream." *Poor* means "needy."

People perspire through the pores in their skin. Pour yourself a glass of water. Your poor body needs it!

Grammar Practice

Using the Right Word 12

- **past, passed; peace, piece; peak, peek, pique; plain, plane; pore, pour, poor**

For each numbered sentence below, write the word "correct" if the underlined word is used correctly. If it is incorrect, write the right word.

Example: Mr. Johnson decided his front walk was in <u>pore</u> condition.
poor

(1) During the <u>passed</u> week, Mr. Jackson replaced his front walk. **(2)** He smashed the old concrete with a sledgehammer until he could pick up each <u>peace</u> with one hand. **(3)** Some neighbors heard the noise and <u>peaked</u> out their windows to see what he was doing. **(4)** At last he was done hammering, and <u>peace</u> returned to the neighborhood.

(5) Mr. Jackson needed help to <u>poor</u> the new cement, so he asked his neighbor, Mr. Gupta. **(6)** <u>Poor</u> Mr. Gupta—he didn't know what he was getting into! **(7)** It was a very hot day, and sweat flowed from every <u>poor</u> of his body. **(8)** Mr. Jackson kindly <u>passed</u> Mr. Gupta a glass of cold lemonade.

(9) Finally, Mr. Jackson carefully smoothed the surface of the wet cement until it was a perfect <u>plain</u>. **(10)** Then he stamped a design that looked like <u>peaks</u> and valleys in the wet cement. **(11)** It was <u>plain</u> to see that the new walk would be quite different from the old one! **(12)** As people <u>past</u> his house, they admired his work. It made Mr. Jackson feel proud.

Next Step: Write two sentences about a project you completed that made you feel proud. Use two of the following words: *past, piece, poor,* and *peak*. Read your sentences aloud to a classmate.

ELPS 5B

732.1
principal, principle

As an adjective, *principal* means "primary." As a noun, it can mean "a school administrator" or "a sum of money." *Principle* means "idea or doctrine."

> **My mom's principal goal is to save money so she can pay off the principal balance on her loan from the bank.**
>
> **Hey, Charlie, I hear the principal gave you a detention.**
>
> **The principle of freedom is based on the principle of self-discipline.**

732.2
quiet, quit, quite

Quiet is the opposite of "noisy." *Quit* means "to stop." *Quite* means "completely or entirely."

> **I quit mowing even though I wasn't quite finished.**
>
> **The neighborhood was quiet again.**

732.3
raise, rays, raze

Raise is a verb meaning "to lift or elevate." *Rays* are thin lines or beams. *Raze* is a verb that means "to tear down completely."

> **When I raise this shade, bright rays of sunlight stream into the room.**
>
> **Construction workers will raze the old theater to make room for a parking lot.**

732.4
real, very, really

Do not use the adjective *real* in place of the adverbs *very* or *really*.

> **The plants scattered throughout the restaurant are not real.**
>
> **Hiccups are very embarrassing.**
>
> **Her nose is really small.**

732.5
red, read

Red is a color; *read*, pronounced the same way, is the past tense of the verb meaning "to understand the meaning of written words and symbols."

> **"I've read five books in two days," said the little boy.**
>
> **The librarian gave him a red ribbon.**

Grammar Practice

Using the Right Word 13

- principal, principle; quiet, quit, quite; raise, rays, raze; real, very, really

For each of the following sentences, write the correct choice from each set of words in parentheses.

Example: While Hugh Jackman is a *(real, really)* person, Wolverine is not.
real

1. Sal wanted to *(quit, quite)* the soccer team, but her mom insisted she play until the end of the season.
2. Tomas heard his parents talking about paying off the *(principal, principle)* on their loan.
3. The sun's *(raise, rays)* finally burst through the heavy cloud cover.
4. City crews will have to *(raise, raze)* the storm-damaged park shelter.
5. Ms. Show said that we must be *(quiet, quite)* during tests.
6. She said, "The *(principal, principle)* reason for my request is so that no one disturbs anyone else."
7. After playing in the snow for several hours, the boys admitted they were *(real, very)* cold.
8. Since there aren't *(quiet, quite)* enough books for everyone in the class, some kids must share.
9. I can better control my anger if I do not *(raise, raze)* my voice.
10. One *(principal, principle)* to live by is "honesty is the best policy."
11. Evan's shoes got *(real, really)* wet as he walked through the deep, dew-covered grass.

Next Step: Write two sentences that show your understanding of *real, really,* and *very*. Share your sentences with a partner.

ELPS 5B

734.1
right, write, rite

Right means "correct or proper"; *right* is the opposite of "left"; it also refers to anything that a person has a legal claim to, as in "copyright." *Write* means "to record in print." *Rite* is a ritual or ceremonial act.

We have to write an essay about how our rights are protected by the Constitution.

Turn right at the next corner.

A rite of passage is a ceremony that celebrates becoming an adult.

734.2
scene, seen

Scene refers to the setting or location where something happens; it also means "sight or spectacle." *Seen* is a form of the verb "see."

The scene of the crime was roped off. We hadn't seen anyone go in or out of the building.

734.3
seam, seem

A *seam* is a line formed by connecting two pieces of material. *Seem* means "appear to exist."

Every Thanksgiving, it seems, I stuff myself so much that my shirt seams threaten to burst.

734.4
sew, so, sow

Sew is a verb meaning "to stitch"; *so* is a conjunction meaning "in order that." The verb *sow* means "to plant."

In Colonial times, the wife would sew the family clothes, and the husband would sow the family garden so the children could eat.

734.5
sight, cite, site

Sight means "the act of seeing" or "something that is seen." *Cite* means "to quote or refer to." A *site* is a location or position (including a Web site on the Internet).

The Alamo at night was a sight worth the trip. I was also able to cite my visit to this historical site in my history paper.

734.6
sit, set

Sit means "to put the body in a seated position." *Set* means "to place." (*Set* is a transitive verb; that means it needs a direct object to complete its meaning.)

How can you just sit there and watch as I set up all these chairs?

Grammar Practice

Using the Right Word 14

■ **right, write, rite; seam, seem; sew, so, sow; sight, cite, site**

For each sentence below, write the word "correct" if the underlined word is used correctly. If it is incorrect, write the right word.

Example: All the computers in the lab seam slow today.
seem

1. Whenever the lab gets a new computer, the computer club has a special rite of initiation.
2. Some computer screen savers are quite a site.
3. Jamal likes using a computer to right letters to his grandmother.
4. Can you find the Write Source Web sight?
5. My computer had crashed, so the teacher restarted it.
6. When you write research reports, make sure you correctly site information from the Internet.
7. Nathan didn't think the Web site's information was rite.
8. Being allowed to enter a chat room is a right of passage for some people.
9. A chat room makes it seam like you're right there talking to someone.
10. Our teacher showed us how to sow a simple case to hold CD's.
11. I stitched the seam twice to make it superstrong.
12. A computer can help a farmer determine the proper time to sew seeds.
13. It can also specify the best site for each crop.

Next Step: Write two sentences that show your understanding of the words *cite* and *site*. Read your sentences aloud to a classmate.

ELPS 5B

736.1
sole, soul

Sole means "single, only one"; *sole* also refers to the bottom surface of a foot or shoe. *Soul* refers to the spiritual part of a person.

Maggie got a job for the sole purpose of saving for a car.

The soles of these shoes are very thick.

"Who told you dogs don't have souls?" asked the kind veterinarian.

736.2
some, sum

Some means "an unknown number or part." *Sum* means "the whole amount."

The sum in the cash register was stolen by some thieves.

736.3
sore, soar

Sore means "painful"; to *soar* means "to rise or fly high into the air."

Craning to watch the eagle soar overhead, we soon had sore necks.

736.4
stationary, stationery

Stationary means "not movable"; *stationery* is the paper and envelopes used to write letters.

Grandpa designed and printed his own stationery.

All of the built-in furniture is stationary, of course.

736.5
steal, steel

Steal means "to take something without permission"; *steel* is a metal.

Early iron makers had to steal recipes for producing steel.

736.6
than, then

Than is used in a comparison; *then* tells when.

Since tomorrow's weather is supposed to be nicer than today's, we'll go to the zoo then.

736.7
their, there, they're

Their is a possessive pronoun, one that shows ownership. (See 766.2.) *There* is an adverb that tells where. *They're* is the contraction for "they are."

They're upset because their dog got into the garbage over there.

736.8
threw, through

Threw is the past tense of "throw." *Through* means "passing from one side to the other" or "by means of."

Through sheer talent and long practice, Nolan Ryan threw baseballs through the strike zone at more than 100 miles per hour.

Grammar Practice

Using the Right Word 15

- **sole, soul; stationary, stationery; than, then; their, there, they're; threw, through**

For each of the following sentences, write the correct choice from each set of words in parentheses.

Example: The *(sole, soul)* of the boot was completely worn out.
sole

1. With only one play left to win the game, the quarterback *(threw, through)* the ball as far as he could.
2. The scouts set up *(their, they're)* tents in a clearing in the forest.
3. Rain began to fall, and *(than, then)* the temperature dropped and turned the rain to snow.
4. Some superheroes can see *(threw, through)* walls.
5. Sanjay, please put that box of books over *(their, there)*.
6. Hoping to strengthen his injured leg, Frank plans to pedal a *(stationary, stationery)* bike for 30 minutes a day.
7. This year, students have to attend school later in June *(than, then)* they did last year.
8. Many people feel that music is good for the *(sole, soul)*.
9. Tonya writes letters on homemade *(stationary, stationery)*.
10. When Mom and Dad get home from work, *(there, they're)* often exhausted.
11. I would rather read a good book *(than, then)* watch daytime television any day.
12. Am I the *(sole, soul)* book lover in this class?

Next Step: Write a sentence that shows your understanding of the words *than* and *they're*. Exchange papers with a classmate and check each other's sentences.

ELPS 5B

738.1
to, too, two

To is the preposition that can mean "in the direction of." (*To* also is used to form an infinitive. See **780.4**.) *Too* is an adverb meaning "very or excessive." *Too* is often used to mean "also." *Two* is the number 2.

Only two of Columbus's first three ships returned to Spain from the New World.

Columbus was too restless to stay in Spain for long.

738.2
vain, vane, vein

Vain means "worthless." It may also mean "thinking too highly of one's self; stuck-up." *Vane* is a flat piece of material set up to show which way the wind blows. *Vein* refers to a blood vessel or a mineral deposit.

The weather vane indicates the direction of wind.

A blood vein determines the direction of flowing blood.

The vain mind moves in no particular direction and thinks only about itself.

738.3
vary, very

Vary is a verb that means "to change." *Very* can be an adjective meaning "in the fullest sense" or "complete"; it can also be an adverb meaning "extremely."

Garon's version of the event would vary from day to day. His very interesting story was the very opposite of the truth.

738.4
waist, waste

Waist is the part of the body just above the hips. The verb *waste* means "to wear away" or "to use carelessly"; the noun *waste* refers to material that is unused or useless.

Don't waste your money on fast-food meals. What a waste to throw away all this food because you're concerned about the size of your waist!

738.5
wait, weight

Wait means "to stay somewhere expecting something." *Weight* is the measure of heaviness.

When I have to wait for the bus, the weight of my backpack seems to keep increasing.

738.6
ware, wear, where

Ware means "a product to be sold"; *wear* means "to have on or to carry on one's body"; *where* asks the question "in what place or in what situation?"

Where can you buy the best cookware to take on a campout—and the best rain gear to wear if it rains?

Grammar Practice

Using the Right Word 16

■ vain, vane, vein; **waist, waste;** wait, weight; **ware, wear, where**

For each of the following sentences, write the correct choice from each set of words in parentheses.

Example: If people need blood in an emergency, they should not have to *(wait, weight)* for it.
wait

1. People may boast about how much blood they give, yet it is not something to be *(vain, vane, vein)* about.
2. Sometimes a nurse who needs to draw some blood searches in *(vain, vane, vein)* for a usable blood vessel.
3. A *(vain, vane, vein)* carries blood from cells back to the heart.
4. The lungs are the place *(ware, wear, where)* blood picks up oxygen.
5. The circulatory system carries some *(waist, waste)* products to the kidneys, which are located near the *(waist, waste)* toward the back of the body.
6. A person's *(wait, weight)* can affect his or her blood pressure.
7. Some medical equipment shows the direction of blood flow like a weather *(vain, vane, vein)* shows the direction of the wind.
8. The hard *(ware, wear, where)* used for blood transfusions can be costly.
9. Red blood cells eventually *(ware, wear, where)* out.
10. Fortunately, healthy people don't have to *(wait, weight)* long for their bones to replace worn-out blood cells.
11. Since the bones continually produce new blood cells, people do not *(waist, waste)* their own blood by donating it.

Next Step: Pick two or three of the words used above that sometimes confuse you. Write a sentence for each word. Read your sentences aloud to a classmate.

ELPS 5B

740.1 **way, weigh**

Way means "path or route" or "a series of actions." *Weigh* means "to measure weight."

What is the correct way to weigh liquid medicines?

740.2 **weather, whether**

Weather refers to the condition of the atmosphere. *Whether* refers to a possibility.

The weather will determine whether I go fishing.

740.3 **week, weak**

A *week* is a period of seven days; *weak* means "not strong."

Last week when I had the flu, I felt light-headed and weak.

740.4 **wet, whet**

Wet means "soaked with liquid." *Whet* is a verb that means "to sharpen."

Of course, going swimming means I'll get wet, but all that exercise really whets my appetite.

740.5 **which, witch**

Which is a pronoun used to ask "what one or ones?" out of a group. A *witch* is a woman believed to have supernatural powers.

Which of the women in Salem in the 1600s were accused of being witches?

740.6 **who, which, that**

When introducing a clause, *who* is used to refer to people; *which* refers to animals and nonliving beings but never to people (it introduces a nonrestrictive, or unnecessary, clause); *that* usually refers to animals or things but can refer to people (it introduces a restrictive, or necessary, clause).

The idea that pizza is junk food is crazy.

Pizza, which is quite nutritious, can be included in a healthful diet.

My mom, who is a dietician, said so.

740.7 **who, whom**

Who is used as the subject in a sentence; *whom* is used as the object of a preposition or as a direct object.

Who asked you to play tennis?

You beat whom at tennis? You played tennis with whom?

NOTE To test for who/whom, arrange the parts of the clause in a subject–verb–direct-object order. *Who* works as the subject, *whom* as the object. (See page 632.)

Grammar Practice

Using the Right Word 17

- **weather, whether; wet, whet; who, which, that; who, whom**

For the following sentences, write a word from the list above to fill in each blank.

Example: "Have you heard today's ____________ forecast?" Jay asked.
weather

1. Steve said, "I did, but I don't know __________ you should get out your skis or not."
2. Last night, Vince Stevens, the meteorologist ________ I usually trust, forecasted clouds but no snow.
3. The forecast ______ is in today's paper, however, predicts heavy, _____ snow.
4. Just thinking about the possibility of a snowstorm will _______ my desire to go skiing.
5. My new skis, ________ I received as a gift, are ready to go!
6. Aunt Winnie, _______ is as big a ski nut as I am, gave them to me for my birthday.
7. Unlike some other athletes, people _______ ski really have to rely on the right ________.
8. The idea ________ I might get to ski today sure is a nice one!
9. __________ or not it snows today, I guess I'll get my gear ready.

Next Step: Write two sentences that show your understanding of the words *who* and *whom*. Share your sentences with a partner.

ELPS 5B

742.1
who's, whose

Who's is the contraction for "who is." *Whose* is a possessive pronoun, one that shows ownership.

Who's the most popular writer today?

Whose bike is this?

742.2
wood, would

Wood is the material that comes from trees; *would* is a form of the verb "will."

Sequoia trees live practically forever, but would you believe that the wood from these giants is practically useless?

742.3
your, you're

Your is a possessive pronoun, one that shows ownership. *You're* is the contraction for "you are."

You're the most important person in your parents' lives.

Grammar Practice

Using the Right Word 18

■ **who's, whose; wood, would; your, you're**

For each of the following sentences, write the correct choice from each set of words in parentheses.

1. *(Whose, Who's)* book is this?
2. The math teacher said that *(your, you're)* the only one who got an *A* on the test.
3. Danica has a pen that's made of *(wood, would).*
4. Dominic, *(whose, who's)* dad is from Italy, speaks Italian.
5. Excuse me, I think you dropped *(your, you're)* calculator.
6. *(Whose, Who's)* going to the basketball game Friday night?
7. I *(wood, would)* go, but I have to baby-sit for my neighbors.

Using the Right Word Review

For each of the following sentences, write the correct choice from each set of words in parentheses.

1. Sanford plays football *(real, very) (good, well).*
2. Shalonda *(heard, herd)* a blue jay this morning.
3. They are noisier *(than, then)* the other birds by her window.
4. I found the missing items *(altogether, all together)* in one place.
5. Donovan puts his homework *(besides, beside)* his shoes so he doesn't forget it.
6. My old dog loves to *(lay, lie)* right on top of a heat vent.
7. This large, empty lot is the *(sight, cite, site)* where the town will *(billed, build)* the new middle school.
8. A peregrine falcon flew *(among, between)* two trees.
9. After 20 minutes had *(past, passed)*, Barry stopped counting the *(amount, number)* of concrete blocks he had to load on the truck.

Understanding Sentences

Sentences

A **sentence** is a group of words that expresses a complete thought. A sentence must have both a subject and a predicate. A sentence begins with a capital letter; it ends with a period, a question mark, or an exclamation point.

I like my teacher this year.

Will we go on a field trip?

We get to go to the water park!

Parts of a Sentence

744.1 Subjects

A subject is the part of a sentence that does something or is talked about.

The kids on my block play basketball at the local park.

We meet after school almost every day.

744.2 Simple Subjects

The simple subject is the subject without the words that describe or modify it. (Also see page 564.)

My friend Chester plays basketball on the school team.

744.3 Complete Subjects

The complete subject is the simple subject and all the words that modify it. (Also see page 563.)

My friend Chester plays basketball on the school team.

744.4 Compound Subjects

A compound subject has two or more simple subjects. (See page 564.)

Chester, Malik, and Meshelle play on our pickup team.

Lou and I are the best shooters.

Practice

Parts of a Sentence 1

Simple, Complete, and Compound Subjects

For each numbered sentence in the paragraphs below, write the complete subject. Then circle the simple subject or the compound subject. (*Remember:* Compound sentences have two subjects.)

Example: Car problems made me late for school.
Car problems

(1) I was on my way to school in my dad's car. **(2)** Suddenly, a light mist came from the vents, and an odd, sweet smell filled the car. **(3)** Dad pulled over and called a tow truck. **(4)** Thinking about yet another trip to the repair shop, he sighed deeply.

(5) A mechanic at the repair shop took a look at the engine. **(6)** Cars are so complex these days! **(7)** How does the mechanic know what to look for? **(8)** In most cases, training programs prepare mechanics for their work. **(9)** A two-year degree from a technical college is required for employment at many automobile dealerships. **(10)** Today's cars call for special training on computerized shop equipment. **(11)** Additionally, mechanics need some knowledge of electronics. **(12)** Of course, they must also work with traditional hand tools. **(13)** Besides a complete knowledge of automobiles, a good mechanic also needs the ability to solve problems.

(14) Dad's mechanic gave him the news. **(15)** "The problem is probably with the heater core." **(16)** Poor, stressed-out Dad had the repair shop fix his car . . . again.

Next Step: Write two sentences about a career that interests you. Exchange papers with a classmate. Underline your partner's complete subjects and circle the simple (or compound) subjects.

Parts of a Sentence . . .

746.1
Predicates

The predicate, which contains the verb, is the part of the sentence that shows action or says something about the subject.

Hunting has reduced the tiger population in India.

746.2
Simple Predicates

The simple predicate is the predicate (verb) without the words that describe or modify it. (See page 564.)

In the past, poachers killed too many African elephants.
Poaching is illegal.

746.3
Complete Predicates

The complete predicate is the simple predicate with all the words that modify or describe it. (See page 563.)

In the past, poachers killed too many African elephants.
Poaching is illegal.

746.4
Direct Objects

The complete predicate often includes a direct object. The direct object is the noun or pronoun that receives the action of the simple predicate—directly. The direct object answers the question *what* or *whom*. (See page 632.)

Many smaller animals need friends who will speak up for them.

The direct object may be compound.

We all need animals, plants, wetlands, deserts, and forests.

746.5
Indirect Objects

If a sentence has a direct object, it may also have an indirect object. An indirect object is the noun or pronoun that receives the action of the simple predicate—indirectly. An indirect object names the person *to whom* or *for whom* something is done. (See page 632.)

I showed the class my multimedia report on endangered species. (*Class* is the indirect object because it says *to whom* the report was shown.)

Remember, in order for a sentence to have an indirect object, it must first have a direct object.

746.6
Compound Predicates

A compound predicate is composed of two or more simple predicates. (See page 564.)

In 1990 the countries of the world met and banned the sale of ivory.

Practice

Parts of a Sentence 2

- Simple, Compound, and Complete Predicates
- Direct and Indirect Objects

For each numbered sentence below, write the complete predicate. (*Remember:* Compound or complex sentences will have two.) Underline any direct objects once and indirect objects twice.

Example: Some people innocently plant weeds.
innocently plant weeds

(1) Kudzu is a vine found in the southern states. **(2)** The climate there encourages the vine's rapid growth—as much as a foot per day! **(3)** The vine climbs trees, signposts, and barns. **(4)** It covers anything in its way.

(5) For Philadelphia's 1876 U.S. Centennial Exposition, the Japanese government created a delightful garden. **(6)** Japanese gardeners sold people the lush, sweet-smelling vine.

(7) Kudzu helped prevent soil erosion, so people planted the vine throughout the South. **(8)** Kudzu now covers seven million acres of land in the region. **(9)** Unfortunately, the thick vines prevent trees from getting sunlight, and valuable forests are dying as a result.

Learning Language **Just as a predicate can be compound, having two or more parts, so can direct objects and indirect objects. A compound direct object is more than one noun, pronoun, or group of words that receives the action of the simple predicate.**

The torrential rains flooded highways and town roads.

Work with a partner to write 3–4 sentences that contain compound direct objects. Take turns reading the sentences aloud.

Parts of a Sentence . . .

748.1
Understood Subjects and Predicates

Either the subject or the predicate (or both) may not be stated in a sentence, but both must be clearly understood.

> [You] **Get involved!** (*You* is the understood subject.)
>
> **Who needs your help? Animals** [do]. (*Do* is the understood predicate.)
>
> **What do many animals face?** [They face] **Extinction.** (*They* is the understood subject, and *face* is the understood predicate.)

748.2
Delayed Subjects

In sentences that begin with *there* followed by a "be" verb, the subject usually follows the verb. (See page 632.)

> **There are** laws **that protect endangered species.** (The subject is *laws; are* is the verb.)

The subject is also delayed in questions.

> **How can** we **preserve the natural habitat?** (*We* is the subject.)

SCHOOL DAZE
John, I've got all the projects. Now which one is yours?
I'm not sure. See if there's one with a missing piece.

748.3
Modifiers

A modifier is a word (adjective, adverb) or a group of words (phrase, clause) that changes or adds to the meaning of another word. (See pages 546–553.)

> Many North American **zoos and aquariums** voluntarily **participate** in breeding programs that help prevent extinction.

The modifiers in this sentence include the following: *many, North American* (adjectives), *voluntarily* (adverb), *in breeding programs* (phrase), *that help prevent extinction* (clause).

Practice

Parts of a Sentence 3

Understood Subjects and Predicates

For the answer to each question below, write the word or words that are not stated but are understood. Identify them as "subject," "predicate," or "both."

Example: *How do we get to Turner Road?*
Turn right at the first stoplight. *You (subject)*

1. *Who is the substitute teacher today?*
   Mr. Ross.
2. *When is our next test?*
   Friday.
3. *May I go outside after lunch?*
   Yes.
4. *How do I cut this?*
   Use a pair of scissors.
5. *What has been added to this popcorn?*
   Oil, butter, and salt.
6. *What did Marva get from Johnny?*
   A box of chocolates.

Delayed Subjects

Rewrite each of the following sentences so that the subject is not delayed.

Example: Would you like to go for a walk?
You would like to go for a walk.

1. Is that a Siamese cat?
2. May I ride my bike to the arcade?
3. Are we having dinner with the Thorsens tonight?
4. After the movie, will Marcus need a ride home?

TEKS 7.19A(iii), 7.19B

Parts of a Sentence . . .

750.1 Clauses

A clause is a group of related words that has both a subject and a verb. (Also see pages 575–577.)

a whole chain of plants and animals is affected
(*Chain* is the subject, and *is affected* is the verb.)

when one species dies out completely
(*Species* is the subject; *dies out* is the verb.)

750.2 Independent Clauses

An independent clause presents a complete thought and can stand alone as a sentence.

This ancient oak tree may be cut down.

This act could affect more than 200 different species of animals!

Why would anyone want that to happen?

750.3 Dependent Clauses

A dependent clause does not present a complete thought and cannot stand as a sentence. A dependent clause *depends* on being connected to an independent clause to make sense. Dependent clauses begin with either a subordinating conjunction *(after, although, because, before, if)* or a relative pronoun *(who, whose, which, that)*. (See pages 762 and 792 for complete lists.)

If this ancient oak tree is cut down, **it could affect more than 200 different species of animals!**

The tree, which experts think could be 400 years old, **provides a home to many different kinds of birds and insects.**

750.4 Adverbial Clauses

An adverbial clause is a clause that acts as an adverb. It contains a subject and a verb and modifies a verb.

Samuel gave me a call when he arrived at the airport.

750.5 Adjectival Clauses

An adjectival clause is always introduced by a relative pronoun—*who, whom, which, whose,* or *that.*

The car that she is driving **is brand new.**

Practice

Parts of a Sentence 4

- Clauses

Some "sentences" in the following paragraphs are actually dependent clauses. Combine these clauses with a nearby independent clause to form a complex sentence.

Example: Before a bee is able to make a pound of beeswax. It must eat about 10 pounds of honey.
Before a bee is able to make a pound of beeswax, it must eat about 10 pounds of honey.

(1) There are three types of bees in a colony, including the queen. Who produces the eggs. **(2)** The male bees are called drones. **(3)** The thousands of female worker bees gather nectar, build the cells of a honeycomb, and make and store honey. **(4)** Worker bees also feed the larvae. **(5)** Until they reach mature size.

(6) Bees know where to find food. **(7)** Because they communicate with each other by "dancing" in a certain pattern. **(8)** Most bees get all of their food from flowers. **(9)** Which provide pollen and nectar. **(10)** The nectar is converted to honey. **(11)** When it reaches the bee's digestive tract.

(12) A beekeeper knows how to care for honeybees so that they produce and store more honey than they need. **(13)** The beekeeper collects the excess honey. **(14)** After the bees have been made sleepy with smoke. **(15)** The bees can then refill the honeycombs, or the beekeeper might melt the honeycomb. **(16)** If she or he wants to use the beeswax.

Next Step: In two columns labeled "relative pronouns" and "subordinating conjunctions," write all of the words that begin the dependent clauses in the paragraphs above.

TEKS 7.19A(iii)

Parts of a Sentence . . .

752.1
Phrases

A phrase is a group of related words that lacks either a subject or a predicate (or both). (See pages 581–582.)

guards the house (The predicate lacks a subject.)

the ancient oak tree (The subject lacks a predicate.)

with crooked old limbs (The phrase lacks both a subject and a predicate.)

The ancient oak tree with crooked old limbs guards the house. (Together, the three phrases form a complete thought.)

752.2
Types of Phrases

Phrases usually take their names from the main words that introduce them (prepositional phrase, noun phrase, verb phrase).

The ancient oak tree (noun phrase)

with crooked old limbs (prepositional phrase)

has stood its guard, (verb phrase)

protecting the little house. (verbal phrase)

Phrases are also named for the function they serve in a sentence (adjectival phrase, adverbial phrase, appositive phrase). An adjectival phrase is a kind of prepositional phrase that modifies a noun or pronoun by telling what kind or which one.

The cat with the short, stubby tail slinked down the alley.

An adverbial phrase is a kind of prepositional phrase that modifies a verb or adverb by telling where, when, or in what way.

The canary flew into the bright blue sky.

An appositive is a noun of pronoun placed after another noun or pronoun to identify or rename the first noun.

The dog, a Golden Retriever, lifted the newspaper in its teeth.

Practice

Parts of a Sentence 5

Phrases

Combine each of the following groups of phrases to write a sentence that forms a complete thought.

Example: of water and land — animals called amphibians — are creatures

Animals called amphibians are creatures of water and land.

1. belong in this classification
salamanders, toads, frogs, and newts

2. to the water
on land
is clear
but their connection
spend most of their lives
these animals

3. will slowly dry out
without a moist environment
any amphibian
a fragile creature

4. in addition, they
need water
to lay their eggs

5. in body shape
go through a change
most amphibians

6. is probably
the everyday frog
the best-known example
with its green skin

7. a frog
in the water
as a tadpole
begins life

8. develops legs and lungs
a baby frog
during its growth period
the tadpole

9. onto land
a fully developed frog
will crawl
at last

Next Step: Label each of the phrases in numbers 3, 6, 7, 8, and 9 above as a "noun phrase," "verb phrase," "adverbial phrase," "adjectival phrase," or "appositive phrase."

Using the Parts of Speech

Nouns

A **noun** is a word that names a person, a place, a thing, or an idea.

Person: **John Ulferts** (uncle) Thing: **"Yankee Doodle"** (song)
Place: **Mississippi** (state) Idea: **Labor Day** (holiday)

Kinds of Nouns

754.1 **Common Nouns**

A common noun is any noun that does not name a specific person, place, thing, or idea. These nouns are not capitalized.

woman **museum** **book** **weekend**

754.2 **Proper Nouns**

A proper noun is the name of a specific person, place, thing, or idea. Proper nouns are capitalized.

Hillary Clinton **Central Park** ***Maniac McGee*** **Sunday**

754.3 **Concrete Nouns**

A concrete noun names a thing that is physical (can be touched or seen). Concrete nouns can be either proper or common.

space station **pencil** **Statue of Liberty**

754.4 **Abstract Nouns**

An abstract noun names something you can think about but cannot see or touch. Abstract nouns can be either common or proper.

Judaism **poverty** **satisfaction** **illness**

754.5 **Collective Nouns**

A collective noun names a group or collection of persons, animals, places, or things.

Persons: **tribe, congregation, family, class, team**
Animals: **flock, herd, gaggle, clutch, litter**
Things: **batch, cluster, bunch**

754.6 **Compound Nouns**

A compound noun is made up of two or more words.

football (written as one word)
high school (written as two words)
brother-in-law (written as a hyphenated word)

Grammar Practice

Nouns 1

Kinds of Nouns

Write the answers to the questions following each paragraph.

After 300 years of Spanish rule, Mexico gained its independence in 1810. Like the United States, Mexico is a federal republic headed by a president. The country is divided into 31 states.

Which of the underlined nouns is . . .

1. a common, concrete noun?
2. a common, abstract noun?
3. a proper, concrete noun?

The population of the entire country is nearly 105 million. A full 89 percent of the people are Roman Catholics. The country's official language is Spanish.

Which of the underlined nouns is . . .

4. a collective noun?
5. a proper, abstract noun?
6. a proper, concrete noun?

Mexico's geography ranges from mountains to desert to low coastal plains. As a result, its climate also varies; there are hot, temperate, and cool regions. Mexico can be an enjoyable place for a family to vacation.

Which of the underlined nouns is . . .

7. a proper, concrete noun?
8. a collective noun?
9. a common, abstract noun?
10. a common, concrete noun?

Nouns . . .

Number of Nouns

The number of a noun is either singular or plural.

756.1 Singular Nouns

A singular noun names one person, place, thing, or idea.

boy **group** **audience** **stage** **concert** **hope**

756.2 Plural Nouns

A plural noun names more than one person, place, thing, or idea.

boys **groups** **audiences** **stages** **concerts** **hopes**

Gender of Nouns

756.3 Noun Gender

Nouns are grouped according to gender: *feminine, masculine, neuter,* and *indefinite*.

Feminine (female): **mother, sister, women, cow, hen**

Masculine (male): **father, brother, men, bull, rooster**

Neuter (neither male nor female): **tree, cobweb, closet**

Indefinite (male or female): **president, duckling, doctor**

Uses of Nouns

756.4 Subject Nouns

A noun that is the subject of a sentence does something or is talked about in the sentence.

The roots of rap can be traced back to West Africa and Jamaica.

756.5 Predicate Nouns

A predicate noun follows a form of the *be* verb *(am, is, are, was, were, being, been)* and renames the subject.

In the 1970s, rap was a street art.

756.6 Possessive Nouns

A possessive noun shows possession or ownership.

Early rap had a drummer's beat but no music.

The rapper's words are set to music.

756.7 Object Nouns

A noun is an object noun when it is used as the direct object, the indirect object, or the object of the preposition.

Some rappers tell people their story about life in the city. (indirect object: *people;* direct object: *story*)

Rap is now a common music choice in this country. (object of the preposition: *country*)

Grammar Practice

Nouns 2

Number and Gender of Nouns

Draw a chart like the one below. Classify the underlined nouns in the following paragraph by writing them in the correct box.

Gender	Singular	Plural
feminine		
masculine		*men*
neuter		
indefinite		

Antarctica was a continent without men or women until explorers and researchers from other parts of the world arrived. Only penguins and seals lived on the land. In December 1911, Roald Amundsen and four other men made their way across Antarctica using skis and dogsleds. They were the first people to reach the South Pole, which is the point in the earth's southern hemisphere where all the lines of longitude start. The group traveled quickly across snow and mountains. When they reached the pole, they set up the Norwegian flag. A month later, a team led by British explorer Robert Scott arrived at the South Pole. It wasn't until 1969, however, that the first woman reached the pole.

Uses of Nouns

Number your paper from 1 to 4. List each underlined noun from the following paragraph and identify it as a "subject noun," a "predicate noun," a "possessive noun," or an "object noun."

Example: Twelve nations signed the International Antarctic Treaty in 1961.
nations, subject noun

The treaty's rules say that people can use Antarctica only for peaceful purposes. The rules also promise freedom to do scientific study. Today, many countries have permanent research stations in Antarctica, and about 4,000 people are full-time residents during its summer months.

TEKS 7.19A(vi), 7.19C

Pronouns

A **pronoun** is a word used in place of a noun. Some examples are *I, you, he, she, it, we, they, his, hers, her, its, me, myself, us, yours,* and so on.

Without pronouns: **Kevin said Kevin would be going to Kevin's grandmother's house this weekend.**

With pronouns: **Kevin said he would be going to his grandmother's house this weekend.**

758.1 Antecedents

An antecedent is the noun that the pronoun refers to or replaces. All pronouns (except interrogative and indefinite pronouns) have antecedents. (See page 534.)

Jamal and Rick tried out for the team, and they both made it.
(*They* refers to *Jamal* and *Rick; it* refers to *team.*)

NOTE Pronouns must agree with their antecedents in number, person, and gender. (See pages 537–538.)

Types of Pronouns

There are several types of pronouns. The most common type is the personal pronoun. (See the chart on page 762.)

758.2 Personal Pronouns

A personal pronoun takes the place of a specific person (or thing) in a sentence. Some common personal pronouns are *I, you, he, she, it, we,* and *they*.

Suriana would not like to live in Buffalo, New York, because she does not like snow.

758.3 Relative Pronouns

A relative pronoun is both a pronoun and a connecting word. It connects a dependent clause to an independent clause in a complex sentence. Relative pronouns include *who, whose, which,* and *that*. (See page 576 and 740.6.)

Buffalo, which often gets more than eight feet of snow in a year, is on the northeast shore of Lake Erie.

The United States city that gets the most snow is Valdez, Alaska.

758.4 Interrogative Pronouns

An interrogative pronoun helps ask a question.

Who wants to go to Alaska?

Which of the cities would you visit?

Whom would you like to travel with?

What did you say?

Grammar Practice

Pronouns 1

Personal, Relative, and Interrogative Pronouns

For each of the following sentences, identify the underlined pronouns as "personal," "relative," or "interrogative."

Example: Great horned owls, which are the second-largest owls in North America, rely on their night vision to find prey in the dark.

relative

1. An owl near Madison, Wisconsin, was starving in the wild because it had gone blind.
2. Who was brave enough to capture the creature?
3. Sue Theys, the woman who netted the owl, suspected that it had cataracts.
4. She and her husband took the owl to the veterinarian.
5. What does a vet do when an owl can't see?
6. Dr. Chris Murphy, a veterinary eye doctor, decided that he could perform surgery on the bird.
7. Dr. Murphy supervised two other doctors, and they implanted a pair of contact lenses into the bird's eyes.
8. Whose were they?
9. The lenses were originally made for another owl that ended up not having the surgery.
10. The Theyses gave the bird antibiotics and fed it mice during its recovery.
11. The great horned owl, whose wingspan can reach 55 inches, eats a variety of other animals.

Next Step: Go back to the previous sentences and write the antecedent for each of the personal and relative pronouns.

Pronouns . . .

Types of Pronouns

760.1
Demonstrative Pronouns

A demonstrative pronoun points out or identifies a noun without naming the noun. When used together in a sentence, *this* and *that* distinguish one item from another, and *these* and *those* distinguish one group from another. (See page 762.)

> This is a great idea; that was a nightmare.
>
> These are my favorite foods, and those are definitely not.

NOTE When these words are used before a noun, they are not pronouns; rather, they are demonstrative adjectives.

> Coming to this picnic was fun—and those ants think so, too.

760.2
Intensive Pronouns

An intensive pronoun emphasizes, or *intensifies*, the noun or pronoun it refers to. Common intensive pronouns include *itself, myself, himself, herself,* and *yourself*.

> Though the chameleon's quick-change act protects it from predators, the lizard itself can catch insects 10 inches away with its long, sticky tongue.
>
> When a chameleon changes its skin color—seemingly matching the background—the background colors themselves do not affect the chameleon's color changes.

NOTE These sentences would be complete without the intensive pronoun. The pronoun simply emphasizes a particular noun.

760.3
Reflexive Pronouns

A reflexive pronoun refers back to the subject of a sentence, and it is always an object (never a subject) in a sentence. Reflexive pronouns are the same as the intensive pronouns—*itself, myself, himself, herself, yourself,* and so on.

> A chameleon protects itself from danger by changing colors. (direct object)
>
> A chameleon can give itself tasty meals of unsuspecting insects. (indirect object)
>
> I wish I could claim some of its amazing powers for myself. (object of the preposition)

NOTE Unlike sentences with intensive pronouns, these sentences would *not* be complete without the reflexive pronouns.

Grammar Practice

Pronouns 2

Demonstrative Pronouns

Write whether the underlined word is a demonstrative adjective or a demonstrative pronoun. *Extra Challenge:* Rewrite any sentence that contains a demonstrative adjective, changing the sentence so that the word is used as a pronoun instead.

Example: This cave is deep and dark.
demonstrative adjective
This is a deep and dark cave.

1. That concert was awful.
2. This is my absolute favorite meal!
3. Those are some of the birds I told you about.
4. This diagram is very confusing.
5. That was an unusual discovery.

Intensive Pronouns

Reflexive Pronouns

For each sentence below, write whether the underlined pronoun is "intensive" or "reflexive."

Example: Have you yourself ever tried inventing something?
intensive

1. Many famous inventors have found themselves doing unusual things to prove their points.
2. Even Benjamin Franklin himself, a remarkable inventor, took risks.
3. I myself would be afraid to fly a kite during a lightning storm.
4. A metal wire on the kite drew the lightning's electricity to itself.
5. Mr. Franklin just wanted to prove something to himself.

Pronouns . . .

Types of Pronouns

762.1 Indefinite Pronouns

An indefinite pronoun is a pronoun that does not have a specific antecedent (the noun or pronoun it replaces). (See page 535.)

Everything **about the chameleon is fascinating.**

Someone **donated a chameleon to our class.**

Anyone **who brings in a live insect can feed our chameleon.**

Types of Pronouns

Personal Pronouns

I, me, mine, my, we, us, our, ours, you, your, yours, they, them, their, theirs, he, him, his, she, her, hers, it, its

Relative Pronouns

who, whose, whom, which, what, that, whoever, whomever, whichever, whatever

Interrogative Pronouns

who, whose, whom, which, what

Demonstrative Pronouns

this, that, these, those

Intensive and Reflexive Pronouns

myself, himself, herself, itself, yourself, yourselves, themselves, ourselves

Indefinite Pronouns

all	both	everything	nobody	several
another	each	few	none	some
any	each one	many	no one	somebody
anybody	either	most	nothing	someone
anyone	everybody	much	one	something
anything	everyone	neither	other	such

Grammar Practice

Pronouns 3

- Indefinite Pronouns

Number your paper from 1 to 3. Write the indefinite pronouns that appear in each of the three paragraphs below.

Example: "Neither of my sisters will believe me," I thought.
neither

"Marisol," I said, "you are someone who is trustworthy. I couldn't tell this to just anyone."

"You have nothing to worry about," Marisol said. "No one will hear a word from me."

I explained, "Something happened last night. I had one of those strange dreams again."

Pronoun Review

For each sentence below, identify the underlined pronoun as "relative," "demonstrative," or "indefinite."

Example: The neighbors have a parrot <u>that</u> talks.
relative

1. Anthony, <u>whose</u> family lives in the blue house, borrowed my bike.
2. <u>Everyone</u> was looking at a stereo in the cafeteria.
3. It was there for the dance, <u>which</u> would take place that evening.
4. Delia pointed and said, "I want to get <u>that</u> for my room."
5. If you asked <u>any</u> of the other kids, they'd say the same thing.
6. <u>This</u> is my favorite song of the CD!

Pronouns . . .

Number of a Pronoun

764.1 **Singular and Plural Pronouns**

Pronouns can be either singular or plural in number.

Singular: **I, you, he, she, it** Plural: **we, you, they**

NOTE The pronouns *you, your,* and *yours* may be singular or plural.

Person of a Pronoun

The person of a pronoun tells whether the pronoun is speaking, being spoken to, or being spoken about. (See page 534.)

764.2 **First Person Pronouns**

A first-person pronoun is used in place of the name of the speaker or speakers.

I **am speaking.** We **are speaking.**

764.3 **Second Person Pronouns**

A second-person pronoun is used to name the person or thing spoken to.

Eliza, will you **please take out the garbage?**

You **better stop grumbling!**

764.4 **Third Person Pronouns**

A third-person pronoun is used to name the person or thing spoken about.

Bill should listen if he **wants to learn the words to this song.**

Charisse said that she **already knows** them**.**

They **will perform the song in the talent show.**

Uses of Pronouns

A pronoun can be used as a subject, as an object, or to show possession. (See the chart on page 766.)

764.5 **Subject Pronouns**

A subject pronoun is used as the subject of a sentence *(I, you, he, she, it, we, they).*

I **like to surf the Net.**

A subject pronoun is also used after a form of the *be* verb *(am, is, are, was, were, being, been)* if it repeats the subject. (See "Predicate Nouns," 756.5.)

"This is she**," Mom replied into the telephone.**

"Yes, it was I**," admitted the child who had eaten the cookies.**

ELPS 3E

Grammar Practice

Pronouns 4

- Number of a Pronoun
- Person of a Pronoun

Write the antecedent for the missing pronoun in each sentence. Is it singular or plural? Is it first, second, or third person? Then, for each blank, write the correct pronoun.

Example: The first time Maggie and I saw the movie *Bambi*, ______ cried.
Maggie and I (plural, first person) we

1. Carlota bought a new leash for ______ dog.
2. Since the leash is leather, ______ will last a long time.
3. Franklin and John have soccer practice, so ______ will be late for dinner.
4. "Boys, you will have to make ______ own meal," Mom said.
5. I don't wake up in the morning until my cat licks ______ nose.
6. Theo isn't very tall, but ______ can really shoot hoops.
7. Grandpa gave this book to Kyle and me, and it is now ______ most prized possession.
8. Darcy, when you grab luggage off the carousel at the airport, make sure it's really ______.
9. Mr. and Mrs. Gunderson are trying to sell ______ house.
10. The towering maple tree has lost all of ______ leaves early this year.
11. I asked Jason to give ______ a ride to school.
12. Jessi and I don't like brussels sprouts, and ______ won't eat lima beans, either.

Next Step: Write a sentence in which you use a singular, second-person pronoun. Write a second sentence using a plural, first-person pronoun. Share your sentences with a partner.

Pronouns . . .

Uses of Pronouns

766.1
Object Pronouns

An object pronoun *(me, you, him, her, it, us, them)* can be used as the object of a verb or preposition. (See **746.4**, **746.5**, and **790.1**.)

I'll call her as soon as I can. (direct object)

Hand me the phone book, please. (indirect object)

She thinks these flowers are from you. (object of the preposition)

766.2
Possessive Pronouns

A possessive pronoun shows possession or ownership. These possessive pronouns function as adjectives before nouns: *my, our, his, her, their, its,* and *your*.

School workers are painting our classroom this summer. Its walls will look much better.

These possessive pronouns can be used after verbs: *mine, ours, hers, his, theirs,* and *yours*.

I'm pretty sure this backpack is mine and that one is his.

NOTE An apostrophe is not needed with a possessive pronoun to show possession.

Uses of Personal Pronouns

	Singular Pronouns			Plural Pronouns		
	Subject Pronouns	Possessive Pronouns	Object Pronouns	Subject Pronoun	Possessive Pronouns	Object Pronouns
First Person	I	my, mine	me	we	our, ours	us
Second Person	you	your, yours	you	you	your, yours	you
Third Person	he	his	him	they	their, theirs	them
	she	her, hers	her			
	it	its	it			

Grammar Practice

Pronouns 5

Uses of Pronouns

For each numbered sentence below, write the underlined pronoun or pronouns and identify each as a "subject pronoun," an "object pronoun," or a "possessive pronoun."

Example: Are you aware of the strange creatures of the sea?
you (subject pronoun)

(1) It is home to lobsters, octopuses, and jellyfish, but one of its most unusual inhabitants has to be the squid. Squid range in size from a few inches to more than 50 feet. **(2)** Ten arms help them swim. **(3)** They move—always backward—by forcing water through a special valve that acts like a jet engine. **(4)** This backward motion probably confuses any fish that might want to eat them. **(5)** A squid can also release an inky cloud that covers its escape.

(6) Even though giant squid live in deep, dark water, their eyes are the largest in the animal kingdom, and they have excellent eyesight. **(7)** This allows them to find food easily. Their one great natural enemy is the sperm whale; however, people also catch tons of squid. **(8)** We use them as bait for other fish and, of course, as food for us, too. **(9)** (My dad loves to eat squid at restaurants.)

Steve O'Shea is a New Zealand zoologist and an expert on squid. **(10)** He and his team of researchers recently caught what they call a "colossal" squid—even larger than the 50-foot giant squid. **(11)** He says, "You are not going to want to meet these in the water." **(12)** I have to believe him!

Next Step: Write two or three sentences about a sea creature. Use the pronoun *it* in its subject, object, and possessive forms. Read your sentences aloud to a classmate.

Verbs

A **verb** is a word that shows action or links a subject to another word in a sentence.

Tornadoes cause tremendous damage. (action verb)

The weather is often calm before a storm. (linking verb)

Types of Verbs

768.1
Action Verbs

An action verb tells what the subject is doing. (See page 540.)

Natural disasters hit the globe nearly every day.

768.2
Linking Verbs

A linking verb connects—or links—a subject to a noun or an adjective in the predicate. The most common linking verbs are forms of the verb *be (is, are, was, were, being, been, am).* Verbs such as *smell, look, taste, feel, remain, turn, appear, become, sound, seem, grow,* and *stay* can also be linking verbs. (See page 540.)

The San Andreas Fault is an earthquake zone in California. (The linking verb *is* connects the subject to the predicate noun *zone.*)

Earthquakes there are fairly common. (The linking verb *are* connects the subject to the predicate adjective *common.*)

768.3
Helping Verbs

A helping verb (also called an auxiliary verb) helps the main verb express tense and voice. The most common helping verbs are *shall, will, should, would, could, must, might, can, may, have, had, has, do, did,* and the forms of the verb *be—is, are, was, were, am, being, been.* (See page 541.)

It has been estimated that 500,000 earthquakes occur around the world every year. (These helping verbs indicate that the tense is present perfect and the voice is passive.)

Fortunately, only about 100 of those will cause damage. (*Will* helps express the future tense of the verb.)

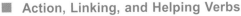

Grammar Practice

Verbs 1

Action, Linking, and Helping Verbs

For the numbered sentences in the following paragraphs, write the underlined verb and identify each as an "action verb," a "linking verb," or a "helping verb."

Example: A boat will not float unless there is enough water.
will (helping verb)

(1) You know that boats need a certain depth of water in order to float. **(2)** What happens when people must take a boat where the water level is too low? **(3)** Engineers can build a dam, which raises the water level on one side of the dam. This enables boats to travel there. **(4)** But how do the boats get from one side of the dam to the other?

A "lock" in the dam allows boats through. **(5)** A lock is a huge container with massive gates on each end, built right into the wall of the dam. **(6)** When a boat approaches the dam, the gates on one end of the lock open so that the boat can enter. Once it's all the way in, the gates close. **(7)** The boat remains steady in the lock while the lock operators either add water (to raise the boat) or remove water (to lower the boat). **(8)** When the water level reaches the water level on the other side of the dam, the opposite gates open, and the boat continues on its way.

(9) Both small boats and large ships can be lifted or lowered in this way. **(10)** The process seems very slow, but boats and ships can go places that would have been impossible to reach without a system of locks.

Next Step: Write 2–3 sentences about being on a boat. Use all three types of verbs. Read your sentences aloud to a classmate.

Verbs . . .

Tenses of Verbs

A verb has three principal parts: *present, past,* and *past participle*. (The part used with the helping verbs *has, have,* or *had* is called the past participle.)

All six of the tenses are formed from these principal parts. The past and past participle of regular verbs are formed by adding *ed* to the present tense. The past and past participle of irregular verbs are formed with different spellings. (See the chart on page 772.)

770.1
Present Tense Verbs

The present tense of a verb expresses action (or a state of being) that is happening now or that happens continually or regularly. (See page 543.)

The universe is gigantic. It takes my breath away.

770.2
Past Tense Verbs

The past tense of a verb expresses action (or a state of being) that was completed in the past. (See page 543.)

To most people many years ago, the universe was the earth, the sun, and some stars. The universe reached only as far as the eye could see.

770.3
Future Tense Verbs

The future tense of a verb expresses action that *will* take place. (See page 543.)

Maybe I will visit another galaxy in my lifetime.

Somebody will find a way to do it.

SCHOOL DAZE
I **know** the answer!
Okay, but I **said** you **will have** to sing the answer . . . go ahead!

Grammar Practice

Verbs 2

- **Present Tense, Past Tense, and Future Tense Verbs**

Make three columns with the headings "Present," "Past," and "Future." Write each of the underlined verbs in the appropriate column.

Imagine that you are standing near a friend and talking. Suddenly, someone tickles you. First, you scream, and then you can't stop laughing. What is going on? Why are people ticklish, anyway?

The answer goes back in time to the beginning of humanity. Feeling a tickle was simply a natural defense. It warned a person that something (say, a spider) was touching the skin.

When feeling a light tickle, hardly anyone will laugh. It's the heavy tickle that causes uncontrollable laughter. The tickle really causes a panic reaction, especially when it is a surprise. Although heavy tickling results in laughter, it is not always a pleasant experience. The sensation of a tickle actually affects the nerves the same way pain does. In fact, tickling that went on and on was a form of torture in the Middle Ages.

Scientists aren't sure why laughing automatically goes along with tickling, but they do know that it has also been seen among apes. Apes who were tickled in the armpits made an uncontrollable sound much like human laughter.

So now you know how you will react the next time you're tickled. First, you will have a brief point of panic (though you probably won't realize it). Then you will laugh, even if you don't think it's funny!

Next Step: Write a sentence in present tense about your thoughts on tickling. Then write it in past and future tenses, too.

TEKS 7.19A(i)

Common Irregular Verbs and Their Principal Parts

The principal parts of the common irregular verbs are listed below. The part used with the helping verbs *has, have,* or *had* is called the **past participle**. (Also see page **541**.)

Present Tense: I write. She hides.
Past Tense: Earlier I wrote. Earlier she hid.
Past Participle: I have written. She has hidden.

Present Tense	Past Tense	Past Participle	Present Tense	Past Tense	Past Participle
am, is, are	was, were	been	lead	led	led
begin	began	begun	lie (recline)	lay	lain
bid (offer)	bid	bid	lie (deceive)	lied	lied
bid (order)	bade	bidden	make	made	made
bite	bit	bitten	ride	rode	ridden
blow	blew	blown	ring	rang	rung
break	broke	broken	rise	rose	risen
bring	brought	brought	run	ran	run
burst	burst	burst	see	saw	seen
buy	bought	bought	set	set	set
catch	caught	caught	shake	shook	shaken
come	came	come	shine (polish)	shined	shined
dive	dived, dove	dived	shine (light)	shone	shone
do	did	done	shrink	shrank	shrunk
draw	drew	drawn	sing	sang, sung	sung
drink	drank	drunk	sink	sank, sunk	sunk
drive	drove	driven	sit	sat	sat
eat	ate	eaten	sleep	slept	slept
fall	fell	fallen	speak	spoke	spoken
fight	fought	fought	spring	sprang, sprung	sprung
flee	fled	fled	steal	stole	stolen
fly	flew	flown	strive	strove	striven
forsake	forsook	forsaken	swear	swore	sworn
freeze	froze	frozen	swim	swam	swum
get	got	gotten, got	swing	swung	swung
give	gave	given	take	took	taken
go	went	gone	tear	tore	torn
grow	grew	grown	throw	threw	thrown
hang (execute)	hanged	hanged	wake	woke, waked	woken, waked
hang (dangle)	hung	hung	wear	wore	worn
hide	hid	hidden, hid	weave	wove	woven
know	knew	known	wring	wrung	wrung
lay (place)	laid	laid	write	wrote	written

TEKS 7.19A(i)
ELPS 3E

Grammar Practice

Verbs 3

Irregular Verbs

For each blank, write the correct form of the irregular verb given in parentheses at the end of each sentence.

Example: Last summer, we spent most of our time at the community pool, and we _______ for hours. *(swim)*
swam

1. We _______ our swimsuits just about everywhere. *(wear)*
2. Always hungry after swimming, we _______ popcorn. *(make)*
3. I don't think I have ever _______ so much popcorn in one summer! *(eat)*
4. When we returned to school, the teachers remarked how we had _______. *(grow)*
5. Diego told us all how he _______ while rock climbing with his dad. *(fall)*
6. He had _______ his leg. *(break)*
7. Dan said, "Our family _______ to Brazil for a few weeks." *(fly)*
8. He _______ some of his souvenirs to show to the class. *(bring)*
9. Teresa reported that her grandmother had _______ her a surprise birthday party. *(throw)*
10. Jaimie explained that her family was bigger now—since her cousin had _______ to live with them. *(come)*
11. Lara stayed at a ranch and _______ a horse every day. *(ride)*
12. Steve said he just _______ as much as he could. *(sleep)*
13. Ms. Logan reminded us, "The school year has _______, so let's get to work." *(begin)*

Next Step: Write some sentences about your summer activities. Use the past tense and past participle of the verbs *see* and *take*. Share your best sentence with a partner.

TEKS 7.19A(i)

Verbs . . .

Tenses of Verbs

774.1
Present Perfect Tense Verbs

The present perfect tense verb expresses action that began in the past but continues or is completed in the present. The present perfect tense is formed by adding *has* or *have* to the past participle. (Also see page 544.)

I have wondered for some time how the stars got their names.

A visible star has emitted light for thousands of years.

774.2
Past Perfect Tense Verbs

The past perfect tense verb expresses action that began in the past and was completed in the past. This tense is formed by adding *had* to the past participle. (Also see page 544.)

I had hoped to see a shooting star on our camping trip.

774.3
Future Perfect Tense Verbs

A future perfect tense verb expresses action that will begin in the future and will be completed by a specific time in the future. The future perfect tense is formed by adding *will have* to the past participle. (Also see page 544.)

By the middle of this century, we probably will have discovered many more stars, planets, and galaxies.

774.4
Present Progressive Tense Verbs

A present progressive tense verb expresses action that is not completed at the time of stating it. The present progressive tense is formed by adding *am, is,* or *are* to the *ing* form of the main verb.

Scientists are learning a great deal from their study of the sky.

774.5
Past Progressive Tense Verbs

A past progressive tense verb expresses action that was happening at a certain time in the past. This tense is formed by adding *was* or *were* to the *ing* form of the main verb.

Astronomers were beginning their quest for knowledge hundreds of years ago.

774.6
Future Progressive Tense Verbs

A future progressive tense verb expresses action that will take place at a certain time in the future. This tense is formed by adding *will be* to the *ing* form of the main verb.

Someday astronauts will be going to Mars.

This tense can also be formed by adding a phrase noting the future *(are going to)* plus *be* to the *ing* form of the main verb.

They are going to be performing many experiments.

Grammar Practice

Verbs 4

Perfect Tense Verbs

For each sentence below, choose the helping verb that best fits the sentence. Then write whether the entire verb tense is "present perfect," "past perfect," or "future perfect."

Example: My family *(has, will have)* taken a driving vacation every year for the past eight years.
has (present perfect)

1. Last year, we *(had, will have)* decided to drive from our home in Ohio to New Mexico.
2. Taking two-lane highways instead of the interstates, we *(had, will have)* wanted to see the "real" America.
3. This year, we're going someplace we *(have, will have)* wanted to see for several years: Maine.
4. By the time we complete this year's vacation, we *(had, will have)* driven in every state except Hawaii.

Progressive Tense Verbs

For each sentence below, identify the underlined verb tense as "present progressive," "past progressive," or "future progressive."

Example: I <u>am looking</u> forward to our time in Maine.
present progressive

1. Originally, we <u>were thinking</u> of going to Montana.
2. I <u>was trying</u> to persuade everyone that we should go someplace we haven't been before.
3. My suggestion worked; now we <u>are planning</u> the route we'll take to Maine.
4. In just a few weeks, we <u>will be loading</u> the car for our trip.
5. For the first time, my brother <u>is going to be driving</u> some of the way.

TEKS 7.19A(i)

Verbs . . .

Forms of Verbs

776.1
Active or Passive Voice

The voice of a verb tells you whether the subject is doing the action or is receiving the action. A verb is in the active voice (in any tense) if the subject is doing the action in a sentence. (See page 542.)

I dream of going to galaxies light-years from Earth.

I will travel in an ultra-fast spaceship.

A verb is in the passive voice if the subject is not doing the action. The action is done *by* someone or something else. The passive voice is always indicated with a helping verb plus a past participle or a past tense verb.

My daydreams often are shattered by reality. (The subject *daydreams* is not doing the action.)

Of course, reality can be seen differently by different people. (The subject *reality* is not doing the action.)

Tense	Active Voice		Passive Voice	
	Singular	Plural	Singular	Plural
Present Tense	I find you find he/she/it finds	we find you find they find	I am found you are found he/she/it is found	we are found you are found they are found
Past Tense	I found you found he found	we found you found they found	I was found you were found he/she/it was found	we were found you were found they were found
Future Tense	I will find you will find he will find	we will find you will find they will find	I will be found you will be found he/she/it will be found	we will be found you will be found they will be found
Present Perfect	I have found you have found he has found	we have found you have found they have found	I have been found you have been found he/she/it has been found	we have been found you have been found they have been found
Past Perfect	I had found you had found he had found	we had found you had found they had found	I had been found you had been found he/she/it had been found	we had been found you had been found they had been found
Future Perfect	I will have found you will have found he will have found	we will have found you will have found they will have found	I will have been found you will have been found he/she/it will have been found	we will have been found you will have been found they will have been found

Grammar Practice

Verbs 5

Active or Passive Voice

Write whether each sentence below is in the active or passive voice.

Example: Marta is going to run in a marathon.
active

1. The distance of a marathon, 26.2 miles, can be driven in about half an hour by someone going 60 miles per hour.
2. Marta has already spent 15 weeks getting ready.
3. She will finish her training in the next six weeks.
4. Marta was told by her doctor that she is in great shape.
5. Stretches are done by all the runners before they compete.
6. First-time competitors are advised by experienced runners to go slow and save up their energy.
7. A runner's endurance is improved by this strategy.
8. During a race, many runners walk for a minute or two to get a little rest.
9. Some people are energized by running a long distance.
10. I would only feel exhausted!
11. Two benefits of running in marathons are increased energy and a sense of accomplishment.

Next Step: Choose two or three of the sentences above that you marked "passive" and rewrite them in the active voice.

Verbs . . .

Forms of Verbs

778.1 Singular and Plural Verbs

A singular subject needs a singular verb. A plural subject needs a plural verb. For action verbs, only the third-person singular verb form is different: *I wonder, we wonder, you wonder, she wonders, they wonder.* Some linking verbs, however, have several different forms.

First Person	**Singular:**	**I am (or was) a good student.**
	Plural:	**We are (or were) good students.**
Second Person	**Singular:**	**You are (or were) a cheerleader.**
	Plural:	**You are (or were) cheerleaders.**
Third Person	**Singular:**	**He is (or was) on the wrestling team.**
	Plural:	**They are (or were) also on the team.**

778.2 Transitive Verbs

A transitive verb is a verb that transfers its action to a direct object. The object makes the meaning of the verb complete. A transitive verb is always an action verb (never a linking verb). (See page 632.)

An earthquake shook San Francisco in 1906. (*Shook* transfers its action to the direct object *San Francisco.* Without *San Francisco* the meaning of the verb *shook* is incomplete.)

The city's people spent many years rebuilding. (Without the direct object *years,* the verb's meaning is incomplete.)

A transitive verb transfers the action directly to a direct object and indirectly to an indirect object.

Fires destroyed the city. (direct object: *city*)

Our teacher gave us the details. (indirect object: *us;* direct object: *details*)

See 746.4 and 746.5 for more on direct and indirect objects.

778.3 Intransitive Verbs

An intransitive verb does not need an object to complete its meaning. (See page 632.)

Abigail was shopping. (The verb's meaning is complete.)

Her stomach felt queasy. (*Queasy* is a predicate adjective describing *stomach;* there is no direct object.)

She lay down on the bench. (Again, there is no direct object. *Down* is an adverb modifying *lay.*)

Grammar Practice

Verbs 6

Transitive Verbs

The following sentences have transitive verbs. Write the direct object from each one.

Example: Ruby keeps her jewelry in a tackle box.
jewelry

1. She especially likes the ring that was her grandmother's.
2. She chose it from her grandma's velvet-lined jewelry box.
3. Ruby wants a real jewelry box, too.
4. Her mom will buy one at a rummage sale.
5. Ruby will put her best rings and bracelets in it.

Intransitive Verbs

For each of the following pairs of sentences, write the letter of the sentence that has an intransitive verb.

Example: **A.** Luke sees well.
B. Luke sees a red-tailed hawk.
A

1. **A.** Ken tasted green peppers in the meat loaf.
   B. The meat loaf tasted funny.
2. **A.** Corinne walked the dog between 3:30 and 4:00 p.m.
   B. Corinne walked briskly along the path.
3. **A.** Mr. Moss speaks quite softly.
   B. Mr. Moss speaks three languages.
4. **A.** He is growing sunflowers in his backyard.
   B. They are growing so big!
5. **A.** Naomi sketches with charcoal and colored pencils.
   B. Naomi sketches pictures of wild animals.

TEKS 7.19A(i)

Verbs . . .

Forms of Verbs

780.1 **Transitive or Intransitive Verbs**

Some verbs can be either transitive or intransitive.

Transitive: **She reads my note.** **Albert ate an apple.**
Intransitive: **She reads aloud.** **Albert ate already.**

Verbals

A **verbal** is a word that is made from a verb but acts as another part of speech. Gerunds, participles, and infinitives are verbals. (Also see page 545.)

780.2 **Gerunds**

A gerund is a verb form that ends in *ing* and is used as a *noun*. A gerund often begins a gerund phrase.

Worrying is useless. (The gerund is the subject noun.)

You should stop worrying about so many things. (The gerund phrase is the direct object.)

780.3 **Participles**

A participle is a verb form ending in *ing* or *ed*. A participle is used as an *adjective* and often begins a participial phrase.

The idea of the earth shaking and splitting both fascinates and frightens me. (The participles modify *earth*.)

Rattling in the cabinets, the dishes were about to crash to the floor. (The participial phrase modifies *dishes*.)

Why doesn't this tired earth just stand still? (The participle modifies *earth*.)

780.4 **Infinitives**

An infinitive is a verb form introduced by *to*. It may be used as a *noun*, an *adjective*, or an *adverb*. It often begins an infinitive phrase.

My need to whisper is due to this secret. (The infinitive is an adjective modifying *need*.)

I am afraid to swim. (The infinitive is an adverb modifying the predicate adjective *afraid*.)

To overcome this fear is my goal. (The infinitive phrase is used as a noun and is the subject of this sentence.)

TEKS 7.19A(i)
ELPS 3E

Grammar Practice

Verbs 7 ■ Verbals

For the sentences below, write the word or words that function as a verbal. The number of each type of verbal is indicated in parentheses at the end of each sentence.

Example: Every living thing needs water to survive. *(1 participle, 1 infinitive)*
living, to survive

1. Living for several weeks without food is possible, but a person would last only a few days without water. *(1 gerund)*
2. Water allows the human body to work better by helping every system run more smoothly. *(1 infinitive, 1 gerund)*
3. Water is a required part of blood circulation and muscle movement. *(1 participle)*
4. To keep cool, the body releases water (sweat) through pores in the skin. *(1 infinitive)*
5. Cushioning joints and organs, water plays an important part in protecting the body from harm. *(1 participle, 1 gerund)*
6. Skin needs water to preserve its softness and flexibility. *(1 infinitive)*
7. Drinking enough water is a key to good health. *(1 gerund)*
8. Without enough water, the body can easily become dehydrated. *(1 participle)*
9. Feeling irritable and restless can be a sign of a lack of fluid. *(1 gerund)*
10. Increased thirst and decreased stretchiness of the skin are other symptoms. *(2 participles)*
11. It is vital to get water into a person with these symptoms. *(1 infinitive)*

Next Step: Write a sentence about being in water. Use one of the verbal forms. Share your sentence with a partner.

Adjectives

An **adjective** is a word used to describe a noun or a pronoun. Adjectives tell *what kind, how many (how much),* or *which one*. They usually come before the word they describe. (See pages 546–549.)

ancient dinosaurs **800 species** **that triceratops**

Adjectives are the same whether the word they describe is singular or plural.

small brain—or—small brains **large tooth—or—large teeth**

782.1 **Articles**

The articles *a, an,* and *the* are adjectives.

A brontosaurus was an animal about 70 feet long.

The huge dinosaur lived on land and ate plants.

782.2 **Proper Adjectives**

A proper adjective is formed from a proper noun, and it is always capitalized. (See 676.1.)

A Chicago museum is home to the skeleton of one of these beasts. (*Chicago* functions as a proper adjective describing the noun *museum.*)

782.3 **Common Adjectives**

A common adjective is any adjective that is not proper. It is not capitalized (unless it is the first word in a sentence).

Ancient mammoths were huge, woolly creatures.

They lived in the ice fields of Siberia.

Special Kinds of Adjectives

782.4 **Demonstrative Adjectives**

A demonstrative adjective points out a particular noun. *This* and *these* point out something nearby; *that* and *those* point out something at a distance.

This mammoth is huge, but that mammoth is even bigger.

NOTE When a noun does not follow *this, these, that,* or *those,* these words are pronouns, not adjectives. (See 760.1.)

782.5 **Compound Adjectives**

A compound adjective is made up of two or more words. (Sometimes it is hyphenated.)

Dinosaurs were egg-laying animals.

The North American Allosaurus had sharp teeth and powerful jaws.

Grammar Practice

Adjectives 1

Proper and Common Adjectives

Write one common adjective and one proper adjective from each sentence below. (Do not include the articles *a, an,* or *the.*)

Example: Guion Bluford, Jr., was the first African American astronaut to travel in space.
first, African American

1. On a hot August day in 1983, the space shuttle *Challenger* blasted off.
2. Bluford was the mission specialist on that *Challenger* expedition.
3. Bluford was a successful pilot in the air force after he graduated from an East Coast college.
4. Then he joined the NASA training program and went through four years of difficult training.
5. In 1991 and 1992, Bluford traveled with the *Discovery* crew on his last two trips into space.

Demonstrative and Compound Adjectives

Write one demonstrative adjective and one compound adjective from each sentence below.

Example: "Alpacas are semi-tame mammals, and this one lives on my uncle's farm," said Abrita, showing a photograph to the class.
this, semi-tame

1. "What an awesome-looking animal! May I see that picture again?" asked Tommy.
2. "These animals live in South American grasslands," she said.
3. "Is this animal classified as a plant-eating mammal?" asked Anne.
4. "Yes," she said, "and notice those two-toed feet! Aren't they funny?"

Adjectives . . .

Special Kinds of Adjectives

784.1 **Indefinite Adjectives**

An indefinite adjective gives approximate, or indefinite, information (*any, few, many, most*, and so on). It does not tell exactly how many or how much.

Some mammoths were heavier than today's elephants.

784.2 **Predicate Adjectives**

A predicate adjective follows a linking verb and describes the subject.

Mammoths were once abundant, but now they are extinct.

Forms of Adjectives

784.3 **Positive Adjectives**

The positive form describes a noun or pronoun without comparing it to anyone or anything else.

The Eurostar is a fast train that runs between London, Paris, and Brussels.

It is an impressive train.

784.4 **Comparative Adjectives**

The comparative form of an adjective *(er)* compares two persons, places, things, or ideas. (See page 547.)

The Eurostar is faster than the Orient Express.

Some adjectives that have more than one syllable show comparisons by their *er* suffix, but many of them use the modifiers *more* or *less*.

It is a speedier commuter train than the Tobu Railway trains in Japan.

This train is more impressive than my commuter train.

784.5 **Superlative Adjectives**

The superlative form (*est* or *most* or *least*) compares three or more persons, places, things, or ideas. (See page 547.)

In fact, the Eurostar is the fastest train in Europe.

It is the most impressive commuter train in the world.

784.6 **Irregular Forms**

Some adjectives use completely different words to express comparison.

good, better, best	**bad, worse, worst**
many, more, most	**little, less, least**

Grammar Practice

Adjectives 2

Indefinite and Predicate Adjectives

To complete each sentence below, write an adjective from the following list to fill in the blanks. The type of adjective to use is given in parentheses.

funny few any most some busy sad

Example: Trevor will go to see just about *(indefinite)* movie.
any

1. I have been very *(predicate)* lately, so I've seen only a *(indefinite)* movies.
2. I really enjoy *(indefinite)* movies that I see with my friends.
3. One that I saw recently was *(predicate)*.
4. In the movie, *(indefinite)* fish get together to find a little lost fish.
5. The little fish is *(predicate)* because he got separated from his dad.

Comparative and Superlative Adjectives

To complete each sentence below, write the correct form of the underlined adjective.

Example: The elm is taller than the maple, and the oak is ________ of all.
tallest

1. Mario has dark hair, but Al has ________ hair than Mario does.
2. Although Penny has many seashells, Sue has ________ seashells than Penny does.
3. Denice has less strength than I do, and Candace has the ________ strength of the three of us.
4. Of course, the Mississippi River is remarkable, but I think the Great Lakes are even ________________ than that.

Adverbs

An **adverb** is a word used to modify a verb, an adjective, or another adverb. It tells *how, when, where, how often,* or *how much*. Adverbs can come before or after the words they modify. (See pages 550–553.)

Dad snores loudly. (*Loudly* modifies the verb *snores*.)

His snores are really explosive. (*Really* modifies the adjective *explosive*.)

Dad snores very loudly. (*Very* modifies the adverb *loudly*.)

Types of Adverbs

There are four basic types of adverbs: *time, place, manner,* and *degree*.

786.1 Adverbs of Time

Adverbs of time tell *when, how often,* and *how long*.

tomorrow often never always

Jen rarely has time to go swimming.

786.2 Adverbs of Place

Adverbs of place tell *where, to where,* or *from where*.

there backward outside

We'll set up our tent here.

786.3 Adverbs of Manner

Adverbs of manner often end in *ly* and tell *how* something is done.

unkindly gently well

Ahmed boldly entered the dark cave.

Some words used as adverbs can be written with or without the *ly* ending. When in doubt, use the *ly* form.

slow, slowly deep, deeply

NOTE Not all words ending in *ly* are adverbs. *Lovely*, for example, is an adjective.

786.4 Adverbs of Degree

Adverbs of degree tell *how much* or *how little*.

scarcely entirely generally very really

Jess is usually the leader in these situations.

Grammar Practice

Adverbs 1

Types of Adverbs

For each numbered, underlined adverb in the paragraph below, write whether it tells "how," "when," "where," "how often," or "how much." Then write whether it is an adverb of "time," "place," "manner," or "degree."

Example: The human ear is rather amazing.
how much; degree

People can hear **very** [1] loud sounds and **extremely** [2] soft sounds. How does an ear hear? The vibration of molecules **constantly** [3] produces sound waves. The waves enter the ear canal and strike the eardrum, causing it to vibrate **rapidly** [4]. These vibrations travel **forward** [5] through the rest of the middle ear, hitting the three tiny bones **there** [6]. Their vibrations make waves in the fluid inside the cochlea, activating tiny, hair-like nerve cells that **immediately** [7] turn the vibrations into electrical signals. The auditory nerve **then** [8] transmits the information to the brain, and the brain interprets the information as sound. When both ears work **together** [9], people can **almost** [10] always tell where a sound is coming from.

Next Step: Use a thesaurus to look up synonyms for three of the underlined adverbs in the paragraph above. Write sentences using these synonyms. Read your best sentence aloud to a classmate.

TEKS 7.19A(iv)

Adverbs . . .

Special Kinds of Adverbs

788.1 Conjunctive Adverbs

A conjunctive adverb can be used as a conjunction and shows a connection or a transition between two independent clauses. Most often, a conjunctive adverb follows a semicolon in a compound sentence; however, it can also appear at the beginning or end of a sentence. (Note that the previous sentence has an example of a conjunctive adverb.)

also	**besides**	**however**	**instead**
meanwhile	**nevertheless**	**therefore**	

Forms of Adverbs

Many adverbs—especially adverbs of manner—have three forms: *positive, comparative,* and *superlative*.

788.2 Positive Adverbs

The positive form describes but does not make a comparison.

Juan woke up late.

He quickly ate some breakfast.

788.3 Comparative Adverbs

The comparative form of an adverb *(er)* compares two things.

Juan woke up later than he usually did. (See page 551.)

Some adverbs that have more than one syllable show comparisons by their *er* suffix, but many of them use the modifiers *more* or *less*.

He ate his breakfast more quickly than usual.

788.4 Superlative Adverbs

The superlative form (*est* or *most* or *least*) compares three or more things. (See page 551.)

Of the past three days, Juan woke up latest on Saturday.

Of the past three days, he ate his breakfast least quickly on Saturday.

788.5 Irregular Forms

Some adverbs use completely different words to express comparison.

Positive	Comparative	Superlative
well	better	best
badly	worse	worst

Grammar Practice

Adverbs 2

Conjunctive Adverbs

Number your paper from 1 to 3. In the following paragraph, find and write the three conjunctive adverbs.

Example: Sojourner Truth did not dwell on her past; instead, she helped others pursue freedom.
instead

We often think of the South when we think of slavery in the United States; however, one of the most famous slaves was a Northern-born woman named Sojourner Truth. She was first sold at the age of 11, going from owner to owner after that. Nevertheless, she remained proud and had a strong faith. She finally gained her freedom and went to New York City. There she took the name Sojourner Truth and preached her faith. Meanwhile, she met and joined others who spoke out for freedom and equality. Their strong voices made a difference for many people.

Forms of Adverbs

For each sentence below, write the correct form (comparative or superlative) of the underlined adverb.

Example: Sojourner Truth worked hard than any of her owners.
harder

1. As a slave, she was treated badly than the animals on a farm.
2. Her first language was Dutch, yet she spoke English well than many others.
3. Sojourner pushed early for equal rights than most other women.
4. Her voice boomed deeply than some men's voices.
5. Of all the speakers' messages, her call for justice was delivered effectively.

TEKS 7.19A(v)

Prepositions

Prepositions are words that show position, direction, or how two words or ideas are related to each other. Specifically, a preposition shows the relationship between its object and some other word in the sentence.

> **Raul hid under the stairs.** (*Under* shows the relationship between *hid* and *stairs.*)

790.1 Prepositional Phrases

A preposition never appears alone; it is always part of a prepositional phrase. A prepositional phrase includes the preposition, the object of the preposition, and the modifiers of the object. (See pages 554–555.)

> **Raul's friends looked in the clothes hamper.** (preposition: *in;* object: *hamper;* modifiers: *the, clothes*)

A prepositional phrase functions as an adjective or as an adverb.

> **They checked the closet with all the winter coats.** (*With all the winter coats* functions as an adjective modifying *closet.*)
>
> **They wandered around the house looking for him.** (*Around the house* functions as an adverb modifying *wandered.*)

NOTE If a word found in the list of prepositions has no object, it is not a preposition. It is probably an adverb.

> **Raul had never won at hide 'n' seek before.** (*Before* is an adverb that modifies *had won.*)

Prepositions

aboard	apart from	beyond	from	like	outside	under
about	around	but	from among	near	outside of	underneath
above	aside from	by	from between	near to	over	until
according to	at	by means of	from under	next to	over to	unto
across	away from	concerning	in	of	owing to	up
across from	back of	considering	in addition to	off	past	up to
after	because of	despite	in front of	on	prior to	upon
against	before	down	in place of	on account of	regarding	with
along	behind	down from	in regard to	on behalf of	since	within
along with	below	during	in spite of	on top of	through	without
alongside	beneath	except	inside	onto	throughout	
alongside of	beside	except for	inside of	opposite	to	
amid	besides	excepting	instead of	out	together with	
among	between	for	into	out of	toward	

Grammar Practice

Prepositions

Write each prepositional phrase that appears in the following paragraphs. Underline the preposition and circle the object of the preposition.

Example: Spiders live everywhere, even in the finest houses.
in the finest houses

Although many people cringe at the sight of spiders, even dangerous spiders don't look for people as prey. Spiders prefer insects, and they eat billions of these pests.

Spiders capture different kinds of insects in the air and on the ground. Sticky spiderwebs trap insects. Some spiders jump out of special burrows to catch grasshoppers. Other spiders stand very still, just waiting for insects that run into their waiting jaws. All spiders have powerful venom that paralyzes their victims. Fortunately, spiders do not prey on humans. They simply go about their business looking for their next insect meal, and people can be glad about that.

For each of the following sentences, write whether the underlined word is a preposition or an adverb.

Example: When I see a spider in my room, I scoop it up and throw it outside.
adverb

1. When my mom sees a spider, she runs around the house, yelling for someone to get rid of it.
2. In the garden, there are quite a few spiders walking about.
3. Yesterday I found a big yellow one under the watering can.
4. Another one was crawling down a sunflower stalk.
5. I wanted to look around for more.
6. However, I had to cut the grass, and I was running behind.

Conjunctions

A **conjunction** connects individual words or groups of words. There are three kinds of conjunctions: *coordinating, correlative,* and *subordinating.* (See pages 556–558.)

792.1 **Coordinating Conjunctions**

A coordinating conjunction connects a word to a word, a phrase to a phrase, or a clause to a clause. The words, phrases, or clauses joined by a coordinating conjunction must be equal, or of the same type.

Polluted rivers and streams can be cleaned up. (Two nouns are connected by *and.*)

Ride a bike or plant a tree to reduce pollution. (Two verb phrases are connected by *or.*)

Maybe you can't invent a pollution-free engine, but you can cut down on the amount of energy you use. (Two equal independent clauses are connected by *but.*)

NOTE When a coordinating conjunction is used to make a compound sentence, a comma always comes before it.

792.2 **Correlative Conjunctions**

Correlative conjunctions are conjunctions used in pairs.

We must reduce not only pollution but also excess energy use.

Either you're part of the problem, or you're part of the solution.

Conjunctions

Coordinating Conjunctions

and, but, or, nor, for, so, yet

Correlative Conjunctions

either, or   neither, nor   not only, but also   both, and   whether, or   as, so

Subordinating Conjunctions

after, although, as, as if, as long as, as though, because, before, if, in order that, provided that, since, so, so that, that, though, till, unless, until, when, where, whereas, while

Grammar Practice

Conjunctions 1

Coordinating Conjunctions

Do this activity with a partner. Each of you must follow the directions in one of the two columns. Then put the columns together to make some funny sentences!

COLUMN A	COLUMN B
1. Write a compound subject connected with the conjunction *or*.	**1.** Write a compound predicate connected with the conjunction *and*.
2. Write one sentence followed by a comma and the conjunction *yet*.	**2.** Write one sentence.
3. Write a compound subject connected with the conjunction *and*.	**3.** Write a compound predicate connected with the conjunction *or*.
4. Write one sentence followed by a comma and the conjunction *but*.	**4.** Write one sentence.

Correlative Conjunctions

Write the correlative conjunctions that make the most sense in the following sentences.

Example: We are going to the beach _______ it's sunny _______ cloudy.
whether, or

1. _______ _______________ dolphins are fish.
2. Dad put up a basketball hoop for ______ my brother _______ me.
3. Josh can _______ shoot three-pointers _______ get nothing but net!
4. Because of his busy schedule, he will join _______ the school team _______ a local league team.

TEKS 7.19A(vii)

Conjunctions . . .

794.1 Subordinating Conjunctions

A subordinating conjunction is a word or group of words that connects two clauses that are not equally important. A subordinating conjunction begins a dependent clause and connects it to an independent clause to make a complex sentence. (See page 579 and the chart on page 792.)

Fuel-cell engines are unusual because **they don't have moving parts.**

Since **fuel-cell cars run on hydrogen, the only waste products are water and heat.**

As you can see in the sentences above, a comma sets off the dependent clause only when it begins the sentence. A comma is usually not used when the dependent clause follows the independent clause.

NOTE Relative pronouns and conjunctive adverbs can also connect clauses. (See 758.3 and 788.1.)

Interjections

An **interjection** is a word or phrase used to express strong emotion or surprise. Punctuation (a comma or an exclamation point) is used to separate an interjection from the rest of the sentence.

Wow, **would you look at that!** Oh no! **He's falling!**

SCHOOL DAZE
Forget it! We aren't using activity money for that.
Yikes, I've told everyone that we could buy a plasma-screen TV for our classroom!

Grammar Practice

Conjunctions 2

Subordinating Conjunctions

Use a subordinating conjunction from the following list and write one complex sentence out of each pair of sentences below.

if while since although when

Example: Ancient people looked at the sky. They saw shapes of animals, people, or objects in the stars.
When ancient people looked at the sky, they saw shapes of animals, people, or objects in the stars.

1. They mapped out the sky as early as 2000 B.C.E. The constellations in the zodiac were named only 2,000 years ago.
2. There are almost 90 known constellations. There are only 12 in the zodiac.
3. People can use the zodiac. They want to find a particular star in one of its constellations.
4. The zodiac is divided into 12 parts. It's easy to divide a 360-degree circle into 30-degree "slices."

Interjections

Use an appropriate interjection in each of the following sentences. Punctuate it with a comma or an exclamation point.

Example: _______ That was some race!
Wow!

1. _______ I dropped the cake.
2. You passed the test? _______
3. _______ I need you here right now!
4. _______ I've discovered the cure for the common cold!

Quick Guide: Parts of Speech

In the English language, there are eight parts of speech. Understanding them will help you improve your writing skills. Every word you write is a part of speech—a noun, a verb, an adjective, and so on. The chart below lists the eight parts of speech.

Noun	A word that names a person, a place, a thing, or an idea **Alex Moya Belize ladder courage**
Pronoun	A word used in place of a noun **I he it they you anybody some**
Verb	A word that shows action or links a subject to another word in the sentence **sing shake catch is are**
Adjective	A word that describes a noun or a pronoun **stormy red rough seven grand**
Adverb	A word that describes a verb, an adjective, or another adverb **quickly today now bravely softer**
Preposition	A word that shows position or direction and introduces a prepositional phrase **around up under over between to**
Conjunction	A word that connects other words or groups of words **and but or so because when**
Interjection	A word (set off by commas or an exclamation point) that shows strong emotion **Stop! Hey, how are you?**

Grammar Practice

Parts of Speech Review

For each numbered sentence below, write whether the underlined word is a "noun," a "pronoun," a "verb," an "adjective," an "adverb," a "preposition," a "conjunction," or an "interjection."

Example: Wow, an Eastern diamondback rattlesnake at Brookfield Zoo gave birth to nine babies last week!
interjection

(1) Our class went on a field trip to the Brookfield Zoo last week. **(2)** This zoo features natural settings for the animals. **(3)** The zoo's designers wanted people to be able to get close to the animals, but they didn't want to use cages or bars. **(4)** So the exhibits are separated from visitors with a high wall and a deep ditch or moat.

(5) We enjoyed looking at all the wonderful animals from around the world. **(6)** We saw Amur tigers, Indian rhinoceroses, Siberian ibexes, orangutans, blue poison frogs, Galapagos tortoises, and giant anteaters. **(7)** We stopped at the elephant house and talked about the amazing size of these animals.

(8) Suddenly Peter yelled, "Watch out! That elephant is going to spray us with water." **(9)** Before any of us could move, the elephant blasted us. **(10)** Those closest to the fence got hit the worst.

(11) "Oh, I'm so sorry," said the guide. **(12)** "She meant no harm."

(13) "Does she always do that?" Jill asked.

(14) The guide answered, "No. I guess she thought that the bunch of you needed to cool off!" **(15)** It *was* a hot day, so no one really complained. **(16)** Later, on the bus, we all laughed about our morning shower.

Next Step: Write a few sentences about a time you visited the zoo. Include all the parts of speech. Share your favorite sentence with a partner.

Credits

Photos: P. cover (yellow coral, bandannas), x, 33, 45, 55, 373, 378, 457, 563 (mask) HMH Collection; cover (red coral), endsheet, v, xvi, 1 (ball), 68, 75, 77, 83, 145, 205, 227, 237, 277, 295, 299, 329, 337, 380 (river), 383 (computer, Jupiter), 384, 387, 390, 485, 552, 586, 609, 617 (rock, coffee pot) ©Photodisc/Getty Images; cover (blue/green coral) ©Digital Vision/Getty Images; cover (coral), 137, 165, 197, 361, 374, 379 (waves), 380 (mud), 381 (sun), 497, 498, 531, 571, 617 (fire) ©Corbis; cover (light), 65 (folders), 504 ©Stockbyte/Getty; back cover, 5 ©Ingram Publishing/Getty Images; vi, ix, 27, 33, 63, 71, 93, 97, 101, 106, 107, 113, 123, 129, 161, 169, 175, 181, 191, 235, 241, 247, 257, 303, 307, 313, 317, 323, 343, 407, 423, 431, 432, 441, 456, 483, 487, 489, 491, 493, 499, 501, 503, 505, 507, 509, 511, 513, 515, 517, 519, 523, 534, 536, 561, 563 (fish), 593, 798 ©Comstock/Getty Images; xiii, 467, 469, 472 ©Gaertner/Alamy; 1 (sign) Harcourt; 10 ©PhotoObjects.net/Jupiter; 11, 16 ©SuperStock RF/SuperStock; 29 ©JUPITERIMAGES/Brand X/Alamy; 57, 60 ©Hemera Technologies/Jupiter; 65 (camera) ©Eyewire/Getty Images; 105 ©Photos.com/Jupiter; 211, 231, 263, 601 ©Getty Images; 271 ©Corbis/Jupiter; 379 (ice) ©Design Pics/Jupiter; 381 (rain) Harcourt School Publishers; 383 (Venus) ©NASA; 481 HMH Collection; 486 ©Alamy; 492 ©ERproductions Ltd/Blend Images/Getty Images; 510 ©Thinkstock/Corbis; 516 ©Steve Skjold/Alamy; 522 ©Ilene MacDonald/Alamy; 524 ©Ablestock.com/Jupiter; 529 ©Comstock/Jupiter; 583, 595 ©Artville/Getty Images; 585 ©Brownstock Inc./Alamy.

Page 526: Copyright © 2010 by Houghton Mifflin Harcourt Publishing Company. Adapted and reproduced by permission from *The American Heritage Student Dictionary*.

Texas Essential Knowledge and Skills (TEKS) for English Language Arts

The TEKS for English Language Arts are the skills you need to master by the end of Grade 7. The first column in the chart below lists the English Language Arts TEKS. The second column shows where these TEKS are taught in *Texas Write Source*.

TEKS 7.14 Writing/Writing Process

Students use elements of the writing process (planning, drafting, revising, editing, and publishing) to compose text. Students are expected to:

A plan a first draft by selecting a genre appropriate for conveying the intended meaning to an audience, determining appropriate topics through a range of strategies (e.g., discussion, background reading, personal interests, interviews), and developing a thesis or controlling idea;	pages 7, 8, 73, 78, 95, 102, 140, 155, 158, 163, 170, 173, 176, 177, 208, 221, 224, 229, 236, 274, 289, 292, 297, 304, 306, 364, 375, 408, 417, 424, 606, 607
B develop drafts by choosing an appropriate organizational strategy (e.g., sequence of events, cause-effect, compare-contrast) and building on ideas to create a focused, organized, and coherent piece of writing;	pages 74, 79, 108–111, 141, 164, 172–174, 178, 179, 209, 242–245, 311, 420, 425, 427, 599, 610, 611, 613
C revise drafts to ensure precise word choice and vivid images; consistent point of view; use of simple, compound, and complex sentences; internal and external coherence; and the use of effective transitions after rethinking how well questions of purpose, audience, and genre have been addressed;	pages 7–9, 38, 74, 107, 112, 114–116, 118, 119, 127, 175, 180, 183, 189, 194, 241, 246, 248, 249, 255, 260, 276, 279, 307, 312, 314–316, 369, 423, 428, 548, 577–579, 601, 634, 635
D edit drafts for grammar, mechanics, and spelling; and	pages 192, 193, 261, 324, 327, 367, 374, 442 pages 6, 10, 22, 34, 42, 59, 60, 154
E revise final draft in response to feedback from peers and teacher and publish written work for appropriate audiences.	pages 18, 19, 30–32, 129, 197, 217, 263, 322, 329, 345, 438, 451, 461, 463 pages 99, 128

*Page References in *Student Edition*
*Page References in *SkillsBook*

TEKS 7.15 Writing/Literary Texts

Students write literary texts to express their ideas and feelings about real or imagined people, events, and ideas. Students are expected to:

A write an imaginative story that: (i) sustains reader interest; (ii) includes well-paced action and an engaging story line;(iii) creates a specific, believable setting through the use of sensory details; (iv) develops interesting characters; and (v) uses a range of literary strategies and devices to enhance the style and tone.	pages 20, 79, 106, 142, 151, 365, 366, 369–372 pages 6, 164
B write a poem using: (i) poetic techniques (e.g., rhyme, scheme, meter); (ii) figurative language (e.g., personification, idioms, hyperbole); and (iii) graphic elements (e.g., word position).	pages 87, 375–381 page 142

TEKS 7.16 Writing

Students write about their own experiences. Students are expected to write a personal narrative that has a clearly defined focus and communicates the importance of or reasons for actions and/or consequences.

pages 103, 105, 110, 111, 141, 142

TEKS 7.17 Writing/Expository and Procedural Texts

Students write expository and procedural or work-related texts to communicate ideas and information to specific audiences for specific purposes. Students are expected to:

A write a multi-paragraph essay to convey information about a topic that: (i) presents effective introduction and concluding paragraphs; (ii) contains a clearly stated purpose or controlling idea; (iii) is logically organized with appropriate facts and details and includes no extraneous information or inconsistencies; (iv) accurately synthesizes ideas from several sources; and (v) uses a variety of sentence structures, rhetorical devices, and transitions to link paragraphs	pages 38, 81, 85, 172–174, 176–180, 182, 183, 185, 209, 210, 217, 276, 321, 397, 412, 416, 424, 428, 432, 433, 436, 437, 439, 444, 579, 594, 595, 600, 602

*Page References in *Student Edition*
*Page References in *SkillsBook*

B	write a letter that reflects an opinion, registers a complaint, or requests information in a business or friendly context;	pages 90, 91, 146, 147, 212, 213, 284–286, 348, 349 page 20
C	write responses to literary or expository texts that demonstrate the writing skills for multi-paragraph essays and provide sustained evidence from the text using quotations when appropriate; and	pages 305, 309, 316, 317, 341, 342, 345, 347–349, 359
D	produce a multimedia presentation involving text and graphics using available technology.	pages 458–463

TEKS 7.18 Writing/Persuasive Texts

Students write persuasive texts to influence the attitudes or actions of a specific audience on specific issues. Students are expected to write a persuasive essay to the appropriate audience that:

A	establishes a clear thesis or position;	pages 229, 240, 243, 275
B	considers and responds to the views of others and anticipates and answers reader concerns and counter-arguments; and	pages 230, 237, 238, 246, 253
C	includes evidence that is logically organized to support the author's viewpoint and that differentiates between fact and opinion.	pages 239, 240, 244, 245, 250–252, 275

*Page References in *Student Edition*
*Page References in *SkillsBook*

TEKS 7.19 Oral and Written Conventions/Conventions

Students understand the function of and use the conventions of academic language when speaking and writing. Students will continue to apply earlier standards with greater complexity. Students are expected to:

A identify, use, and understand that function of the following parts of speech in the context of reading, writing, and speaking:
- (i) verbs (perfect and progressive tenses) and participles;
- (ii) appositive phrases;
- (iii) adverbial and adjectival phrases and clauses;
- (iv) conjunctive adverbs (e.g., consequently, furthermore, indeed);
- (v) prepositions and prepositional phrases and their influence on subject-verb agreement;
- (vi) relative pronouns (e.g., whose, that, which);
- (vii) subordinating conjunctions (e.g., because, since); and
- (viii) transitions for sentence to sentence or paragraph to paragraph coherence.

pages 116, 125, 126, 193, 258, 259, 325, 326, 442, 443, 533, 544, 545, 554–558, 560, 569, 574, 576, 581, 582, 590, 601, 602, 615, 634, 635, 750–753, 758, 759, 772–777, 780, 781, 788–791, 794, 795

pages 77–91, 127–130, 133, 134, 153, 154, 169, 170, 173, 174, 187–192, 195, 196

B write complex sentences and differentiate between main versus subordinate clauses; and

pages 260, 560, 579, 750, 751

pages 75, 76, 123–128

C use a variety of complete sentences (e.g., simple, compound, complex) that include properly placed modifiers, correctly identified antecedents, parallel structures, and consistent tenses.

pages 124, 324, 442, 534, 537, 543, 567, 570, 575, 584, 621, 758, 759

pages 10, 103, 104, 159–162

TEKS 7.20 Oral/Written Conventions/Handwriting, Capitalization, and Punctuation

Students write legibly and use appropriate capitalization and punctuation conventions in their compositions. Students are expected to:

A use conventions of capitalization; and

pages 531, 676–685

pages 49–52

B recognize and use punctuation marks including:
- (i) commas after introductory words, phrases, and clauses; and
- (ii) semicolons, colons, and hyphens.

pages 195, 445, 650–657, 668–671

pages 11–18, 29, 30, 41–43

*Page References in *Student Edition*
*Page References in *SkillsBook*

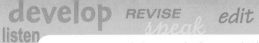

TEKS 7.21 Oral and Written Conventions/Spelling

Students spell correctly. Students are expected to spell correctly, including using various resources to determine and check correct spellings. — pages 261, 327, 525, 698–707; pages 59, 60

TEKS 7.22 Research/Research Plan

Students ask open-ended research questions and develop a plan for answering them. Students are expected to:

A brainstorm, consult with others, decide upon a topic, and formulate a major research question to address the major research topic; and — pages 163, 208, 384, 398, 408–411, 420

B apply steps for obtaining and evaluating information from a wide variety of sources and create a written plan after preliminary research in reference works and additional text searches. — pages 170, 384, 386, 388, 389, 392–395, 411, 413, 421; pages 104, 122

TEKS 7.23 Research/Gathering Sources

Students determine, locate, and explore the full range of relevant sources addressing a research question and systematically record the information they gather. Students are expected to:

A follow the research plan to gather information from a range of relevant print and electronic sources using advanced search strategies; — pages 384, 412, 413, 415

B categorize information thematically in order to see the larger constructs inherent in the information; — pages 384, 413, 414, 416

C record bibliographic information (e.g. author, title, page number) for all notes and sources according to a standard format; and — pages 384, 395, 397, 400, 415, 422, 429, 430

D differentiate between paraphrasing and plagiarism and identify the importance of citing valid and reliable sources. — pages 171, 396, 400, 412, 414, 463

*Page References in *Student Edition*
*Page References in *SkillsBook*

TEKS 7.24 Research/Synthesizing Information

Students clarify research questions and evaluate and synthesize collected information. Students are expected to:

A	narrow or broaden the major research question, if necessary, based on further research and investigation; and	pages 385, 418, 419
B	utilize elements that demonstrate the reliability and validity of the sources used (e.g., publication date, coverage, language, point of view) and explain why one source is more useful than another.	pages 385, 387–389, 415, 421

TEKS 7.25 Research/Organizing and Presenting Ideas

Students organize and present their ideas and information according to the purpose of the research and their audience. Students are expected to synthesize the research into a written or an oral presentation that:

A	draws conclusions and summarizes or paraphrases the findings in a systematic way;	pages 317, 385, 396, 399, 434, 438, 439, 450, 451, 462
B	marshals evidence to explain the topic and gives relevant reasons for conclusions;	pages 186, 187, 385, 417, 428, 432, 452, 453
C	presents the findings in a meaningful format; and	pages 184, 385, 435, 454, 459, 461
D	follows accepted formats for integrating quotations and citations into the written text to maintain a flow of ideas.	pages 243, 309, 422, 424–427, 433

*Page References in *Student Edition*
*Page References in *SkillsBook*

English Language Proficiency Standards (ELPS)

The English Language Proficiency Standards (ELPS) outline expectations for students who are learning English. The first column in the chart below lists selected ELPS for English Language Arts. The second column shows where these ELPS are taught in *Texas Write Source.*

ELPS 2 Cross-curricular second language acquisition/listening

The ELL listens to a variety of speakers including teachers, peers, and electronic media to gain an increasing level of comprehension of newly acquired language in all content areas. ELLs may be at the beginning, intermediate, advanced, or advanced high stage of English language acquisition in listening. In order for the ELL to meet grade-level learning expectations across the foundation and enrichment curriculum, all instruction delivered in English must be linguistically accommodated (communicated, sequenced, and scaffolded) commensurate with the student's level of English language proficiency. The student is expected to:

D monitor understanding of spoken language during classroom instruction and interactions and seek clarification as needed.	pages 468, 471, 474, 475, 489

*Page References in *Student Edition*
*Page References in *SkillsBook*

ELPS 3 Cross-curricular second language acquisition/speaking

The ELL speaks in a variety of modes for a variety of purposes with an awareness of different language registers (formal/informal) using vocabulary with increasing fluency and accuracy in language arts and all content areas. ELLs may be at the beginning, intermediate, advanced, or advanced high stage of English language acquisition in speaking. In order for the ELL to meet grade-level learning expectations across the foundation and enrichment curriculum, all instruction delivered in English must be linguistically accommodated (communicated, sequenced, and scaffolded) commensurate with the student's level of English language proficiency. The student is expected to:

A	practice producing sounds of newly acquired vocabulary such as long and short vowels, silent letters, and consonant clusters to pronounce English words in a manner that is increasingly comprehensible;	pages 481, 495, 513
G	express opinions, ideas, and feelings ranging from communicating single words and short phrases to participating in extended discussions on a variety of social and grade-appropriate academic topics; and	pages 6, 9, 12, 15 18, 19, 27, 29–32, 40, 42, 47, 62, 63, 147, 160, 193, 237, 250, 294, 360, 408, 412, 414, 416, 466, 472, 479, 482, 484, 486–488, 490–494, 496, 498–500, 502, 504–506, 511, 512, 514, 516–518, 522, 523, 528, 640
H	narrate, describe, and explain with increasing specificity and detail as more English is acquired.	pages 6, 19, 40, 42, 47, 58, 85, 125, 153, 160, 162, 168, 186, 187, 189, 193, 259, 294, 297, 325, 360, 387, 388, 396, 414, 415, 421, 469, 482, 486–488, 491–494, 498–500, 504–506, 510–512, 516–518, 522, 523, 528

*Page References in *Student Edition*
*Page References in *SkillsBook*

ELPS 4 Cross-curricular second language acquisition/reading

The ELL reads a variety of texts for a variety of purposes with an increasing level of comprehension in all content areas. ELLs may be at the beginning, intermediate, advanced, or advanced high stage of English language acquisition in reading. In order for the ELL to meet grade-level learning expectations across the foundation and enrichment curriculum, all instruction delivered in English must be linguistically accommodated (communicated, sequenced, and scaffolded) commensurate with the student's level of English language proficiency. The student is expected to:

C develop basic sight vocabulary, derive meaning of environmental print, and comprehend English vocabulary and language structures used routinely in written classroom materials.

pages 12, 16–18, 20, 34, 35, 37, 38, 40, 46–48, 108, 160, 176, 178, 214, 216, 226, 242, 476, 477, 480, 481, 483, 484, 489, 490, 495, 496, 501, 503, 507, 508, 513, 519, 520, 528, 641, 642, 644, 646, 648, 650, 652, 654, 656, 658, 660, 662, 664, 666, 668, 670 , 672, 674

pages 3, 5, 7, 9, 11, 13, 15, 17, 19, 21, 23, 25, 29, 31, 33, 35, 37, 39, 41, 43, 44

ELPS 5 Cross-curricular second language acquisition/writing

The ELL writes in a variety of forms with increasing accuracy to effectively address a specific purpose and audience in all content areas. ELLs may be at the beginning, intermediate, advanced, or advanced high stage of English language acquisition in writing. In order for the ELL to meet grade-level learning expectations across foundation and enrichment curriculum, all instruction delivered in English must be linguistically accommodated (communicated, sequenced, and scaffolded) commensurate with the student's level of English language proficiency. The student is expected to:

B write using newly acquired basic vocabulary and content-based grade-level vocabulary; and

pages 164, 171, 179, 195, 204, 242, 270, 336, 484, 533–537, 541, 553, 560, 708–714, 716–742

pages 61–65

*Page References in *Student Edition*
*Page References in *SkillsBook*

G	narrate, describe, and explain with increasing specificity and detail to fulfill content area writing needs as more English is acquired.	pages 172, 174, 204, 207, 215, 217, 219, 223, 228–230, 238, 245, 246, 270, 273, 274, 279, 283, 285, 286, 291, 292, 298, 306, 336, 341, 349, 363, 369, 371, 374, 394, 470, 531, 536, 543, 544, 548, 549, 552, 556, 566, 588–590, 593–595, 599, 661, 663, 665, 675, 747 page 170

Index

This **index** will help you find specific information in this book. Words that are in italic are from the "Using the Right Word" section. The colored boxes contain information you will use often.

A

D

E

H

I

J

K

L

N

Q

R

Y